EYEWITNESS HANDBOOKS

WILD FLOWERS

OF BRITAIN AND NORTHWEST EUROPE

EYEWITNESS HANDBOOKS

WILD FLOWERS

OF BRITAIN AND NORTHWEST EUROPE

CHRISTOPHER GREY-WILSON

Photography by
NEIL FLETCHER

Editorial Consultant
FRANCIS ROSE

DORLING KINDERSLEY
London • New York • Stuttgart

A DORLING KINDERSLEY BOOK

Important Notice
Care has been taken in the preparation of this book not to harm wild plants. Threatened species have been photographed either by using cultivated specimens or by using techniques that will leave plants intact.

Project Editor Angeles Gavira
Project Art Editor Elaine Hewson
Series Editor Jonathan Metcalf
Series Art Editor Peter Cross
Production Controller Caroline Webber

First published in Great Britain in 1995 by Dorling Kindersley Limited, 9 Henrietta Street, London WC2E 8PS

A CIP catalogue record for this book is available from the British Library

ISBN 0-7513-1024-7 flexibound

Computer page make-up by
Adam Moore and Mark Bracey
Text film output by
The Right Type, Great Britain
Reproduced by Colourscan, Singapore
Printed and bound by
Kyodo Printing Co., Singapore

CONTENTS

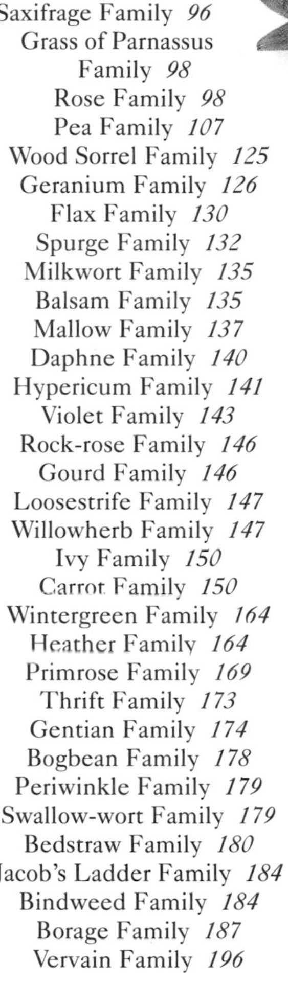

AUTHOR'S INTRODUCTION

The health of the countryside is to be found in the abundance and variety of wildlife, and wild flowers play a vital role in maintaining the natural balance. Studying and getting to know them provides a hobby that can last a lifetime; learning the skills necessary to identify them can prove a challenging and fascinating pastime which brings many rewards.

THE CONTRASTING CONDITIONS that exist in northwest Europe have evolved a complex variety of habitats, each with its own unique associations of plants. The Atlantic region is dominated by broad-leaved deciduous woodland, while the inner montane areas and northern Europe are characterized by evergreen coniferous woodland. In contrast, the treeless tundra in and near the Arctic Circle forms an uninterrupted landscape, stretching vast distances and broken only by lakes and outcrops of bare rocks or higher mountain chains.

CLIMATIC ZONES

Three principal climate types dominate northwest Europe. Variations in temperature, rainfall, available sunlight, and the relief of the land are all critical factors that influence the distribution and variety of plants in an area.

BOREAL & ARCTIC

Winters are long and dark, often with subzero temperatures and much snow. Summers are short, with long days and short nights. High mountains experience even greater seasonal contrasts.

ATLANTIC

Wet and mild with the heaviest rainfall to the west, especially on the higher ground. Relatively mild winters and warm summers are the norm, with rain possible throughout most of the year.

CENTRAL EUROPEAN

Has a harsher climate than that of the Atlantic. This region, away from the temperate influence of the Atlantic Ocean, has greater seasonal extremes, with colder winters and hotter, often rather dry, summers.

The Importance of Wild Flowers

The close association of plants and animals is essential to the natural balance of life. Plants play an absolutely vital role in our environment: without wild flowers most of the associated animals, insects, small mammals, and a myriad of microscopic creatures would become extinct, as plants provide much of their food. Compare the bustle of insect life along a flowery hedgerow to a similar one where the use of herbicides has reduced the plants to a few spray-tolerant species that are shunned by most insects, and you will notice a considerable difference.

The interest in wildflower gardening, the re-establishment of wildflower meadows and waysides, together with the replanting of hedgerows and woodland, are evidence of an ever-growing awareness of the important role wild flowers play in our lives, and of the realization that so much of our native flora has been lost in recent years due to land development and modern farming practices. With increased leisure time, more people are finding that visiting the countryside, whether walking along a lane, or following a mountain trail, is a relaxing and fulfilling pastime, and many have become eager to learn about wild flowers and how to identify them. Not all will want to study the fauna and flora in detail, but most will be delighted by the variety of flowers and creatures that are to be casually observed.

Wildlife Reserve
Wildflower meadows, like the one above, provide havens for insects and other small creatures.

Flower Garden
The seeds of a large range of wild flowers are widely available. Planting wild-flower areas in your garden not only provides interest and colour for much of the year, it is also a good way of conserving the native and naturalized plants of a region.

Yellow Corydalis

THE PLANT KINGDOM

Living organisms are divided by biologists into a number of universally accepted categories. The basic division separates out five large groups called kingdoms, of which plants represent a single kingdom, Plantae. This, like the other kingdoms, is progressively broken down into smaller units. Thus Plantae is next divided into ten phyla, of which the phylum Angiospermophyta (the angiosperms) includes all the flowering plants – the subject of this book. Other phyla include the Coniferophyta (the conifers) and Sphenophyta (the horsetails). Further subdivisions group the plants into classes, orders, and families. This book covers the two orders that make up the angiosperms: monocotyledons and dicotyledons. The family is usually the starting unit of identification. The next division is the genus, which in turn divides into the basic unit of identification, species. This system produces tiers of hierarchy, otherwise known as a family tree. The diagram below explains these tiers.

A FAMILY TREE

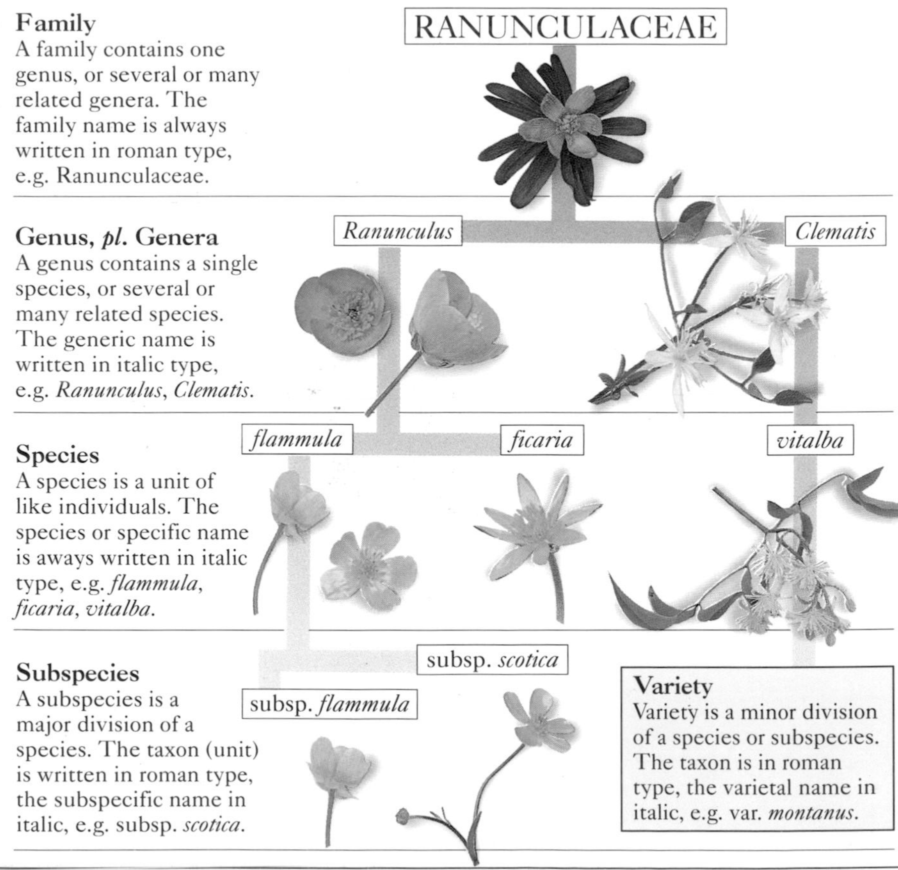

Family
A family contains one genus, or several or many related genera. The family name is always written in roman type, e.g. Ranunculaceae.

Genus, *pl.* Genera
A genus contains a single species, or several or many related species. The generic name is written in italic type, e.g. *Ranunculus*, *Clematis*.

Species
A species is a unit of like individuals. The species or specific name is aways written in italic type, e.g. *flammula*, *ficaria*, *vitalba*.

Subspecies
A subspecies is a major division of a species. The taxon (unit) is written in roman type, the subspecific name in italic, e.g. subsp. *scotica*.

Variety
Variety is a minor division of a species or subspecies. The taxon is in roman type, the varietal name in italic, e.g. var. *montanus*.

HOW THIS BOOK WORKS

THIS BOOK is divided into two main parts, the two recognized orders of flowering plants, Dicotyledons and Monocotyledons. These two groups are further divided into families, each one introduced by a family heading. The order in which the plants occur in this book follows that set out by the major reference work *Flora Europaea*. To aid in the identification of the plants, many of the entries have a Related Species section after the habitat information, consisting of a brief description of how similar species differ and can be distinguished from the featured plant. Photographic close-ups, called details, are often included to show particular parts of the plant more clearly. The annotated example below shows how a typical species entry is organized.

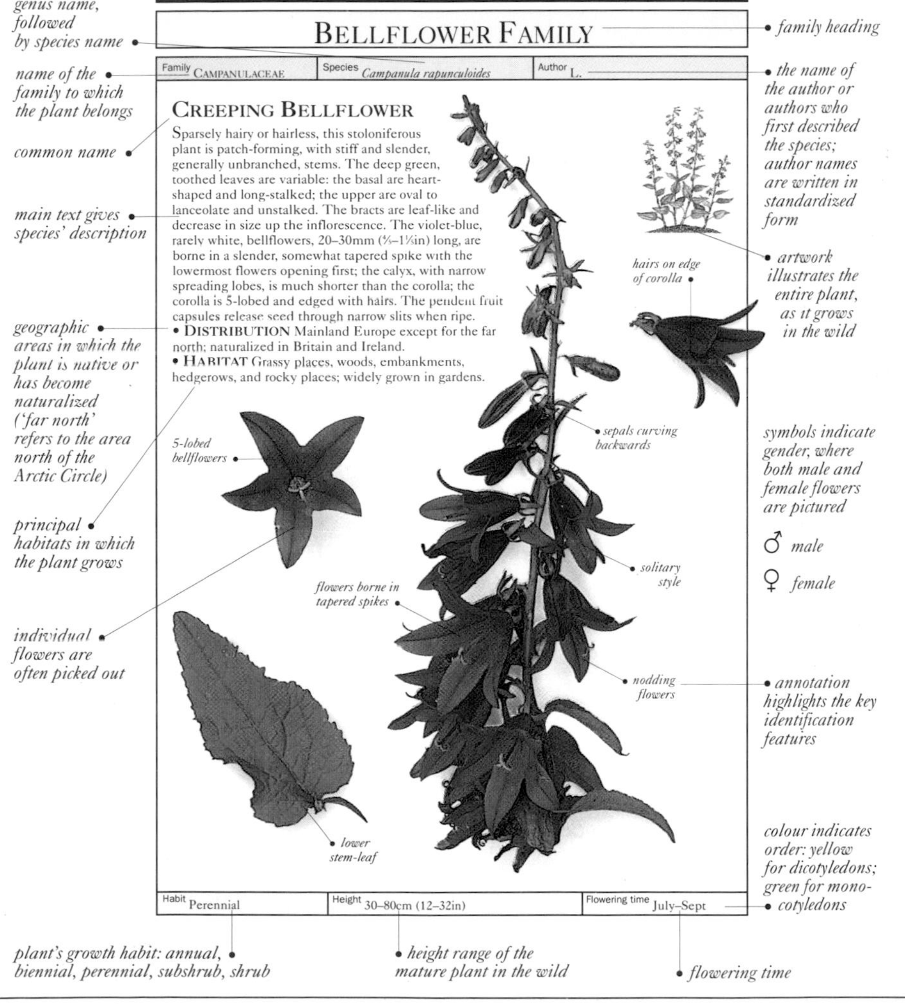

Life Cycle

Like all living organisms, flowering plants have a precise and definable life cycle. Most follow a complete cycle from seed and seedling to adult plant, when they produce the flowers and fruit, although there are variations on the theme. A minority of plants reproduce vegetatively (without the production of seed) or apomictically (producing viable seed without fertilization). The diagram below describes the life cycle of a typical dicotyledon.

Seed

Seeds vary greatly in size, from the fine dust of the orchids to the large seeds of many legumes (peas). Seeds contain all the genetic information characteristic of a given species. They may be short-lived and need to germinate rapidly, or they may remain dormant in the soil for years until conditions are right for germination. Many seeds have a rich food reserve (endosperm) that helps to sustain them and nourish the seedling.

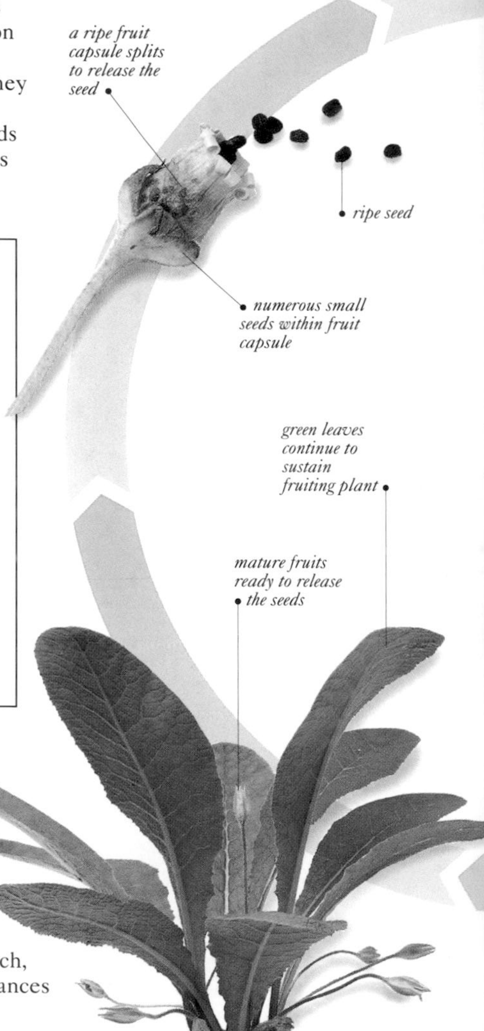

Main Wild Flower Habits

The habit of flowering plants has evolved along a number of distinct lines.
Annuals: Plants that complete their life cycle in a single year and then die.
Biennials: Plants that germinate in the first year, persist over winter, then flower, seed, and die in the second year.
Perennials: Plants that flower year after year, over-wintering above or below ground.
Subshrubs: Low and shrub-like plants with at least some woody stems that do not die back to ground level each autumn, or die back only in part.
Shrubs: Plants with woody persistent stems and branches. Once they reach maturity, they flower year after year.

Fruit

The entire purpose of the plant is the ultimate development of the fruit. Fruits are the net product of pollination and fertilization and constitute the last phase in the plant's growth cycle. The seeds they contain represent future generations for the species. Fruits are very variable in shape, structure, and texture but each, in its own way, is designed to maximize the chances for the survival and dispersal of the seeds.

SEEDLING

Although many species produce numerous seeds, only a very small minority of seeds germinate, and of these relatively few go on to become mature flowering plants. The seedling phase is a very hazardous stage in a plant's life as it is vulnerable to desiccation, trampling, and the depredations of insects and other creatures such as slugs and snails.

dicotyledon seedling

roots develop in advance of the leaves

COTYLEDONS

Flowering plants are divided into two main orders based on their seedling characteristics. Dicotyledons (dicots) have two seed leaves, called cotyledons; these are generally above ground, but not always so. Monocotyledons (monocots) have only one cotyledon, which is usually above ground. As the true leaves appear, the cotyledons generally wither away, their function of protecting the growing point of the plant and helping to nourish the developing seedling having been completed.

MONOCOTYLEDON

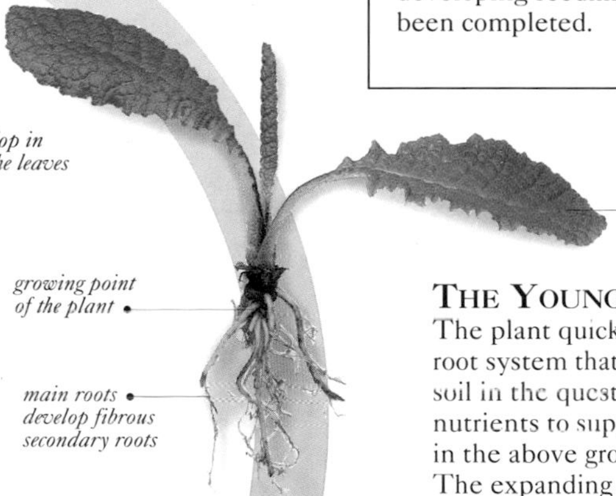

developing leaves contain chlorophyll

growing point of the plant

main roots develop fibrous secondary roots

THE YOUNG PLANT

The plant quickly develops an intricate root system that delves deep into the soil in the quest for moisture and vital nutrients to support the growing leaves in the above ground portion of the plant. The expanding green leaves harness the sun's energy through chlorophyll (the leaf's green pigment); from this they are able to manufacture the sugars that provide the energy to support the growing plant. Many plants cannot flower until they reach a certain size.

large corollas attract pollinators

large leaf surface of mature plant

extensive roots of mature plant

THE MATURE PLANT

When the plant is large enough, it matures and reaches its flowering phase. Species have quite specific flowering times that, in order to maximize the chances of survival, are frequently related to the availability of suitable insect pollinators, although other elemental factors such as available light and temperature are also significant. Pollination is usually followed by fertilization, which in turn leads to the development of the fruit.

Plant Profile

The different parts of a plant all perform vital functions. The root system supports and sustains the portion of the plant above ground. The stems allow the plant to compete with its neighbours for space and light. The leaves transform the sun's energy into food to sustain the plant. They vary greatly in size, shape, and arrangement and so can be a great aid to identificaton. The flowers are usually the most obvious manifestation of the plant and their presence indicates that the plant is in its reproductive stage; this leads to the production of the fruit and seeds.

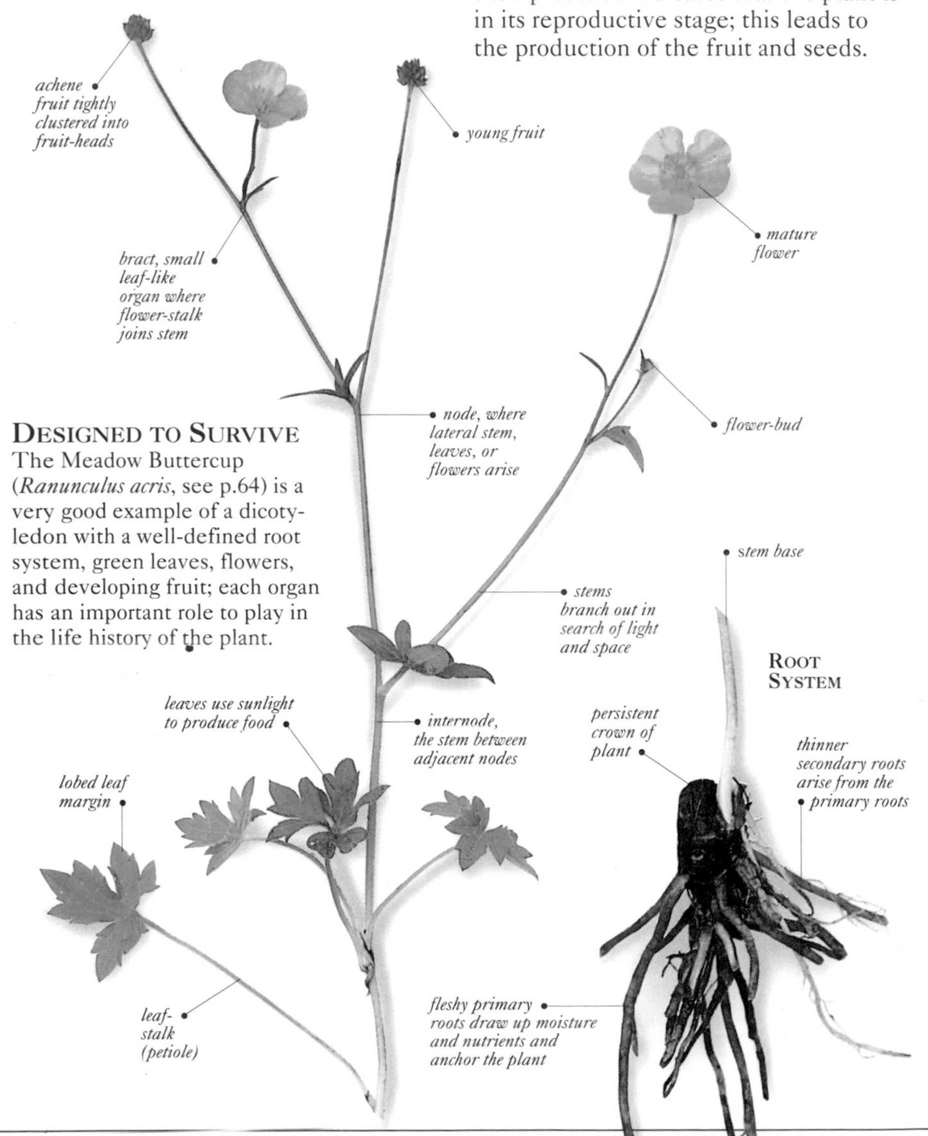

Designed to Survive

The Meadow Buttercup (*Ranunculus acris*, see p.64) is a very good example of a dicotyledon with a well-defined root system, green leaves, flowers, and developing fruit; each organ has an important role to play in the life history of the plant.

FLOWER

The outer whorl of a typical flower consists of sepals (collectively the calyx); some flowers have an extra calyx (epicalyx) below the true one. Within the sepals are the petals (collectively the corolla). Within these lie the male organs of the plant, the stamens (collectively the androecium), which consist of a stalk (filament) and an anther containing the pollen. Inside the androecium lies the female part of the flower, the gynoecium, made up of an ovary that contains the unfertilized seeds (ovules), and a style with one or several stigmas at the tip. The stigma receives the pollen. One or more of these organs may be missing from some flowers.

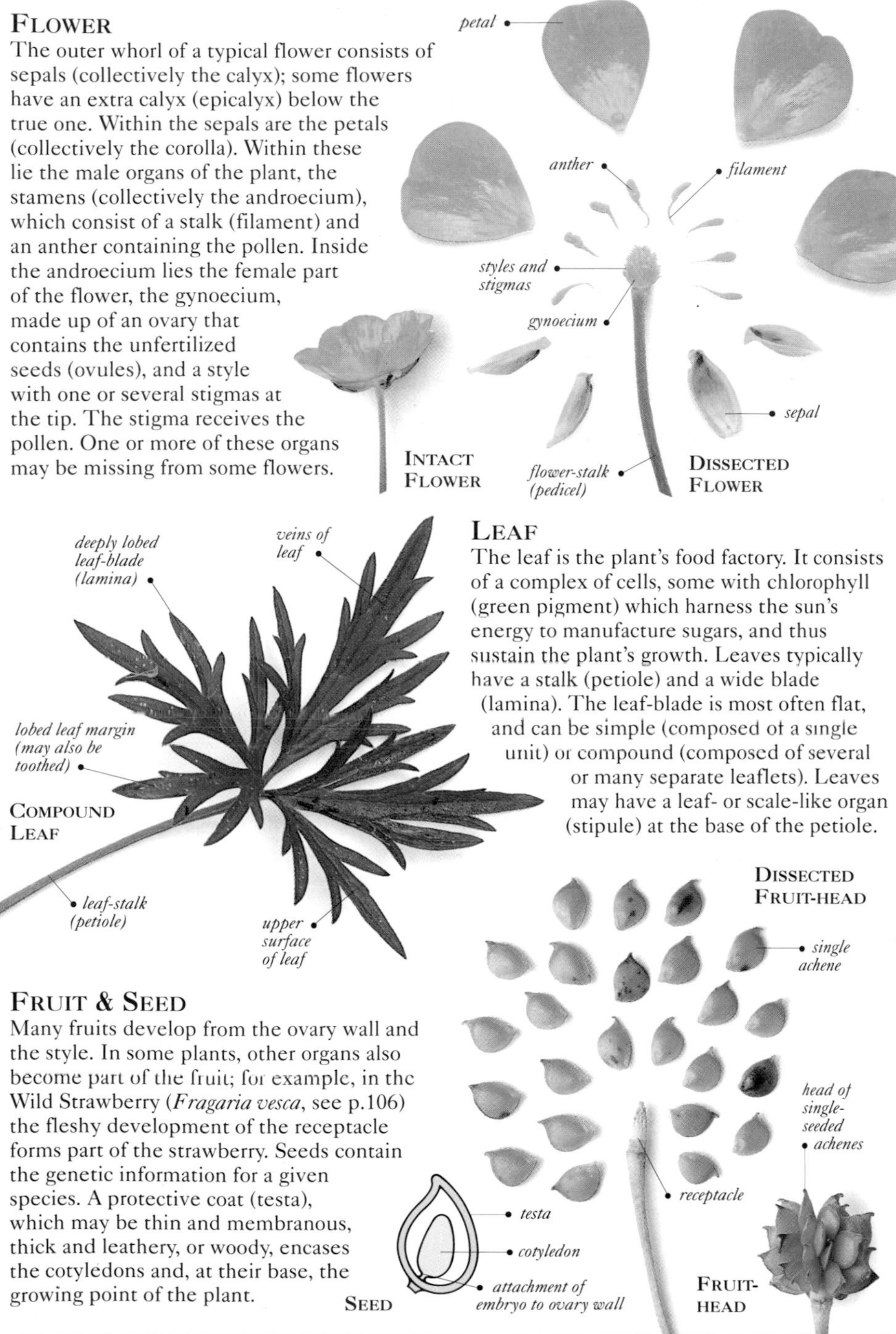

LEAF

The leaf is the plant's food factory. It consists of a complex of cells, some with chlorophyll (green pigment) which harness the sun's energy to manufacture sugars, and thus sustain the plant's growth. Leaves typically have a stalk (petiole) and a wide blade (lamina). The leaf-blade is most often flat, and can be simple (composed of a single unit) or compound (composed of several or many separate leaflets). Leaves may have a leaf- or scale-like organ (stipule) at the base of the petiole.

FRUIT & SEED

Many fruits develop from the ovary wall and the style. In some plants, other organs also become part of the fruit; for example, in the Wild Strawberry (*Fragaria vesca*, see p.106) the fleshy development of the receptacle forms part of the strawberry. Seeds contain the genetic information for a given species. A protective coat (testa), which may be thin and membranous, thick and leathery, or woody, encases the cotyledons and, at their base, the growing point of the plant.

Growth Types

A PLANT'S mode of growth (erect, prostrate, etc.) and its habit (annual, biennial, etc.) are often typical of a particular species or group of plants, or even to entire genera. Because the growth types are often so characteristic, they can be an important clue to recognizing the type of plant, and can be a prime factor in accurate naming. Look at the plant carefully and note whether stems are present and, if so, whether they are soft or woody, spreading or upright, clambering or stiff, to help you distinguish between annuals, biennials, perennials, subshrubs, and shrubs (see also p.10). The illustrations and captions below describe the principal modes of growth.

◁ AQUATIC
The leaves and flowers of these plants may float, or they may project above the water surface. The plants mostly grow with their roots anchored to the mud, and have very long stems or leaf-stalks (petioles).

PROSTRATE △
Plants in exposed places are often low-lying, to minimize wind damage. The stems spread out on the ground. The flowers are close to, or slightly above, the foliage.

STEMLESS ▷
Many plants, like the Cowslip, have no obvious stem and the leaves are borne in a basal rosette with the flower stems arising from them. The leaf-rosettes may be solitary or grouped together.

CLIMBING ▷
These clamber up other plants, walls, fences, or available supports in a number of ways. The stems may twine around a support, or clasp it by means of leaf tendrils or a mass of short and closely adhering stem roots.

SPREADING △
Many perennial plants have stems that spread out from the base. The flowers are usually borne on short upright stems. The way in which these plants grow means that they often intermingle to form dense undergrowth.

◁ ERECT
Stiff and upright stems are characteristic of some plants, especially many biennials and perennials. Foxgloves and mulleins are typical examples of this group. Some of these plants have several erect stems arising from a common base.

LEAF TYPES

EVOLUTION has equipped plants with a remarkable diversity of leaf forms, shapes, and arrangements. The leaf margin can vary from entire (untoothed) to toothed or variously lobed, while the surface of the leaf-blade can be smooth or rough, hairless, or adorned with hairs of varying types, warts, or scales. These features are usually characteristic of a given species.

LEAF ARRANGEMENTS

Alternate leaves are arranged singly along the stem, sometimes strictly alternately but usually spiralling. Opposite leaves are in opposing pairs, with the pairs at right angles to each other. Leaves may also grow in whorls of three or more.

ALTERNATE OPPOSITE WHORLED

SIMPLE LEAVES

These are leaves with a single leaf-blade that may be unlobed or lobed, and with or without a toothed margin. Simple leaves come in an enormous number of shapes: only a few common examples are shown here.

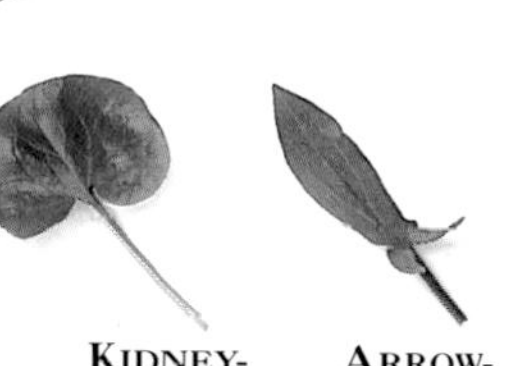

KIDNEY-SHAPED ARROW-SHAPED

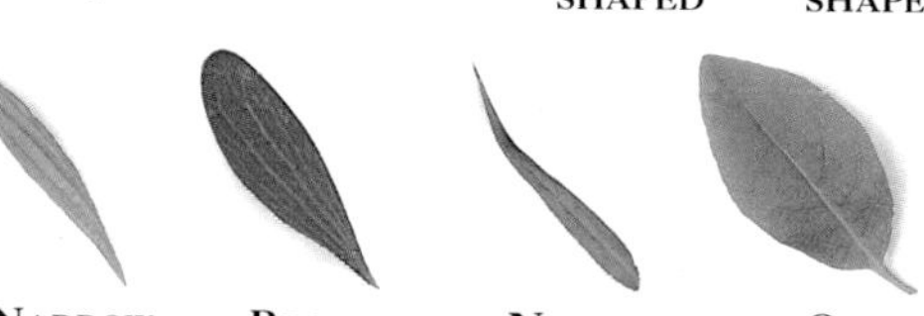

NARROW-ELLIPTICAL BROAD-ELLIPTICAL NARROW-LANCEOLATE OVAL

OVATE SHALLOWLY HEART-SHAPED PALMATELY LOBED PINNATELY LOBED

COMPOUND LEAVES

These are leaves composed of two or more discrete leaflets. They may have leaflets arranged along a simple axis (rachis) or a more complex arrangement composed of lateral rachises and numerous leaflets.

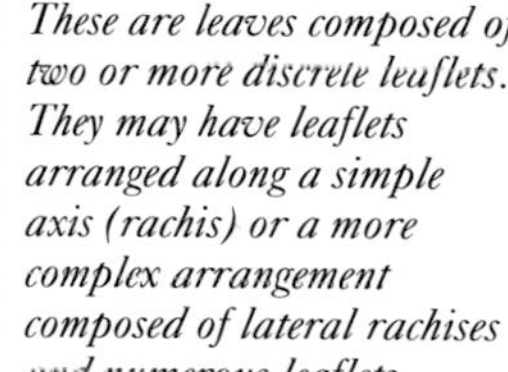

PEDATE

DIGITATE PINNATE

TRIFOLIATE PINNATE WITH TENDRIL BIPINNATE

MONOCOT LEAVES

While they essentially fit into the above categories, many monocot leaves have a distinctive look. They are usually simple shapes with an untoothed (entire) margin and veins that often run parallel or almost parallel to each other.

HEART-SHAPED LINEAR ARROW-SHAPED ELLIPTICAL SPEAR-SHAPED

FLOWER TYPES

FLOWERING is the sexual phase of the plant's life cycle. Most flowers are hermaphrodite (have male and female parts), but the flowers of some species are either male or female (unisexual) with both sexes borne on the same plant (monoecious) or on separate plants (dioecious). Whether they are unisexual or hermaphrodite, the flowers may be solitary or grouped in inflorescences.

INFLORESCENCE TYPES

SOLITARY FLOWERS
Flowers borne singly, either from the base of the plant or from a leaf-axil, and not in a formal inflorescence.

SPIKE
Numerous unstalked flowers borne along a simple axis, generally with the lowermost flower opening first.

RACEME
Essentially like a spike but with individual flowers clearly stalked. One of the commonest types of inflorescence.

PANICLE
A compound inflorescence that may be either a branched raceme or a regularly branched cyme.

CYME
Each branch ends with a flower. Spiralled or scorpioid cymes have the flowers arranged along a spiral axis.

UMBEL
Flat-topped or domed with flowers arising on stems originating at the same place, like the spokes of an umbrella.

CORYMB
Rather like an umbel, but with the branches arising at different levels along the stem, not at the same point.

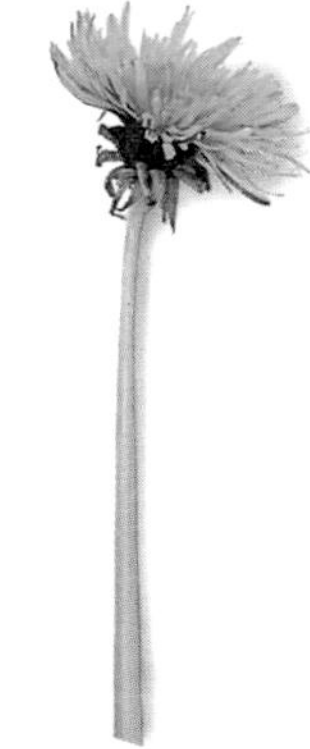

HEAD (CAPITULUM)
A highly modified inflorescence with many flowers (florets) massed together on a disc-like structure (involucre).

FLOWER FORMS

REGULAR FLOWERS

Technically called actinomorphic flowers, these have more than one plane of symmetry. The flower parts are all similar within each whorl, with even petals and even sepals and so on. There are, however, variations in the way the flower parts are arranged. Those of the Marsh Marigold (*Caltha palustris*, see p.60) are all separate from one another, while the Cowslip (*Primula veris*, see p.169) has the sepals and petals joined into two separate tubes, both of which are lobed at the top. Red Campion (*Silene dioica*, see p.53) has the sepals fused together into a tube, while the petals are separate with a long narrow claw that reaches down to the base of the calyx-tube.

MARSH MARIGOLD

COWSLIP

RED CAMPION

IRREGULAR FLOWERS

These are technically referred to as zygomorphic flowers and have a single plane of symmetry. Pea-flowers, like the Bush Vetch (*Vicia sepium*, see p.111), have sepals that are fused below into a short tube, while the petals (except for the basal two) are separate from one another. In the Foxglove (*Digitalis purpurea*, see p.224) the sepals are separate, while the petals are fused into a distinctive tube, so that it is impossible to distinguish the number of petals. Most members of the mint family, such as White Deadnettle (*Lamium album*, see p.202) for instance, have the petals fused into a two-lipped flower.

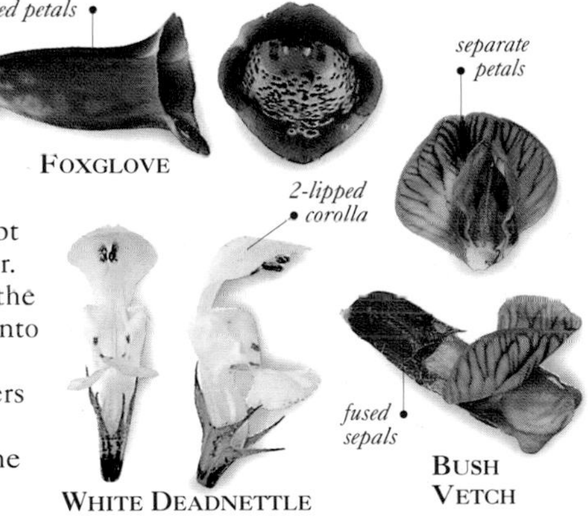

FOXGLOVE

WHITE DEADNETTLE

BUSH VETCH

MONOCOT FLOWERS

While they can be either regular or irregular, monocot flowers generally have a distinctive appearance. The parts are usually arranged in threes, whereas in dicots the parts most often occur in fours, fives, or more. In the Snowdrop (*Galanthus nivalis*, see p.292) there are three large outer petal-like sepals and three shorter inner petals. In the Flowering Rush (*Butomus umbellatus*, see p.278) the three sepals are shorter than the three larger and more conspicuous petals. Orchid flowers (see p.298) are more specialized, with three similar sepals and three petals; the upper two petals are small and inconspicuous, whereas the lower one forms a conspicuous lip.

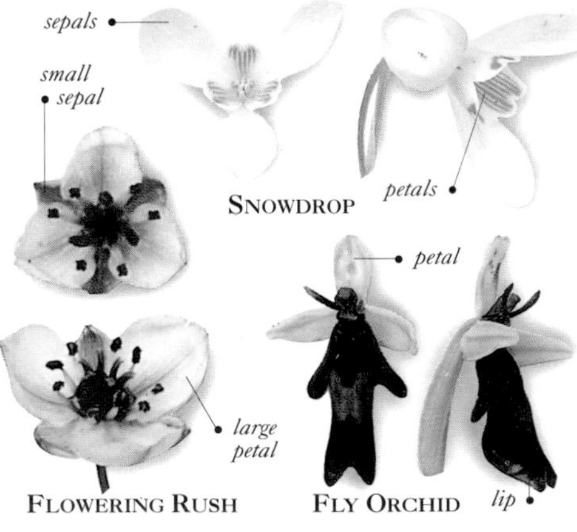

SNOWDROP

FLOWERING RUSH

FLY ORCHID

FRUIT TYPES

FRUITS RANGE from simple single-seeded organs to complex fleshy fruits or capsules containing the seeds in one or several chambers. Fruits can be adorned with feathery appendages, or hooks or spines, and may be smooth or lobed, hairless or hairy. They split in a variety of ways to expel the seeds. The fruit type is fundamental in identifying different genera and species.

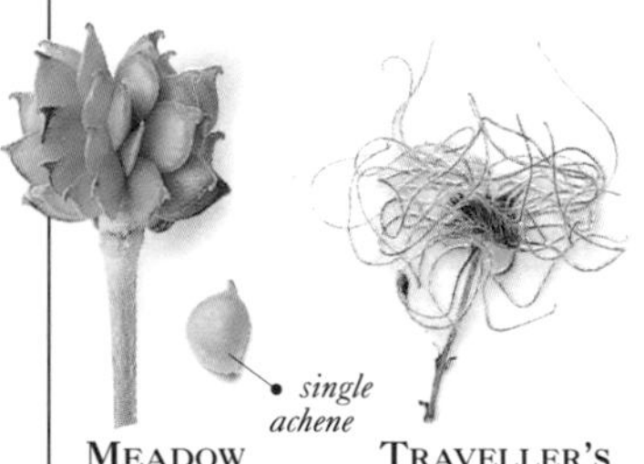

MEADOW BUTTERCUP

TRAVELLER'S JOY

HERB BENNET

◁ ACHENE

This is a single-seeded fruit that does not split when mature but falls away from the plant in a single piece. Achenes may be blunt or pointed, or adorned with a feathery or hooked style. They often occur clustered in heads, the product of a single flower. Achenes are perhaps the simplest type of fruit and are typical of plants such as the buttercups and geums.

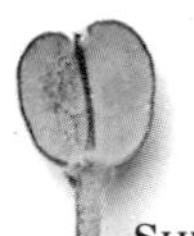

SHEPHERD'S PURSE

WILD CABBAGE

BROAD-LEAVED EVERLASTING-PEA

◁ POD OR LEGUME

The simplest pod consists of a single chamber with the seeds arranged along one margin. When ripe, the pod splits lengthwise into two to release the seeds.

LOMENTUM ▷

A pod that splits transversely into a number of similar single-seeded units when ripe. Lomentums are usually in clusters, each pod being the product of a single flower.

HORSESHOE VETCH

△ SILICULA AND ◁ SILIQUA

A fruit with two parallel chambers divided by a membrane (septum) and containing one or more seeds. The fruit usually splits lengthwise into two when ripe. Siliquas are narrow and much longer than they are broad; siliculas are short and scarcely longer than broad.

▽ CAPSULE

Basically consists of a vessel with one or several uniform compartments, often containing numerous seeds. Capsules split (dehisce) in various ways: some lengthwise into a number of valves, others along a cap or a ring of pores or slits at the base or at the top of the capsule.

COLUMBINE

◁ FOLLICLE

Consists of a series of pod-like structures that are joined together for part or all of their length. Each follicle splits lengthwise along one edge to expel the seeds. Follicles often occur in small clusters of 4 or 5, e.g. Columbine.

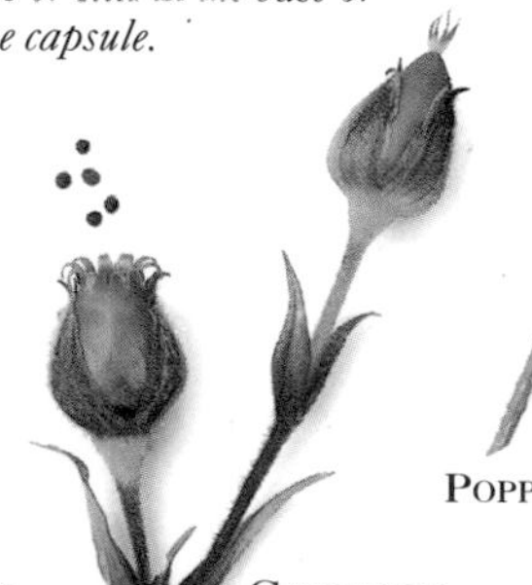

STINKING IRIS

CATCHFLY

POPPY

WHITE DEADNETTLE

◁ NUTLET
A single-seeded fruit with a hard, often woody, coat. It falls to the ground as a single unit when ripe. Labiates and borages usually have four nutlets inside each calyx.

HOGWEED

◁ MERICARP
Consists of a dry, single-seeded unit that splits away from a two- to several-seeded fruit. Mericarps are characteristic of certain families such as carrot and mallow.

BERRY ▷
Consists of a fleshy or succulent, non-dehiscent (non-splitting) fruit in which the woody coated seeds are embedded in the flesh of the fruit. Most berries are eaten by animals; only the fleshy part is digested, the seeds are not harmed.

BLACK BRYONY

DRUPELET ▷
A collection of small berry-like structures that each contain one seed and together form a fleshy fruit that is the product of a single flower, e.g. Raspberry.

RASPBERRY

SEED DISPERSAL

Seeds or fruits are dispersed in a variety of ways. Gravity, wind, animals (including humans), and water all play their role in the seed dispersal of different plants. Light seeds are more buoyant than large heavy ones and are likely to be carried greater distances by air currents. To disperse successfully seeds must reach the correct habitat in which the species can thrive. The success rate in most species is low, with relatively few seeds germinating and growing on to become mature plants.

EXPLOSIVE △
Some plants, such as Himalayan Balsam, have fruit capsules that split quite violently and elastically in order to fling the seeds, often for some distance, away from the parent plant.

MECHANICAL ▷
The seeds are simply knocked out of the fruit by disturbance or under the force of gravity. The poppy capsule acts like a pepper pot, spilling seeds out of pores close to the cap.

ANIMAL ▷
Some fruits and seeds have a sticky coat or barbed hooks that attach them to fur and clothing and so can be transported large distances before they finally work free or are brushed off.

INSECT ▷
Insects and small mammals often carry away the seeds or fruits of some species for food, and those that don't get eaten may eventually germinate.

WIND ▷
This is a prime agent in seed dispersal. The seeds of plants such as Dandelion have a light, feathery appendage (a pappus) that allows the wind to blow them off the plant and transport them effortlessly to new locations.

HABITATS

Any region will have a variety of different places (habitats) in which plants are able to grow, and each habitat generally has its own harmonious association of plants and animals. Some species may be restricted to one habitat type, while others can thrive in a variety of habitats. Temperature, rainfall, altitude, rock and soil types, and coastal or inland conditions, are all important factors in determining the types of plants to be found in a particular place.

DECIDUOUS WOODLAND

Broad-leaved deciduous trees, often of several species, are typical of the woodland of the Atlantic and central European regions. A well-developed shrub layer grows beneath the trees and, because light is good in the spring, many herbs flower on the woodland floor before the leaves of the trees fully develop. Different woodland types develop on different soils: beech, for example, on shallow alkaline soils, and pedunculate oak on heavy alkaline clays.

BLUEBELL

BLUEBELL WOOD
*Bluebells (*Scilla non-scripta, *see p.285) flower before the leaves of the trees cast deep shade.*

CONIFEROUS WOODLAND

At higher altitudes and in the northern Boreal and central European regions, needle-leaved, mostly evergreen, conifers form extensive woodland, in places mixed with some deciduous trees, particularly birch. Conifers are generally associated with extremely acid soils which are unsuitable for most other plants. In addition, these woods are dark and sombre so that the shrub and herbaceous floras are usually poor. Such conditions favour mosses and plants that live on dead organic matter.

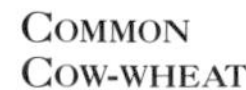

COMMON COW-WHEAT

POOR LIGHT
*Coniferous woods cast a permanent shade that only a few plants like Common Cow-wheat (*Melampyrum pratense, *see p.228) tolerate.*

SUMMER ABUNDANCE
*A medley of flowers such as Common Fleabane (*Pulicaria dysenterica, *see p.250) typify mature hedgerows, and are a boon to wildlife.*

HEDGEROW

Hedgerows are artificially created boundaries between fields and along roadsides and tracks. They often mark the limit of estates and plots, or were originally established to contain livestock. Because they present various aspects (face different directions, so they may have shaded, sunny, dry, or moist aspects) and exhibit different types of niche (conditions in which a plant thrives) they can support a wide variety of plants and small animals. Hedges also provide corridors and refugios along which both plants and animals can migrate. Young hedgerows generally have only a few principal plant species, whereas other hedgerows may be very ancient and are characterized by a richness of species. It is therefore possible to roughly estimate the age of hedgerows by the number of different woody plants that they contain.

COMMON FLEABANE

GRASSLAND

Essentially a very open habitat, much of Europe's grassland has been artificially created over the centuries. Modern grassland is poor in species due to farming practices, but ancient meadows used for hay production or grazing, where artificial fertilizers and herbicides have not been applied, can be rich and floriferous. The constituent elements of meadows are greatly influenced by soil type, rainfall, and altitude, so a marked difference often exists between the flora of mountain meadows and that of lowland ones.

BUZZING WITH LIFE
*Unspoilt meadows harbour a great variety of plants including Red Clover (*Trifolium pratense, *see p.120) and marsh orchids; they attract a wide variety of insects and small mammals.*

RED CLOVER

SIDE BY SIDE
*Common Poppy (*Papaver rhoeas, *see p.68) and crops can grow together if no herbicides are used.*

ARABLE

Arable land is an artificial habitat, but one in which certain wild plants are able to thrive. Thus a wheat field can also be a colourful blaze of red poppies, blue cornflowers, and yellow corn marigolds. Typical arable land plants are annuals, as the land is ploughed each year. Unfortunately, in many regions arable flowers have been severely reduced in recent years by the heavy and mostly unnecessary use of herbicides. Arable land can, if properly managed, provide an important habit for animals and plants, while allowing the farmer to produce a healthy crop at the same time.

COMMON POPPY

HEATH

This habitat is characteristic of areas close to the Atlantic Ocean where the natural woodland has been cleared by man, and extensive communities of Gorse and ericaceous plants, like Heather and Bilberry, have developed. Heaths are primarily formed on acid soils where there is a very heavy rainfall. They are maintained by grazing and burning, as well as by the continued clearance of young trees. Left to itself, heathland would return to woodland.

HEATHER

HEATHLAND
*Ericaceous shrubs like Heather (*Calluna vulgaris, *see p.166) are typical heath flora.*

FENS, BOGS, AND MARSHES

Marshes develop on ground that is seasonally or permanently wet but not peaty. Fens, on the other hand, are peaty and usually form where the drainage water is rich in calcium and minerals. In contrast, communities on wet acid peats are called bogs. In the north of the region, where peat forms on the surface just above the water level, very extensive mires have developed. Each of these types of landscape is variable and they sometimes merge into one another. Modern farming, especially land-drainage, has severely reduced these habitats.

BUTTERBUR

WET HABITATS
*Butterbur (*Petasites hybridus, *see p.258) is one of a host of moisture-loving plants that colonize and thrive in wet situations.*

GOLDEN SAMPHIRE

SALT MARSHES
*Golden Samphire (*Inula crithmoides, *see. p 249) competes with other salt-tolerant plants on mudflats.*

SAND DUNES
*Sea Holly (*Eryngium maritimium, *see p.151) often grows alongside Marram Grass.*

COASTAL

Coastal habitats are very exposed to wind and to salt spray, yet they can be surprisingly dry. Sand dunes and shingle are essentially inhospitable and unstable environments. Sand dunes, for example, shift in the wind, although they can be anchored by grasses and other plants (Marram Grass is often used to stabilize them). Despite the harsh conditions, dunes and shingle can harbour a surprising number of specialized plants. The same is true of extensive salt marshes or mudflats close to the sea or along river estuaries. Coastal cliffs form another habitat type that has its own unique associations of plants.

ALPINE

Mountains provide a wide variety of habitats in which a number of highly specialized plant communities have successfully developed. All the usual habitats are present, such as woodland, meadows, hedgerows, lakes, and rivers, as well as alpine fens and heaths. The most specialized plant communities are found above the tree line, where there are often extensive areas of rocky meadows, stream margins, and snow hollows, and where the mountains provide large areas of exposed rocks, screes, moraines, and cliffs.

BIRD'S-EYE PRIMROSE

MOUNTAIN FLORAS
*At altitude plants are usually sparse but can form unique communities of alpine species, e.g. Bird's-eye Primrose (*see p.170*) or Alpine Pasque-flower.*

FINDING AND OBSERVING

THE ONLY EFFECTIVE WAY to learn the various features of the plants you come across in the countryside is by careful observation and by reference to a good identification guide. Diligent searching will often reward you with new or rare plants and will reveal the natural variations present in all plant species. Notes on the colour, size, and shape of the flowers, leaves, and fruit of each plant you see and a description of the habitat in which they are growing will soon build into useful records that can be added to year after year.

PRESERVATION

Even when you find a rich community of plants, like these oxlips, you should never dig wild flowers up, and should only pick one if absolutely essential; in this way they will remain for others to enjoy. A good rule to follow when trying to identify a flower is to take the book to the plant and not the plant to the book.

BASIC EQUIPMENT

You only need a minimal amount of equipment to identify and record the plants you find in the wild.

CONSERVATION AND THE LAW

Many plants are protected and to dig them up is an offence punishable by law. Some countries, such as Britain, prohibit the removal of any plants from the wild. In the light of increased habitat destruction, such laws are necessary to protect wild plants from humans. The Lady's Slipper Orchid, *Cypripedium calceolus* (right), is now confined to a single colony in Britain where it is closely guarded; it is a threatened species in most of Europe.

IDENTIFICATION KEY

THIS KEY is designed to enable you to identify a species or group of closely allied species by means of a series of simple questions about the visual characteristics of the flowers and fruit. The final lists are illustrated with a representative flower and direct you to the relevant pages in the main part of the book, where detailed information allows confirmation of the identification.

DICOTYLEDON OR MONOCOTYLEDON?

DICOTYLEDONS

Dicotyledons (dicots) are the major group of flowering plants and have seedlings with two seed leaves (cotyledons) above or below ground. The leaves have a network of secondary veins. The flowers vary in shape and construction but mostly have distinct sepals and petals, often in fours, fives, sevens, or more, occasionally less. The stems of dicots have continuous rings of vessels.

see below

MONOCOTYLEDONS

Monocotyledons (monocots) are a smaller group that is characterized by plants with a single seed leaf (cotyledon). The leaves have parallel veins without a network of secondary veins. The flower parts are usually in multiples of three; the perianth may or may not be divisible into distinct sepals and petals. The stem vessels are in discrete bundles scattered throughout the stem, or towards its perimeter.

see pp.32–33

DICOTYLEDONS

COROLLA SPURRED

Aconitum **61**
Aquilegia **68**
Corydalis **71–2**
Fumaria **72**
Impatiens **135–36**
Viola odorata **143**
Viola **144**
Viola arvensis **145**
Misopates, Linaria **221–22**
Kickxia, Cymbalaria, Erinus **223**
Centranthus **237**

COROLLA NOT SPURRED

AGGREGATED FLOWERS

see pp.26–27

PETALS FREE

see pp.28–29

PETALS FUSED OR PARTLY FUSED

see pp.30–31

AGGREGATED

FLOWERS TINY, OFTEN IN

SPIKES,

PANICLES,

OR CATKINS

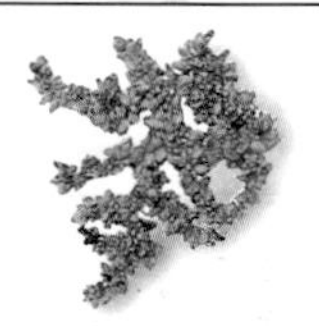

Humulus, Urtica, Viscum **34–35**
Polygonum, Fallopia, Oxyria, Rumex, Beta, Chenopodium, Halimione, Atriplex, Salicornia, Suaeda, Salsola **36–45**
Mercurialis **132**
Plantago **233–34**

FLOWERS IN UMBELS

Euphorbia **132–34**
Hedera, Sanicula **150**
Astrantia, Chaerophyllum, Anthriscus, Myrrhis, Smyrnium, Conopodium, Pimpinella, Aegopodium, Crithmum, Seseli, Oenanthe, Foeniculum, Bupleurum, Conium, Apium, Sison, Levisticum, Angelica, Heracleum, Aethusa, Pastinaca, Torilis, Daucus **152–63**

STAMENS FREE AND OBVIOUS

Detail

Eryngium **151**,
Dipsacus, Succisa, Scabiosa, Knautia **238–40**
Jasione **243**

THISTLE-LIKE

Carlina **262**
Serratula, Carduus, Cirsium, Onopordon **263–67**
Silybum **270**

CORNFLOWER-LIKE

Centaurea **268–69**

AGGREGATED

FLOWERS IN DISTINCT HEADS

FLOWERS IN CLUSTERS

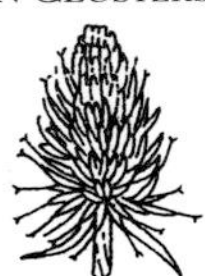

STAMENS FUSED AND PARTLY HIDDEN

DAISY-LIKE

DANDELION-LIKE

RAYLESS

Solidago, Bellis, Aster, Erigeron, Conyza **245–48**
Inula crithmoides **249**
Antennaria, Pulicaria, Bidens, Anthemis, Achillea **250–53**
Matricaria, Chamomilla **254**
Tanacetum parthenium **255**
Leucanthemum, Chrysanthemum **256–57**

Petasites, Tussilago, Doronicum **258–59**
Senecio squalidus **260**
Senecio jacobaea **261**

Cichorium, Tragopogon, Hypochoeris, Sonchus, Lactuca, Taraxacum, Lapsana, Picris, Crepis, Pilosella, Hieracium **270–76**

Phyteuma **243**

Eupatorium **244**
Inula conyza **249**
Bidens **251**
Otanthus **253**
Tanacetum vulgare **255**
Artemisia **257**
Senecio vulgaris **260**
Arctium **262**

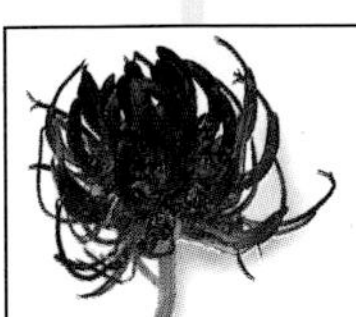

PETALS FREE

PETALS 2 (NOT MONOCOTS)

Circaea **147**

PETALS 4

APPARENTLY NO SEPALS

Clematis **63**
Chrysosplenium **97**
Sanguisorba **101**

SEPALS 2

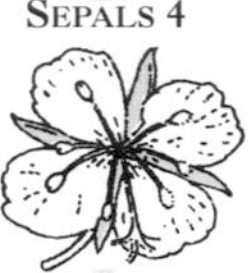

Papaveraceae
(Poppy Family) **69–71**

SEPALS 4

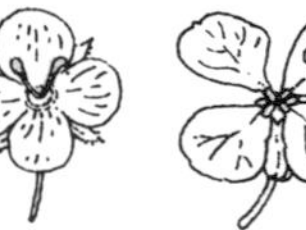

STAMENS 2 TO 4

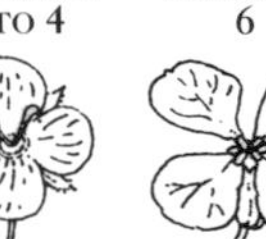

Alchemilla **106**
Veronica **225–27**

STAMENS 6

Cruciferae
(Cress Family) **73–91**

STAMENS 8 OR MORE

Rhodiola **95**
Potentilla erecta **105**
Oenothera, Chamerion, Epilobium **148–49**
Vaccinium **167**
Adoxa **235**

APPARENTLY NO SEPALS

Helleborus **58**
Nigella **59**
Caltha **60**

Montia, Arenaria, Moehringia, Honkenya, Stellaria, Cerastium, Spergula, Spergularia **46–9**
Ranunculus **64–5**
Ranunculus

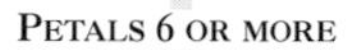

PETALS FREE

PETALS 5

PETALS 6 OR MORE

SEPALS PRESENT

TERRESTRIAL PLANTS

WATER PLANTS

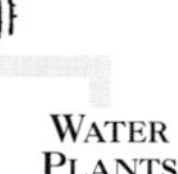

SEPALS JOINED AT LEAST HALFWAY

SEPALS FREE OR ALMOST FREE

PEAFLOWERS

NON-PEAFLOWERS

NO EPICALYX

EPICALYX

Leguminosae (Pea Family) **107–24**

Lychnis, Agrostemma, Silene, Saponaria, Petrorhagia, Dianthus **50–6** Lythrum **147**

Potentilla **103–04** Potentilla rupestris **105** Fragaria **106** Malva, Althaea, Lavatera **137–39** Geum **102–03**

Nymphaea, Nuphar **57**

sceleratus **66** Ranunculus, Myosurus **67** Sedum, Rhodiola, Saxifraga **94–7** Parnassia, Filipendula, Rubus, Agrimonia **98–101**

Oxalis, Geranium **125–29** Erodium, Limun **130–31** Hypericum, Viola, Helianthemum, Bryonia **141–46** Pyrola **164** Sambucus **236**

Lysimachia **171** Reseda, Drosera **92–3** Anagallis **172**

Carpobrotus **45** Eranthis **59** Trollius **60** Anemone **62**

Pulsatilla **62** Adonis **63–4** Ranunculus ficaria **66** Mahonia **68** Dryas **102** Lythrum **147** Reseda, Drosera **92–3**

Petals Fused or Partly Fused

Flowers 1- to 2-lipped

Corolla 1-lipped

Aristolochia **36**
Polygala **135**
Ajuga **196**
Teucrium **197**

Corolla 2-lipped

Fruit 4 Nutlets

Echium **188**
Melittis, Marrubium, Galeopsis, Scutellaria, Ballota, Lamiastrum, Lamium, Stachys, Glechoma, Prunella, Melissa, Acinos, Clinopodium, Lycopus, Calamintha, Origanum, Thymus, Mentha, Salvia **198–213**

Fruit a Capsule

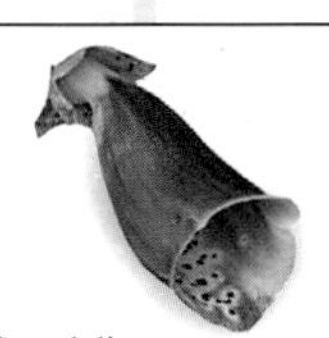

Corydalis, Fumaria **71–2**
Mimulus, Scrophularia, Antirrhinum, Misopates, Linaria, Kickxia, Cymbalaria, Erinus, Digitalis **219–24**
Melampyrum, Parentucellia, Odontites, Euphrasia, Pedicularis, Rhinanthus, Lathraea, Orobanche, Pinguicula **228–33**

Fruit a Berry

Lonicera **235**

Flowers Trumpet or Funnel-shaped

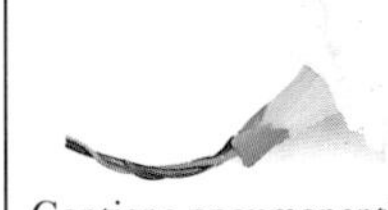

Gentiana pneumonanthe **176**
Calystegia, Convolvulus **185–86**
Buglossoides **187**
Datura, Gratiola **216**

PETALS FUSED OR PARTLY FUSED

FLOWERS NOT LIPPED

FLOWERS WITH A SPREADING LIMB, WITH OR WITHOUT A TUBE

FLOWERS TUBULAR OR BELL-SHAPED

COROLLA FRINGED (WATER PLANTS)

COROLLA NOT FRINGED (TERRESTRIAL PLANTS)

COROLLA WITHOUT A TUBE

COROLLA WITH A TUBE

Menyanthes,
Nymphoides **178**

Cyclamen,
Lysimachia **170–71**
Borago **192**
Solanum **215**
Verbascum **217–18**

Asarum **35**
Umbilicus **93**
Erica, Calluna,
Daboecia,
Arctostaphylos,
Vaccinium **164–8**
Glaux **172**
Gentiana **175**
Echium, Cerinthe,
Pulmonaria,
Symphytum **188–90**
Mentha **210–11**
Atropa,
Hyoscyamus **214**
Campanula **241–42**

Daphne **140**
Primula **169–70**
Armeria, Limonium,
Centaurium **173–74**
Gentiana verna **176**
Gentiana,
Blackstonia **177**
Vinca, Vincetoxicum,
Sherardia, Asperula,
Galium, Cruciata,
Rubia, Polemonium,
Cuscuta **179–184**
Lithospermum **187**
Anchusa,
Pentaglottis **191–92**
Myosotis, Lappula,
Omphalodes,
Cynoglossum,

Verbena **193–96**
Valeriana,
Centranthus **236–37**

MONOCOTYLEDONS

LEAVES HEART-SHAPED

FLOWERS CONSPICUOUS

FLOWERS WITHOUT LIP OR SPUR

SEPALS 3 OR 4, PETALS 3 OR 4

STAMENS 3

OVARY BELOW PETALS, SEPALS AND PETALS FREE

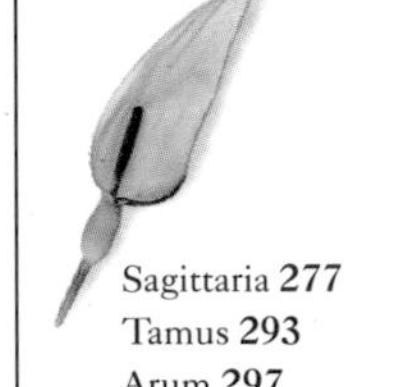

Sagittaria **277**
Tamus **293**
Arum **297**

Alisma, Butomus, Hydrocharis, **278–79**
Paris **290**

Iris, Crocosmia **294–96**

Leucojum, Galanthus, Narcissus **291–93**

MONOCOTYLEDONS

LEAVES OVAL TO LINEAR

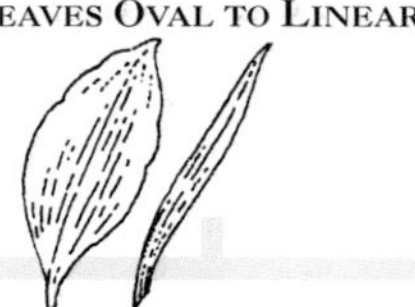

FLOWERS MINUTE, OFTEN IN DENSE SPIKES

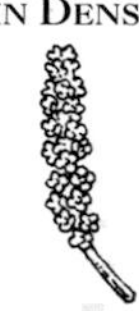

FLOWERS WITH LIP AND/OR SPUR

SEPALS AND PETALS SIMILAR

STAMENS 6

OVARY ABOVE PETALS, SEPALS AND PETALS FREE

OVARY ABOVE PETALS, SEPALS AND PETALS JOINED

Narthecium, Anthericum, Colchicum, Fritillaria, Ornithogalum, Tulipa, Scilla **280–84**
Scilla verna **285**
Allium **287–88**

Scilla non-scripta **285**
Muscari **286**
Convallaria, Polygonatum **289**

Orchidaceae (Orchid family) **298–307**

Aponogeton, Potamogeton **279–80**
Ruscus **290**
Sparganium **296**
Typha **297**

DICOTYLEDONS

HEMP FAMILY

Family CANNABACEAE	Species *Humulus lupulus*	Author L.

HOP

This is a climbing, rough-haired plant. The leaves have 3 to 5 coarsely toothed lobes. Male and female flowers are on separate plants: the male are green, 4–5mm (⅙–⅕in) long, in loose pendent panicles, the female pale green in pendent, cone-like clusters. The ripe fruit, 25–30mm (1–1⅕in) long, is pale brown.

• **DISTRIBUTION** S. Britain and most of mainland Europe, except for the far north.

• **HABITAT** Hedgerows, woodland margins, scrub, old walls, abandoned cultivation, fen carrs.

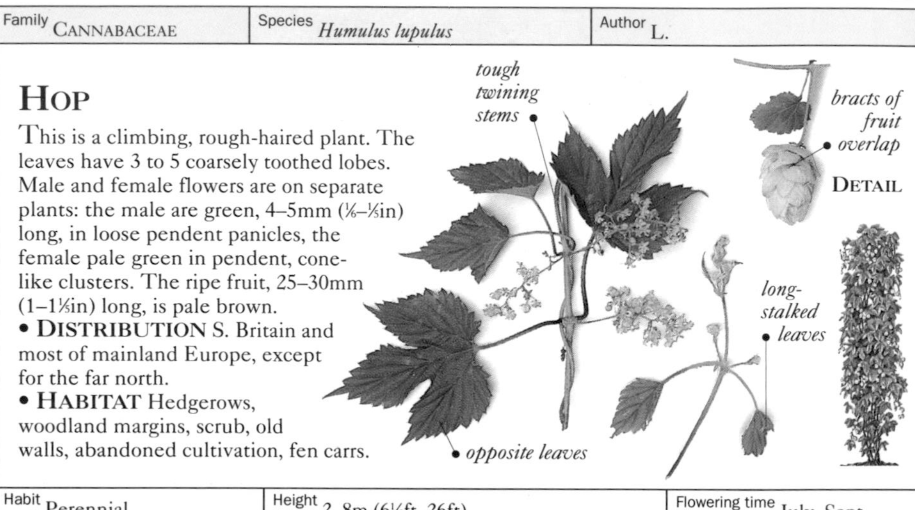

Habit Perennial	Height 2–8m (6½ft–26ft)	Flowering time July–Sept

NETTLE FAMILY

Family URTICACEAE	Species *Urtica dioica*	Author L.

STINGING NETTLE

Also called Common Nettle, this plant has stinging hairs on the stems and leaves; the stems are branched or unbranched, with vigorous basal stolons. The leaves are lanceolate to heart-shaped. The 4- to 5-parted male and female flowers are borne on separate plants; the male are in long, pendent, catkin-like spikes, while the female are in small clusters. The fruit is a small achene.

• **DISTRIBUTION** Throughout the region, except for Spitsbergen.

• **HABITAT** Meadows, fields, cultivated and waste land, roadsides, woodland, scrub, and farmyards, especially on phosphate-rich soils.

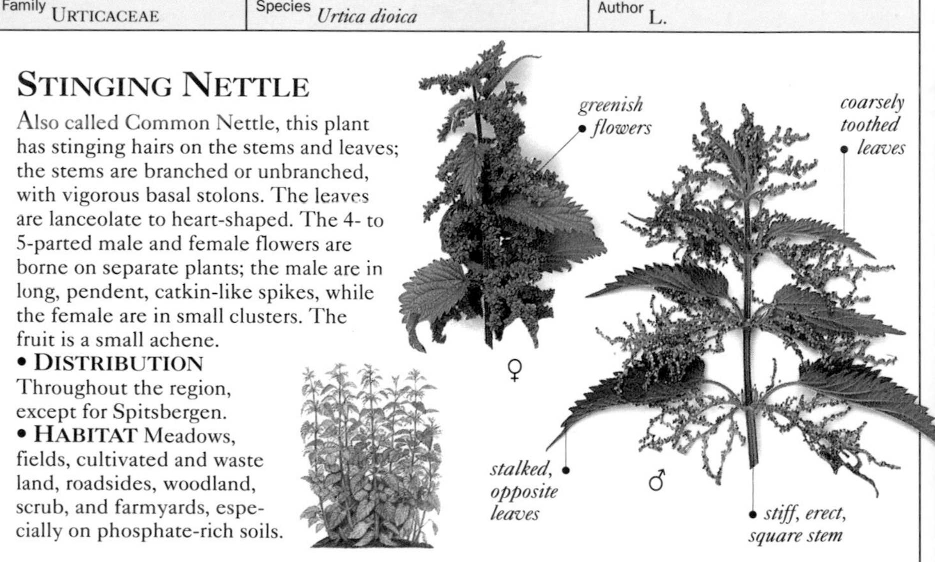

Habit Perennial	Height 50–150cm (20–60in)	Flowering time June–Sept

MISTLETOE FAMILY

Family LORANTHACEAE	Species *Viscum album*	Author L.

MISTLETOE

This semi-parasitic evergreen forms rounded masses. The stems are jointed at the nodes. The yellowish green leaves, 20–80mm (⅘–3⅕in) long, are broadest above the middle and untoothed. Small green flowers are borne in tiny clusters at the shoot tips, with male and female on separate plants. Male flowers have 4 petals and 4 anthers; females have 4 sepals, 4 petals, and a one-celled ovary. The berries are 6–10mm (¼–⅖in) across.

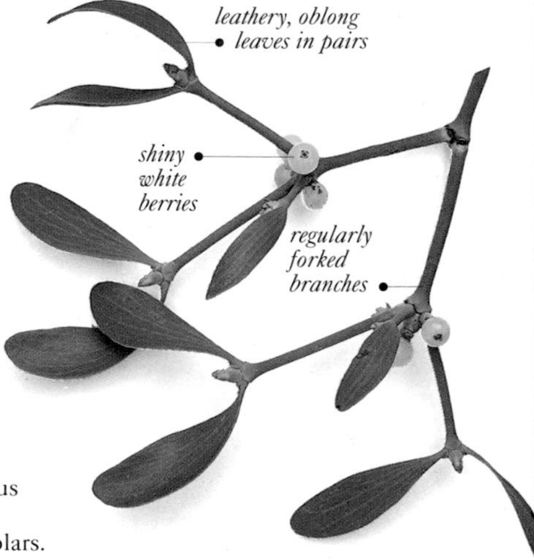

• **DISTRIBUTION** Throughout, except for Ireland and the far north; naturalized in Scotland.

• **HABITAT** On deciduous trees, especially apples, hawthorns, limes, and poplars.

Habit Shrub	Height Up to 2m (6½ft)	Flowering time Feb–Apr

BIRTHWORT FAMILY

Family ARISTOLOCHIACEAE	Species *Asarum europaeum*	Author L.

ASARABACCA

This patch-forming evergreen has rhizomes that creep on the surface of the soil and root down. The scaly stems, up to 10cm (4in) in length, usually bear one pair of leaves. The leaves, 2.5–10cm (1–4in) across, are firm, untoothed, and grow on long hairy stalks. Hidden below the leaves, the solitary, terminal flowers are nodding and purplish brown, with 12 stamens. The petals are not differentiated. The fruit, a small, many-seeded capsule, splits irregularly when ripe.

• **DISTRIBUTION** Throughout, except for Ireland and the far north.

• **HABITAT** Moist, shaded places in woodland, especially under deciduous trees. Sometimes in gardens.

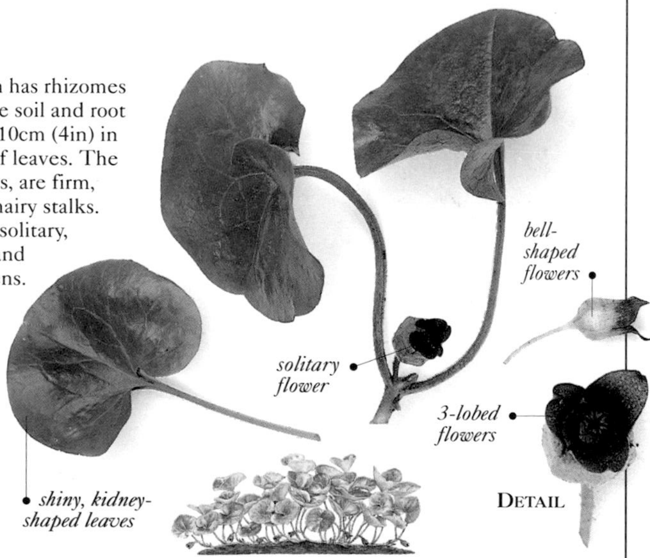

Habit Perennial	Height 5–15cm (2–6in)	Flowering time Mar–Aug

Family ARISTOLOCHIACEAE	Species *Aristolochia clematitis*	Author L.

BIRTHWORT

Birthwort is a herbaceous plant with spreading underground rhizomes. Usually unbranched, the stems are erect and smooth or slightly ridged. The alternate leaves, 3–15cm (1⅕–6in) long, are blunt, untoothed, and hairless, with stalks up to 50mm (2in) long. The yellow flowers, 20–30mm (⅘–1⅕in) long, have a brownish limb and form small clusters of up to 8 in the leaf-axils. The fruit capsule, 2–5cm (⅘–2in) long, varies from egg-shaped to pear-shaped, and splits apart when ripe.

• **DISTRIBUTION** Naturalized throughout the region, except for Ireland and the far north. Native to E. and S.E. Europe.

• **HABITAT** Rough ground, waste places, scrub, and abandoned cultivation.

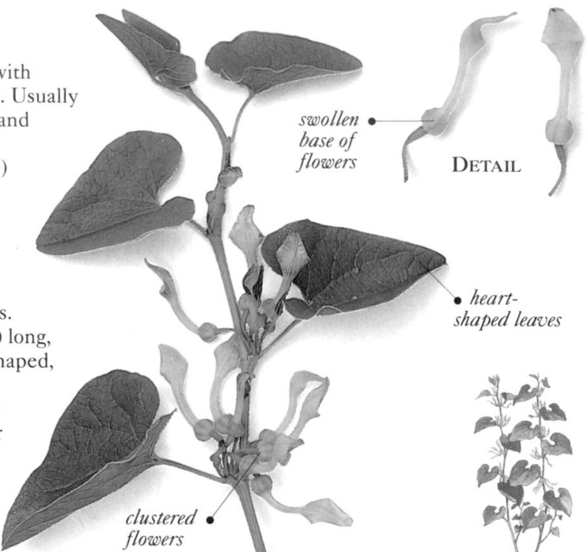

Habit Perennial	Height 60–100cm (24–40in)	Flowering time June–Sept

DOCK FAMILY

Family POLYGONACEAE	Species *Persicaria bistorta*	Author (L.) Samp.

COMMON BISTORT

Also known as *Polygonum bistorta*, this hairless, herbaceous plant spreads by stout underground rhizomes. The stems are thin, erect, and unbranched. The leaves are 5–15cm (2–6in) long, alternate, and hairless. Only the lower leaves have winged stalks; the upper leaves are smaller and more triangular in shape. The small pink flowers are aggregated into dense terminal clusters and have 5 petals and 8 stamens. The fruit is a small, one-seeded, triangular nut.

• **DISTRIBUTION** Throughout the region, but probably only naturalized in S. Britain and Ireland.

• **HABITAT** Damp grassy places, particularly old meadows and pastures, and occasionally along road verges or in open woodland; often grown in gardens.

Habit Perennial	Height 20–100cm (8–40in)	Flowering time June–Oct

Family POLYGONACEAE	Species *Persicaria maculosa*	Author Gray

REDSHANK

Also known as *Polygonum persicaria*, this stout plant has erect to somewhat spreading stems. The leaves are lanceolate, up to 15cm (6in) long and, although usually glabrous, are sometimes finely downy on the underside; the upper surface often has a conspicuous blackish blotch. The pale to deep pink flowers are small but are borne in short, dense spikes; each flower usually has 5 petals and 8 stamens. The fruit, 2–3mm ($\frac{1}{12}$–$\frac{1}{8}$in) across, is a shiny black achene.

• **DISTRIBUTION** Throughout.
• **HABITAT** Bare, waste, and cultivated ground; often a weed of arable land, and often near water.
• **RELATED SPECIES** *Persicaria lapathifolia*, Pale Persicaria, has unblotched leaves and green-white, glandular petals. It grows in similar habitats throughout.

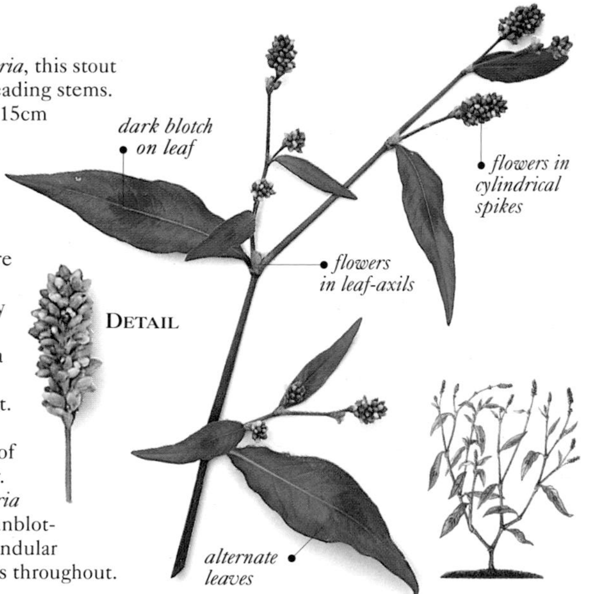
dark blotch on leaf
flowers in cylindrical spikes
DETAIL
flowers in leaf-axils
alternate leaves

Habit Perennial	Height 20–80cm (8–32in)	Flowering time June–Oct

Family POLYGONACEAE	Species *Polygonum aviculare*	Author L.

KNOTGRASS

This variable plant can have erect, spreading, or sometimes scrambling, branched stems. The leaves, up to 50mm (2in) long, are lanceolate to oval, narrowed at the base, untoothed, and glabrous; those on the main stem are much larger than those on the lateral branches. The silvery ochreae at the leaf bases are faintly veined and have a rather ragged edge. The small, whitish, pinkish, or greenish flowers are solitary, or in small clusters; each flower has 8 stamens. The fruit is a small, dull, pitted achene.

• **DISTRIBUTION** Throughout.
• **HABITAT** Cultivated, bare, and waste ground, roadsides, and seashores.
• **RELATED SPECIES** *Polygonum boreale*, Northern Knotgrass, has leaves broadest above the middle, with the leaf-stalk extending beyond the ochrea. It grows in N. Britain, the Shetland Islands, and Scandinavia.

alternate leaves
flowers at leaf-axils
DETAIL
flowers with a 5-lobed perianth
stipule-like ochrea

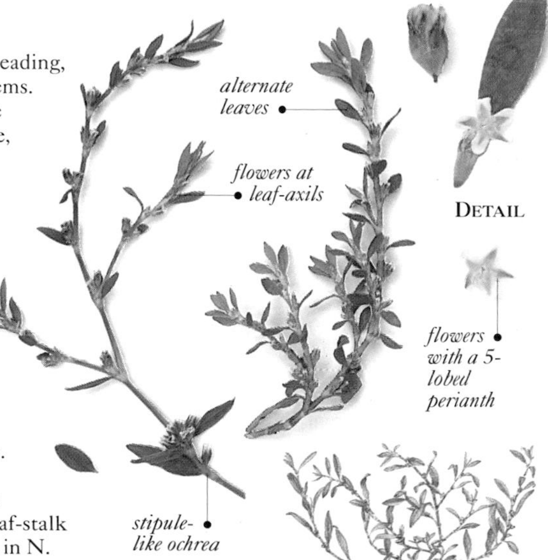

Habit Annual	Height 10–70cm (4–28in)	Flowering time June–Nov

Family POLYGONACEAE	Species *Persicaria hydropiper*	Author (L.) Spach

WATER-PEPPER

Also known as *Polygonum hydropiper*, this hairless plant has spreading to erect stems. It has a hot, peppery taste when chewed. The alternate leaves are lanceolate and pointed, untoothed, and scarcely stalked; the ochrea is brown and fringed. The small flowers, 3–4mm ($\frac{1}{8}$–$\frac{1}{6}$in) across, are pink or occasionally greenish white, and are borne in slender spikes which often nod at the tip; the perianth is 5-parted and dotted with glands. The fruit is a small, dull brown nutlet.

• **DISTRIBUTION** Throughout, except for the Faeroes, Iceland, and Spitsbergen.

• **HABITAT** Damp sites, meadows, marshes, or shallow water; often in shaded places.

• **RELATED SPECIES** *Persicaria laxiflora* (syn. *Polygonum mite*), Tasteless Water-pepper, is a tasteless plant with non-glandular flowers and shiny black nutlets. Its habitats and distribution are similar to Water-pepper's, but it is absent from much of Scandinavia.

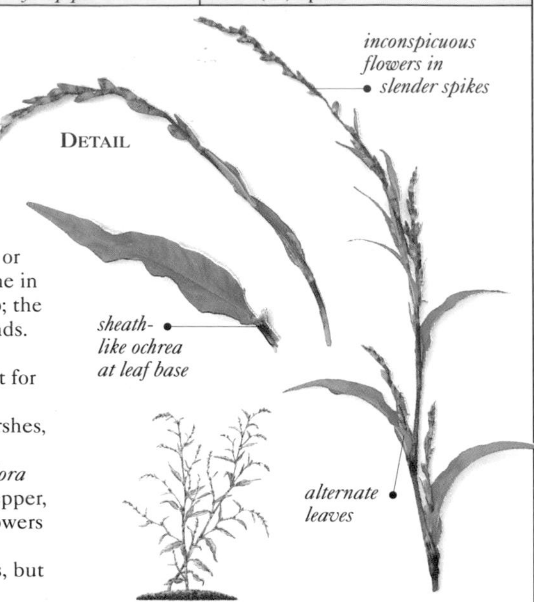

Habit Annual	Height 30–75cm (12–30in)	Flowering time June–Sept

Family POLYGONACEAE	Species *Fallopia convolvulus*	Author (L.) A. Löve

BLACK BINDWEED

Also known as *Polygonum convolvulus*, this finely hairy plant has slender, twining, sometimes trailing, stems. The leaves are alternate, mealy beneath, untoothed, and have a blunt or rather pointed apex and a slender stalk. Borne in loose, slightly leafy spikes at the leaf-axils, the small greenish white or greenish pink flowers, only 1–2mm ($\frac{1}{25}$–$\frac{1}{12}$in) across, have 5 winged perianth segments. The fruit, 4–7mm ($\frac{1}{6}$–$\frac{2}{9}$in) long, is clustered and short-stalked, containing dull black triangular nutlets.

• **DISTRIBUTION** Common almost throughout, apart from Spitsbergen.

• **HABITAT** Cultivated, especially arable, land; roadsides, waste ground, and rubbish tips.

• **RELATED SPECIES** *Fallopia aubertii*, Russian Vine, is a much taller woody perennial with denser, white flowers. It is widely naturalized; native to C. Asia.

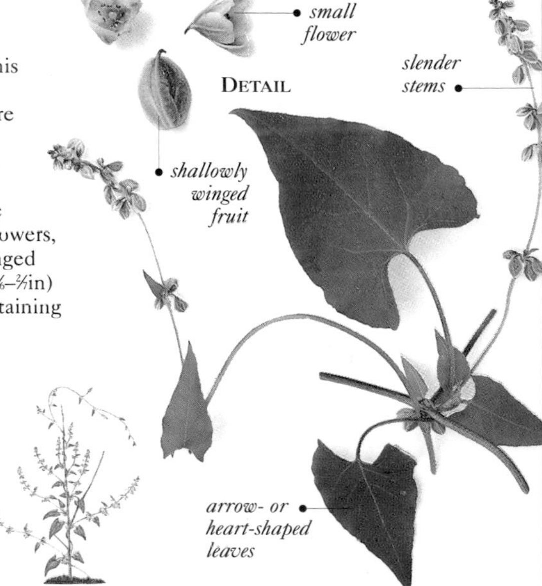

Habit Annual	Height Up to 1.5m (5ft)	Flowering time July–Oct

Family POLYGONACEAE	Species *Oxyria digyna*	Author (L.) Hill

MOUNTAIN SORREL

Most of the leaves of this hairless, herbaceous plant are borne in a basal tuft. The stems are erect and solitary or grouped together, but have few branches. The untoothed leaves, up to 30mm (1⅕in) across, are deep green, with long, slender stems. The greenish flowers are borne in branched racemes that elongate as the fruit develops. The 4 petals are sepal-like, the inner 2 enlarging in fruit; there are 6 stamens. The fruit, 3–4mm (⅛–⅙in) long, is a 2-sided, winged achene.

• **DISTRIBUTION** The mountains of the region, but not C. or S. Britain, and rare in Ireland.

• **HABITAT** Damp rocky mountain habitats, especially on granitic rocks, by streamsides; occasionally at lower altitudes where it has been washed down by a stream.

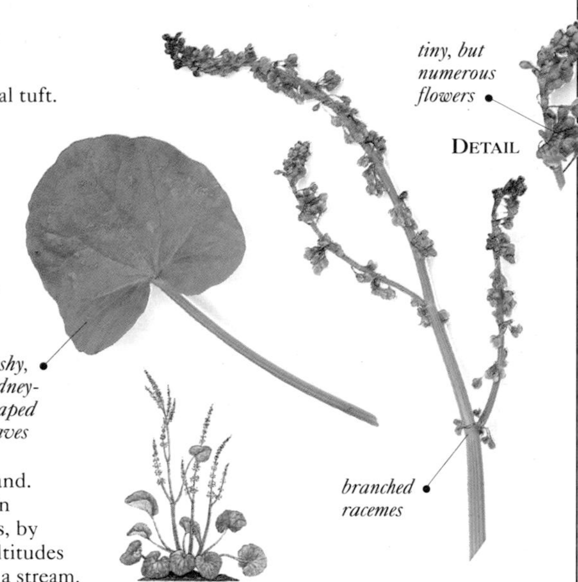

Habit Perennial	Height 10–30cm (4–12in)	Flowering time June–Aug

Family POLYGONACEAE	Species *Rumex acetosella*	Author L.

SHEEP'S SORREL

This very variable, hairless plant has slender, spreading to erect stems. The acid-tasting leaves are linear to oblong, untoothed, and mostly 10–40mm (⅖–1⅗in) long, with a pair of spreading or forward-pointing basal lobes. The tiny greenish flowers are unisexual, with male and female flowers borne on separate plants. Male flowers have 3 sepals, 3 petals, and 6 stamens; female flowers are similar but have an ovary in the centre and no stamens. The fruit, to 1.5mm (1/16in) long, is a triangular achene.

• **DISTRIBUTION** Throughout.

• **HABITAT** Dry meadows and other grassy places, bare ground, open heathy sites, coastal sands; mainly well-drained, acid soils.

• **RELATED SPECIES** *Rumex tenuifolius* has narrower leaves; stem-leaves are no more than 2mm (1/12in) wide. It inhabits dry, sandy places throughout.

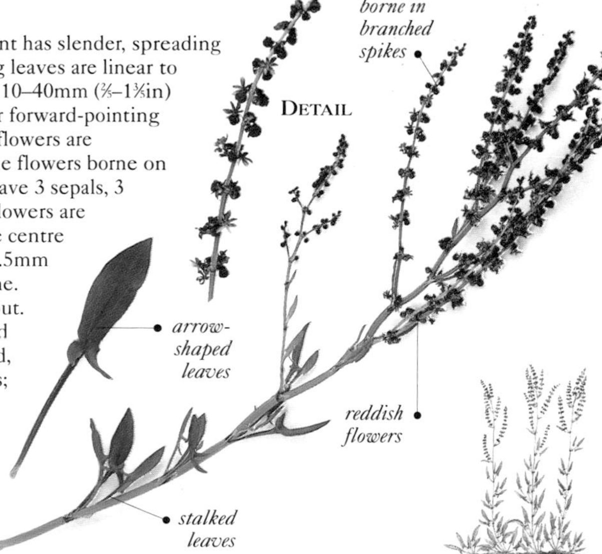

Habit Perennial	Height 5–30cm (2–12in)	Flowering time May–Aug

Family POLYGONACEAE	Species *Rumex crispus*	Author L.

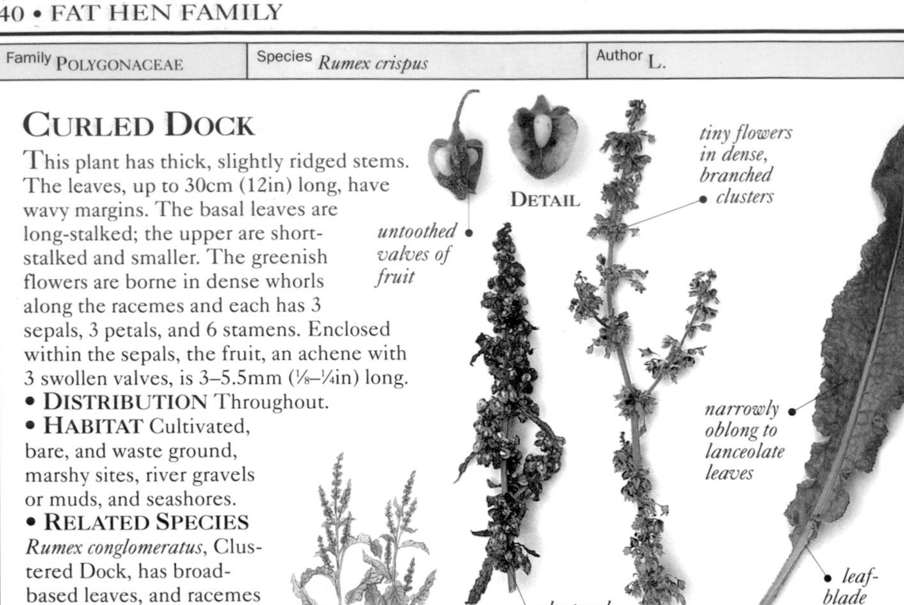

CURLED DOCK

This plant has thick, slightly ridged stems. The leaves, up to 30cm (12in) long, have wavy margins. The basal leaves are long-stalked; the upper are short-stalked and smaller. The greenish flowers are borne in dense whorls along the racemes and each has 3 sepals, 3 petals, and 6 stamens. Enclosed within the sepals, the fruit, an achene with 3 swollen valves, is 3–5.5mm (⅛–¼in) long.

• **DISTRIBUTION** Throughout.

• **HABITAT** Cultivated, bare, and waste ground, marshy sites, river gravels or muds, and seashores.

• **RELATED SPECIES** *Rumex conglomeratus*, Clustered Dock, has broad-based leaves, and racemes that are leafy almost to the top. It grows throughout.

Habit Perennial	Height 30–150cm (12–60in)	Flowering time June–Oct

FAT HEN FAMILY

Family CHENOPODIACEAE	Species *Beta vulgaris*	Author L.

SEA BEET

Also known as *Beta maritima*, this hairless plant is often red-tinged. The stems are spreading to erect and usually branched. The leaves are slightly fleshy and oval to lanceolate; the lower leaves are larger and often have a heart-shaped base. Borne in small clusters in branched spikes, the green or purplish red flowers have a perianth of 5 sepal-like segments, and 5 stamens. The fruit has corky, swollen, perianth segments.

• **DISTRIBUTION** Throughout, except for the far north.

• **HABITAT** Coastal shingle beaches, dry salt marshes, and occasionally old sea walls or grassy embankments.

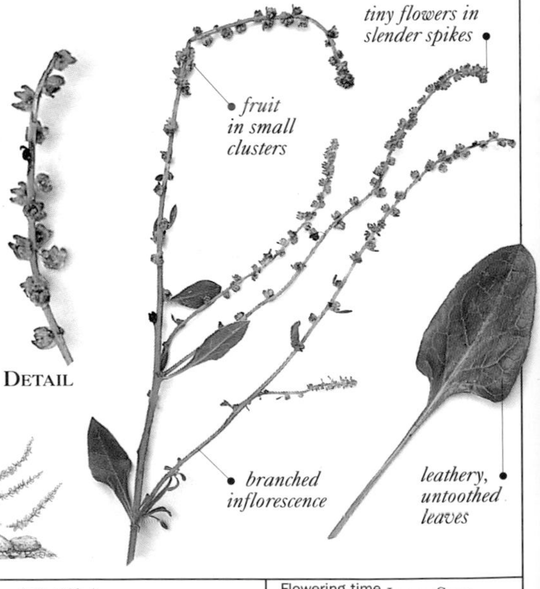

DETAIL

tiny flowers in slender spikes

fruit in small clusters

branched inflorescence

leathery, untoothed leaves

Habit Annual or perennial	Height 30–150cm (12–60in)	Flowering time June–Sept

Family CHENOPODIACEAE	Species *Chenopodium bonus-henricus*	Author L.

GOOD KING HENRY

This rather variable plant is mealy when young. The stems and leaves are often flushed with red. The alternate leaves are somewhat fleshy, triangular to diamond-shaped with a wavy or lobed margin, and untoothed or with only a few marginal teeth; the lowermost leaves are long-stalked, while the upper are short-stalked. The small flowers are green, although often flushed with pink or red, and are borne in dense, branched spikes; the 3 to 5 tepals are fused to about halfway; the stamens usually number 4 or 5. The fruit has one small seed and is surrounded by the persistent tepals.
• **DISTRIBUTION** Throughout the region, except for the far north.
• **HABITAT** Cultivated, bare, and waste ground, fields, hedgerows, farmyards, and roadsides; often on nitrogen-rich soils.

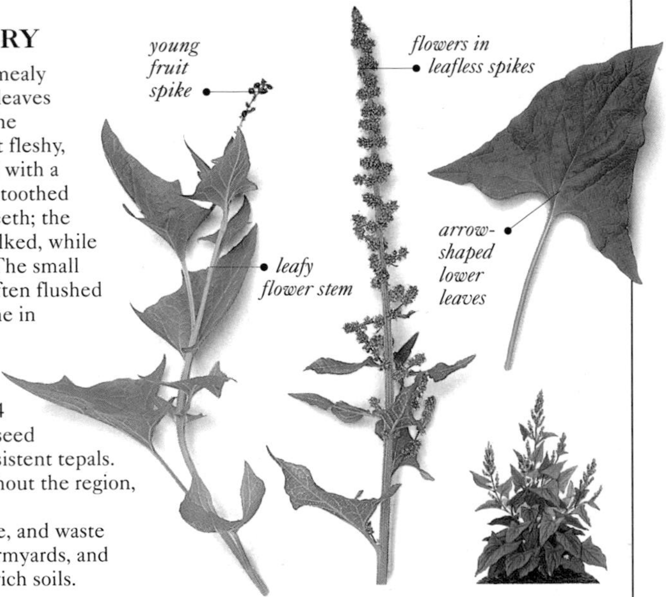

Habit Annual	Height 25–50cm (10–20in)	Flowering time May–Aug

Family CHENOPODIACEAE	Species *Chenopodium album*	Author L.

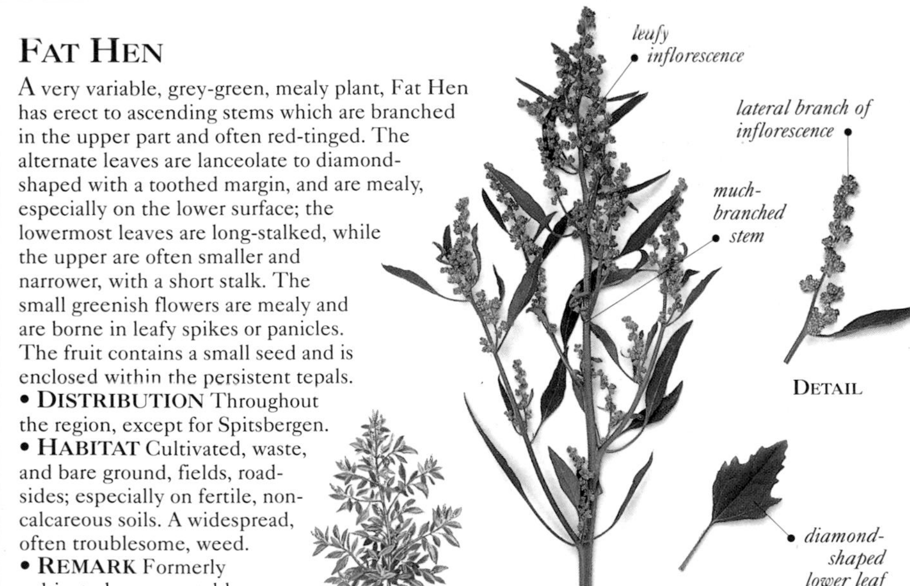

FAT HEN

A very variable, grey-green, mealy plant, Fat Hen has erect to ascending stems which are branched in the upper part and often red-tinged. The alternate leaves are lanceolate to diamond-shaped with a toothed margin, and are mealy, especially on the lower surface; the lowermost leaves are long-stalked, while the upper are often smaller and narrower, with a short stalk. The small greenish flowers are mealy and are borne in leafy spikes or panicles. The fruit contains a small seed and is enclosed within the persistent tepals.
• **DISTRIBUTION** Throughout the region, except for Spitsbergen.
• **HABITAT** Cultivated, waste, and bare ground, fields, roadsides; especially on fertile, non-calcareous soils. A widespread, often troublesome, weed.
• **REMARK** Formerly cultivated as a vegetable.

Habit Annual	Height 40–150cm (16–60in)	Flowering time June–Oct

Family CHENOPODIACEAE	Species *Chenopodium rubrum*	Author L.

RED GOOSEFOOT

This spreading to erect, hairless plant is little- to much-branched and often red-tinged, especially when in fruit. The alternate leaves are lanceolate to diamond-shaped and often markedly lobed. The tiny greenish or reddish flowers are borne in simple or branched spikes, each flower with a 2- to 5-lobed perianth and 4 to 5 stamens. The fruit is an achene surrounded by the unaltered perianth.

• **DISTRIBUTION** Throughout the region, but absent from most of the far north.

• **HABITAT** Cultivated, arable, and bare land, coasts, manure heaps, refuse dumps; occasionally dried reservoir or lake margins; often gregarious.

• **RELATED SPECIES** *Chenopodium chenopodioides*, Saltmarsh Goosefoot, is more spreading, with leaves barely toothed and red beneath. It grows in mainland Europe (except Scandinavia), and E. and S.E. England.

Habit Annual	Height 5–90cm (2–36in)	Flowering time July–Oct

Family CHENOPODIACEAE	Species *Atriplex portulacoides*	Author L.

SEA PURSLANE

Also known as *Halimione portulacoides*, this shrub has much-branched stems that become brownish when older and often root down to the ground. Mostly opposite and short-stalked, the leaves, 10–40mm (⅖–1⅗in) long, are oblong or elliptical, thick, mealy, and rather fleshy. Borne in short, almost leafless panicles, the tiny greenish yellow flowers are mostly unisexual, with 5 perianth segments and 5 stamens. The fruit is a small achene held within 2 enlarged 3-lobed bracts, which are fused together almost to the top.

• **DISTRIBUTION** Throughout the region as far north as C. Scotland and Denmark.

• **HABITAT** Coastal sites, particularly the drier parts of salt marshes, sandy and muddy places, pool and channel margins, and occasionally sea-cliffs. Often forms large and conspicuous colonies, frequently in association with other salt marsh plants.

Habit Shrub	Height 20–80cm (8–32in) rarely more	Flowering time July–Oct

Family CHENOPODIACEAE	Species *Atriplex littoralis*	Author L.

GRASS-LEAVED ORACHE

The leaves of this branched, hairless plant are linear to narrow-oblong and toothed or untoothed; the lower leaves are short-stalked, while the upper are unstalked. The greenish flowers are borne in small clusters that make up unisexual spikes. Male flowers have 5 perianth segments and 5 stamens; female flowers are borne on the same plant and have only 2 large persistent bracts surrounding the ovary. The fruit is enclosed within 2 diamond-shaped, toothed bracts, which are spongy at the base and 3–6mm (⅛–¼in) long.

• **DISTRIBUTION** Throughout, except for N. Scandinavia; rare in Ireland and N. Scotland.

• **HABITAT** Coastal sites, especially on the upper parts of salt marshes and in rough grassy places; occasionally inland on saline or muddy habitats.

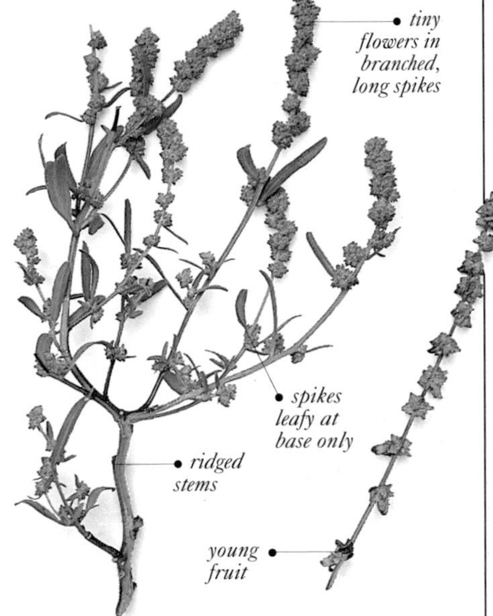

Habit Annual	Height 40–150cm (16–60in)	Flowering time July–Oct

Family CHENOPODIACEAE	Species *Atriplex prostrata*	Author Boucher ex DC.

SPEAR-LEAVED ORACHE

Also known as *Atriplex hastata*, this prostrate to erect plant is mealy and green when young, but often reddens with age. The stems are strongly ridged. The alternate leaves are not mealy when mature and have 2 basal lobes at right angles to the leaf-stalk. The tiny greenish flowers are borne in dense, branched spikes that are leafy in the lower part; male flowers have 5 perianth segments and 5 stamens; female flowers have only 2 persistent bracts around the ovary. The fruit is enclosed within 2 triangular, toothed bracts, 2–6mm (1/12–¼in) long.

• **DISTRIBUTION** Throughout the region, except for N. Scandinavia.

• **HABITAT** Cultivated, bare, and waste ground, and saline habitats, both coastal and inland.

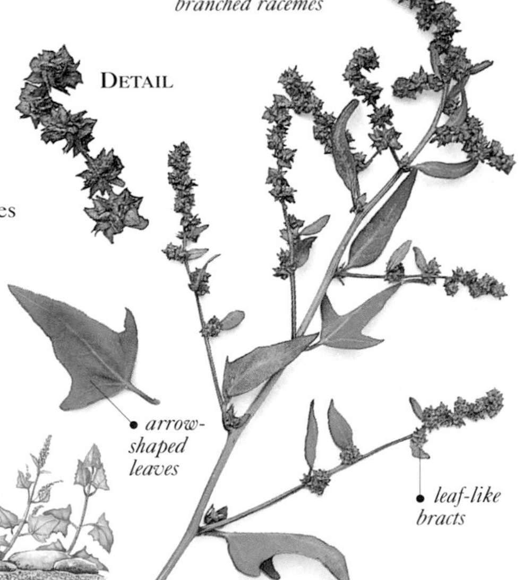

Habit Annual	Height 5–150cm (2–60in)	Flowering time July–Oct

Family CHENOPODIACEAE	Species *Salicornia europaea*	Author L.

COMMON GLASSWORT

This very variable, erect to prostrate, fleshy, and hairless plant bears long, ascending branches. The translucent stems are jointed, and opposite pairs of scale-like leaves are fused across them. The plant is blue- or grass-green but is sometimes flushed with red at flowering time. The inconspicuous flowers are borne singly or in threes on the surface of the fleshy, branched spikes; the terminal spikes are 10–50mm (⅖–2in) long. Each flower has one or 2 stamens. The fruit is inconspicuous.

• **DISTRIBUTION** Throughout the region.

• **HABITAT** Coastal mudflats and salt marshes; occasionally inland on motorway verges and sandy ground.

• **RELATED SPECIES** *Salicornia ramosissima*, Purple Glasswort, is up to 40cm (16in) tall, much-branched, and usually turns dark purple. The terminal spikes are up to 30mm (1⅕in) long. It has similar distribution and habitats to the above.

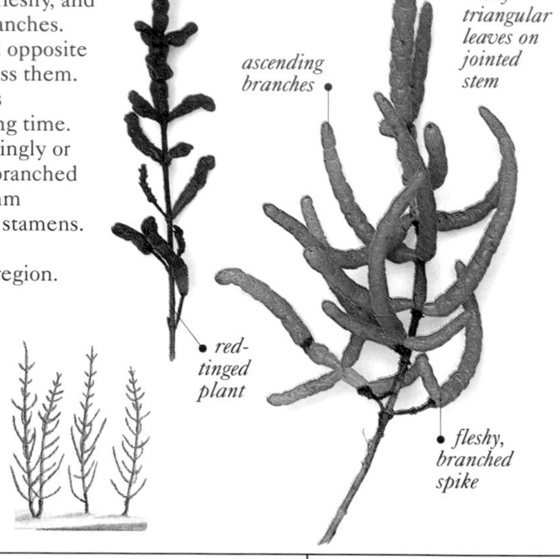

Habit Annual	Height 10–30cm (4–12in)	Flowering time Aug–Sept

Family CHENOPODIACEAE	Species *Suaeda maritima*	Author (L.) Dumort.

ANNUAL SEABLITE

This is a highly variable, erect or prostrate, hairless plant. The branched stems are bluish green at first but become purple, then bright red late in the season. The alternate leaves, 10–50mm (⅖–2in) long, are linear, fleshy, and pointed. The inconspicuous, green flowers, solitary or 2 or 3 together, are hermaphrodite; each flower has 5 fleshy perianth segments, 5 stamens, and 2 styles. The fruit is a small, greenish or reddish achene.

• **DISTRIBUTION** Throughout, except for N. Scandinavia.

• **HABITAT** Coastal sites, especially muddy salt marshes.

• **RELATED SPECIES** *Suaeda vera*, Shrubby Seablite, is a greyish sub-shrub up to 120cm (48in) tall, with smaller leaves. It grows in similar habitats in S. England and France.

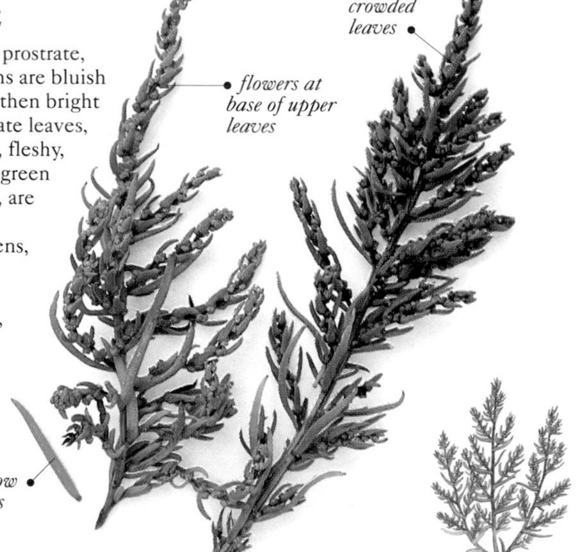

Habit Annual	Height 10–50cm (4–20in)	Flowering time July–Sept

Family CHENOPODIACEAE	Species *Salsola kali*	Author L.

PRICKLY SALTWORT

This branched, stiff, and prickly plant has spreading to erect stems. The alternate, linear leaves, 10–40mm (⅖–1⅗in) long, are bluish green and widest at or near the base. The tiny green flowers are sometimes flushed with pink, and each has 5 perianth segments, 5 stamens, and 2 stigmas. The small fruit is hidden by the flower parts.
• **DISTRIBUTION** Throughout the region, except N. Scandinavia.
• **HABITAT** Sandy coastal beaches, on the drift line, and occasionally on waste places inland. Often in association with *Atriplex* species or *Cakile maritima*, Sea Rocket (see p.89).

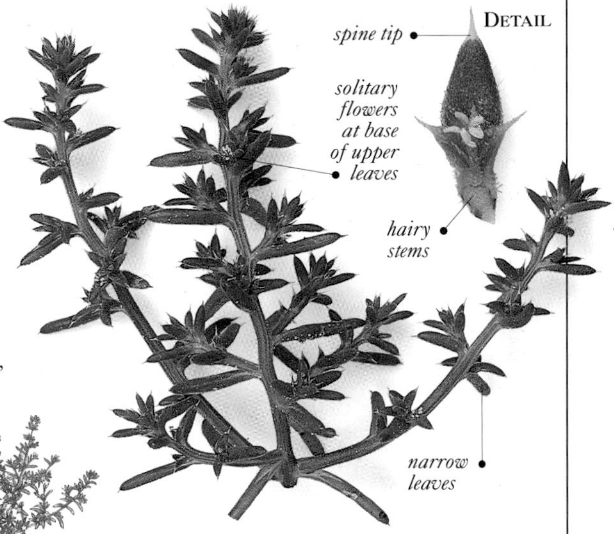

Habit Annual	Height 20–100cm (8–40in)	Flowering time July–Oct

MESEMBRYANTHEMUM FAMILY

Family PORTULACACEAE	Species *Carpobrotus edulis*	Author (L.) N.E.Br.

HOTTENTOT FIG

This prostrate to trailing plant is hairless and has woody, angled stems. The paired, fleshy leaves, 40–90mm (1⅗–3⅗in) long, are oblong. The large, showy, multipetalled flowers, 70–90mm (2⅘–3⅗in) across, are borne at the shoot-tips and have numerous stamens; the linear petals are yellow or bright pinkish purple. The fruit is fleshy, fig-like, and non-splitting.
• **DISTRIBUTION** Naturalized in W. France, S. and S.W. England, Wales, and S. and E. Ireland. Native to South Africa.
• **HABITAT** Coastal rocks, sands, and cliffs.
• **RELATED SPECIES** *Carpobrotus acinaciformis* has leaves that are thicker in the middle, and larger pinkish purple flowers. It grows in S.W. England and the Scilly Isles. It is also native to South Africa.

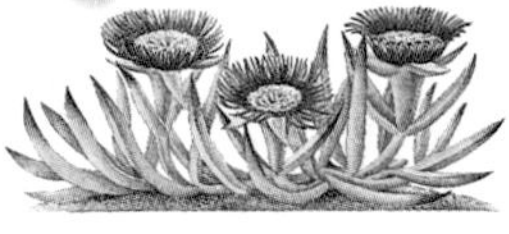

Habit Perennial	Height Spreading to 3m (10ft)	Flowering time May–Aug

Purslane Family

Family PORTULACACEAE	Species *Claytonia perfoliata*	Author Donn ex Willd.

Spring Beauty

Also known as *Montia perfoliata*, this low, hairless, tufted plant is fleshy and fragile, with erect stems. The leaves, mostly basal, are oval or diamond-shaped, untoothed, and usually pale green. Borne in lax clusters, the flowers, 4–5mm (1/6–1/5in) across, are surrounded by a ruff of leaves, and may have slightly notched petals; each flower has 5 stamens. The fruit is a small, many-seeded capsule.

• **DISTRIBUTION** Naturalized in W. Britain, Ireland, and mainland Europe, but not Norway and Sweden.

• **HABITAT** Waste, bare, and cultivated land, in dry, light, sandy places; often on acid soils.

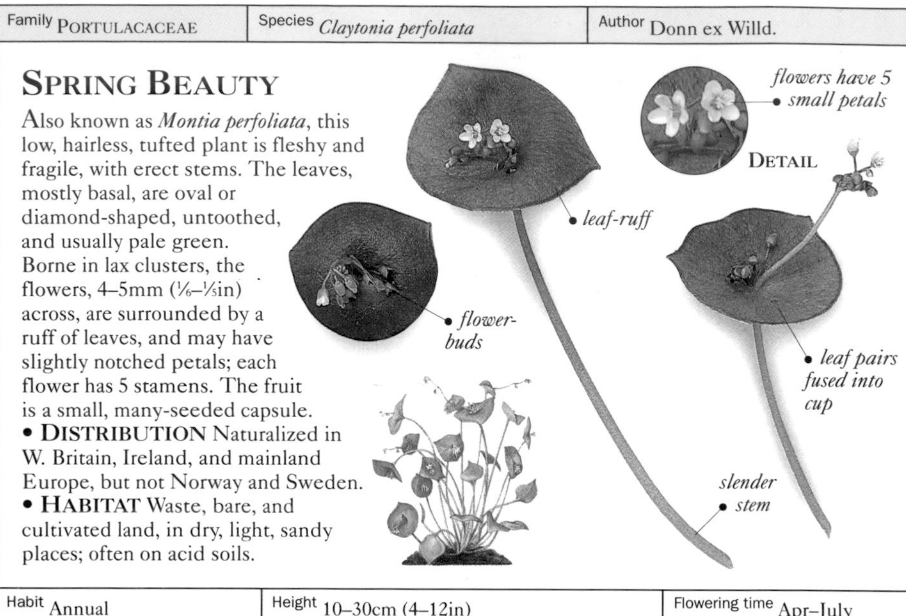

Habit Annual	Height 10–30cm (4–12in)	Flowering time Apr–July

Pink Family

Family CARYOPHYLLACEAE	Species *Arenaria serpyllifolia*	Author L.

Thyme-leaved Sandwort

This prostrate to rather bushy plant is rough-haired and often rather greyish. The stems are slender and much-branched. The leaves, 2.5–8mm (1/10–1/3in) long, are broadly oval to lanceolate, pointed, and 3- to 5-veined. Borne in spreading cymes, the white flowers, 5–8mm (1/5–1/3in) across, have unnotched petals, pointed sepals, and 10 stamens. The fruit capsule is slightly longer than the persistent sepals and splits by 6 teeth at the apex.

• **DISTRIBUTION** Throughout, except the far north of the region.

• **HABITAT** Dry and bare sandy or chalky places, fields, downs, and occasionally old walls.

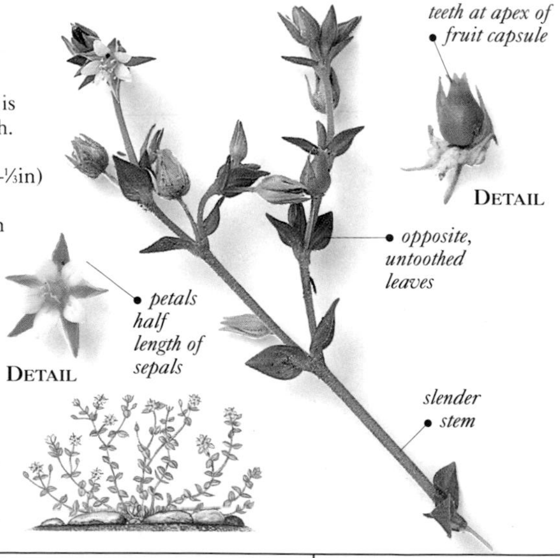

teeth at apex of fruit capsule

DETAIL

opposite, untoothed leaves

petals half length of sepals

DETAIL

slender stem

Habit Annual	Height 10–30cm (4–12in)	Flowering time Apr–Sept

Family CARYOPHYLLACEAE | Species *Moehringia trinervia* | Author (L.) Clairv.

THREE-NERVED SANDWORT

Also known as *Arenaria trinervia*, this plant has trailing or straggling stems. The oval to elliptical leaves are 3- to 5-veined. The white flowers, 4–7mm (⅙–2⁄7in) across, are solitary or several on hairy stalks, and have 5 sepals and 5 unnotched petals. The many-seeded capsule splits by 4 or 6 teeth.

• **DISTRIBUTION** Throughout the region, except for the far north.

• **HABITAT** Woodland, hedgerows, other shaded places; rarer in open sites.

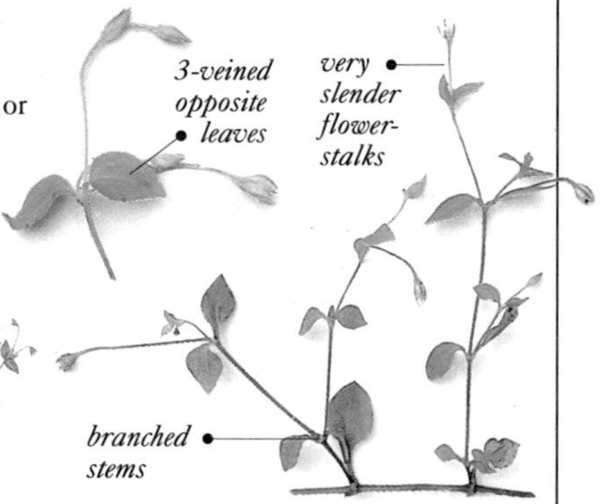

3-veined opposite leaves

very slender flower-stalks

branched stems

Habit Annual or biennial | Height 10–40cm (4–16in) | Flowering time May–July

Family CARYOPHYLLACEAE | Species *Honkenya peploides* | Author Ehrh.

SEA SANDWORT

This is a mat- or patch-forming, slightly succulent, hairless, often yellowish green plant. The spreading, branched stems root down at the nodes. The leaves are untoothed and very short-stalked or unstalked. The solitary or clustered flowers, 6–10mm (¼–⅖in) across, have 5 sepals and 5 shorter petals. The fruit opens by 3 valves and contains many seeds.

• **DISTRIBUTION** Throughout the region.

• **HABITAT** Coastal sands, rocks, and shingle; tolerant of salt-spray.

greenish white flower

DETAIL

small fruit capsule

oval, pointed, opposite leaves

Habit Perennial | Height 4–15cm (1⅗–6in) | Flowering time May–Aug

Family CARYOPHYLLACEAE | Species *Stellaria holostea* | Author L.

GREATER STITCHWORT

This patch-forming, rough-feeling plant has straggling, much-branched, spreading to ascending stems. The leaves are narrow-lanceolate, untoothed, and mostly unstalked. Borne in loose clusters, the flowers are 18–30mm (5⁄7–1⅕in) across, with petals longer than the sepals. The fruit capsule splits by 6 teeth.

• **DISTRIBUTION** Throughout the region, except for the far north.

• **HABITAT** Grassy places, field boundaries, hedgerows, embankments, and woodland margins.

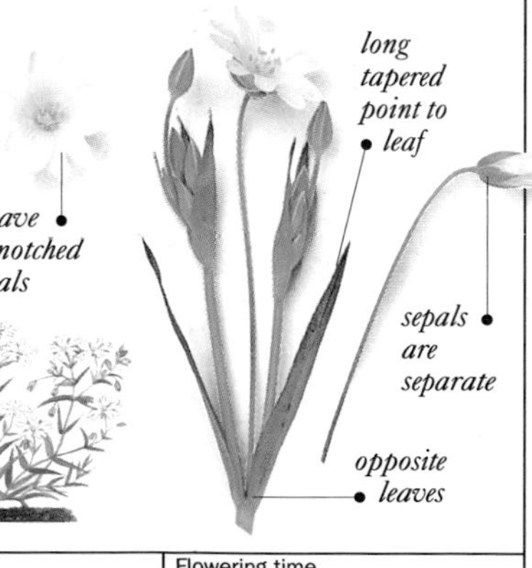

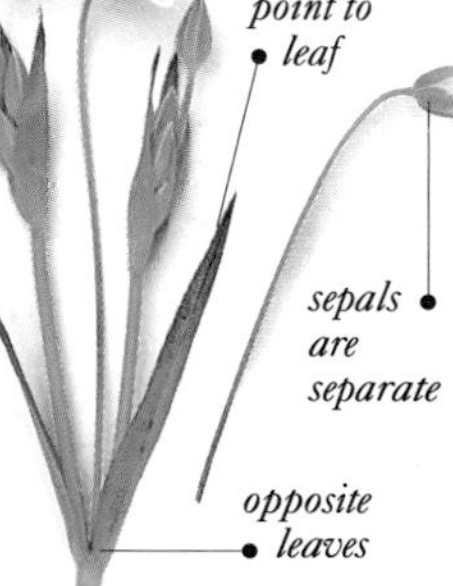

Habit Perennial | Height 30–60cm (12–24in) | Flowering time Apr–June

Family CARYOPHYLLACEAE	Species *Stellaria media*	Author (L.) Villars

COMMON CHICKWEED

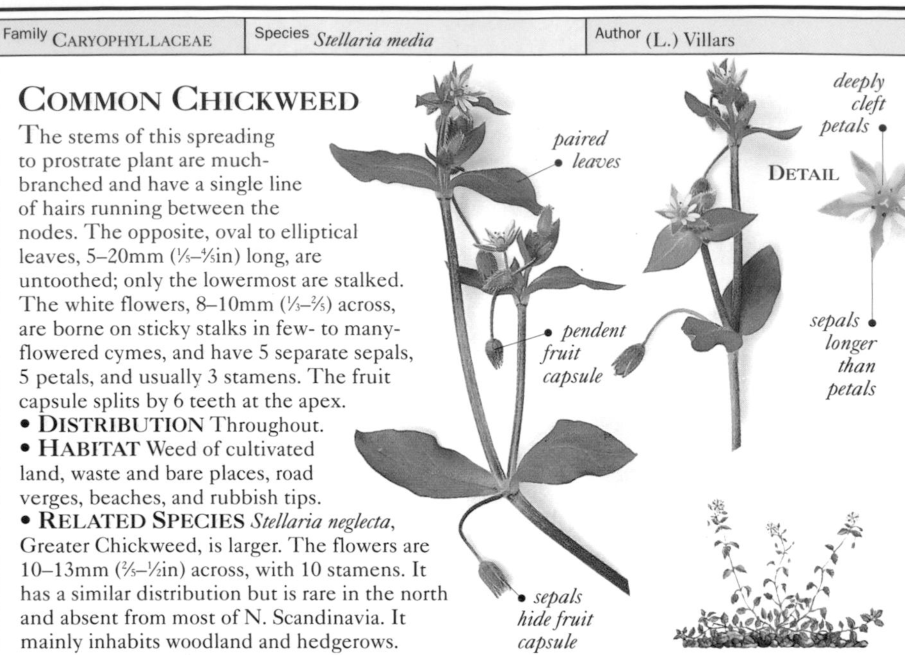

The stems of this spreading to prostrate plant are much-branched and have a single line of hairs running between the nodes. The opposite, oval to elliptical leaves, 5–20mm (⅕–⅘in) long, are untoothed; only the lowermost are stalked. The white flowers, 8–10mm (⅓–⅖) across, are borne on sticky stalks in few- to many-flowered cymes, and have 5 separate sepals, 5 petals, and usually 3 stamens. The fruit capsule splits by 6 teeth at the apex.

• **DISTRIBUTION** Throughout.

• **HABITAT** Weed of cultivated land, waste and bare places, road verges, beaches, and rubbish tips.

• **RELATED SPECIES** *Stellaria neglecta*, Greater Chickweed, is larger. The flowers are 10–13mm (⅖–½in) across, with 10 stamens. It has a similar distribution but is rare in the north and absent from most of N. Scandinavia. It mainly inhabits woodland and hedgerows.

Habit Annual	Height 5–35cm (2–14in)	Flowering time Year round

Family CARYOPHYLLACEAE	Species *Cerastium arvense*	Author L.

FIELD MOUSE-EAR

The spreading stems of this very variable, somewhat hairy plant are often matted; vegetative shoots often root at the nodes. The leaves, 10–30mm (⅖–1⅕) long, are narrow-lanceolate and blunt-tipped. The bracts have membranous, hairy margins. The white flowers, 12–20mm (½–⅘in) across, are in cymes, and have deeply notched petals which are twice as long as the separate sepals. The fruit capsule splits by 10 teeth at the apex.

• **DISTRIBUTION** Throughout the region, but absent from the far north and scarcer in the west of Britain and Ireland.

• **HABITAT** Dry open places, grassland, hedgebanks, and road verges; to 3,100m (10,150ft).

Habit Perennial	Height 5–30cm (2–12in)	Flowering time Apr–Aug

Family CARYOPHYLLACEAE	Species *Cerastium fontanum*	Author Baumg.

COMMON MOUSE-EAR

This slightly hairy, loosely tufted plant has leafy stems and ascending flowering shoots. The lanceolate leaves are 5–20mm (⅕–⅘in) long. In spreading cymes, the flowers, 6–10mm (¼–⅖in) across, have deeply notched petals. The fruit capsule splits by 10 teeth at the apex.

• **DISTRIBUTION** Throughout the region.

• **HABITAT** Grassy and moist places, sand dunes, and shingle banks; usually on calcareous or neutral soils.

sepals as long as petals
white-edged bracts
deeply notched petals
unstalked leaves

Habit Perennial	Height 5–30cm (2–12in)	Flowering time Apr–Nov

Family CARYOPHYLLACEAE	Species *Spergula arvensis*	Author L.

CORN SPURREY

The stems of this plant have glandular hairs near the top. The leaves, 10–30mm (⅖–1⅕) long, are grooved beneath. The white flowers, 4–8mm (⅙–⅓in) across, have 5 or 10 stamens. Borne on long slender stalks, the pendent fruit capsules split into 5 valves.

• **DISTRIBUTION** Throughout.

• **HABITAT** Mostly sandy arable and cultivated land, and waste and bare ground.

Habit Annual	Height 5–60cm (2–24in)	Flowering time May–Sept

Family CARYOPHYLLACEAE	Species *Spergularia marina*	Author (L.) Griseb.

LESSER SAND-SPURREY

This plant's fleshy, linear leaves, mostly 6–15mm (¼–⅗in) long, have short, whitish, glandular-hairy stipules. The flowers, 5–8mm (⅕–⅓in) across, have separate sepals and up to 5 stamens. The pendent fruit capsules, 3.5–5mm (1/7–⅕in) long, split into 3 valves.

• **DISTRIBUTION** Throughout the region.

• **HABITAT** Coastal sands, dry salt marshes, and sometimes saline soils inland.

Habit Annual, rarely perennial	Height 5–20cm (2–8in)	Flowering time May–Sept

Family CARYOPHYLLACEAE	Species *Lychnis flos-cuculi*	Author L.

RAGGED ROBIN

This loosely tufted plant has slender, erect stems which may be branched or unbranched, hairless or slightly hairy. The leaves are in pairs; the basal are spoon-shaped to oval and stalked; those on the stem are narrow-lanceolate, pointed, and unstalked. The bright purplish pink, occasionally white, flowers, 30–40mm (1⅕–1⅗in) across, are in loose spreading cymes; the sepals are fused into a 5-toothed tube. The fruit capsule splits by 5 teeth at the apex.

• **DISTRIBUTION** Throughout.

• **HABITAT** Damp meadows, marshes, streamsides, fens, and wet woodland; often on peaty or mineral-rich soils.

• **RELATED SPECIES** *Lychnis viscaria*, Sticky Catchfly, has stems that are sticky below each node, and smaller flowers in a denser inflorescence; petals are only notched. It inhabits dry rocky places throughout, but is absent from N. Scandinavia, Ireland, and E. Britain.

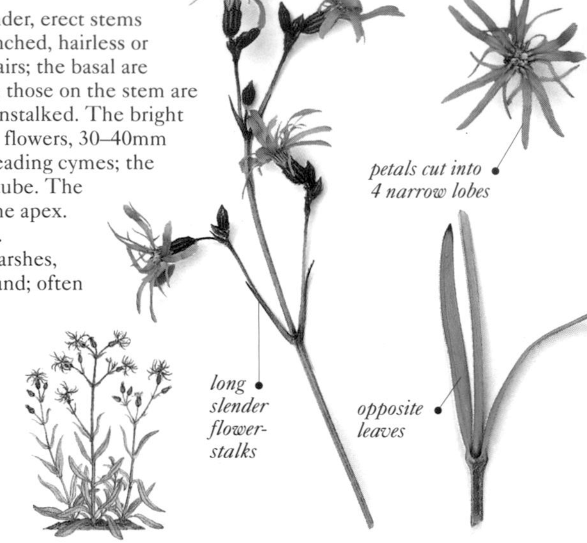

Habit Perennial	Height 20–70cm (8–28in)	Flowering time May–Aug

Family CARYOPHYLLACEAE	Species *Lychnis alpina*	Author L.

ALPINE CATCHFLY

Commonly grown in gardens as an alpine, this tufted, hairless, or slightly hairy plant has erect, non-sticky, unbranched stems. The opposite leaves, mostly basal, are spoon-shaped to linear and untoothed; the lowermost leaves are stalked. The stems have only 2 to 3 pairs of leaves. The pale purple, occasionally white, flowers, 8–12mm (⅓–½in) across, are borne in dense heads in which the smaller flowers are often only female. The sepals are fused into a short, 5-toothed tube and the petals are deeply notched to about half way. The many-seeded fruit capsule, 4–5mm (⅙–⅕in) long, splits by 5 teeth at the apex.

• **DISTRIBUTION** Native to Scandinavia, Iceland, and the Alps. A very rare and protected species in N. Britain.

• **HABITAT** Mountain rocks, mountain meadows, and stony areas; generally on soils rich in heavy metals or serpentine.

Habit Perennial	Height 5–20cm (2–8in)	Flowering time June–Aug

Family CARYOPHYLLACEAE	Species *Agrostemma githago*	Author L.

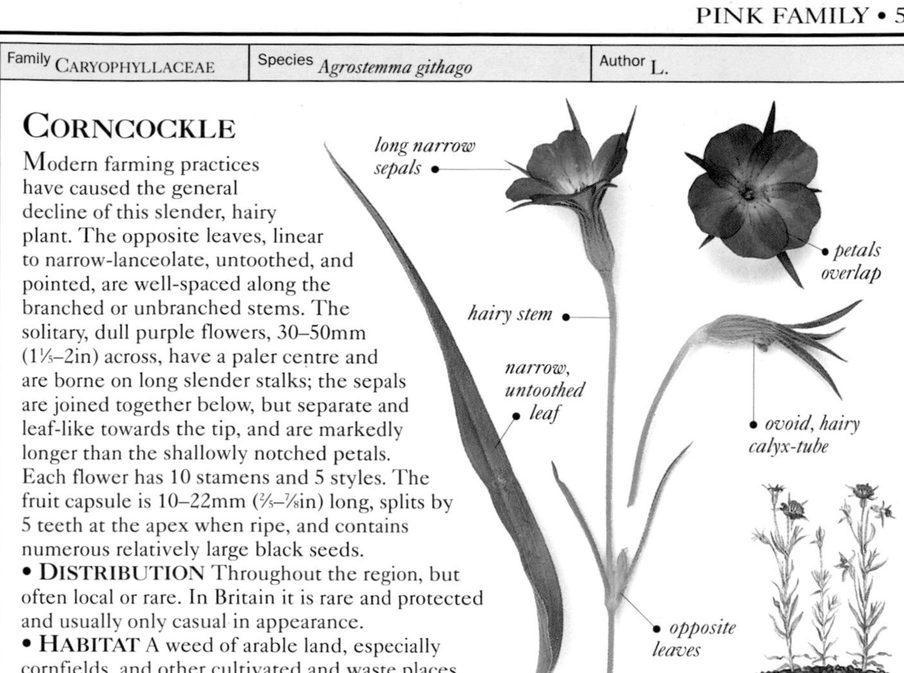

CORNCOCKLE

Modern farming practices have caused the general decline of this slender, hairy plant. The opposite leaves, linear to narrow-lanceolate, untoothed, and pointed, are well-spaced along the branched or unbranched stems. The solitary, dull purple flowers, 30–50mm (1⅕–2in) across, have a paler centre and are borne on long slender stalks; the sepals are joined together below, but separate and leaf-like towards the tip, and are markedly longer than the shallowly notched petals. Each flower has 10 stamens and 5 styles. The fruit capsule is 10–22mm (⅖–⅞in) long, splits by 5 teeth at the apex when ripe, and contains numerous relatively large black seeds.

• **DISTRIBUTION** Throughout the region, but often local or rare. In Britain it is rare and protected and usually only casual in appearance.

• **HABITAT** A weed of arable land, especially cornfields, and other cultivated and waste places.

Habit Annual	Height 60–100cm (24–40in)	Flowering time May–Aug

Family CARYOPHYLLACEAE	Species *Silene nutans*	Author L.

NOTTINGHAM CATCHFLY

This stickily-hairy plant has erect, generally unbranched, stems. The lower leaves are oblong to spoon-shaped and stalked; the upper are narrow-lanceolate, pointed, and stalkless. The petals of the nodding white flowers are often greenish or reddish on the reverse; the sepals are fused into a 5-toothed tube 9–12mm (⅜–½in) long and sticky with glandular hairs.

• **DISTRIBUTION** Throughout the region, except for N. Scandinavia, N. Britain, and Ireland.

• **HABITAT** Dry rocky and grassy places, sea-cliffs, shingle, and fields.

• **RELATED SPECIES** *Silene italica*, Italian Catchfly, has ascending flowers and broader, less deeply notched petals. It is casual or naturalized.

petals curl up during day

DETAIL

unripe fruit

flowers in loose, one-sided panicle

deeply cleft petals

stalked leaves

Habit Perennial	Height 20–60cm (8–24in)	Flowering time May–Aug

Family	Species	Author
CARYOPHYLLACEAE	*Silene vulgaris*	Garcke

BLADDER CAMPION

This variable, hairless, greyish plant has erect shoots arising from a woody base; all the shoots flower. The leaves are oval to elliptical and untoothed; only the lowermost are stalked. The fragrant white flowers, 16–18mm (5/8–5/7in) across, are borne in branched cymes; the 5 petals are deeply notched and do not overlap. The fruit is a many-seeded capsule with 6 teeth.

• **DISTRIBUTION** Throughout the region, except for some of the northernmost islands.

• **HABITAT** Grassy places and open and rough ground; generally on dry calcareous soils.

• **RELATED SPECIES** *Silene uniflora* (syn. *S. maritima*), Sea Campion, is fleshier and forms mats of flowering and non-flowering shoots; flowers are larger, with broad overlapping petal-lobes. It inhabits coastal rocks, cliffs, and shingle, and lake-shores and mountains inland throughout the region.

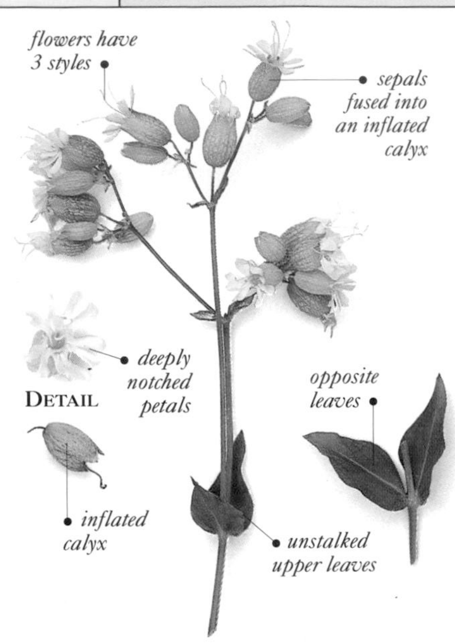

Habit	Height	Flowering time
Perennial	40–80cm (16–32in)	May–Sept

Family	Species	Author
CARYOPHYLLACEAE	*Silene acaulis*	(L.) Jacq.

MOSS CAMPION

This low-growing plant is mat- or cushion-forming and rather moss-like. The small bright green leaves are linear and pointed, opposite, and crowded on short stems. The solitary, pale to deep pink flowers are 6–10mm (1/4–2/5in) across, and are borne on very short, slender stalks; the calyx is bell-shaped and often flushed with red or purple; the stamens protrude beyond the mouth of the flower. The small fruit capsule contains many tiny seeds.

• **DISTRIBUTION** Throughout the region, except for Belgium, Holland, and Denmark; in Britain confined to N. Wales, the Lake District, Scotland, and Northern Ireland.

• **HABITAT** Mountain rocks and scree, or short alpine turf; only on the higher mountains in the south of its range, and often local.

• **REMARK** The flowers may be hermaphrodite, male, or female.

DETAIL
5 notched petals
slender flower-stalk
protruding stamens
short-stalked flowers
moss-like tufts
leafy shoots with paired leaves

Habit	Height	Flowering time
Perennial	3–8cm (1 1/5–3 1/5in)	June–Aug

Family CARYOPHYLLACEAE	Species *Silene dioica*	Author (L.) Clairv.

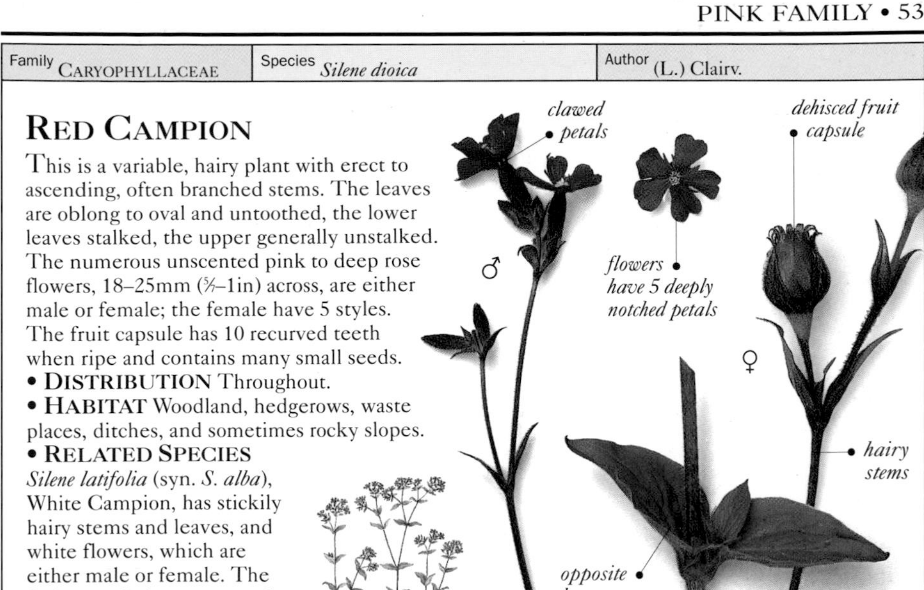

RED CAMPION

This is a variable, hairy plant with erect to ascending, often branched stems. The leaves are oblong to oval and untoothed, the lower leaves stalked, the upper generally unstalked. The numerous unscented pink to deep rose flowers, 18–25mm (¾–1in) across, are either male or female; the female have 5 styles. The fruit capsule has 10 recurved teeth when ripe and contains many small seeds.

• **DISTRIBUTION** Throughout.

• **HABITAT** Woodland, hedgerows, waste places, ditches, and sometimes rocky slopes.

• **RELATED SPECIES** *Silene latifolia* (syn. *S. alba*), White Campion, has stickily hairy stems and leaves, and white flowers, which are either male or female. The fruit capsule has erect teeth. It grows along roadsides, and hedgerows throughout, except for the far north.

Habit Perennial or biennial	Height 50–100cm (20–40in)	Flowering time May–Nov

Family CARYOPHYLLACEAE	Species *Silene conica*	Author L.

SAND CATCHFLY

This stickily hairy, rather greyish plant has erect to somewhat spreading, simple or branched stems. The leaves are linear to narrow-lanceolate and untoothed; the lowermost are stalked. The rose-pink or white flowers, 4–5mm (⅙–⅕in) across, are solitary or in small clusters.

• **DISTRIBUTION** S. and E. Britain (local), France, Holland, and Germany; naturalized and native in Britain.

• **HABITAT** Sandy and waste places; frequently growing on sand dunes.

• **RELATED SPECIES** *Silene gallica*, Small-flowered Catchfly, has non-inflated 10-veined calyces, and flowers borne in one-sided, branched spikes. It grows in similar habitats and on arable land in the Channel Islands and W. France.

flowers have 5 slightly notched petals

calyx is 20- to 30-veined

flask-shaped calyx

fruit capsule within inflated, ribbed calyx

unstalked upper leaf

opposite leaves

untoothed leaf margin

Habit Annual	Height 20–35cm (8–14in)	Flowering time May–Aug

Family CARYOPHYLLACEAE	Species *Saponaria officinalis*	Author L.

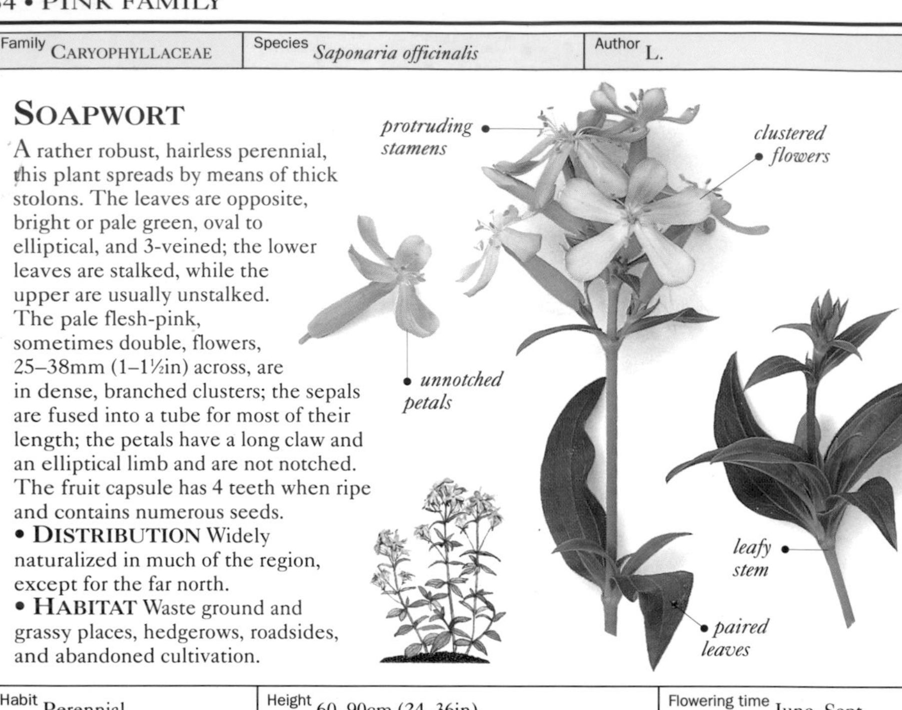

SOAPWORT

A rather robust, hairless perennial, this plant spreads by means of thick stolons. The leaves are opposite, bright or pale green, oval to elliptical, and 3-veined; the lower leaves are stalked, while the upper are usually unstalked. The pale flesh-pink, sometimes double, flowers, 25–38mm (1–1½in) across, are in dense, branched clusters; the sepals are fused into a tube for most of their length; the petals have a long claw and an elliptical limb and are not notched. The fruit capsule has 4 teeth when ripe and contains numerous seeds.

• **DISTRIBUTION** Widely naturalized in much of the region, except for the far north.

• **HABITAT** Waste ground and grassy places, hedgerows, roadsides, and abandoned cultivation.

Habit Perennial	Height 60–90cm (24–36in)	Flowering time June–Sept

Family CARYOPHYLLACEAE	Species *Petrorhagia nanteulii*	Author (Burnat) P. Ball & Heyw.

CHILDING PINK

This rather slight, tufted plant has slender stems which are hairless or minutely hairy. The leaves are linear, 3-veined, and taper to a fine point. The pink flowers, 5–6mm (⅕–¼in) across, are borne in small, dense heads surrounded by brownish, papery, overlapping bracts. The small fruit capsule splits by 4 teeth at the apex.

• **DISTRIBUTION** Britain as far north as S. Scotland, and France; occasionally casual elsewhere.

• **HABITAT** Dry grassy, sandy, and gravelly sites; often near the sea.

• **RELATED SPECIES** *Petrorhagia prolifera*, Proliferous Pink, has hairier stems and longer leaf-sheaths; the seed surface is netted, not warted. It grows in E. England (very rare) and on mainland Europe as far north as S. Sweden.

Habit Annual	Height 20–50cm (8–20in)	Flowering time June–Aug

Family CARYOPHYLLACEAE	Species *Dianthus armeria*	Author L.

DEPTFORD PINK

The stiff erect stems of this short, tufted, and hairy plant are unbranched or slightly branched. The paired, dark green leaves are linear to narrowly triangular, pointed, and untoothed. The unscented bright pink or reddish pink flowers are 10–15mm (⅖–⅗in) across. The narrow petal-limbs are generally spotted and have a slightly toothed margin; the tubular calyx is 15–20mm (⅗–⅘in) long and bears 2 pairs of equally long, leaf-like scales at the base. The fruit capsule splits at the top into 4 teeth and contains numerous small seeds.

• **DISTRIBUTION** S. Sweden and Denmark southwards, and S. Britain, but introduced further north. Often local and rather rare.

• **HABITAT** Dry grassy places, hedgerows, and road verges; generally on sandy or calcareous soils.

Habit Annual or biennial	Height 30–60cm (12–24in)	Flowering time June–Aug

Family CARYOPHYLLACEAE	Species *Dianthus carthusianorum*	Author L.

CARTHUSIAN PINK

The flowering stems of this tufted, hairless plant are erect and rather stiff. The green, tapered leaves, up to 5mm (⅕in) wide, are linear and well-spaced along the flowering stems. Borne in tight terminal clusters, the flowers, 18–20mm (¾–⅘in) across, are deep pink to purple, or more rarely white; the petals are unspotted, and the calyx is surrounded by long, brown, pointed bracts. The fruit capsule has 4 teeth.

• **DISTRIBUTION** Holland, France, and Germany; casual or a garden escape in Britain.

• **HABITAT** Dry grassy and rocky sites, and sometimes open woodland.

• **RELATED SPECIES** *Dianthus gratianopolitanus*, Cheddar Pink, is smaller with grey leaves and solitary flowers. It has a similar distribution but also grows in Belgium and one locality in Britain (Somerset), where it is protected; inhabits rocky places.

Habit Perennial	Height 20–60cm (8–24in)	Flowering time May–Aug

Family CARYOPHYLLACEAE	Species *Dianthus deltoides*	Author L.

MAIDEN PINK

Loosely tufted, and often rather matted, this minutely hairy plant has numerous sterile vegetative shoots as well as ascending to erect flowering stems. The opposite, bluish green leaves are linear-oblong, with a blunt apex. The flowers are spotted in the centre, 15–20mm (⅗–⅘in) across, solitary or 2 or 3 borne together, and scentless; the calyx is tubular, with 5 slender teeth and long-pointed basal scales half its length; the 5 petals have a fringed limb and a long slender claw. The fruit capsule splits by 4 teeth at the top and contains many small seeds.

• **DISTRIBUTION** Throughout, except for the far north and Ireland; in Britain, absent from C. Scotland northwards.

• **HABITAT** Dry, sandy grassland, banks, rocky slopes; on calcareous or slightly acid soils.

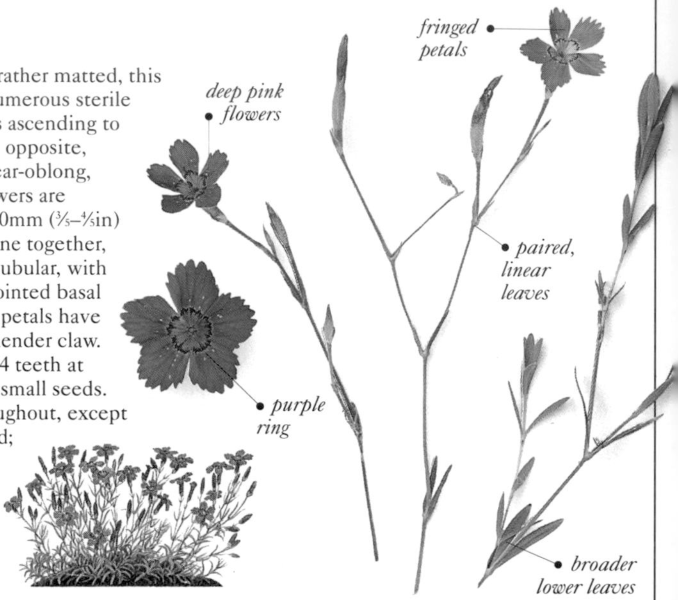

fringed petals
deep pink flowers
paired, linear leaves
purple ring
broader lower leaves

Habit Perennial	Height 10–30cm (4–12in)	Flowering time June–Sept

Family CARYOPHYLLACEAE	Species *Dianthus gratianopolitanus*	Author Villars

CHEDDAR PINK

This densely tufted, rather greyish, hairless plant has creeping vegetative shoots and more or less erect flowering stems. The linear leaves have untoothed margins which are rough to the touch. The pink flowers, 20–30mm (⅘–1⅕in) across, are solitary; the calyx is narrow and tubular, with 5 triangular teeth at the apex and short, paired, basal scales about a quarter of its length; the petals have a toothed limb that is bearded at the base, and a long, narrow claw. The fruit capsule splits by 4 teeth at the apex and contains many small seeds.

• **DISTRIBUTION** S.W. England (rare) and mainland Europe as far north as C. Germany, but not in Holland.

• **HABITAT** Rocky sites, particularly cliff crevices and screes; usually on limestone.

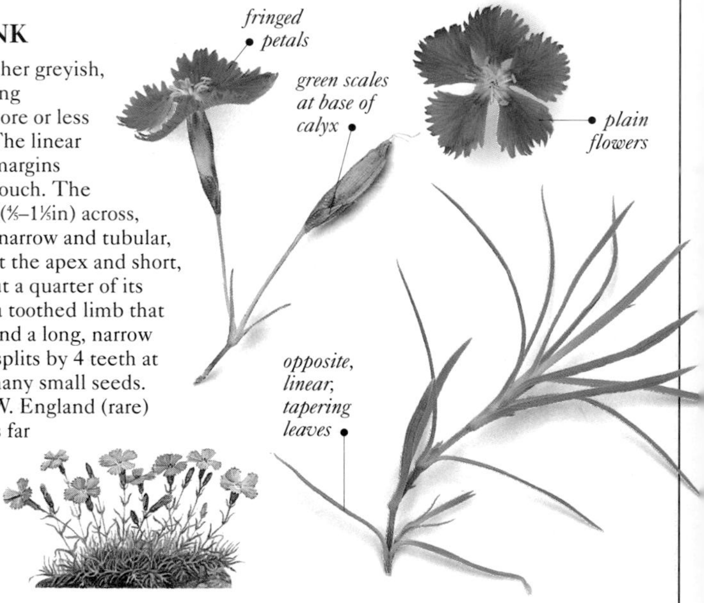

fringed petals
green scales at base of calyx
plain flowers
opposite, linear, tapering leaves

Habit Perennial	Height 10–20cm (4–8in)	Flowering time May–July

WATER-LILY FAMILY

Family NYMPHAEACEAE	Species *Nymphaea alba*	Author L.

WHITE WATER-LILY

This robust, aquatic, hairless plant has a rhizomatous stock. The leaves, mostly floating or held just above or below the water surface, are circular in outline and split to the stalk at one point. The flowers, 10–20cm (4–8in) across, are held just above the water surface, each with 20 or more fleshy oval petals, and 4 to 6 sepals which are similar to the petals but greenish. The fruit is a spongy capsule which develops below the water surface.

• **DISTRIBUTION** Throughout, except for the Faeroes, Iceland, and Spitsbergen; widely cultivated in ponds.

• **HABITAT** Still and slow-moving fresh water: rivers, streams, lakes, ponds, ditches, and dykes.

Habit Perennial	Height Aquatic	Flowering time June–Sept

Family NYMPHAEACEAE	Species *Nuphar lutea*	Author (L.) Smith

YELLOW WATER-LILY

This is a robust, rhizomatous, and hairless aquatic plant. The leaves are of 2 kinds: submerged leaves are thin and translucent, rounded, and short-stalked; floating leaves are deep green and thick, oval, deeply cleft to the long stalk at one point, with an untoothed margin. The yellow flowers are held above the water surface on stout stalks, each flower is 12–40mm (½–1⅗in) across, with 5 to 6 large overlapping sepals and several smaller petals; the stamens are numerous. The fruit capsule is flask-shaped.

• **DISTRIBUTION** Throughout the region, except for the Faeroes, Iceland, and Spitsbergen.

• **HABITAT** Still and slow-moving fresh water: rivers and streams, lakes and ponds, ditches and dykes; in water up to 5m (16½ft) deep.

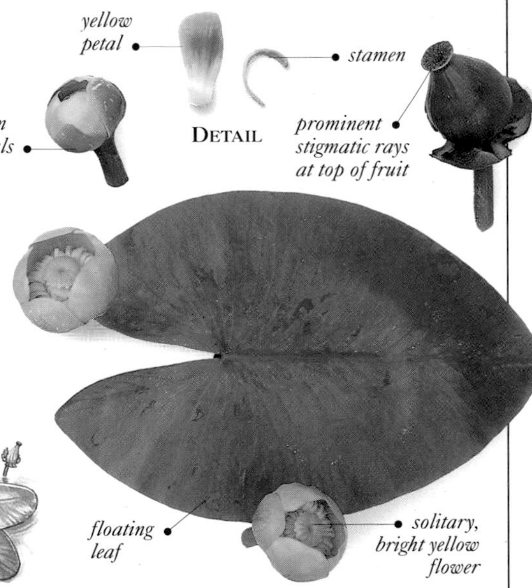

Habit Perennial	Height Aquatic	Flowering time June–Sept

BUTTERCUP FAMILY

Family RANUNCULACEAE	Species *Helleborus foetidus*	Author L.

STINKING HELLEBORE

This is a rather robust, unpleasant smelling, hairless plant with leafy overwintering stems. The leaves, all on the stems, are alternate, leathery, deep green, and palmately lobed with up to 12 lobes; upper leaves and bracts have a smaller blade and a broad and rather prominent stalk. The nodding green flowers, 10–30mm (⅖–1⅕in) across, are rimmed with purple; the sepals, usually 5, are conspicuous. The fruit is a cluster of generally 3 many-seeded follicles. The plant is poisonous.
• **DISTRIBUTION** England and Wales to Holland and Germany southwards.
• **HABITAT** Woods, coppices, and scrub; on stony open calcareous soils. Widely grown in gardens and often becoming naturalized.

bell-shaped flowers in terminal clusters

dry, dehiscent fruit

DETAIL

narrow-elliptical, toothed leaf-lobes

simple bract

Habit Perennial	Height 40–80cm (16–32in)	Flowering time Jan–May

Family RANUNCULACEAE	Species *Helleborus viridis*	Author L.

GREEN HELLEBORE

This tufted, hairless plant often has 2 non-overwintering basal leaves. The rather dull deep green leaves are palmately lobed into 5 to 7 main segments. The bracts are leaf-like but smaller and unstalked. The yellowish green flowers are saucer-shaped, 30–50mm (1⅕–2in) across, and half-nodding; the sepals are conspicuous, oval, and spread widely apart. The fruit consists of 2 to 5 many-seeded follicles. The plant is poisonous.
• **DISTRIBUTION** England and Wales to Holland and Germany southwards.
• **HABITAT** Woodland, coppices, and scrub, on deep loamy calcareous soils.
• **REMARK** In W. Europe the plant is subsp. *occidentalis*. Elsewhere in Europe it is referable to subsp. *viridis*.

Habit Perennial	Height 30–40cm (12–16in)	Flowering time Feb–Apr

Family RANUNCULACEAE	Species *Eranthis hyemalis*	Author (L.) Salisb.

WINTER ACONITE

This is a small, hairless plant. The main leaves are basal, circular in outline, palmately lobed, and long-stalked, while 3 stem-leaves form a whorl and are smaller and stalkless; all are shiny bright green. The bright yellow flowers, 20–30mm (⅘–1⅕in) across, appear before the basal leaves, are nodding in bud, becoming erect as they mature, and each have 6 oval, petal-like sepals.

• **DISTRIBUTION** Widely naturalized, except in Ireland and most of Scandinavia. Widely cultivated. Native of C. and E. Europe.

• **HABITAT** Moist deciduous woodland, hedgebanks, and churchyards; on humus-rich soils.

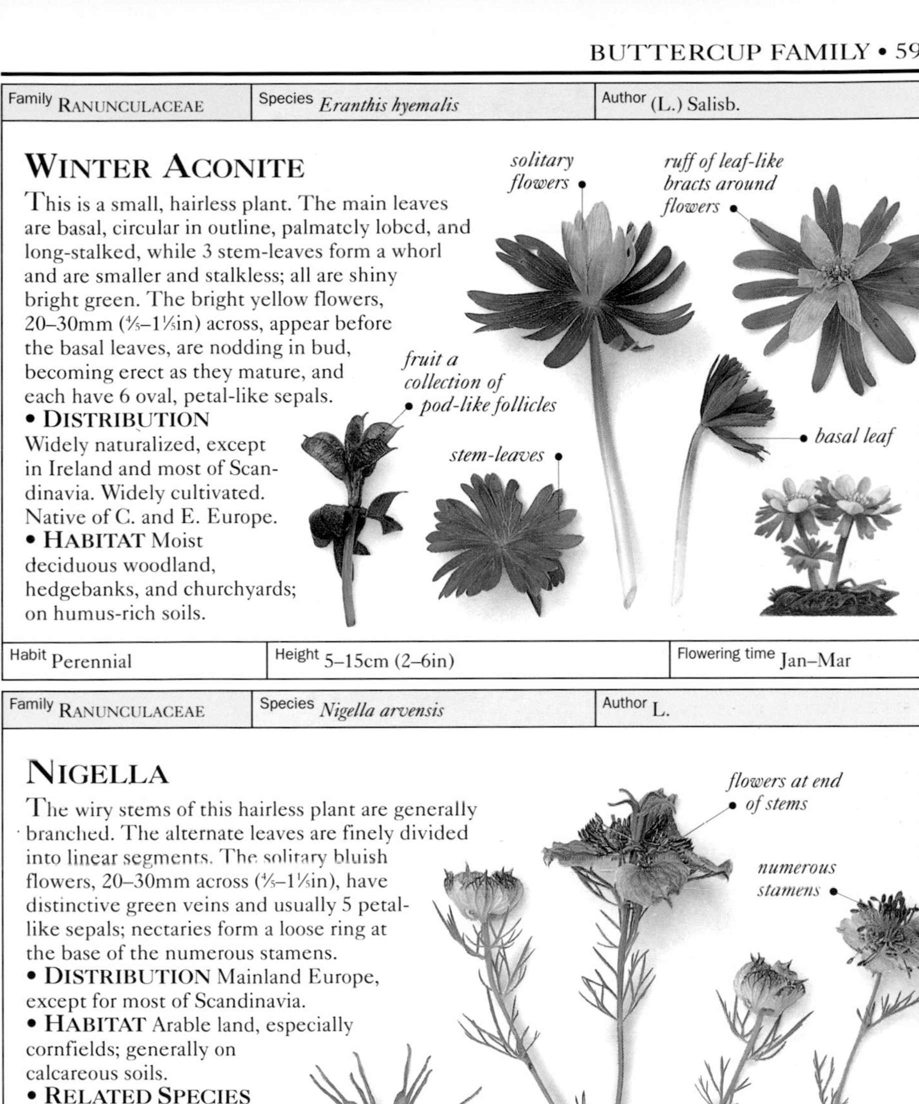

Habit Perennial	Height 5–15cm (2–6in)	Flowering time Jan–Mar

Family RANUNCULACEAE	Species *Nigella arvensis*	Author L.

NIGELLA

The wiry stems of this hairless plant are generally branched. The alternate leaves are finely divided into linear segments. The solitary bluish flowers, 20–30mm across (⅘–1⅕in), have distinctive green veins and usually 5 petal-like sepals; nectaries form a loose ring at the base of the numerous stamens.

• **DISTRIBUTION** Mainland Europe, except for most of Scandinavia.

• **HABITAT** Arable land, especially cornfields; generally on calcareous soils.

• **RELATED SPECIES** *Nigella damascena*, Love-in-a-mist, has brighter blue flowers with a ruff of leaves below and a swollen head of united follicles. It has a similar distribution; casual on waste ground in Britain.

flowers at end of stems

numerous stamens

fruit a collection of narrow follicles

feathery leaves

nectary petals

DETAIL

Habit Annual	Height 30–50cm (12–20in)	Flowering time June–July

Family RANUNCULACEAE	Species *Trollius europaeus*	Author L.

GLOBEFLOWER

This rather robust, tufted, hairless plant has erect, scarcely branched stems. The deep green leaves are palmately lobed with 5 to 7 main segments which are further lobed and toothed; the basal leaves are long-stalked, while the upper are short-stalked or unstalked. The flowers are lemon-yellow, 25–50mm (1–2in) across, with about 10 broadly overlapping and incurved "petals"; the stamens are numerous. The fruit is a collection of many-seeded follicles which split along the inner side. The plant is poisonous.

• **DISTRIBUTION** Much of the region, mainly in the uplands; in Britain confined to Wales, N. England, and Scotland.

• **HABITAT** Damp grassy meadows, cliffs, open woodland, and stream margins; widely cultivated in gardens, including forms with golden yellow and orange flowers.

Habit Perennial	Height 40–70cm (16–28in)	Flowering time May–Aug

Family RANUNCULACEAE	Species *Caltha palustris*	Author L.

MARSH MARIGOLD

Also known as Kingcup, this is a variable, tufted, hairless, and rhizomatous plant, with erect to spreading stems which sometimes root at the lower nodes. The leaves, mainly basal, are heart-shaped and toothed; the basal leaves are long-stalked, while the stem-leaves are rather few and similar to the basal, but short-stalked. Borne in loose, branched clusters, the flowers are saucer-shaped, 15–50mm (⅗–2in) across, with 5 to 8 oval, spreading "petals". The fruit is a cluster of many-seeded follicles which split along the inner margin. The plant is poisonous.

• **DISTRIBUTION** Throughout the region, except for Spitsbergen.

• **HABITAT** Damp places, marshes, bogs, pond and stream margins, seepage zones, ditches, wet woodland; grown in gardens, including a form with double flowers.

Habit Perennial	Height 20–60cm (8–24in)	Flowering time Mar–Aug

Family RANUNCULACEAE	Species *Aconitum napellus*	Author L.

MONK'S HOOD

Rather robust, and almost hairless, this plant has stiff, erect stems which are generally unbranched, except in the inflorescence. The alternate leaves are rounded in outline but divide into 5 to 7 toothed lobes. The deep blue or reddish violet flowers have numerous stamens and 5 petal-like parts; the upper part is larger and forms a hood containing 2 spurred nectaries. The plant is poisonous.

• **DISTRIBUTION** S. Britain, Belgium, France, and Germany; widely cultivated and often naturalized.

• **HABITAT** Damp woodland, meadows, scrub, and stream margins.

• **RELATED SPECIES** *Aconitum vulparia*, Wolfsbane, has pale yellow flowers. It is native in mainland Europe, except for Scandinavia.

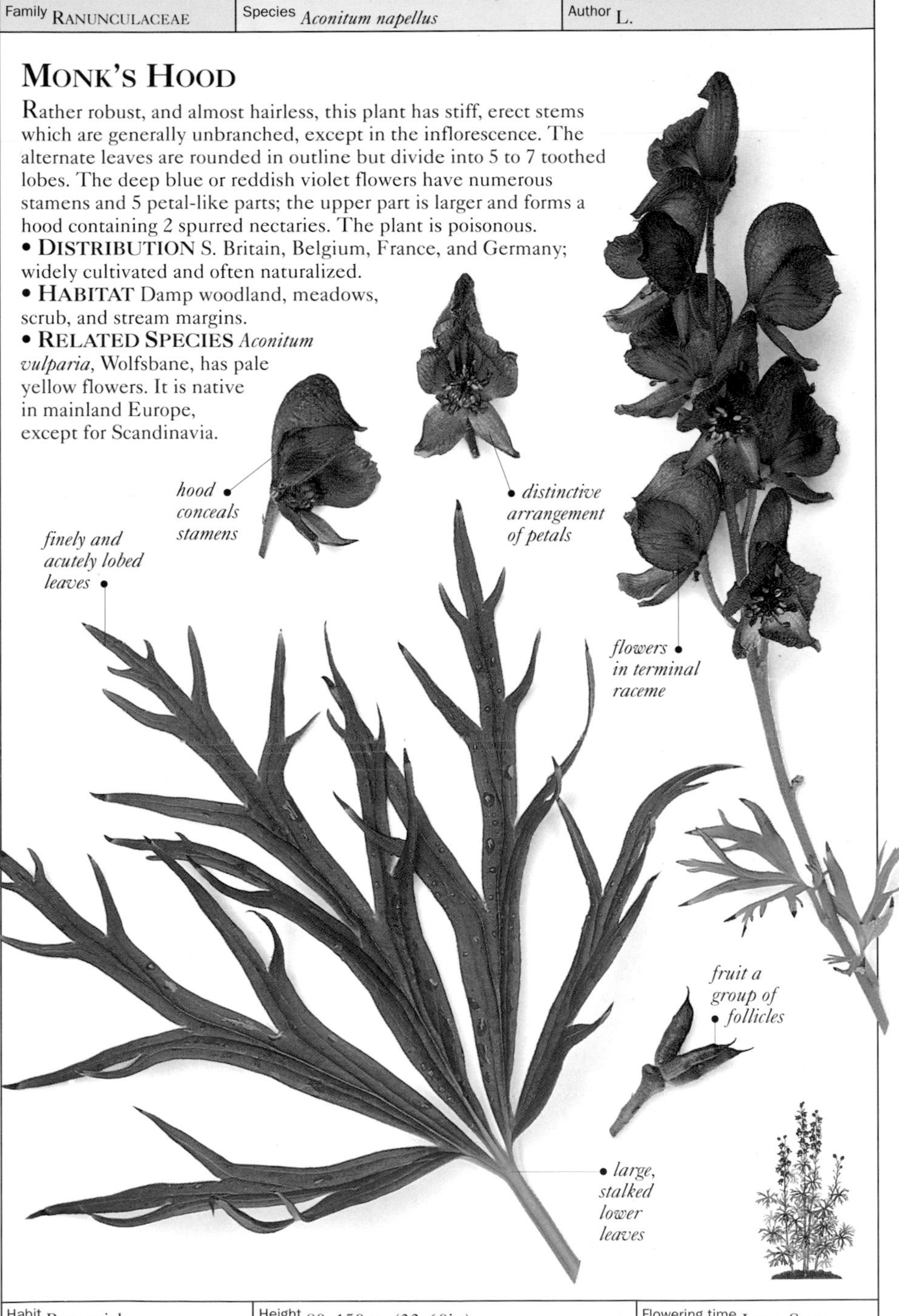

Habit Perennial	Height 80–150cm (32–60in)	Flowering time June–Sept

Family RANUNCULACEAE	Species *Anemone nemorosa*	Author L.

WOOD ANEMONE

Also often called Windflower, this familiar plant is patch-forming and almost hairless. The basal leaves, generally appearing after the flowers, have deeply lobed, toothed divisions and are long-stalked; the stem-leaves are similar but are short-stalked. The solitary flowers, 20–40mm ($\frac{4}{5}$–$1\frac{3}{5}$in) across, are half-nodding to erect, white, and often flushed with pink or blue on the outside; each flower has 6 to 12 oval "petals". The fruit is a nodding head of small achenes.

• **DISTRIBUTION** Throughout the region, except for the far north.

• **HABITAT** Woodland, coppices, scrub, hedgerows, sometimes meadows in wetter areas; on a variety of soils.

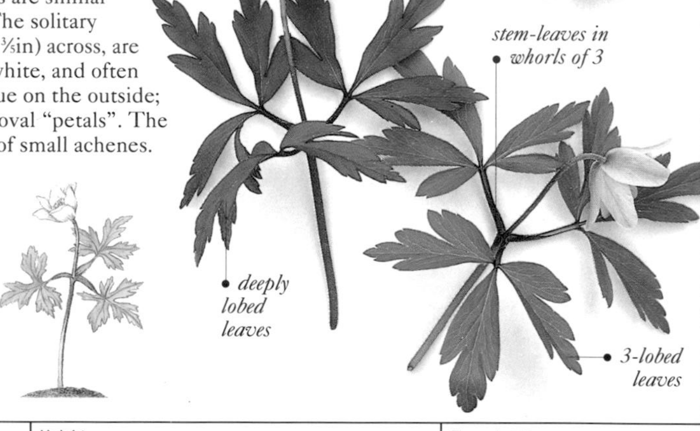

Habit Perennial	Height 5–30cm (2–12in)	Flowering time Mar–May

Family RANUNCULACEAE	Species *Pulsatilla vulgaris*	Author Miller

PASQUE-FLOWER

Also known as *Anemone pulsatilla*, this hairy plant forms discrete tufts, with the flowers appearing with the young leaves. The leaves are all basal and are pinnately cut into many linear segments. The bracts are similar to the leaves but are unstalked and borne in a close whorl just below the flowers. The solitary pale to dark purple flowers, 55–85mm ($2\frac{1}{5}$–$3\frac{2}{5}$in) across, are erect at first but gradually become half-nodding; the "petals", usually 6, are twice as long as the numerous yellow stamens. The fruit is a dense head of feathered achenes.

• **DISTRIBUTION** C. and E. England (rather rare), Belgium, Holland, W. France, Germany, Denmark, S. Sweden.

• **HABITAT** Dry grassy places, downland, and low turf over neutral to mildly acid soils, to 1,200m (3,950ft); widely cultivated in gardens.

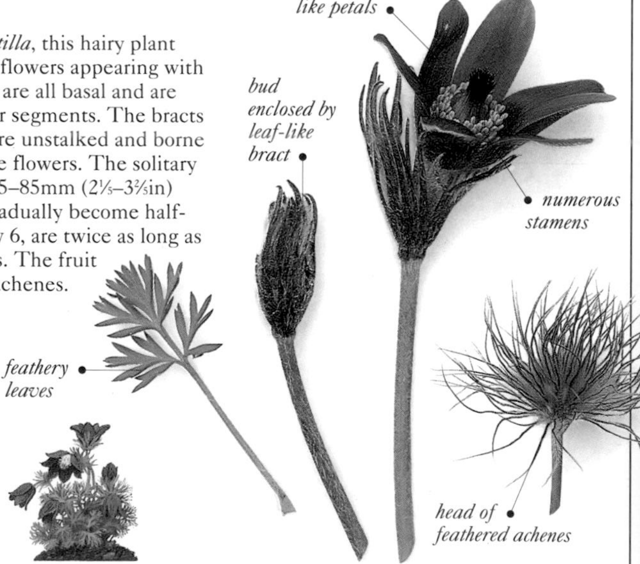

Habit Perennial	Height 15–30cm (6–12in)	Flowering time Apr–June

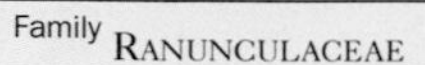

Family RANUNCULACEAE	Species *Clematis vitalba*	Author L.

TRAVELLER'S JOY

This rampant deciduous plant climbs by means of twisting and clinging leaf-stalks which persist after the leaves have fallen. The stems become thick and woody with age. The leaves are opposite and pinnate, with oval to lanceolate toothed leaflets. The fragrant greenish white to cream flowers, 18–20mm (⅝–¾in) across, have 4 petal-like sepals which are hairy underneath. The fruit consists of a dense cluster of feathered achenes (hence the other common name often used for this plant, Old Man's Beard).

• **DISTRIBUTION** S. England and Wales, Holland to C. Germany southwards; naturalized elsewhere in the region including Scotland and Ireland.

• **HABITAT** Hedgerows, scrub, woodland, old walls; mostly on calcareous soils.

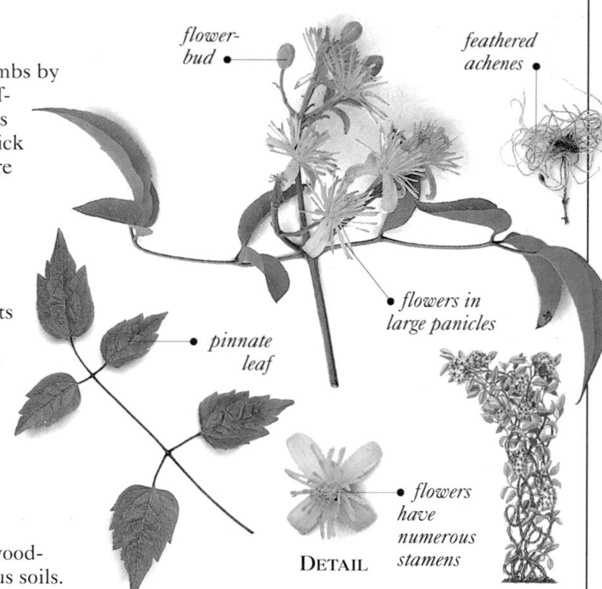

Habit Woody climber	Height 4–30m (13–100ft)	Flowering time July–Sept

Family RANUNCULACEAE	Species *Adonis vernalis*	Author L.

YELLOW PHEASANT'S-EYE

This tufted, more or less hairless plant has slender, erect, unbranched stems forming large clumps in older plants. The stems are scaly at the base. The leaves are 3-pinnate, with very narrow, pointed segments, and are usually rather pale or yellowish green. The large flowers, 40–80mm (1⅗–3⅕in) across, have 10 to 12 elliptical, shiny petals and a ruff of leaves immediately beneath; sepals are present; stamens are numerous. The fruit is a dense head of hairy achenes.

• **DISTRIBUTION** C. and S. France, S. Germany, S. Sweden (Gotland), and the mountains of C. Europe. Always local.

• **HABITAT** Dry grassy places, occasionally scrub; sometimes cultivated.

Habit Perennial	Height 15–25cm (6–10in)	Flowering time Apr–May

Family RANUNCULACEAE	Species *Adonis annua*	Author L.

PHEASANT'S EYE

The stems of this erect plant are thin and may be branched or unbranched. The feathery leaves are alternate up the stem and are divided into thread-like segments. The bright red buttercup-like flowers are 15–25mm (⅗–1in) across, and usually have 5 to 8 petals and 5 spreading, hairless sepals. The fruit consists of a head of achenes.

• **DISTRIBUTION** Native in France and Germany but naturalized or casual in Britain and S. Scandinavia; now very rare in Britain. Declining due to farming.

• **HABITAT** Arable land, especially cornfields; waste and disturbed land, and rubbish tips; cultivated in gardens.

• **RELATED SPECIES** *Adonis flammea* has larger flowers with petals pressed close to the hairy sepals. It grows in similar habitats from N. France and C. Germany southwards.

Habit Annual	Height 10–40cm (4–16in)	Flowering time June–Aug

Family RANUNCULACEAE	Species *Ranunculus acris*	Author L.

MEADOW BUTTERCUP

This is a variable, usually hairy, plant. The basal leaves are cut into 3 to 7, toothed, wedge-shaped segments; the upper leaves are much smaller and unstalked. The flowers, 15–25mm (⅗–1in) across, terminate the branched stems and have 5 sepals and 5 petals. The fruit is a cluster of small achenes, each with a hooked beak. The plant is poisonous.

• **DISTRIBUTION** Throughout the region, where various varieties are recognized. Often abundant.

• **HABITAT** Damp meadows and pastures, road verges, open woodland, and ditches.

• **RELATED SPECIES** *Ranunculus repens*, Creeping Buttercup, has creeping runners, and basal leaves with 3 main segments. It has similar habitats and distribution to the above.

Habit Perennial	Height 30–100cm (12–40in)	Flowering time Apr–Sept

Family RANUNCULACEAE	Species *Ranunculus bulbosus*	Author L.

BULBOUS BUTTERCUP

Common and very variable, this hairy plant has erect stems that are swollen and bulb-like at the base and branched in the upper part. The long-stalked leaves are mainly basal, 3-lobed, and toothed; the upper leaves are smaller and short-stalked. Borne on furrowed stalks, the flowers, 20–30mm ($\frac{4}{5}$–$1\frac{1}{5}$in) across, each have 5 downturned sepals and 5 petals.

• **DISTRIBUTION** Throughout, except for the Faeroes, Iceland, and Spitsbergen.

• **HABITAT** Meadows, pastures, roadsides, hedgerows, river- and stream-banks, fixed sand dunes.

• **RELATED SPECIES** *Ranunculus sardous*, Hairy Buttercup, is slighter, with a scarcely swollen stem base, and shiny leaves. The flowers are paler. Its distribution and habitats are similar.

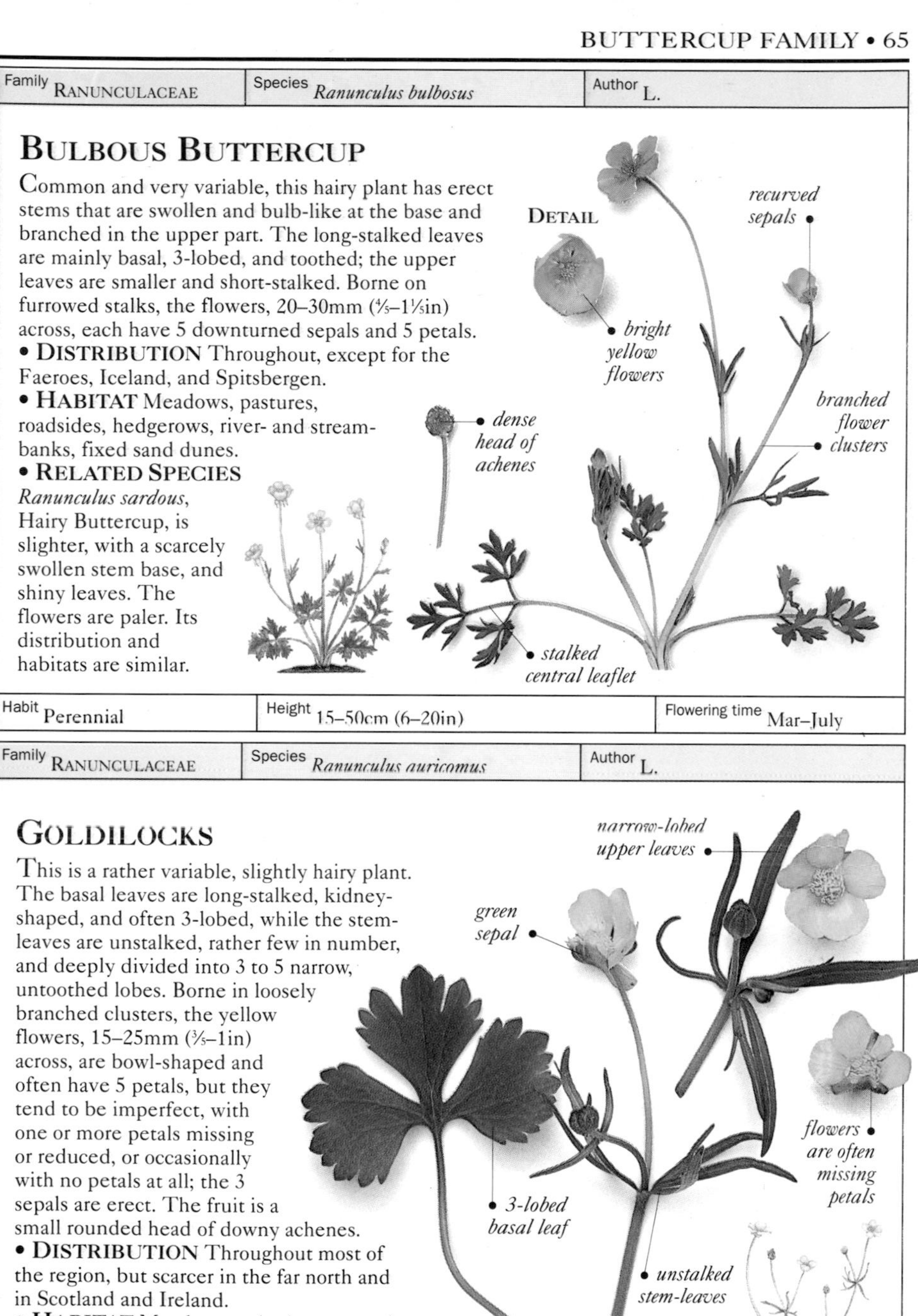

Habit Perennial	Height 15–50cm (6–20in)	Flowering time Mar–July

Family RANUNCULACEAE	Species *Ranunculus auricomus*	Author L.

GOLDILOCKS

This is a rather variable, slightly hairy plant. The basal leaves are long-stalked, kidney-shaped, and often 3-lobed, while the stem-leaves are unstalked, rather few in number, and deeply divided into 3 to 5 narrow, untoothed lobes. Borne in loosely branched clusters, the yellow flowers, 15–25mm ($\frac{3}{5}$–1in) across, are bowl-shaped and often have 5 petals, but they tend to be imperfect, with one or more petals missing or reduced, or occasionally with no petals at all; the 3 sepals are erect. The fruit is a small rounded head of downy achenes.

• **DISTRIBUTION** Throughout most of the region, but scarcer in the far north and in Scotland and Ireland.

• **HABITAT** Meadows and other grassy sites (although scarce), old woodland, hedgerows, and rocky places; often on heavy calcareous or neutral soils and in quite deep shade.

Habit Perennial	Height 20–40cm (8–16in)	Flowering time Apr–May

Family RANUNCULACEAE	Species *Ranunculus sceleratus*	Author L.

CELERY-LEAVED BUTTERCUP

The thick, hollow, furrowed stems of this almost hairless plant are erect and usually branched. The lower leaves are stalked and divided into 3 lobed and toothed segments, while the upper leaves are mostly just 3-lobed; all leaves are shiny green. The numerous flowers are relatively small, 5–10mm (⅕–⅖in) across, and are borne in branched clusters; the 5 downturned sepals are as long as the petals. The fruit consists of numerous small hairless achenes in an oblong head, each with a short blunt beak. The plant is poisonous.

• **DISTRIBUTION** Throughout most of the region, except for the far north; mostly on coastal sites in the northern part of its range.

• **HABITAT** Marshes, open muddy places in meadows, tracksides, ditches, pond, lake, and river margins.

small petals

oblong head of achenes

DETAIL

thick stem

basal leaf

Habit Annual	Height 30–60cm (12–24in)	Flowering time May–Sept

Family RANUNCULACEAE	Species *Ranunculus ficaria*	Author L.

LESSER CELANDINE

This is a variable, tuberous-rooted, and hairless plant, with short fleshy stems. Mostly basal or sub-basal, the shiny deep green leaves are uncut and long-stalked and often have dark markings in the form of spots or blotches. The solitary terminal flowers, 20–30mm (⅘–1⅕in) across, each have 8 to 12 narrow-elliptical yellow petals which bleach as they age, and only 3 sepals. The fruit is a small head of hairless achenes.

• **DISTRIBUTION** Throughout, except for the far north of the region. Many forms are cultivated in gardens.

• **HABITAT** Damp grassy places, woodland, hedgerows, ditches, stream and river margins; in sun and partial shade.

• **REMARK** Subsp. *bulbifera* is a widespread and more slender form bearing small bulbils in the leaf-axils and producing few fertile seeds.

shiny yellow petals

flowers with sepals and petals

DETAIL

head of achenes

heart-shaped leaf-blade

Habit Perennial	Height 5–25cm (2–10in)	Flowering time Mar–May

Family RANUNCULACEAE	Species *Ranunculus flammula*	Author L.

LESSER SPEARWORT

This hairless plant can be erect, spreading, or prostrate; in prostrate forms the stems root down at some of the nodes. The smooth, often reddish, stems bear a few alternate leaves. The basal leaves are oblong or lanceolate and usually untoothed. The flowers, 7–20mm (2/7–4/5in) across, grow in loose clusters on furrowed stalks and are rarely solitary.

• **DISTRIBUTION** Throughout.

• **HABITAT** Wet places, meadows, marshes, flushes, pool and lake margins; mainly on neutral or calcareous soils.

• **RELATED SPECIES** *Ranunculus lingua*, Greater Spearwort, has erect, hollow stems, larger flowers, and grows almost throughout.

Habit Perennial	Height 10–50cm (4–20in)	Flowering time May–Sept

Family RANUNCULACEAE	Species *Myosurus minimus*	Author L.

MOUSETAIL

This is a small, hairless, and rather fleshy plant. The leaves are pale to mid-green and are untoothed. Borne on leafless stems, the solitary pale yellowish green flowers are 4–5mm (1/6–1/5in) across, and have 5 to 7 petal-like sepals which bear short basal spurs. The true petals, also 5 to 7, are in the form of tubular nectaries at the base of the stamens. The achenes are borne in a long, tail-like spike.

• **DISTRIBUTION** Throughout, except for the far north; in Britain, mainly confined to C. and S. England. Generally scarce and declining in most areas due to farming.

• **HABITAT** Damp places, sandy arable land, path margins, and bare and waste places; to 1,400m (4,600ft).

head of achenes develops into long tail

DETAIL

spurred sepals

leaves all linear and basal

Habit Annual	Height 3–14cm (1 1/5–5 1/2in)	Flowering time Mar–June

Family RANUNCULACEAE	Species *Aquilegia vulgaris*	Author L.

COLUMBINE

This is a rather stiff, hairy plant with erect, branched stems. The leaves are mainly basal and are a dull green, with broad, 2- to 3-lobed leaflets. The blue or purplish, occasionally pink or white, flowers are 30–50mm (1⅕–2in) across. The 5 petal-like sepals are the same colour as the true petals; each petal bears a pronounced, hooked spur. The fruit is a collection of follicles, often 5 in number. The plant is poisonous.

• **DISTRIBUTION** Throughout, except for the far north. Widely cultivated in gardens.

• **HABITAT** Damp meadows, hedgerows, open woodland, scrub, and fens; generally on calcareous soils to 2,000m (6,550ft) altitude.

• **REMARK** Cultivated forms often become naturalized and may be mistaken for the true wild plant.

Habit Perennial	Height 50–90cm (20–36in)	Flowering time May–July

BARBERRY FAMILY

Family BERBERIDACEAE	Species *Mahonia aquifolium*	Author (Pursh) Nutt.

OREGON GRAPE

Often forming dense shrubberies, this stoloniferous evergreen has stout, woody, scarcely branched stems. The leaves are leathery and pinnate, with 5 to 9 holly-like leaflets. The fragrant small yellow flowers cluster into large terminal heads; each flower has 4 to 6 stamens and 6 to 9 petals. The fleshy, rounded berries are bluish green at first but turn purplish black when ripe.

• **DISTRIBUTION** Naturalized locally in Britain, Holland, and Germany. Native to W. North America.

• **HABITAT** Woodland, scrub, hedgebanks, and abandoned cultivation; generally found growing in shaded or semi-shaded places.

Habit Shrub	Height 50–150cm (20–60in)	Flowering time Mar–May

POPPY FAMILY

Family PAPAVERACEAE	Species *Papaver somniferum*	Author L.

OPIUM POPPY

This is a stiffly erect, hairless or somewhat bristly plant. The alternate leaves are fleshy, bluish green, lobed, and undulated. The large, mauve to purple, lilac, or occasionally white flowers, 8–18cm (3⅕–7in) across, are bowl-shaped and solitary, the 4 broad petals often with a dark basal blotch. The large, many-seeded fruit capsules are globe-like and smooth, with pores just below the stigmatic cap through which the seeds escape.

• **DISTRIBUTION** Naturalized widely over the region except for the far north. Native of E. Europe and W. Asia.

• **HABITAT** In bare and waste places and on cultivated land.

• **REMARK** The seeds of this poppy are edible and are used in breads and cakes. The latex produced by the plant is the source of opium and its derivatives.

Habit Annual	Height 10–90cm (4–36in)	Flowering time June–Aug

Family PAPAVERACEAE	Species *Papaver rhoeas*	Author L.

COMMON POPPY

Usually branched, the stems of this plant have stiff, spreading hairs. The leaves are deep green and pinnately lobed. The large, deep scarlet flowers, 75–100mm (3–4in) across, often have a black blotch at the base of each petal and are occasionally plain pink, white, mauve, or even bicoloured; the stamens are numerous, with bluish anthers. When ripe, the smooth, rounded fruit capsule releases its seeds through a ring of pores just below the stigmatic cap.

• **DISTRIBUTION** Throughout the region, except for the far north.

• **HABITAT** Cultivated land, particularly arable fields, waste and disturbed places, and roadsides.

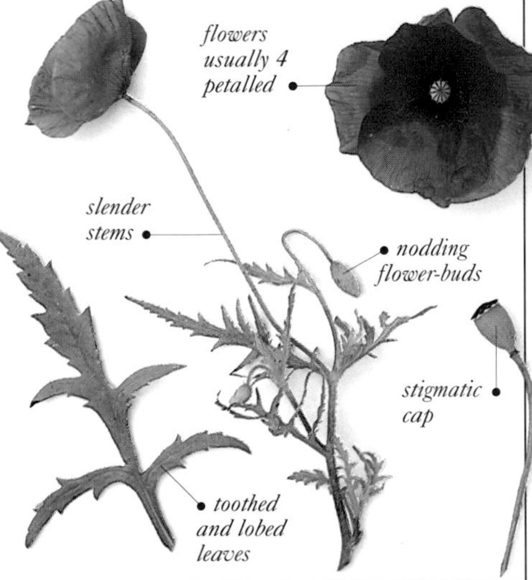

Habit Annual	Height 20–80cm (8–32in)	Flowering time June–Oct

Family PAPAVERACEAE	Species *Meconopsis cambrica*	Author (L.) Vig.

WELSH POPPY

This almost hairless, tufted plant has slender, somewhat branched stems. The leaves, often rather pale green, have rounded or oblong divisions. The solitary yellow flowers, 40–80mm (1⅗–3⅕in) across, are borne on long slender stems and are nodding in bud; each flower has 2 sepals, which fall as the flowers open, and numerous stamens. The fruit is an erect capsule and contains many fine seeds.

• **DISTRIBUTION** Native in Wales, S.W. England, Ireland, and W. France; sometimes naturalized elsewhere in the region.

• **HABITAT** Shaded or semi-shaded places among rocks, beneath trees, and along old walls, hedgebanks, or streamsides.

pinnately lobed leaves

short style

4 petals

spindle-shaped fruit capsule

numerous stamens

Habit Perennial	Height 40–60cm (16–24in)	Flowering time June–Aug

Family PAPAVERACEAE	Species *Glaucium flavum*	Author Crantz

YELLOW HORNED POPPY

The stems of this robust, greyish plant are erect to arched and often branched. The basal leaves are stalked, pinnately lobed, and have an undulating surface; the upper stem-leaves are smaller and unstalked. The solitary yellow flowers, 60–90mm (2⅖–3⅗in) across, have 2 sepals which fall as soon as the flower opens; the 4 petals occasionally have a dark basal blotch. The fruit is a smooth, many-seeded capsule and splits lengthways when ripe.

• **DISTRIBUTION** Throughout, as far north as C. Scotland and S. Norway.

• **HABITAT** Coastal sands and shingle, sea-cliffs, and more rarely on waste ground inland. On very well-drained soils.

flowers have numerous stamens

long slender fruit-pod

upper leaves clasp stem

lobed, fleshy basal leaves

Habit Biennial or perennial	Height 50–90cm (20–36in)	Flowering time June–Sept

Family PAPAVERACEAE	Species *Chelidonium majus*	Author L.

GREATER CELANDINE

Rather succulent and brittle, this tufted, slightly hairy plant exudes orange latex when cut. The leaves, in a basal rosette at first, are pale greyish green and pinnately lobed, with rounded segments; the stem-leaves are alternate and similar, although slightly smaller. Borne in small umbels of 2 to 6, the yellow poppy-like flowers are 15–25mm (⅗–1in) across, with 2 hairy sepals and 4 petals. The fruit capsule is linear and hairless, splitting into 2 to release numerous seeds.

• **DISTRIBUTION** Throughout, except for Iceland and most of the smaller islands; often gregarious; probably not native.

• **HABITAT** Open woodland, coppices, hedgerows, open and bare ground, and the base of old walls; cultivated in gardens, including forms with double flowers.

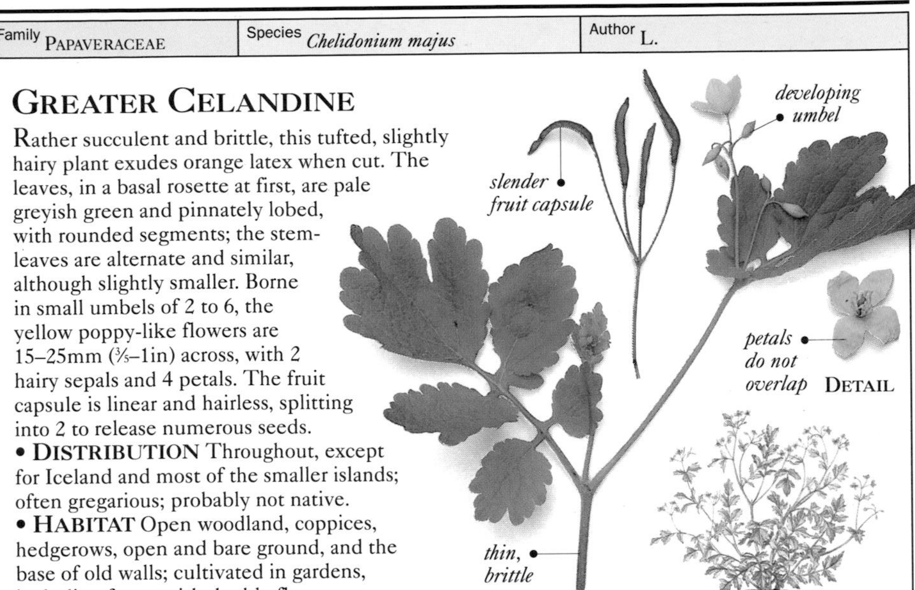

Habit Perennial	Height 40–90cm (16–36in)	Flowering time Apr–Oct

FUMITORY FAMILY

Family FUMARIACEAE	Species *Ceratocapnos claviculata*	Author (L.) Lidén

CLIMBING CORYDALIS

Also known as *Corydalis claviculata*, this scrambling and climbing, hairless plant is rather delicate, with slender, pale green, much-branched stems. The pale green, alternate leaves are 2-pinnate and terminate in a branched clinging tendril; the leaflets are elliptical to oval and untoothed. The small fumitory flowers are cream, 4–6mm (⅙–¼in) long, and are borne in lateral racemes of 6 to 8; the corolla is short-spurred. The fruit, an elliptical capsule 9–10mm (⅜–⅖in) long, is brown when ripe, splits lengthwise, and contains 2 or 3 seeds.

• **DISTRIBUTION** Throughout the region as far north as S. Norway.

• **HABITAT** Rocky and woody places, scrub, old walls, and other shaded habitats. Generally local and often associated with areas of ancient woodland; usually on acid soils.

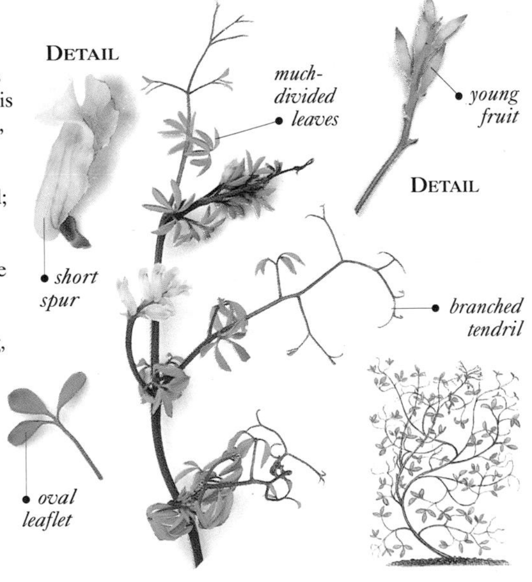

Habit Annual	Height 30–75cm (12–30in)	Flowering time June–Sept

Family FUMARIACEAE	Species *Pseudofumaria lutea*	Author (L.) Borkh.

YELLOW CORYDALIS

Also known as *Corydalis lutea*, this greyish green plant has branched stems. The leaves have many narrow-oblong, untoothed segments. The flowers are 12–20mm (½–⅘in) long; the corolla has a spurred base. The fruit capsule contains black seeds.

• **DISTRIBUTION** Naturalized in Britain and mainland Europe as far north as Scandinavia.

• **HABITAT** Moist, shaded places, especially walls and rocks.

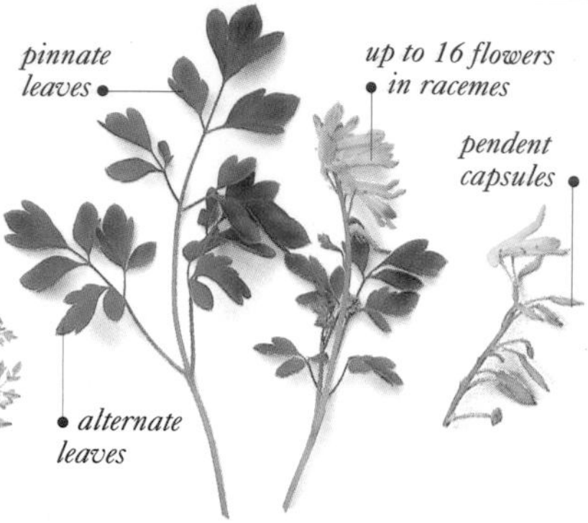

pinnate leaves

up to 16 flowers in racemes

pendent capsules

alternate leaves

Habit Perennial	Height 15–30cm (6–12in)	Flowering time May–Oct

Family FUMARIACEAE	Species *Fumaria capreolata*	Author L.

WHITE RAMPING-FUMITORY

This is a robust, sprawling to clambering, hairless plant. The leaves are much-divided into numerous wedge-shaped or oblong segments. The white or cream flowers, 10–14mm (⅖–⁴⁄₇in) long, have a reddish black apex and 2 small, toothed sepals. The fruit is borne on a short, recurved stalk.

• **DISTRIBUTION** Britain, Ireland, Belgium, France, and Germany; naturalized elsewhere.

• **HABITAT** Arable, waste, and disturbed land, and hedgebanks.

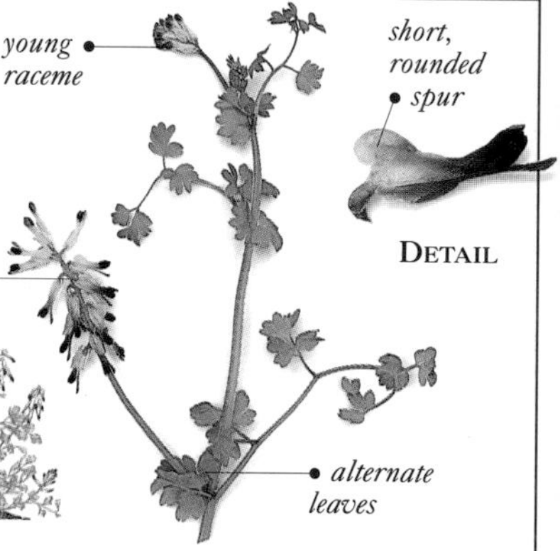

young raceme

short, rounded spur

DETAIL

long-stalked racemes

alternate leaves

Habit Annual	Height 20–80cm (8–32in)	Flowering time May–Sept

Family FUMARIACEAE	Species *Fumaria officinalis*	Author L.

COMMON FUMITORY

This is a weak, spreading to scrambling, rather succulent plant. The alternate leaves are much-divided and lobed, with narrow, flat divisions; most leaves have slender stalks. In lateral and terminal racemes, the purplish pink flowers, 7–9mm (²⁄₇–⅜in) long, have a reddish black tip. The fruit, 2–2.5mm (¹⁄₁₂–¹⁄₁₀in) across, is single-seeded.

• **DISTRIBUTION** Throughout the region, except for Spitsbergen.

• **HABITAT** Cultivated, disturbed, and waste land, roadsides.

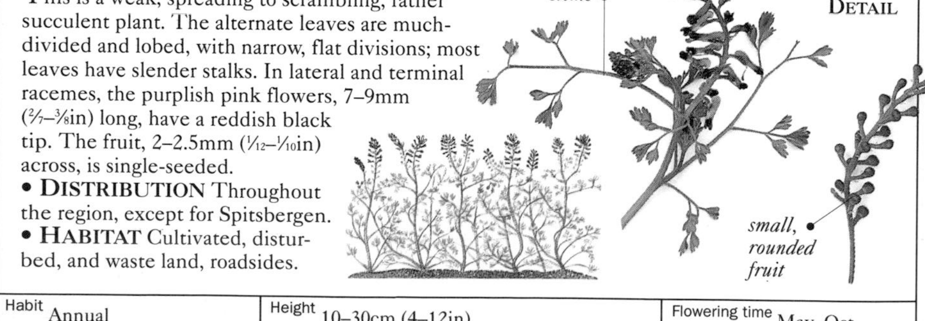

Habit Annual	Height 10–30cm (4–12in)	Flowering time May–Oct

Cress Family

Family CRUCIFERAE	Species *Sisymbrium officinale*	Author (L.) Scop.

Hedge Mustard

This is a rough-haired or hairless plant with spreading side branches. The leaves are alternate; the lower are stalked with a large end lobe; the upper are unstalked. The small yellow flowers, 3–4mm (⅛–⅙in) across, are borne in racemes that elongate as the fruit develops; each flower has 4 separate sepals and petals. The siliquas, 10–20mm (⅖–⅘in) long, are pressed close to the stem.

• **DISTRIBUTION** Throughout the region, except for the far north.

• **HABITAT** Waste and bare ground, hedgerows and roadsides, or arable land.

• **RELATED SPECIES** *Sisymbrium orientale*, Eastern Rocket, has larger flowers, and longer fruit more than 40mm (1⅗in) long. It is naturalized throughout much of the region.

slender, erect siliqua

racemes elongating in fruit

DETAIL

petals not notched

pinnately lobed lower leaves

Habit Annual or biennial	Height 40–100cm (16–40in)	Flowering time May–Sept

Family CRUCIFERAE	Species *Alliaria petiolata*	Author (M.Bieb.) Camara & Grande

Garlic Mustard

Generally unbranched, this hairy plant has stiff, slender stems. The alternate leaves are toothed and stalked and smell distinctly of garlic when crushed. The white flowers, 3–5mm (⅛–⅕in) across, are borne in racemes that grow longer as the fruit develops; each flower has 4 sepals and petals and 6 stamens. When ripe, the siliquas, 20–70mm (⅘–2⅘in) long, split lengthways.

• **DISTRIBUTION** Native throughout the region, except for the far north, and often casual in the northernmost part of its range.

• **HABITAT** Cultivated, waste, and bare ground, hedgerows, open woodland, scrub, and roadsides; on calcareous soils. Sometimes growing in large colonies.

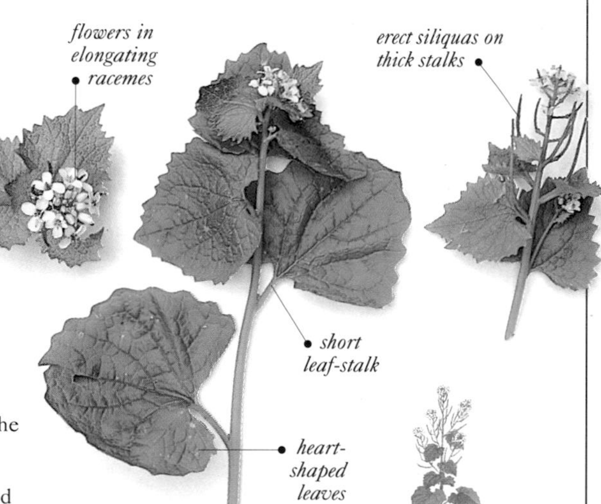

Habit Biennial	Height 60–120cm (24–48in)	Flowering time Apr–June

Family CRUCIFERAE	Species *Arabidopsis thaliana*	Author (L.) Heynh.

THALE CRESS

The slender stems of this slightly hairy plant are branched or unbranched, with a few alternate, usually unstalked, stem-leaves. The stalked basal leaves form a rosette, and are elliptical, toothed or untoothed. The flowers, 3–4mm (1/8–1/6in) across, have 4 free sepals and 4 free petals, and are borne in loose racemes that elongate as the fruit develops. The siliquas, 5–20mm (1/5–4/5in) long, are linear, straight or slightly curved, and hairless.

• **DISTRIBUTION** Throughout the region, except for much of the north; scarce in Ireland and Scotland.

• **HABITAT** Cultivated, waste, rocky, and bare places, banks, hedgerows, and old walls; generally on dry sandy soils.

• **RELATED SPECIES** *Arabidopsis suecica* has more strongly toothed, or lobed, basal leaves, and fruit 20–30mm (4/5–1 1/5in) long. It is confined to Scandinavia.

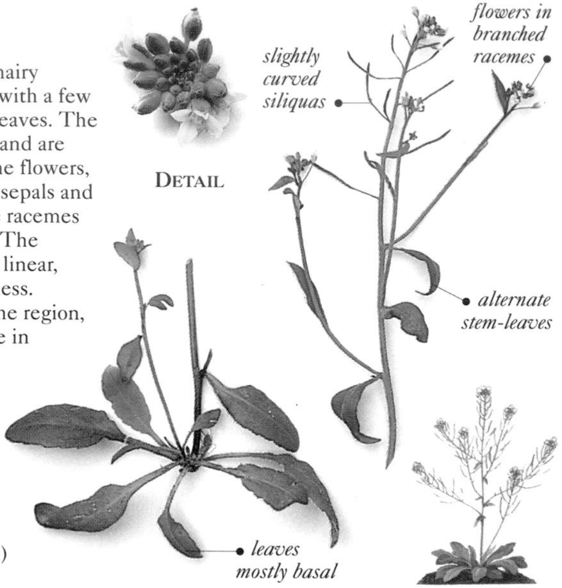

Habit Annual or biennial	Height 10–30cm (4–12in)	Flowering time Mar–Oct

Family CRUCIFERAE	Species *Isatis tinctoria*	Author L.

WOAD

Cultivated as a source of blue dye in the Middle Ages, this is a rather robust, greyish, and almost hairless plant. The stiff stem is branched towards the top and bears alternate leaves. The basal leaves are lanceolate and stalked, whereas the stem-leaves are unstalked; all leaves are untoothed. The yellow flowers, 3–4mm (1/8–1/6in) across, are borne in dense panicles. The pendent siliculas are oblong, flattened, and 11–27mm (3/7–1 1/12in) long.

• **DISTRIBUTION** Naturalized or casual throughout, apart from the far north, but often very local. Native to E. Europe and W. Asia.

• **HABITAT** Cultivated and waste places, rocks and cliffs; on dry soils. Formerly widely cultivated and often a relict of former cultivation.

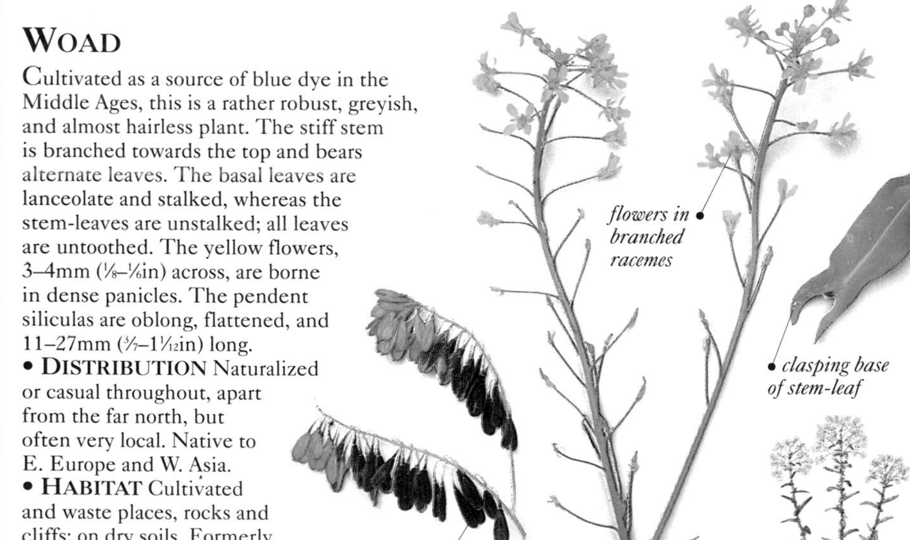

Habit Biennial	Height 80–150cm (32–60in)	Flowering time July–Aug

Family CRUCIFERAE	Species *Erysimum cheiranthoides*	Author L.

TREACLE-MUSTARD

The stems of this erect, hairy plant are square and usually branched. The lower leaves wither before the plant starts to flower; the upper are persistent, more pointed, and ascending. Borne in racemes that elongate as the fruit develops, the yellow flowers, 5–6mm (⅕–¼in) across, each have 4 separate sepals and petals. The siliquas are 10–50mm (⅖–2in) long, slightly hairy, somewhat curved, and almost square in cross-section.

• **DISTRIBUTION** Throughout the region, except for the far north; probably only naturalized in Britain and Ireland.

• **HABITAT** Cultivated, bare, and waste ground, and road verges. Found particularly on sandy, well-drained soils.

• **RELATED SPECIES** *Erysimum hieracifolium* has deeply toothed greyish leaves and larger flowers, 8–10mm (⅓–⅖in) across. The siliquas are held parallel to the stem. It inhabits rocky places and woods in mainland Europe, except for N. Scandinavia.

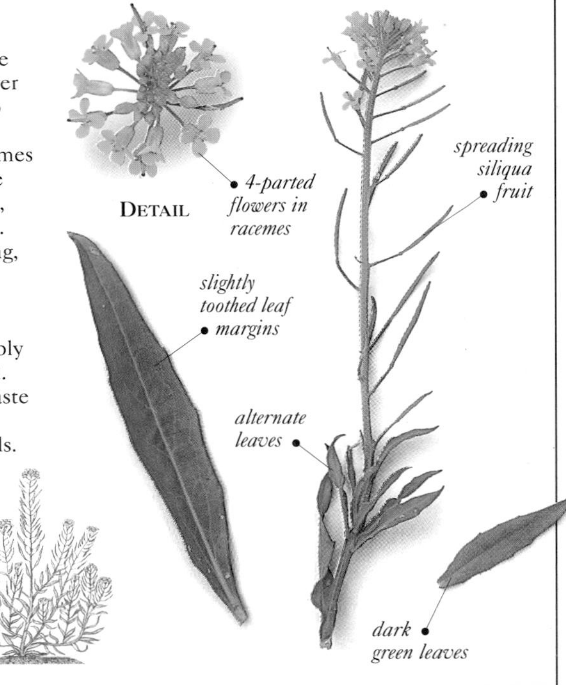

Habit Annual	Height 30–60cm (12–24in)	Flowering time June–Aug

Family CRUCIFERAE	Species *Hesperis matronalis*	Author L.

DAME'S VIOLET

This hairy or hairless plant is branched only in the inflorescence. The alternate leaves are lanceolate, toothed, and short-stalked; the upper leaves are smaller than the lower. The scented flowers are white or purple, 15–20mm (⅗–⅘in) across, and are borne in racemes; the stigma is 2-lobed. The ascending siliquas, 25–100mm (1–4in) long, contain many seeds, and split lengthways when ripe.

• **DISTRIBUTION** Naturalized widely, except in the far north. Native from C. France southwards.

• **HABITAT** Damp or semi-shaded places, streamsides, waste land, hedgerows, roadsides, and often near settlements. Cultivated in gardens.

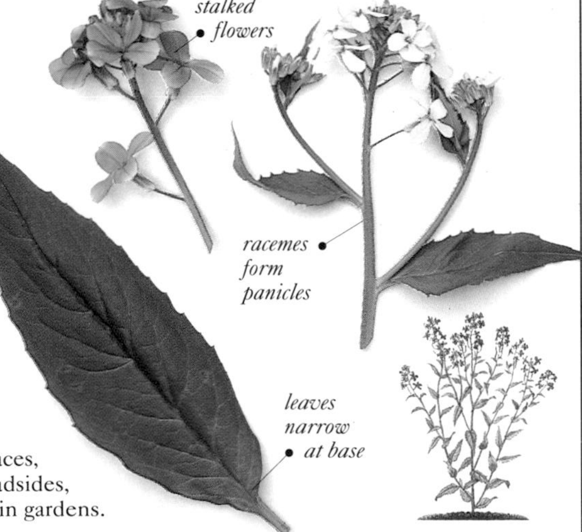

Habit Biennial or perennial	Height 70–120cm (28–48in)	Flowering time May–Aug

Family CRUCIFERAE	Species *Cheiranthus cheiri*	Author (L.) Crantz

WALLFLOWER

Also known as *Erysimum cheiri*, this plant is variably hairy, with rather stiff, branched stems that often become woody towards the bottom. The leaves are alternate and oblong to lanceolate, with a short stalk or no stalk; the uppermost leaves are generally narrower than the lower ones. The sweetly fragrant yellow or orange flowers are 10–20mm (⅖–⅘in) across, and are borne in dense racemes that elongate as the fruit develops; each flower has 4 sepals and 4 petals. The fruit is a slender, flattened, many-seeded siliqua up to 75mm (3in) long.

• **DISTRIBUTION** Widely naturalized in Britain, Belgium, Holland, France, Germany. Native to S.E. Europe.

• **HABITAT** Old walls, cliffs, rocky sites, embankments. Grown in gardens; garden escapes have larger flowers and are yellow, red, purple, mauve, or white.

Habit Perennial	Height 20–60cm (8–24in)	Flowering time Mar–June

Family CRUCIFERAE	Species *Matthiola incana*	Author (L.) R. Br.

HOARY STOCK

This plant is densely covered in white woolly hairs and has erect to ascending stems. The alternate leaves are lanceolate, mostly unlobed, and untoothed. The fragrant, purple or pink, occasionally white, flowers, 25–30mm (1–1⅕in) across, are borne in loose racemes; each flower has 4 sepals and 4 petals. The linear siliquas, up to 16cm (6¼in) long, are downy, with a pair of short horns at the tip.

• **DISTRIBUTION** S. Britain and W. France; occasionally naturalized elsewhere.

• **HABITAT** Rocky coastal sites, especially cliffs, and shingle; sometimes inland on old walls; cultivated in gardens.

• **RELATED SPECIES** *Matthiola sinuata*, Sea Stock, has lobed, rather undulate leaves. The fruit is sticky with yellow or black glands. It inhabits sea-cliffs and dunes in S. Britain, S. Ireland, and W. France.

Habit Perennial	Height 40–80cm (16–32in)	Flowering time May–Aug

Family CRUCIFERAE	Species *Armoracia rusticana*	Author Gaertn., Mey. & Scherb.

HORSE-RADISH

This robust, hairless, and rhizomatous plant has erect stems branched towards the top. The leaves are primarily basal, oblong to elliptical, toothed, long-stalked, and occasionally lobed; stem-leaves are smaller and short-stalked. The white flowers, 8–9mm (⅓–⅜in) across, are numerous, each with 4 sepals and 4 petals. The fruit is a rounded and somewhat inflated silicula, 4–6mm (⅙–¼in) across.

• **DISTRIBUTION** Widely naturalized throughout the region, except for the far north. Native to S. Russia.

• **HABITAT** Grassy places, waste and cultivated land, railway embankments, roadsides, and streamsides.

• **REMARK** The fruit is rarely formed in the region. Although the root has long been used for a sauce, it is poisonous if used in quantity.

finely toothed leaf margin

flowers borne in large panicles

basal leaf

large deep green leaves

Habit Perennial	Height 50–120cm (20–48in)	Flowering time May–June

Family CRUCIFERAE	Species *Rorippa nasturtium-aquaticum*	Author (L.) Hayek

WATERCRESS

Also known as *Nasturtium officinale*, this familiar hairless plant has rather succulent stems and leaves with a characteristic peppery taste; the stems are usually branched and sometimes float on water, or creep and root in mud. The alternate leaves are pinnate, shiny deep green, with rounded or elliptical leaflets. The flowers, 4–6mm (⅙–¼in) across, are borne in racemes that elongate as the fruit develops; each flower has 4 sepals and 4 petals. The fruit is a narrow-elliptical, somewhat curved, siliqua, up to 18mm (⅝in) long.

• **DISTRIBUTION** Throughout the region, except for the far north.

• **HABITAT** Shallow, clear freshwater rivers and streams, lakes, ponds, ditches and dykes, wet flushes, and muddy places; widely cultivated and used as a salad vegetable.

DETAIL

white flower

Habit Perennial	Height 30–70cm (12–28in)	Flowering time May–Oct

Family CRUCIFERAE	Species *Barbarea vulgaris*	Author R. Br.

WINTERCRESS

Only the upper parts of the erect stems of this hairless plant are branched. The rather shiny deep green leaves are variable: the lower have 2 to 5 pairs of lateral lobes and a large end leaflet, while the upper are unlobed, unstalked, and clasp the stem. The small bright yellow flowers, 7–9mm (2/7–3/8in) across, are borne in racemes that elongate in fruit; each flower has 4 separate sepals and petals. The narrow siliquas are 15–30mm (3/5–1 1/5in) long and are held stiffly erect.

• **DISTRIBUTION** Throughout the region, except for the far north.

• **HABITAT** Damp places, roadsides, streambanks, hedgerows, and waste places.

Habit Biennial or perennial	Height 40–100cm (16–40in)	Flowering time May–Aug

Family CRUCIFERAE	Species *Cardamine bulbifera*	Author (L.) Crantz

CORALROOT BITTERCRESS

This is a hairless, rhizomatous plant. The lower leaves have one to 3 pairs of toothed lateral leaflets, while the upper leaves are toothed but undivided; all leaves are alternate. Most upper leaves bear purplish brown bulbils which drop off to form new plants. The pale purple or lilac flowers are 12–18mm (1/2–5/7in) across. The smooth, ascending siliquas, 20–35mm (4/5–1 2/5) long, are very rare.

• **DISTRIBUTION** Throughout the region, except for Ireland and the far north.

• **HABITAT** Deciduous, often beech, woodland, embankments, and streamsides; on calcareous or loamy soils.

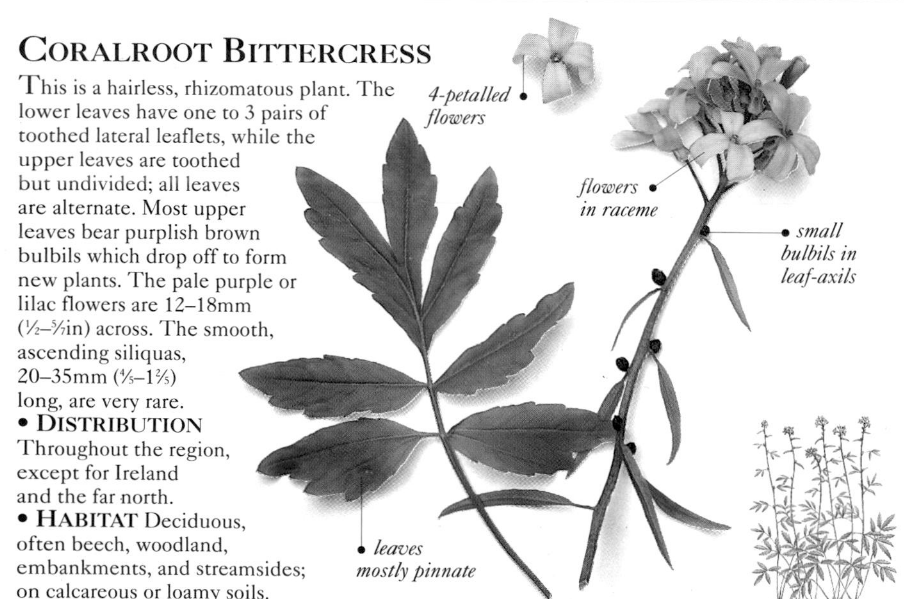

Habit Perennial	Height 30–75cm (12–30in)	Flowering time May–June

Family CRUCIFERAE	Species *Cardamine amara*	Author L.

LARGE BITTERCRESS

This is a rhizomatous and hairless plant with slightly branched or unbranched, erect to ascending, angular stems; the stolons are slender. The leaves are all pinnate and alternate along the stem, not in a basal rosette, and have 2 to 5 pairs of oval, toothed leaflets; the upper leaves generally have narrower leaflets. The flowers, 12mm (½in) across, are usually white, although occasionally purple, and are borne in a loose raceme. The fruit, a slender ascending siliqua, is 20–40mm (⅘–1⅗in) long.

• **DISTRIBUTION** Grows throughout the region, except for the far north, but often local, especially in Wales and Ireland.

• **HABITAT** Damp places, particularly in pastures, woodland, marshes, fens, and along the margins of rivers and streams.

slender fruit

blackish violet anthers

DETAIL

alternate leaves

Habit Perennial	Height 20–60cm (8–24in)	Flowering time Apr–June

Family CRUCIFERAE	Species *Cardamine pratensis*	Author L.

CUCKOO FLOWER

This hairless plant is also known as Lady's Smock. The deep green leaves have up to 10 pairs of toothed or untoothed leaflets. The basal leaves are aggregated into a loose rosette. The pale lilac-pink, or occasionally white, flowers are 12–18mm (½–⅗in) across and are borne in loose racemes that elongate as the fruit develops. The slender siliquas are 25–40mm (1–1⅗in) long.

• **DISTRIBUTION** Throughout, except for the far north of the region.

• **HABITAT** Moist grassy places such as meadows, marshes, open woodland, roadsides, and hedgerows.

Habit Perennial	Height 20–60cm (8–24in)	Flowering time Apr–June

Family CRUCIFERAE	Species *Cardamine impatiens*	Author L.

NARROW-LEAVED BITTERCRESS

This is a hairless plant, with erect, leafy stems. The pinnate leaves have 5 to 9 pairs of often 3-lobed leaflets, and pointed stipules. The tiny whitish or greenish flowers are only 3–4mm (⅛–⅙in) across, and have 4 or no petals. The slender siliquas, 20–30mm (⅘–1⅕in) long, burst explosively when ripe.

• **DISTRIBUTION** Throughout the region, except for Ireland, much of N. Britain, and N. Scandinavia.

• **HABITAT** Damp sites, woodland, streambanks, rocky places, and screes.

Habit Annual or biennial	Height 20–60cm (8–24in)	Flowering time May–Aug

Family CRUCIFERAE	Species *Cardamine hirsuta*	Author L.

HAIRY BITTERCRESS

This plant has hairless stems. The alternate, pinnate leaves have up to 5 pairs of leaflets which are hairy on the upper surface; the lower leaves form a basal rosette. The white flowers are 3–4mm (⅛–⅙in) across. The smooth siliquas are 20–25mm (⅘–1in) long.

• **DISTRIBUTION** Throughout.

• **HABITAT** Bare, waste, cultivated, and rocky ground.

Habit Annual or biennial	Height 5–30cm (2–12in)	Flowering time Feb–Nov

Family CRUCIFERAE	Species *Arabis hirsuta*	Author (L.) Scop.

HAIRY ROCKCRESS

This hairy plant is branched only on the upper part of the stem, if at all. The leaves are oval to lanceolate, toothed or untoothed, and hairy; only the lowermost are stalked. The white flowers, 3–5mm (⅛–⅕in) across, are borne in racemes that elongate as the linear siliquas, 15–40mm (⅗–1⅗in) long, develop.

• **DISTRIBUTION** Throughout, except for the far north.

• **HABITAT** Dry places, grassland, sand dunes, rocks, and old walls, especially on calcareous soils.

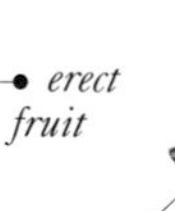

Habit Biennial or perennial	Height 30–60cm (12–24in)	Flowering time May–Aug

Family CRUCIFERAE	Species *Lunaria annua*	Author L.

HONESTY

The branched stems of this robust, hairy plant form a leafy rosette in the first year. The deep green leaves are coarsely toothed; only the lower are stalked. The flowers, 25–30mm (1–1⅕in) across, are reddish purple, mauve, or occasionally white. The flat round to oval fruit is 30–55mm (1⅕–2⅕in) long, and splits to reveal a typical, silvery inner septum which persists long after the seeds are shed.

• **DISTRIBUTION** Naturalized or casual throughout the region, except for the north. Native of S.E. Europe.

• **HABITAT** Cultivated land, waste ground, and roadsides.

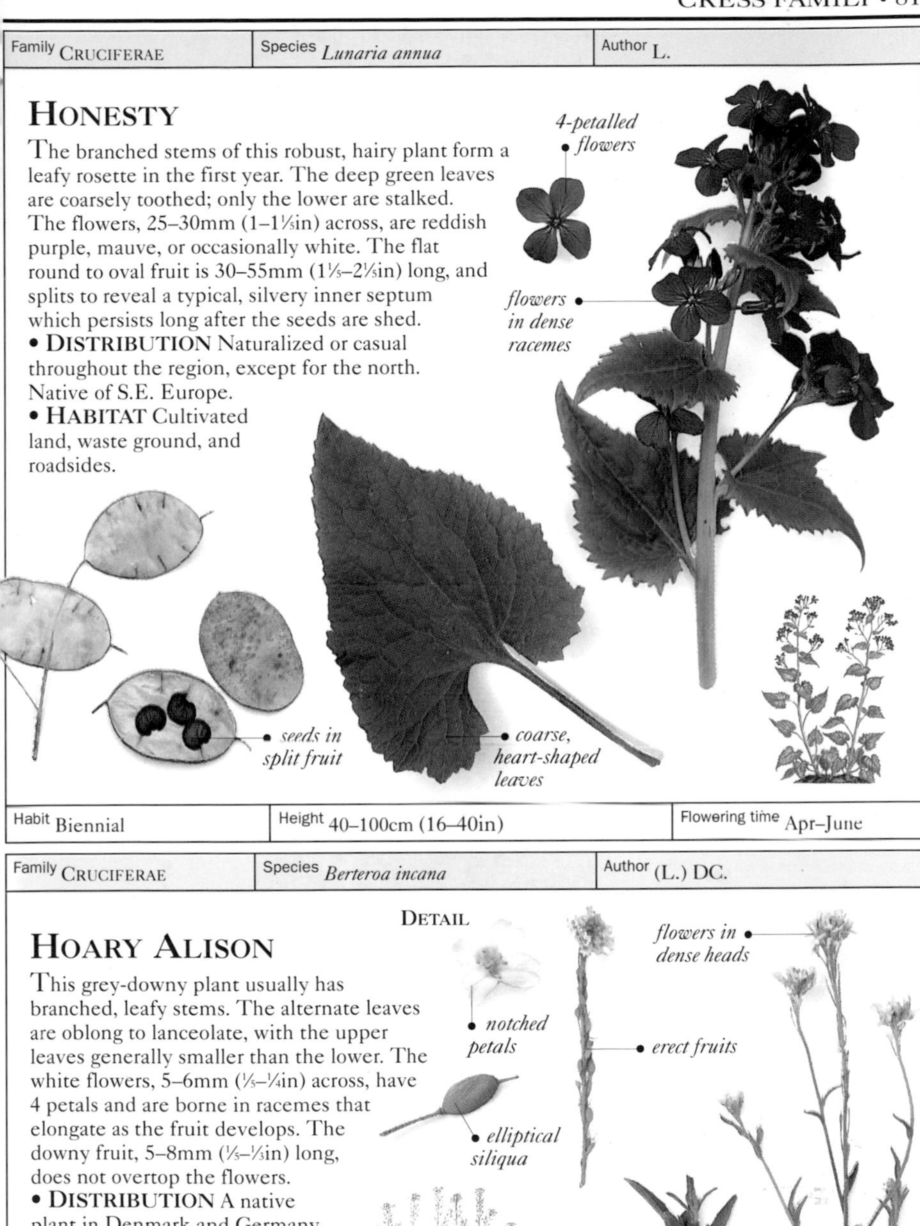

Habit Biennial	Height 40–100cm (16–40in)	Flowering time Apr–June

Family CRUCIFERAE	Species *Berteroa incana*	Author (L.) DC.

HOARY ALISON

This grey-downy plant usually has branched, leafy stems. The alternate leaves are oblong to lanceolate, with the upper leaves generally smaller than the lower. The white flowers, 5–6mm (⅕–¼in) across, have 4 petals and are borne in racemes that elongate as the fruit develops. The downy fruit, 5–8mm (⅕–⅓in) long, does not overtop the flowers.

• **DISTRIBUTION** A native plant in Denmark and Germany. Naturalized throughout, except for Iceland, N. Scandinavia, Ireland, and N. Britain.

• **HABITAT** Arable land, waste ground, and grassy places, on dry, often rather poor, soils.

DETAIL

notched petals

elliptical siliqua

flowers in dense heads

erect fruits

undivided leaves

Habit Annual or perennial	Height 30–60cm (12–24in)	Flowering time June–Oct

Family CRUCIFERAE	Species *Lobularia maritima*	Author (L.) Desv.

SWEET ALISON

This is a hairy, greyish or whitish plant. The linear-lanceolate leaves are pointed, with an untoothed margin. Borne in clusters that slowly lengthen as the fruit develops, the sweetly scented white flowers, 5–6mm (⅕–¼in) across, have 4 sepals and 4 petals. The silicula fruit is oval and generally downy.

• **DISTRIBUTION** Naturalized in Britain and much of Europe, except the north. Native of S. Europe.

• **HABITAT** Dry and waste sites, coastal sands and rocks.

Habit Annual	Height 5–20cm (2–8in)	Flowering time June–Sept

Family CRUCIFERAE	Species *Draba aizoides*	Author L.

YELLOW WHITLOW-GRASS

This rather variable, tufted or cushion-forming, hairless plant has leafless flower scapes. The leaves are deep green, linear-lanceolate, and edged with stiff bristles. The flowers, 5–7mm (⅕–²⁄₇in) across, are borne in dense clusters that lengthen as the fruit develops.

• **DISTRIBUTION** Wales (Gower Peninsula), the mountains of Belgium, France, and Germany.

• **HABITAT** Mountain rocks, cliffs, and screes, on calcareous rocks, and rarely old walls; grown in gardens.

Habit Perennial	Height 5–15cm (2–6in)	Flowering time Mar–May

Family CRUCIFERAE	Species *Erophila verna*	Author (L.) DC.

COMMON WHITLOW-GRASS

This is a rather variable, slightly hairy, tufted plant, with leafless flower scapes. The greyish leaves are lanceolate to elliptical, with a toothed margin. The small white or pinkish flowers are 3–5mm (⅛–⅕in) across, and are borne in loose racemes; each flower is on a slender stalk and has 4 deeply notched petals. The fruit is a narrow-elliptical, hairless silicula.

• **DISTRIBUTION** Throughout, apart from the Arctic region and the Faeroes.

• **HABITAT** Open, bare, and rocky ground, old walls, and sand dunes; most frequently on light soils.

Habit Annual or biennial	Height 4–10cm (1⅗–4in)	Flowering time Mar–June

Family CRUCIFERAE	Species *Cochlearia officinalis*	Author L.

COMMON SCURVY-GRASS

This variable, fleshy, hairless plant has leafy stems. The basal leaves are long-stalked, with an entire margin; the upper are unstalked, clasp the stem, and are often lobed. The flowers, 8–10mm (1/3–2/5in) across, have 4 unnotched petals. The rounded silicula fruit is 4–7mm (1/6–2/7in) across.

• **DISTRIBUTION** Throughout, except for the far north and Finland.

• **HABITAT** Coastal rocks and salt marshes, sea walls, motorway verges subjected to salting, mountain rocks.

Habit Biennial or perennial	Height 10–40cm (4–16in)	Flowering time Apr–Aug

Family CRUCIFERAE	Species *Capsella bursa-pastoris*	Author (L.) Medicus

SHEPHERD'S-PURSE

This very common plant is extremely variable, hairy or not, with erect, often branched, stems. The basal leaves are borne in a loose rosette, pinnately lobed, and stalked, while the upper leaves are unstalked and clasp the stem with heart-shaped bases. The flowers are 2–3mm (1/12–1/8in) across; the 4 petals are occasionally absent. The silicula fruit, 6–9mm (1/4–3/8in) long, is characteristically heart-shaped.

• **DISTRIBUTION** Throughout the region.

• **HABITAT** A widespread weed of cultivated, bare, and waste ground.

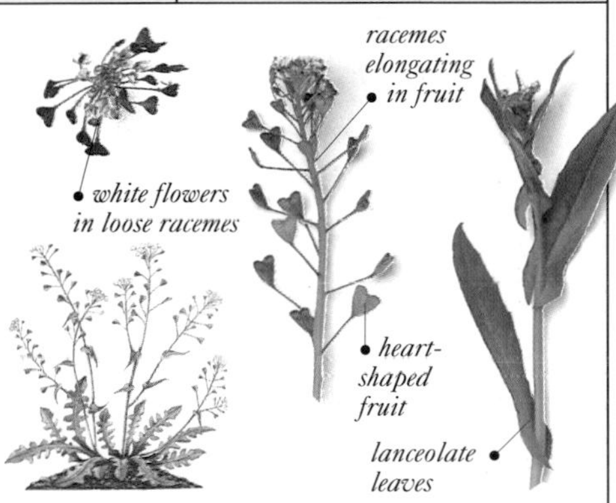

Habit Annual or biennial	Height 15–40cm (6–16in)	Flowering time Year-round

Family CRUCIFERAE	Species *Teesdalia nudicaulis*	Author (L.) R.Br.

SHEPHERD'S CRESS

This is a small and hairless plant with the leaves mainly in a basal rosette. The basal leaves are oval to elliptical, pinnately lobed, and stalked; the stem-leaves are few and much smaller. Borne in loose racemes, the white flowers, only 2mm (1/12in) across, have 4 unnotched petals. The oval silicula is blunt-ended or slightly notched.

• **DISTRIBUTION** Throughout the region; often local.

• **HABITAT** Open sandy and gravelly places, heaths, and disturbed land; frequently on acid soils.

Habit Annual	Height 15–40cm (6–16in)	Flowering time May–Oct

Family CRUCIFERAE	Species *Thlaspi arvense*	Author L.

FIELD PENNY-CRESS

This variable and hairless plant is foul-smelling when crushed. The stems are erect and leafy and are usually branched in the upper part. The lower leaves, not borne in a rosette, are oblong, usually toothed, and stalked, while the upper leaves are similar but clasp the stem with unstalked bases. Borne in racemes that elongate as the fruit develops, the white flowers, 10–15mm (⅖–⅗in) across, have 4 sepals and 4 petals, the latter usually slightly notched. The flat, rounded silicula fruit measures 10–15mm (⅖–⅗in) across, is deeply notched at the top, broadly winged, and borne on ascending stalks.

• **DISTRIBUTION** Throughout, except for the far north.

• **HABITAT** Cultivated, especially arable, land, waste places, and disturbed ground.

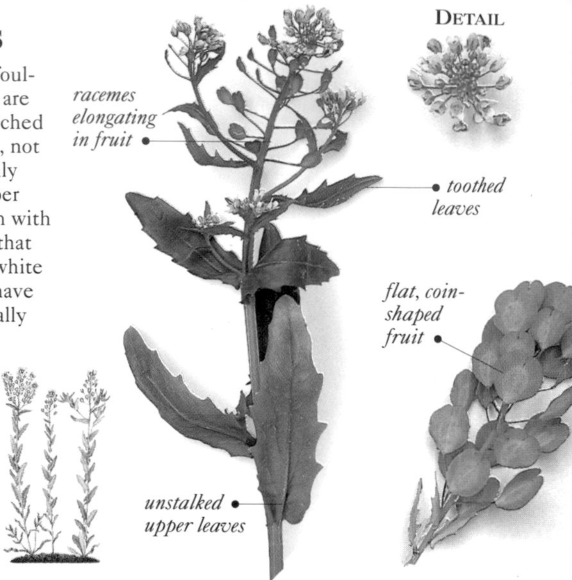

Habit Annual	Height 30–60cm (12–24in)	Flowering time May–Aug

Family CRUCIFERAE	Species *Iberis amara*	Author L.

WILD CANDYTUFT

The erect, leafy stems of this slightly hairy plant are usually branched in the upper part. The fleshy, alternate leaves are elliptical to lanceolate, with a lobed or sometimes toothed margin; the lower leaves are stalked. The white or purplish flowers, 6–8mm (¼–⅓in) across, are borne in rather flat-headed clusters that elongate as the fruit begins to develop; each flower has 4 unequal petals, 2 long and 2 short. The silicula fruit, 3–5mm (⅛–⅕in) long, is flat and heart-shaped, with triangular wings.

• **DISTRIBUTION** S. England, Holland to Germany southwards.

• **HABITAT** Arable and cultivated land, dry hillsides, open woodland, and grassland; generally on calcareous soils, especially where there are rabbits.

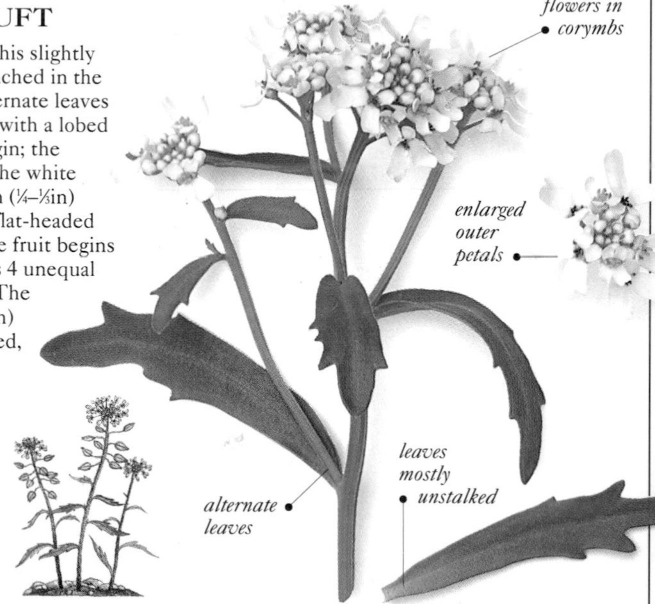

Habit Annual	Height 15–30cm (6–12in)	Flowering time May–Sept

Family CRUCIFERAE	Species *Biscutella laevigata*	Author L.

BUCKLER MUSTARD

This is a very variable, tufted, and hairy plant, with erect to ascending stems which are generally branched in the upper half. The leaves, mostly basal, are green or grey-green and are linear to lanceolate, usually with a lobed or toothed margin but sometimes entire, and have a slender stalk; the stem-leaves are few, often only 2, smaller than the basal, and often unstalked. The small yellow flowers, 6–10mm (1/4–2/5in) across, are borne in branched racemes; each flower has 4 sepals and 4 petals; the petals are not notched. The flat fruit is 4–8mm (1/6–1/3in) across and consists of 2 disc-like lobes arranged side by side like a pair of spectacles.

• **DISTRIBUTION** Belgium, France, and Germany.

• **HABITAT** Dry limestone rocks and open bare places; sometimes on cultivated land or on waste ground.

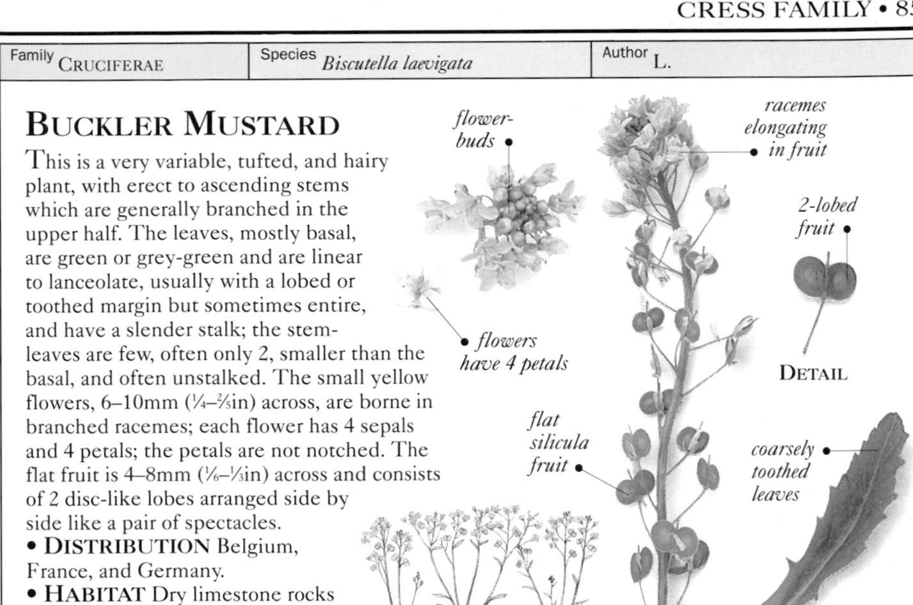

Habit Perennial	Height 10 25cm (4–10in)	Flowering time May–July

Family CRUCIFERAE	Species *Lepidium campestre*	Author (L.) R. Br.

FIELD PEPPERWORT

This rather greyish, hairy plant has erect to spreading stems which are usually branched in the upper part. The basal leaves are oval, stalked, and untoothed, but sometimes slightly lobed, while the upper leaves are lanceolate, clasp the stem with unstalked bases, and normally have toothed margins. The white flowers, only 2mm (1/12in) across, are borne in branched racemes that elongate as the fruit develops; the petals are scarcely longer than the sepals. The silicula fruit, 5–6mm (1/5–1/4in) long, are oval, winged, notched in the upper part, and covered in minute scales.

• **DISTRIBUTION** Throughout the region; a naturalized plant in the Faeroes and Iceland.

• **HABITAT** Cultivated, waste, and disturbed land, roadsides, embankments, occasionally old walls; a widespread weed of open, dry places.

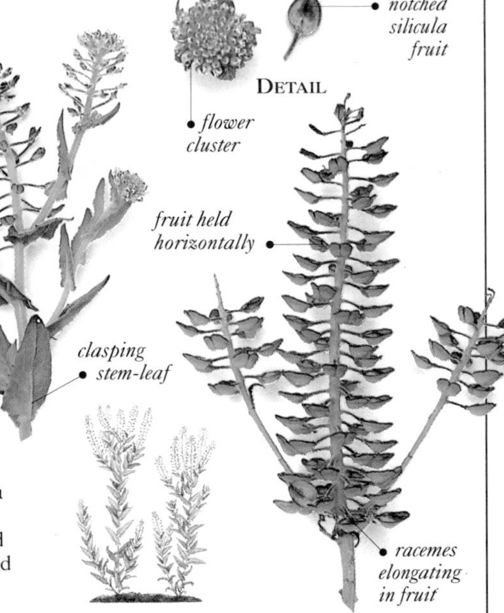

Habit Annual or biennial	Height 30–60cm (12–24in)	Flowering time May–Aug

Family CRUCIFERAE	Species *Cardaria draba*	Author (L.) Desv.

HOARY CRESS

Also known as *Lepidium draba*, this hairless, or slightly hairy, plant has branches on the upper parts of the stems. The leaves are deeply and coarsely toothed; the lower leaves are oblong and stalked, while most of the greyish, alternate stem-leaves are unstalked. The white flowers, 5–6mm (1/5–1/4in) across, are borne in umbel-like clusters that elongate as the fruit develops; the petals are not notched. The indehiscent siliculas, 3–4.5mm (1/8–1/5in) long, have a projecting style.

• **DISTRIBUTION** Naturalized throughout, except for the far north.

• **HABITAT** Cultivated, waste, and disturbed land, roads, tracksides, hedgerows, and coastal sands; generally on calcareous or neutral soils.

flowers in branched heads

plant in fruit

stem-leaves clasp stem

DETAIL

kidney-shaped silicula

Habit Perennial	Height 30–90cm (12–36in)	Flowering time May–June

Family CRUCIFERAE	Species *Coronopus didymus*	Author (L.) Smith

LESSER SWINECRESS

This spreading to prostrate, delicate, slightly hairy plant smells strongly when crushed. The finely divided, alternate leaves are stalked and have linear or elliptical segments. The tiny flowers, 1mm (1/25in) across, are borne in lateral racemes opposite the upper leaves; the sepals are longer than the petals. The siliculas are 1.5–2mm (1/16–1/12in) long.

• **DISTRIBUTION** Naturalized throughout the region, except for the far north.

• **HABITAT** Cultivated, bare, and waste land.

• **RELATED SPECIES** *Coronopus squamatus*, Swinecress, is a more substantial plant, with larger, sharp-warted fruit. It is native to much of the region in similar habitats.

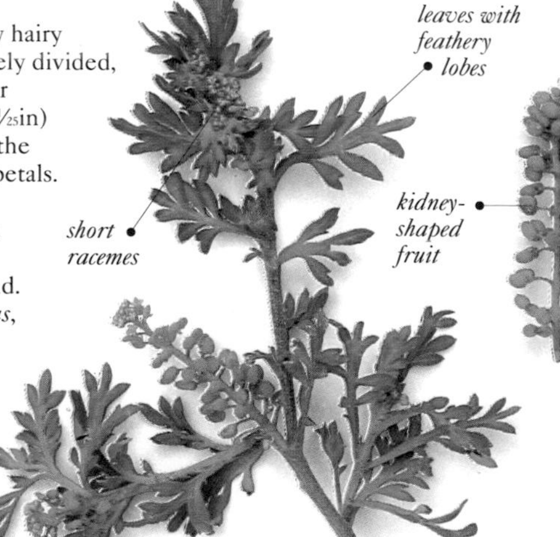

Habit Annual or biennial	Stem length Up to 30cm (12in)	Flowering time June–Sept

Family CRUCIFERAE	Species *Brassica oleracea*	Author L.

WILD CABBAGE

The stems of this rather robust, hairless plant become woody at the base and bear prominent leaf-scars. The large, undulating, glaucous, and fleshy basal leaves are pinnately lobed and stalked, while the upper leaves are unstalked. The large yellow flowers are 30–40mm (1⅕–1⅗in) across, and are borne in long, branched racemes. The siliquas, 50–70mm (2–2⅘in) long, are fleshy and cylindrical, and bear a prominent conical beak.
• **DISTRIBUTION** Native in Britain and France; naturalized in Holland and Germany.
• **HABITAT** Rocky maritime places, particularly calcareous sea-cliffs.

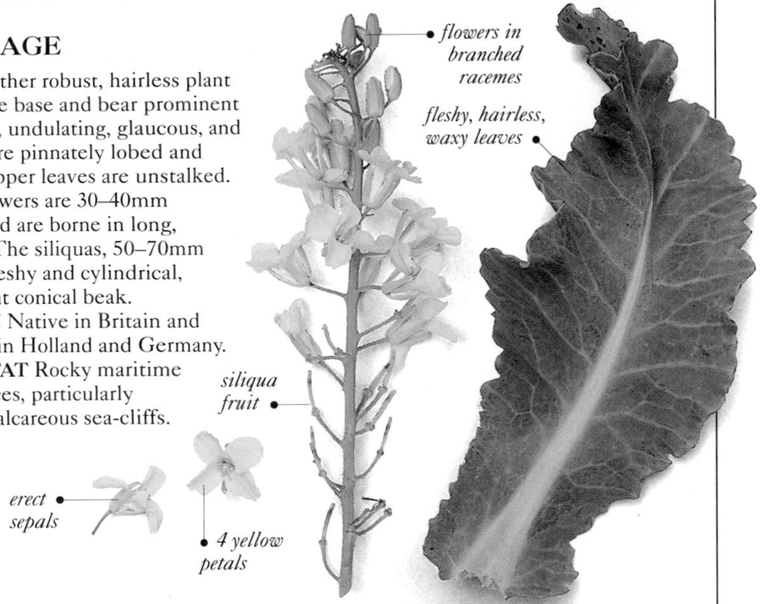

flowers in branched racemes
fleshy, hairless, waxy leaves
siliqua fruit
erect sepals
4 yellow petals

Habit Biennial or perennial	Height 60–200cm (24–80in)	Flowering time May–Sept

Family CRUCIFERAE	Species *Brassica napus*	Author L.

RAPE

The stems of this slightly bristly plant are usually branched. The leaves are greyish; the basal leaves are stalked, while the stem-leaves are alternate and clasp the stem. The yellow flowers, 15–25mm (⅗–1in) across, are borne in long racemes. The siliquas are cylindrical, 50–100mm (2–4in) long, with a prominent slender beak.
• **DISTRIBUTION** Naturalized throughout, except for the far north.
• **HABITAT** Cultivated, bare, and waste places, field margins, roadsides, and ditches.
• **RELATED SPECIES** *Brassica rapa*, Turnip, has bright green, bristly, basal leaves and flower-buds overtopped by the open flowers. It has similar distribution and habitats to *B. napus*, but is native to the region, not naturalized.

Habit Annual or biennial	Height 50–150cm (20–60in)	Flowering time May–Aug

Family CRUCIFERAE	Species *Brassica nigra*	Author (L.) Koch.

BLACK MUSTARD

This tall, rather greyish plant has bristly lower stems and branched upper stems. The leaves are alternate and somewhat bristly; the lower are broad and pinnately lobed, with toothed lobes, while the upper are smaller and unlobed, with non-clasping bases. The yellow flowers, 12–15mm (½–⅗in) across, are borne in long narrow racemes. The relatively small siliquas are 10–25mm (⅖–1in) long and are pressed close to the stem.

• **DISTRIBUTION** Throughout, except for much of the north; casual in many places.

• **HABITAT** Cultivated, bare, and waste ground, ditches, riversides, and sea-cliffs. Cultivated for its seeds, the source of black mustard.

• **RELATED SPECIES** *Brassica juncea* has large greyish lower leaves with up to 3 pairs of lobes. The fruit is ascending, not pressed close to the stem. It is naturalized in Holland and Germany.

distinctive beak of erect siliqua
4 sepals
DETAIL
flower-buds
narrow base of stem-leaves
narrow-oblong middle leaf

Habit Annual	Height 40–100cm (16–40in)	Flowering time June–Aug

Family CRUCIFERAE	Species *Sinapis arvensis*	Author L.

CHARLOCK

This is a bristly plant. The lower leaves are large, lyre-shaped, lobed and toothed, or unlobed; the upper are lanceolate, not lobed, nor clasping the stem. The flowers, 15–20mm (⅗–⅘in) across, are borne in elongating racemes; the sepals and petals are roughly equal in length. The siliquas, 25–45mm (1–1⅘in) long, are beaded and bristly, with a tapered beak.

• **DISTRIBUTION** Throughout the region, except for the far north.

• **HABITAT** Cultivated, bare, or waste ground, roadsides, and rubbish tips; often on calcareous soils.

• **RELATED SPECIES** *Sinapis alba*, White Mustard, has all the leaves pinnately lobed. It is naturalized throughout the region.

elongating racemes
prominently beaked fruit
DETAIL
unnotched yellow petals
lobed leaves, rough with hairs

Habit Annual	Height 40–100cm (16–40in)	Flowering time Apr–Oct

Family CRUCIFERAE	Species *Eruca vesicaria*	Author (L.) Cav.

ROCKET

This bristly or hairless plant has spreading to erect, branched stems. The alternate leaves are deeply pinnately lobed; the upper leaves are smaller than the lower. The flowers, 20–30mm (⅘–1⅕in) across, are whitish or yellowish with persistent sepals; petals have deep violet "pencil-line" veins. The thick siliquas, 10–25mm (⅖–1in) long, have a pronounced, narrow, triangular beak and 2 valves with a single midvein.

• **DISTRIBUTION** Naturalized in scattered localities in Britain, Ireland, Germany, and Norway, and perhaps elsewhere.

• **HABITAT** Waste, disturbed, and cultivated land.

• **REMARK** Long cultivated as a salad vegetable, making its origins obscure.

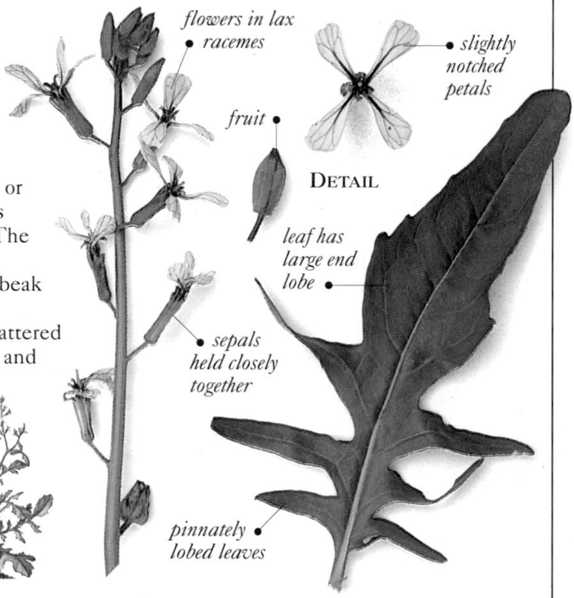

flowers in lax racemes

slightly notched petals

fruit

DETAIL

leaf has large end lobe

sepals held closely together

pinnately lobed leaves

Habit Annual	Height 30–100cm (12–40in)	Flowering time May–Aug

Family CRUCIFERAE	Species *Cakile maritima*	Author Scop.

SEA ROCKET

This bluish or greyish hairless plant has spreading to erect, often branched, stems. The alternate leaves vary from linear to pinnately lobed. The lilac, pink, or white flowers, 6–14mm (¼–⅘in) across, are borne in racemes that elongate as the fruit develops. The fruit, 10–25mm (⅖–1in) long, has an egg-shaped upper part, and a lower part with 2 projections.

• **DISTRIBUTION** Throughout the region as far north as C. Scandinavia.

• **HABITAT** Coastal sands and shingle, often close to the drift line, and occasionally on coastal rocks.

• **RELATED SPECIES** *Cakile edentula* can be distinguished by the lack of basal projections on the lower part of the fruit. It grows in Arctic regions.

Habit Annual	Height 20–50cm (8–20in)	Flowering time June–Sept

Family CRUCIFERAE	Species *Rapistrum rugosum*	Author (L.) Bergeret

BASTARD CABBAGE

The stems of this erect annual are bristly, at least in the lower part of the plant, and branched towards the top. The leaves are stalked and pinnately lobed to coarsely toothed. The pale yellow flowers, 8–10mm (⅓–⅖in) across, are borne in clusters in branched racemes that elongate as the fruit develops; the petals are not notched. The 2-parted silicula has a short beak at the tip, is 3–10mm (⅛–⅖in) long overall, and breaks transversely, the globose, ribbed, fertile upper part falling away from the narrower lower part when ripe.

• **DISTRIBUTION** A native plant in C. and S. France, but introduced, casual, or naturalized elsewhere in the region, except for Scandinavia.

• **HABITAT** Cultivated, bare, and waste ground; sometimes gregarious.

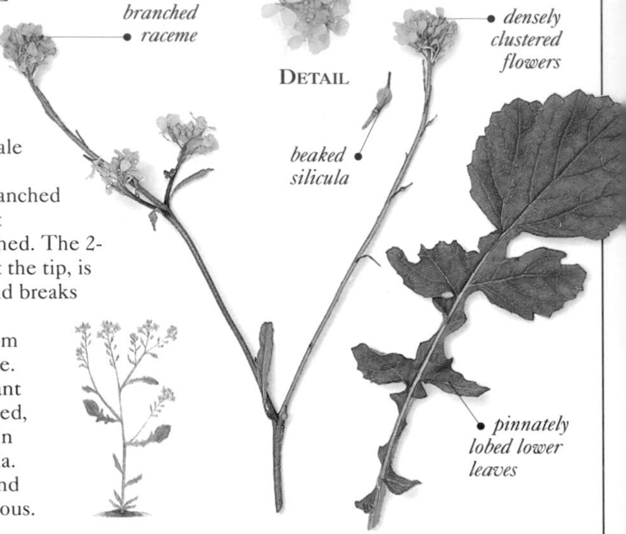

branched raceme

DETAIL

densely clustered flowers

beaked silicula

pinnately lobed lower leaves

Habit Annual	Height 40–80cm (16–32in)	Flowering time May–Sept

Family CRUCIFERAE	Species *Raphanus raphanistrum*	Author L.

WILD RADISH

A rough, bristly plant, Wild Radish has ascending to erect, branched stems. The leaves are deep green; the lower leaves are pinnately lobed and stalked; the upper ones are unlobed but toothed, and often unstalked. Borne in loose, branched racemes, the flowers, 15–30mm (⅗–1⅕in) across, vary in colour from white to yellow, or occasionally pale mauve, and usually have violet veins on the petals. The siliquas, 30–90mm (1⅕–3⅗in) long, are beaded, jointed, and strongly veined.

• **DISTRIBUTION** Throughout the region, except for the far north, but probably not native in much of N.W. Europe.

• **HABITAT** Cultivated, bare, and waste land, and occasionally rubbish tips; mainly on clay soils.

• **REMARK** Cultivated forms have a swollen root.

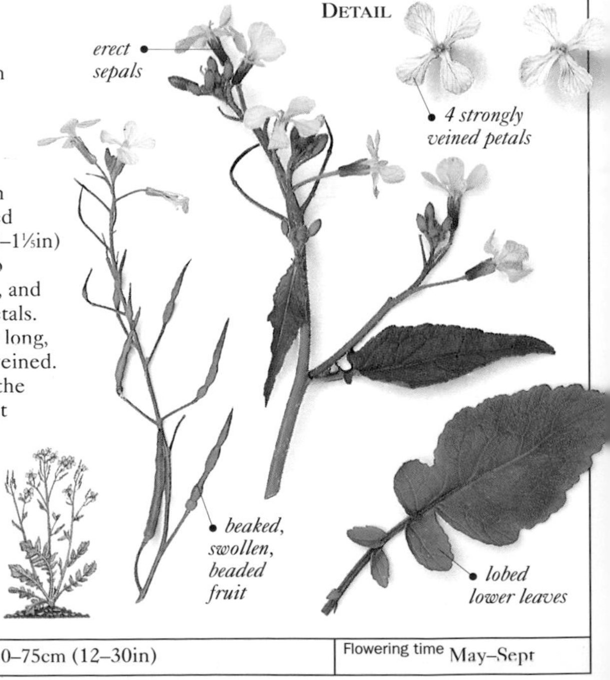

DETAIL

erect sepals

4 strongly veined petals

beaked, swollen, beaded fruit

lobed lower leaves

Habit Annual	Height 30–75cm (12–30in)	Flowering time May–Sept

Family CRUCIFERAE	Species *Crambe maritima*	Author L.

SEA KALE

This large, clump-forming, hairless plant has thick, branched stems. The leaves are lobed, with undulating margins; the lower leaves are stalked. The white flowers, 10–15mm (⅖–⅗in) across, are borne in large, broad panicles. The siliculas, 8–14mm (⅓–⁴⁄₇in) long, are fleshy, somewhat inflated, and elliptical to rounded in outline.

• **DISTRIBUTION** Atlantic and Baltic coasts of W and N.W. Europe, but often local. Declining in many regions, but increasing on the south coast of England.

• **HABITAT** Coastal sands, shingle beaches, and rocks; sometimes sea-cliffs, but favouring the shoreline.

Habit Perennial	Height 30–75cm (12–30in)	Flowering time June–Aug

MIGNONETTE FAMILY

Family RESEDACEAE	Species *Reseda luteola*	Author L.

WELD

The stiff and slender stems of this hairless plant are often branched towards the top. The leaves are linear to lanceolate, unlobed, and untoothed, forming a basal rosette in the first year. The yellowish green flowers, 4–5mm ($\frac{1}{6}$–$\frac{1}{5}$in) across, are borne in spikes, each flower with 4 sepals and 4 deeply lacerated petals. The fruit capsule, 3–4mm ($\frac{1}{8}$–$\frac{1}{6}$in) long, is erect, 3-lobed, and contains many small seeds.

• **DISTRIBUTION** Throughout the region, except for the far north, but often very local.

• **HABITAT** Grassy places, arable land, waste places, field boundaries, disturbed land, and old quarries; generally on calcareous soils.

• **RELATED SPECIES** *Reseda alba*, White Mignonette, has pinnately lobed leaves and white flowers with 5 to 6 sepals and petals. It is naturalized or casual in Britain, Holland, and Germany.

Habit Biennial	Height 80–150cm (32–60in)	Flowering time June–Sept

Family RESEDACEAE	Species *Reseda lutea*	Author L.

WILD MIGNONETTE

This is a hairless, branched, often rather bushy plant. The leaves mostly have one or 2 pairs of lobes near the base, the terminal lobe being larger and elliptical. The yellow flowers, 7–9mm ($\frac{2}{7}$–$\frac{3}{8}$in) across, are borne in long, tapered spikes; each flower has 6 sepals and 6 petals. The 3-lobed fruit capsule, 7–12mm ($\frac{2}{7}$–$\frac{1}{2}$in) long, is open-ended from the start.

• **DISTRIBUTION** Throughout the region, as far north as S. Scandinavia.

• **HABITAT** Cultivated, disturbed, and waste land, roadsides, and field boundaries; on calcareous soils.

• **RELATED SPECIES** *Reseda phyteuma*, Corn Mignonette, has white flowers and pendent fruit. It is naturalized in N. France, Britain, Holland, Germany.

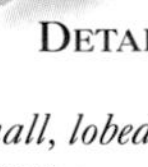

Habit Biennial or perennial	Height 30–75cm (12–30in)	Flowering time June–Sept

SUNDEW FAMILY

Family DROSERACEAE	Species *Drosera rotundifolia*	Author L.

COMMON SUNDEW

This is a small, hairy, insectivorous plant which is often difficult to spot among other herbage. The leaves are borne in a loose basal rosette and are long-stalked, with a rounded blade covered in glistening, sticky, stalked glands that entrap small insects and other creatures. The white flowers, 5mm (⅕in) across, occur in loose, leafless spikes held high above the spreading leaves; each flower has 5 to 8 sepals and petals. The fruit is a small many-seeded capsule.

• **DISTRIBUTION** Throughout the region, except for Spitsbergen, much of S. and E. England, and France.

• **HABITAT** Acid, peaty sites like wet heaths, moors, and sphagnum bogs.

• **RELATED SPECIES** *Drosera intermedia*, Oblong-leaved Sundew, has oblong leaves. It has similar habitats and distribution.

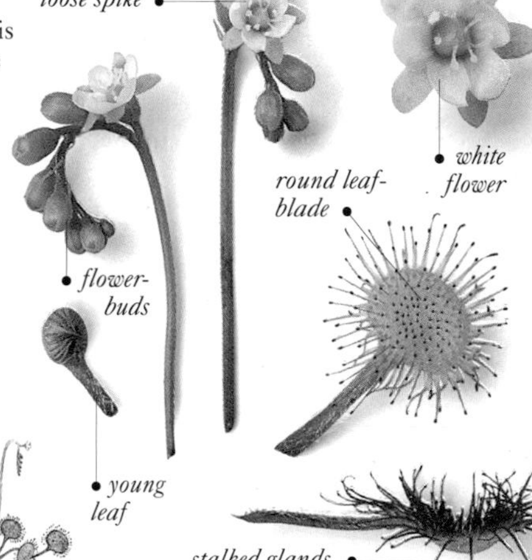

Habit Perennial	Height 5–15cm (2–6in)	Flowering time June–Aug

STONECROP FAMILY

Family CRASSULACEAE	Species *Umbilicus rupestris*	Author (Salisb.) Dandy

NAVELWORT

This succulent, hairless plant has erect, usually unbranched, stems. The leaves are mostly basal and are circular in outline, with a long stalk attached to the middle beneath; stem-leaves are few, becoming progressively smaller up the stem. The greenish white or straw-coloured flowers, 8–10mm (⅓–⅖in) long, are narrow-bell-shaped, pendent, and 5-parted, with the petals fused into a tube for most of their length. The fruit consists of a small group of follicles containing tiny seeds.

• **DISTRIBUTION** Britain (except N. Scotland), Ireland, and France; mostly western.

• **HABITAT** Walls, cliffs, and other rocky places, rooftops, and stony hedgebanks; to an altitude of 2,800m (9,200ft).

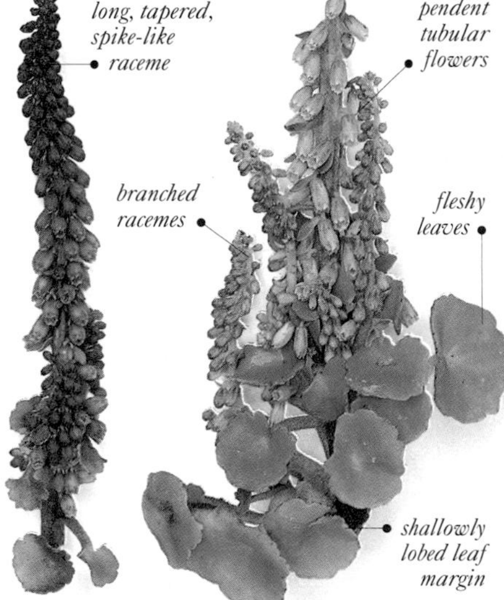

Habit Perennial	Height 15–40cm (6–16in)	Flowering time June–Aug

Family CRASSULACEAE	Species *Sedum acre*	Author L.

BITING STONECROP

Also called Wallpepper, this hairless plant forms rather fleshy yellowish green mats. The stems spread and often root down. The alternate leaves, 3–6mm (⅛–¼in) long, are roughly egg-shaped. The flowers, 10–12mm (⅖–½in) across, have 5 sepals, 5 petals, and 10 stamens. The fruit consists of 5 small follicles forming a small star.

• **DISTRIBUTION** Throughout the region, except for Spitsbergen.

• **HABITAT** Dry rocky and sandy places, embankments, old walls and roof-tops, and shingle beaches.

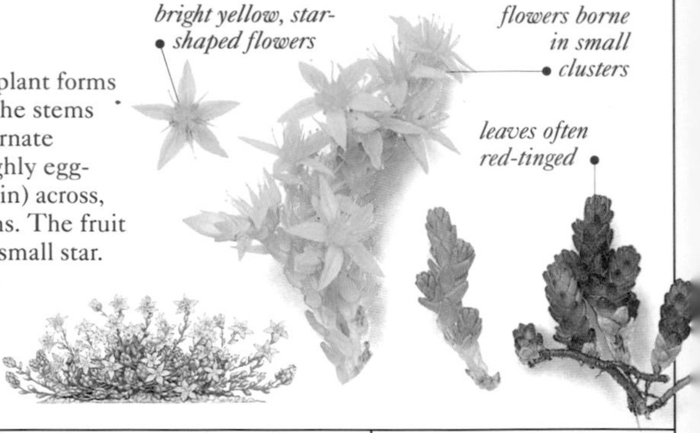

bright yellow, star-shaped flowers

flowers borne in small clusters

leaves often red-tinged

Habit Perennial	Height 4–10cm (1⅗–4in)	Flowering time May–July

Family CRASSULACEAE	Species *Sedum album*	Author L.

WHITE STONECROP

A mat-forming, fleshy plant, its rather straggling stems root down at intervals; the flowering stems are erect to ascending. The leaves are alternate, bright green, and rather shiny. The flowers, 6–9mm (¼–⅜in) across, are borne in loose, flat-topped clusters; carpels are pink. The fruit is a collection of small erect follicles.

• **DISTRIBUTION** Throughout, except for the Faeroes and the far north; only naturalized in the north.

• **HABITAT** Rocky places, screes, cliffs, moraines, roadsides, old walls.

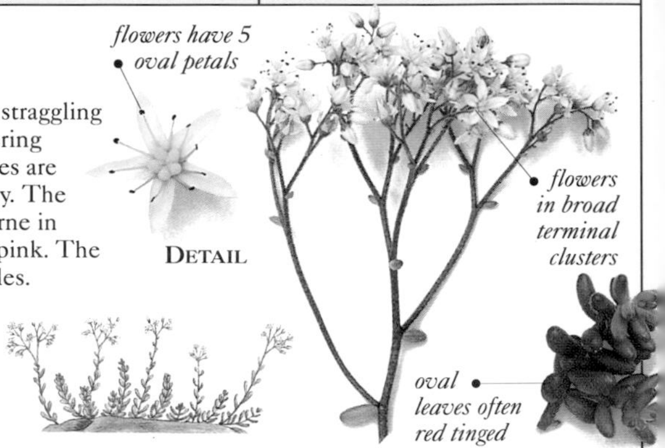

flowers have 5 oval petals

DETAIL

flowers in broad terminal clusters

oval leaves often red tinged

Habit Perennial	Height 8–20cm (3⅕–8in)	Flowering time June–Aug

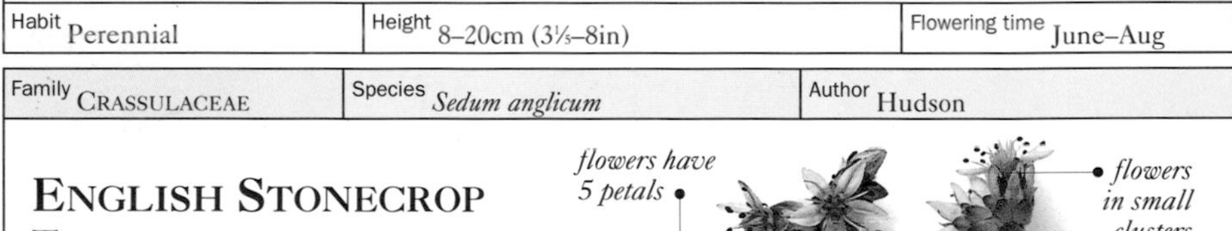

Family CRASSULACEAE	Species *Sedum anglicum*	Author Hudson

ENGLISH STONECROP

This hairless, bluish green plant is generally mat-forming. The alternate leaves are oval, fleshy, and 3–5mm (⅛–⅕in) long. Borne in few-flowered clusters, the flowers, 9–12mm (⅜–½in) across, are white flushed with pink beneath and have 5 petals and 10 black anthers.

• **DISTRIBUTION** Throughout, except for Germany, Iceland, and the far north.

• **HABITAT** Rocky and dry grassy places, embankments, and sand dunes or shingle; mostly on acid soils on lowland and in the mountains.

Habit Perennial	Height 4–13cm (1⅗–5in)	Flowering time June–Sept

Family CRASSULACEAE	Species *Sedum telephium*	Author L.

ORPINE

This tufted, greyish, succulent plant has erect, leafy stems; all stems are flowering. The alternate leaves are fleshy, oblong to almost round, toothed, and 50–80mm (2–3⅕in) long. The bright reddish purple, greenish yellow, or whitish flowers are 8–10mm (⅓–⅖in) across.

• **DISTRIBUTION** Throughout, except for the Faeroes and the far north.

• **HABITAT** Woodland, hedgerows, embankments and grassy places, and occasionally rocky terrain; usually on rather light sandy soils.

• **RELATED SPECIES** *Sedum anacampseros*, Love-restoring Stonecrop, has sterile procumbent shoots, untoothed leaves, and pink to mauve flowers in a rounded panicle. It is a naturalized or casual plant in the region.

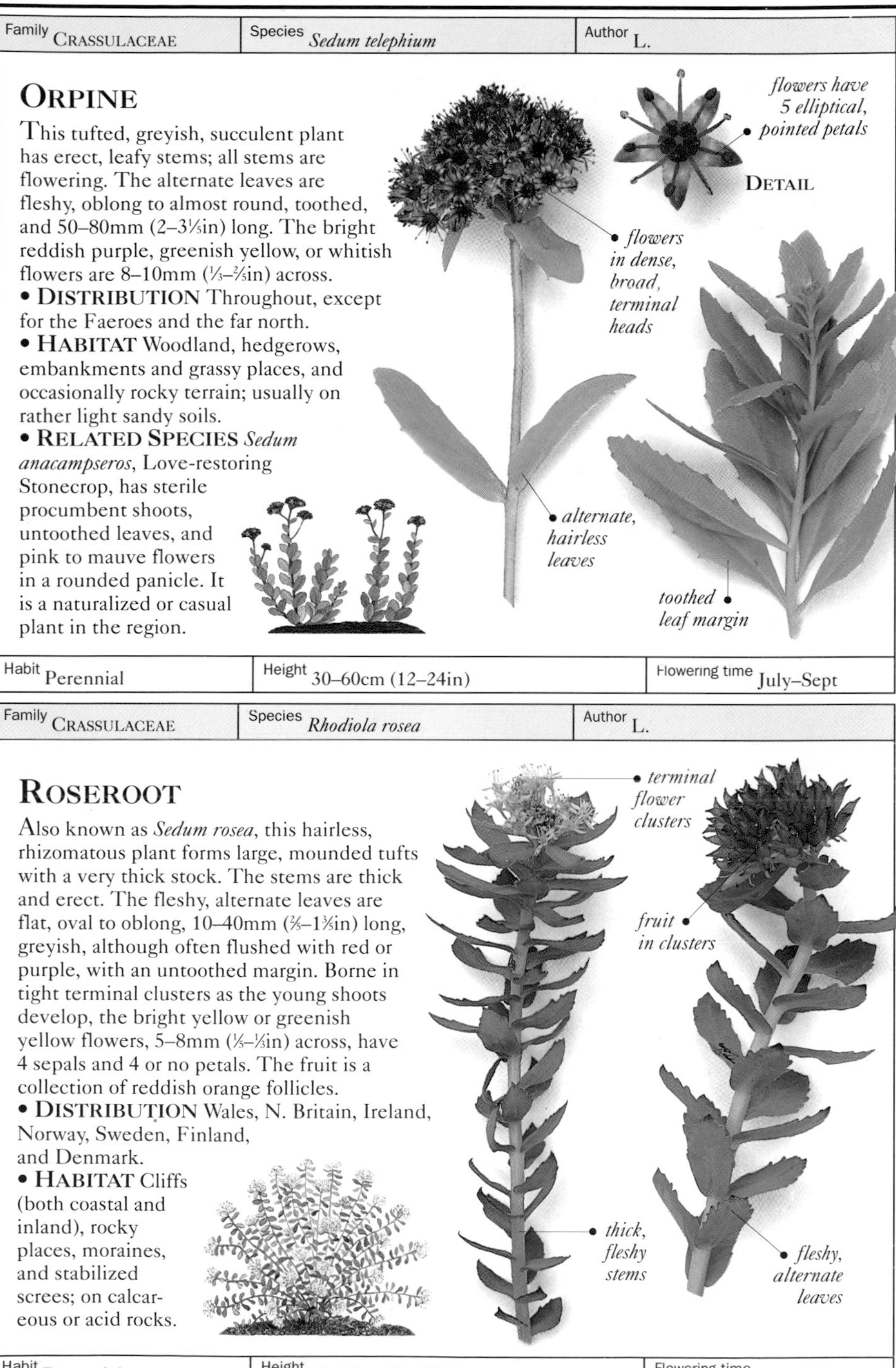

Habit Perennial	Height 30–60cm (12–24in)	Flowering time July–Sept

Family CRASSULACEAE	Species *Rhodiola rosea*	Author L.

ROSEROOT

Also known as *Sedum rosea*, this hairless, rhizomatous plant forms large, mounded tufts with a very thick stock. The stems are thick and erect. The fleshy, alternate leaves are flat, oval to oblong, 10–40mm (⅖–1⅗in) long, greyish, although often flushed with red or purple, with an untoothed margin. Borne in tight terminal clusters as the young shoots develop, the bright yellow or greenish yellow flowers, 5–8mm (⅕–⅓in) across, have 4 sepals and 4 or no petals. The fruit is a collection of reddish orange follicles.

• **DISTRIBUTION** Wales, N. Britain, Ireland, Norway, Sweden, Finland, and Denmark.

• **HABITAT** Cliffs (both coastal and inland), rocky places, moraines, and stabilized screes; on calcareous or acid rocks.

Habit Perennial	Height 20–35cm (8–14in)	Flowering time May–July

SAXIFRAGE FAMILY

Family SAXIFRAGACEAE	Species *Saxifraga tridactylites*	Author L.

RUE-LEAVED SAXIFRAGE

This small, stickily hairy plant is often a reddish colour. The leaves are somewhat fleshy; the lowermost are spoon-shaped, unlobed, stalked, and generally withered by flowering time, while the rest of the leaves are very short-stalked or unstalked, with 3 to 5 deep, elliptical to oval, untoothed lobes. The white flowers, 4–6mm (⅙–¼in) across, are borne on long stalks, in loose, leafy cymes; each flower has 5 slightly notched petals. The fruit is a small 2-parted capsule.

• **DISTRIBUTION** Throughout, except for the far north; often local.

• **HABITAT** Dry, rocky, and bare places, sandy heaths, sand dunes, field margins, and occasionally old walls; often on calcareous soils.

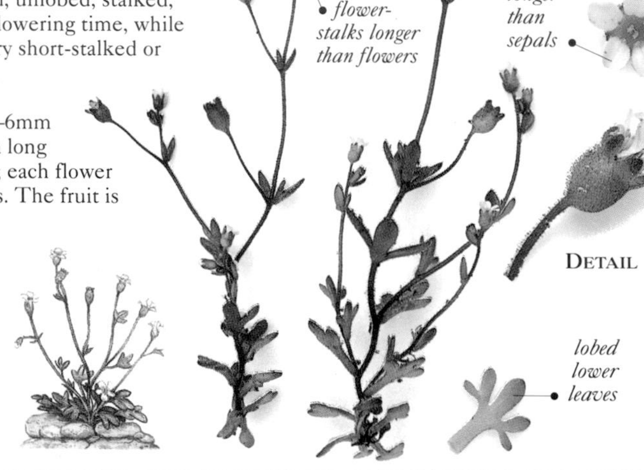

Habit Annual	Height 5–15cm (2–6in)	Flowering time June–Sept

Family SAXIFRAGACEAE	Species *Saxifraga granulata*	Author L.

MEADOW SAXIFRAGE

This variable, hairy plant is branched towards the top. The leaves are mainly borne in a basal rosette, the lowermost with bulbils in the leaf-axils just below ground level; the leaf-blade is rounded in outline with a kidney-shaped base. The white flowers are 18–30mm (⅗–1⅕in) across. The fruit is a small 2-parted capsule.

• **DISTRIBUTION** Throughout the region, except for the far north and Iceland.

• **HABITAT** Grassy places and road verges; on well-drained neutral or calcareous soils.

• **RELATED SPECIES** *Saxifraga rivularis*, Highland Saxifrage, has 3- to 5-lobed basal leaves, and smaller flowers often veined or flushed with pink. It inhabits mountain sites in N. Britain, Iceland, and S. Norway.

Habit Perennial	Height 20–50cm (8–20in)	Flowering time Apr–June

Family SAXIFRAGACEAE	Species *Saxifraga aizoides*	Author L.

YELLOW SAXIFRAGE

This tufted, slightly hairy, leafy plant has spreading to ascending sterile and flowering shoots. The linear to narrow-elliptical leaves have small spaced-out teeth on the margin. The yellow to orange flowers, 5–10mm (⅕–⅖in) across, often have red spots on the petals. The fruit capsule is 2-parted.

• **DISTRIBUTION** Throughout the region, except for the Faeroes and most of lowland Europe.

• **HABITAT** Damp mountain rocks, streamsides, and wet flushes; to an altitude of 3,150m (10,350ft).

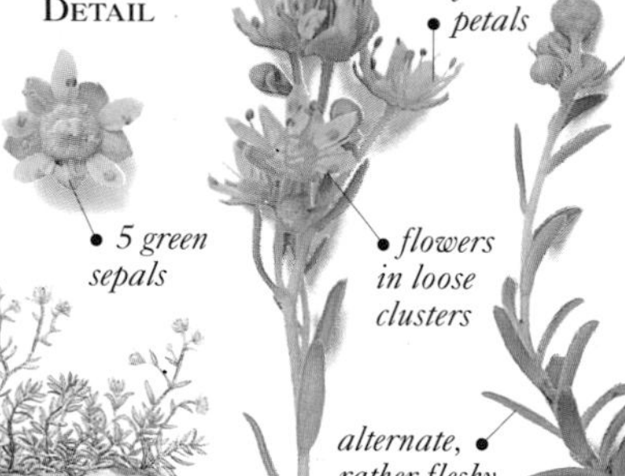

Habit Perennial	Height 10–25cm (4–10in)	Flowering time June–Sept

Family SAXIFRAGACEAE	Species *Saxifraga stellaris*	Author L.

STARRY SAXIFRAGE

This slightly hairy stoloniferous plant forms loose to dense tufts. The leaves are oblong to oval, often broadest above the middle, and scarcely stalked. The white star-shaped flowers, 10–15mm (⅖–⅗in) across, have 5 narrow-elliptical petals. The fruit, a 2-parted capsule, contains many tiny seeds.

• **DISTRIBUTION** Throughout the region, except for S. Britain, Holland, Belgium, and Denmark.

• **HABITAT** Wet rocks and rock ledges, flushes, stream banks, and marshes; to 1,900m (6,250ft).

DETAIL

2 yellow spots near base of petals

flowers generally in loose panicles

all leaves in basal rosette

toothed leaf margin

Habit Perennial	Height 8–20cm (3⅕–8in)	Flowering time June–Aug

Family SAXIFRAGACEAE	Species *Chrysoplenium oppositifolium*	Author L.

OPPOSITE-LEAVED GOLDEN SAXIFRAGE

This somewhat hairy, creeping, mat-forming plant has spreading shoots that root down at intervals. The stems are square. The leaves are oblong to rounded, with a bluntly toothed margin and a stalk equalling the blade. The flowers, 2–3mm (1/12–⅛in) across, have 4 sepals and 4 stamens, but no petals.

• **DISTRIBUTION** Throughout the region, except for the far north.

• **HABITAT** Wet rocks, damp woodland, wet flushes, streamsides; mostly on acid soils; often forms extensive local colonies.

yellowish flowers

opposite leaves

yellowish leafy bracts around flowers

Habit Perennial	Height 5–15cm (2–6in)	Flowering time Apr–July

GRASS OF PARNASSUS FAMILY

Family PARNASSIACEAE	Species *Parnassia palustris*	Author L.

GRASS OF PARNASSUS

This tufted and hairless plant has erect, unbranched stems. The leaves are heart-shaped, mostly basal, untoothed, and stalked; the single stem-leaf is similar but is unstalked and clasps the stem. The solitary flowers, 15–30mm (⅗–1⅕in) across, have 5 branched staminodes alternating with 5 fertile stamens. The 4-lobed fruit capsule contains many seeds.

• **DISTRIBUTION** Throughout, except for the far north; often very local and rare in the south, but sometimes forming large colonies.

• **HABITAT** Moist grassy places, marshes, fens, and streamside flushes; generally on base-rich soils; on lowland and mountains to 2,500m (8,200ft).

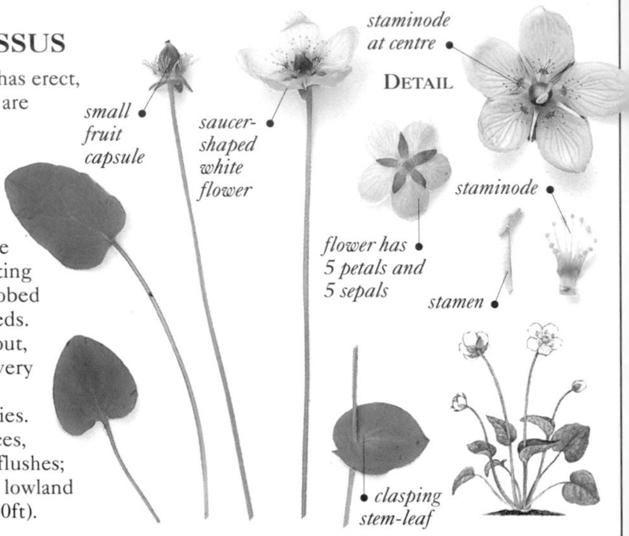

small fruit capsule

saucer-shaped white flower

staminode at centre

DETAIL

staminode

flower has 5 petals and 5 sepals

stamen

clasping stem-leaf

Habit Perennial	Height 10–30cm (4–12in)	Flowering time June–Sept

ROSE FAMILY

Family ROSACEAE	Species *Filipendula ulmaria*	Author (L.) Maxim.

MEADOWSWEET

The stiff stems of this tufted plant are generally unbranched except in the inflorescence. The leaves have up to 5 pairs of leaflets. Borne in wide-branched clusters, the fragrant cream flowers, 4–8mm (⅙–⅓in) across, have separate sepals and petals; the petals usually number 5, sometimes 6.

• **DISTRIBUTION** Throughout, except for Spitsbergen.

• **HABITAT** Moist sites in fens, marshes, meadows, ditches, roadsides, woodland fringes, and stream margins; often in extensive colonies.

• **RELATED SPECIES** *Aruncus dioica*, Goatsbeard, has 2-pinnate leaves and thin inflorescence branches. It grows in Belgium to Germany southwards; naturalized in Britain.

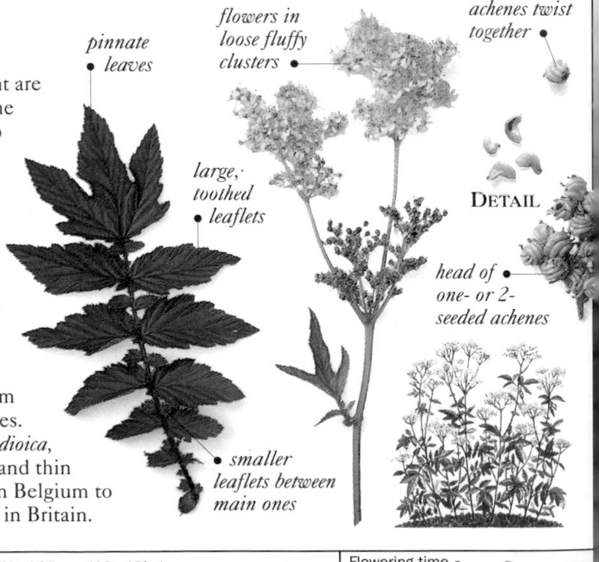

pinnate leaves

flowers in loose fluffy clusters

achenes twist together

large, toothed leaflets

DETAIL

head of one- or 2-seeded achenes

smaller leaflets between main ones

Habit Perennial	Height 70–120cm (28–48in)	Flowering time June–Sept

Family ROSACEAE	Species *Filipendula vulgaris*	Author Moench

DROPWORT

This tufted, hairless plant has stiff, erect, unbranched, leafy stems. The alternate leaves are pinnate, with small leaflets between the main ones; the main leaflets are oblong to elliptical, deeply cut, and dark green above but paler beneath. Leaflet-like stipules are present at the base of each leaf. Borne in rather flat-headed cymes, the pale cream or whitish flowers, 8–16mm (⅓–⅝in) across, are flushed with purple beneath and usually have 6 petals. The fruit consists of a head of usually 4 to 12 small, one- to 2-seeded achenes.

• **DISTRIBUTION** Grows throughout the region, except for the far north; a rare plant in N. Scotland and Ireland.

• **HABITAT** Meadows, roadsides, and downs; grows on calcareous soils to an altitude of 1,500m (4,900ft).

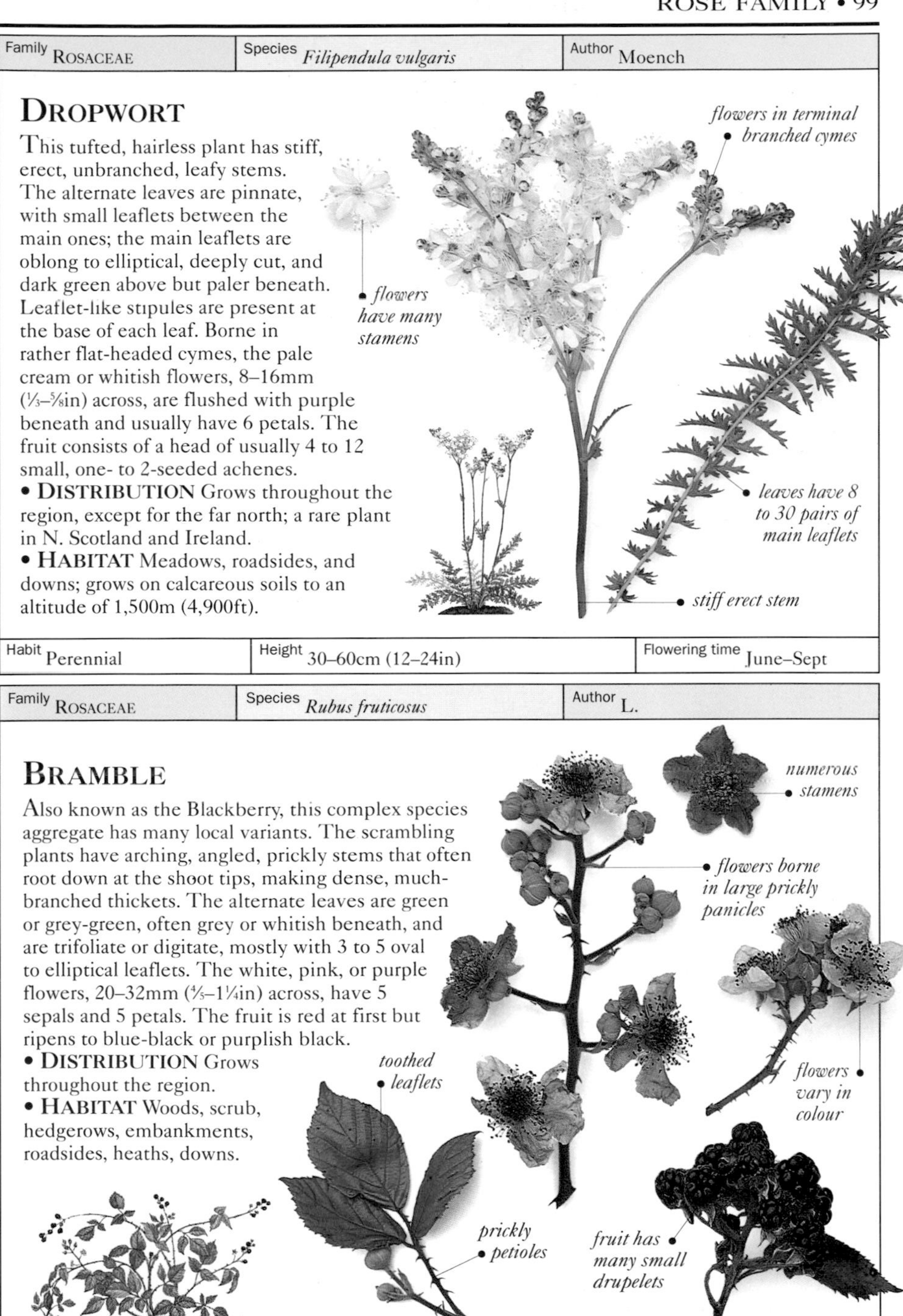

Habit Perennial	Height 30–60cm (12–24in)	Flowering time June–Sept

Family ROSACEAE	Species *Rubus fruticosus*	Author L.

BRAMBLE

Also known as the Blackberry, this complex species aggregate has many local variants. The scrambling plants have arching, angled, prickly stems that often root down at the shoot tips, making dense, much-branched thickets. The alternate leaves are green or grey-green, often grey or whitish beneath, and are trifoliate or digitate, mostly with 3 to 5 oval to elliptical leaflets. The white, pink, or purple flowers, 20–32mm (⅘–1¼in) across, have 5 sepals and 5 petals. The fruit is red at first but ripens to blue-black or purplish black.

• **DISTRIBUTION** Grows throughout the region.

• **HABITAT** Woods, scrub, hedgerows, embankments, roadsides, heaths, downs.

Habit Subshrub	Height 1–3m (3¼–10ft)	Flowering time May–Sept

Family ROSACEAE	Species *Rubus idaeus*	Author L.

RASPBERRY

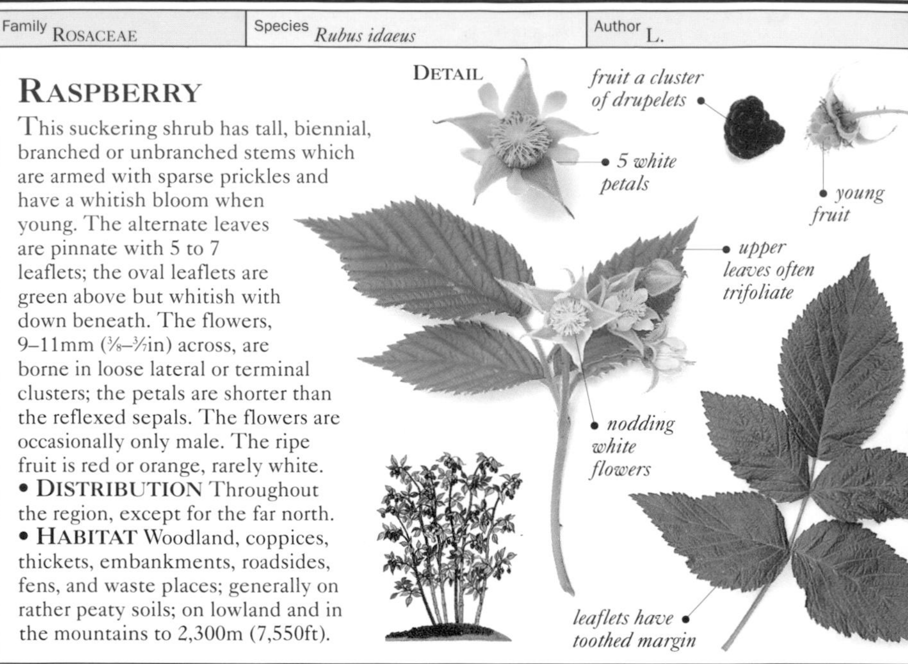

This suckering shrub has tall, biennial, branched or unbranched stems which are armed with sparse prickles and have a whitish bloom when young. The alternate leaves are pinnate with 5 to 7 leaflets; the oval leaflets are green above but whitish with down beneath. The flowers, 9–11mm (3/8–3/7in) across, are borne in loose lateral or terminal clusters; the petals are shorter than the reflexed sepals. The flowers are occasionally only male. The ripe fruit is red or orange, rarely white.

• **DISTRIBUTION** Throughout the region, except for the far north.

• **HABITAT** Woodland, coppices, thickets, embankments, roadsides, fens, and waste places; generally on rather peaty soils; on lowland and in the mountains to 2,300m (7,550ft).

Habit Perennial	Height 70–150cm (28–60in)	Flowering time May–Aug

Family ROSACEAE	Species *Rubus caesius*	Author L.

DEWBERRY

The weak arching stems of this low subshrub root down at the tips, bear scattered prickles, and have a bluish or greyish bloom, especially when young. The alternate leaves are trifoliate; the leaflets are oval to elliptical with a toothed margin and are hairy or hairless on the underside. Scale-like stipules are present at the base of each leaf. The flowers are white, or occasionally pale pink, 20–25mm (4/5–1in) across, and borne in small lateral or terminal clusters; the 5 sepals and 5 petals are roughly equal in length. The fruit is bluish black with a waxy bloom when ripe.

• **DISTRIBUTION** Throughout, except for the far north; scarce in N. Britain.

• **HABITAT** Scrub and grassland; often on chalky soils but also on sand dunes and rocks.

fruit a cluster of drupelets
5-petalled flowers
upper leaves sometimes simple
finely prickly stems
trifoliate leaves

Habit Subshrub	Height 10–30cm (4–12in)	Flowering time May–Sept

Family ROSACEAE	Species *Agrimonia eupatoria*	Author L.

AGRIMONY

The leafy stems of this slender and hairy plant are erect and branched or unbranched. The alternate leaves are pinnate, with 3 to 6 main pairs of toothed leaflets, and smaller intermediate leaflets. The yellow flowers, 5–8mm (⅕–⅓in) across, have 5 separate sepals and petals and up to 20 stamens. The fruit bears hooked bristles which readily attach themselves to soft materials such as fur and clothes and help to disperse the plant to new locations.

• **DISTRIBUTION** Throughout most of the region, except for the far north.

• **HABITAT** Dry grassy places, roadsides, field boundaries, and hedgerows; on mildly acid to calcareous soils.

• **RELATED SPECIES** *Agrimonia procera*, Fragrant Agrimony, has leaves sticky with glands on the underside, and fragrant flowers. The fruit is more bell-shaped, with spreading bristles. Its distribution is similar but it is generally more local and is confined to acid soils.

Habit Perennial	Height 50–100cm (20–40in)	Flowering time June–Aug

Family ROSACEAE	Species *Sanguisorba minor*	Author Scop.

SALAD BURNET

This is a tufted, greyish, hairless or slightly hairy plant, with stems generally branched towards the top. The leaves are stalked and mostly basal, with 3 to 12 pairs of rounded to elliptical, toothed leaflets; stipules are present at the leaf bases. The small flowers, borne in rounded heads 10–20mm (⅖–⅘in) across, have 4 sepals and no petals; the female flowers have reddish styles, and the male flowers have yellow anthers. The fruit consists of one or 2 achenes enclosed within the base of the hardened calyx.

• **DISTRIBUTION** Throughout, except for the far north of the region.

• **HABITAT** Dry grasslands, rocky places, and roadside embankments; on calcareous or neutral soils.

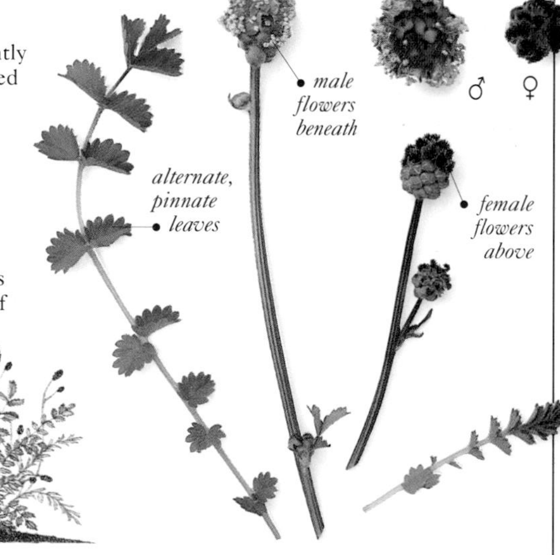

Habit Perennial	Height 20–80cm (8–32in)	Flowering time May–Sept

Family ROSACEAE	Species *Dryas octopetala*	Author L.

MOUNTAIN AVENS

An evergreen, this subshrubby avens has creeping stems which become woody at the base. The oblong leaves, 6–25mm (¼–1in) long, are alternate, toothed, stalked, and white-felted underneath. Borne on long hairy stalks, the solitary white flowers, 20–40mm (⅘–1⅗in) across, have 8 or more oval to elliptical petals and a calyx with 7 to 10 lobes. The numerous achenes are wind-dispersed.

• **DISTRIBUTION** Ireland, mid-Wales, N. Britain, Scandinavia, and the mountains of France and Germany.

• **HABITAT** Rock crevices and ledges, mountain heaths, sea-cliffs, and sand dunes; on calcareous or neutral soils.

Habit Subshrub	Height Up to 1m (3¼ft)	Flowering time May–July

Family ROSACEAE	Species *Geum rivale*	Author L.

WATER AVENS

The stems of this tufted and hairy plant are erect to ascending and are branched only towards the top. The basal leaves are pinnate, with 3 to 6 pairs of rounded to oval, lobed and toothed leaflets, the end lobe being the largest; the stem-leaves are smaller and usually trifoliate. Borne on arched stalks, the dull pink to cream flowers, 8–15mm (⅓–⅗in) across, have an epicalyx and a purplish brown calyx. The fruit is a collection of achenes with hooked and slightly feathered styles.

• **DISTRIBUTION** Throughout the region, except for Spitsbergen.

• **HABITAT** Moist sites, marshes, ditches, wet woodland, meadows, and rock ledges; often in the shade and on calcareous or base-rich soils.

Habit Perennial	Height 30–50cm (12–20in)	Flowering time Apr–Sept

Family ROSACEAE	Species *Geum urbanum*	Author L.

HERB BENNET

The slender erect to spreading stems of this hairy, tufted plant are branched towards the top. The alternate leaves are mainly basal and pinnate, with up to 5 oval to rounded, lobed and toothed leaflets; the upper leaves are much smaller, often 3-lobed, and have a pair of conspicuous leaf-like stipules at the base. The solitary yellow flowers are erect, 8–15mm (⅓–⅗in) across, and usually have 5 spreading petals and 5 sepals. The fruit-heads consist of numerous hairy achenes.

• **DISTRIBUTION** Throughout the region, except for the far north.

• **HABITAT** Woodland, hedgerows, and other shaded places; on lowlands and mountains to an altitude of 1,850m (6,050ft).

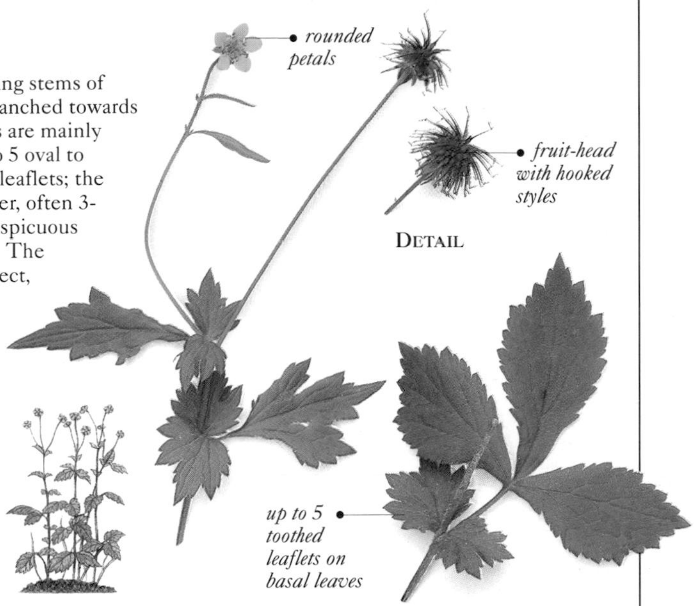

rounded petals

fruit-head with hooked styles

DETAIL

up to 5 toothed leaflets on basal leaves

Habit Perennial	Height 40–70cm (16–28in)	Flowering time May–Sept

Family ROSACEAE	Species *Potentilla palustris*	Author (L.) Scop.

MARSH CINQUEFOIL

Also known as *Comarum palustre,* this tufted, slightly hairy plant has erect to ascending stems, branched only towards the top, and spreads by means of rather woody rhizomes. The alternate leaves have 5, occasionally 7, oblong to elliptical leaflets, and papery stipules at the base of each leaf-stalk. Borne in branched clusters, the purplish to maroon flowers, 20–30mm (⅘–1⅕in) across, have 5 sepals and 5 petals, an epicalyx, and numerous stamens. The fruit consists of a tight head of achenes surrounded by the persistent calyx.

• **DISTRIBUTION** Throughout, although often very local in the south of its range.

• **HABITAT** Wet meadows, swamps, fens, bogs, and ditches; on a variety of soil types.

sepals much larger than petals

leaves with 5 toothed leaflets

trifoliate upper leaves

Habit Perennial	Height 30–50cm (12–20in)	Flowering time May–July

Family ROSACEAE	Species *Potentilla anserina*	Author L.

SILVERWEED

The creeping runners of this hairy perennial root down to produce new plants at intervals. The leaves, borne in rosettes, are green or greyish above, silvery below, and pinnate, with 15 to 25 oblong leaflets, generally with smaller leaflets between the main ones. The solitary yellow flowers, 15–20mm ($\frac{3}{5}$–$\frac{4}{5}$in) across, are borne in the axils of stolon leaves on slender, erect, leafless stalks. The sepals are half the length of the petals and there are usually 5 of each; an epicalyx is also present. The fruit consists of a tight head of achenes.

• **DISTRIBUTION** Throughout the region; often gregarious and in large colonies.

• **HABITAT** Grassy places, cultivated and waste ground, pathways, abandoned cultivation, roadsides, sand dunes, and open woodland.

Habit Perennial	Height 5–25cm (4–10in)	Flowering time May–Aug

Family ROSACEAE	Species *Potentilla reptans*	Author L.

CREEPING CINQUEFOIL

Low, creeping, and invasive, this hairy plant spreads by means of long slender runners that root down at the nodes. The green leaves have 5 to 7 oblong, toothed leaflets and are borne in rosettes or scattered along the stolons. The yellow flowers are 17–25mm ($\frac{2}{3}$–1in) across, and are borne on long slender stalks; each flower has 5 sepals, 5 petals, and an epicalyx. The fruit consists of a tight cluster of achenes.

• **DISTRIBUTION** Throughout the region, except for the far north.

• **HABITAT** Cultivated, bare, and waste ground, grassy places, tracksides, road verges, open woodland, and sand dunes; on various soil types.

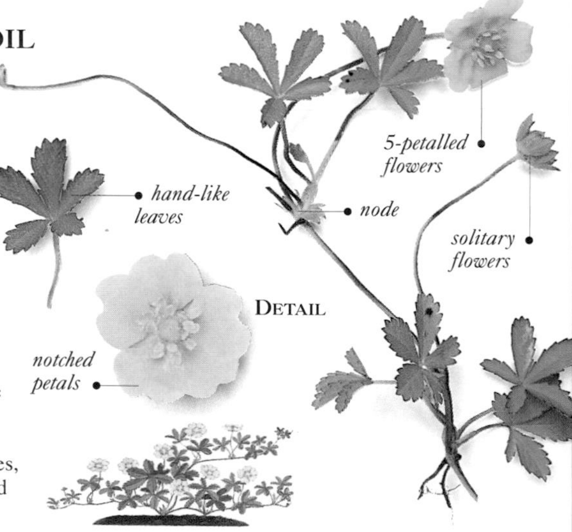

Habit Perennial	Height 5–10cm (2–4in)	Flowering time June–Sept

Family ROSACEAE	Species *Potentilla rupestris*	Author L.

Rock Cinquefoil

A tufted, hairy plant, its erect stems are branched towards the top. The pinnate leaves are mostly in a basal rosette, with 5 to 7 pairs of rounded to oval, toothed leaflets; the stem-leaves have 3 leaflets, and a pair of leafy stipules at the base. The white flowers, 16–28mm (5/8–1 1/8in) across, are borne in loose clusters; an epicalyx is present.

• **DISTRIBUTION** Mountains of the region, as far north as Norway and S. Sweden. Protected in Britain.

• **HABITAT** Rocky places.

• **RELATED SPECIES** *Potentilla alba*, White Cinquefoil, has leaves with 5 leaflets and flowers with notched petals. It grows on mountains in France and Germany.

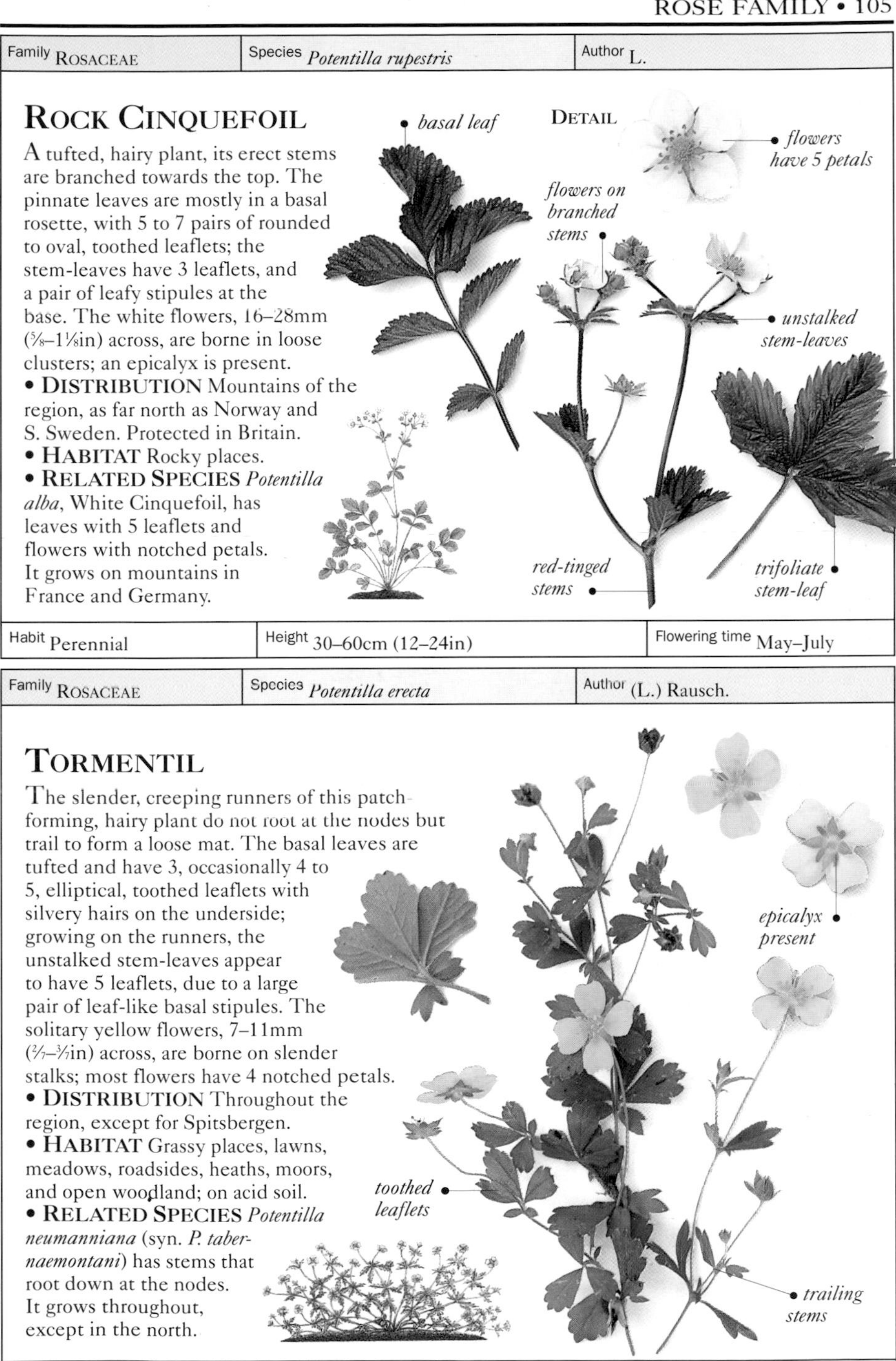

Habit Perennial	Height 30–60cm (12–24in)	Flowering time May–July

Family ROSACEAE	Species *Potentilla erecta*	Author (L.) Rausch.

Tormentil

The slender, creeping runners of this patch-forming, hairy plant do not root at the nodes but trail to form a loose mat. The basal leaves are tufted and have 3, occasionally 4 to 5, elliptical, toothed leaflets with silvery hairs on the underside; growing on the runners, the unstalked stem-leaves appear to have 5 leaflets, due to a large pair of leaf-like basal stipules. The solitary yellow flowers, 7–11mm (2/7–3/7in) across, are borne on slender stalks; most flowers have 4 notched petals.

• **DISTRIBUTION** Throughout the region, except for Spitsbergen.

• **HABITAT** Grassy places, lawns, meadows, roadsides, heaths, moors, and open woodland; on acid soil.

• **RELATED SPECIES** *Potentilla neumanniana* (syn. *P. tabernaemontani*) has stems that root down at the nodes. It grows throughout, except in the north.

Habit Perennial	Height 3–10cm (1 1/5–4in)	Flowering time May–Sept

Family ROSACEAE	Species *Alchemilla vulgaris*	Author L.

LADY'S MANTLE

This is a very variable, tufted, and hairy plant. Mostly borne in basal clusters, the leaves are rounded in outline, with rounded lobes and small teeth along the margin; the stem-leaves are smaller and short-stalked or unstalked. The greenish yellow flowers, 3–4mm (1/8–1/6in) across, have 4 partly fused sepals, but no petals.

• **DISTRIBUTION** Throughout the region; scarce in S.E. England.

• **HABITAT** Grassy and rocky places, meadows, woodland margins, stream-sides, and rock ledges; growing both at low altitudes and in the mountains.

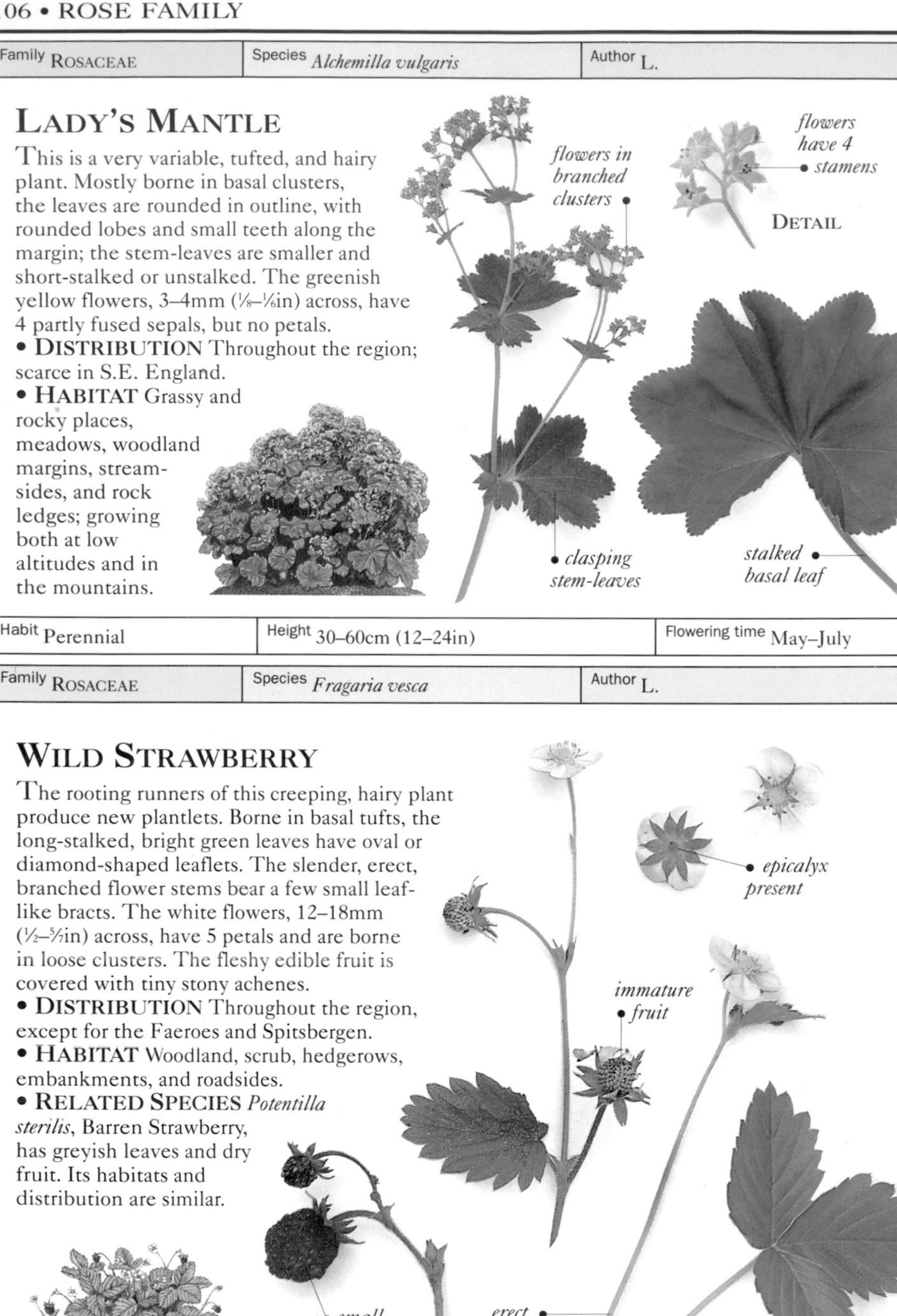

Habit Perennial	Height 30–60cm (12–24in)	Flowering time May–July

Family ROSACEAE	Species *Fragaria vesca*	Author L.

WILD STRAWBERRY

The rooting runners of this creeping, hairy plant produce new plantlets. Borne in basal tufts, the long-stalked, bright green leaves have oval or diamond-shaped leaflets. The slender, erect, branched flower stems bear a few small leaf-like bracts. The white flowers, 12–18mm (1/2–5/7in) across, have 5 petals and are borne in loose clusters. The fleshy edible fruit is covered with tiny stony achenes.

• **DISTRIBUTION** Throughout the region, except for the Faeroes and Spitsbergen.

• **HABITAT** Woodland, scrub, hedgerows, embankments, and roadsides.

• **RELATED SPECIES** *Potentilla sterilis*, Barren Strawberry, has greyish leaves and dry fruit. Its habitats and distribution are similar.

Habit Perennial	Height 10–25cm (4–10in)	Flowering time Apr–July

PEA FAMILY

Family LEGUMINOSAE	Species *Cytisus scoparius*	Author (L.) Link

BROOM

This much-branched deciduous shrub has slender, erect stems which are green and ridged, with long divisions, and are hairy in the first year. The small, alternate leaves are simple or trifoliate, with untoothed leaflets. The strongly scented, relatively large peaflowers are golden yellow, sometimes marked with red or mauve, 16–18mm (5/8–5/7in) long, and borne in leafy spikes; the sepals are united into a short tube. The fruit, an oblong pod, turns black when ripe, and is hairy on the fringes but hairless on the sides.

• **DISTRIBUTION** Throughout, except the far north.

• **HABITAT** Dry heaths and grassy places, roadsides, embankments, open woodland, and scrub.

• **REMARK** *Cytisus scoparius* subsp. *maritimus* grows on coastal cliffs and shingle and is often procumbent.

DETAIL

stem with young leaves

stamens protrude after flower is pollinated

flat fruit-pod

DETAIL

tough but slender stems

Habit Shrub	Height 1–2.5m (3¼–8ft)	Flowering time Apr–June

Family LEGUMINOSAE	Species *Genista tinctoria*	Author L.

DYER'S GREENWEED

This prostrate to more or less erect, non-spiny subshrub is rather variable in general growth habit. The alternate leaves are simple, oval to lanceolate, and may be hairy; tiny stipules are present at the base of each leaf. The yellow peaflowers are 8–15mm (1/3–3/5in) long and are borne in stalked spikes. The fruit consists of a small, hairless, narrow-oblong pod.

• **DISTRIBUTION** Throughout, except for the far north; absent from Ireland and N. Scotland.

• **HABITAT** Grassy places, old meadows, roadsides, embankments, rough ground, and scrub.

• **RELATED SPECIES** *Genista pilosa*, Hairy Greenweed, has dark green, hairy leaves and smaller flowers, 8–10mm (1/3–2/5in) long. It inhabits heathland, cliff-tops, and rocky places in Wales, S. England, Denmark, and Germany southwards; it is a very rare plant in Britain.

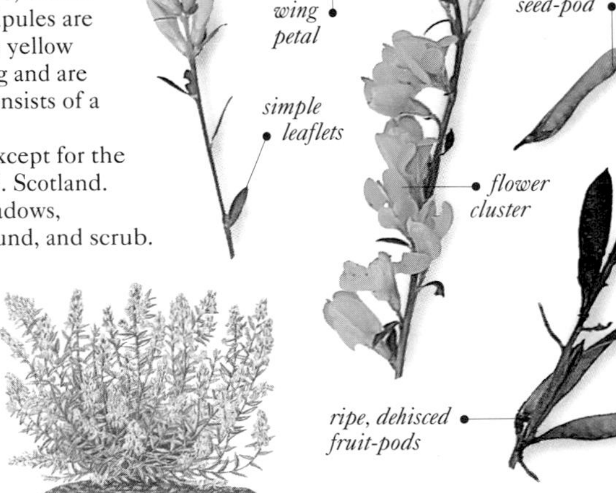

Habit Subshrub	Height 30–60cm (12–24in)	Flowering time May–July

Family LEGUMINOSAE	Species *Chamaespartium sagittale*	Author (L.) P. Gibbs

WINGED BROOM

Also known as *Genista sagittalis*, this mat-forming subshrub has long, spreading, green stems that give rise to ascending to erect, strongly winged flowering shoots; the vegetative, sterile, shoots often root down at the lower nodes. The alternate leaves are small and rather inconspicuous, simple, and lanceolate to elliptical. The yellow peaflowers, 10–12mm (2/5–1/2in) long, are borne in dense but small terminal heads; the wing petals are slightly shorter than the keel petal.

• **DISTRIBUTION** S.E. Belgium, France, and Germany; often rather local.

• **HABITAT** Meadows, rocky places, open woodland, calcareous downs, and roadsides, to an altitude of 1,900m (6,250ft); also cultivated in gardens.

Habit Subshrub	Height 10–40cm (4–16in)	Flowering time May–July

Family LEGUMINOSAE	Species *Lupinus polyphyllus*	Author Lindley

GARDEN LUPIN

This minutely hairy plant has stiff, erect, usually unbranched, stems. The leaves have 9 to 17 radiating lanceolate leaflets, which are deep green above and sparsely silky-hairy beneath. The scented flowers, 12–14mm (1/2–4/7in) long, are blue, pink, purple, white, or rarely yellow, but are often bicoloured. The oblong fruit-pod, 25–40mm (1–1 3/5in) long, is sparsely hairy.

• **DISTRIBUTION** Naturalized throughout, except for the far north.

• **HABITAT** Grassy places, roadsides, embankments, abandoned cultivation; widely grown in gardens.

• **RELATED SPECIES** *Lupinus nootkatensis*, Nootka Lupin, is hairier with 6 to 8 leaflets per leaf. It is naturalized in Scotland, Orkney, and Norway.

Habit Perennial	Height 70–120cm (28–48in)	Flowering time June–Aug

Family LEGUMINOSAE	Species *Galega officinalis*	Author L.

GOAT'S RUE

The stems of this hairless or slightly hairy plant are slender and erect, and may be branched. The alternate leaves are pinnate, with 4 to 8 pairs of oblong to lanceolate leaflets which have untoothed margins and a pointed apex; green leaflet-like stipules are present at the base of each leaf. The white to pale lilac or purple, often bi-coloured flowers are 10–15mm (2/5–3/5in) long; the calyx has 5 bristle-like teeth. The fruit-pod is cylindrical, 20–50mm (4/5–2in) long, and constricted between each seed.

• **DISTRIBUTION** France and S. Germany; naturalized elsewhere in N.W. Europe including C. and S. Britain.

• **HABITAT** Damp grassy places, roadsides, river- and stream-banks, and along ditches; cultivated in gardens.

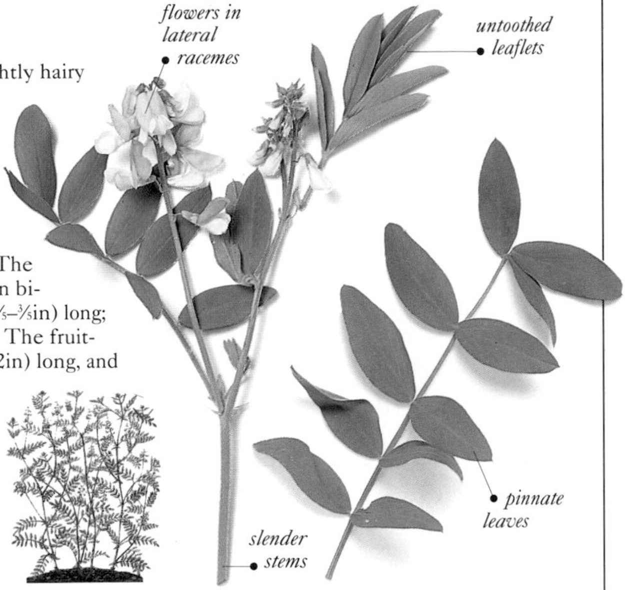

flowers in lateral racemes

untoothed leaflets

pinnate leaves

slender stems

Habit Subshrub	Height 80–150cm (32–60in)	Flowering time July–Sept

Family LEGUMINOSAE	Species *Astragalus glycyphyllos*	Author L.

WILD LIQUORICE

This is a rather straggling, slightly hairy or hairless plant with erect, unbranched or somewhat branched stems. The alternate leaves are pinnate, with 4 to 7 pairs of oval to elliptical, untoothed leaflets which are often rather pale green. The pale cream or whitish green peaflowers are 11–15mm (3/7–3/5in) long and are borne in dense, short, lateral racemes. The fruit is a slightly curved, narrow-oblong, hairless pod measuring 30–40mm (1 1/5–1 3/5in) in length.

• **DISTRIBUTION** Throughout the region, except for Ireland and the far north, but confined to the mountains in the south of its range; absent from N. Scotland

• **HABITAT** Rough grassy places, open woodland, scrub, and roadside embankments; usually on calcareous soils.

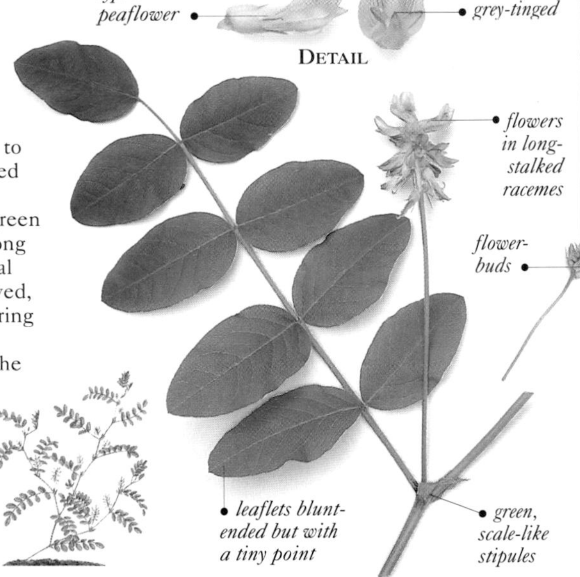

Habit Perennial	Height 80–150cm (32–60in)	Flowering time June–Aug

Family LEGUMINOSAE	Species *Vicia tetrasperma*	Author (L.) Schreber

SMOOTH TARE

This hairless plant climbs by means of leaf-tendrils. The stems are ridged but unwinged. The pinnate leaves have 3 to 6 pairs of linear leaflets and a terminal, usually unbranched, tendril. The peaflowers, 4–8mm (⅙–⅓in) long, are solitary or paired and are borne on long slender stalks. The fruit-pod is oval, brown when ripe, and often contains 4 seeds.

• **DISTRIBUTION** Throughout, except the Faeroes and the far north; naturalized in Ireland and Scotland.

• **HABITAT** Grassy sites, hedgerows, scrub, roadsides.

• **RELATED SPECIES** *Vicia parviflora* (syn. *V. tenuissima*), Slender Tare, has up to 5 flowers per raceme, and pods with 4 to 8 seeds. It grows in C. and S. Britain to Holland and Belgium southwards.

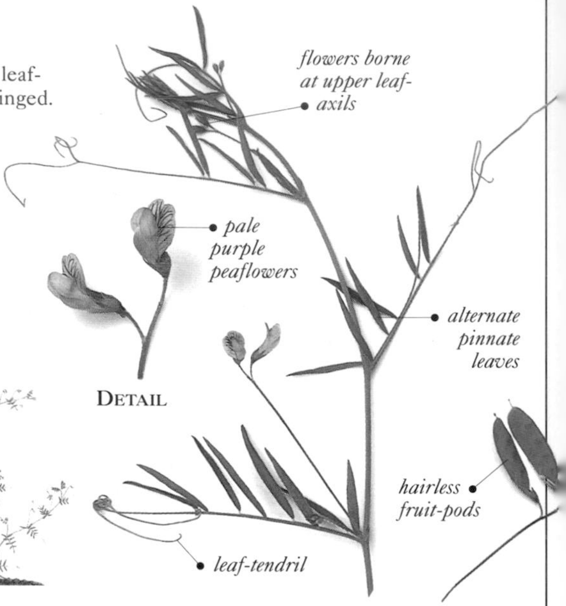

flowers borne at upper leaf-axils

pale purple peaflowers

DETAIL

alternate pinnate leaves

hairless fruit-pods

leaf-tendril

Habit Annual	Height 20–60cm (8–24in)	Flowering time May–Aug

Family LEGUMINOSAE	Species *Vicia cracca*	Author L.

TUFTED VETCH

This is a clambering and climbing, somewhat hairy or hairless plant with slender, branched, and slightly ridged stems. The alternate, pinnate leaves have 6 to 15 pairs of linear to oblong leaflets. The peaflowers are bluish violet and 8–12mm (⅓–½in) long. The fruit-pod is narrow-oblong, 10–25mm (⅖–1in) long, hairless, and brown when ripe.

• **DISTRIBUTION** Throughout the region, except for Spitsbergen.

• **HABITAT** Grassy places, meadows, hedgerows, scrub, woodland margins, roadsides, and coastal rocks and shingle.

• **RELATED SPECIES** *Vicia tenuifolia*, Fine-leaved Vetch, has narrower, linear-lanceolate leaflets and larger, paler, lilac or bluish lilac flowers. It grows in similar habitats on mainland Europe as far north as S. Sweden; naturalized in England and Scotland.

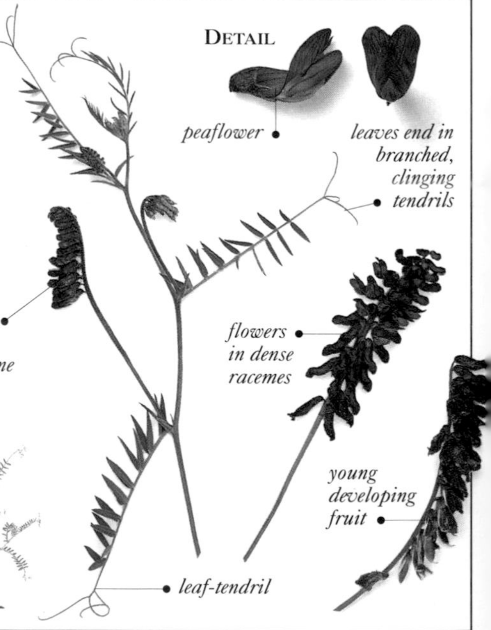

DETAIL

peaflower

leaves end in branched, clinging tendrils

flowers in long, one-sided raceme

flowers in dense racemes

young developing fruit

leaf-tendril

Habit Perennial	Height 80–200cm (32–80in)	Flowering time June–Aug

Family LEGUMINOSAE	Species *Vicia hirsuta*	Author (L.) Gray

HAIRY TARE

This hairy plant has slender unwinged stems. The alternate, pinnate leaves have stipules and 4 to 10 pairs of leaflets. Whitish, lilac-tinted peaflowers, 3–5mm (⅛–⅕in) long, are borne in stalked racemes of up to 8 flowers. The fruit-pod, 6–11mm (¼–3⁄7in) long, is black when ripe and usually contains 2 seeds.
• **DISTRIBUTION** Throughout, except the Faeroes and Spitsbergen.
• **HABITAT** Woodland margins, grassy meadows, scrub, hedgerows, and cultivated land; on calcareous to slightly acid soils.
• **RELATED SPECIES** *Vicia parviflora*, Slender Tare, has leaves with only 2 to 5 pairs of leaflets and larger pale purple flowers. It grows in C. Britain and Belgium southwards.

DETAIL
long calyx-teeth
branched tendrils at end of leaves
raceme of unripe fruit-pods
hairy, pendent fruit-pod
linear leaflets
DETAIL

Habit Annual	Height 30–80cm (12–32in)	Flowering time May–Aug

Family LEGUMINOSAE	Species *Vicia sepium*	Author L.

BUSH VETCH

This slender-stemmed, usually hairy, scrambling plant climbs by means of slender tendrils. The alternate, pinnate leaves bear toothed stipules. The purplish blue peaflowers, 12–15mm (½–⅗in) long, are borne in short-stalked clusters of 2 to 6. The hairless fruit-pod is black when ripe and 20–35mm (⅘–1⅖in) long.
• **DISTRIBUTION** Throughout the region, except the Faeroes and Spitsbergen.
• **HABITAT** Rough grassy places, meadows, scrub, roadsides, and hedgerows; on calcareous to slightly acid soils.
• **RELATED SPECIES** *Vicia sativa*, Common Vetch, has a dark spot on its stipules, oval to elliptical leaflets, and larger, often paired, flowers. The fruit-pod is yellowish or brownish when ripe. Its distribution and habitats are similar to those of the above.

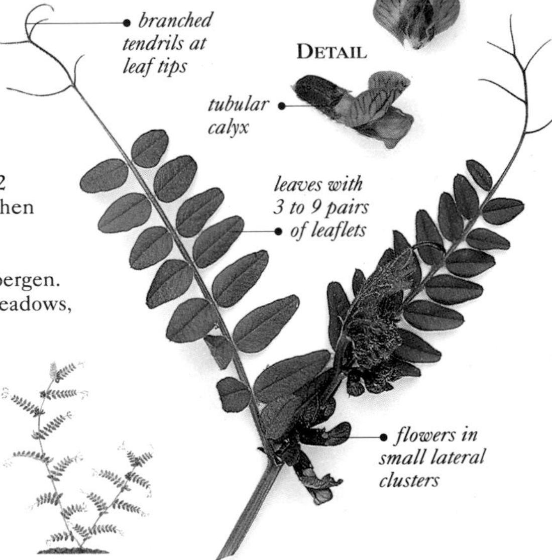

Habit Perennial	Height 20–60cm (8–24in)	Flowering time May–Nov

Family LEGUMINOSAE	Species *Vicia sativa*	Author L.

COMMON VETCH

This variable, clambering, and somewhat hairy plant has slender, ridged stems. The alternate, pinnate leaves have 3 to 8 pairs of oval leaflets; the stipules are toothed and have a prominent dark spot. The pink to reddish purple, occasionally white or bicoloured, peaflowers, 18–30mm ($\frac{5}{7}$–$1\frac{1}{5}$in) long, are solitary or paired. The slender fruit-pod, 25–70mm (1–$2\frac{4}{5}$in) long, is brown to black when ripe.

• **DISTRIBUTION** Throughout, but mainly naturalized in the north.

• **HABITAT** Cultivated and waste ground, scrub, grassy places, roadsides, and banks.

• **RELATED SPECIES** *Vicia lutea*, Yellow Vetch, has pale yellow flowers, often tinged with pink, and broader, shorter, hairy pods. It grows in coastal sites and rough grassland in Britain and France.

fruit-pod usually hairy

leaves have a terminal, branched tendril

DETAIL

calyx teeth are equal

peaflowers in leaf-axils

immature fruit-pod

Habit Annual	Height Up to 1.5m (5ft)	Flowering time Apr–Sept

Family LEGUMINOSAE	Species *Lathyrus vernus*	Author (L.) Bernh.

SPRING VETCHLING

The stems of this hairless or slightly hairy, clump-forming plant are erect to ascending and not winged. The alternate leaves are pinnate, with 2 to 4 pairs of pointed leaflets. The reddish purple to blue, occasionally pink, peaflowers are 13–20mm ($\frac{1}{2}$–$\frac{4}{5}$in) long. The fruit-pod is 40–60mm ($1\frac{3}{5}$–$2\frac{2}{5}$in) long and hairless.

• **DISTRIBUTION** Mainland Europe, except for the far north; widely grown in gardens, especially in Britain.

• **HABITAT** Woodland, scrub, semi-shaded banks; often on calcareous soils; to 1,900m (6,230ft).

• **RELATED SPECIES** *Lathyrus niger*, Black Pea, is taller. The leaves have 3 to 6 pairs of blunt leaflets; the flowers are smaller. Its distribution is similar; rare in Britain.

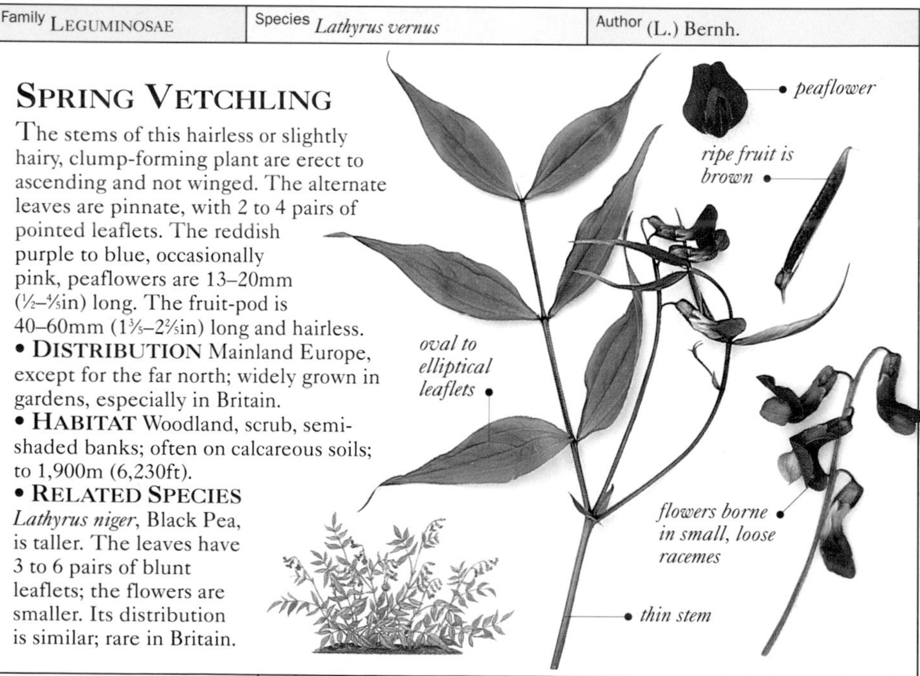

Habit Perennial	Height 20–45cm (8–18in)	Flowering time Apr–June

Family LEGUMINOSAE	Species *Lathyrus japonicus*	Author Willd.

SEA PEA

Also known as *Lathyrus maritimus*, this is a sprawling, usually hairless, and rather fleshy, grey-green plant, with angled but unwinged stems. The pinnate leaves carry 2 to 5 pairs of untoothed, elliptical leaflets and a branched or unbranched terminal tendril; stipules are leaflet-like and also untoothed. The purple peaflowers, 18–22mm (5/7–⅞in) long, gradually change to blue and are borne in short, lateral racemes of 2 to 10. The fruit is a hairless pod, 30–50mm (1⅕–2in) long, which turns brown when ripe.

• **DISTRIBUTION** Along the coasts of N.W. Europe. Locally decreasing in Britain and in Ireland.

• **HABITAT** Coastal shingles, rocks, and sand dunes; occasionally inland along stony lake margins. It is an early colonizer of fresh shingle, often forming large colonies.

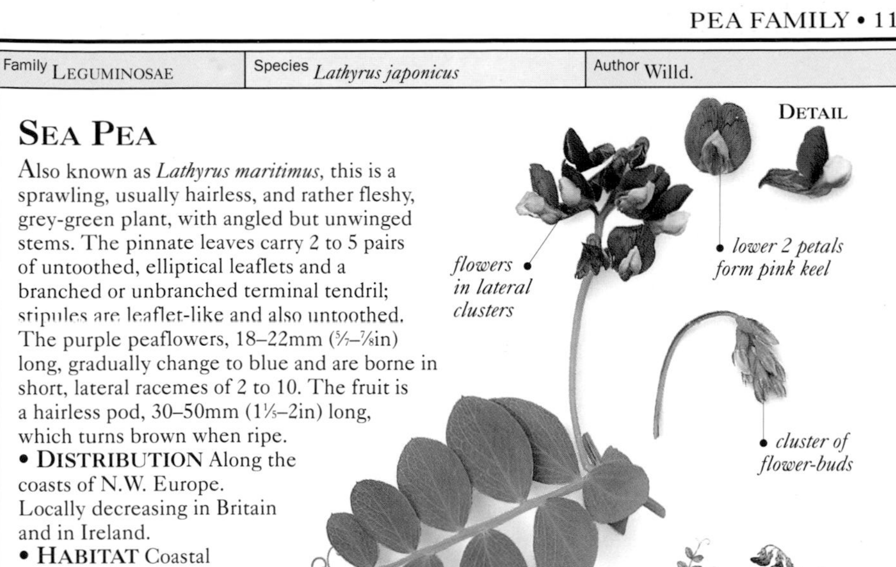

Habit Perennial	Stem length Up to 90cm (36in)	Flowering time June–Aug

Family LEGUMINOSAE	Species *Lathyrus linifolius* var. *montanus*	Author (Reichard) Baessler

BITTER VETCH

This is a hairless plant with slender, winged, erect stems. The leaves are pinnate, ending in a point, not a tendril, and each have 2 to 4 pairs of linear to narrow-elliptical, untoothed leaflets; the stipules clasp the stem with heart-shaped bases. The crimson to reddish purple peaflowers, 10–16mm (⅖–⅝in) long, change to blue as they age, and are borne in lateral, long-stalked racemes of usually 2 to 6 flowers. The fruit-pod is hairless, 25–45mm (1–1⅘in) long, and reddish brown when ripe.

• **DISTRIBUTION** Throughout the region, except for the Faeroes and Iceland; scarce in parts of Ireland and E. England.

• **HABITAT** Grassy places, road verges, banks, open woodland and woodland margins, scrub, and hedgerows; often on acid soils; in the mountains, to an altitude of 2,200m (7,220ft).

Habit Perennial	Height 20–40cm (8–16in)	Flowering time Apr–July

Family LEGUMINOSAE	Species *Lathyrus pratensis*	Author L.

MEADOW VETCHLING

This clambering and hairless plant has thin, winged stems. The alternate leaves have a single pair of narrow-lanceolate to elliptical, pointed leaflets, and terminate in a tendril. The peaflowers, 10–18mm (⅖–5⁄7in) long, are borne in long-stalked racemes, usually well clear of the leaves. The fruit-pod, 20–40mm (⅘–1⅗in) long, is hairless or slightly hairy, black when ripe, and usually contains 4 to 9 seeds.

• **DISTRIBUTION** Growing throughout much of the region, except for the far north; sometimes local.

• **HABITAT** Rough grassy places, meadows, roadsides, embankments, hedgerows, open woodland, scrub, coastal rocks, and occasionally dunes; on calcareous to slightly acid soils.

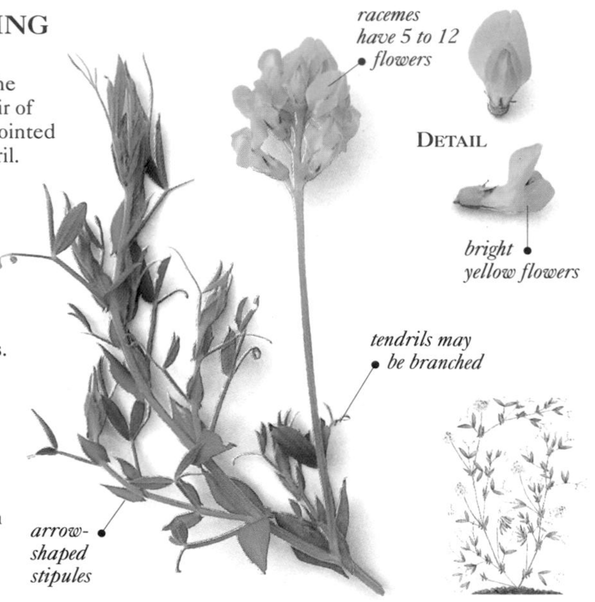

Habit Perennial	Height 50–120cm (20–48in)	Flowering time May–Aug

Family LEGUMINOSAE	Species *Lathyrus latifolius*	Author L.

BROAD-LEAVED EVERLASTING-PEA

This robust, clambering or sprawling plant has broad, winged, often branched, stems. The leaves have one pair of linear to elliptical leaflets. In long-stalked, lateral racemes, the peaflowers, 20–30mm (⅘–1⅕in) across, are magenta-purple or pink, rarely white. The hairless, many-seeded fruit-pod, 5–11cm (2–4¼in) long, is dark brown when ripe.

• **DISTRIBUTION** France; widely naturalized in Britain, Belgium, Holland, and Germany.

• **HABITAT** Grassy sites, embankments, roadsides, woodland margins, fields, hedgerows, and scrub.

• **RELATED SPECIES** *Lathyrus heterophyllus*, Norfolk Everlasting-pea, has 2 or 3 pairs of leaflets and smaller flowers. It grows in France, Germany, and S. Sweden, and is naturalized on dunes in W. Norfolk (England).

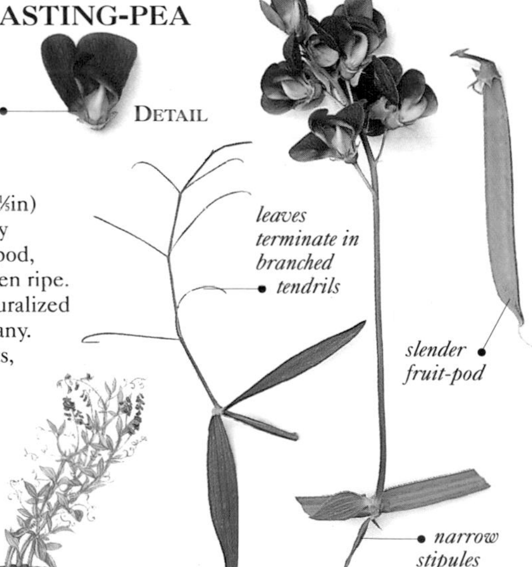

Habit Perennial	Height Up to 3m (10ft)	Flowering time June–Sept

Family LEGUMINOSAE	Species *Lathyrus nissolia*	Author L.

GRASS VETCHLING

The stems of this slender, hairless or slightly hairy plant are unwinged. The leaves are reduced to a single, pointed blade; the stipules are small and rather inconspicuous. The crimson peaflowers, 8–18mm (1/3–5/7in) across, are solitary or paired. The narrow fruit-pod is 30–60mm (1⅕–2⅖in) long, may be hairy or hairless, and turns a pale brown colour when ripe.

• **DISTRIBUTION** Throughout, except for Ireland, Scandinavia, and Iceland, but local or only casual in the north of the region.

• **HABITAT** Grassy places, banks, field boundaries; occasionally along woodland margins.

• **RELATED SPECIES** *Lathyrus hirsutus*, Hairy Vetchling, has paired leaflets and tendrils. The pods are silky with hairs. It is native in Germany, France, Belgium; naturalized in England and S. Scotland.

DETAIL

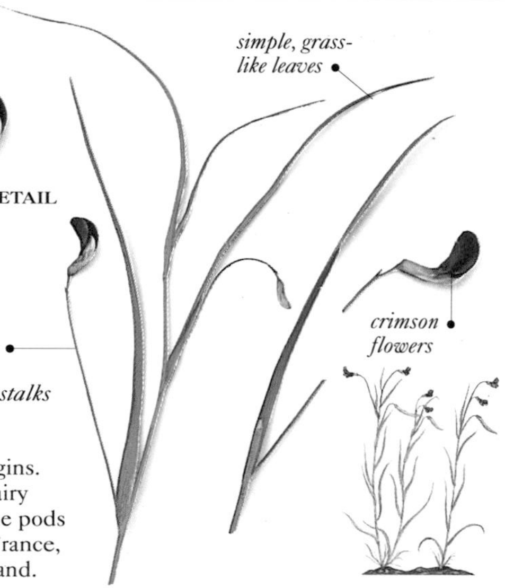

simple, grass-like leaves

flowers on long slender stalks

crimson flowers

Habit Annual	Height 30–90cm (12–36in)	Flowering time May–July

Family LEGUMINOSAE	Species *Lathyrus aphaca*	Author L.

YELLOW VETCHLING

This clambering, hairless plant has slender, unwinged, often branched, stems. The true leaves are reduced to simple, unbranched tendrils, while the paired stipules, 6–50mm (¼–2in) long, are large and leaf-like. The flowers, 10–16mm (⅖–⅝in) long, are borne on long, slender stems and are usually solitary, but occasionally paired. The hairless fruit-pod is 20–35mm (⅘–1⅖in) long, and brown when ripe.

• **DISTRIBUTION** C. and E. France. Naturalized in S. Britain, Belgium, Holland, and Germany; casual in other parts of the region.

• **HABITAT** Dry places, grassy banks, meadows, rough grassy habitats, woodland margins, scrub, and roadsides.

• **REMARK** In this unusual species the function of the leaves is taken over by leaf-like stipules.

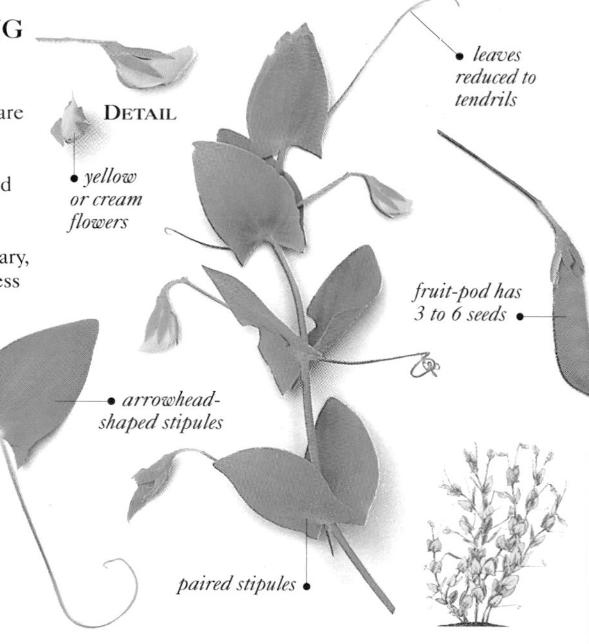

Habit Annual	Height Up to 60cm (24in)	Flowering time May–Aug

Family LEGUMINOSAE	Species *Melilotus officinalis*	Author (L.) Lam.

RIBBED MELILOT

This is a hairless plant with slender, unbranched or somewhat branched, erect to slightly spreading stems. The leaves are alternate. The leaflets of the lower leaves are oval and sharply toothed; those of the upper are narrower. The stipules are usually untoothed. Borne in slender, lateral racemes, the peaflowers are 4–7mm (⅙–²⁄₇in) long, with the wing petals longer than the keel petal. The fruit-pods are 3–5mm (⅛–⅕in) long, transversely ridged, one-seeded, and brown when ripe.

• **DISTRIBUTION** Holland and Germany southwards; naturalized in Britain, Ireland, and Denmark.

• **HABITAT** Cultivated, waste, and bare land, open grassy places; sometimes roadsides.

• **RELATED SPECIES** *Melilotus altissima* has mostly 2-seeded, net-veined, hairy black pods. It inhabits damp areas as far north as S. Sweden.

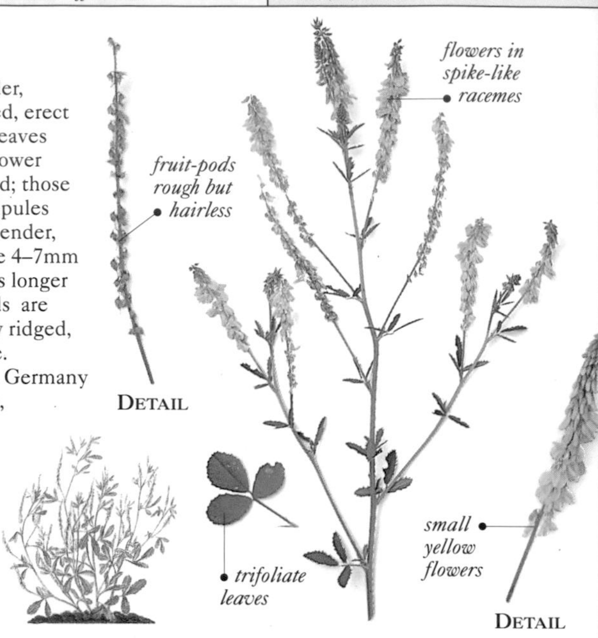

Habit Biennial or perennial	Height 80–150cm (32–60in)	Flowering time July–Sept

Family LEGUMINOSAE	Species *Melilotus albus*	Author Medicus

WHITE MELILOT

This hairless plant has slender, erect, leafy stems. The alternate leaves have oval to elliptical, sharply toothed leaflets; the stipules are linear and untoothed. The peaflowers, 4–5mm (⅙–⅕in) long, are borne in dense, lateral racemes; the standard petal is slightly longer than the others. The fruit-pod, 3–5mm (⅛–⅕in) long, is netted on the outside or sometimes ribbed, greyish brown when ripe, and hairless.

• **DISTRIBUTION** Native in mainland Europe as far north as C. Scandinavia, but naturalized further north in the region and in Britain and Ireland.

• **HABITAT** Cultivated, especially arable, land; waste and bare ground, roadsides, grassy places. It is a fairly frequent weed in some parts.

• **RELATED SPECIES** *Melilotus indicus*, Small Melilot, has yellow flowers and is the smallest of any European melilot. The fruit-pods are olive-green when ripe.

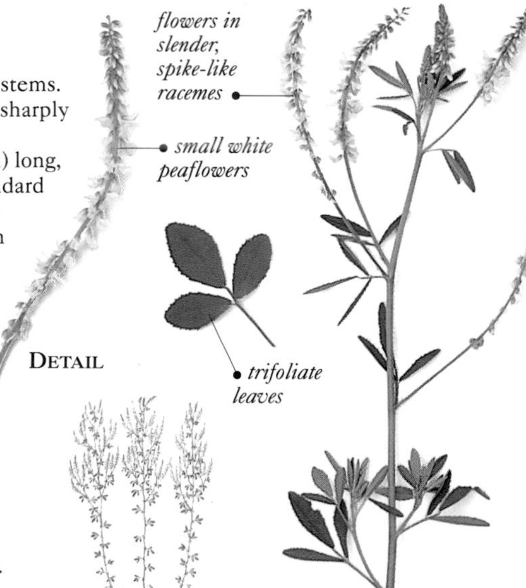

Habit Annual or biennial	Height 80–150cm (32–60in)	Flowering time July–Sept

Family LEGUMINOSAE	Species *Ononis repens*	Author L.

COMMON RESTHARROW

This is a spreading to more or less prostrate, glandular-hairy plant. The branched stems are woody at the base, often rooting down, and sometimes have weak spines. The alternate leaves have one or 3, toothed leaflets, which are usually notched at the top. The pink or purplish peaflowers, 15–20mm ($\frac{3}{5}$–$\frac{4}{5}$in) long, are borne in leafy, terminal racemes. The hairy fruit-pods, 5–8mm ($\frac{1}{5}$–$\frac{1}{3}$in) long, contain one or 2 seeds.

• **DISTRIBUTION** Throughout, except for the far north, the Faeroes, and Iceland.

• **HABITAT** Rough grassy places, meadows, pastures, downs, and roadsides.

• **RELATED SPECIES** *Ononis spinosa* (syn. *O. campestris*), Spiny Restharrow, is a stiffly spiny, small shrub. The stems have 2 opposite lines of hairs. It has a similar distribution to Common Restharrow but grows on heavier soils.

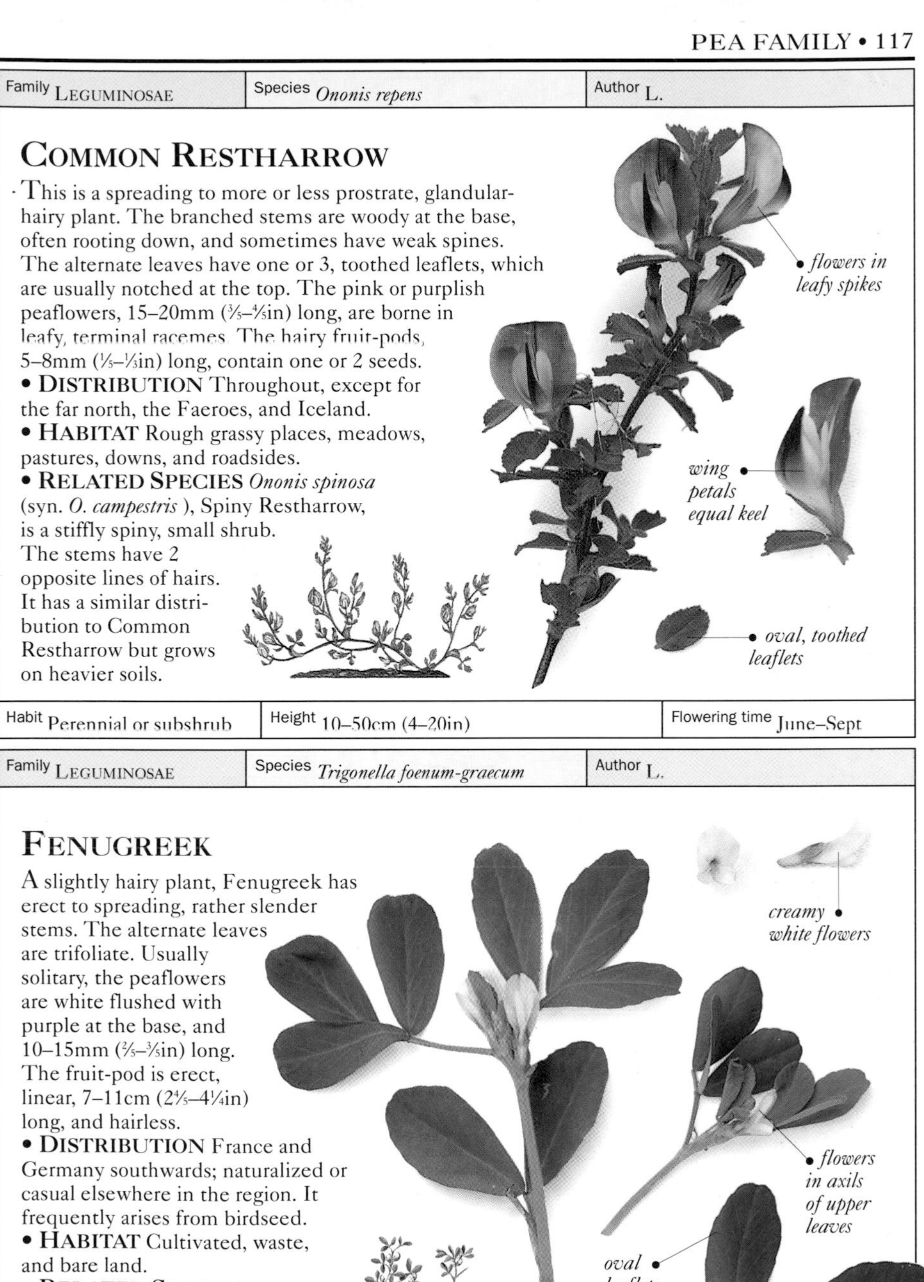

Habit Perennial or subshrub	Height 10–50cm (4–20in)	Flowering time June–Sept

Family LEGUMINOSAE	Species *Trigonella foenum-graecum*	Author L.

FENUGREEK

A slightly hairy plant, Fenugreek has erect to spreading, rather slender stems. The alternate leaves are trifoliate. Usually solitary, the peaflowers are white flushed with purple at the base, and 10–15mm ($\frac{2}{5}$–$\frac{3}{5}$in) long. The fruit-pod is erect, linear, 7–11cm ($2\frac{4}{5}$–$4\frac{1}{4}$in) long, and hairless.

• **DISTRIBUTION** France and Germany southwards; naturalized or casual elsewhere in the region. It frequently arises from birdseed.

• **HABITAT** Cultivated, waste, and bare land.

• **RELATED SPECIES** *Trigonella monspeliaca* is hairy, with smaller flowers in small clusters and much smaller fruit-pods. It grows in similar habitats in Belgium and France.

Habit Annual	Height 20–50cm (8–20in)	Flowering time Apr–June

Family LEGUMINOSAE	Species *Medicago lupulina*	Author L.

BLACK MEDICK

This is a low, often hairy, plant with spreading to scrambling, slender stems. The alternate leaves are trifoliate, with rounded to oblong or diamond-shaped, toothed or untoothed leaflets; the stipules are slightly toothed. The small yellow flowers, only 2–3mm (1/12–1/8in) long, are borne in clusters on long slender stalks. The fruit-pod, 1.5–3mm (1/16–1/8in) long, is kidney-shaped, slightly coiled, and may be hairy.

• **DISTRIBUTION** Throughout, except for Spitsbergen; scarcer and often coastal in the north of its natural range.

• **HABITAT** Grassy places; generally grows on short turf, on well-drained, calcareous soils.

flowers in crowded clusters

trifoliate leaves

fruit-pod is black when ripe

narrow, triangular stipules

Habit Annual	Stem length Up to 80cm (32in)	Flowering time Apr–Sept

Family LEGUMINOSAE	Species *Medicago sativa*	Author L.

LUCERNE

This is a very variable, hairy plant with erect to spreading stems. The alternate leaves are trifoliate, with the leaflets toothed towards the tip. The violet to blue flowers, 7–11mm (2/7–3/7in) long, are borne in short racemes. The fruit-pods, 5–6mm (1/5–1/4in) across, are spiralled with a hole in the centre, and may be hairy.

• **DISTRIBUTION** Throughout, except for the far north; scarcer in the north of its range.

• **HABITAT** Cultivated, waste, and bare ground, roadsides, rough grassy places, rubbish tips.

• **REMARK** Subsp. *falcata*, Sickle Medick, has yellow flowers and straight to curved fruit-pods. It is native in mainland Europe; in England it is restricted to East Anglia; naturalized elsewhere in the region.

Habit Perennial	Height 40–90cm (16–36in)	Flowering time June–July

Family	Species	Author
LEGUMINOSAE	*Trifolium repens*	L.

WHITE CLOVER

This very variable, practically hairless, patch-forming plant spreads by means of creeping stems that root down at the nodes. The alternate leaves are trifoliate, with 3 oval to elliptical, finely toothed leaflets which are bright green but generally with a paler or darker central V-shaped mark. The white or pink, rarely red, sweetly scented peaflowers, 7–10mm (2⁄7–⅖in) long, are borne in dense rounded heads on a long thin stalk. The narrow fruit-pod contains only 3 or 4 seeds.

• **DISTRIBUTION** Throughout the region, except for the far north.

• **HABITAT** Meadows, fields, road verges, hedgebanks, and other grassy places; often forming extensive colonies; on a variety of soils to an altitude of 2,750m (9,000ft).

• **REMARK** Plants from the higher mountains are smaller, with shorter stems and fewer flowers to each inflorescence.

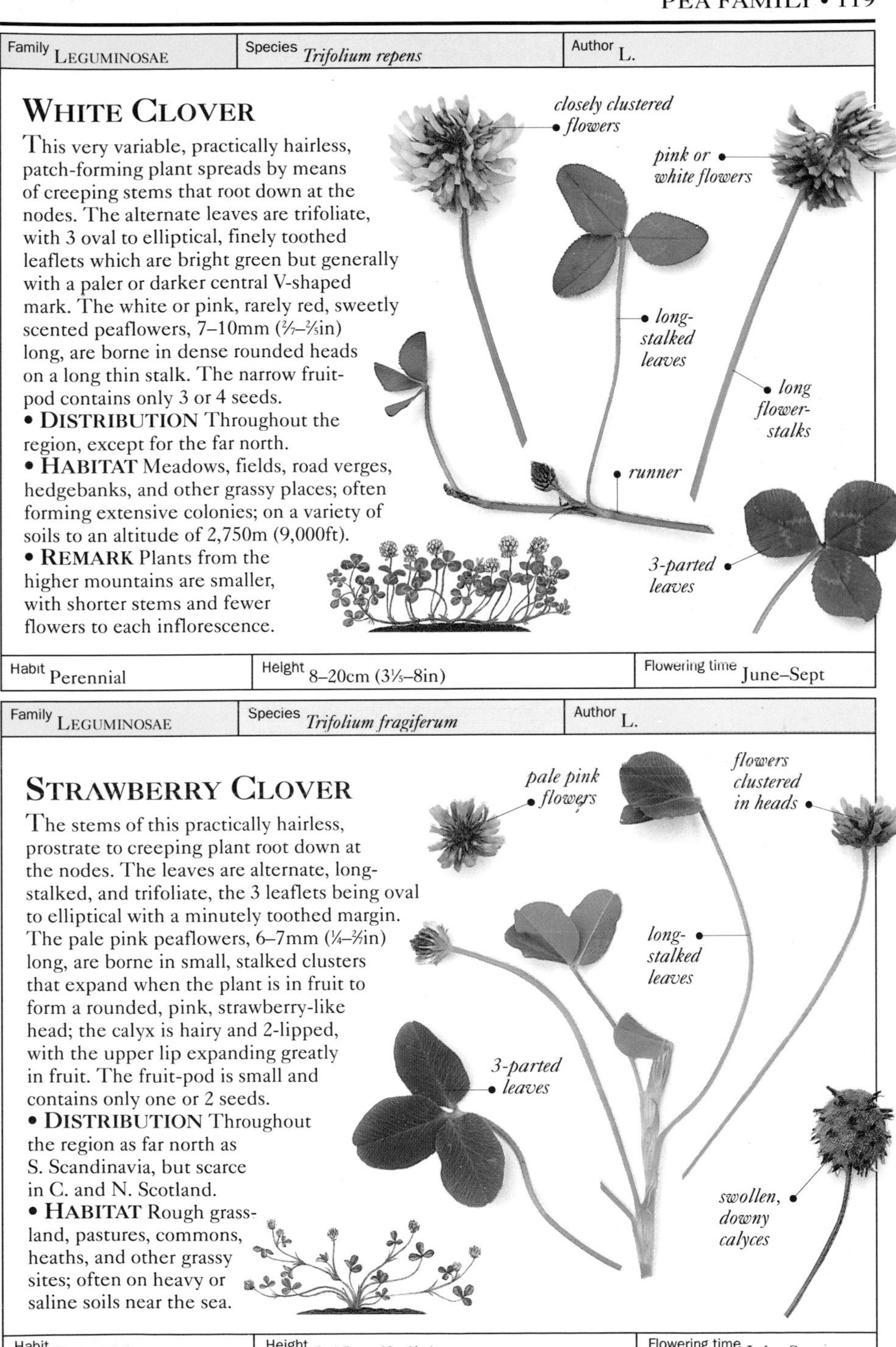

Habit	Height	Flowering time
Perennial	8–20cm (3⅕–8in)	June–Sept

Family	Species	Author
LEGUMINOSAE	*Trifolium fragiferum*	L.

STRAWBERRY CLOVER

The stems of this practically hairless, prostrate to creeping plant root down at the nodes. The leaves are alternate, long-stalked, and trifoliate, the 3 leaflets being oval to elliptical with a minutely toothed margin. The pale pink peaflowers, 6–7mm (¼–⅖in) long, are borne in small, stalked clusters that expand when the plant is in fruit to form a rounded, pink, strawberry-like head; the calyx is hairy and 2-lipped, with the upper lip expanding greatly in fruit. The fruit-pod is small and contains only one or 2 seeds.

• **DISTRIBUTION** Throughout the region as far north as S. Scandinavia, but scarce in C. and N. Scotland.

• **HABITAT** Rough grassland, pastures, commons, heaths, and other grassy sites; often on heavy or saline soils near the sea.

Habit	Height	Flowering time
Perennial	5–15cm (2–6in)	July–Sept

Family LEGUMINOSAE	Species *Trifolium scabrum*	Author L.

ROUGH CLOVER

The slender stems of this hairy plant are spreading to ascending. The trifoliate leaves have rather thick, finely toothed, oval leaflets; the stipules are oval with a fine point. The whitish or sometimes pinkish flowers, 4–7mm (⅙–²⁄₇in) long, are borne in clusters at the leaf-axils; the petals are shorter than the spine-tipped calyx. The oblong, one-seeded fruit-pod is hidden within the persistent calyx.

• **DISTRIBUTION** Throughout the region, but absent from Scandinavia and Iceland, and a rare plant in N. Scotland and most of Ireland.

• **HABITAT** Sandy places and short grassland in open situations, especially near the sea.

Habit Annual	Height 5–20cm (2–8in)	Flowering time May–July

Family LEGUMINOSAE	Species *Trifolium pratense*	Author L.

RED CLOVER

This is a very variable, tufted, and hairy plant with spreading to erect stems. The trifoliate leaves have oval to elliptical leaflets; the triangular stipules are often wide-based. The reddish purple to pink flowers, 12–15mm (½–⅗in) long, are borne in dense, rounded heads. The fruit-pod has a thickened rim and is mostly hidden within the persistent calyx.

• **DISTRIBUTION** Throughout the region, except for parts of the far north, but widely grown as a forage crop and often naturalized.

• **HABITAT** Grassy places, rough and waste ground, and roadsides; on lowland and in the mountains to 3,150m (10,350ft).

Habit Perennial	Height 20–60cm (8–24in)	Flowering time May–Sept

Family LEGUMINOSAE	Species *Trifolium campestre*	Author Schreber

HOP TREFOIL

This hairy plant has slender, erect to spreading stems. The trifoliate leaves have oval, finely toothed leaflets. The yellow flowers, 4–5mm (⅙–⅕in) long, are borne in rounded clusters on a common stalk. The fruit-pod, hidden within the persistent calyx, has a single seed.

• **DISTRIBUTION** Throughout, except for the far north.

• **HABITAT** Dry, grassy places, road verges, tracksides, and sand dunes.

• **RELATED SPECIES** *Trifolium aureum*, Large Hop Trefoil, is larger, with the central leaflet unstalked; the flowers are longer. It inhabits woods, scrub, and waste places in mainland Europe, except for the far north, and is naturalized in parts of Britain.

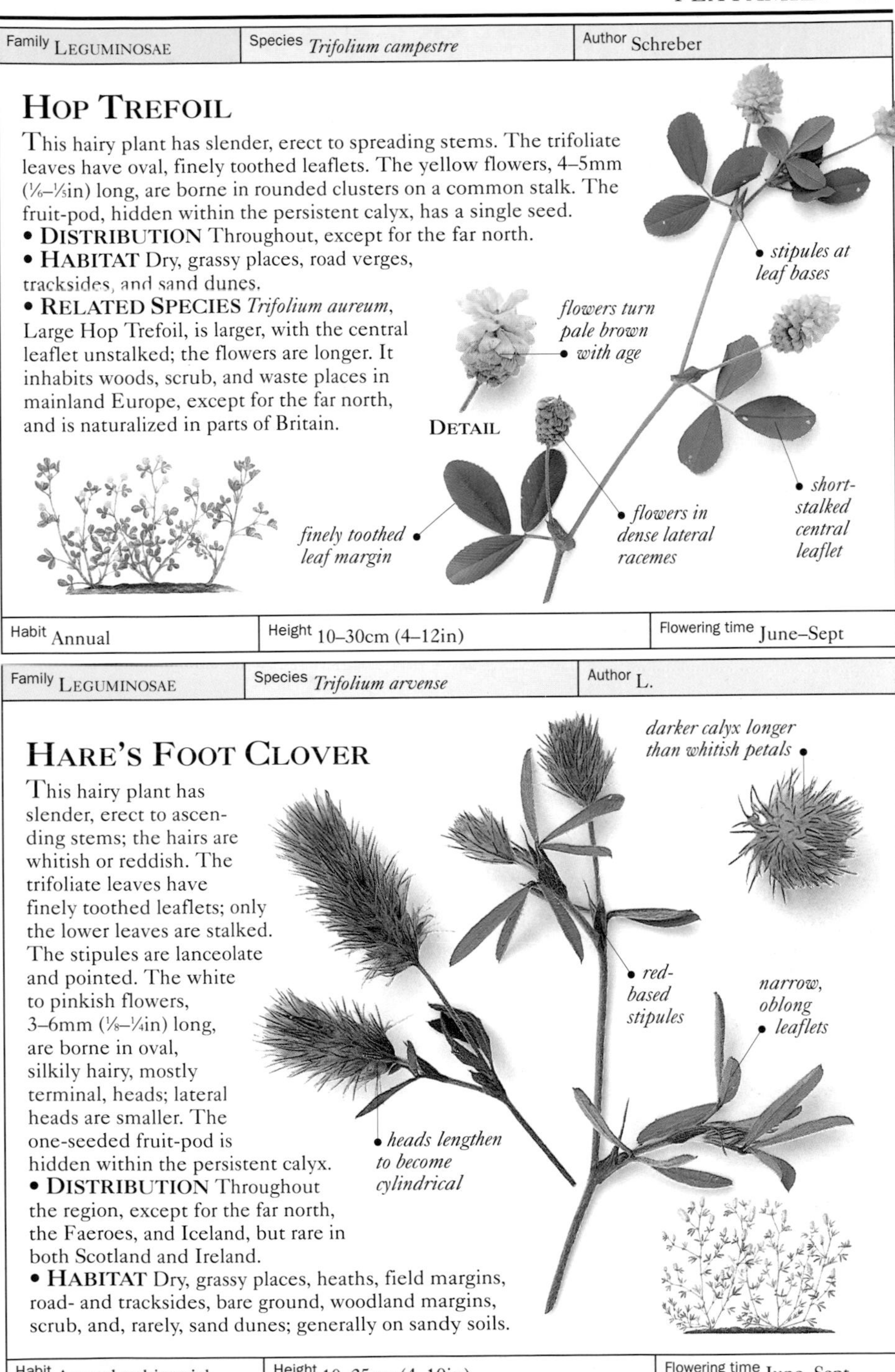

Habit Annual	Height 10–30cm (4–12in)	Flowering time June–Sept

Family LEGUMINOSAE	Species *Trifolium arvense*	Author L.

HARE'S FOOT CLOVER

This hairy plant has slender, erect to ascending stems; the hairs are whitish or reddish. The trifoliate leaves have finely toothed leaflets; only the lower leaves are stalked. The stipules are lanceolate and pointed. The white to pinkish flowers, 3–6mm (⅛–¼in) long, are borne in oval, silkily hairy, mostly terminal, heads; lateral heads are smaller. The one-seeded fruit-pod is hidden within the persistent calyx.

• **DISTRIBUTION** Throughout the region, except for the far north, the Faeroes, and Iceland, but rare in both Scotland and Ireland.

• **HABITAT** Dry, grassy places, heaths, field margins, road- and tracksides, bare ground, woodland margins, scrub, and, rarely, sand dunes; generally on sandy soils.

Habit Annual or biennial	Height 10–25cm (4–10in)	Flowering time June–Sept

Family LEGUMINOSAE	Species *Lotus corniculatus*	Author L.

COMMON BIRD'S-FOOT TREFOIL

This variable, spreading to almost prostrate, rarely hairy plant has solid stems that become woody at the base. The leaves are alternate and pinnate, with lanceolate to rounded leaflets which are 4–18mm (⅙–⅖in) long and pointed or slightly notched at the apex; the lower pair of leaflets are close to the stem and stipule-like. The peaflowers, 10–16mm (⅖–⅝in) long, are bright yellow or sometimes orange-yellow, and often streaked with red; the flower-buds are reddish. The fruit-pod, 15–30mm (⅗–1⅕in) long, is dark brownish black when ripe.

• **DISTRIBUTION** Throughout the region, except for Spitsbergen; probably only naturalized in Iceland.

• **HABITAT** Grassy places, meadows, fields, roadsides, heathland, open scrub, and sand dunes.

• **REMARK** Forms growing in coastal areas are frequently dwarf, almost completely hairless, and have small, rather fleshy, leaflets.

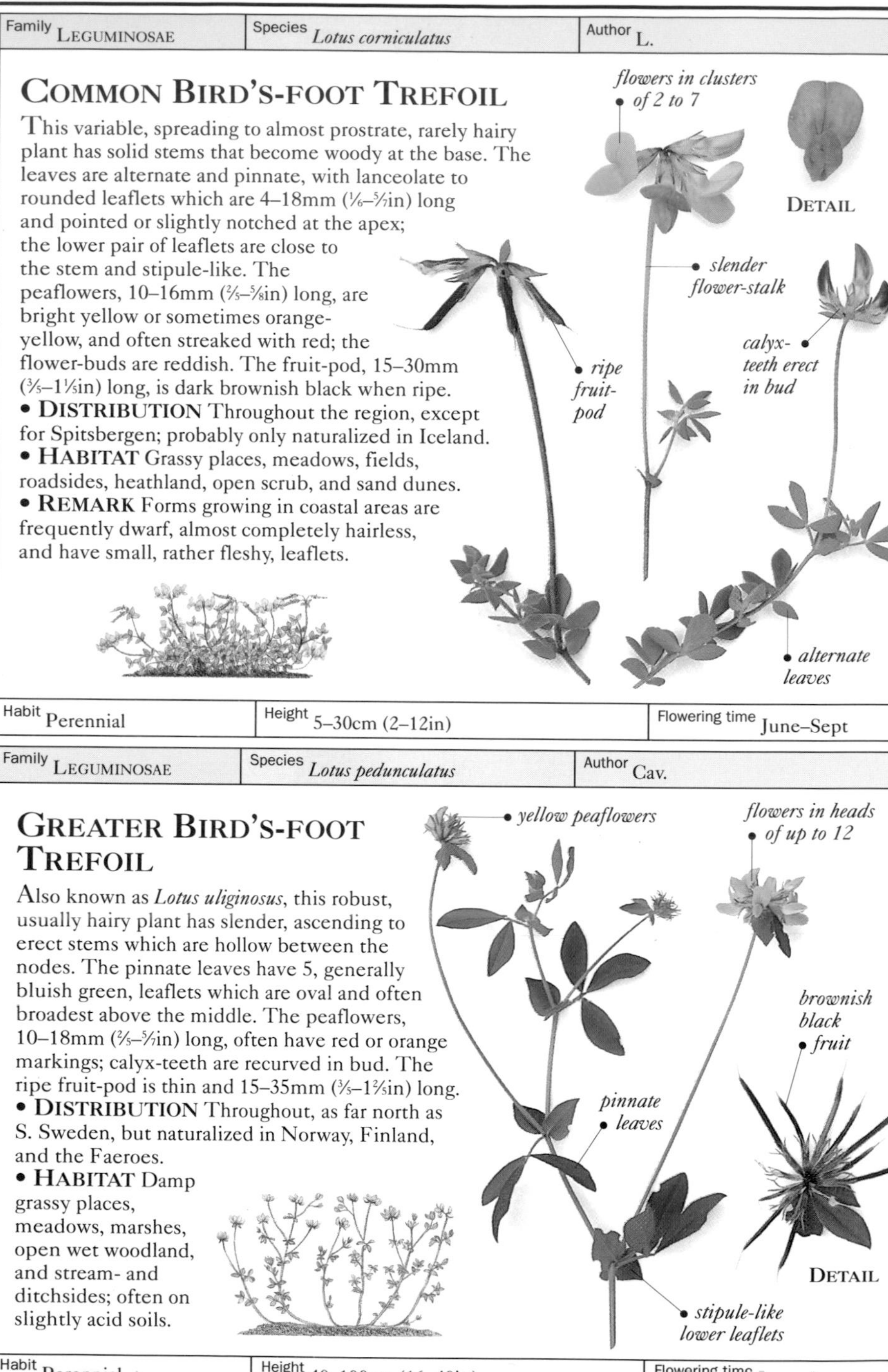

Habit Perennial	Height 5–30cm (2–12in)	Flowering time June–Sept

Family LEGUMINOSAE	Species *Lotus pedunculatus*	Author Cav.

GREATER BIRD'S-FOOT TREFOIL

Also known as *Lotus uliginosus*, this robust, usually hairy plant has slender, ascending to erect stems which are hollow between the nodes. The pinnate leaves have 5, generally bluish green, leaflets which are oval and often broadest above the middle. The peaflowers, 10–18mm (⅖–⅔in) long, often have red or orange markings; calyx-teeth are recurved in bud. The ripe fruit-pod is thin and 15–35mm (⅗–1⅖in) long.

• **DISTRIBUTION** Throughout, as far north as S. Sweden, but naturalized in Norway, Finland, and the Faeroes.

• **HABITAT** Damp grassy places, meadows, marshes, open wet woodland, and stream- and ditchsides; often on slightly acid soils.

Habit Perennial	Height 40–100cm (16–40in)	Flowering time June–Aug

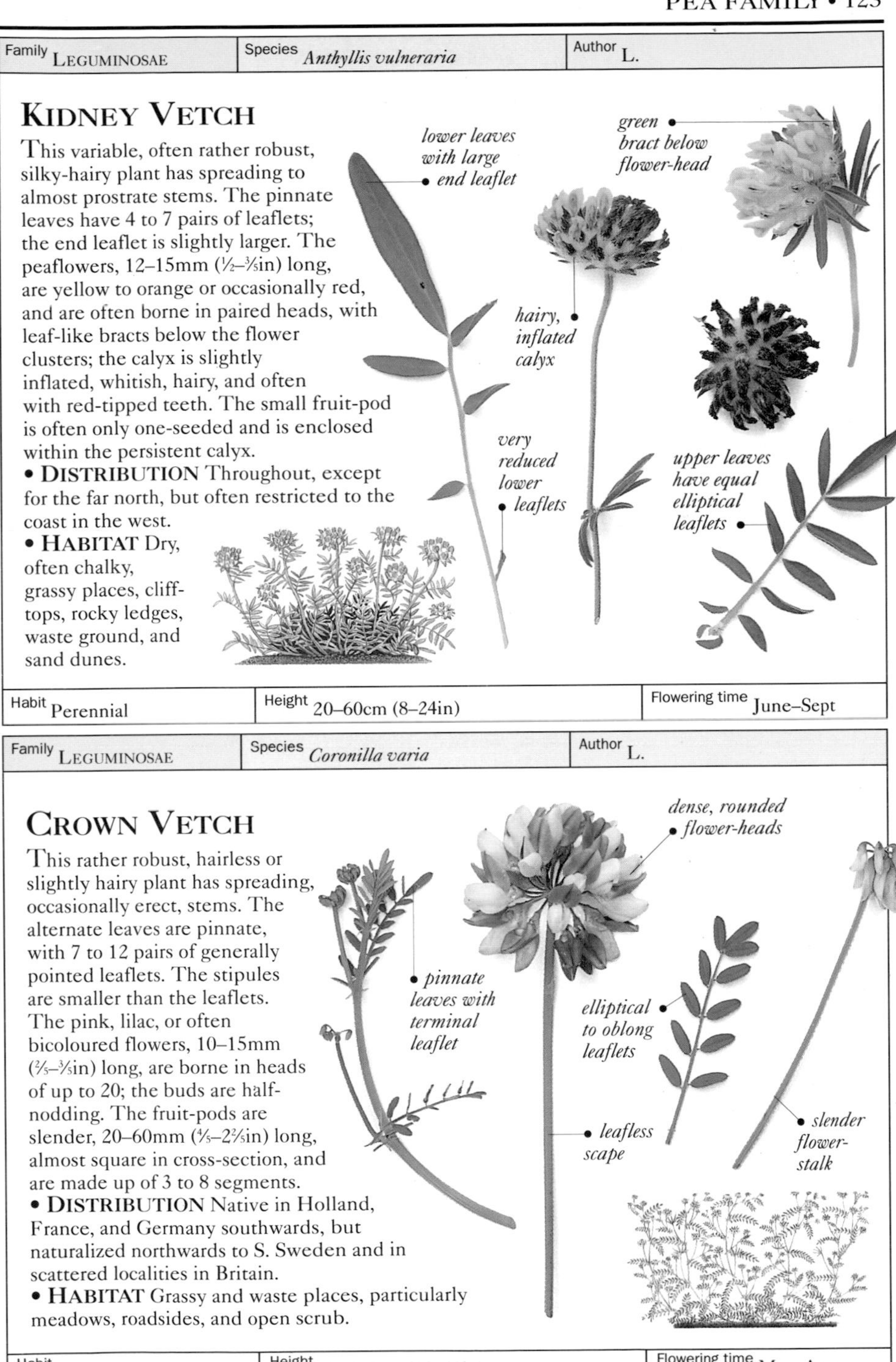

Family	Species	Author
LEGUMINOSAE	*Anthyllis vulneraria*	L.

KIDNEY VETCH

This variable, often rather robust, silky-hairy plant has spreading to almost prostrate stems. The pinnate leaves have 4 to 7 pairs of leaflets; the end leaflet is slightly larger. The peaflowers, 12–15mm (½–⅗in) long, are yellow to orange or occasionally red, and are often borne in paired heads, with leaf-like bracts below the flower clusters; the calyx is slightly inflated, whitish, hairy, and often with red-tipped teeth. The small fruit-pod is often only one-seeded and is enclosed within the persistent calyx.

• **DISTRIBUTION** Throughout, except for the far north, but often restricted to the coast in the west.

• **HABITAT** Dry, often chalky, grassy places, cliff-tops, rocky ledges, waste ground, and sand dunes.

Habit	Height	Flowering time
Perennial	20–60cm (8–24in)	June–Sept

Family	Species	Author
LEGUMINOSAE	*Coronilla varia*	L.

CROWN VETCH

This rather robust, hairless or slightly hairy plant has spreading, occasionally erect, stems. The alternate leaves are pinnate, with 7 to 12 pairs of generally pointed leaflets. The stipules are smaller than the leaflets. The pink, lilac, or often bicoloured flowers, 10–15mm (⅖–⅗in) long, are borne in heads of up to 20; the buds are half-nodding. The fruit-pods are slender, 20–60mm (⅘–2⅖in) long, almost square in cross-section, and are made up of 3 to 8 segments.

• **DISTRIBUTION** Native in Holland, France, and Germany southwards, but naturalized northwards to S. Sweden and in scattered localities in Britain.

• **HABITAT** Grassy and waste places, particularly meadows, roadsides, and open scrub.

Habit	Height	Flowering time
Perennial	30–100cm (12–40in)	May–Aug

Family LEGUMINOSAE	Species *Hippocrepis comosa*	Author L.

HORSESHOE VETCH

The slender stems of this generally low, hairless plant are prostrate to ascending. The alternate leaves are pinnate, with 3 to 8 pairs of linear to oval leaflets which are often broadest above the middle and sometimes notched at the apex; green narrow-triangular stipules are present at the base of each leaf. The yellow peaflowers, 6–10mm (¼–⅖in) long, are borne in long-stalked clusters from the axils of the upper leaves; the standard petal has a distinct claw. The fruit-pod, up to 30mm (1⅕in) in length overall, is twisted, with 3 to 6 small horseshoe-shaped segments.

• **DISTRIBUTION** England to Holland and Germany southwards; absent from Scotland and Ireland; often local.

• **HABITAT** Dry and sunny grassy places, and cliff-tops; invariably over chalk or limestone.

Habit Perennial	Height 15–30cm (6–12in)	Flowering time Apr–July

Family LEGUMINOSAE	Species *Onobrychis viciifolia*	Author Scop.

SAINFOIN

This hairless or slightly hairy plant has slender erect to ascending stems which are unbranched or slightly branched in the upper half. The alternate leaves are pinnate with 6 to 14 pairs of oblong to linear, untoothed leaflets. The flowers, 10–14mm (⅖–⅘in) long, have deeper purple veins, particularly on the standard petal, and are borne in racemes from the axils of the upper stem-leaves. The fruit-pod, 5–8mm (⅕–⅓in) long, has distinctive toothed sides.

• **DISTRIBUTION** Widely naturalized in the region as far north as S. Sweden. Native to C. and S. Europe and S. England.

• **HABITAT** Grassy and waste places, cultivated land; generally on calcareous soils. Widely grown for fodder, especially in former times.

Habit Perennial	Height 30–70cm (12–28in)	Flowering time June–Sept

WOOD SORREL FAMILY

Family OXALIDACEAE	Species *Oxalis acetosella*	Author L.

WOOD SORREL

This low, patch-forming, slightly hairy plant has slender creeping rhizomes. The pale green leaves are trifoliate. The solitary flowers, 8–15mm (⅓–⅗in) long, are half-nodding, bell-shaped, and are borne on slender stalks with a pair of small bracts in the upper part. Smaller cleistogamous flowers are often borne after the perfect flowers finish in the early summer. The angled fruit capsule, 3–4mm (⅛–⅙in) long, explodes when ripe to expel the numerous small seeds.

• **DISTRIBUTION** Throughout the region, except for Spitsbergen.

• **HABITAT** Woodland, scrub, rocky places, hedgerows, and embankments; generally on humus-rich soils, on lowland and in the mountains to an altitude of 2,100m (6,900ft).

mauve or lilac veins usually on petals

tiny bracts

drooping, heart-shaped leaflets

Habit Perennial	Height 4–10cm (1⅕–4in)	Flowering time Apr–June

Family OXALIDACEAE	Species *Oxalis articulata*	Author Savigny

PINK SORREL

This is a tufted and hairy plant. The leaves are all basal and trifoliate, with even sized heart-shaped leaflets which are covered in orange or brownish dots. The pink flowers, 12–20mm (½–⅘in) across, are borne in umbels on a long slender stalk.

• **DISTRIBUTION** Naturalized in parts of S. Britain, Ireland, and France; widely cultivated in gardens. A native plant of E. temperate South America.

• **HABITAT** Waste places, disturbed ground, roadsides, and coastal sands.

• **RELATED SPECIES** *Oxalis debilis*, Large-flowered Pink Sorrel, is bulbous and its leaves have translucent dots on the underside. The flowers are pinkish purple. Its distribution is similar to the above. Native to South America. It grows mainly in cultivated and waste places.

Habit Perennial	Height 15–35cm (6–14in)	Flowering time May–Oct

GERANIUM FAMILY

Family GERANIACEAE	Species *Geranium pratense*	Author L.

MEADOW CRANE'S-BILL

The stems of this tufted, hairy plant are erect, branched, and leafy. The leaves are round in outline but cut into 5 to 7 deeply toothed and lobed segments; the lower and basal leaves are stalked. The bright violet-blue flowers, 25–30mm (1–1⅕in) across, are cup-shaped, with 5 rounded petals, and are often paired in branched clusters. The beaked fruit splits into 5 one-seeded portions.

• **DISTRIBUTION** Throughout the region, except for the far north.

• **HABITAT** Meadows and pastures, roadsides, and woodland margins; on base-rich and calcareous soils in lowland areas and in the mountains to 1,900m (6,250ft).

Habit Perennial	Height 60–100cm (24–40in)	Flowering time June–Sept

Family GERANIACEAE	Species *Geranium sanguineum*	Author L.

BLOODY CRANE'S-BILL

This is a hairy, spreading to almost prostrate plant with branched stems. The leaves are round in outline but are deeply divided into 5 to 7 lobed segments; all the leaves are stalked. The bright reddish purple flowers, 25–30mm (1–1⅕in) across, are often solitary, although sometimes paired. The flower-stalks are hairy, with a pair of small bracts in the middle. The fruit is beaked and splits into 5 one-seeded portions.

• **DISTRIBUTION** N. and W. Britain, C. Ireland, and most of mainland Europe, excluding Holland and the far north of the region.

• **HABITAT** Rocky habitats, open woodland, and occasionally sand dunes, on basic soils; on lowland and in the mountains to an altitude of 1,900m (6,250ft). Often grown in gardens.

Habit Perennial	Height 10–30cm (4–12in)	Flowering time July–Aug

Family GERANIACEAE	Species *Geranium sylvaticum*	Author L.

WOOD CRANE'S-BILL

This tufted, hairy plant, has erect, branched stems. The leaves are rounded in outline and cut into 5 to 9 lobed segments. The flowers, 22–26mm (⅞–1in) across, vary from bluish to reddish purple or reddish violet, and are often in pairs in branched clusters. The fruit is beaked and splits into 5 one-seeded portions.

• **DISTRIBUTION** Throughout, except for Spitsbergen, but mainly on the mountains in the south of the region.

• **HABITAT** Woodland, scrub, hedgerows, damp meadows, rocky habitats, and streamsides.

• **REMARK** Subsp. *rivulare* is a shorter form which has white flowers veined with red and occurs in E. France.

flowers often have whitish centre

DETAIL

palmately lobed leaves

flowers mostly in pairs

Habit Perennial	Height 30–70cm (12–28in)	Flowering time June–July

Family GERANIACEAE	Species *Geranium phaeum*	Author L.

DUSKY CRANE'S-BILL

This hairy, tufted plant has erect, branched stems. The rounded leaves are cut just over halfway into broad, toothed segments; only the lower leaves are stalked. The dark purple-black, sometimes pinkish mauve or white, flowers, 15–20mm ($\frac{3}{5}$–$\frac{4}{5}$in) across, are mostly paired, and are borne in branched clusters; the petals have a pointed apex. The fruit is beaked and hairy.

• **DISTRIBUTION** Native in France and S. Germany, but widely naturalized in Britain, Ireland, and elsewhere in the region, as far north as S. Sweden.

• **HABITAT** Shaded and often damp places, woodland, copses, scrub, and hedgerows.

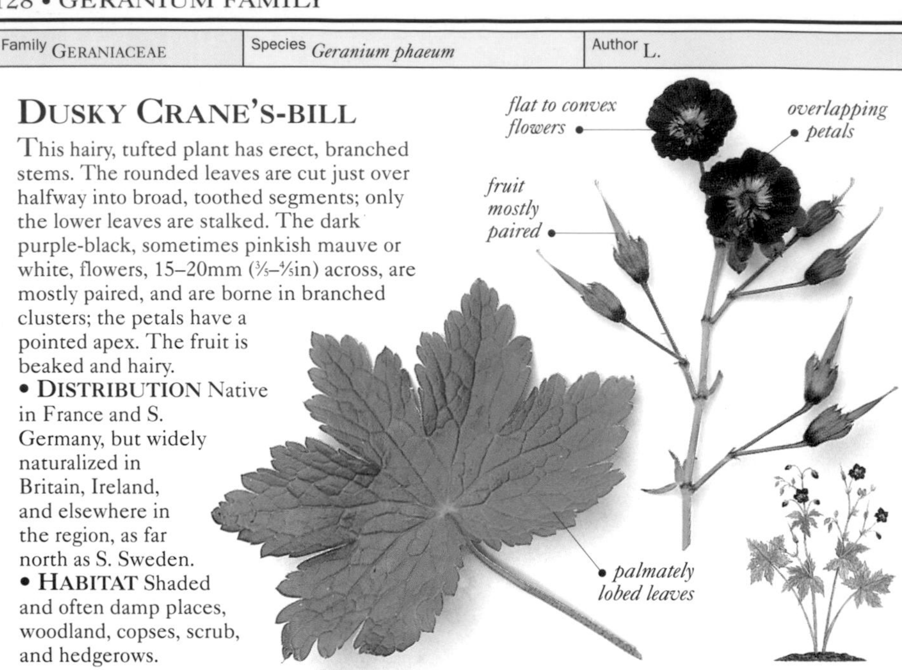

Habit Perennial	Height 50–80cm (20–32in)	Flowering time May–July

Family GERANIACEAE	Species *Geranium pyrenaicum*	Author Burm. f.

HEDGEROW CRANE'S-BILL

This is a hairy, tufted plant, with erect, branched stems. The leaves are rounded in outline and cut to about halfway into 5 to 7 lobes; the upper leaves are unstalked. The small purple or pinkish flowers are 14–18mm ($\frac{4}{7}$–$\frac{5}{7}$in) across. The hairy, beaked fruit is borne on a slender, downturned stalk and splits into 5 one-seeded portions when ripe.

• **DISTRIBUTION** C. and S. Britain and France; naturalized elsewhere on mainland Europe as far north as S. Sweden.

• **HABITAT** Grassy places, meadows, field margins, hedgerows, cultivated and waste land.

• **RELATED SPECIES** *Geranium bohemicum* has more deeply divided leaves, and violet-blue flowers with darker veins. It inhabits meadows, open woodland, and scrub in S. Scandinavia, E. France, and S. Germany.

deeply notched petals

flowers paired, in branched clusters

paired leaves

wedge-shaped lobes, toothed at top

Habit Perennial	Height 40–60cm (16–24in)	Flowering time June–Aug

Family GERANIACEAE	Species *Geranium molle*	Author L.

DOVE'S FOOT CRANE'S-BILL

This hairy plant has spreading to almost prostrate, branched stems with long, whitish hairs. The stalked, grey-green, rounded or kidney-shaped leaves are cut to about halfway into 5 to 7 lobed segments; the upper leaves are alternate. The pinkish purple flowers, 6–10mm (¼–⅖in) across, are paired and borne in loose clusters.

• **DISTRIBUTION** Throughout the region, except for the far north.

• **HABITAT** Cultivated, waste, and bare land, grassy places, and sand dunes.

• **RELATED SPECIES** *Geranium pusillum*, Small-flowered Crane's-bill, has densely hairy stems, and narrower leaf-segments; the flowers are smaller, and pale lilac.

notched petals

each leaf segment is 3-lobed at top

hairless, beaked fruit

deeply lobed leaves

Habit Annual	Height 5–20cm (2–8in)	Flowering time May–Sept

Family GERANIACEAE	Species *Geranium robertianum*	Author L.

HERB ROBERT

This hairy, strong-smelling herb is often tinged with red. The stems are spreading to erect, and branched towards the top. The stalked leaves have 3 or 5 deeply lobed segments, cut almost to the midrib; the upper leaves are mostly 3-lobed. The bright pink, occasionally white, flowers, 14–18mm (4/7–5/7in) across, have orange pollen, and distinctly clawed petals with a rounded apex.

• **DISTRIBUTION** Throughout, except for the far north.

• **HABITAT** Woodland, shady banks, the base of old walls, rocky and coastal habitats.

• **REMARK** Forms vary. British coastal forms with prostrate stems are usually called subsp. *maritimum*. Subsp. *celticum* has larger, paler flowers and grows in coastal rock crevices in S. Wales and W. Ireland.

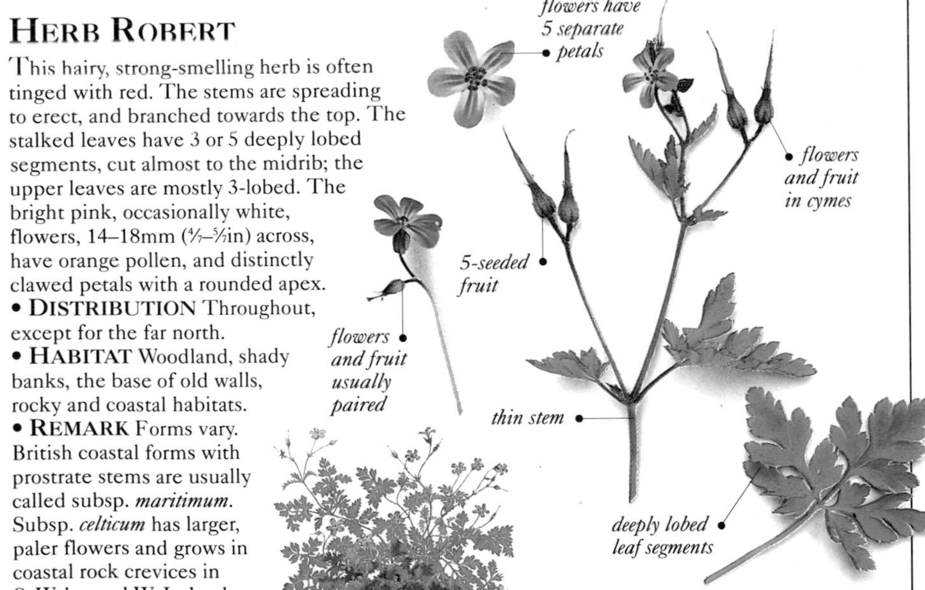

Habit Annual or biennial	Height 10–50cm (4–20in)	Flowering time May–Sept

Family GERANIACEAE	Species *Erodium cicutarium*	Author (L.) L'Hér.

COMMON STORK'S-BILL

This variable, low, hairy plant has a basal tuft of leaves, and spreading to prostrate stems. The feathery leaves are pinnately lobed, with toothed leaflets. In umbels of up to 12, the flowers, 7–18mm (2/7–5/7in) across, are purplish pink or occasionally white; the petals are elliptical, with the upper 2 in each flower often slightly larger and bearing a dark basal spot. The fruit has a long beak and is hairy.

• **DISTRIBUTION** Throughout the region, except for the far north; often rather local.

• **HABITAT** Dry grassy and bare places, and disturbed ground.

• **RELATED SPECIES** *Erodium moschatum*, Musk Stork's-bill, smells of musk. The larger flowers, 16–24mm (5/8–1in) across, have plain petals.

Habit Annual or biennial	Height 10–60cm (4–24in)	Flowering time June–Sept

FLAX FAMILY

Family LINACEAE	Species *Linum catharticum*	Author L.

FAIRY FLAX

Slender and hairless, this plant often has a single stem, branched towards the top. The untoothed leaves are opposite, unstalked, and one-veined. The flowers, 4–6mm (1/6–1/4in) across, are borne in loose clusters and are nodding in bud. The 5 sepals are pointed and have glandular-hairy margins; the 5 petals are elliptical; the sepals and petals are all separate. The fruit capsule, 2–3mm (1/12–1/8in) long, is borne on a long, slender stalk and splits into 10 valves when ripe.

• **DISTRIBUTION** Throughout the region, except for Spitsbergen.

• **HABITAT** Dry calcareous grassland, grassy heaths and mountain meadows, moors, cliffs, and sand dunes; to an altitude of 2,350m (7,700ft).

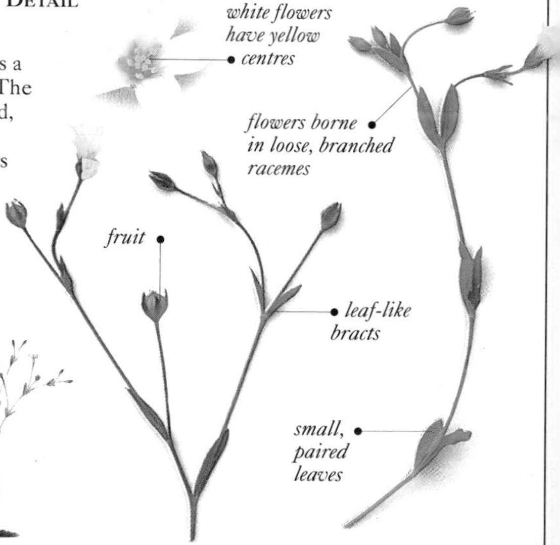

DETAIL

white flowers have yellow centres

flowers borne in loose, branched racemes

fruit

leaf-like bracts

small, paired leaves

Habit Annual	Height 8–25cm (3–10in)	Flowering time May–Sept

Family LINACEAE	Species *Linum perenne*	Author L.

PERENNIAL FLAX

This tufted, hairless plant has slender, erect to somewhat spreading stems. The rather crowded alternate leaves are linear to lanceolate, pointed and one-veined. The large dark blue flowers, 20–26mm (⅘–1in) across, are borne in leafy racemes. The 5 thin, silky petals are rounded at the apex; the 5 sepals are short. The fruit capsule is erect and rounded with a short beak.

• **DISTRIBUTION** Growing throughout most of E. Britain, E. France, and S. Germany.

• **HABITAT** Dry, grassy meadows, waysides, and other grassy places on calcareous soils.

• **RELATED SPECIES** *Linum austriacum* has one- to 3-veined middle stem-leaves. The fruit is borne on a downturned stalk. It grows in similar habitats in France and Germany; naturalized in Denmark. *L. leoni* is smaller, up to 30cm (12in) tall, with stems bearing up to 6 flowers. The fruit-stalks are generally downturned. It is native in France and W. Germany.

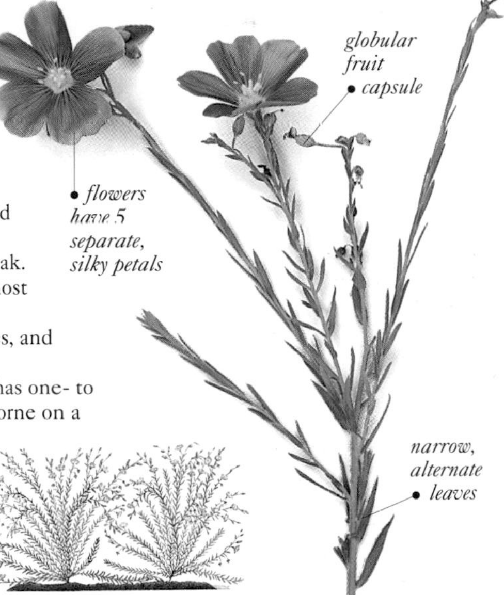

Habit Perennial	Height 30–60cm (12–24in)	Flowering time May–July

Family LINACEAE	Species *Linum bienne*	Author Miller

PALE FLAX

This hairless plant has several slender, erect stems, branched towards the top. The untoothed leaves are alternate and one- to 3-veined, with a pointed apex. The pale blue or bluish lilac flowers, 16–24mm (⅔–1in) across, are borne in loose cymes; the 5 sepals are all equal, pointed, and shorter than the petals. The fruit capsule, 4–6mm (⅙–¼in) across, is rounded with a short beak at the top.

• **DISTRIBUTION** C. and S. Britain, and France; often local and close to the sea.

• **HABITAT** Dry grassy habitats on neutral or calcareous soils.

• **RELATED SPECIES** *Linum usitatissimum*, Flax, is annual and generally has a solitary stem and 3-veined leaves. The flowers are larger and clear blue. It is occasionally naturalized or casual in the region.

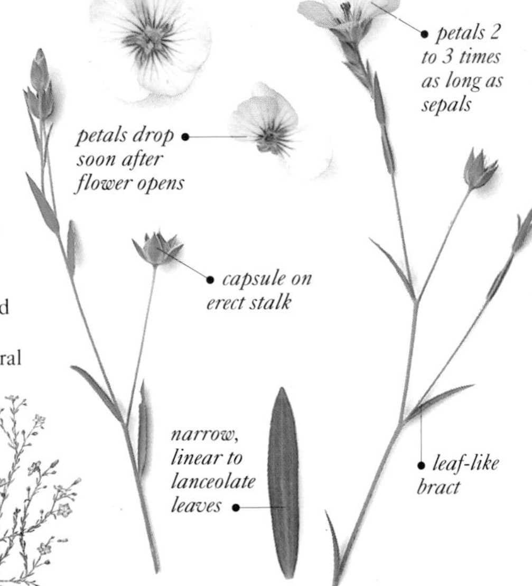

Habit Biennial or perennial	Height 30–60cm (12–24in)	Flowering time May–Sept

Spurge Family

Family EUPHORBIACEAE	Species *Mercurialis perennis*	Author L.

Dog's Mercury

This hairy plant has thin, erect, unbranched stems and spreads by means of thin underground rhizomes. The paired leaves are oval to elliptical and up to 80mm (3⅕in) long; the lowermost leaves are much reduced and scale-like. The flowers are male or female and are borne on separate plants: male flowers are in long, erect spikes, with 8 to 15 stamens; female flowers are solitary or 2 or 3 together, nodding on short stalks at the upper leaf-axils. The small fruit is covered in hairs and attaches itself to clothing, fur, etc.

- **Distribution** Throughout the region, but very rare in Ireland.
- **Habitat** Shaded places, particularly woodland, copses, hedgerows, and shaded rocks.

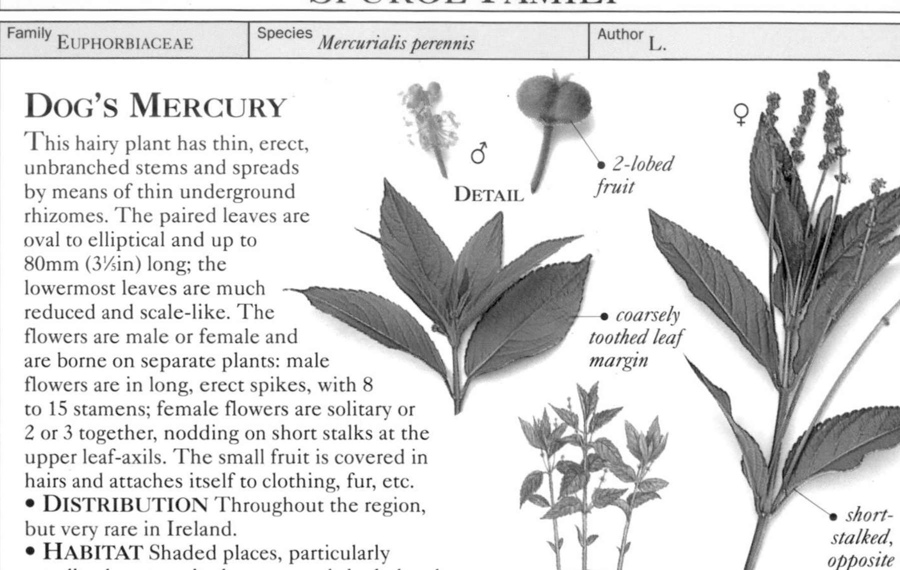

Habit Perennial	Height 15–40cm (6–16in)	Flowering time Feb–Apr

Family EUPHORBIACEAE	Species *Euphorbia hyberna*	Author L.

Irish Spurge

Clump-forming and often slightly hairy, this plant has erect to ascending stems which exude a milky latex when cut. The leaves are usually broadest above the middle, unstalked, and untoothed. The yellowish green leaf-like bracts form a ruff around the flower clusters. Borne in umbel-like inflorescences, the small yellowish green flowers each have 4 kidney-shaped, brown or yellowish glands. The 3-lobed fruit capsule, 5–6mm (⅕–¼in) across, is covered in oblong warts.

- **Distribution** S.W. England, S.W. Ireland, W. and S.W. France.
- **Habitat** Damp, often shaded, grassy or wooded places, hedgerows, and river and stream margins.
- **Related Species** *Euphorbia palustris*, Marsh Spurge, is taller, with non-flowering leafy branches.

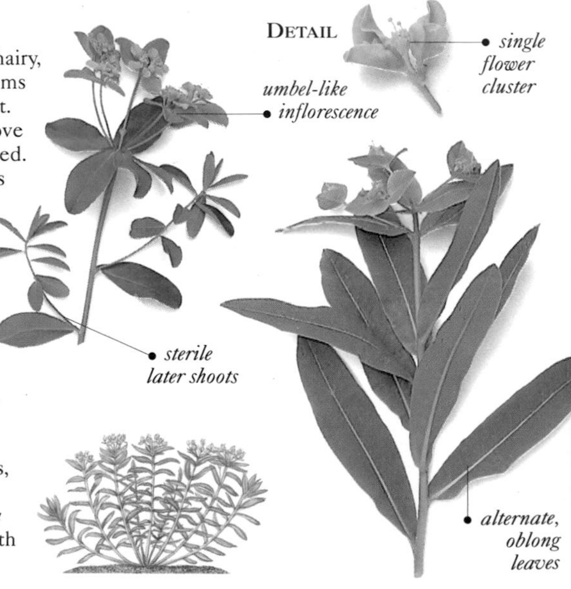

Habit Perennial	Height 40–60cm (16–24in)	Flowering time Apr–July

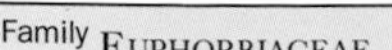

Family EUPHORBIACEAE	Species *Euphorbia helioscopia*	Author L.

SUN SPURGE

The stems of this more or less hairless plant produce a white latex when cut. The oval leaves are tapered towards the base and broadest above the middle, with the margin finely toothed in the upper half. The bracts are similar to the leaves but are yellowish and in whorls. The greenish yellow flowers are surrounded by 4 glands. The 3-lobed fruit capsule is smooth. The plant is poisonous.

• **DISTRIBUTION** Throughout the region, except for the far north.

• **HABITAT** Cultivated, waste, and disturbed land, and roadsides.

• **RELATED SPECIES** *Euphorbia platyphyllos*, Broad-leaved Spurge, is taller; the main umbel has 5 spokes; the capsule is covered in warts. It grows in S. Britain, Belgium, France, Germany.

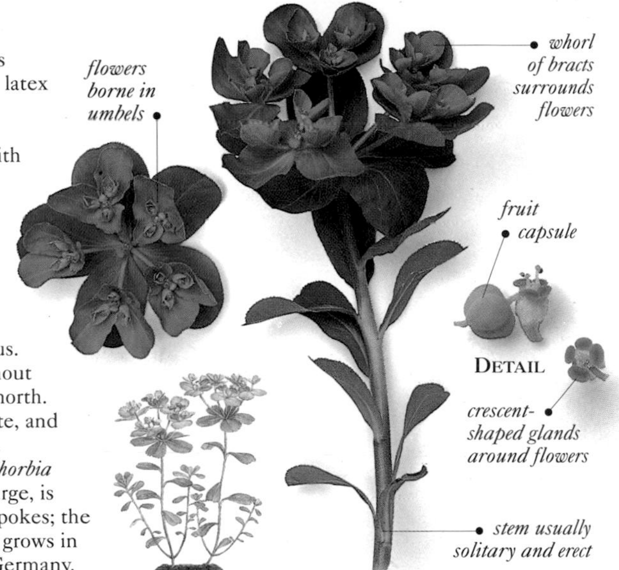

Habit Annual	Height 20–50cm (8–20in)	Flowering time May–Aug

Family EUPHORBIACEAE	Species *Euphorbia peplus*	Author L.

PETTY SPURGE

The stems of this hairless green plant are erect and produce a white latex when cut. The alternate leaves are rounded to oval, untoothed, and short-stalked. The bracts are similar to the leaves and are generally born in threes. The umbels usually have 3 spokes. The small green flowers have 4 kidney-shaped glands which are each adorned with a pair of slender horns. The smooth, 3-lobed fruit capsule has 2 keels on the back of each lobe. The plant is poisonous.

• **DISTRIBUTION** Native throughout the region, as far north as C. Scandinavia.

• **HABITAT** Arable, disturbed, and waste land; a weed in gardens.

• **RELATED SPECIES** *Euphorbia exigua*, Dwarf Spurge, is greyish, with linear to narrow-elliptical leaves and bracts.

Habit Annual	Height 10–40cm (4–16in)	Flowering time Apr–Oct

Family EUPHORBIACEAE	Species *Euphorbia paralias*	Author L.

SEA SPURGE

The stems of this fleshy, hairless plant branch at the base and produce a white latex when cut. The leaves are oval. The bracts are similar to the leaves, but are whorled. The flowers have kidney-shaped glands with a pair of pointed horns. The fruit capsule is 3-lobed. The plant is poisonous.

• **DISTRIBUTION** Coastal areas of S. and W. Britain and Ireland, Holland, Belgium, and France.

• **HABITAT** Coastal sands, sand dunes, rocks, and fine shingle.

• **RELATED SPECIES** *Euphorbia portlandica*, Portland Spurge, has less fleshy, more spreading leaves, with a prominent midrib beneath. It has a similar distribution (not Holland or Belgium) and habitats.

Habit Perennial	Height 20–50cm (8–20in)	Flowering time June–Oct

Family EUPHORBIACEAE	Species *Euphorbia cyparissias*	Author L.

CYPRESS SPURGE

A tufted and rhizomatous, hairless plant, its erect, branched stems produce a white latex when cut. The alternate, linear, rather dull green leaves are densely crowded; the leaves later become yellowish or reddish. The bracts are bright yellow-green, kidney-shaped, and often paired or in threes. The flowers have kidney-shaped glands, each with a pair of short horns. The 3-lobed fruit capsule has a granular surface. The plant is poisonous.

• **DISTRIBUTION** Holland and Germany southwards, but widely naturalized in Britain, C. Ireland, and parts of Scandinavia.

• **HABITAT** Rough grassy and rocky sites, roadsides, and scrub; to 2,650m (8,700ft) in the south of its range.

main umbels have 9 to 18 spokes

small yellow-green flowers

crowded leaves make stems look like small conifers

bracts turn red

Habit Perennial	Height 20–50cm (8–20in)	Flowering time Apr–July

MILKWORT FAMILY

Family POLYGALACEAE	Species *Polygala vulgaris*	Author L.

COMMON MILKWORT

This rather dainty, hairless or slightly hairy plant has a woody stock and ascending to erect shoots. The leaves are oval to elliptical and untoothed; the upper leaves are narrower than the lower. The blue, pink, or white flowers, 5–8mm (⅕–⅓in) long, are borne in dense racemes with up to 40 flowers; each one has 5 sepals, the inner 2 much larger and wing-like; the corolla has 3 fused petals which are fringed at the end. The fruit is a small 2-lobed capsule.

• **DISTRIBUTION** Throughout, except for Iceland and Spitsbergen.

• **HABITAT** Grassy places (usually short turf over calcareous soils), heaths, and sand dunes.

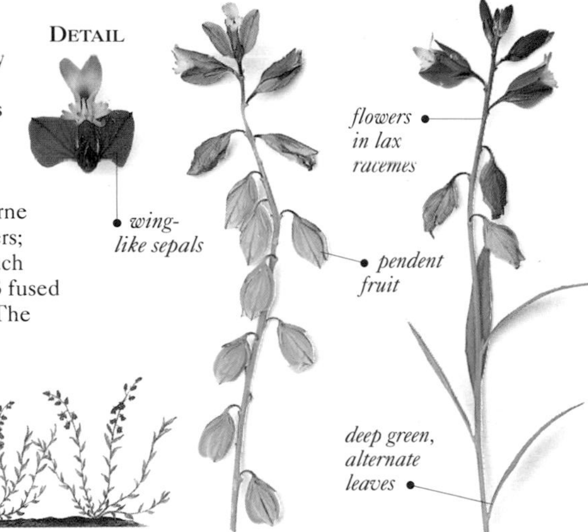

Habit Perennial	Height 10–30cm (4–12in)	Flowering time May–Sept

BALSAM FAMILY

Family BALSAMINACEAE	Species *Impatiens parviflora*	Author DC.

SMALL BALSAM

This hairless, rather succulent plant has erect, branched or unbranched stems. The alternate leaves are elliptical to oval, long-stalked, and toothed, usually with one or several pairs of glands towards the base of the stalk; the upper leaves are larger than the lower. The creamy white or pale yellow flowers, 6–14mm (¼–⅗in) across, have 3 sepals, the lateral 2 small and scale-like but the lower one drawn out into a short spur. The fruit capsules explode to expel the seeds.

• **DISTRIBUTION** Widely naturalized in the region, except for the far north. Native to C. Asia.

• **HABITAT** Moist and damp places, woodland, cultivated land, lanes, waste and disturbed ground.

Habit Annual	Height 20–70cm (8–28in)	Flowering time July–Nov

Family BALSAMINACEAE	Species *Impatiens glandulifera*	Author Royle

HIMALAYAN BALSAM

Also known as Policeman's Helmet, this hairless plant is robust and rather fleshy. The leaves are opposite or in whorls of 3 to 5 and are lanceolate to elliptical. Nectary-like stipules are present at the base of the leaf-stalks. The pink, red, purple, mauve, or white flowers, 25–40mm (1–1⅗in) long, have a sickly scent and are often spotted in the "throat"; the lower sepal is pouched, with a short incurved spur; the upper petal is helmet-like, while the other 2 petals form a lip. The spindle-shaped fruit capsule explodes when ripe to expel the seeds.

• **DISTRIBUTION** Naturalized throughout the region as far north as C. Scandinavia. Native to the Himalayas.

• **HABITAT** Damp places along river- and streamsides, ditches, dykes, and waste and cultivated land.

DETAIL

COLOUR VARIATIONS

Habit Annual	Height 1–3m (3¼–10ft)	Flowering time July–Oct

MALLOW FAMILY

Family MALVACEAE	Species *Malva moschata*	Author L.

MUSK MALLOW

A rough-haired plant, Musk Mallow has stiff, erect stems. The alternate leaves are more or less rounded in outline but are cut into 5 to 7 rather pointed, pinnately lobed segments; the upper leaves are more deeply and narrowly divided than the lower leaves. The large, bright pink to white flowers, 30–60mm (1⅕–2⅖in) across, are solitary at the upper leaf-axils; the calyx has a distinct epicalyx of 3 linear lobes. The fruit consists of a ring of nutlets surrounded by the persistent calyx.

• **DISTRIBUTION** Britain, Ireland, Belgium, Holland, France, and Germany.

• **HABITAT** Grassy habitats, field margins, meadows, roadsides, and hedgerows.

notched petals

5-lobed calyx

deeply lobed upper leaves

lower leaves less deeply divided

Habit Perennial	Height 50–80cm (20–32in)	Flowering time July–Aug

Family MALVACEAE	Species *Malva sylvestris*	Author L.

COMMON MALLOW

This is a robust, hairy plant, with erect, very occasionally sprawling, stems. The alternate leaves are rounded in outline, but have 3 to 7 shallow, blunt, toothed lobes; all the leaves are stalked. Borne in clusters of 2 or more at the upper leaf-axils, the flowers are 20–50mm (⅘–2in) across, and have 5 deeply notched pink to purple petals with darker coloured veins; the 3 epicalyx segments are elliptical. The fruit consists of a ring of one-seeded segments.

• **DISTRIBUTION** Throughout the region, except for the far north.

• **HABITAT** Grassy places, meadows, rough and waste ground, roadsides, and railway embankments.

petals have thin dark veins

flowers in clusters at leaf-axils

palmately lobed leaves

fruit a ring of nutlets

Habit Perennial	Height 50–100cm (20–40in)	Flowering time June–Sept

Family MALVACEAE	Species *Malva neglecta*	Author Wallr.

DWARF MALLOW

Generally rather sprawling, this hairy plant has procumbent to ascending, often branched, stems. The kidney-shaped to rounded leaves have 5 to 7 shallow, rounded, toothed lobes; the leaf-stalks have 2 small scale-like stipules. The whitish to pale lilac flowers, 15–25mm (⅗–1in) across, are borne in lateral clusters of 3 to 6; the flowers have a calyx and an epicalyx. The fruit is a ring of almost smooth mericarps within the persistent calyx.

• **DISTRIBUTION** Throughout the region, except for the far north.

• **HABITAT** Fields, bare and waste ground, roadsides, coasts; usually on rather dry soils.

• **RELATED SPECIES** *Malva parviflora*, Least Mallow, has smaller flowers and netted mericarps. It grows in similar habitats in France; naturalized in many parts of the region.

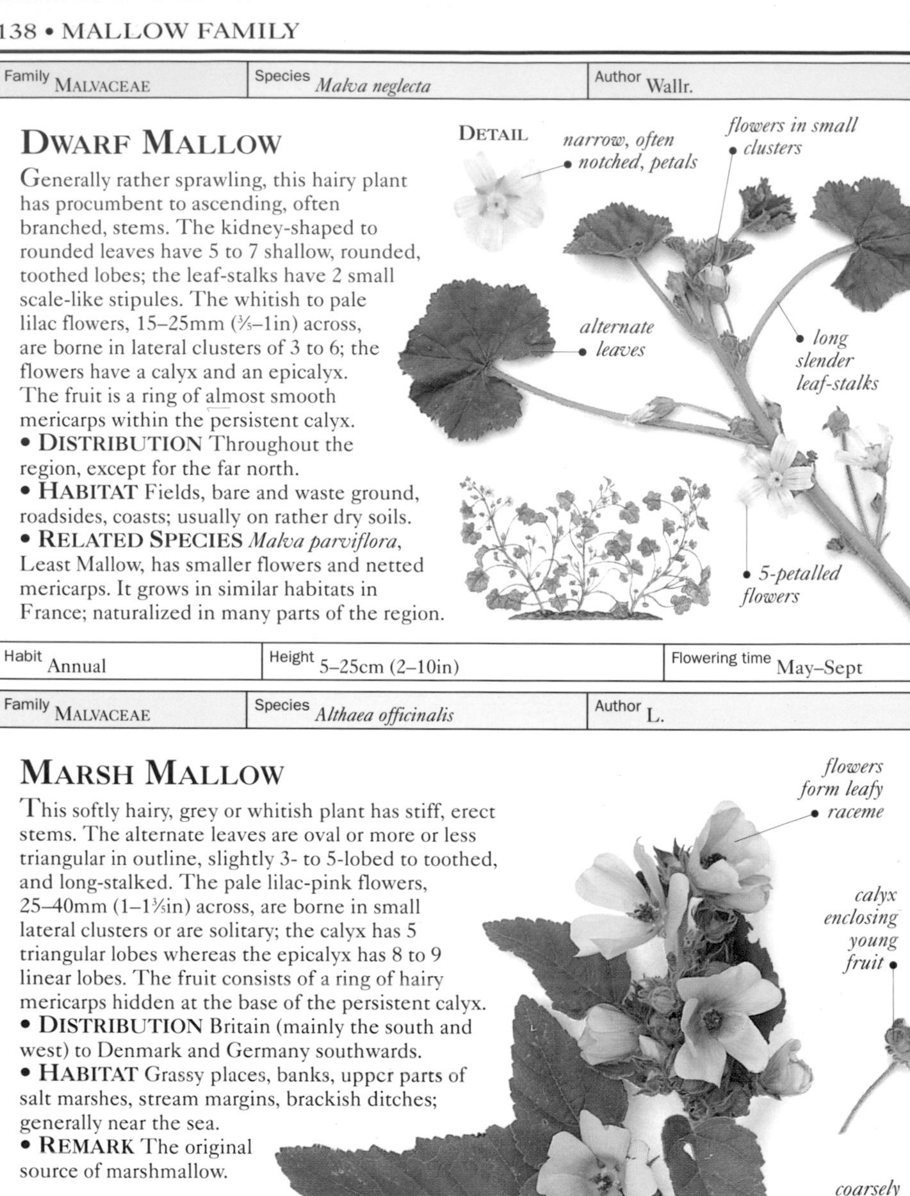

Habit Annual	Height 5–25cm (2–10in)	Flowering time May–Sept

Family MALVACEAE	Species *Althaea officinalis*	Author L.

MARSH MALLOW

This softly hairy, grey or whitish plant has stiff, erect stems. The alternate leaves are oval or more or less triangular in outline, slightly 3- to 5-lobed to toothed, and long-stalked. The pale lilac-pink flowers, 25–40mm (1–1⅗in) across, are borne in small lateral clusters or are solitary; the calyx has 5 triangular lobes whereas the epicalyx has 8 to 9 linear lobes. The fruit consists of a ring of hairy mericarps hidden at the base of the persistent calyx.

• **DISTRIBUTION** Britain (mainly the south and west) to Denmark and Germany southwards.

• **HABITAT** Grassy places, banks, upper parts of salt marshes, stream margins, brackish ditches; generally near the sea.

• **REMARK** The original source of marshmallow.

Habit Perennial	Height 80–150cm (32–60in)	Flowering time Aug–Sept

Family MALVACEAE	Species *Lavatera arborea*	Author L.

TREE MALLOW

A robust plant, its stout stems become woody at the base and, although somewhat hairy when young, become hairless, like the leaves, on ageing. The large leaves are rounded in outline and stalked, with 5 to 7 shallow, toothed lobes. The bright pinkish purple flowers, 30–40mm (1⅕–1⅗in) across, are borne in clusters of 2 to 7 at the upper leaf-axils; the epicalyx-lobes are longer than those of the calyx. The fruit is a ring of hairy or hairless nuts held within the persistent calyx.

• **DISTRIBUTION** Coastal S. Britain, W. Ireland, and W. France; naturalized locally or casual in other parts of the region.

• **HABITAT** Coastal rocks and cliffs, and stony ground; more rarely along hedgerows, on stabilized dunes, or on waste land. Widely grown in gardens.

Habit Biennial	Height 1.5–3m (5–10ft)	Flowering time June–Sept

DAPHNE FAMILY

Family THYMELAEACEAE	Species *Daphne mezereum*	Author L.

MEZEREON

A stiffly branched deciduous shrub, Mezereon has erect to spreading greyish brown branches; young shoots are hairy. The leaves are oblong to lanceolate with an untoothed margin and a short stalk. The fragrant pinkish purple flowers are borne along the branches before the leaves emerge; the 4 petals are united in the lower half into a short tube. The fruit is a small oval berry. The plant is very poisonous.

• **DISTRIBUTION** C. and S. Britain (scarce), and mainland Europe except the far north; scarcer now due to land clearance.

• **HABITAT** Woods, scrub, and pastures on calcareous soils, to 2,600m (8,550ft); mountain forms are shorter and more spreading; also cultivated in gardens.

untoothed leaves

ripe, shiny bright red berries

flowers in small clusters

pale green alternate leaves

Habit Shrub	Height 50–200cm (20–80in)	Flowering time Feb–May

Family THYMELAEACEAE	Species *Daphne laureola*	Author L.

SPURGE-LAUREL

This evergreen shrub has ascending branches with the leaves clustered in the upper part of the stems. The leaves are oblong, often broadest above the middle, with an untoothed margin and short stalk. The half-nodding, greenish yellow, honey-scented flowers, 8–12mm (⅓–½in) long, are borne in crowded racemes among the leaves. The fruit is a small oval berry. The plant is poisonous.

• **DISTRIBUTION** C. and S. Britain, Belgium to Germany southwards; naturalized in Denmark and perhaps elsewhere in the region.

• **HABITAT** Woodland, hedgerows, and sometimes rocky sites; on calcareous or clay soils to 1,600m (5,250ft).

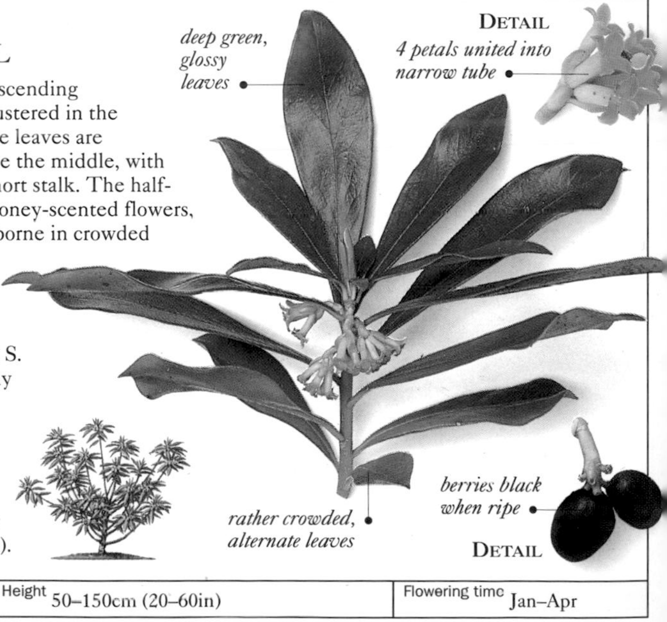

deep green, glossy leaves

DETAIL *4 petals united into narrow tube*

rather crowded, alternate leaves

berries black when ripe DETAIL

Habit Shrub	Height 50–150cm (20–60in)	Flowering time Jan–Apr

HYPERICUM FAMILY

Family HYPERICACEAE	Species *Hypericum androsaemum*	Author L.

TUTSAN

This semi-evergreen, hairless shrub has much-branched, 2-ridged stems. The opposite pairs of leaves are unstalked, oval to oblong, slightly aromatic when crushed, and sometimes clasping the stem. The pale yellow flowers, 18–22mm (5/7–7/8in) across, have 5 oval petals; the sepals are longer than the petals. The fleshy, berry-like fruit, 7–10mm (2/7–2/5in) long, is reddish at first but purplish black when ripe.
• **DISTRIBUTION** Britain, Ireland, Belgium, and France; widely cultivated in gardens and naturalized elsewhere.
• **HABITAT** Damp places in deciduous woodland, scrub, hedgerows, or rocky habitats.

flowers in terminal clusters

DETAIL

stamens form 5 bundles

sepals enlarged and persistent in fruit

Habit Small shrub	Height 50–80cm (20–32in)	Flowering time June–Aug

Family HYPERICACEAE	Species *Hypericum elodes*	Author L.

MARSH ST. JOHN'S-WORT

This hairy, creeping plant often forms dense mats floating in water. Its flower stems are erect and root at the base; the stems are round and often swollen between the nodes. The opposite leaves are oval or almost round and half-clasp the stem. Borne in small clusters, the yellow flowers, 12–15mm (½–3/5in) across, are bell-shaped, with 5 petals; the sepals are erect, with red marginal glands. The small fruit capsule is surrounded by the persistent petals and stamens and splits open when ripe.
• **DISTRIBUTION** Grows in Britain, Holland, Germany, Belgium, and France.
• **HABITAT** Damp or wet places, in shallow water or on heaths, bogs, marshes, ponds, and pond margins; on acid soils.

Habit Perennial	Height 20–40cm (8–16in)	Flowering time June–Sept

Family HYPERICACEAE	Species *Hypericum tetrapterum*	Author Fries

SQUARE-STALKED ST. JOHN'S-WORT

Also known as *Hypericum acutum*, this tufted, hairless plant has erect stems that spread and root at the base; they are square, with 4 narrow wings. Borne in pairs, the leaves are oval to elliptical with unstalked bases that partly clasp the stem; the leaf-surface has pale translucent dots. The flowers, 9–10mm (3/8–2/5in) across, have 5 pale yellow petals sometimes veined with red, and 5 narrow green sepals; the many stamens are borne in 5 bundles. The fruit is a small many-seeded capsule.

• **DISTRIBUTION** Throughout, except for Norway, Finland, and the far north.

• **HABITAT** Damp places, particularly in meadows, marshes, and fens, and along pond and river margins.

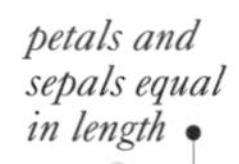

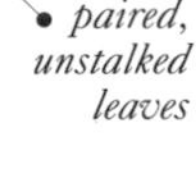

Habit Perennial	Height 50–90cm (20–36in)	Flowering time June–Sept

Family HYPERICACEAE	Species *Hypericum perforatum*	Author L.

PERFORATE ST. JOHN'S-WORT

This hairless plant has stiff, erect stems that spread and root at the base. The oval to linear leaves are unstalked, untoothed, and have large translucent dots on the surface. The flowers, 18–22mm (5/7–7/8in) across, have 5 petals, and many stamens in 5 bundles. The fruit is a small many-seeded capsule.

• **DISTRIBUTION** Throughout the region, except for the far north.

• **HABITAT** Woods, scrub, dry fields and other grassy places, banks, road verges, and hedgerows.

• **RELATED SPECIES** *Hypericum maculatum*, Imperforate St. John's-wort, has square, 4-ridged stems, and undotted leaves. It grows in damper sites.

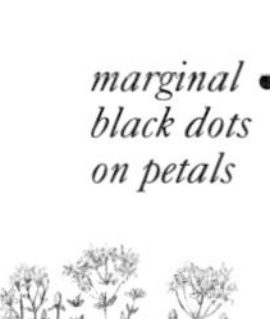

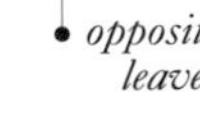

Habit Perennial	Height 40–80cm (16–32in)	Flowering time May–Sept

VIOLET FAMILY

Family VIOLACEAE	Species *Viola odorata*	Author L.

SWEET VIOLET

This low-growing, slightly hairy plant forms patches by means of long runners that root down at intervals. The leaves are in a basal tuft and are long-stalked, the stipules are oval and usually fringed. Borne on long stalks with a pair of small bracts in the middle, the sweetly scented flowers are dark violet, or white, and 13–15mm (½–⅗in) across. The small fruit capsule is 3-parted.

• **DISTRIBUTION** Throughout the region, except for the far north.

• **HABITAT** Woodland, coppices, scrub, and hedgerows; neutral or calcareous soils.

• **RELATED SPECIES** *Viola alba*, White Violet, has non-rooting runners and pure white, rarely pale violet, flowers. It is native in S. England, France, Germany, and S. Sweden.

solitary flowers

white form has pale violet spur

bract

5 separate petals

toothed, heart-shaped leaves

stipules at leaf bases

Habit Perennial	Height 7.5–15cm (3–6in)	Flowering time Feb–May

Family VIOLACEAE	Species *Viola reichenbachiana*	Author Jordan ex Boreau

EARLY DOG-VIOLET

This is a slightly hairy plant with basal tufts of leaves from which arise leafy lateral flowering stems. The leaves are broad and heart-shaped, with a toothed margin and a long stalk; those on the lateral stems are smaller than those on the main stem. The stipules are narrow-lanceolate and have a fringed margin. The solitary, unscented flowers, 12–18mm (½–⅗in) across, are violet, with a straight dark violet spur behind; each flower has 5 separate petals. The fruit capsule is hairless, 3-parted, and many seeded.

• **DISTRIBUTION** Found throughout the region, except for the far north.

• **HABITAT** Woods, coppices, scrub, hedgerows, and other shady places; to an altitude of 1,800m (5,900ft).

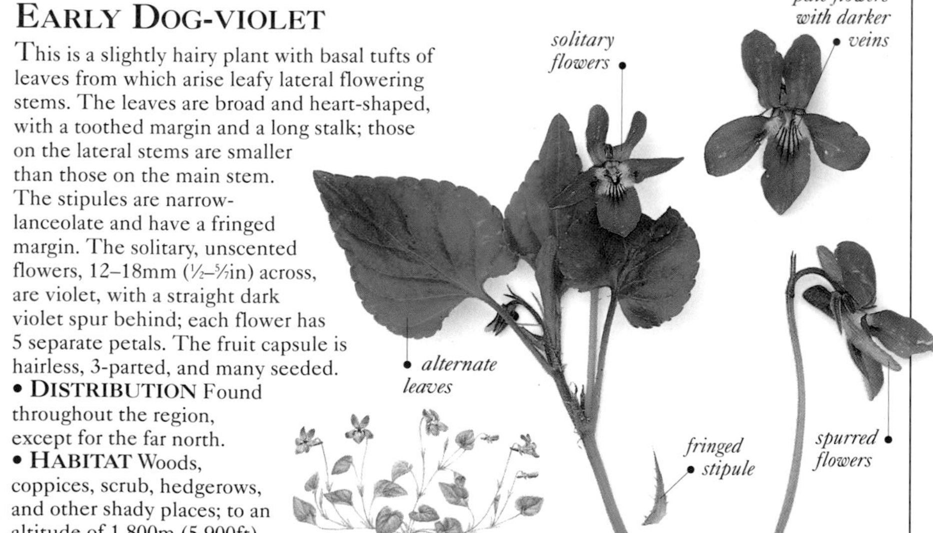

Habit Perennial	Height 10–20cm (4–8in)	Flowering time Mar–June

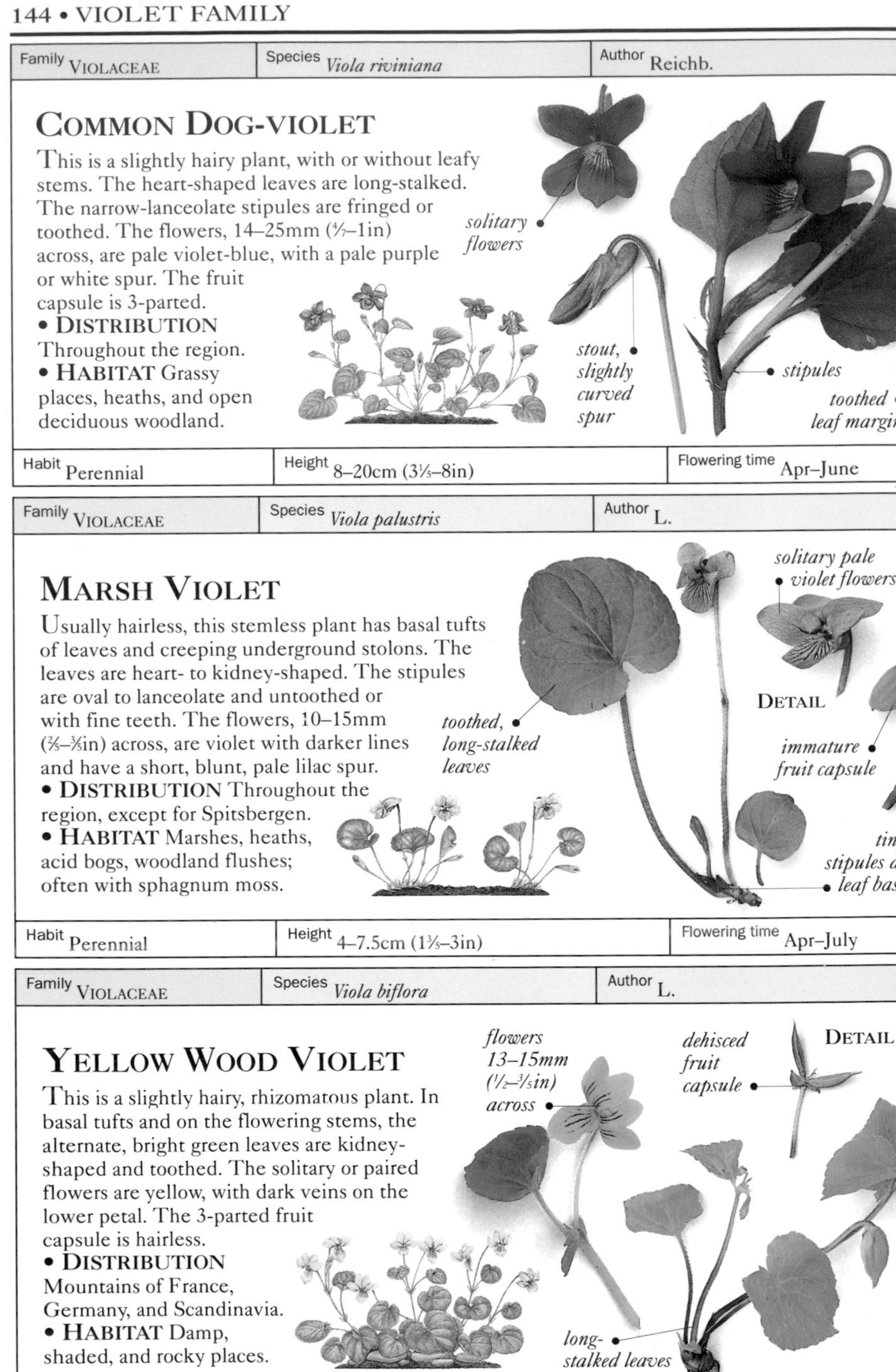

Family VIOLACEAE	Species *Viola riviniana*	Author Reichb.

COMMON DOG-VIOLET

This is a slightly hairy plant, with or without leafy stems. The heart-shaped leaves are long-stalked. The narrow-lanceolate stipules are fringed or toothed. The flowers, 14–25mm (4/7–1in) across, are pale violet-blue, with a pale purple or white spur. The fruit capsule is 3-parted.

• **DISTRIBUTION** Throughout the region.

• **HABITAT** Grassy places, heaths, and open deciduous woodland.

Habit Perennial	Height 8–20cm (3 1/5–8in)	Flowering time Apr–June

Family VIOLACEAE	Species *Viola palustris*	Author L.

MARSH VIOLET

Usually hairless, this stemless plant has basal tufts of leaves and creeping underground stolons. The leaves are heart- to kidney-shaped. The stipules are oval to lanceolate and untoothed or with fine teeth. The flowers, 10–15mm (2/5–3/5in) across, are violet with darker lines and have a short, blunt, pale lilac spur.

• **DISTRIBUTION** Throughout the region, except for Spitsbergen.

• **HABITAT** Marshes, heaths, acid bogs, woodland flushes; often with sphagnum moss.

Habit Perennial	Height 4–7.5cm (1 3/5–3in)	Flowering time Apr–July

Family VIOLACEAE	Species *Viola biflora*	Author L.

YELLOW WOOD VIOLET

This is a slightly hairy, rhizomatous plant. In basal tufts and on the flowering stems, the alternate, bright green leaves are kidney-shaped and toothed. The solitary or paired flowers are yellow, with dark veins on the lower petal. The 3-parted fruit capsule is hairless.

• **DISTRIBUTION** Mountains of France, Germany, and Scandinavia.

• **HABITAT** Damp, shaded, and rocky places.

Habit Perennial	Height 7.5–20cm (3–8in)	Flowering time May–Aug

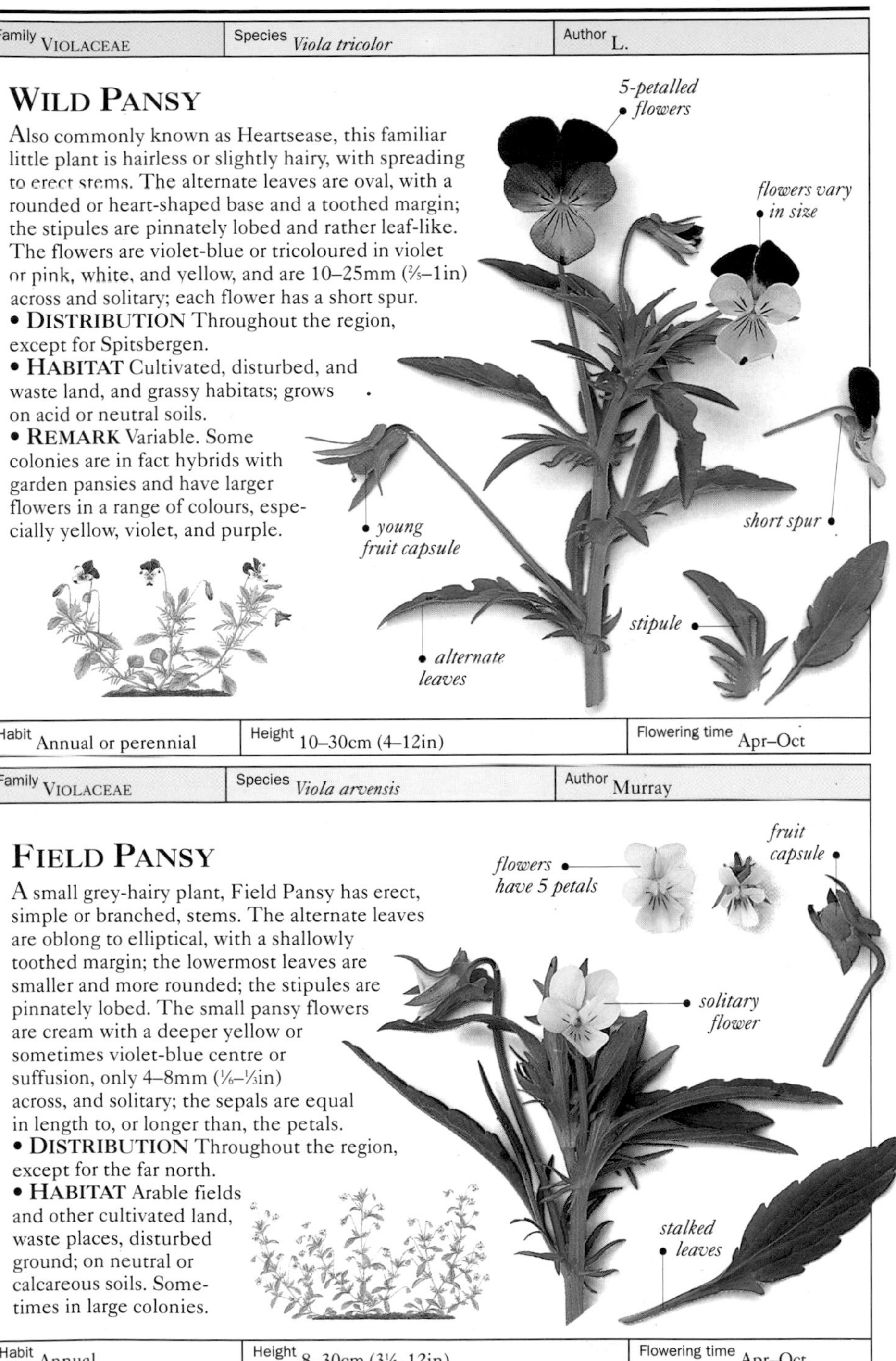

Family VIOLACEAE	Species *Viola tricolor*	Author L.

WILD PANSY

Also commonly known as Heartsease, this familiar little plant is hairless or slightly hairy, with spreading to erect stems. The alternate leaves are oval, with a rounded or heart-shaped base and a toothed margin; the stipules are pinnately lobed and rather leaf-like. The flowers are violet-blue or tricoloured in violet or pink, white, and yellow, and are 10–25mm (⅖–1in) across and solitary; each flower has a short spur.

• **DISTRIBUTION** Throughout the region, except for Spitsbergen.

• **HABITAT** Cultivated, disturbed, and waste land, and grassy habitats; grows on acid or neutral soils.

• **REMARK** Variable. Some colonies are in fact hybrids with garden pansies and have larger flowers in a range of colours, especially yellow, violet, and purple.

Habit Annual or perennial	Height 10–30cm (4–12in)	Flowering time Apr–Oct

Family VIOLACEAE	Species *Viola arvensis*	Author Murray

FIELD PANSY

A small grey-hairy plant, Field Pansy has erect, simple or branched, stems. The alternate leaves are oblong to elliptical, with a shallowly toothed margin; the lowermost leaves are smaller and more rounded; the stipules are pinnately lobed. The small pansy flowers are cream with a deeper yellow or sometimes violet-blue centre or suffusion, only 4–8mm (⅙–⅓in) across, and solitary; the sepals are equal in length to, or longer than, the petals.

• **DISTRIBUTION** Throughout the region, except for the far north.

• **HABITAT** Arable fields and other cultivated land, waste places, disturbed ground; on neutral or calcareous soils. Sometimes in large colonies.

Habit Annual	Height 8–30cm (3⅕–12in)	Flowering time Apr–Oct

ROCK-ROSE FAMILY

Family CISTACEAE	Species *Helianthemum nummularium*	Author (L.) Miller

COMMON ROCK-ROSE

This variable evergreen plant has slender prostrate to ascending stems. The leaves are elliptical to oblong, green above but white with hairs beneath, and untoothed; small stipules are present at the base of the short leaf-stalks. The bright yellow, sometimes cream or orange, flowers are borne in racemes of up to 12. The fruit is a small many-seeded capsule.

• **DISTRIBUTION** Throughout, except the far north.

• **HABITAT** Grassy sites, short-turf downs, banks, and rocky places; on calcareous soils to 2,800m (9,200ft).

• **RELATED SPECIES** *Helianthemum apenninum*, White Rock-rose, has greyer leaves and white flowers.

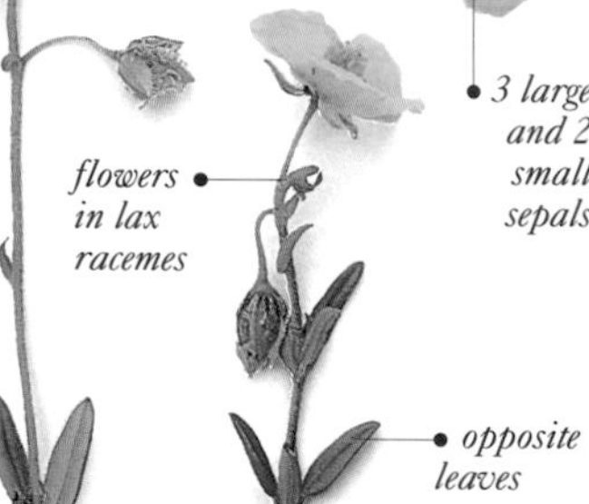

Habit Subshrub	Stem length Up to 50cm (20in)	Flowering time June–Sept

GOURD FAMILY

Family CUCURBITACEAE	Species *Bryonia dioica*	Author Jacq.

WHITE BRYONY

This vigorous rough-haired climber has a tuberous rootstock. The stems are slender and branch by means of simple coiled tendrils borne near the base of each leaf. The alternate leaves are long-stalked and palmately lobed, usually with 5 main lobes. The greenish white flowers are 10–18mm (⅖–⁵⁄₇in) across; the female flowers are smaller and are borne in small lateral clusters; the male are on separate plants in half-drooping clusters. The fruit, a small berry 6–10mm (¼–⅖in) across, is green at first but red when ripe.

• **DISTRIBUTION** S. Britain, Holland, and Germany southwards.

• **HABITAT** Hedgerows, woodland margins, scrub; on calcareous or base-rich soils, at low altitudes.

5-parted flowers with darker veins

♂

♀

DETAIL

alternate leaves

coiled stem-tendril

berry fruit

Habit Perennial	Height 2–4m (6½–13ft)	Flowering time May–Sept

LOOSESTRIFE FAMILY

Family LYTHRACEAE	Species *Lythrum salicaria*	Author L.

PURPLE LOOSESTRIFE

This is a rather robust, clump-forming, grey-hairy plant. The stems are rigid and erect, branched only in the upper part, and have 4 or more raised lines. The leaves are oval to lanceolate, toothed, unstalked, and opposite or in whorls of 3, although the uppermost are sometimes alternate. The bright purple flowers, 10–15mm (⅖–⅗in) across, are borne in whorls that make up long racemes; each flower has 6 petals, and usually 12 stamens in 2 groups of 6 at different levels within the flower. The fruit is a many-seeded capsule.

• **DISTRIBUTION** Throughout the region, except for the far north.

• **HABITAT** Damp sites, river, stream, and lake margins, canals, ditches, dykes, and marshes; on neutral or calcareous soils.

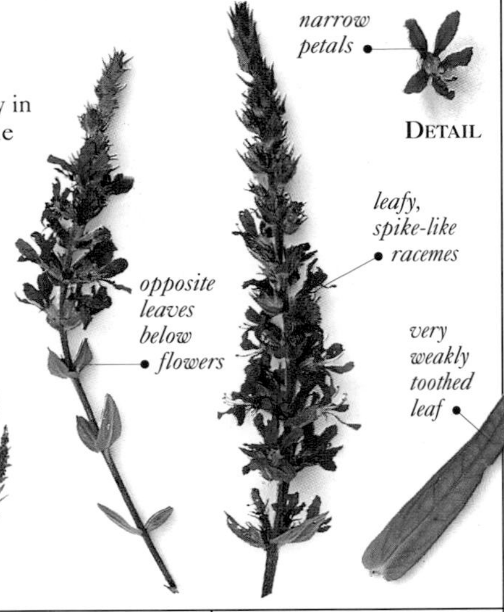

Habit Perennial	Height 70–150cm (28–60in)	Flowering time June–Aug

WILLOWHERB FAMILY

Family ONAGRACEAE	Species *Circaea lutetiana*	Author L.

ENCHANTER'S NIGHTSHADE

Spreading and slightly hairy, this plant has erect flowering stems and a vigorous, creeping rhizomatous stock; the stems are slender and may be branched. The opposite leaves are stalked and oval to elliptical, with a truncated or somewhat heart-shaped base. The white or pinkish flowers, 4–7mm (⅙–⅖in) across, have 2 sepals and 2 petals, the latter deeply notched. The fruit is a semi-pendent achene with whitish bristles.

• **DISTRIBUTION** Throughout the region, except for the far north.

• **HABITAT** Woodland, coppices, scrub, cultivated land, and shaded habitats.

• **RELATED SPECIES** *Circaea alpina*, Alpine Enchanter's Nightshade, has hairy, not glandular, flower-stalks and sepals. It grows in more upland sites.

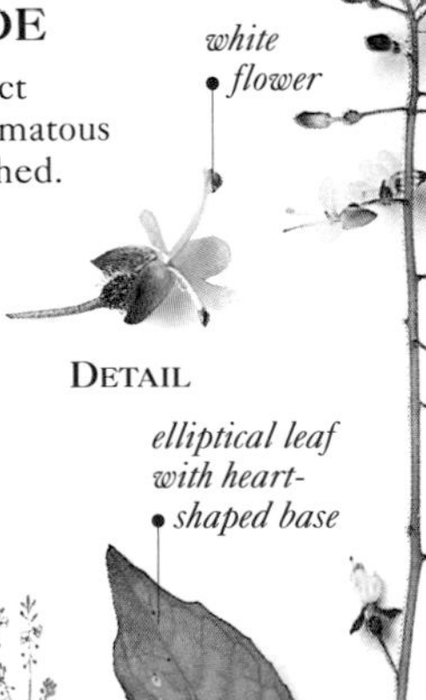

Habit Perennial	Height 30–60cm (12–24in)	Flowering time June–Aug

Family ONAGRACEAE	Species *Oenothera biennis*	Author L.

COMMON EVENING-PRIMROSE

Slightly hairy and fairly robust, this plant has stiff, erect stems. The green or bluish green leaves, in a basal rosette in the first year, are alternate, lanceolate, and slightly toothed, gradually decreasing in size up the stem; old basal leaves are often veined with red. Borne in leafy racemes, the flowers, 40–50mm (1⅗–2in) across, with 4 petals and 4 reflexed sepals, open in the evening but remain closed or partially closed during the day. The fruit capsule contains numerous small seeds.

• **DISTRIBUTION** Naturalized in most of the region, except for the far north. Native to North America.

• **HABITAT** Open habitats, waste and disturbed land, roadsides, embankments, and sand dunes.

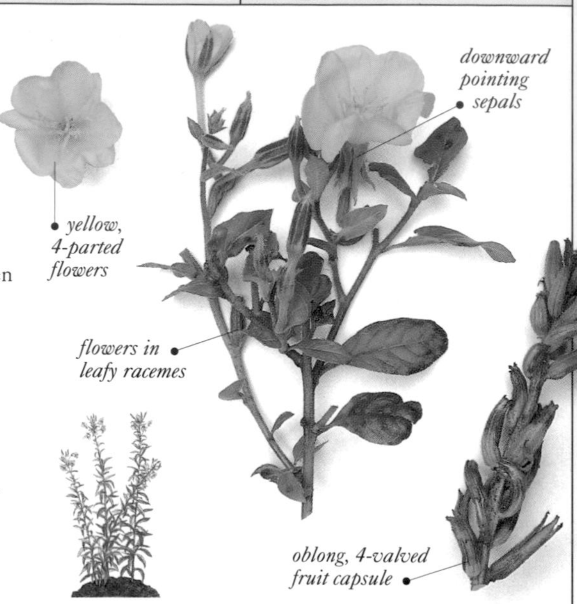

Habit Annual or biennial	Height 80–150cm (32–60in)	Flowering time June–Sept

Family ONAGRACEAE	Species *Chamerion angustifolium*	Author (L.) Holub.

ROSEBAY WILLOWHERB

Also known as *Epilobium angustifolium*, this vigorous plant spreads, using slender rhizomes, to form extensive patches. The alternate leaves are lanceolate and pointed, with a slightly toothed margin. The violet or rose-purple flowers, 20–30mm (⅘–1⅕in) across, have 4 sepals and 4 slightly notched petals, and are borne in racemes. The fruit capsule splits into 4 valves to release numerous, light, fluffy seeds.

• **DISTRIBUTION** Throughout the region, except for Spitsbergen.

• **HABITAT** Woodland margins and rides, roadsides, waste land, old building sites, railway embankments, riverbanks, and river margins.

• **RELATED SPECIES** *Chamerion latifolium*, Broad-leaved Willowherb is smaller, with up to 7 larger flowers in a raceme. It inhabits rocky sites in the Arctic.

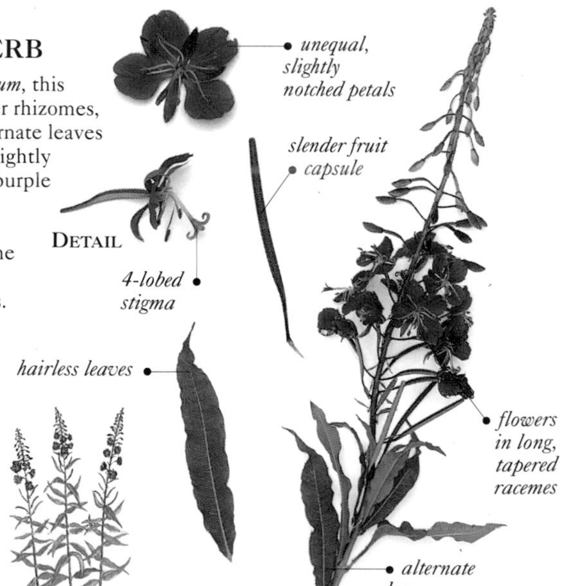

Habit Perennial	Height 80–150cm (32–60in)	Flowering time June–Sept

Family ONAGRACEAE	Species *Epilobium hirsutum*	Author L.

GREAT WILLOWHERB

This rather robust, very hairy, rhizomatous plant has erect stems and often forms extensive patches. The leaves, mostly opposite or occasionally whorled, are oblong to lanceolate, coarsely toothed, and unstalked, often clasping the stem with their base. Borne in leafy racemes, the bright purplish pink flowers, 15–25mm (3/5–1in) across, have 4 sepals and 4 longer, notched petals. The slender, hairy fruit capsules split into 4 segments when ripe to release the numerous, light, hairy seeds.

• **DISTRIBUTION** Grows throughout the region, except for the far north, the Faeroes, and Iceland.

• **HABITAT** Wet and damp places, river- and stream-sides, lake margins, ditches, and dykes; generally in open places, due to its intolerance of shade.

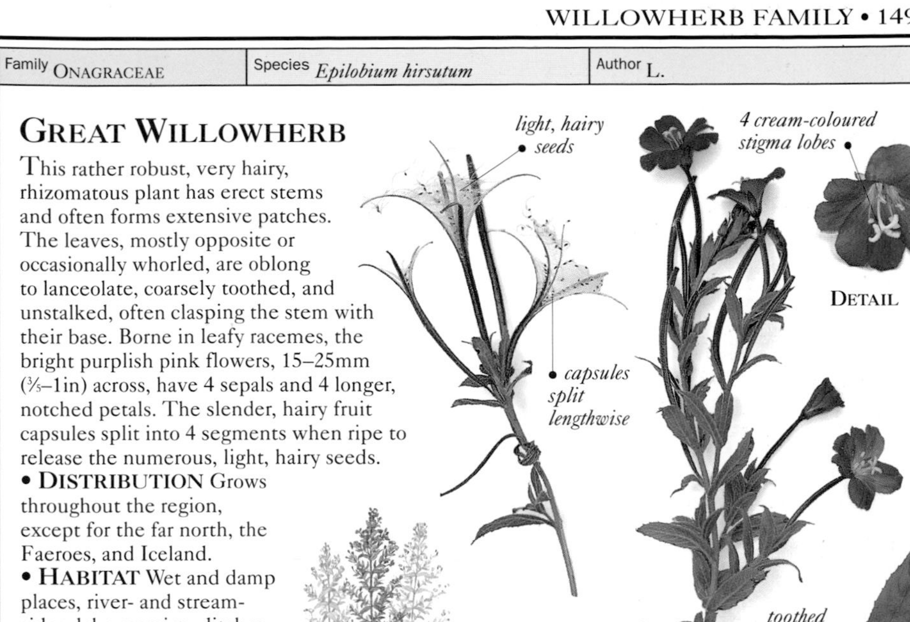

Habit Perennial	Height 80–180cm (32–72in)	Flowering time June–Sept

Family ONAGRACEAE	Species *Epilobium montanum*	Author L.

BROAD-LEAVED WILLOWHERB

This slightly hairy plant spreads by means of overwintering leafy buds at the base of the erect, leafy stems. The leaves are unstalked and mostly opposite, but the uppermost are alternate. The purplish pink flowers, 6–12mm (1/4–1/2in) across, are borne in leafy racemes, and each has 4 notched petals longer than the sepals.

• **DISTRIBUTION** Throughout, except for Iceland and Spitsbergen.

• **HABITAT** Cultivated and waste land, woodland, ditches, hedgerows, and rocky places; often in the shade.

• **RELATED SPECIES** *Epilobium obscurum*, Short-fruited Willowherb, has leafy stolons. The flowers are 7–10mm (2/7–2/5in) across, with a club-shaped stigma. It inhabits wetter sites but has a similar distribution.

Habit Perennial	Height 30–75cm (12–30in)	Flowering time May–Aug

IVY FAMILY

Family ARALIACEAE	Species *Hedera helix*	Author L.

IVY

A vigorous, woody, evergreen climber, Ivy clings by means of short stem-roots. The leathery, alternate leaves are stalked, untoothed, and deep green; those of young plants are 3- to 5-lobed, while those of mature plants are elliptical to heart-shaped. The greenish yellow flowers, 7–9mm (2/7–3/8in) across, are borne in small, rather dense umbels. The green berries turn brown then black when ripe.

• **DISTRIBUTION** Grows throughout the region, except for the far north.

• **HABITAT** On trees and rocks in woodland and on cliffs, old walls and buildings, hedgerows; often in dense shade. Sometimes creeping over the ground.

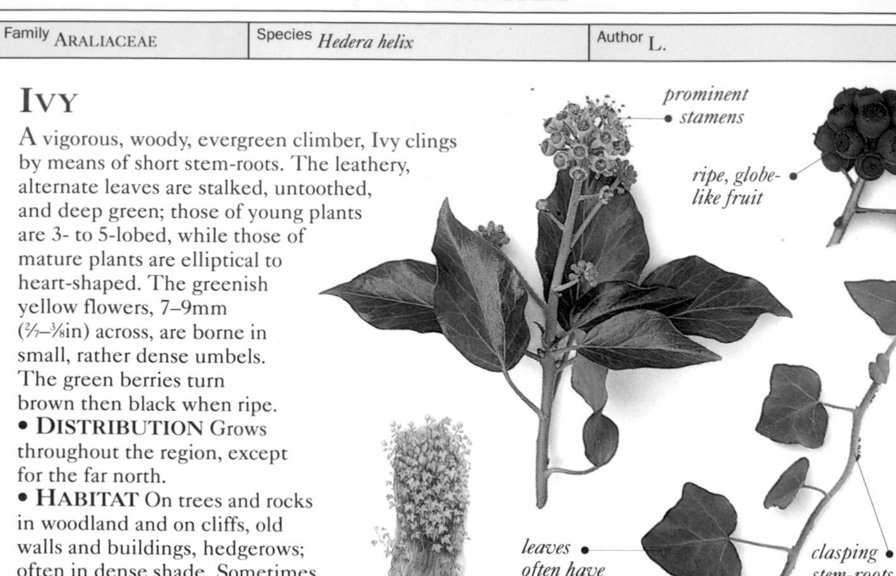

Habit Woody climber	Height Up to 30m (100ft)	Flowering time Sept–Nov

CARROT FAMILY

Family UMBELLIFERAE	Species *Sanicula europaea*	Author L.

SANICLE

A hairless plant, its stems are erect and usually branched. The shiny green leaves have 3 to 5 wedge-shaped, toothed lobes, the teeth terminating in a short bristle. The lower leaves are long-stalked; the upper are unstalked. Borne in clusters, the small white, pinkish, or greenish white flowers form uneven umbels; the outer flowers of each cluster are male, the inner are female. The fruit is oval, 2-parted, and 4–5mm (1/6–1/5in) long.

• **DISTRIBUTION** Throughout, except for the far north of the region.

• **HABITAT** Damp, shaded deciduous woodland, often of ash or beech; generally on humus-rich soils.

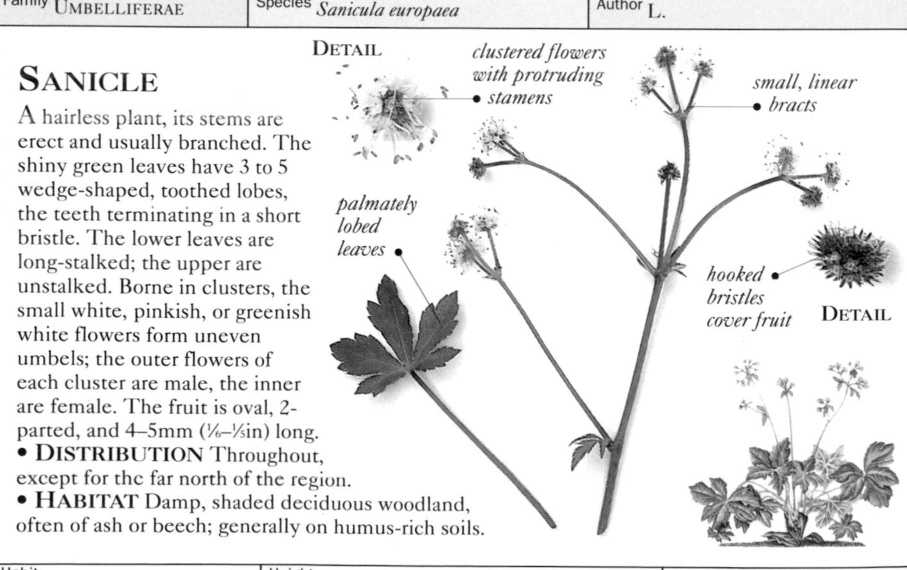

Habit Perennial	Height 20–50cm (8–20in)	Flowering time May–Aug

Family UMBELLIFERAE	Species *Eryngium maritimum*	Author L.

SEA HOLLY

This tough, leathery, bluish green plant has stiff, erect stems. The leaves are roughly rounded or heart-shaped in outline, but 3- to 5-lobed, with an undulate surface, a densely spiny margin, and whitish veins and edges. The tiny powder-blue flowers are borne in rounded heads 15–30mm (3/5–1 1/5in) across. The small 2-parted fruit is covered in overlapping scales.

• **DISTRIBUTION** Coastal Europe as far north as S. Sweden.

• **HABITAT** Sands and shingles; occasionally among rocks.

• **RELATED SPECIES** *Eryngium planum*, Blue Eryngo, has smaller, narrower bracts and oblong, spineless, lower leaves. It is native in C. and S. Germany and is naturalized in S. Britain.

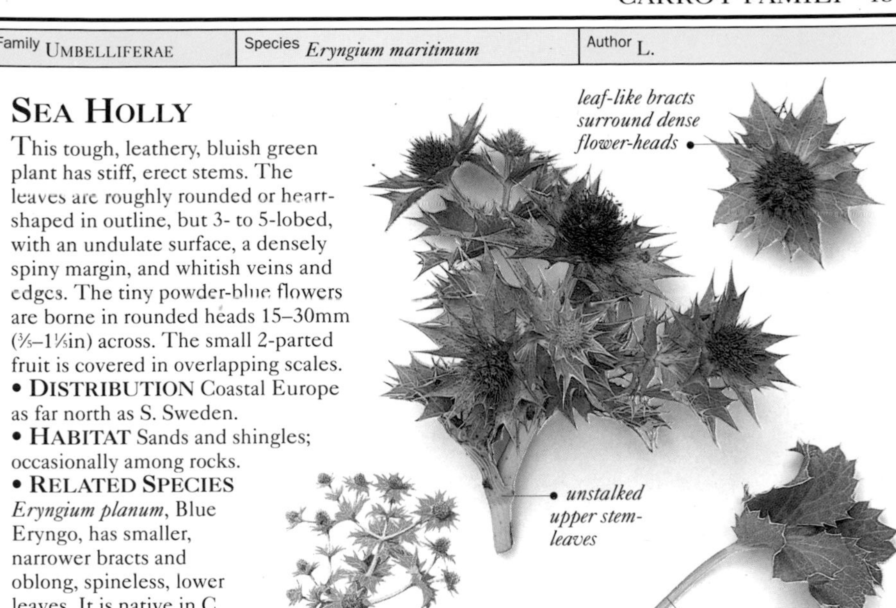

Habit Perennial	Height 30–60cm (12–24in)	Flowering time June–Sept

Family UMBELLIFERAE	Species *Eryngium campestre*	Author L.

FIELD ERYNGO

A tough, leathery, hairless plant, its stiff, erect stems are branched in the upper half. The basal leaves, usually persistent, are long-stalked and oval in outline, with 3 lobes that are themselves further lobed. The upper leaves are unstalked, with narrower lobes. The pale greenish white flower-heads, 10–15mm (2/5–3/5in) across, form a flat-topped inflorescence. The 2-parted fruit is covered in dense, overlapping scales.

DISTRIBUTION Holland to Germany southwards, and in S. Britain.

HABITAT Dry grassy places and rough grassland; often near the coast.

linear, spiny bracts around flower-head

flowers in dense, thistle-like heads

strongly spiny leaf margin

Habit Perennial	Height 40–75cm (16–30in)	Flowering time July–Aug

Family UMBELLIFERAE	Species *Astrantia major*	Author L.

GREAT MASTERWORT

A tufted, hairless, often rather robust plant, its erect stems are branched towards the top. The leaves, mostly basal, are rounded in outline, with 3 to 5 toothed lobes; the basal leaves are long-stalked but the upper are usually unstalked. The flower-heads, 20–35mm (⅘–1⅖in) across, are pinkish, whitish, or greenish, and are surrounded by a ruff of bracts which are whitish with green, pink, or purple tips and green veins. The fruit is ridged and 6–8mm (¼–⅓in) long.
• **DISTRIBUTION** C. and S. France and Germany; naturalized in parts of Britain, Denmark, Finland, and possibly elsewhere.
• **HABITAT** Meadows, open woods, shady places; mostly in the mountains to 2,000m (6,550ft).

DETAIL

2-parted fruit

thin flower-stalks

pin-cushion flower-head

linear, pointed bracts

lanceolate to elliptical lobes

Habit Perennial	Height 50–80cm (20–32in)	Flowering time May–Sept

Family UMBELLIFERAE	Species *Chaerophyllum temulum*	Author L.

ROUGH CHERVIL

Also known as *Chaerophyllum temulentum*, this rough-haired plant has erect, branched stems which are purple or purple-spotted. The feathery leaves are dark green or purplish, and 2- to 3-pinnate, with numerous small oval segments. The small white flowers, 2mm (1/12in) across, form broad, compound umbels which are drooping in bud; the secondary umbels have linear, hairy bracts. The 2-parted fruit, 4–7mm (⅙–2/7in) long, is ridged and tapers towards the top.
• **DISTRIBUTION** Throughout the region, as far north as S. Sweden; scarce in Ireland.
• **HABITAT** Rough grassy places, woodland margins, and hedgerows; on well-drained soils.

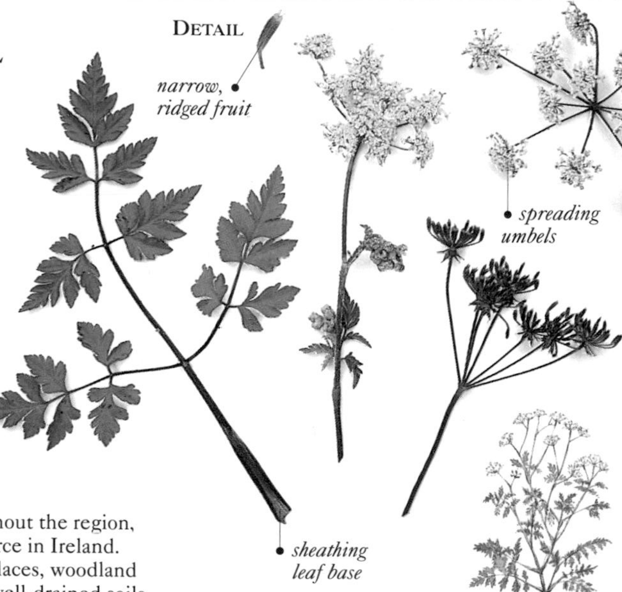

Habit Biennial	Height 60–100cm (24–40in)	Flowering time May–Aug

Family UMBELLIFERAE	Species *Anthriscus sylvestris*	Author (L.) Hoffm.

COW-PARSLEY

This slightly hairy plant has a tuberous rootstock. The leaves are 3-pinnate, with many lanceolate to triangular, pointed segments; leaf-stalks have sheathing bases. The flowers, 3–4mm (1/8–1/6in) across, are borne in umbels. The 2-parted fruit, 7–10mm (2/7–2/5in) long, has a terminal beak.

• **DISTRIBUTION** Throughout the region, except for the far north.

• **HABITAT** Grassy places, meadows, roadsides, hedgerows, woodland margins; generally growing at rather low altitudes.

• **RELATED SPECIES** *Anthriscus cerefolium*, Garden Chervil, has hairy spokes to the umbels. It is naturalized or casual in Britain and mainland Europe as far north as Denmark.

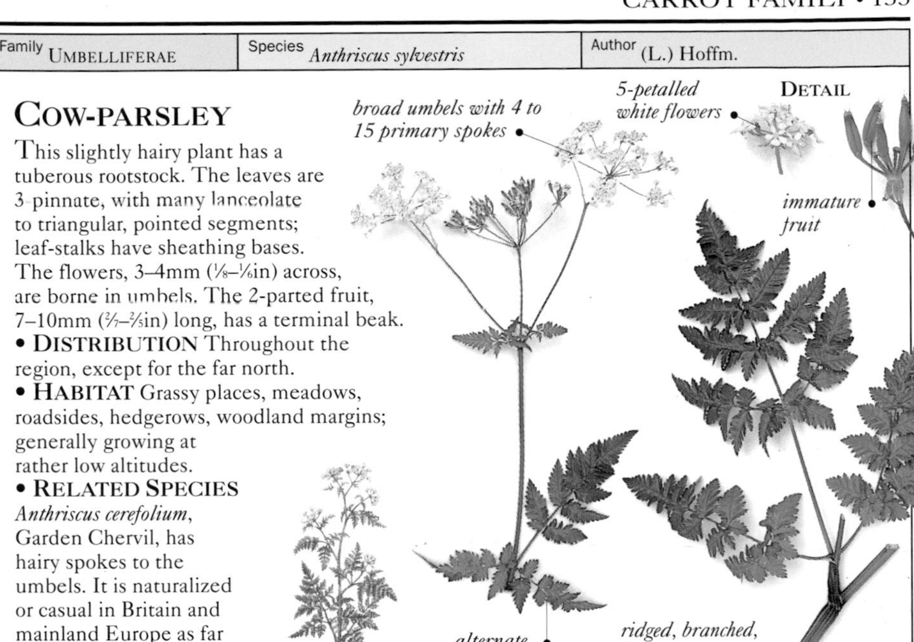

Habit Perennial	Height 80–150cm (32–60in)	Flowering time Apr–June

Family UMBELLIFERAE	Species *Myrrhis odorata*	Author (L.) Scop.

SWEET CICELY

This softly hairy, rather robust plant has a tuberous rootstock and thick, erect, branched stems which smell of aniseed if crushed. The leaves are quite large and 2- to 3-pinnate, with many lanceolate, deeply toothed lobes; the basal leaves have conspicuous pale sheathing stalks. Borne in wide umbels with 4 to 20 main spokes and no bracts, the flowers have 5 petals; the petals of the outer flowers are uneven. The 2-parted fruit is shiny and dark brown when ripe.

• **DISTRIBUTION** France and Germany; widely naturalized elsewhere, especially in N. Britain and Ireland.

• **HABITAT** Damp pastures and meadows, roadsides, woodland margins, scrub, and streamsides; mainly in the uplands and mountains.

narrow, elliptical, ridged fruit

small white flowers

DETAIL

alternate pale green leaves

leaves have many pinnately lobed segments

Habit Perennial	Height 80–180cm (32–72in)	Flowering time May–July

Family UMBELLIFERAE	Species *Smyrnium olusatrum*	Author L.

ALEXANDERS

This is a robust, often gregarious, hairless plant which is pungent when crushed. The stem is erect and branched, becoming stout and hollow with age, with the upper branches opposite. The leaves are 3-ternate, with broad elliptical to oval, toothed leaflets, and leaf bases with inflated sheaths; the upper leaves are chrome-yellow with large sheathing bases and a reduced blade. The yellow or greenish yellow flowers are borne in broad umbels without bracts; each flower has 5 even petals. The 2-parted fruit is 7–8mm (2/7–1/3in) long, and is black when ripe.

• **DISTRIBUTION** N.W. France southwards; widely naturalized in Britain and Holland, especially near the coast.

• **HABITAT** Hedgerows, roadsides, ditches, damp sand dunes, and coastal cliffs and rocks.

umbels have 7 to 15 main spokes

yellow flowers

DETAIL

flowers in large, broad umbels

egg-shaped fruit with slender ridges

shiny green leaf

Habit Biennial	Height 80–150cm (32–60in)	Flowering time Apr–June

Family UMBELLIFERAE	Species *Conopodium majus*	Author (Gouan) Loret

PIGNUT

This scarcely hairy plant has a globose underground tuber and a slender, erect, slightly ridged stem that eventually becomes hollow. The alternate leaves are 2- to 3-pinnate, the lower with elliptical to lanceolate untoothed lobes, the upper with narrow, often linear, lobes. The flowers, 1–3mm (1/25–1/8in) across, are borne in umbels, often with just one or 2 linear bracts; the 5 notched petals are often brown-veined on the back. The oblong, hairless, 2-parted fruit, 3–4mm (1/8–1/6in) long, has slight ridges.

• **DISTRIBUTION** Britain, France, and Norway; naturalized in the Faeroes and occasionally elsewhere.

• **HABITAT** Rough grassy places, field banks, roadsides, open woodland, hedgerows, and heaths; on light, dry, acid soils.

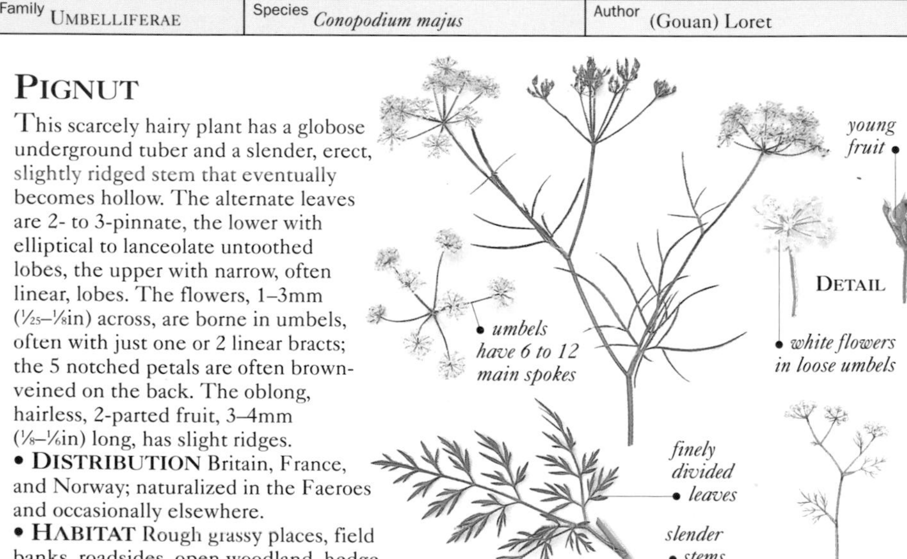

Habit Perennial	Height 20–40cm (8–16in)	Flowering time May–July

Family UMBELLIFERAE	Species *Pimpinella major*	Author (L.) Hudson

GREATER BURNET-SAXIFRAGE

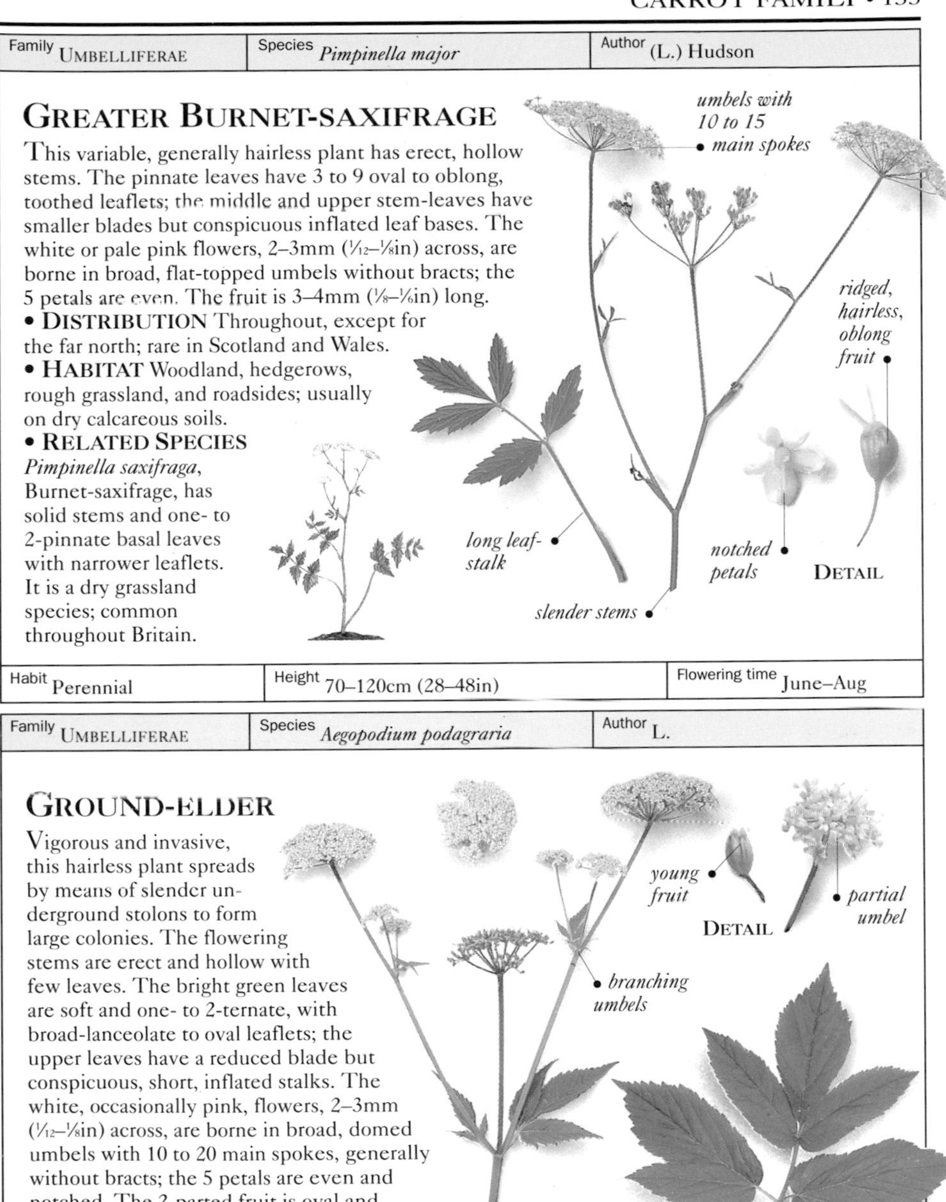

This variable, generally hairless plant has erect, hollow stems. The pinnate leaves have 3 to 9 oval to oblong, toothed leaflets; the middle and upper stem-leaves have smaller blades but conspicuous inflated leaf bases. The white or pale pink flowers, 2–3mm (1/12–1/8in) across, are borne in broad, flat-topped umbels without bracts; the 5 petals are even. The fruit is 3–4mm (1/8–1/6in) long.

- **DISTRIBUTION** Throughout, except for the far north; rare in Scotland and Wales.
- **HABITAT** Woodland, hedgerows, rough grassland, and roadsides; usually on dry calcareous soils.
- **RELATED SPECIES** *Pimpinella saxifraga*, Burnet-saxifrage, has solid stems and one- to 2-pinnate basal leaves with narrower leaflets. It is a dry grassland species; common throughout Britain.

Habit Perennial	Height 70–120cm (28–48in)	Flowering time June–Aug

Family UMBELLIFERAE	Species *Aegopodium podagraria*	Author L.

GROUND-ELDER

Vigorous and invasive, this hairless plant spreads by means of slender underground stolons to form large colonies. The flowering stems are erect and hollow with few leaves. The bright green leaves are soft and one- to 2-ternate, with broad-lanceolate to oval leaflets; the upper leaves have a reduced blade but conspicuous, short, inflated stalks. The white, occasionally pink, flowers, 2–3mm (1/12–1/8in) across, are borne in broad, domed umbels with 10 to 20 main spokes, generally without bracts; the 5 petals are even and notched. The 2-parted fruit is oval and hairless, with narrow ridges.

- **DISTRIBUTION** Throughout the region, except for the far north.
- **HABITAT** Cultivated and waste ground, open woodland, roadsides, and shady places; mostly at low altitudes and often on damp calcareous soils.

Habit Perennial	Height 30–90cm (12–36in)	Flowering time May–Aug

Family UMBELLIFERAE	Species *Crithmum maritimum*	Author L.

ROCK SAMPHIRE

A fleshy, greyish, hairless plant, its branched, erect to spreading stems become woody at the base. The leaves are triangular in outline, and one- to 2-pinnate, with segments that smell of polish when crushed. The yellowish green flowers, 2mm (1/12in) across, are borne in wide umbels up to 60mm (2⅖in) across; the bracts are lanceolate. The small, 2-parted fruit, 3.5–6mm (1/7–¼in) long, is ridged, yellow or purplish when ripe, and rather spongy.

• **DISTRIBUTION** Coastal Europe as far north as Holland and Britain, but absent from the north and much of the east coast of the latter.

• **HABITAT** Mainly on coastal rocks, sands, and shingles, but also on sea-cliffs.

Habit Perennial	Height 20–45cm (8–18in)	Flowering time June–Oct

Family UMBELLIFERAE	Species *Seseli libanotis*	Author (L.) Koch

MOON CARROT

This variable, hairy or hairless plant has erect, ridged, solid stems with a sheath of fibres at the base. The leaves are one- to 3-pinnate, with linear to sickle-shaped leaflets. Bracts are numerous, linear, and pointed. The flowers, 1–1.5mm (1/25–1/16in) across, are white or pink; the petals are hairy on the back. The 2-parted fruit is 2.5–4mm (1/10–⅙in) long.

• **DISTRIBUTION** Throughout the region, except for Ireland, Holland, and the far north; confined to the south in England.

• **HABITAT** Generally rough grassland and open scrub on calcareous soils.

• **RELATED SPECIES** *Seseli montanum* is a shorter, hairless perennial without bracts; the fruit is oblong, with sharp ridges. It inhabits rocky and grassy, chalky places.

Habit Biennial or perennial	Height 30–60cm (12–24in)	Flowering time July–Sept

Family UMBELLIFERAE	Species *Oenanthe aquatica*	Author (L.) Poiret

FINE-LEAVED WATER-DROPWORT

Robust and semi-aquatic, this rather pale green, hairless plant spreads by stolons. The thick stems are hollow and grooved. The basal leaves are submerged and have thread-like divisions; the aerial leaves are 3-pinnate, with oval, pointed, toothed leaflets. The white flowers are only 2mm (1/12in) across, but are borne in broad umbels with 5 to 15 primary spokes; the 5 petals are notched. The 2-parted fruit, 3.5–4.5mm (1/8–1/5in) long, is ridged and slightly curved.

• **DISTRIBUTION** Throughout the region, except for the far north.

• **HABITAT** Wet places, river, stream, and canal margins, ditches; usually in shallow, mineral-rich waters.

• **RELATED SPECIES** *Oenanthe fluviatilis*, River Water-dropwort, has partly floating stems, and longer fruit. It grows throughout the region, except Scandinavia.

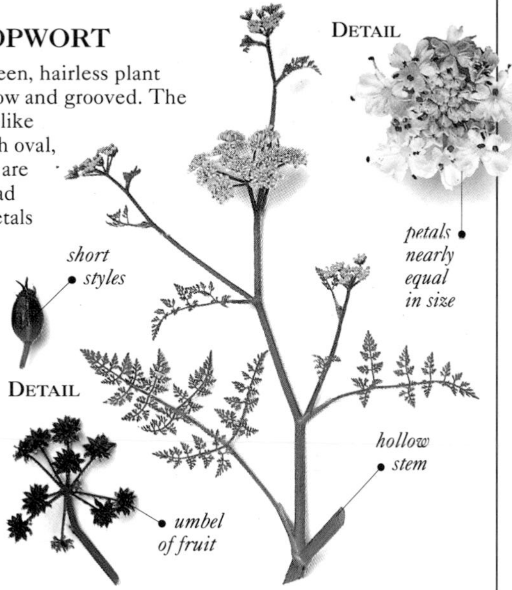

DETAIL

petals nearly equal in size

short styles

DETAIL

hollow stem

umbel of fruit

Habit Perennial	Height 1–1.5m (3¼–5ft)	Flowering time June–Sept

Family UMBELLIFERAE	Species *Foeniculum vulgare*	Author Miller

FENNEL

Strongly pungent when crushed, this is a robust, tufted, and hairless plant. Its stiff, erect stems, branched in the upper part, are rough, shiny, and eventually become hollow. The grey or bronze foliage is pinnately lobed into numerous thread-like segments; the upper leaves are much smaller. The flowers are 2–3mm (1/12–1/8in) across, and are borne in umbels, without bracts. The 2-parted fruit, 4–10mm (1/6–2/5in) long, is oblong and ridged.

• **DISTRIBUTION** Britain and France; naturalized in Belgium, Holland, and Germany.

• **HABITAT** Cultivated and waste ground, roadsides, rocky places, and cliffs; often near the sea.

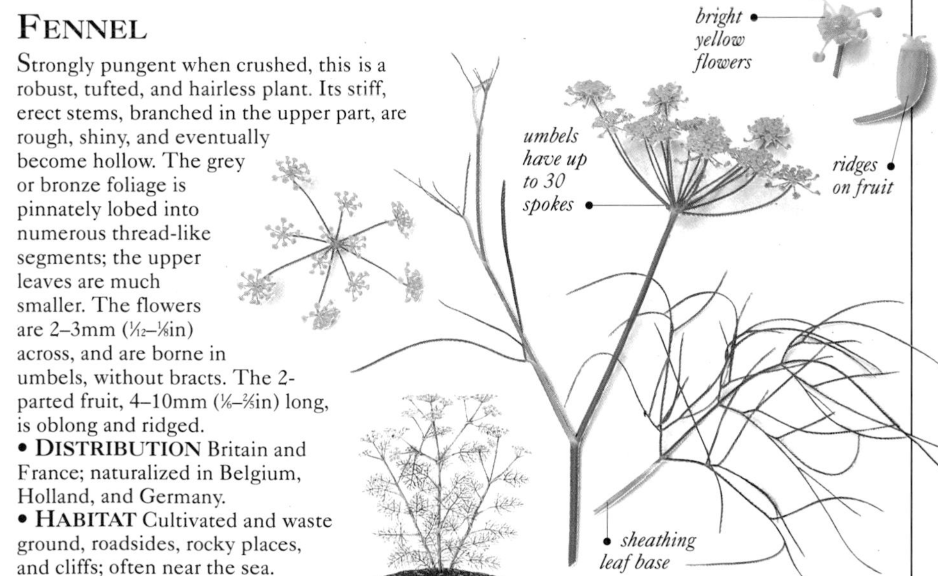

Habit Perennial	Height 1.5–2.5m (5–8ft)	Flowering time July–Oct

Family UMBELLIFERAE	Species *Bupleurum rotundifolium*	Author L.

THOROW-WAX

This is a greyish, somewhat fleshy, hairless plant that is often flushed with purple. The slender erect stems are branched or not. The alternate leaves are oval to rounded and untoothed; the lower leaves are narrower and short-stalked; the upper are broader and completely encircle the stem. The flowers have 5 tiny petals with an inrolled tip and are borne in small tight umbels with 5 to 10 main spokes; each umbel is surrounded by 5 to 6 conspicuous, oval, yellowish green bracts that form a cup around the flowers. The 2-parted fruit is oblong, 3–3.5mm (⅛–⅐in) long, with slender ridges.

• **DISTRIBUTION** Belgium, France, and Germany; naturalized in Holland and at one time in England (now believed to be extinct).

• **HABITAT** Arable fields and waste and dry open places.

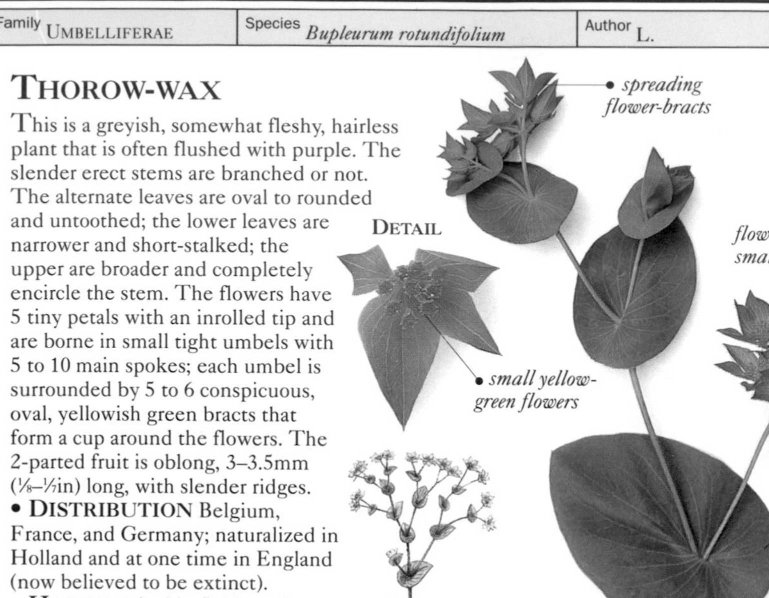

Habit Annual	Height 15–30cm (6–12in)	Flowering time June–July

Family UMBELLIFERAE	Species *Bupleurum falcatum*	Author L.

SICKLE-LEAVED HARE'S-EAR

This variable, hairless plant has a solitary or several erect stems. The leaves are rather thick and leathery, untoothed, and mostly basal; basal leaves are oval to elliptical, 3- to 5-veined, and long-stalked, while stem-leaves are smaller, narrower, often sickle-shaped, and half-clasping the stem with unstalked bases. The bracts, 2 to 5 to each partial umbel, are small and linear-lanceolate. The small yellow flowers are borne in umbels. The fruit is 2-parted, oblong, 3–4mm (⅛–⅙in) long, and ridged.

• **DISTRIBUTION** S.E. England (but rare and confined to Essex), Belgium, France, and Germany.

• **HABITAT** Damp or dry grassland, roadsides and ditches, and waste places; occasionally along hedgerows.

partial umbel

DETAIL

umbels have 3 to 15 main spokes

stems branch in upper part

slender leaves

prominent ridges on fruit

DETAIL

fruiting umbels

Habit Perennial	Height 50–100cm (20–40in)	Flowering time July–Oct

Family UMBELLIFERAE	Species *Conium maculatum*	Author L.

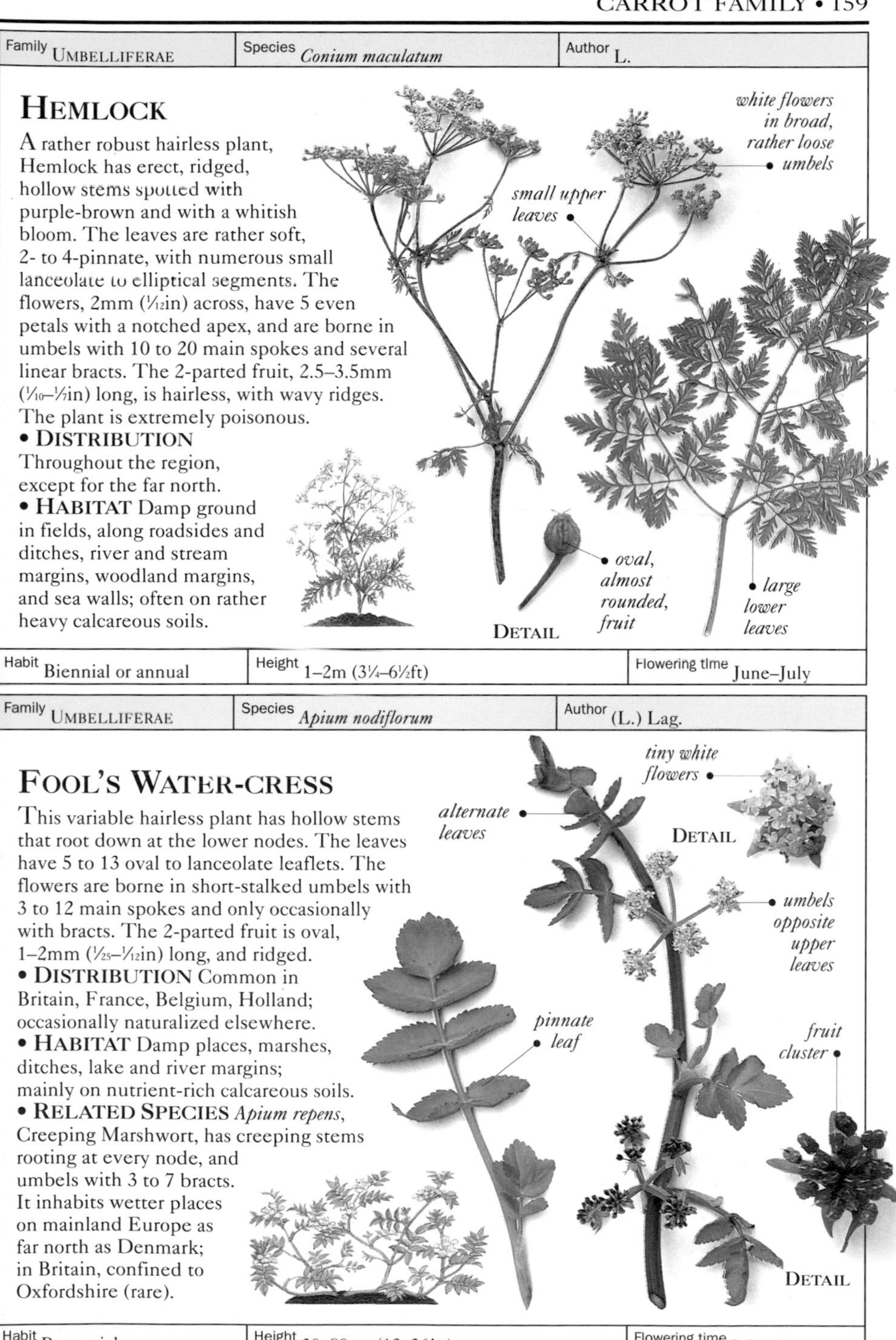

HEMLOCK

A rather robust hairless plant, Hemlock has erect, ridged, hollow stems spotted with purple-brown and with a whitish bloom. The leaves are rather soft, 2- to 4-pinnate, with numerous small lanceolate to elliptical segments. The flowers, 2mm ($\frac{1}{12}$in) across, have 5 even petals with a notched apex, and are borne in umbels with 10 to 20 main spokes and several linear bracts. The 2-parted fruit, 2.5–3.5mm ($\frac{1}{10}$–$\frac{1}{7}$in) long, is hairless, with wavy ridges. The plant is extremely poisonous.

• **DISTRIBUTION** Throughout the region, except for the far north.

• **HABITAT** Damp ground in fields, along roadsides and ditches, river and stream margins, woodland margins, and sea walls; often on rather heavy calcareous soils.

Habit Biennial or annual	Height 1–2m (3¼–6½ft)	Flowering time June–July

Family UMBELLIFERAE	Species *Apium nodiflorum*	Author (L.) Lag.

FOOL'S WATER-CRESS

This variable hairless plant has hollow stems that root down at the lower nodes. The leaves have 5 to 13 oval to lanceolate leaflets. The flowers are borne in short-stalked umbels with 3 to 12 main spokes and only occasionally with bracts. The 2-parted fruit is oval, 1–2mm ($\frac{1}{25}$–$\frac{1}{12}$in) long, and ridged.

• **DISTRIBUTION** Common in Britain, France, Belgium, Holland; occasionally naturalized elsewhere.

• **HABITAT** Damp places, marshes, ditches, lake and river margins; mainly on nutrient-rich calcareous soils.

• **RELATED SPECIES** *Apium repens*, Creeping Marshwort, has creeping stems rooting at every node, and umbels with 3 to 7 bracts. It inhabits wetter places on mainland Europe as far north as Denmark; in Britain, confined to Oxfordshire (rare).

Habit Perennial	Height 30–90cm (12–36in)	Flowering time July–Aug

Family UMBELLIFERAE	Species *Sison amomum*	Author L.

STONE PARSLEY

Described as smelling of petrol and nutmeg when crushed, this is a hairless plant, with thin, erect, ridged stems branched only in the upper part. The lower leaves are pinnate with 5 to 9 pairs of oblong, toothed leaflets; the upper leaves are smaller and bract-like. The linear bracts are much shorter than the spokes of the umbel. The white flowers, only 1–2mm (1/25–1/12in) across, are borne in loose umbels with 3 to 6 spokes; each flower has 5 even petals with incurved tips, but no sepals. The 2-parted fruit, 1.5–3mm (1/16–1/8in) long, is rounded to oblong and ridged.

• **DISTRIBUTION** C. and S. Britain, and France; rare and often only casual further north.

• **HABITAT** Grassy places, banks, roadsides, hedgerows, and occasionally waste ground.

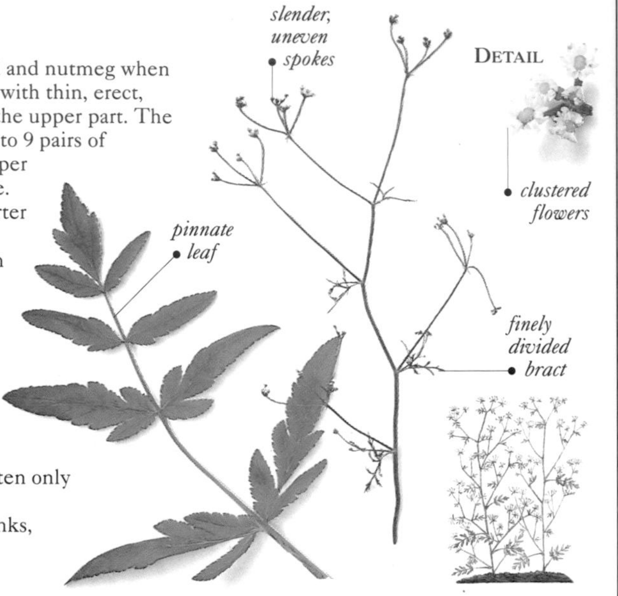

slender, uneven spokes

DETAIL

clustered flowers

pinnate leaf

finely divided bract

Habit Biennial	Height 50–100cm (20–40in)	Flowering time July–Sept

Family UMBELLIFERAE	Species *Levisticum officinale*	Author Koch.

LOVAGE

This robust, clump-forming plant has a strong celery smell when crushed. The stems are stout but hollow, with the lower branches alternate and the upper ones opposite or whorled. The leaves are hairless, 2- to 3-pinnate, and roughly triangular in outline, with elliptical to wedge-shaped, irregularly toothed or untoothed leaflets. The yellow-green flowers are borne in dense umbels. The 2-parted fruit is oblong, 4–7mm (1/6–2/7in) long, strongly ridged, and yellow or brown when ripe.

• **DISTRIBUTION** Naturalized throughout, except for the far north. Native of Iran.

• **HABITAT** Grassy and waste places, abandoned cultivation, roadsides, and hedgerows.

• **REMARK** Grown as a herb to flavour food and for salads.

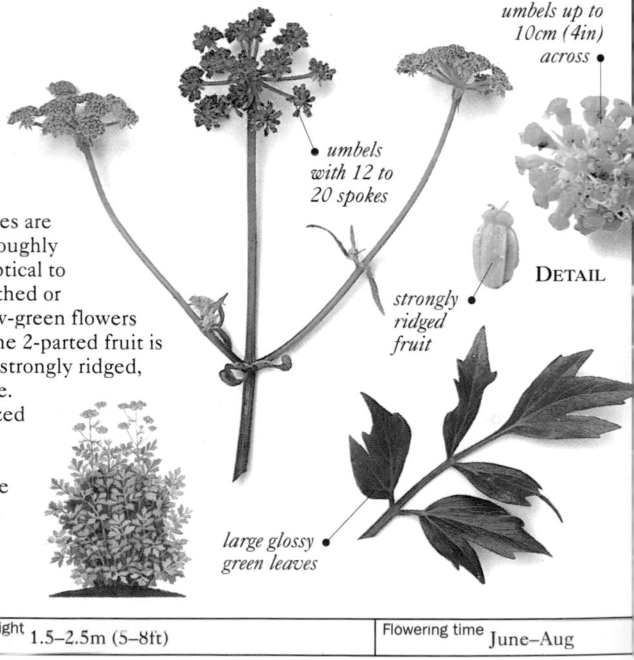

umbels up to 10cm (4in) across

umbels with 12 to 20 spokes

DETAIL

strongly ridged fruit

large glossy green leaves

Habit Perennial	Height 1.5–2.5m (5–8ft)	Flowering time June–Aug

Family UMBELLIFERAE	Species *Angelica sylvestris*	Author L.

WILD ANGELICA

This robust, almost hairless plant has erect, hollow, ridged stems which are branched towards the top and often flushed with purple. The large, 2- to 3-pinnate leaves have oval to oblong, finely toothed segments; the upper leaves are much reduced, with large, inflated sheath-bases. The white or pink flowers form large umbels 3–15cm (1⅕–6in) across. The bracts are few and soon fall. The 2-parted fruit is 4–5mm (⅙–⅕) long and has membranous wings.

• **DISTRIBUTION** Native throughout the region, except for the far north.

• **HABITAT** Damp places in meadows, marshes, fens, open woodland, and along roadsides and riverbanks.

Habit Perennial	Height 1–2.5m (3¼–8ft)	Flowering time July–Oct

Family UMBELLIFERAE	Species *Heracleum sphondylium*	Author L.

HOGWEED

This variable, rough-haired plant has stout, erect, hollow stems. The large basal leaves are pinnate with broad, lobed and toothed segments; the upper leaves are much reduced, with a large, inflated base. The white, rarely pink or greenish, flowers are borne in umbels up to 15cm (6in) across; the petals are notched. The 2-parted fruit is flattened and broadly winged.

• **DISTRIBUTION** Native throughout the region, except for the far north.

• **HABITAT** Grassy places, woods, roadsides, embankments.

• **RELATED SPECIES** *Heracleum mantegazzianum*, Giant Hogweed, grows to 5m (16½ft) tall, has much larger umbels, and is dangerous to touch. It is naturalized in W. Europe; native of the Caucasus.

Habit Biennial	Height 1–2.5m (3¼–8ft)	Flowering time Apr–Sept

Family UMBELLIFERAE	Species *Aethusa cynapium*	Author L.

FOOL'S PARSLEY

This variable, generally robust, hairless plant has erect hollow stems. The leaves are 2-pinnate with oval to elliptical lobed leaflets. The flowers, 2mm (1/12in) across, have 5 even petals with inrolled tips, and are borne in slightly domed umbels with 10 to 20 main spokes. Bracts are absent, but 3 to 5 linear and pendent secondary bracts (bracteoles) are present. The 2-parted fruit is 3–4mm (1/8–1/6in) long, with prominent keel-like ridges. The plant is poisonous.

• **DISTRIBUTION** Throughout, except for the far north; in Britain, found mainly in the south and southwest.

• **HABITAT** Cultivated land, including gardens, waste land, farmyards, open woodland, and roadsides; mostly at rather low altitudes.

Habit Annual or biennial	Height 60–100cm (24–40in)	Flowering time June–Oct

Family UMBELLIFERAE	Species *Pastinaca sativa*	Author L.

WILD PARSNIP

This rather robust, hairy plant has a strong smell, especially when crushed. The stems are erect, often branched, hollow, and ridged. The deep green leaves are pinnate, with 5 to 11 oval, toothed leaflets; the lower leaves are long-stalked, while the upper have very reduced blades and an ensheathing base. The yellow flowers, 1.5mm (1/16in) across, are borne in broad umbels which each have 9 to 20 rather uneven main spokes. If present, the bracts number no more than 2 and soon fall. The 2-parted fruit, 5–7mm (1/5–2/7in) long, is elliptical, with narrowly winged ridges.

• **DISTRIBUTION** C. and S. Britain to Holland and Germany southwards; naturalized in Ireland.

• **HABITAT** Grassland, scrub, roadsides; usually on dry calcareous soils.

Habit Biennial	Height 60–100cm (24–40in)	Flowering time July–Aug

Family UMBELLIFERAE	Species *Torilis japonica*	Author (Houtt.) DC.

UPRIGHT HEDGE-PARSLEY

The stems of this rough-haired plant are solid, ridged, and branched. The leaves are one- to 3-pinnate with oval to lanceolate segments; the upper leaves are much reduced and often trifoliate. The white, pink, or pale purplish flowers, 2–3mm (1/12–1/8in) across, are borne in umbels with 4 to 6, sometimes more, bracts; the 5 petals are somewhat unequal with inrolled tips. The 2-parted oval fruit, 3–4mm (1/8–1/6in) long, has curved spines.
• **DISTRIBUTION** Throughout, except the far north; rare or absent in N. Scotland.
• **HABITAT** Grassy places, woodland margins, and scrub; generally on light dry soils.
• **RELATED SPECIES** *Torilis arvensis*, Spreading Hedge-parsley, has one or no bracts per umbel and straight spines on the fruit. Inhabits arable land in S.E. England (rare) and W. Europe.

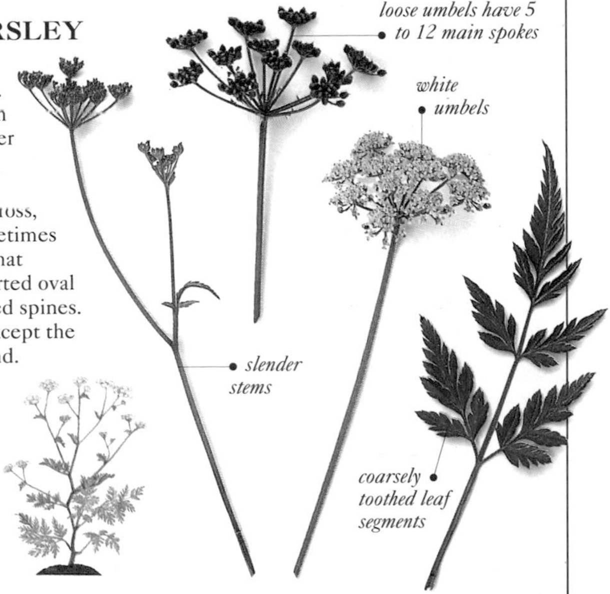

loose umbels have 5 to 12 main spokes
white umbels
slender stems
coarsely toothed leaf segments

Habit Annual or biennial	Height 50–120cm (20–48in)	Flowering time July–Sept

Family UMBELLIFERAE	Species *Daucus carota*	Author L.

WILD CARROT

A very variable, hairy or hairless plant, Wild Carrot has simple or widely branched, erect stems, which are solid and usually ridged. The narrowly cut leaves are 2- to 3-pinnate and rather feathery, with numerous linear to lanceolate segments; uppermost leaves are often much reduced and bract-like. The white flowers are borne in broad, rather flat umbels, with numerous main spokes that become incurved in fruit; the centre flower of the umbel is sometimes purple. Bracts are conspicuous and often 3-lobed. The 2-parted fruit, 2–4mm (1/12–1/6in) long, is oval with rows of barbed spines.
• **DISTRIBUTION** Throughout the region, except for the far north.
• **HABITAT** Downs, cliffs, dry meadows, field boundaries, roadsides; often coastal.

Habit Biennial	Height 50–100cm (20–40in)	Flowering time June–Aug

WINTERGREEN FAMILY

Family PYROLACEAE	Species *Pyrola rotundifolia*	Author L.

ROUND-LEAVED WINTERGREEN

This is a hairless spreading and patch-forming plant with slender creeping rhizomes and erect flowering stems. The leaves, mainly basal or on the lower part of the stem, are deep green and rather leathery, rounded to oval, and long-stalked; the upper leaves are small and bract-like. The pure white flowers, 8–12mm (⅓–½in) across, are borne in racemes, and are saucer-shaped and nodding, with 5 spreading petals, a distinctive S-shaped style, and 10 stamens. The fruit is a small capsule containing numerous tiny seeds.

• **DISTRIBUTION** Locally distributed throughout the region, except for the far north.

• **HABITAT** Damp woodland, bogs, fens, rocky places, and hollows in sand dunes; to an altitude of 1,450m (4,750ft).

Habit Perennial	Height 10–25cm (4–10in)	Flowering time June–Sept

HEATHER FAMILY

Family ERICACEAE	Species *Erica ciliaris*	Author L.

DORSET HEATH

Often rather straggly, this evergreen is much-branched, with hairy young shoots. In whorls of 3, the leaves are linear to narrow-lanceolate, with untoothed margins rolled under, glandular-hairy above and along the edge, and whitish beneath. The bright reddish purple, rarely white, flowers are slightly curved and 8–12mm (⅓–½in) long; the stamens do not protrude. The small fruit capsule contains many tiny seeds.

• **DISTRIBUTION** S. and S.W. Britain, W. Ireland, and W. and C. France.

• **HABITAT** Open woodland, moist heath; on acid soils; often gregarious.

• **RELATED SPECIES** *Erica mackaiana*, Mackay's Heath, has leaves in whorls of 4, and flowers in terminal clusters. Restricted to Ireland.

Habit Shrub	Height 30–60cm (12–24in)	Flowering time May–Oct

Family ERICACEAE	Species *Erica tetralix*	Author L.

CROSS-LEAVED HEATH

This is a rather straggly, small shrub with thin, woody, much-branched stems, and an overall greyish appearance. The young shoots are hairy. The small leaves, 2–5mm (1/12–1/5in) long, are hairy, at least when young. The rounded bell-shaped, pale pink or rarely white flowers, 6–9mm (1/4 3/8in) long, are borne in small clusters; the stamens do not protrude. The fruit is a small, dry, many-seeded, downy capsule.

DETAIL

• **DISTRIBUTION** Native throughout much of the region, except for the far north.
• **HABITAT** Wet moors and heaths, bogs, pine woodland, occasionally drier heaths; on acid soils, on lowland and in the mountains to 2,200m (7,200ft).
• **RELATED SPECIES** *Erica terminalis*, Corsican Heath, is larger, with leaves mostly in whorls of 4, and bright pink flowers with recurved corolla-lobes. Naturalized in parts of Ireland.

Habit Evergreen shrub	Height 30–70cm (12–28in)	Flowering time June–Oct

Family ERICACEAE	Species *Erica cinerea*	Author L.

BELL HEATHER

This dwarf shrub has branched, woody stems; young shoots are hairy. The linear leaves, 4–7mm (1/6–2/7in) long, are borne in whorls of 3 and are green or more often bronze. The bright magenta-purple, rarely white, flowers, 5–7mm (1/5–2/7in) long, are borne in leafy racemes or panicles and occasionally in smaller, more compact, clusters; the stamens do not protrude. The fruit is a small, dry, hairless capsule.

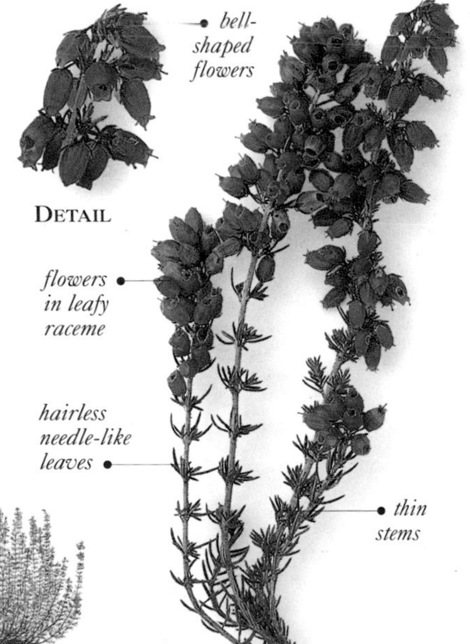

• **DISTRIBUTION** Throughout, except for much of the north and east of the region.
• **HABITAT** Dry places on heaths and moors, and open pine woodland; on acid soils, on lowland and mountains to 1,500m (4,900ft).
• **RELATED SPECIES** *Erica vagans*, Cornish Heath, is hairless, with leaves in whorls of 4 to 5, and smaller lilac, pink, or white flowers. It is native in S.W. England, N.W. Ireland, and W. France; occasionally naturalized elsewhere. Also native in N. Spain.

Habit Evergreen shrub	Height 20–60cm (8–24in)	Flowering time July–Sept

Family ERICACEAE	Species *Calluna vulgaris*	Author (L.) Hull

HEATHER

Also known as Ling, this small, almost hairless shrub is spreading to upright, often forming a carpet. The thin, much-branched stems soon become woody. The tiny, scale-like leaves are in pairs, with strongly rolled-back margins. The pale purple to pinkish purple, or occasionally white, flowers are borne in slender, branched racemes or panicles. The 4 sepals are separate and petal-like, while the true petals are smaller and fused together in the lower quarter; the 8 stamens do not protrude. The small, many-seeded fruit capsule splits when ripe.

• **DISTRIBUTION** Throughout the region, except for Spitsbergen.

• **HABITAT** Moors, bogs, heaths, open pine and birch woodland, banks, roadsides, and stabilized sand dunes; grows on acid soils. It often forms extensive colonies.

DETAIL

flowers 3–4mm (1/8–1/6in) long

woody stems

leaves crowded and closely pressed against stems

Habit Shrub	Height 20–80cm (8–32in)	Flowering time July–Sept

Family ERICACEAE	Species *Daboecia cantabrica*	Author (Hudson) K. Koch

ST. DABOEC'S HEATH

This small, somewhat hairy, and rather straggly shrub has branched, wiry stems forming a loose dome shape. The alternate leaves, 8–14mm (1/3–4/7in) long, are lanceolate to oblong, with strongly rolled-back margins, and are dark green and glandular-hairy on the upper surface, and white with felt beneath. The purplish pink, rarely white, flowers, 9–14mm (3/8–4/7in) long, are bell-shaped, narrowed and 4-lobed at the distal end, and are borne in loose terminal racemes, with a bract to each flower; the 8 stamens do not protrude; the calyx consists of 4 linear, glandular-hairy lobes. The fruit is a small, dry, many-seeded capsule.

• **DISTRIBUTION** Restricted to W. Ireland and W. France. Also known from N.W. Spain.

• **HABITAT** Open woodland, heaths, peaty and rocky moors; on acid soils. Widely grown in gardens but not naturalizing.

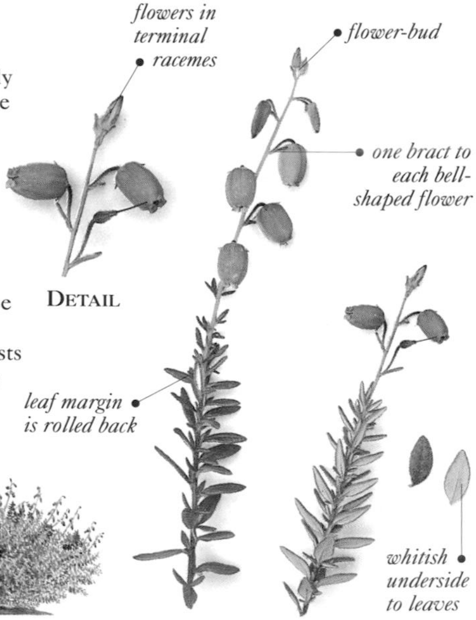

flowers in terminal racemes

flower-bud

one bract to each bell-shaped flower

DETAIL

leaf margin is rolled back

whitish underside to leaves

Habit Dwarf shrub	Height 40–70cm (16–28in)	Flowering time May–Oct

Family ERICACEAE	Species *Arctostaphylos uva-ursi*	Author (L.) Sprengel

BEARBERRY

This spreading evergreen has prostrate, rooting branches. The leaves are oval, often broadest above the middle, deep green, and leathery, with an untoothed, flat margin. The flowers are greenish white to pale pink, bell-shaped, 5–6mm (⅕–¼in) long, and borne in small terminal clusters. The berries are 6–8mm (¼–⅓in) across.

• **DISTRIBUTION** Throughout the region, except the far north.

• **HABITAT** Open woodland, moors, heaths; generally in exposed upland places on thin, peaty, acid soils.

• **RELATED SPECIES** *Arctostaphylos alpina*, Mountain Bearberry, has non-leathery leaves which wither in the autumn, white flowers tinged with green, and black berries. It grows on mountain moors in N. Scotland and mainland Europe, except the far north.

petals fused for most of length

leathery alternate leaves

half-drooping flower clusters

shiny red, ripe berries

Habit Shrub	Height 10–30cm (4–12in)	Flowering time July–Sept

Family ERICACEAE	Species *Vaccinium oxycoccus*	Author L.

CRANBERRY

This is a prostrate creeping evergreen with rooting stems. The small, alternate leaves are oval, untoothed, and deep green above but white beneath. The flowers, 6–10mm (¼–⅖in) across, have 4 reflexed petals, are long-stalked, and are borne singly or in groups of 2 to 4. The rounded or pear-shaped berries, 8–10mm (⅓–⅖in) across, are red or brownish when ripe and often speckled; they are edible.

• **DISTRIBUTION** Throughout the region, except for the far north and most of S. England.

• **HABITAT** Bogs, moors, heaths, and open wet woodland; often creeping among sphagnum moss.

• **RELATED SPECIES** *Vaccinium microcarpum*, Small Cranberry, has hairless flower-stalks and much smaller berries. *V. macrocarpon*, American Cranberry, sometimes a garden escape, has larger berries.

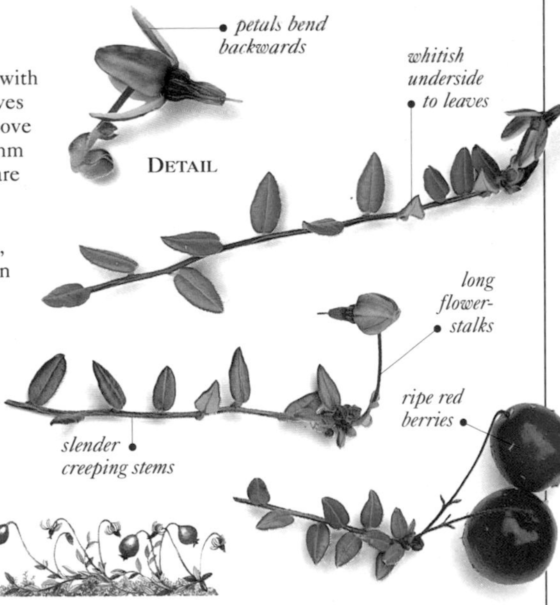

Habit Subshrub	Height 3–7cm (1⅕–2⅘in)	Flowering time June–Aug

Family ERICACEAE	Species *Vaccinium vitis-idaea*	Author L.

COWBERRY

A spreading to ascending or creeping, often matted, evergreen subshrub, Cowberry often forms substantial colonies. The young stems are minutely hairy. The alternate leaves are oblong, often broadest above the middle, with downturned, untoothed or minutely toothed margins. The bell-shaped, white or pale pink flowers are 5–8mm (⅕–⅓in) long; the corolla has pointed lobes. The ripe berry, 5–10mm (⅕–⅖in) across, is red.

• **DISTRIBUTION** Throughout the region; absent from much of S. Britain and lowland France.

• **HABITAT** Moors, heaths, tundra, open coniferous woodland; lowland and mountains, usually on poor, thin, acid, often peaty, soils.

• **REMARK** It hybridizes with *Vaccinium myrtillus*, Bilberry (see below), where the two species grow very close to one another.

DETAIL

bell-shaped flower

flowers in drooping terminal clusters

dark green leathery leaves

leaves dotted with glands beneath

rounded red berries

Habit Subshrub	Height 30–70cm (12–28in)	Flowering time June–Aug

Family ERICACEAE	Species *Vaccinium myrtillus*	Author L.

BILBERRY

This hairless, creeping, deciduous shrub has much-branched, angled stems. The alternate leaves are bright green, oval to elliptical, with a flat, toothed margin and a short stalk. The urn-shaped flowers are pale green flushed with pink, 4–6mm (⅙–¼in) long, and solitary, or occasionally paired. The fruit is a fleshy berry 6–10mm (¼–⅖in) across.

• **DISTRIBUTION** Throughout the region, except for Spitsbergen.

• **HABITAT** Heaths, moors, and deciduous or coniferous woodland; on lowland and mountains, on dry acid soils.

• **RELATED SPECIES** *Vaccinium uliginosum*, Bog Bilberry, has rounded stems, untoothed bluish green leaves, and white flowers flushed with pink. The berry is bluish black. It inhabits damper soils throughout the region.

urn-shaped flowers

ripe, bluish black berry

COLOUR VARIANTS

white bloom on ripe berry

toothed, deciduous leaves

3-angled stems

Habit Shrub	Height 20–50cm (8–20in)	Flowering time Apr–June

PRIMROSE FAMILY

Family PRIMULACEAE	Species *Primula vulgaris*	Author Hudson

PRIMROSE

This soft-haired plant has basal rosettes of bright green oblong leaves. The solitary, fragrant flowers, 20–40mm (⁴⁄₅–1³⁄₅in) across, are pale yellow, rarely pink or white, generally with orange markings in the centre. The slender flower-stalks are soft-haired. The fruit capsule is many seeded.

- **DISTRIBUTION** Throughout, except for Finland, Iceland, and the far north of the region.
- **HABITAT** Grassy banks, open woodland, meadows, embankments, roadsides, ditches, and sea-cliffs.
- **RELATED SPECIES** *Primula elatior*, Oxlip, has wider leaves, and flowers in a nodding, one-sided umbel. It inhabits moister sites in ancient woodland south from E. England and Denmark.

Habit Perennial	Height 5–12cm (2–4³⁄₄in)	Flowering time Jan–May

Family PRIMULACEAE	Species *Primula veris*	Author L.

COWSLIP

This soft-haired, stemless plant has basal rosettes of leaves. The leaves are oblong, toothed, broadest near the base, and abruptly narrowed into the stalk. The sweetly fragrant, deep yellow, nodding flowers are 7–14mm (²⁄₇–⁴⁄₇in) across, have orange markings in the centre, and are borne in one-sided umbels of up to 30 flowers, on long, slender scapes. The fruit is a many-seeded capsule.

- **DISTRIBUTION** Grows throughout the region, except for the far north.
- **HABITAT** Open dry grassy places, meadows, roadsides, and embankments; often on calcareous soils.
- **REMARK** Where Primrose (see above) and Cowslip grow together, the hybrid *Primula* x *polyantha*, False Oxlip, often occurs. Crosses of both species with *P. elatior*, Oxlip, also occur.

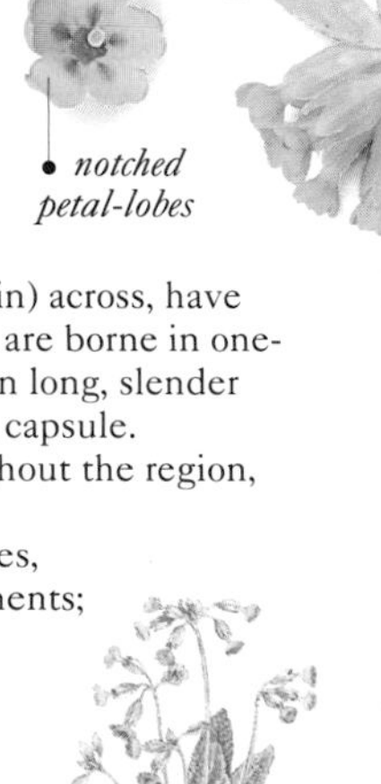

Habit Perennial	Height 10–30cm (4–12in)	Flowering time Apr–May

Family PRIMULACEAE	Species *Primula farinosa*	Author L.

BIRD'S-EYE PRIMROSE

Small and mealy, this plant forms small tufts with one or several basal leaf-rosettes and whitish, leafless flower stems. The leaves are elliptical to almost spoon-shaped, with a finely toothed or untoothed margin. The flowers, 8–16mm (⅓–⅝in) across, are purple or lilac-pink, occasionally white, with a yellow "eye"; the corolla has 5 notched lobes fused below into a long slender tube.

• **DISTRIBUTION** N. England, S. Scotland, and mainland Europe as far north as Denmark and S. Sweden.

• **HABITAT** Damp places on grassland, and peaty or stony ground; in the mountains to 3,000m (9,850ft).

• **RELATED SPECIES** *Primula scotica*, Scottish Primrose, is smaller, with wider leaves and darker, purple flowers with overlapping petal-lobes. It inhabits damp grassy places, especially above sea-cliffs, and grassy dunes in N. Scotland and Orkney only.

flowers in umbel

long calyx-tube

notched petal-lobes

green upper surface of leaf

mealy white underside of leaf

Habit Perennial	Height 7–15cm (2⅘–6in)	Flowering time May–Aug

Family PRIMULACEAE	Species *Cyclamen hederifolium*	Author Aiton

IVY-LEAVED SOWBREAD

This is a somewhat glandular, hairless plant, with basal leaves and flowers, arising from a large tuberous stock at or just below the surface of the soil. The long-stalked leaves are heart-shaped to oval, generally lobed and toothed, purple or reddish beneath, and variegated with green, grey, or silver above. The pale pink, rarely white, solitary flowers, 12–25mm (½–1in) long, are marked with magenta close to the mouth, which has small projections; the 5 petal-lobes are bent backwards and are slightly twisted. The fleshy fruit capsule develops close to the ground on a tightly coiled stalk.

• **DISTRIBUTION** Naturalized in scattered localities in Britain, parts of France, and perhaps elsewhere in the region. Native to S. and S.E. Europe and to S.W. Asia.

• **HABITAT** Woodland, scrub, and rocky places; grown in gardens.

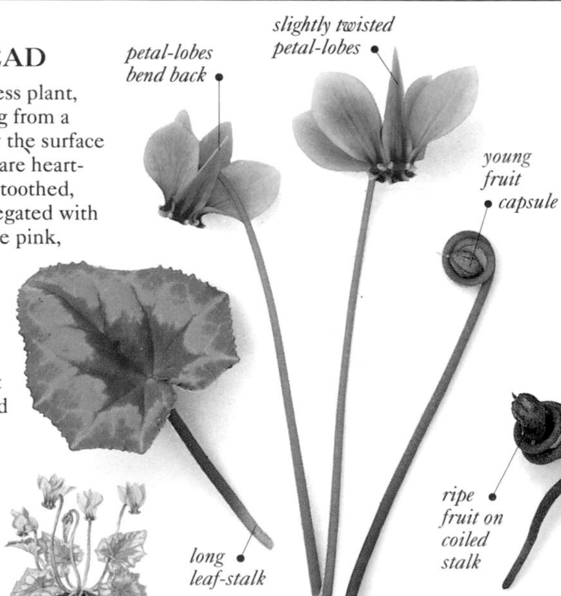

Habit Perennial	Height 5–12.5cm (2–5in)	Flowering time Aug–Nov

Family PRIMULACEAE	Species *Lysimachia nemorum*	Author L.

YELLOW PIMPERNEL

This creeping, bright green, hairless plant has slender stems rooting down at intervals. The leaves are lanceolate to almost rounded, untoothed, short-stalked, and generally pointed. The solitary, long-stalked flowers, 10–15mm (⅖–⅗in) across, are bright yellow and star-shaped, with 5 petals fused together near the base; the sepals are narrow, linear, pointed, and not overlapping. The small, many-seeded fruit capsule splits into 5 valves when ripe.

• **DISTRIBUTION** Throughout the region, except for the far north; often local.

• **HABITAT** Damp, shaded places, woodland and copses, ditches, and occasionally along hedgerows or riverbanks. Cultivated in gardens.

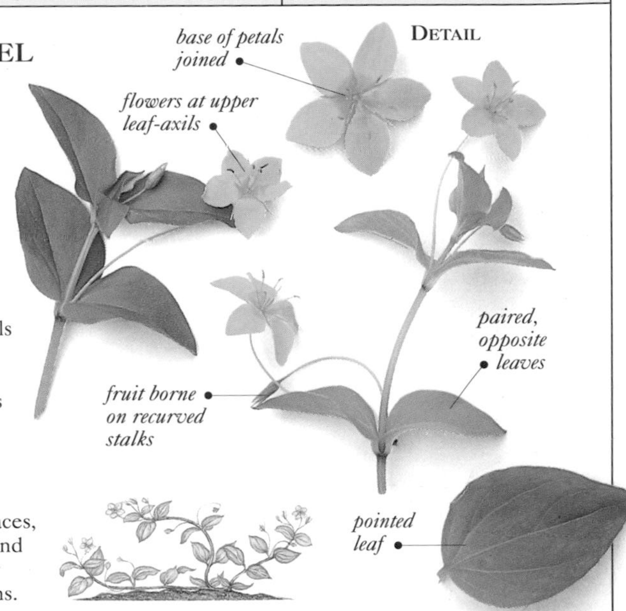

Habit Perennial	Stem length Up to 40cm (16in)	Flowering time May–July

Family PRIMULACEAE	Species *Lysimachia nummularia*	Author L.

CREEPING JENNY

This creeping evergreen is hairless, with slender stems rooting down at intervals. The leaves are rounded to oval, with a blunt apex, untoothed, and covered in tiny black dots. The solitary, yellow flowers, 8–18mm (⅓–⅗in) across, are borne on long, slender stalks. The sepals are oval, pointed, and slightly overlapping; the oval petal-lobes are covered in tiny black dots. Borne on curved to erect stalks, the many-seeded fruit capsules split into 5 valves when ripe.

• **DISTRIBUTION** Throughout, except for the far north of the region.

• **HABITAT** Damp, primarily shaded places, open woodland, lake shores, stream margins, ditches, and damp hedgerows. Widely grown in gardens.

Habit Perennial	Stem length Up to 60cm (24in)	Flowering time May–July

Family PRIMULACEAE	Species *Glaux maritima*	Author L.

SEA-MILKWORT

This is a low-growing, often mat-forming, rather fleshy, hairless plant, with spreading stems that root down at the nodes. The small elliptical to narrow-oval leaves are mostly opposite, unstalked, and 4–12mm (⅙–½in) long. The pale pink to purple, or sometimes white flowers, 3–6mm (⅛–¼in) across, are borne on very short stalks; the petals are absent. The fruit is a small 5-valved capsule.

• **DISTRIBUTION** Coastal Europe, including Ireland; occasionally inland.

• **HABITAT** Fine shingle and sand, rocky places, and dry salt marshes.

Habit Perennial	Height 1–5cm (⅖–2in)	Flowering time May–Sept

Family PRIMULACEAE	Species *Anagallis arvensis*	Author L.

SCARLET PIMPERNEL

This spreading plant has weak, prostrate to ascending, square stems. The opposite leaves are oval to lanceolate, untoothed, and unstalked. The solitary, red, occasionally pink or blue, flowers, 4–7mm (⅙–2⁄7in) across, are 5-parted; the petals have hairy margins. The fruit is a small, many-seeded, rounded capsule, which splits open by a small lid when ripe.

• **DISTRIBUTION** Throughout the region, except for the far north.

• **HABITAT** Cultivated, waste, and disturbed land, field margins, and coastal dunes; mainly light sandy or chalky soils.

Habit Annual	Height 5–20cm (2–8in)	Flowering time May–Oct

Family PRIMULACEAE	Species *Anagallis tenella*	Author (L.) L.

BOG PIMPERNEL

Generally mat-forming, this plant has slender creeping stems that root down at intervals. The leaves are mainly opposite, elliptical to rounded, untoothed, and short-stalked. The flowers, 6–10mm (¼–⅖in) across, are pink, occasionally white, 5-parted, with oval, hairless petals. The many-seeded fruit capsule has a small cap-like lid.

• **DISTRIBUTION** Britain (except for most of the east), and the Faeroes.

• **HABITAT** Bogs, marshes, damp meadows, woodland rides, flushes; on peaty, weakly acid, or alkaline soils.

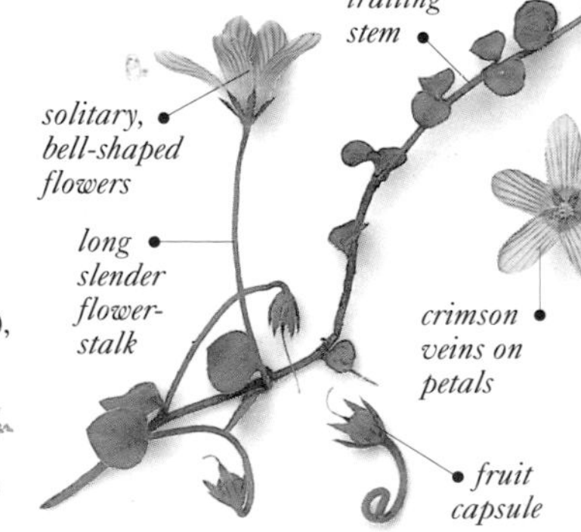

Habit Perennial	Height 2–5cm (⅘–2in)	Flowering time May–Sept

THRIFT FAMILY

Family PLUMBAGINACEAE	Species *Armeria maritima*	Author (Miller) Willd.

THRIFT

This is a very variable, low, densely tufted, hairy plant, forming rounded cushions. The leaves are deep green, linear, and usually one-veined. The fragrant pink, red, or white flowers are borne on leafless, hairy scapes and form dense heads, 15–25mm (⅗–1in) across, with a tubular sheath below each flower-head; the 5 petals are rounded and fused together into a short tube. The small, one-seeded fruit is dry and has a papery wall.

• **DISTRIBUTION** Throughout the region, except for Spitsbergen.

• **HABITAT** Coastal meadows, cliffs, and salt marshes, and inland on mountain rocks.

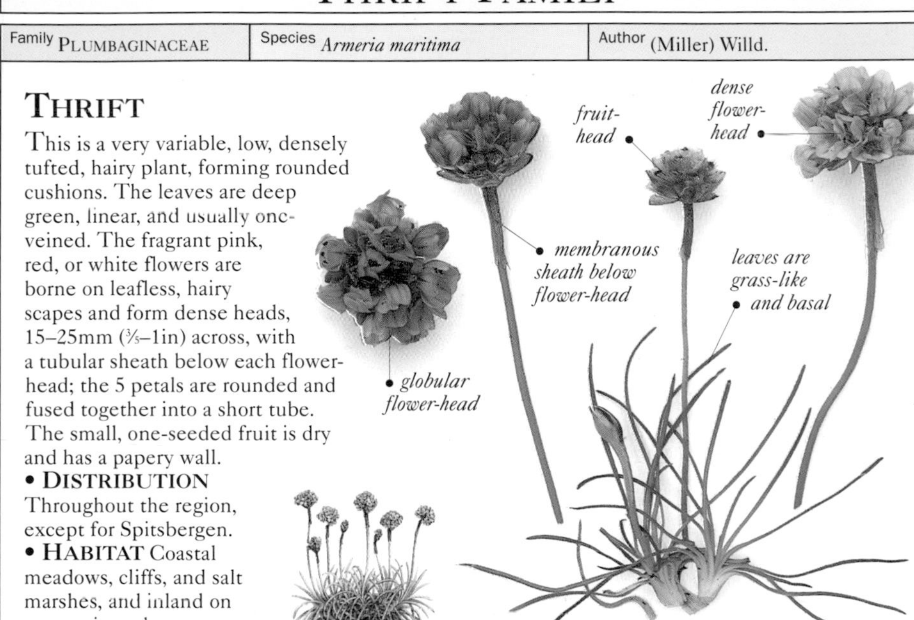

Habit Perennial	Height 5–30cm (2–12in)	Flowering time Apr–Aug

Family PLUMBAGINACEAE	Species *Limonium vulgare*	Author Miller

COMMON SEA-LAVENDER

This is a hairless plant which often forms a carpet on the ground. The stems are slender, wiry, round, and erect, with scarce leaves. Mainly basal, the leaves are elliptical to spoon-shaped, pinnately veined, untoothed, and long-stalked, and die away in the autumn. The small reddish or lavender-lilac flowers, 6–8mm (¼–⅓in) long, have yellow anthers and are borne in spreading, rather crowded, branched spikes. The fruit is a one-seeded capsule with a persistent papery calyx.

• **DISTRIBUTION** Throughout the region as far north as S. Sweden.

• **HABITAT** Muddy salt marshes. Often forming large colonies.

Habit Perennial	Height 20–50cm (8–20in)	Flowering time July–Sept

GENTIAN FAMILY

Family GENTIANACEAE	Species *Centaurium erythraea*	Author Rafn

COMMON CENTAURY

This very variable and hairless plant has a single, or sometimes several, erect stems which are branched in the upper part. The opposite leaves are elliptical to oval with 3 to 7 veins; the lower leaves are in a rosette and are usually short-stalked. Borne in distinctive flat-topped clusters, the purple or pink, occasionally white, flowers are salver-shaped, 9–15mm (⅜–⅗in) across, and have 5 or 6 petals that are fused below into a long slender tube. The fruit capsule is 2-parted and many-seeded.

• **DISTRIBUTION** Throughout the region, except for Norway, Finland, and the far north.

• **HABITAT** Grassy places, open ground, woodland margins, scrub, and mountain slopes.

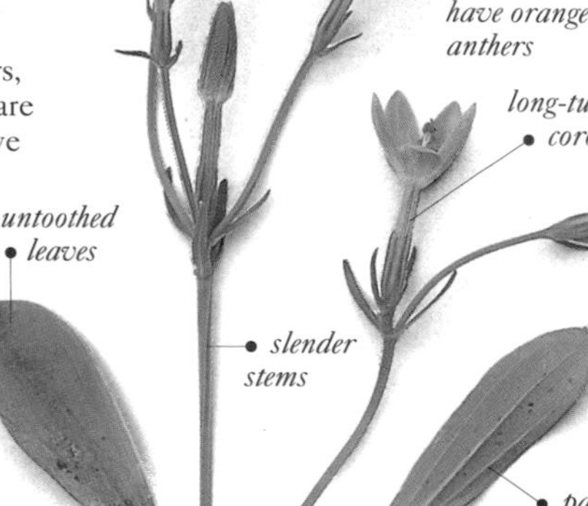

Habit Biennial	Height 5–50cm (2–20in)	Flowering time June–Sept

Family GENTIANACEAE	Species *Centaurium pulchellum*	Author (Swartz) Druce

LESSER CENTAURY

This rather short, hairless plant has no basal rosette of leaves. The slender stems are branched in the upper part or unbranched. The opposite leaves are lanceolate to oval, with an untoothed margin and a somewhat pointed apex; each has 3 to 7 main veins. The pinkish purple, occasionally white, salver-shaped flowers, 5–9mm (⅕–⅜in) long, are borne in wide-spreading clusters which are occasionally few-flowered in poorer specimens. The fruit consists of a narrow, 2-parted capsule containing numerous tiny seeds.

• **DISTRIBUTION** Throughout the region, except for the Faeroes, Iceland, and the far north; absent from much of N. Britain and Ireland.

• **HABITAT** Damp grassy, generally open, ground, especially near the sea.

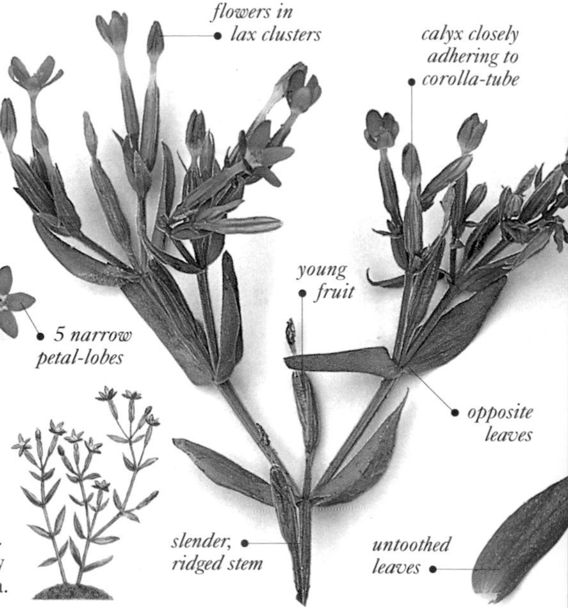

Habit Annual	Height 5–20cm (2–8in)	Flowering time June–Sept

Family GENTIANACEAE	Species *Gentiana asclepiadea*	Author L.

WILLOW GENTIAN

This graceful, hairless plant has slender, erect to arching, unbranched stems. The green leaves are unstalked, lanceolate to oval, and untoothed. The mid- to deep blue or purple, occasionally white, flowers are 35–50mm (1⅗–2in) long, with 5 pointed lobes, and often a purple-spotted throat. The fruit capsule splits lengthwise into 2 when ripe, to release a mass of dust-like seed.

• **DISTRIBUTION** C. and E. France, and Germany; naturalized in S.E. England and perhaps elsewhere.

• **HABITAT** Damp places, meadows, open woodland, stream-banks, and rocky places; primarily in the mountains, to 2,200m (7,200ft). Various forms are widely grown in gardens.

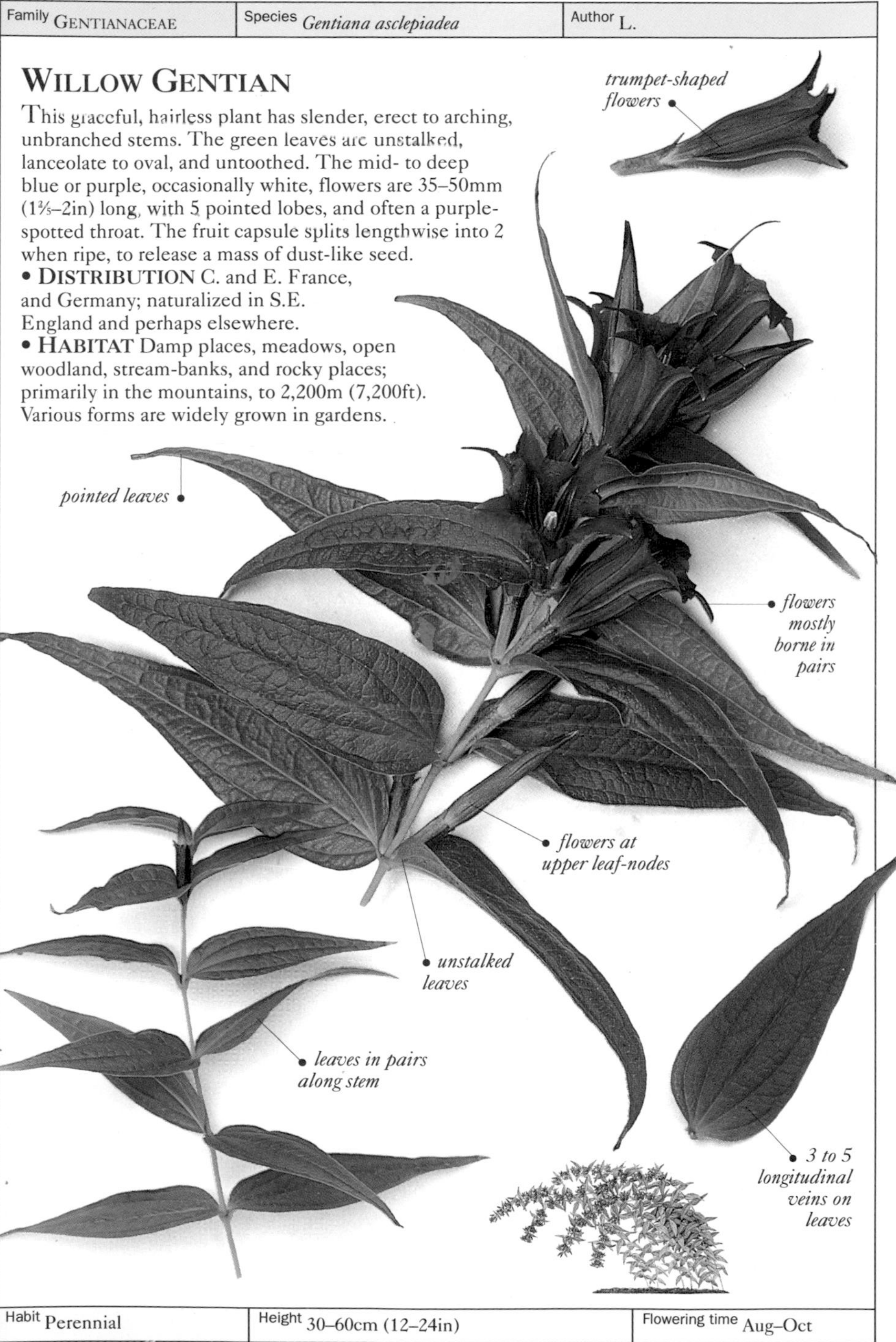

Habit Perennial	Height 30–60cm (12–24in)	Flowering time Aug–Oct

Family GENTIANACEAE	Species *Gentiana verna*	Author L.

SPRING GENTIAN

This hairless herb is tufted or mat-forming, with very short, erect stems, generally with only one or 2 pairs of leaves. The bright green leaves are paired, oval to lanceolate, untoothed, and short-stalked or unstalked. The bright blue, rarely white, flowers, 12–18mm (½–⅗in) across, are solitary and salver-shaped, with 5 small, fringed lobes between the 5 main corolla-lobes, a white stigma, and a tubular calyx.

• **DISTRIBUTION** Native in N. England, W. Ireland, C. and E. France, and S. Germany.

• **HABITAT** Mountain rocks and meadows, heaths, fixed calcareous dunes, glacial deposits.

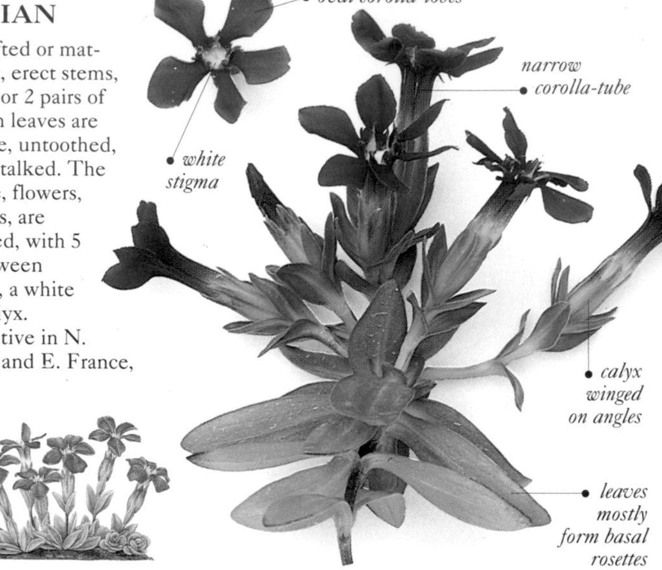

Habit Perennial	Height 1–7.5cm (⅖–3in)	Flowering time Apr–June

Family GENTIANACEAE	Species *Gentiana pneumonanthe*	Author L.

MARSH GENTIAN

The stems of this hairless plant are green, erect, and leafy. The leaves are linear to oblong, untoothed, and one-veined. The large, blue, green-striped flowers, 25–45mm (1–1⅘in) long, are solitary or up to 10 in the upper leaf-axils. The ripe fruit capsule splits into 2 to release the dust-like seed.

• **DISTRIBUTION** Throughout the region, except for the far north and most of the islands; local; decreasing in England.

• **HABITAT** Moist places on heaths and marshes, on peaty, acid soils.

• **RELATED SPECIES** *Gentiana cruciata*, Cross Gentian, has a basal leaf-rosette, and smaller, 4-lobed flowers which are borne in whorls at the upper nodes. It inhabits scrub, dry grassland, and open woodland.

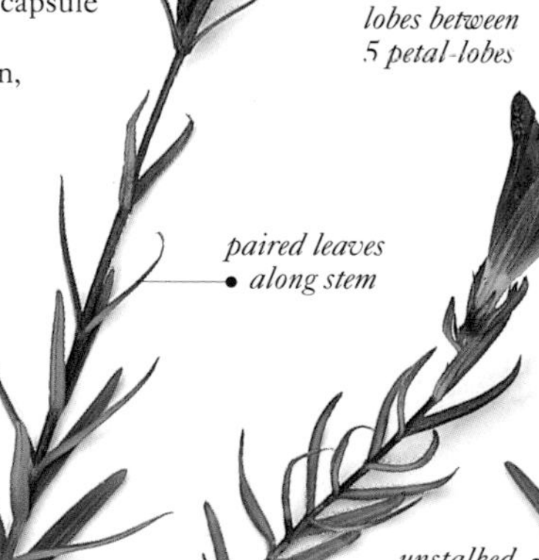

Habit Perennial	Height 20–50cm (8–20in)	Flowering time July–Oct

Family GENTIANACEAE	Species *Gentianella amarella*	Author (L.) Boerner

AUTUMN GENTIAN

This variable, hairless herb has thin, erect stems, branched in the upper part, if at all. The leaves are oval to lanceolate and untoothed; basal leaves are usually in a rosette. The blue, dull purple, pink, or whitish flowers are salver-shaped, 14–22mm ($\frac{4}{7}$–$\frac{7}{8}$in) long, and generally 5-lobed. The fruit capsule splits into 2 when ripe.

• **DISTRIBUTION** Mainly the western fringes of Europe, except Iceland and the far north.

• **HABITAT** Dry, grassy meadows and pastures, cliffs, and sand dunes; often on calcareous soils.

• **RELATED SPECIES** *Gentianella campestris*, Field Gentian, has a 4-lobed corolla; the calyx has 2 wide and 2 narrow lobes. It grows on neutral or acid soils.

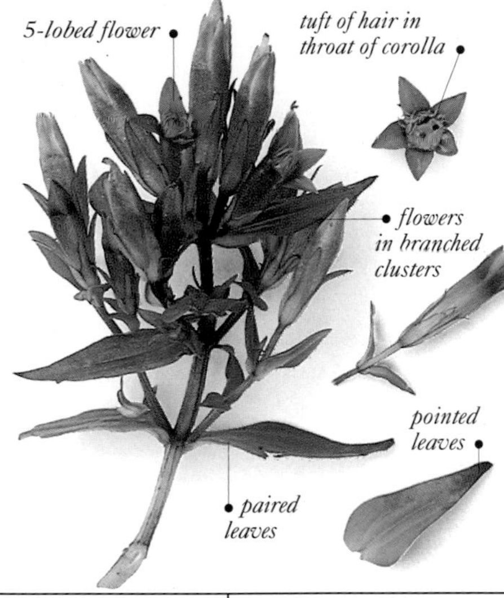

Habit Annual or biennial	Height 10–30cm (4–12in)	Flowering time June–Oct

Family GENTIANACEAE	Species *Blackstonia perfoliata*	Author (L.) Hudson

YELLOW-WORT

This greyish, hairless plant has slender, erect, leafy stems which are unbranched or branched towards the top. The paired leaves are variable; the basal ones are oval, borne in a loose rosette, and often withered by flowering time, whereas the stem-leaves are broader, often triangular, and fused together around the stem. The flowers, 8–15mm ($\frac{1}{3}$–$\frac{3}{5}$in) across, are salver-shaped; the corolla has 6 to 8 petal-lobes and a short tube; the calyx-lobes equal the petals in number. The fruit capsule is 2-parted, with many tiny seeds.

• **DISTRIBUTION** Britain and S. Ireland, Holland to S. Germany southwards.

• **HABITAT** Calcareous grassland, rocky places, and sand dunes, on the coast and inland.

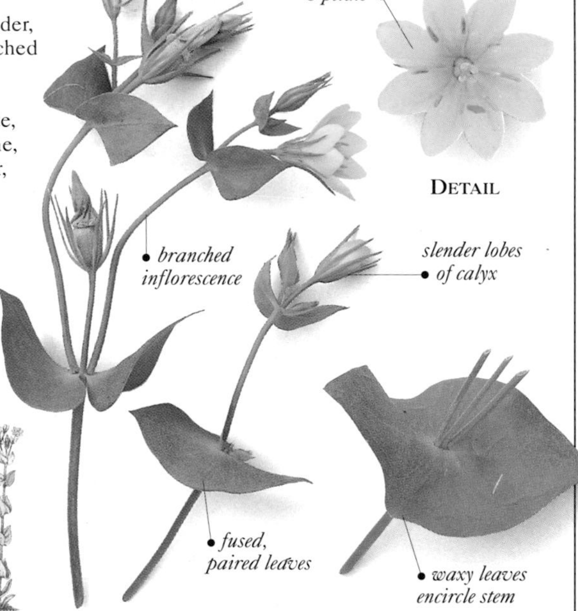

Habit Annual	Height 20–50cm (8–20in)	Flowering time June–Oct

BOGBEAN FAMILY

Family MENYANTHACEAE	Species *Menyanthes trifoliata*	Author L.

BOGBEAN

This is a vigorous, hairless, aquatic or semi-aquatic plant with long, thick, rather spongy, prostrate or floating stems that root at the nodes. The alternate leaves are trifoliate and rather pale green, with elliptical to oval or diamond-shaped, untoothed leaflets, and a long stalk. The whitish flowers are flushed with pink on the outside and are 14–16mm (4/7–5/8in) across, star-shaped, and borne in rather loose, erect racemes above the surface of the water; each flower has 5 sepals and 5 petals, the latter with a fringe of long white hairs. The fruit consists of an egg-shaped capsule which splits by 2 valves when ripe.
• **DISTRIBUTION** Throughout the region, except for parts of the far north; often rather local.
• **HABITAT** In water or on moist ground such as bogs, fens, marshes, pools, and lake margins; on lowland and in the mountains to 1,800m (5,900ft).

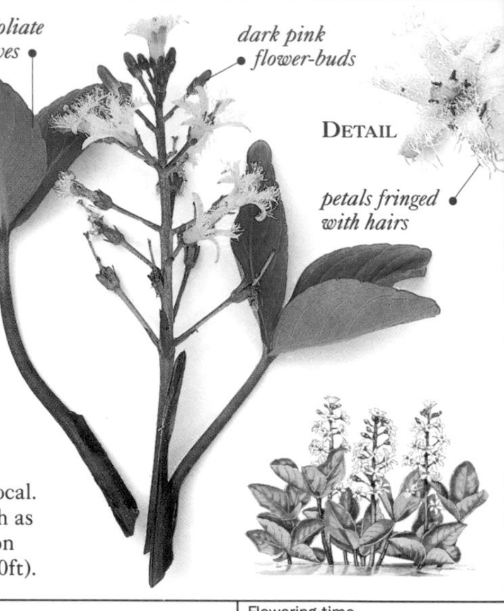

Habit Perennial	Height 10–35cm (4–14in)	Flowering time Apr–June

Family MENYANTHACEAE	Species *Nymphoides peltata*	Author Kuntze

FRINGED WATER-LILY

This aquatic, hairless plant has long, slender, spreading stems that float on or lie beneath the water surface. The alternate floating leaves are deep green and shiny, sometimes purple-blotched above but usually purplish beneath, rounded to kidney-shaped, split at the base to the long stalk, and have an untoothed margin. The solitary or clustered yellow flowers, 30–40mm (1⅕–1⅗in) across, are saucer-shaped, and are held just above the water surface; the 5 joined petals have a fringed margin (hence the plant's common name). The fruit consists of a small egg-shaped capsule containing several seeds.
• **DISTRIBUTION** Britain, Belgium, Holland, France, and Germany; naturalized in Scandinavia; in Britain, absent from N. Scotland. Generally rather local.
• **HABITAT** Ponds, lakes, lake margins, and ditches, in still and slow-moving fresh water.

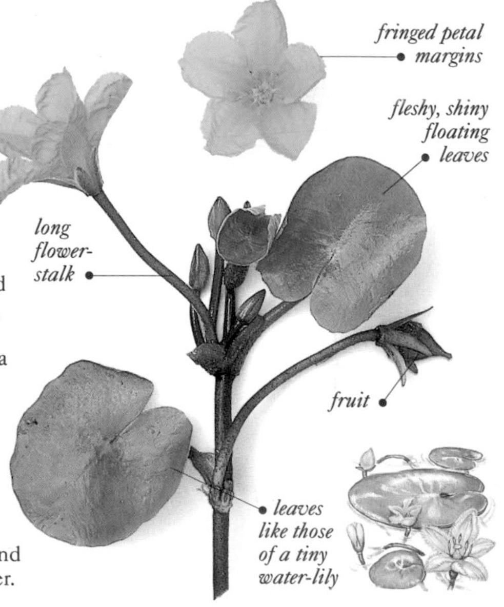

Habit Perennial	Height 5–10cm (2–4in)	Flowering time July–Sept

PERIWINKLE FAMILY

Family APOCYNACEAE	Species *Vinca major*	Author L.

GREATER PERIWINKLE

This vigorous evergreen has slender, arching, leafy stems which often root down at the tip. The paired, shiny, deep green, sometimes variegated, leaves have a short stalk and a hairy margin. The solitary flowers, 30–50mm (1⅕–2in) across, are borne on a slender stalk. The forked, 2-lobed fruit is rare.

- **DISTRIBUTION** Naturalized in Britain, Ireland, parts of France, and perhaps elsewhere in the region.
- **HABITAT** Open woodland, scrub, abandoned cultivation, hedgerows.
- **RELATED SPECIES** *Vinca minor*, Lesser Periwinkle, has hairless, oval to elliptical leaves, and smaller reddish purple to pink flowers. It grows as far north as Denmark.

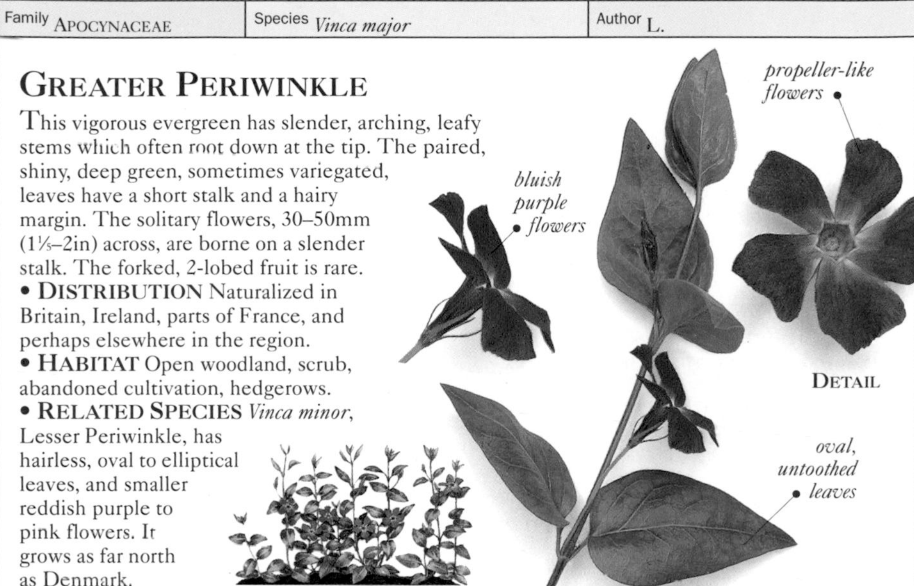

Habit Perennial	Stem length Up to 1.5m (5ft)	Flowering time Mar–May

SWALLOW-WORT FAMILY

Family ASCLEPIADACEAE	Species *Vincetoxicum hirundinaria*	Author Medicus

SWALLOW-WORT

This tufted, hairless or slightly hairy plant has erect, leafy stems. The lanceolate to heart-shaped leaves are untoothed and short-stalked. In loose clusters of 6 to 8 at the upper leaf-axils, the greenish yellow or greenish white flowers are 5–10mm (⅕–⅖in) across, each with 5 stamens. The paired or solitary, spindle-shaped fruit, 50–60mm (2–2⅖in) long, contains large seeds with a tuft of hair on one end. The plant is poisonous.

- **DISTRIBUTION** Mainland Europe north to S. Sweden.
- **HABITAT** Woodland, rocky places, hedgerows, scrub; usually on calcareous soils, to 1,800m (5,900ft).

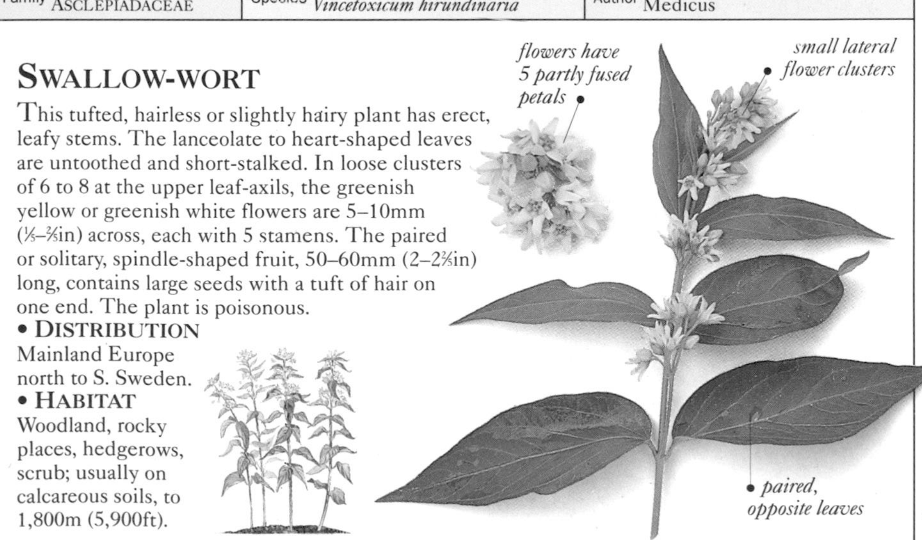

Habit Perennial	Height 40–80cm (16–32in)	Flowering time June–Sept

BEDSTRAW FAMILY

Family RUBIACEAE	Species *Sherardia arvensis*	Author L.

FIELD MADDER

This small bristly herb has slender, spreading to ascending, square stems which are much-branched from the base. The oval to lanceolate leaves are pointed and unstalked. The violet, pale purple, pink, or mauvish flowers, 3mm (⅛in) across, are borne in terminal clusters of up to 10; the corolla is salver-shaped, with a long, slender tube and 4 spreading lobes. The rounded fruit is 2-lobed, bristly, and surrounded by 4 to 6 enlarged sepal-teeth.

• **DISTRIBUTION** Throughout, except for the far north; generally local in the north of its range.

• **HABITAT** Cultivated land, especially arable; waste and bare ground, and thin grassy habitats.

Habit Annual	Height 5–40cm (2–16in)	Flowering time May–Sept

Family RUBIACEAE	Species *Asperula arvensis*	Author L.

BLUE WOODRUFF

This more or less hairless herb has thin, erect, branched stems. The lanceolate to almost linear leaves are one-veined and pointed. The blue or bluish purple flowers, 3–4mm (⅛–⅙in) across, are borne in dense terminal clusters surrounded by a ruff of narrow bracts; the corolla has a slender tube and 4 spreading lobes. The small, rounded, one- to 2-lobed fruit is smooth and brown when ripe.

• **DISTRIBUTION** France, Holland, and S. Germany; naturalized in scattered localities in Britain and Scandinavia.

• **HABITAT** Arable and thin grassy land, waste places, and rubbish tips.

Habit Annual	Height 20–50cm (8–20in)	Flowering time Apr–July

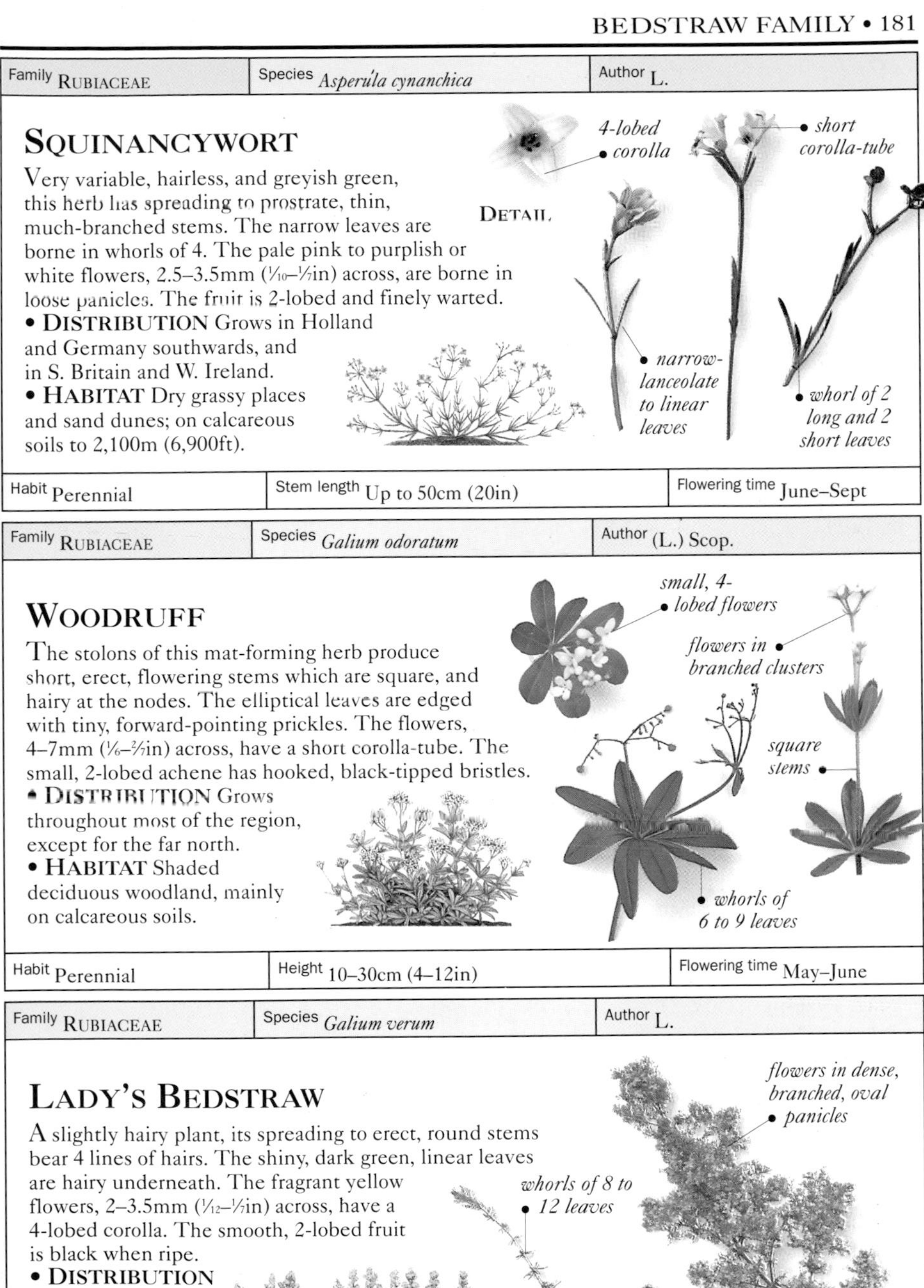

Family RUBIACEAE	Species *Asperula cynanchica*	Author L.

SQUINANCYWORT

Very variable, hairless, and greyish green, this herb has spreading to prostrate, thin, much-branched stems. The narrow leaves are borne in whorls of 4. The pale pink to purplish or white flowers, 2.5–3.5mm (1/10–1/7in) across, are borne in loose panicles. The fruit is 2-lobed and finely warted.

• **DISTRIBUTION** Grows in Holland and Germany southwards, and in S. Britain and W. Ireland.

• **HABITAT** Dry grassy places and sand dunes; on calcareous soils to 2,100m (6,900ft).

Habit Perennial	Stem length Up to 50cm (20in)	Flowering time June–Sept

Family RUBIACEAE	Species *Galium odoratum*	Author (L.) Scop.

WOODRUFF

The stolons of this mat-forming herb produce short, erect, flowering stems which are square, and hairy at the nodes. The elliptical leaves are edged with tiny, forward-pointing prickles. The flowers, 4–7mm (1/6–2/7in) across, have a short corolla-tube. The small, 2-lobed achene has hooked, black-tipped bristles.

• **DISTRIBUTION** Grows throughout most of the region, except for the far north.

• **HABITAT** Shaded deciduous woodland, mainly on calcareous soils.

Habit Perennial	Height 10–30cm (4–12in)	Flowering time May–June

Family RUBIACEAE	Species *Galium verum*	Author L.

LADY'S BEDSTRAW

A slightly hairy plant, its spreading to erect, round stems bear 4 lines of hairs. The shiny, dark green, linear leaves are hairy underneath. The fragrant yellow flowers, 2–3.5mm (1/12–1/7in) across, have a 4-lobed corolla. The smooth, 2-lobed fruit is black when ripe.

• **DISTRIBUTION** Throughout, except for the far north.

• **HABITAT** Dry grassland, roadsides, banks, sand dunes.

Habit Perennial	Height 20–80cm (8–32in)	Flowering time June–Sept

Family RUBIACEAE	Species *Galium mollugo*	Author L.

HEDGE BEDSTRAW

Vigorous and usually hairless, this plant has long, smooth, square stems arising from a reddish stock and underground stolons. The pale green, oblong to elliptical leaves are borne in whorls of 6 to 8 and have a sharply pointed apex. The small white flowers, 2–3mm (1/12–1/8in) across, are borne in loose, branched panicles. The 2-lobed, smooth or wrinkled fruit is black when ripe.

• **DISTRIBUTION** Throughout the region, except for the far north and much of Scandinavia; often local.

• **HABITAT** Open woodland, scrub, hedgerows, meadows, and other grassy places.

• **RELATED SPECIES** *Galium sylvaticum*, Wood Bedstraw, is rather greyish green, with rounded stems, and flowers nodding in bud. The fruit is bluish green. It inhabits woodland and scrub from Holland to Germany southwards.

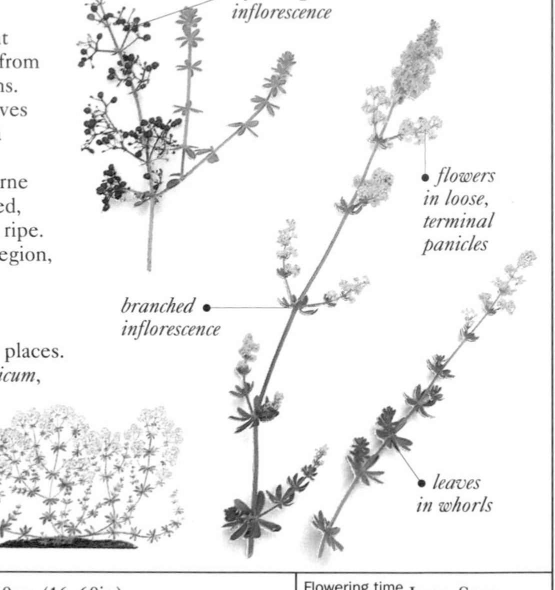

Habit Perennial	Height 40–150cm (16–60in)	Flowering time June–Sept

Family RUBIACEAE	Species *Galium aparine*	Author L.

CLEAVERS

Also called Goosegrass, this vigorous, often scrambling, yet brittle plant has square, branched stems. The stems and leaf margins are adorned with backward-pointing prickles. Borne in whorls of 6 to 9, the narrow-elliptical leaves are broadest above the middle and sharply pointed. The tiny, dull white flowers, less than 2mm (1/12in) across, are borne in small clusters at the base of the upper leaves. The green fruit is covered in dense, hooked bristles which attach them to soft materials like animal fur and human clothing.

• **DISTRIBUTION** Throughout the region, except for the far north.

• **HABITAT** Cultivated, waste, and disturbed land, open woodland, scrub, hedgerows, and coastal shingles.

• **RELATED SPECIES** *Galium spurium*, False Cleavers, has greenish yellow flowers. The fruit is black when ripe. It has a similar distribution to Cleavers but is mostly casual in Britain and Ireland.

Habit Annual	Height 50–300cm (1⅔–10ft)	Flowering time May–Sept

Family RUBIACEAE	Species *Cruciata laevipes*	Author Opiz

CROSSWORT

This tufted or clump-forming plant is softly hairy, with a creeping rootstock. The erect to ascending stems are usually branched near the base. The leaves are elliptical to oval, with 3 main veins. The pale yellow flowers are honey-scented; the corolla is 4-lobed, with a short tube and 4 stamens. The fruit consists of one or 2 smooth rounded nutlets on short recurved stalks and is black when ripe.

• **DISTRIBUTION** Throughout the region, except for the far north, Ireland, and N. Scotland.

• **HABITAT** Grassy places, meadows and pastures, road verges, hedgerows, and scrub; usually on calcareous soils.

• **RELATED SPECIES** *Cruciata glabra* is a hairless plant except for the young leaves. It grows in Holland to Germany southwards.

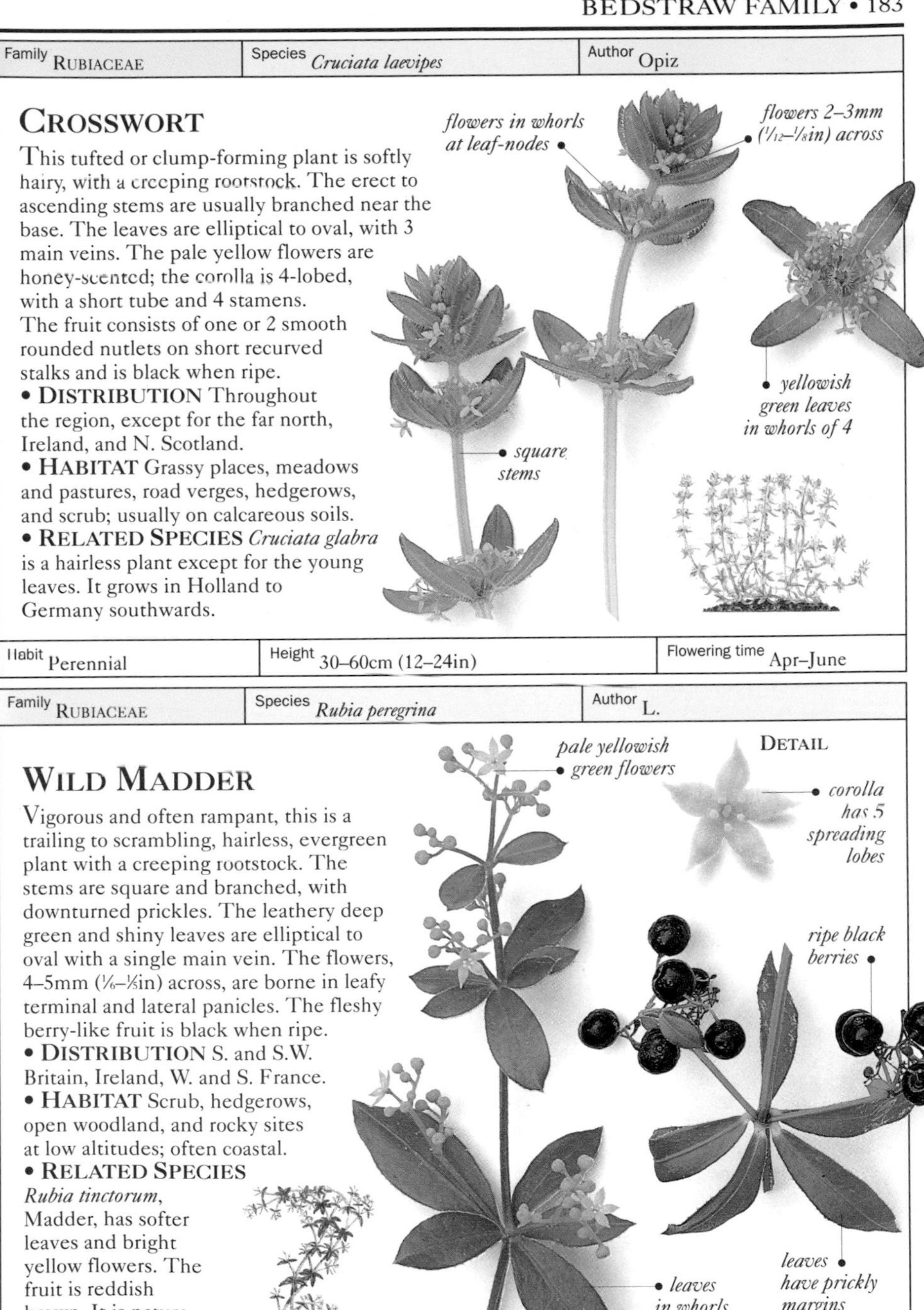

Habit Perennial	Height 30–60cm (12–24in)	Flowering time Apr–June

Family RUBIACEAE	Species *Rubia peregrina*	Author L.

WILD MADDER

Vigorous and often rampant, this is a trailing to scrambling, hairless, evergreen plant with a creeping rootstock. The stems are square and branched, with downturned prickles. The leathery deep green and shiny leaves are elliptical to oval with a single main vein. The flowers, 4–5mm (1/6–1/5in) across, are borne in leafy terminal and lateral panicles. The fleshy berry-like fruit is black when ripe.

• **DISTRIBUTION** S. and S.W. Britain, Ireland, W. and S. France.

• **HABITAT** Scrub, hedgerows, open woodland, and rocky sites at low altitudes; often coastal.

• **RELATED SPECIES** *Rubia tinctorum*, Madder, has softer leaves and bright yellow flowers. The fruit is reddish brown. It is naturalized in France and Germany.

Habit Perennial	Height 50–150cm (20–60in)	Flowering time June–Aug

JACOB'S LADDER FAMILY

Family POLEMONIACEAE	Species *Polemonium caeruleum*	Author L.

JACOB'S LADDER

The stems of this tufted, somewhat hairy plant are erect, angled, and usually branched towards the top. The alternate leaves are pinnate, with up to 12 pairs of leaflets. Borne in dense terminal clusters, the blue, rarely white, flowers, 20–30mm (⅘–1⅕in) across, have 5 sepals and 5 petals. The fruit is a small, many-seeded capsule.
• **DISTRIBUTION** N. England and mainland Europe except for the far north, but probably only naturalized in Belgium, Holland, and Denmark.
• **HABITAT** Damp meadows and rocks to 2,300m (7,550ft); often on limestone. Widely grown in gardens.
• **RELATED SPECIES** *Polemonium acutifolium* has less than 9 pairs of leaflets per leaf; the petals are more pointed. It grows in Arctic Europe.

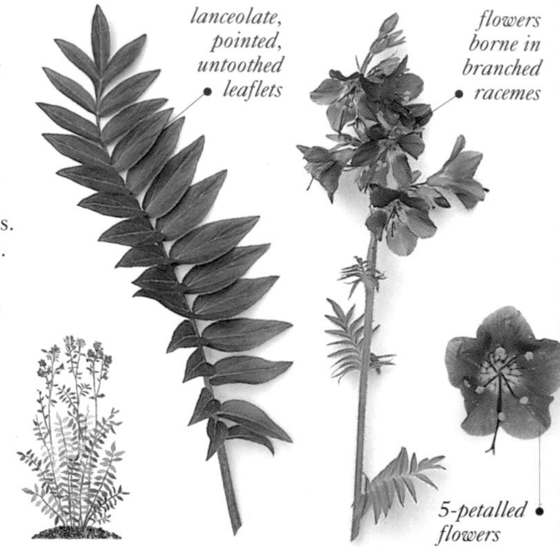

Habit Perennial	Height 50–100cm (20–40in)	Flowering time May–Aug

BINDWEED FAMILY

Family CONVOLVULACEAE	Species *Cuscuta epithymum*	Author (L.) L.

COMMON DODDER

This parasitic plant has no green leaves and forms a tangled mass of reddish or purplish thread-like stems. The leaves are reduced to tiny scattered scales along the stems. The small flowers, 3–4mm (⅛–⅙in) across, are pale pink and scented, with protruding stamens. The fruit is a small capsule that splits transversely.
• **DISTRIBUTION** Throughout, except for the far north of the region.
• **HABITAT** Parasitic on various hosts, particularly *Ulex europaeus*, Gorse, *Calluna vulgaris*, Heather (see p.166), and various clovers.
• **RELATED SPECIES** *Cuscuta europaea*, Greater Dodder, is stouter, with flowers often 4-parted; the styles are shorter than the ovary. Its distribution is similar, but it parasitizes nettles and hops.

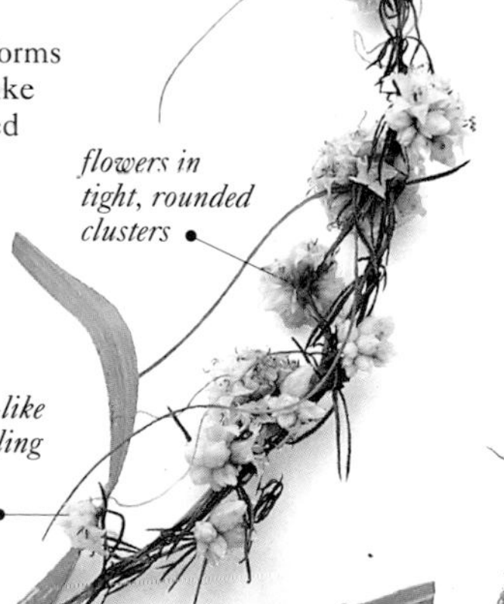

DETAIL

Habit Annual	Stem length Up to 60cm (24in)	Flowering time June–Oct

Family CONVOLVULACEAE	Species *Calystegia soldanella*	Author (L.) R. Br.

SEA BINDWEED

This trailing and crawling, hairless plant has stems that sometimes twine rather weakly, and spreads by means of branched underground stolons. The alternate leaves are kidney-shaped, long-stalked, and untoothed. The large solitary flowers, 30–50mm (1⅕–2in) across, are pinkish or purplish, often with white stripes; the petals are fused together into a funnel shape; the calyx consists of 5 lobes and is enclosed by 2 large and overlapping, pouched, sepal-like bracts that are slightly shorter than the sepals. The fruit is a many-seeded capsule.

• **DISTRIBUTION** Coasts of Europe as far north as Denmark; often rare or local. In Britain, absent from N. Scotland and mostly decreasing, but protected.

• **HABITAT** Coastal sands and shingle, stabilized sand dunes; rarely among rocks.

• *young leaf*

• *whitish stripes on petals*

reddish green stems •

• *funnel-shaped corolla*

• *alternate leaves*

fleshy leaves •

• *sepal-like bracts*

Habit Perennial	Stem length Up to 1m (3¼ft)	Flowering time June–Aug

Family CONVOLVULACEAE	Species *Calystegia silvatica*	Author (Kit. ex Schrader) Griseb.

GREAT BINDWEED

This is a vigorous, stoloniferous, hairless plant, with twining and climbing stems. The alternate leaves are rather thin, bright green, arrow-shaped, stalked, and untoothed. The large, funnel-shaped flowers, 50–90mm (2–3⅗in) across, are solitary and white, although occasionally striped with pale pink; the calyx consists of 5 sepals surrounded by 2 large, somewhat overlapping, pouched bracts. The fruit is a many-seeded capsule.

• **DISTRIBUTION** Naturalized in Britain, Ireland, and parts of W. Europe. Native to S. and S.E. Europe.

• **HABITAT** Cultivated land and waste land, hedgerows, and around old buildings.

slender, twining stems

large bracts conceal sepals

yellow centre of flower

pointed leaves

Habit Perennial	Height Up to 3m (10ft)	Flowering time July–Sept

Family CONVOLVULACEAE	Species *Convolvulus arvensis*	Author L.

BINDWEED

This is a hairy or hairless, twining or scrambling plant, with slender stems. The arrow-shaped to oblong, alternate leaves are stalked, untoothed, and usually plain green. The solitary flowers, 10–25mm (⅖–1in) across, are plain white or pink, or pink striped with white, and are funnel-shaped and weakly scented; the calyx is 5-lobed and is not enclosed within the bracts. The 2 tiny bracts are located halfway along the slender flower-stalks. The flowers, like those of all bindweeds, are short-lived and only open during the day, also closing in dull weather. The fruit is a rounded, many-seeded capsule.

• **DISTRIBUTION** Throughout the region, except for the far north; mostly on lowland.

• **HABITAT** A widespread weed of cultivated and waste land, grassy and rocky places, hedgerows, and coastal rocks and shingle; to 1,850m (6,050ft).

Habit Perennial	Height Up to 1.5m (5ft)	Flowering time June–Sept

BORAGE FAMILY

Family BORAGINACEAE	Species *Lithospermum officinale*	Author L.

COMMON GROMWELL

This tufted, somewhat rhizomatous, hairy plant has erect flowering stems branched in the upper half. The alternate leaves are oval to lanceolate and untoothed; only the lower are stalked. The flowers are yellowish, creamish, or greenish white, 3–6mm (⅛–¼in) long, and in small, spiralled clusters; the 5 petals are rounded and fused below into a short tube. The fruit consists of 4 shiny white nutlets located at the bottom of the persistent calyx.

• **DISTRIBUTION** Throughout, except the far north; rare in N. Britain.

• **HABITAT** Scrub, hedgerows, woodland margins; on limy soils.

• **RELATED SPECIES** *Lithospermum arvense* (syn. *Buglossoides arvensis*) Corn or Field Gromwell, is an annual with indistinct lateral leaf-veins and brown nutlets.

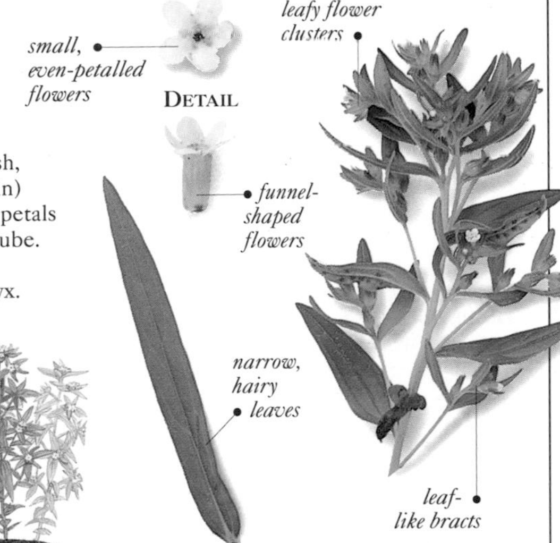

Habit Perennial	Height 40–80cm (16–32in)	Flowering time May–Aug

Family BORAGINACEAE	Species *Lithospermum purpurocaeruleum*	Author L.

PURPLE GROMWELL

Also known as *Buglossoides purpurocaerulea*, this tufted, hairy, rhizomatous plant has spreading to prostrate, leafy, sterile shoots and erect, generally unbranched, flowering stems. The leaves are alternate, lanceolate to elliptical, and pointed; the upper leaves are unstalked. In leafy clusters that elongate as the fruit develops, the salver-shaped flowers, 14–19mm (4/7–¾in) long, open reddish purple but change to bright blue; the 5 elliptical petals are fused into a long slender tube. The fruit consists of 4, rarely 2, nutlets, located at the base of the persistent calyx.

• **DISTRIBUTION** S. Britain, Belgium, and C. Germany southwards; rare further north.

• **HABITAT** Woodland margins and scrub; mainly on calcareous soils.

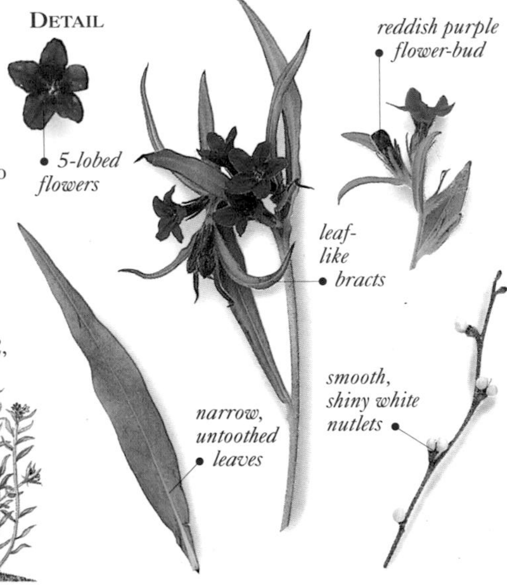

Habit Perennial	Height 40–60cm (16–24in)	Flowering time Apr–June

Family BORAGINACEAE	Species *Echium vulgare*	Author L.

VIPER'S BUGLOSS

This bristly-haired plant has a solitary stem or several stems and forms a leafy rosette in the first year or two. The leaves are lanceolate to elliptical and untoothed; the lower are stalked, but the upper are unstalked and smaller. The flowers are bright blue, violet-blue, or purple, 15–20mm (⅗–⅘in) long, and borne in coiled cymes that make up a large terminal panicle; the corolla is hairy, with a tube and 5 spreading lobes. The fruit consists of 4 nutlets hidden at the base of the persistent calyx.

• **DISTRIBUTION** Throughout, except for the far north.

• **HABITAT** Dry open places, grassy banks, road verges, cliffs, shingle, and dunes.

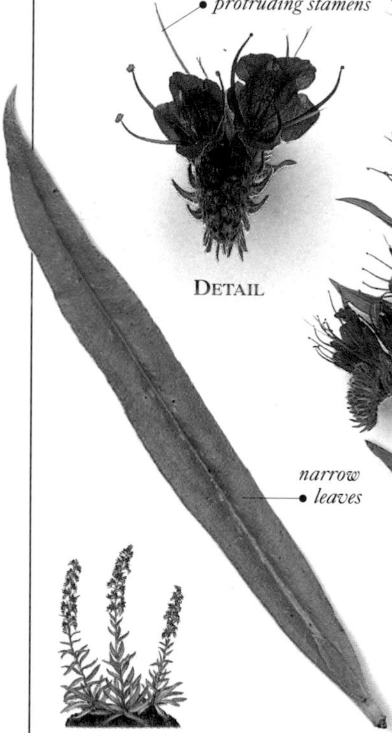

Habit Biennial usually	Height 50–100cm (20–40in)	Flowering time June–Sept

Family BORAGINACEAE	Species *Cerinthe glabra*	Author Miller

SMOOTH HONEYWORT

This somewhat fleshy, hairless plant has slender, generally branched, stems. The leaves are alternate and untoothed; the lower leaves are oblong and stalked, while the upper are heart-shaped, with unstalked bases. The flowers are yellow tubular-bells, 8–13mm (⅓–½in) long, generally with 5 red spots in the throat and with 5 short recurved lobes. The fruit consists of 4 nutlets on downcurved stalks.

• **DISTRIBUTION** C. France and S. Germany southwards, but casual further north.

• **HABITAT** Meadows, woodland, and damp, often shaded, sites; usually on calcareous soils.

• **RELATED SPECIES** *Cerinthe minor*, Lesser Honeywort, has white-spotted leaves, and pointed, non-recurved corolla-lobes. Its distribution is similar, but it is less common generally.

tubular flower

4 nutlets

loosely coiled, leafy flower clusters

upper leaves clasp stem

leaves alternate along stem

Habit Biennial or perennial	Height 25–50cm (10–20in)	Flowering time May–July

Family BORAGINACEAE	Species *Pulmonaria officinalis*	Author L.

COMMON LUNGWORT

This is a rough-haired, clump-forming and spreading plant. The leaves are untoothed and green, with pronounced white blotches. The basal leaves are heart-shaped, with a long stalk, while the upper leaves are smaller, somewhat narrower, and unstalked. Borne in small terminal clusters, the flowers, 13–18mm (½–⅝in) long, are pink in bud but open reddish violet or bluish violet; the corolla has 5 rounded lobes and a slender tube. The fruit consists of 4 small nutlets hidden at the base of the persistent calyx.

• **DISTRIBUTION** Native in mainland Europe as far north as S. Sweden; naturalized in scattered locations in Britain. Widely cultivated in gardens.

• **HABITAT** Woodland, scrub, hedgebanks, and other damp, shady sites; on humus-rich soils.

Habit Perennial	Height 18–30cm (7–12in)	Flowering time Mar–May

Family BORAGINACEAE	Species *Symphytum officinale*	Author L.

COMMON COMFREY

This variable, robust, clump-forming plant has erect, partly winged stems. All the leaves are rough with hairs; the basal ones are large, coarse, oval to lanceolate, and stalked, the upper oval and half-clasping the stem with unstalked bases. The flowers, 12–18mm (1/2–5/7in) long, are purplish violet to pink, or whitish; the corolla has 5 short, recurved lobes and a protruding style. The nutlets are shiny.

• **DISTRIBUTION** Throughout, except for the far north, but naturalized in Ireland and in much of the north of its range.

• **HABITAT** Damp meadows, marshes, fens, ditches, roadsides, river and stream margins.

• **RELATED SPECIES** *Symphytum* x *uplandicum*, Russian Comfrey, has narrowly winged stems and blue or violet flowers that are pink in bud. The nutlets are dull.

flowers may be pink

flowers in coiled cymes

funnel-shaped flowers

untoothed leaf margin

leaf base forms wing along stem

Habit Perennial	Height 80–150cm (32–60in)	Flowering time May–July

Family BORAGINACEAE	Species *Symphytum orientale*	Author L.

WHITE COMFREY

This softly hairy plant has erect, branched, unwinged stems and forms a large leafy rosette in the first year. The leaves are a pale green; the lower leaves are oval to heart-shaped and stalked; the upper ones are narrower, mostly unstalked, and half-clasp the stem. The white corolla has 5 straight, short lobes and a protruding style. The fruit consists of 4 dull, granular nutlets.

• **DISTRIBUTION** Locally naturalized in Britain and Scotland.

• **HABITAT** Shady places, hedgerows, open woodland, abandoned cultivation, and occasionally on damp meadows.

• **RELATED SPECIES** *Symphytum tuberosum*, Tuberous Comfrey, is perennial with ellip tical to lanceolate leaves and pale yellow flowers. It is native in Britain, France, and Germany.

Habit Biennial or perennial	Height 40–70cm (16–28in)	Flowering time Apr–May

Family BORAGINACEAE	Species *Anchusa arvensis*	Author (L.) M. Bieb.

BUGLOSS

Also known as *Lycopsis arvensis*, this bristly plant has ascending to erect stems. The rough, alternate leaves are lanceolate to narrow-elliptical, with undulating and toothed margins; the lower leaves are stalked, but the upper are unstalked and clasp the stem with heart-shaped bases. The bright blue, occasionally whitish, flowers are salver-shaped, 4–6mm (1/6–1/4in) across, and borne in forked, leafy, spiralled clusters; the corolla has 5 rounded lobes fused together into a tube that is clearly curved in the middle. The fruit consists of 4 netted nutlets hidden at the base of the calyx, which enlarges as the fruit develops.

• **DISTRIBUTION** Throughout, except for the far north; locally common.

• **HABITAT** Cultivated, waste, and bare land, and heaths; often growing close to the sea and at low altitudes; on acid and calcareous soils.

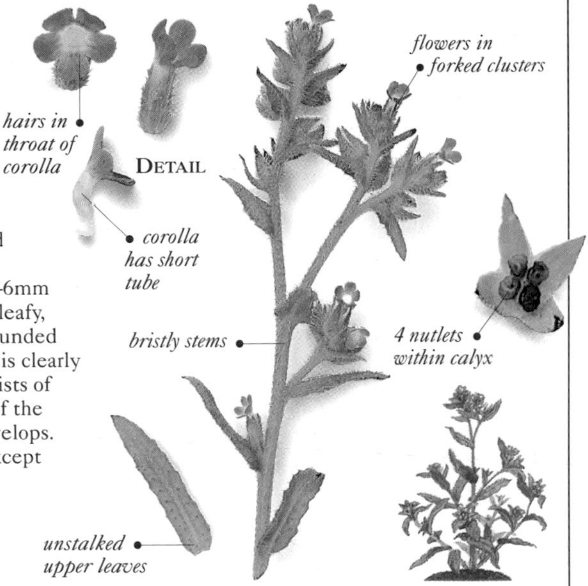

hairs in throat of corolla

DETAIL

corolla has short tube

flowers in forked clusters

bristly stems

4 nutlets within calyx

unstalked upper leaves

Habit Annual	Height 20–70cm (8–28in)	Flowering time Apr–Sept

Family BORAGINACEAE	Species *Anchusa officinalis*	Author L.

ALKANET

This bristly plant has unbranched, erect stems. The leaves are lanceolate and 10–20mm (2/5–4/5in) wide at the most; only the lower leaves are stalked. The salver-shaped flowers, 7–15mm (2/7–3/5in) across, are violet, bluish red, or occasionally cream or white, and are borne in branched, spiralled clusters that elongate in fruit; the calyx is split for only half its length. The fruit consists of 4 conical nutlets which are hidden at the base of the persistent calyx.

• **DISTRIBUTION** Throughout mainland Europe as far north as S. Scandinavia; naturalized or casual in parts of Britain.

• **HABITAT** Meadows, other grassy sites, waste places; often on calcareous soils.

• **RELATED SPECIES** *Anchusa azurea*, Garden Anchusa, has larger violet or deep blue flowers with the calyx divided to the base.

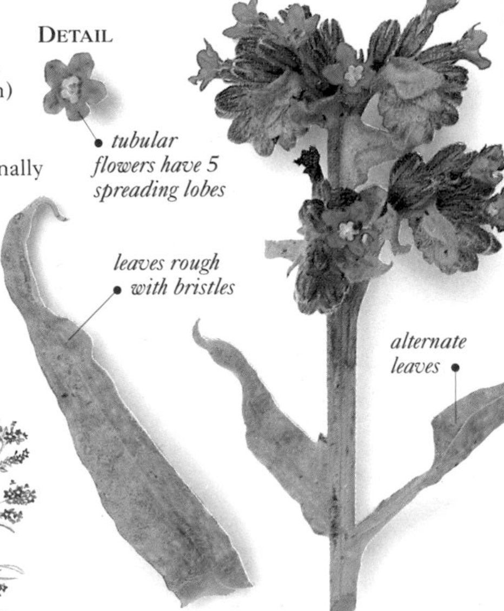

Habit Perennial	Height 80–150cm (32–60in)	Flowering time May–Sept

Family BORAGINACEAE	Species *Pentaglottis sempervirens*	Author (L.) Tausch ex L. Bailey

GREEN ALKANET

Also known as *Anchusa sempervirens*, this bristly plant has erect, branched, leafy stems. The leaves are lanceolate to oval and rather abruptly narrowed at the base, with a wavy margin; the upper leaves are unstalked, while the lower are stalked and initially form a rosette. Borne in branched, leafy clusters, the flowers are bright blue, 8–10mm (⅓–⅖in) across, with a white scaly throat; the corolla has spreading, rounded lobes and a short straight tube. The fruit consists of 4 ridged nutlets hidden at the base of the persistent calyx.

• **DISTRIBUTION** Native in France; naturalized in Britain and Belgium.

• **HABITAT** Grassy and waste places, rough ground, woodland, hedgerows, and abandoned cultivation; often close to habitation.

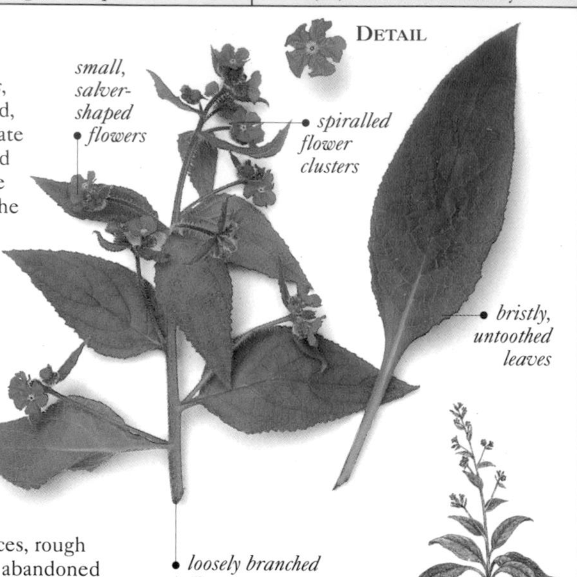

Habit Perennial	Height 50–100cm (20–40in)	Flowering time Apr–July

Family BORAGINACEAE	Species *Borago officinalis*	Author L.

BORAGE

A rough-bristly plant, this herb has a thick, erect, branched stem. Initially in a rosette, the basal leaves are oval to oblong, untoothed, narrowed below into a stalk, with a wavy margin; the upper leaves are smaller and unstalked. The bright blue, rarely white, flowers, 20–25mm (⅘–1in) across, are half-nodding and are borne in branched, slightly coiled clusters; the stamens are purple-black. The fruit consists of 4 nutlets located at the base of the persistent calyx.

• **DISTRIBUTION** C. and S. France; naturalized in Britain, Holland, and N. France, casual elsewhere.

• **HABITAT** Arable, waste, and disturbed land, abandoned cultivation; dry, sunny places.

Habit Annual	Height 30–60cm (12–24in)	Flowering time May–Sept

Family BORAGINACEAE	Species *Myosotis arvensis*	Author (L.) Hill

FIELD FORGET-ME-NOT

This variable, greyish green plant, is tufted and softly hairy. The stems are slender and branched in the upper half. The leaves are elliptical and generally broadest above the middle; the basal leaves are borne in a lax rosette, while the stem-leaves are alternate, the lower ones blunt, the upper more pointed. The pale grey-blue flowers, 3–4mm (1/8–1/6in) across, are borne in branched, coiled clusters that elongate as the fruit begins to develop. The fruit consists of 4 dark brown nutlets hidden at the base of the persistent calyx.

• **DISTRIBUTION** Throughout the region, except for Spitsbergen.

• **HABITAT** Dry open places, fields, cultivated land, coastal habitats, especially sand dunes; to 2,000m (6,550ft).

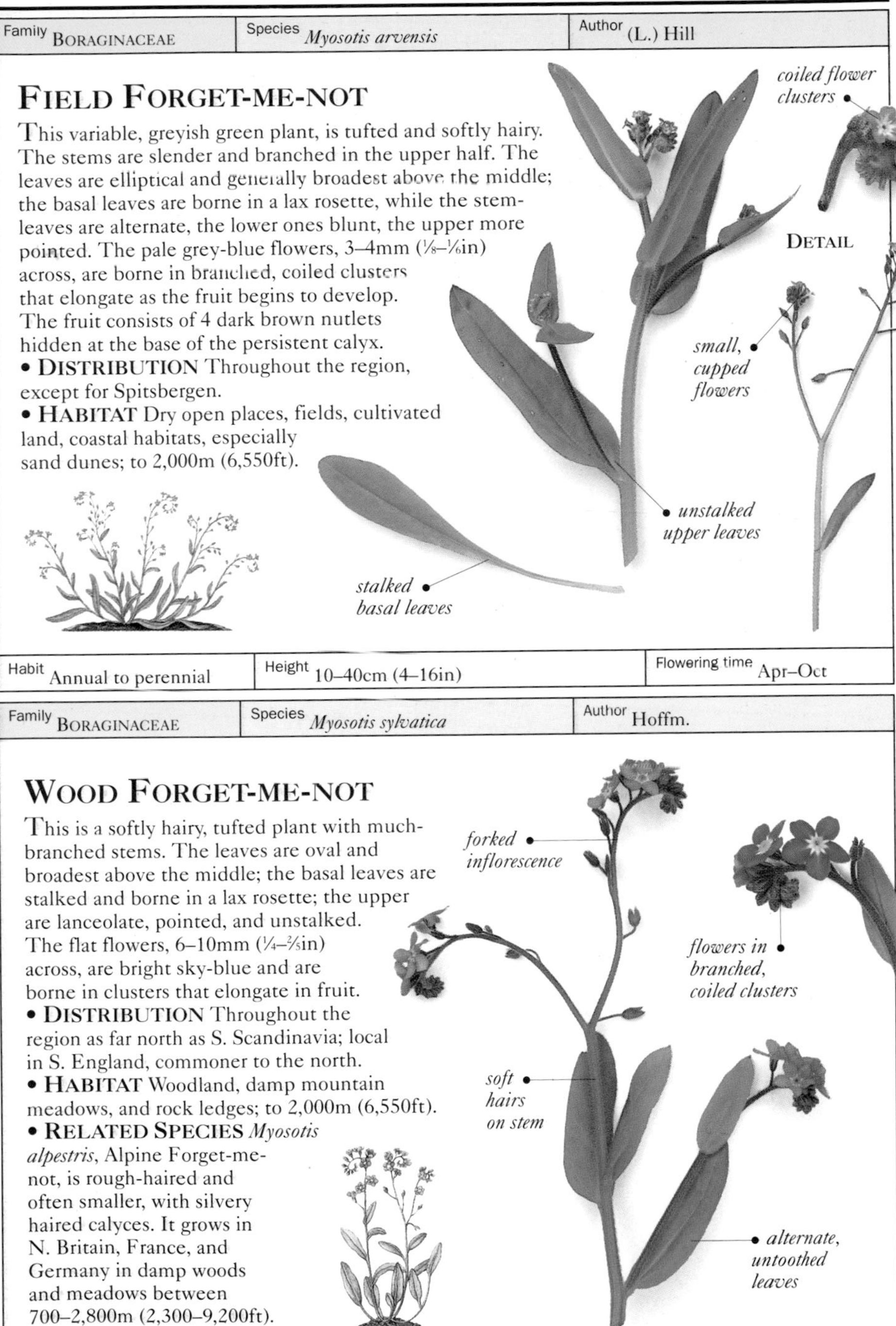

Habit Annual to perennial	Height 10–40cm (4–16in)	Flowering time Apr–Oct

Family BORAGINACEAE	Species *Myosotis sylvatica*	Author Hoffm.

WOOD FORGET-ME-NOT

This is a softly hairy, tufted plant with much-branched stems. The leaves are oval and broadest above the middle; the basal leaves are stalked and borne in a lax rosette; the upper are lanceolate, pointed, and unstalked. The flat flowers, 6–10mm (1/4–2/5in) across, are bright sky-blue and are borne in clusters that elongate in fruit.

• **DISTRIBUTION** Throughout the region as far north as S. Scandinavia; local in S. England, commoner to the north.

• **HABITAT** Woodland, damp mountain meadows, and rock ledges; to 2,000m (6,550ft).

• **RELATED SPECIES** *Myosotis alpestris*, Alpine Forget-me-not, is rough-haired and often smaller, with silvery haired calyces. It grows in N. Britain, France, and Germany in damp woods and meadows between 700–2,800m (2,300–9,200ft).

Habit Perennial	Height 30–50cm (12–20in)	Flowering time Apr–July

Family BORAGINACEAE	Species *Myosotis scorpioides*	Author L.

WATER FORGET-ME-NOT

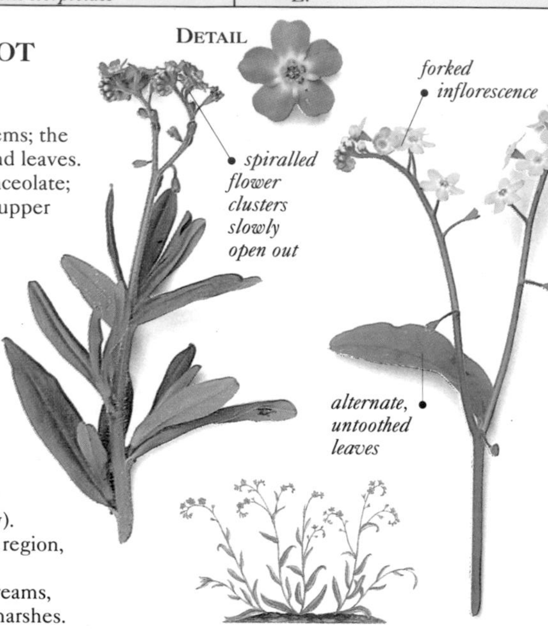

This spreading plant has numerous branching and rooting rhizomes and ascending, usually hairy, flowering stems; the hairs are pressed close to the stems and leaves. The alternate leaves are oblong to lanceolate; the lower ones are stalked, while the upper are unstalked. Borne in loosely coiled clusters, the salver-shaped flowers, 4–10mm (⅙–⅖in) across, are usually sky-blue but may occasionally be pink or white; the corolla has 5 spreading, rounded lobes which make a rather flat limb and unite into a short tube; the calyx-tube has short triangular teeth which are up to one-third its length. The fruit consists of 4 black nutlets hidden at the base of the persistent calyx (a x10 hand lens is needed to see this clearly).
• **DISTRIBUTION** Throughout the region, except for Spitsbergen.
• **HABITAT** Wet places by rivers, streams, and lakes, ditches, damp fields, and marshes.

Habit Perennial	Height 30–60cm (12–24in)	Flowering time May–Sept

Family BORAGINACEAE	Species *Lappula squarrosa*	Author (Retz.) Dumort.

BUR FORGET-ME-NOT

This rough-haired, greyish plant has erect, generally branched stems; the hairs are pressed close to the stems and leaves. The leaves are narrow-lanceolate to elliptical, untoothed, and short-stalked to unstalked. The pale blue flowers, 2–4mm (1/12–⅙in) across, are borne in leafy, branched clusters; the corolla has 5 short, rounded lobes which form a slightly cupped limb and unite into a short tube. The fruit consists of 4 small, barbed nutlets hidden at the base of the persistent calyx.
• **DISTRIBUTION** France and S. Sweden; widely naturalized or casual over much of the region. Often introduced in wool or grains.
• **HABITAT** Dry places, cultivated, waste, and disturbed land, coastal habitats, and rubbish tips.

Habit Annual or biennial	Height 30–50cm (12–20in)	Flowering time June–Aug

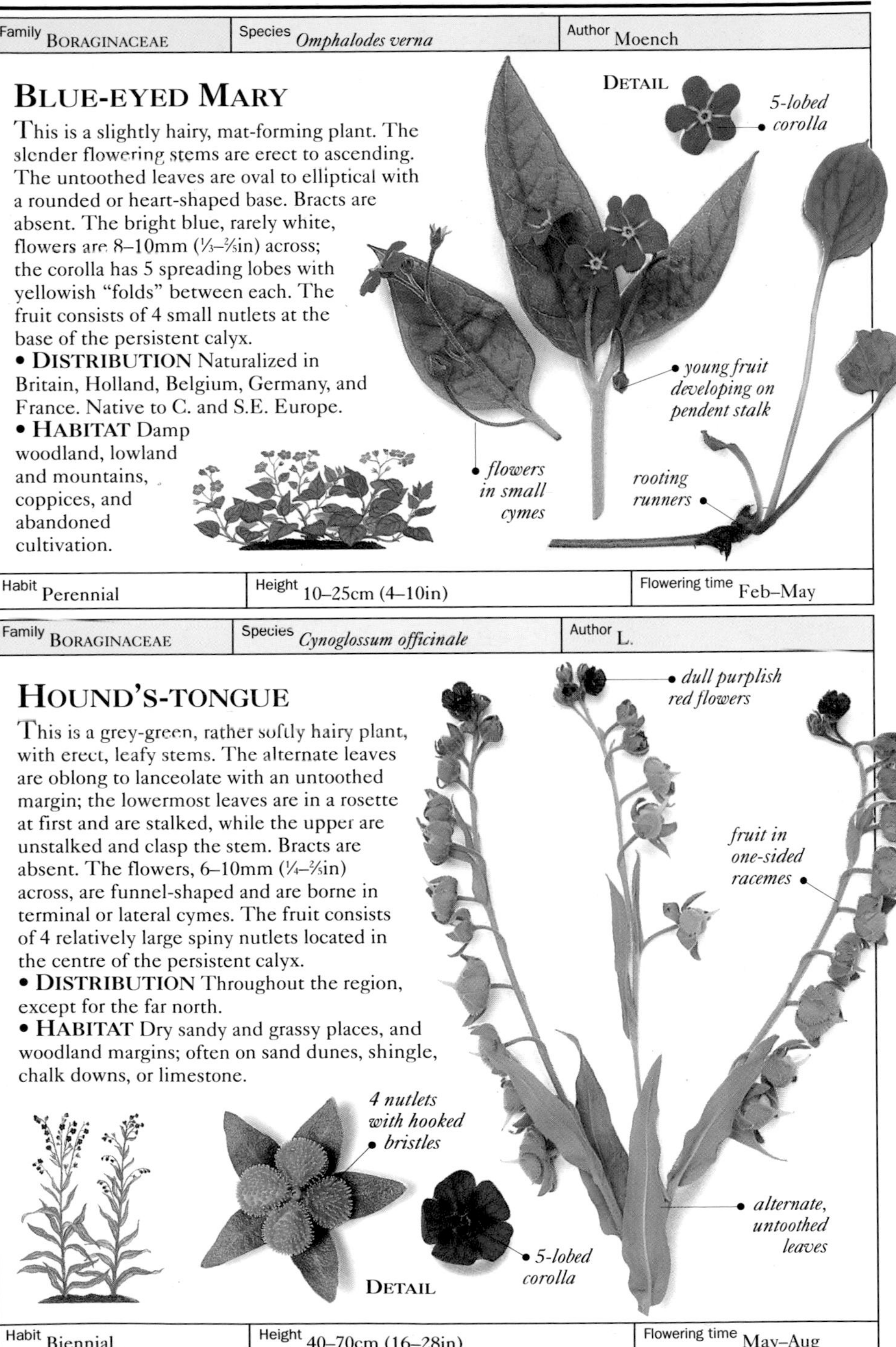

Family BORAGINACEAE | Species *Omphalodes verna* | Author Moench

BLUE-EYED MARY

This is a slightly hairy, mat-forming plant. The slender flowering stems are erect to ascending. The untoothed leaves are oval to elliptical with a rounded or heart-shaped base. Bracts are absent. The bright blue, rarely white, flowers are 8–10mm (⅓–⅔in) across; the corolla has 5 spreading lobes with yellowish "folds" between each. The fruit consists of 4 small nutlets at the base of the persistent calyx.

• **DISTRIBUTION** Naturalized in Britain, Holland, Belgium, Germany, and France. Native to C. and S.E. Europe.

• **HABITAT** Damp woodland, lowland and mountains, coppices, and abandoned cultivation.

Habit Perennial | Height 10–25cm (4–10in) | Flowering time Feb–May

Family BORAGINACEAE | Species *Cynoglossum officinale* | Author L.

HOUND'S-TONGUE

This is a grey-green, rather softly hairy plant, with erect, leafy stems. The alternate leaves are oblong to lanceolate with an untoothed margin; the lowermost leaves are in a rosette at first and are stalked, while the upper are unstalked and clasp the stem. Bracts are absent. The flowers, 6–10mm (¼–⅔in) across, are funnel-shaped and are borne in terminal or lateral cymes. The fruit consists of 4 relatively large spiny nutlets located in the centre of the persistent calyx.

• **DISTRIBUTION** Throughout the region, except for the far north.

• **HABITAT** Dry sandy and grassy places, and woodland margins; often on sand dunes, shingle, chalk downs, or limestone.

Habit Biennial | Height 40–70cm (16–28in) | Flowering time May–Aug

Vervain Family

Family Verbenaceae	Species *Verbena officinalis*	Author L.

Vervain

This erect, rough-haired plant has stiff, branched, square stems. The paired leaves are deep green; the lower are deeply lobed or toothed, and often pinnately lobed; the upper are smaller and lobed or unlobed. Small clusters of pale pink flowers elongate into slender, branched spikes as the fruit develops; the corolla is weakly 2-lipped, with 5 shallowly notched lobes.

• **Distribution** Grows throughout, except for most of Scotland, Scandinavia, the Faeroes, and Iceland.

• **Habitat** Rocky, bare, and waste ground, rough grassy places, and roadsides; mainly on well-drained soils.

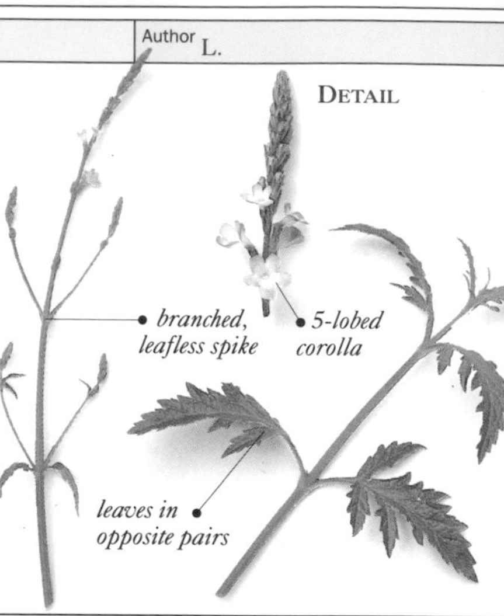

Habit Perennial	Height 50–75cm (20–30in)	Flowering time June–Oct

Mint Family

Family Labiatae	Species *Ajuga reptans*	Author L.

Bugle

This hairy, spreading plant forms mats of leaves with its long, leafy stolons. The square stems are hairy on only 2 opposing faces. The leaves are oval, toothed or more or less untoothed, and green or bronze; only the lowermost are stalked. The leaf-like bracts are mostly flushed with blue, or occasionally copper. The blue, sometimes pink or white, flowers, 14–17mm ($\frac{4}{7}$–$\frac{2}{3}$in) long, are borne in leafy spikes.

• **Distribution** Throughout; not the far north.

• **Habitat** Damp sites in woodland and on grassland; occasionally hedgerows and other shady places.

• **Related Species** *Ajuga pyramidalis*, Pyramidal Bugle, has no stolons. The stems are hairy all round. It grows in N. Britain, N. Europe, and the mountains in the south of the region.

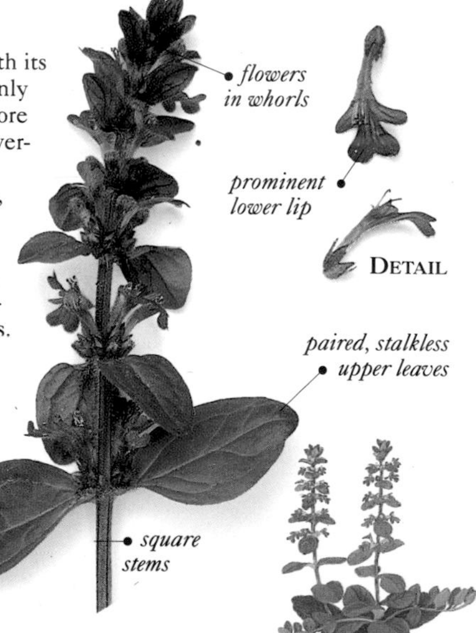

long-stalked basal leaves

leafy stolons

Habit Perennial	Height 10–30cm (4–12in)	Flowering time Apr–June

Family LABIATAE	Species *Teucrium scorodonia*	Author L.

WOOD SAGE

This tufted, hairy plant is almost subshrubby, with erect, branched stems which become woody at the base. The leaves are heart-shaped to oval, finely toothed, and stalked; the upper leaves are somewhat smaller than the lower ones. The small one-lipped flowers, 8–9mm (⅓–⅜in) long, are pale greenish yellow or whitish and are borne in leafless spikes; the corolla is hairy and contains maroon anthers which protrude on long filaments. The fruit consists of 4 small nutlets located at the base of the persistent calyx.

• **DISTRIBUTION** Throughout the region as far north as S. Norway.

• **HABITAT** Dry places, woodland, hedgerows, shingles, and sand dunes.

• **RELATED SPECIES** *Teucrium scordium*, Water Germander, smells of garlic when crushed and bears purplish flowers in interrupted, leafy spikes. It has a similar distribution to Wood Sage but is rare and very local in England and Ireland.

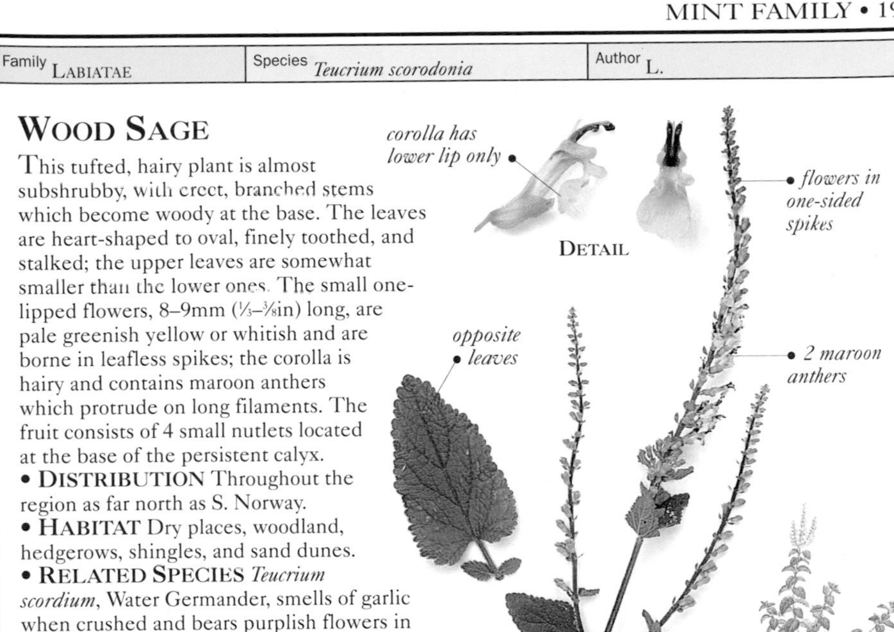

Habit Perennial	Height 30–50cm (12–20in)	Flowering time July–Sept

Family LABIATAE	Species *Teucrium montanum*	Author L.

MOUNTAIN GERMANDER

This mat-forming, subshrubby plant has spreading, rather woody stems which often root down at the nodes. The leaves are leathery, narrow-elliptical, untoothed, grey-green above but white-felted beneath, with the edges rolled under. Borne in flattish heads, the one-lipped flowers are cream or pale yellow and 12–15mm (½–⅗in) long; the lip of the corolla has 2 small lateral lobes and a large end lobe. The fruit consists of 4 small nutlets hidden at the base of the persistent calyx.

• **DISTRIBUTION** France, S. Germany.

• **HABITAT** Dry grassy, rocky, and stony places, to 2,400m (7,900ft).

• **RELATED SPECIES** *Teucrium chamaedrys*, Wall Germander, is a more tufted plant, with cut leaves, and pink or purplish flowers in leafy spikes. It inhabits open calcareous sites, dry places, and old walls in Britain, Belgium, France, and Germany.

DETAIL

long style

one-lipped corolla

leaf is white below

paired leaves

Habit Subshrub	Height 5–15cm (2–6in)	Flowering time May–Aug

Family LABIATAE	Species *Melittis melissophyllum*	Author L.

BASTARD BALM

Tufted, hairy, and rather strong-smelling, this plant has ascending to erect, usually unbranched stems which die down in the autumn. The leaves are stalked and oblong to heart-shaped, with a coarsely toothed margin. The flowers, 25–40mm (1–1⅗in) long, are pink, mauve, purple, white, or bicoloured, and are mostly paired or in groups of 3 or 4; the corolla-tube is much longer than the 5-toothed calyx. The fruit consists of 4 nutlets located at the base of the persistent calyx.

• **DISTRIBUTION** France and S.W. Britain, but occasionally naturalized elsewhere in the region; cultivated in gardens.

• **HABITAT** Wooded places, hedgerows, roadsides, shaded rocks, and other shady sites, avoiding limy soils; on lowland and in the mountains.

Habit Perennial	Height 40–70cm (16–28in)	Flowering time May–July

Family LABIATAE	Species *Marrubium vulgare*	Author L.

WHITE HOREHOUND

Smelling of thyme when crushed, this white-downy plant has erect stems, often bearing numerous short, non-flowering shoots. The leaves are oval to rounded, often with a slightly heart-shaped base, and are toothed along the margin. The 2-lipped flowers are white, 12–15mm (½–⅗in) long, and borne in dense whorls at the base of the upper leaves; the calyx has 10 short, hooked lobes; the lower lip of the corolla is 3-lobed and the upper lip is 2-lobed. The fruit consists of 4 small nutlets that are hidden at the base of the persistent calyx.

• **DISTRIBUTION** Throughout, except for the far north of the region; scarce in Britain, absent from N. Scotland, and probably only naturalized in Ireland.

• **HABITAT** Dry, grassy and waste places, rough ground, and short grassland; generally on calcareous soils.

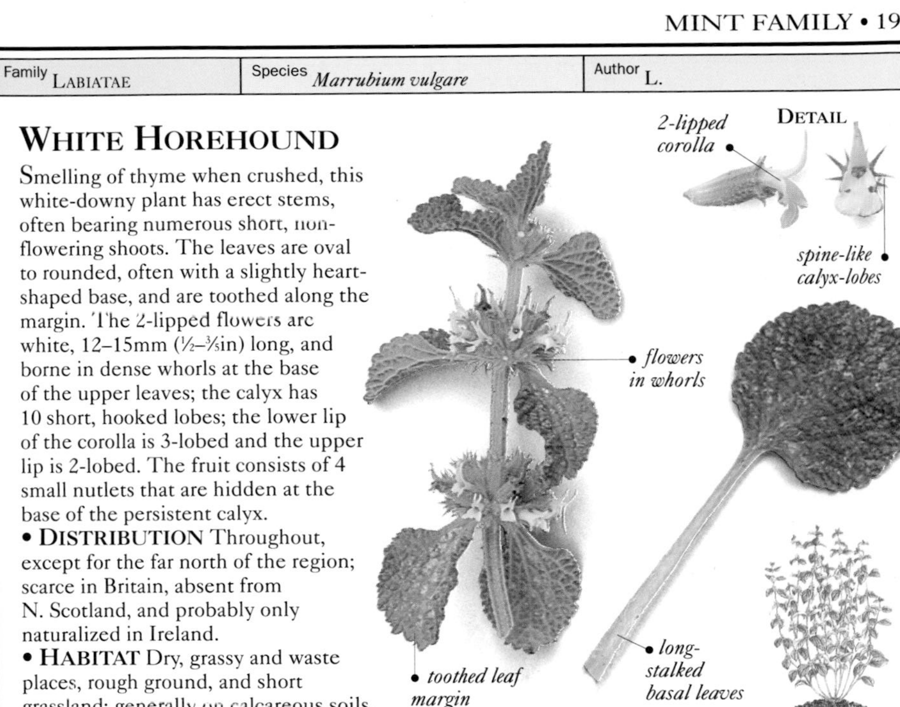

Habit Perennial	Height 40–60cm (16–24in)	Flowering time June–Sept

Family LABIATAE	Species *Galeopsis tetrahit*	Author L.

COMMON HEMP-NETTLE

The stems of this rough-haired plant are erect, branched, swollen at the nodes, and hairy on 2 opposing sides. The leaves are lanceolate to oval, toothed, and stalked (the uppermost only shortly so). The flowers, 15–20mm (⅗–⅘in) long, are pinkish purple with darker markings, but occasionally all yellowish or whitish. The fruit consists of 4 small nutlets hidden at the base of the persistent calyx.

• **DISTRIBUTION** Throughout the region, except for Spitsbergen.

• **HABITAT** Open woods, woodland margins, arable land, heaths, and open places.

• **RELATED SPECIES** *Galeopsis angustifolia*, Red Hemp-nettle, has stems not swollen at the nodes, linear-lanceolate leaves, and flowers bearing yellow markings on the lower lip. It grows in S. Britain, Ireland, and France.

DETAIL

flowers at upper leaf-nodes

2-lipped corolla

opposite leaves

DETAIL

square stem

spine-toothed calyces

Habit Annual	Height 40–80cm (16–32in)	Flowering time July–Oct

Family LABIATAE	Species *Scutellaria galericulata*	Author L.

SKULLCAP

This hairy, occasionally hairless, tufted plant has a shortly spreading stock. The stems are square, erect, and branched or unbranched. The leaves are lanceolate to oval with a rounded or heart-shaped base, and are short-stalked or unstalked. The bright violet-blue or blue, rarely pink, flowers are 2-lipped and 10–18mm (⅖–⅝in) long. The fruit consists of 4 small nutlets.

• **DISTRIBUTION** Throughout the region, except for the far north.

• **HABITAT** Damp places in meadows, along river- and stream-banks, fens, and ditches.

• **RELATED SPECIES** *Scutellaria altissima*, Somerset Skullcap, is taller. The bluish flowers have a white lower lip. The lower leaves have stalks over 10mm (⅖in) long. It is naturalized locally in S. England, France, and perhaps elsewhere.

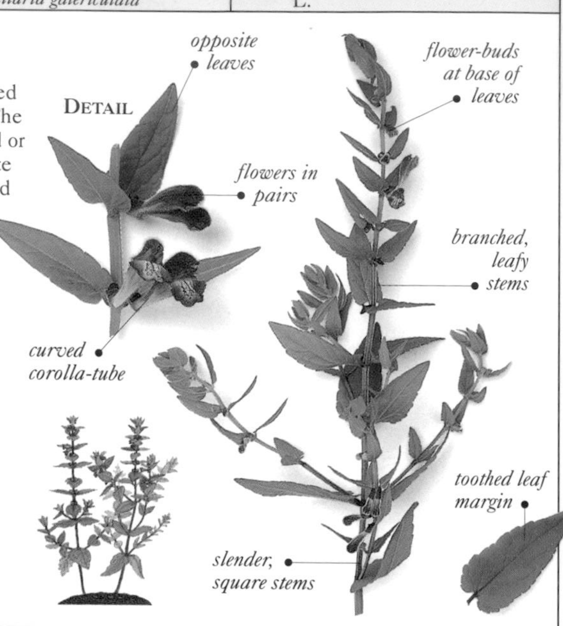

Habit Perennial	Height 30–50cm (12–20in)	Flowering time June–Sept

Family LABIATAE	Species *Scutellaria minor*	Author Hudson

LESSER SKULLCAP

The stems of this slender and somewhat hairy plant are erect to spreading and usually branched. The opposite leaves are oval to lanceolate with a rounded or heart-shaped base; the leaf margins are untoothed or with one or 2 small teeth on each side close to the base. The bracts are similar to the leaves. The pink 2-lipped flowers, 6–10mm (¼–⅖in) long, are borne in pairs at the upper nodes; the corolla has a straight tube; the calyx is hairy or hairless. The fruit consists of 4 small nutlets at the base of the calyx.

• **DISTRIBUTION** England, Wales, S. Ireland, and mainland Europe as far north as S. Sweden.

• **HABITAT** Damp places on heathland, open woodland, and woodland rides; primarily on thin, peaty, acid soils.

Habit Perennial	Height 10–25cm (4–10in)	Flowering time July–Oct

Family LABIATAE	Species *Ballota nigra*	Author L.

BLACK HOREHOUND

This very variable, almost hairless plant has a strong, rather unpleasant smell. The stems are erect to somewhat straggling, square, and branched. The leaves are oval to narrow-oblong, narrowed or heart-shaped at the base, toothed, and short-stalked. The reddish mauve to lilac flowers, 12–14mm (½–⅘in) long, are borne in dense whorls at the upper leaf-nodes; the calyx is funnel-shaped with triangular, finely pointed lobes.

• **DISTRIBUTION** E. France and Germany; scarcer and probably naturalized in N. Britain.

• **HABITAT** Open scrub, hedgerows, dry rough grassy places, and roadsides; on neutral or calcareous soils; often gregarious.

• **REMARK** Plants with slightly larger lilac to white flowers and shorter calyx-teeth are called subsp. *foetida* and can be found in similar habitats throughout the region, except for the Faeroes, Iceland, and much of Scandinavia; they are commoner in the south in Britain and local in Ireland.

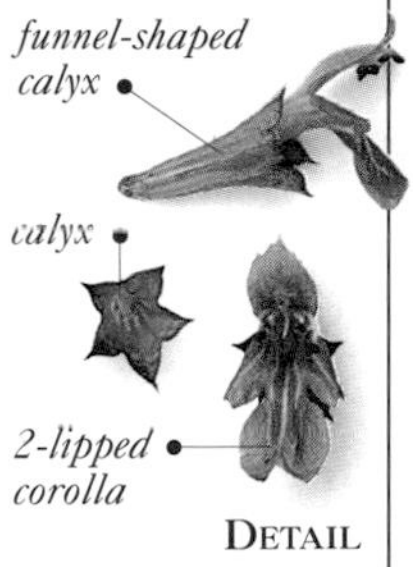

funnel-shaped calyx
calyx
2-lipped corolla
DETAIL
opposite leaves
flower whorl

Habit Perennial	Height 50–100cm (20–40in)	Flowering time June–Sept

Family LABIATAE	Species *Lamiastrum galeobdolon*	Author (L.) Ehrend. & Polatschek

YELLOW ARCHANGEL

Also known as *Lamium galeobdolon*, this is a strong-smelling, hairy, stoloniferous plant with leafy runners that root down at the nodes. The paired leaves are dark green, oval to almost triangular, coarsely toothed, and mostly stalked. In whorls at the upper leaf-nodes, the bright yellow flowers are 17–21mm (⅔–⅚in) long, with greenish brown markings on the lower lip.

• **DISTRIBUTION** Mainland Europe to S. Sweden, and E. England (Lincolnshire).

• **HABITAT** Woodland, bushy places, coppices, and other shady habitats; on heavy clay or chalky soils.

• **REMARK** Subsp. *montanum* is more robust, with the flower stems hairy all round. It grows in much of Britain, Ireland, and mainland Europe.

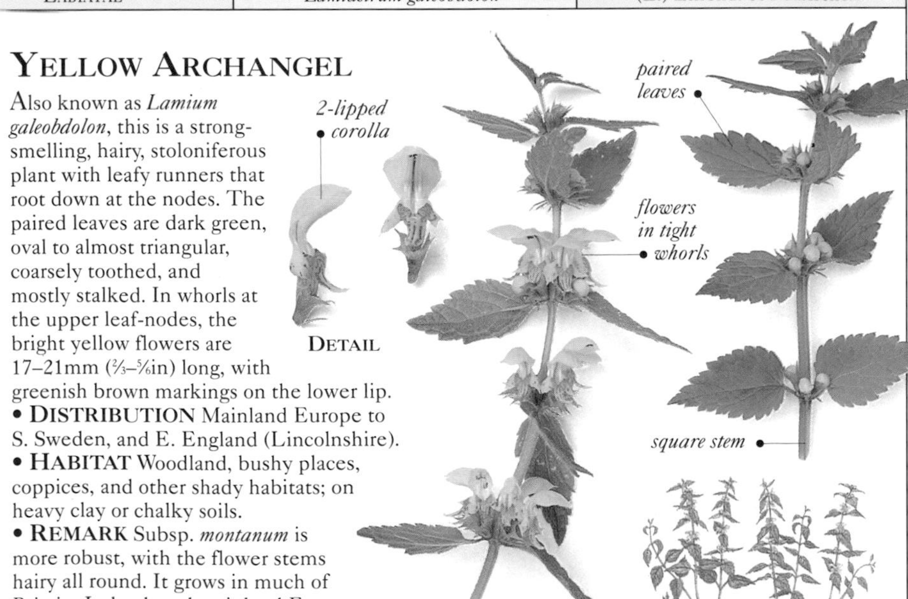

Habit Perennial	Height 30–60cm (12–24in)	Flowering time Apr–July

Family LABIATAE	Species *Lamium album*	Author L.

WHITE DEAD-NETTLE

This robust, patch-forming, faintly aromatic, and hairy plant has vigorous spreading and rooting runners. The vegetative stems are spreading but the flowering stems are mostly erect. The paired leaves are oval to heart-shaped with a pointed apex; the upper are short-stalked or practically unstalked. The 2-lipped flowers, 18–25mm ($\frac{5}{7}$–1in) long, are borne in tight whorls; the corolla has a tube that is bent towards the base, and a very hairy, hood-like upper lip. The fruit consists of 4 small nutlets hidden at the base of the persistent calyx.

• **DISTRIBUTION** Throughout, except for the far north; rare in much of N. Scotland.

• **HABITAT** Grassy and rough ground, cultivated land, open woodland, roadsides, hedgerows, and farmyards; to 2,300m (7,550ft) altitude.

Habit Perennial	Height 20–50cm (8–20in)	Flowering time Apr–Nov

Family LABIATAE	Species *Lamium maculatum*	Author (L.) L.

SPOTTED DEAD-NETTLE

This variable, patch-forming, hairy plant generally has leafy rooting runners. The sterile leafy shoots are more or less prostrate but the flowering stems are ascending. The leaves often have a whitish, sometimes pinkish, patch in the centre; the lower leaves are long-stalked, the upper short-stalked. The pinkish purple, rarely white or purplish brown, flowers are 20–35mm ($\frac{4}{5}$–1$\frac{2}{5}$in) long and borne in whorls. The fruit consists of 4 small nutlets hidden at the base of the calyx.

• **DISTRIBUTION** Belgium and Germany southwards; widely naturalized in Britain and parts of Scandinavia.

• **HABITAT** Grassy and waste places, woodland margins, roadsides, and rubbish tips.

DETAIL
curved corolla-tube
flowers at base of upper leaves
paired green leaves
long-stalked lower leaves
toothed, oval to triangular leaves

Habit Perennial	Height 20–80cm (8–32in)	Flowering time Apr–Oct

Family LABIATAE	Species *Lamium purpureum*	Author L.

RED DEAD-NETTLE

This is a relatively small, aromatic, hairy plant, generally with a single branched stem. The paired leaves are oval to almost heart-shaped, and coarsely toothed; the lower leaves are long-stalked; the upper are short-stalked and often flushed with purple. The pinkish purple flowers, 10–18mm (2/5–5/7in) long, are borne in loose whorls at the upper nodes. The fruit consists of 4 tiny nutlets hidden at the base of the persistent calyx.

• **DISTRIBUTION** Grows throughout the region, except for Spitsbergen.

• **HABITAT** Cultivated, disturbed, and waste land, and roadsides; often common and a frequent weed of gardens.

• **RELATED SPECIES** *Lamium hybridum*, Cut-leaved Dead-nettle, has deeply saw-toothed leaves. It has a similar distribution, often growing with Red Dead-nettle.

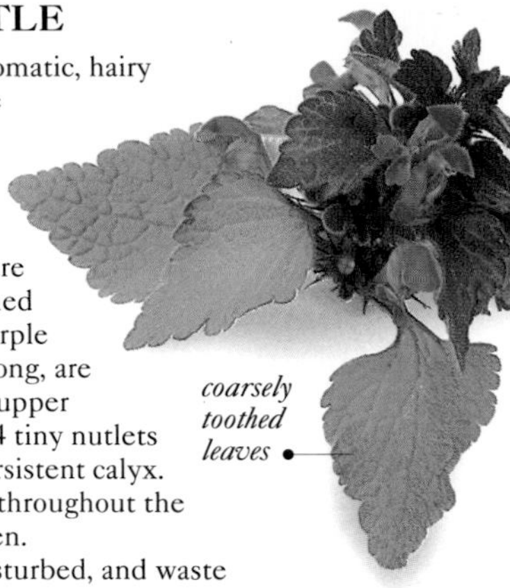

arched upper corolla-lip
straight corolla-tube
DETAIL 
coarsely toothed leaves
purple-flushed upper leaves

Habit Annual	Height 8–25cm (3 1/5–10in)	Flowering time Mar–Dec

Family LABIATAE	Species *Lamium amplexicaule*	Author L.

HENBIT DEAD-NETTLE

This is a hairy, thin-stemmed, scarcely branched plant. The paired leaves are rounded to oval and coarsely toothed; the lower leaves are long-stalked, while the upper are unstalked and clasp the stem. The pinkish purple flowers, 14–20mm (4/7–4/5in) long, are borne in lax whorls at the upper leaf-nodes; the calyx, 5–7mm (1/5–2/7in) long, is hairy. The fruit consists of 4 tiny nutlets hidden at the base of the calyx.

• **DISTRIBUTION** Throughout, except for the Faeroes and Spitsbergen.

• **HABITAT** Cultivated, waste, and disturbed ground in open situations.

• **RELATED SPECIES** *Lamium confertum* (syn. *L. molucellifolium*), Northern Dead-nettle, has a longer calyx with closely pressed hairs. It grows in similar habitats in N. Britain, the Faeroes, N. Germany, and Scandinavia.

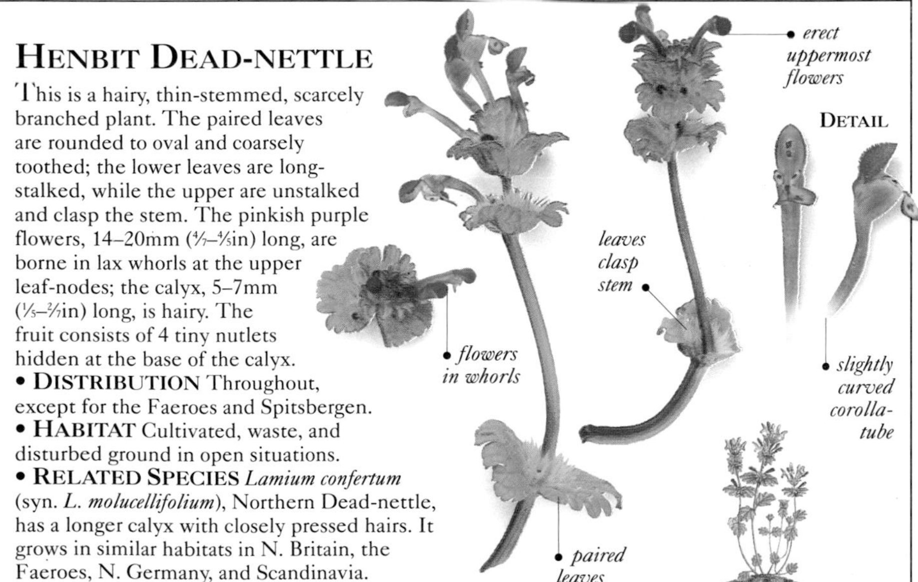

Habit Annual	Height 8–25cm (3 1/5–10in)	Flowering time Mar–Dec

Family LABIATAE	Species *Stachys alpina*	Author L.

LIMESTONE WOUNDWORT

This softly hairy, rather grey plant has square, erect stems covered in glandular hairs. The paired leaves are oblong or oval with coarsely toothed margins; the lower leaves are long-stalked, while the upper are short-stalked or unstalked. The pink or purple flowers are 15–22mm (3/5–7/8in) long, and are borne in dense whorls at the base of the upper leaves; the calyx is tubular with unequal teeth. The fruit consists of 4 small nutlets hidden at the base of the persistent calyx.

• **DISTRIBUTION** Britain (rare in Wales and W. England), Belgium, France, and Germany.

• **HABITAT** Open woodland and damp rocky places in hills and mountains to 2,000m (6,550ft); mainly over limestone.

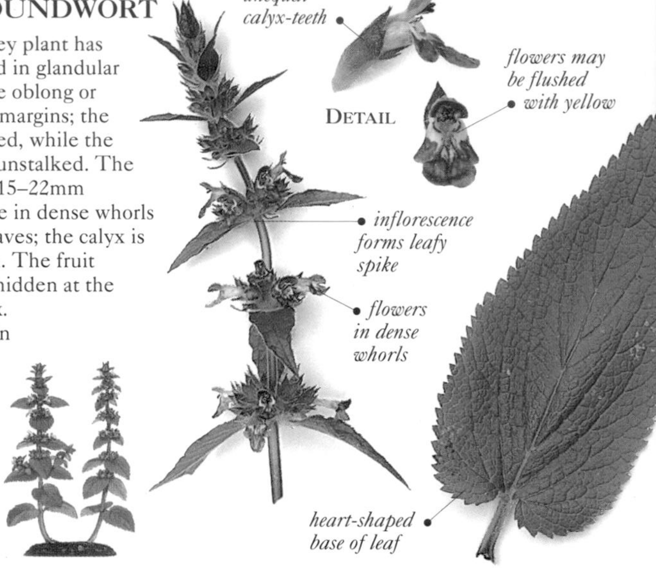

Habit Perennial	Height 60–100cm (24–40in)	Flowering time June–Aug

Family LABIATAE	Species *Stachys sylvatica*	Author L.

HEDGE WOUNDWORT

This evil-smelling, glandular-hairy plant has creeping and rooting rhizomes on the soil surface. The paired leaves are sparsely hairy and narrow to broadly heart-shaped; the lower leaves are long-stalked, the upper are short-stalked. The dull reddish purple, 2-lipped flowers, 13–18mm (1/2–5/7in) long, are borne in whorls at the base of the upper leaves. The fruit consists of 4 small nutlets hidden at the base of the persistent calyx.

• **DISTRIBUTION** Throughout the region, except for the Faeroes, Iceland, and Spitsbergen.

• **HABITAT** Woodland, hedgerows, roadsides, margins of cultivation, and waste ground; mostly in shade.

• **RELATED SPECIES** *Stachys palustris*, Marsh Woundwort, has unstalked upper leaves, paler flowers, and grows in wetter sites.

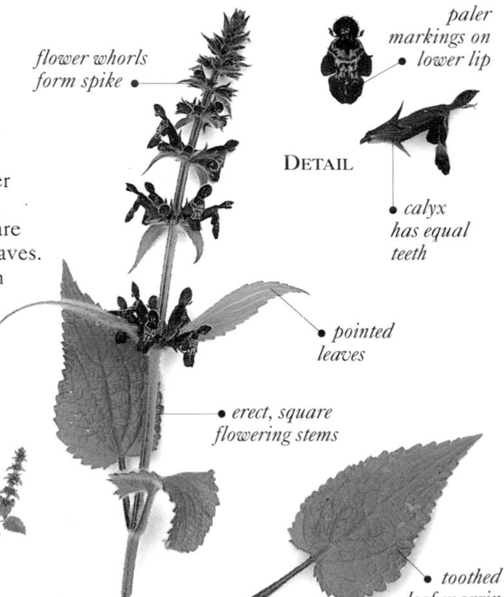

Habit Perennial	Height 60–100cm (24–40in)	Flowering time June–Sept

Family LABIATAE	Species *Stachys officinalis*	Author (L.) Trev. St. Leon

BETONY

This is a somewhat hairy, tufted plant, with erect, square stems and sterile, persistent leaf-rosettes; the stems bear 2 to 4 pairs of leaves. The leaves are deep green, oval to oblong, and coarsely toothed; the lower leaves are long-stalked, while the upper are unstalked or short-stalked. The bright reddish purple flowers are 12–18mm (½–⅔in) long, and are borne in dense whorls which make up an oblong spike, with the lower whorl often rather distant from the other flowers; the corolla is 2-lipped. The fruit consists of 4 small nutlets hidden at the base of the persistent calyx.

• **DISTRIBUTION** Throughout the region, as far north as S. Scandinavia.

• **HABITAT** Dry grassy places, heaths, hedgerows, cliff-tops, embankments, and open woodland; on both acid and calcareous soils. When in exposed coastal locations this plant can be very dwarf.

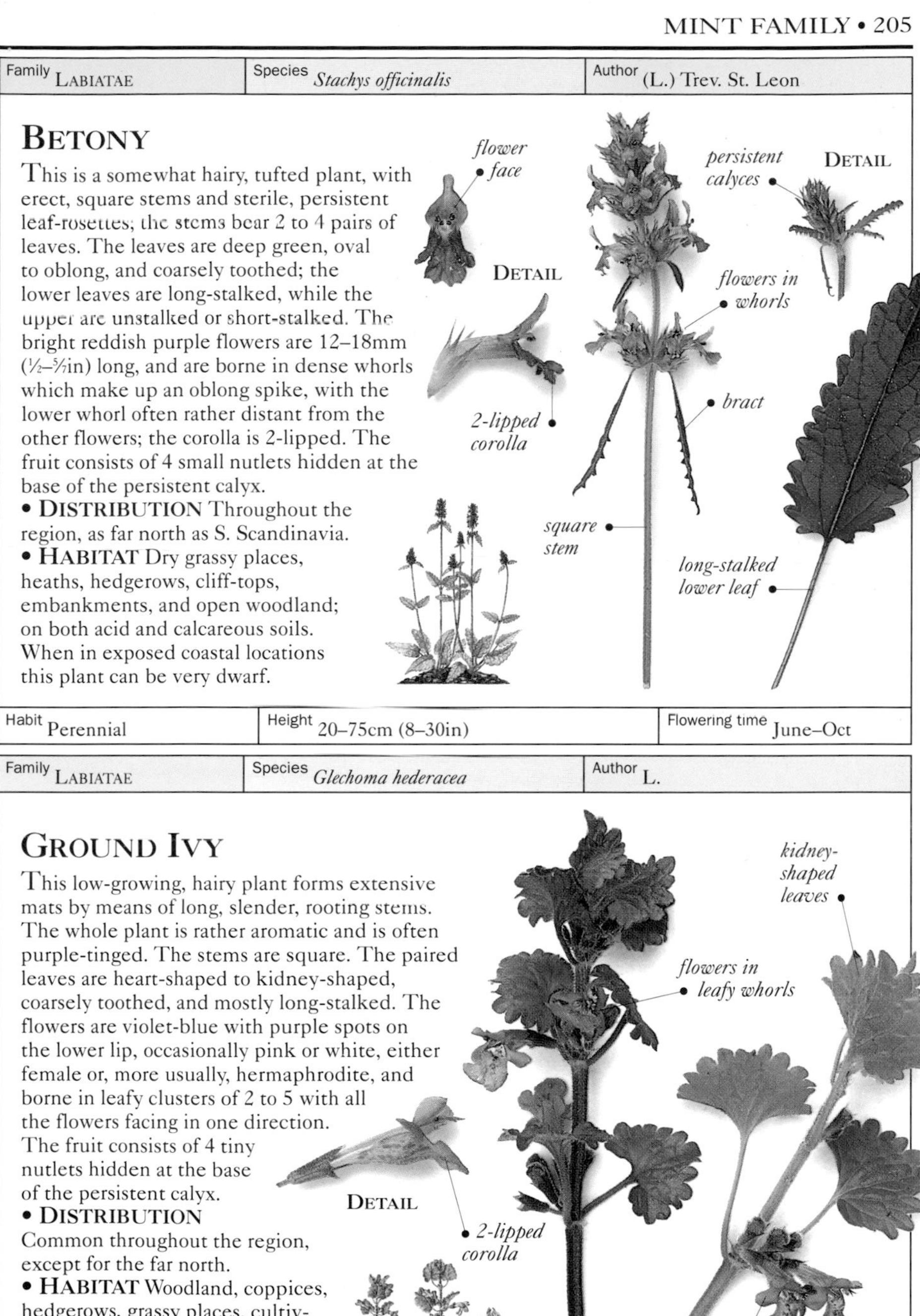

Habit Perennial	Height 20–75cm (8–30in)	Flowering time June–Oct

Family LABIATAE	Species *Glechoma hederacea*	Author L.

GROUND IVY

This low-growing, hairy plant forms extensive mats by means of long, slender, rooting stems. The whole plant is rather aromatic and is often purple-tinged. The stems are square. The paired leaves are heart-shaped to kidney-shaped, coarsely toothed, and mostly long-stalked. The flowers are violet-blue with purple spots on the lower lip, occasionally pink or white, either female or, more usually, hermaphrodite, and borne in leafy clusters of 2 to 5 with all the flowers facing in one direction. The fruit consists of 4 tiny nutlets hidden at the base of the persistent calyx.

• **DISTRIBUTION** Common throughout the region, except for the far north.

• **HABITAT** Woodland, coppices, hedgerows, grassy places, cultivated and waste ground; primarily on heavy damp soils; sometimes an invasive weed of cultivation.

Habit Perennial	Height 10–25cm (4–10in)	Flowering time Mar–Sept

Family LABIATAE	Species *Prunella vulgaris*	Author L.

SELF-HEAL

This is a patch-forming, generally hairy plant, with creeping and rooting stems but more or less erect flowering shoots. The leaves are oval to diamond-shaped and toothed or untoothed. The flowers, 13–15mm (½–⅗in) long, are bluish violet, or occasionally pink or white. The fruit consists of 4 nutlets hidden at the base of the persistent calyx.

• **DISTRIBUTION** Throughout the region, except for the far north.

• **HABITAT** Grassy places, roadsides, cultivated land, and open woods.

• **RELATED SPECIES** *Prunella laciniata*, Cut-leaved Self-heal, has deeply cut leaves, and cream, white, or rarely pale pink flowers. It is native from Belgium to Germany southwards.

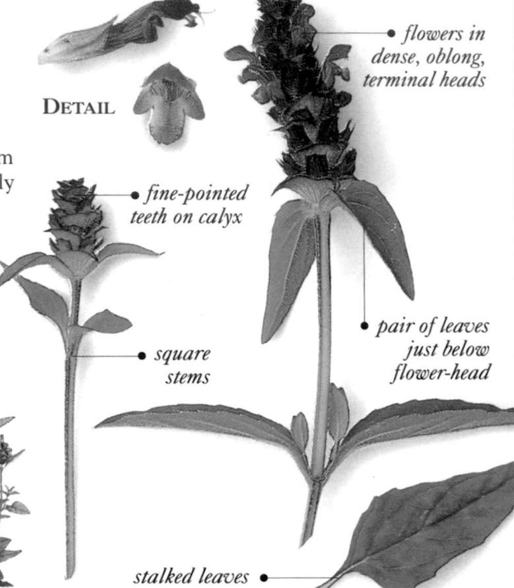

Habit Perennial	Height 15–30cm (6–12in)	Flowering time June–Nov

Family LABIATAE	Species *Melissa officinalis*	Author L.

BALM

Smelling strongly of lemon when crushed, this is a tufted, hairy plant, with erect and stiff, square, thin stems which are generally branched in the upper part. The paired leaves are yellowish green overall and oval to diamond-shaped, the lower often having a heart-shaped base. The small whitish or pale yellow flowers, 8–15mm (⅓–⅗in) long, often turn pink on ageing, and are borne in loose whorls at the base of the upper leaves; the corolla is 2-lipped with the upper lip erect and the lower 3-lobed.

• **DISTRIBUTION** Native in C. and S. France and much of S. Europe; widely naturalized in much of the region as far north as S. Sweden.

• **HABITAT** Waste places, hedgerows, dry banks, scrub, and shaded places; at low altitudes. Often grown in gardens, including a form with yellow leaves.

Habit Perennial	Height 50–100cm (20–40in)	Flowering time July–Sept

Family LABIATAE	Species *Acinos arvensis*	Author (Lam.) Dandy

BASIL THYME

Also known as *Clinopodium acinos*, this aromatic, hairy plant has thin stems that branch near the base. The small, paired leaves are oval to lanceolate, netted with veins, and blunt-tipped or pointed, with a few or no marginal teeth. The bright violet flowers, 7–10mm (²⁄₇–²⁄₅in) long, have white markings on the lower lip of the corolla and are borne in small clusters of usually 2 to 6 at the base of the upper leaves; the corolla has an erect upper lip.

• **DISTRIBUTION** Throughout, except for the Faeroes, Iceland, and Spitsbergen.

• **HABITAT** Dry open calcareous places such as open chalky downs, bare or sparsely grassy arable land, or rocky sites.

• **RELATED SPECIES** *Acinos alpinus*, Alpine Calamint, is a tufted perennial, with flowers 12–20mm (½–⁴⁄₅in) long. It inhabits the mountains of France and Germany.

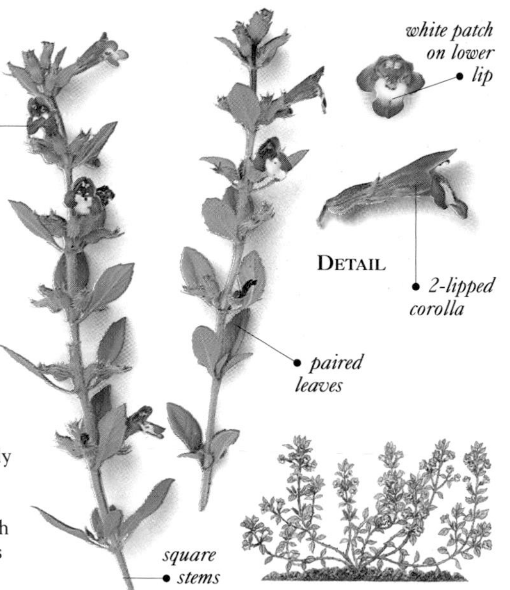

Habit Annual	Height 10–25cm (4–10in)	Flowering time May–Sept

Family LABIATAE	Species *Clinopodium vulgare*	Author L.

WILD BASIL

This slightly aromatic, softly hairy plant has thin, unbranched or somewhat branched, square stems. The paired leaves are oval to lanceolate, up to 50mm (2in) long, toothed, and short-stalked. The dark pinkish purple flowers, 12–22mm (½–⅞in) long, are borne in rather dense whorls at the base of the upper leaves; the calyx, often tinged with purple, has long slender teeth and is covered in hair; the 2-lipped corolla has an erect upper lip and a 3-lobed lower lip. The fruit consists of 4 small nutlets hidden at the base of the persistent calyx.

• **DISTRIBUTION** Throughout much of the region, except for the far north; uncommon in Ireland, absent from most of N. Scotland.

• **HABITAT** Dry places, particularly open woodland, scrub, hedgerows, banks, and grassy meadows, at low altitudes; usually on light calcareous soils.

• **REMARK** Not culinary basil.

Habit Perennial	Height 40–75cm (16–30in)	Flowering time July–Sept

Family LABIATAE	Species *Clinopodium menthifolium*	Author (Host) Stace

Wood Calamint

Also known as *Calamintha sylvatica*, this hairy plant spreads by means of a stoloniferous rootstock. The stems are square, erect, generally branched, and with long hairs. The opposite leaves, which smell of mint when crushed, are dark green, oval, stalked, and have a toothed margin. The pink or lilac 2-lipped flowers, 15–22mm (⅗–⅞in) long, often have darker spots and are borne in loose whorls in leafy spikes; the calyx has 5 slender teeth, and hairs in the "mouth". The fruit consists of 5 small nutlets hidden at the base of the persistent calyx.

• **DISTRIBUTION** S. England (rare and confined to the Isle of Wight), France, and W. Germany (local); occasionally naturalized elsewhere.

• **HABITAT** Open woodland, grassy banks, and hedgerows; on calcareous soils.

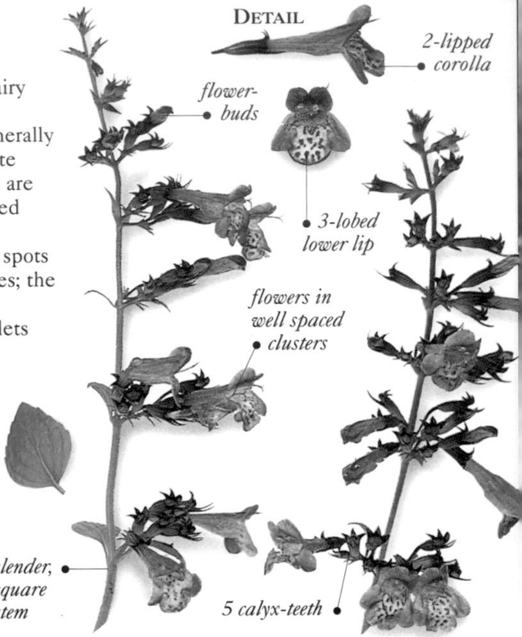

Habit Perennial	Height 40–60cm (16–24in)	Flowering time July–Oct

Family LABIATAE	Species *Lycopus europaeus*	Author L.

Gipsywort

This tufted, slightly hairy, non-aromatic plant has stiff, branched or unbranched, erect stems. The paired plain green leaves are mostly stalked and are oval to elliptical in outline but deeply and jaggedly toothed, the lower more so than the upper. Borne in dense, rather distant whorls at the base of the upper leaves, the small white flowers, only 3–5mm (⅛–⅕in) long, have tiny purple dots; the calyx has spine-like teeth, and the corolla has 4 more or less even lobes and 2 protruding stamens. The fruit consists of 4 nutlets hidden at the base of the persistent calyx.

• **DISTRIBUTION** Grows throughout most of the region except for the far north; scarcer in Scotland and Ireland.

• **HABITAT** Wet places in woodland, ditches, marshes, river, stream, and lake margins.

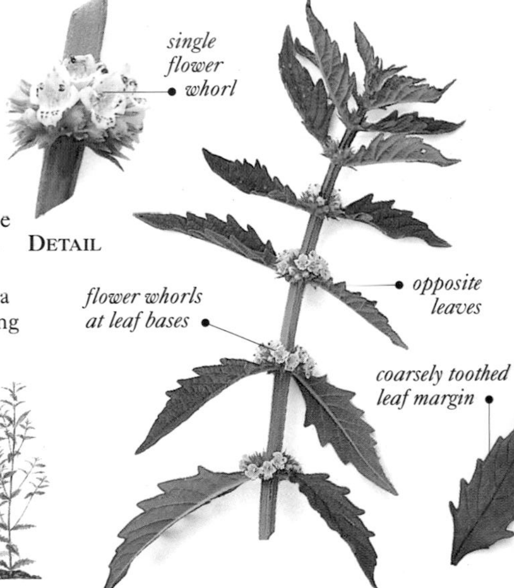

Habit Perennial	Height 60–100cm (24–40in)	Flowering time July–Sept

Family LABIATAE	Species *Origanum vulgare*	Author L.

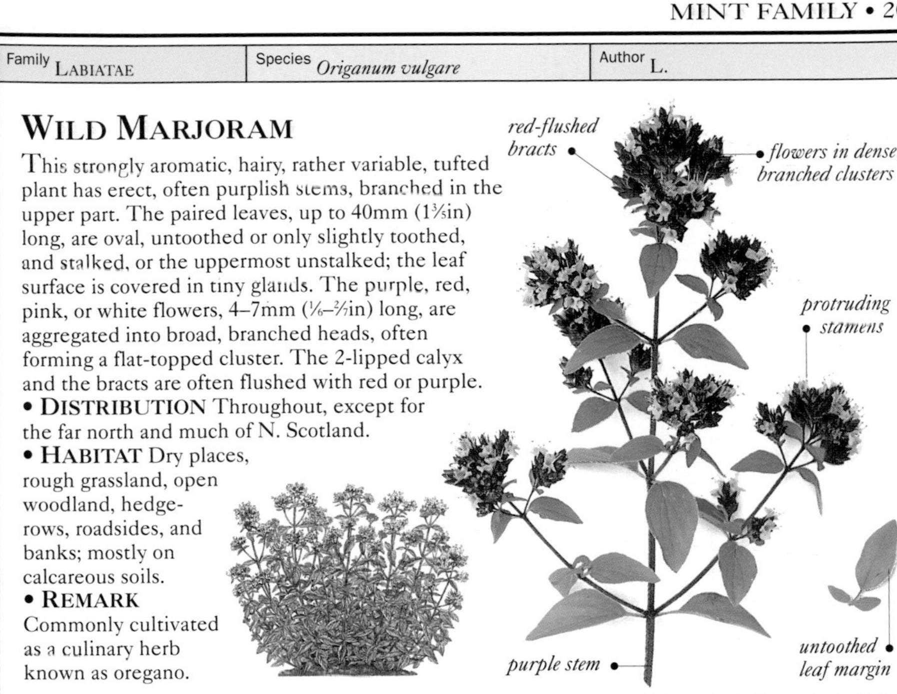

WILD MARJORAM

This strongly aromatic, hairy, rather variable, tufted plant has erect, often purplish stems, branched in the upper part. The paired leaves, up to 40mm (1⅗in) long, are oval, untoothed or only slightly toothed, and stalked, or the uppermost unstalked; the leaf surface is covered in tiny glands. The purple, red, pink, or white flowers, 4–7mm (⅙–⅖in) long, are aggregated into broad, branched heads, often forming a flat-topped cluster. The 2-lipped calyx and the bracts are often flushed with red or purple.

• **DISTRIBUTION** Throughout, except for the far north and much of N. Scotland.

• **HABITAT** Dry places, rough grassland, open woodland, hedgerows, roadsides, and banks; mostly on calcareous soils.

• **REMARK** Commonly cultivated as a culinary herb known as oregano.

Habit Perennial	Height 30–60cm (12–24in)	Flowering time July–Sept

Family LABIATAE	Species *Thymus polytrichus*	Author A. Kerner ex Borbas

WILD THYME

Also known as *Thymus praecox*, this aromatic plant has spreading, leafy stems with short ascending shoots bearing the flowers; the stems are square and hairy on 2 opposing sides, and root down to form a dense mat. The small leaves, not more than 8mm (⅓in) long, are oval to almost rounded, untoothed, and hairy towards the base along the margin. The small pinkish purple flowers, only 5–6mm (⅕–¼in) long, are borne in small, rounded heads.

• **DISTRIBUTION** Throughout the region, except for Denmark, Finland, and Sweden.

• **HABITAT** Dry sandy and rocky places, short turf, heaths, banks, and often on closely grazed areas.

flowers in dense heads

protruding stamens

flat leaves

DETAIL

flowers have 4 stamens: 2 long, 2 short

tiny, paired, oval leaves

Habit Dwarf shrub	Height 4–10cm (1⅗–4in)	Flowering time May–Sept

Family LABIATAE	Species *Mentha arvensis*	Author L.

CORN MINT

This hairy, patch-forming plant, occasionally with a solitary stem, has a strong peppery, rather sickly smell, especially when crushed. The stems are square, erect to ascending, and terminate in leaves, not flowers. The opposite leaves are oval to elliptical, with a rather shallowly toothed margin and mostly with a short stalk. The 2-lipped flowers, 3–4mm (⅛–⅙in) long, are pink, lilac, or white, with protruding stamens, and are borne in dense whorls at the base of the upper leaves. The fruit consists of 4 small nutlets at the base of the persistent 5-toothed calyx.

• **DISTRIBUTION** Grows throughout the region, except for the far north.

• **HABITAT** Arable fields, damp places such as pond margins, tracks, open woodland, and ditches.

Habit Perennial or annual	Height 30–60cm (12–24in)	Flowering time July–Sept

Family LABIATAE	Species *Mentha aquatica*	Author L.

WATER MINT

This very strongly aromatic plant is hairy or almost hairless, and often flushed with purple. The leaves are oval to lanceolate, coarsely toothed, and stalked, with a blunt or pointed apex. The lilac-pink flowers, 4–6mm (⅙–¼in) long, are borne in dense heads, often with one or several flower whorls below; the corolla has 4 more or less equal lobes and 4 protruding stamens. The fruit consists of 4 tiny nutlets at the base of the calyx.

• **DISTRIBUTION** Throughout, except for the far north.

• **HABITAT** Wet places like marshes, swamps, and wet meadows, river, stream, and lake margins, and ditches.

• **REMARK** Hybrid species of mint are common in the region and can unfortunately make identification difficult.

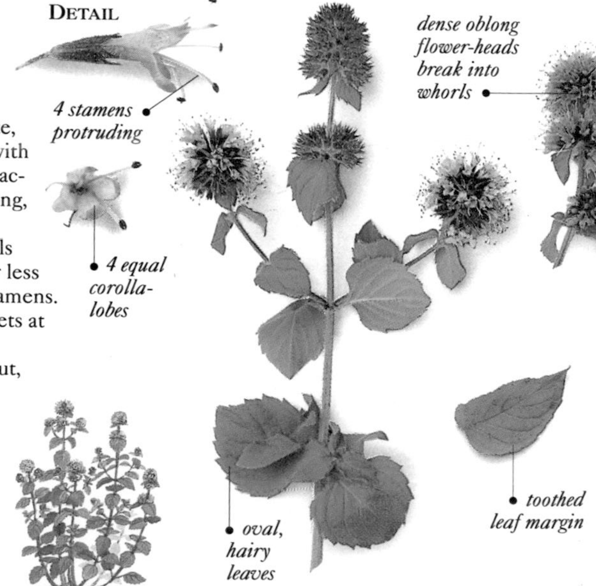

Habit Perennial	Height 40–90cm (16–36in)	Flowering time July–Sept

Family LABIATAE	Species *Mentha pulegium*	Author L.

PENNYROYAL

This aromatic, somewhat hairy plant has creeping and rooting leafy runners and erect to ascending leafy flowering stems. The leaves are short-stalked, narrow-elliptical to oval, often hairy beneath, and with an untoothed or slightly toothed margin in the lower half. The lilac flowers, 4–6mm (⅙ ¼in) long, are borne at the base of the middle and upper leaves; the corolla has 4 lobes and 4 protruding stamens.

• **DISTRIBUTION** Throughout, except for much of Scandinavia; scarce in S. Britain and Ireland.

• **HABITAT** Damp grazed sites, meadows, ditches, along lake and pool margins, and in damp hollows on dunes.

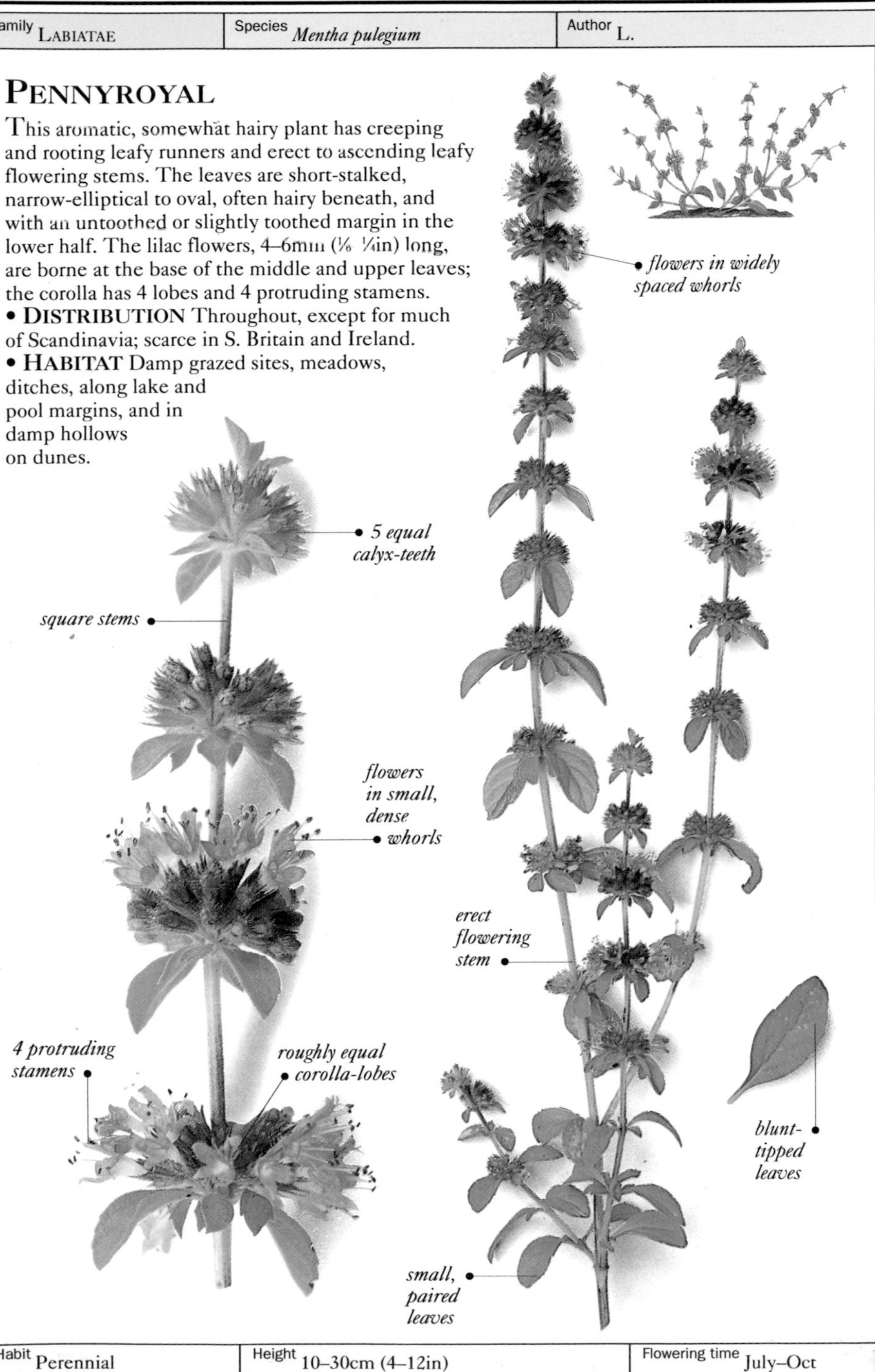

Habit Perennial	Height 10–30cm (4–12in)	Flowering time July–Oct

Family LABIATAE	Species *Salvia glutinosa*	Author L.

JUPITER'S DISTAFF

This tufted plant is sticky with glandular hairs. The stems are branched or unbranched, square, and erect. The paired leaves are arrow-shaped or heart-shaped, bright green, and stalked; the upper leaves are smaller and narrower than the lower. The bracts are small and green, the lowermost being leaf-like. Borne in whorls that form a long raceme, the yellow flowers, 30–40mm (1⅕–1⅗in) long, are marked with reddish brown and have 2 stamens and a glandular hairy calyx. The fruit consists of 4 nutlets hidden at the base of the persistent calyx.

• **DISTRIBUTION** France and S. Germany; naturalized in parts of England and Scotland.

• **HABITAT** Woods, copses, hedgerows, and roadsides; primarily in the mountains to an altitude of 1,800m (5,900ft).

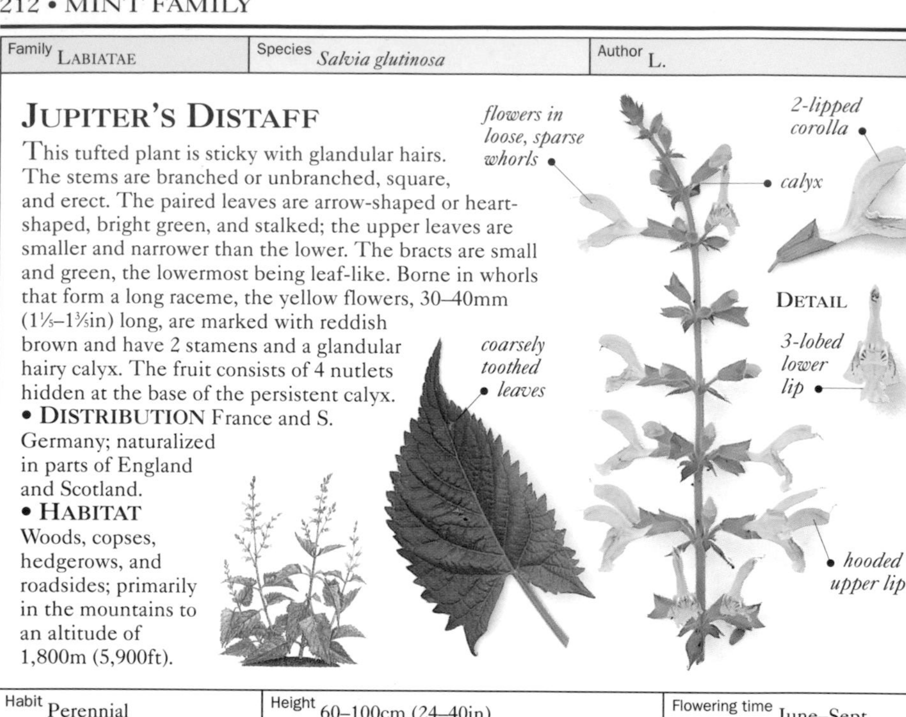

Habit Perennial	Height 60–100cm (24–40in)	Flowering time June–Sept

Family LABIATAE	Species *Salvia pratensis*	Author L.

MEADOW CLARY

A variable, tufted, slightly aromatic, hairy plant, Meadow Clary has square, branched stems which are often flushed with red or purple. The deep green leaves are oval to oblong with a slightly heart-shaped base and a rough and somewhat wrinkled upper surface; the lower leaves are long-stalked, while the upper are smaller and generally unstalked. The bracts are small, the lowermost being leaf-like. The violet-blue, occasionally pink or white, flowers are 20–30mm (⅘–1⅕in) long and are borne in loose, close whorls of up to 6 flowers, forming a long raceme; the calyx is often flushed with red or purple; the corolla has a hooded upper lip and only 2 stamens.

• **DISTRIBUTION** S. Britain and mainland Europe as far north as S. Sweden.

• **HABITAT** Meadows and other grassy places, roadsides, scrub, and woodland margins; on calcareous soils.

2-lipped corolla

DETAIL

long, forked style

flowers in whorls

long-stalked, coarsely toothed lower leaf

small bract

Habit Perennial	Height 50–80cm (20–32in)	Flowering time June–July

Family LABIATAE	Species *Salvia verticillata*	Author L.

WHORLED CLARY

This is a tufted, hairy plant with a rather unpleasant smell. The stems are erect, branched, and often purple-flushed. The paired leaves are oval to lyre-shaped, with a heart-shaped or squarish base and a coarsely toothed margin; the lower leaves are stalked, while the upper ones are unstalked and often flushed with purple. The small bracts may be green, brown, or purplish. The lilac-blue or purplish flowers, 8–15mm (⅓–⅗in) long, are borne in spaced, dense whorls of up to 30 flowers; the corolla has a hooded upper lip and 2 stamens.

- **DISTRIBUTION** C. and S. France, but widely naturalized in the rest of the region as far north as S. Sweden.
- **HABITAT** Dry grassy and waste places, rough ground along roads and railways, stony places, and pathways.

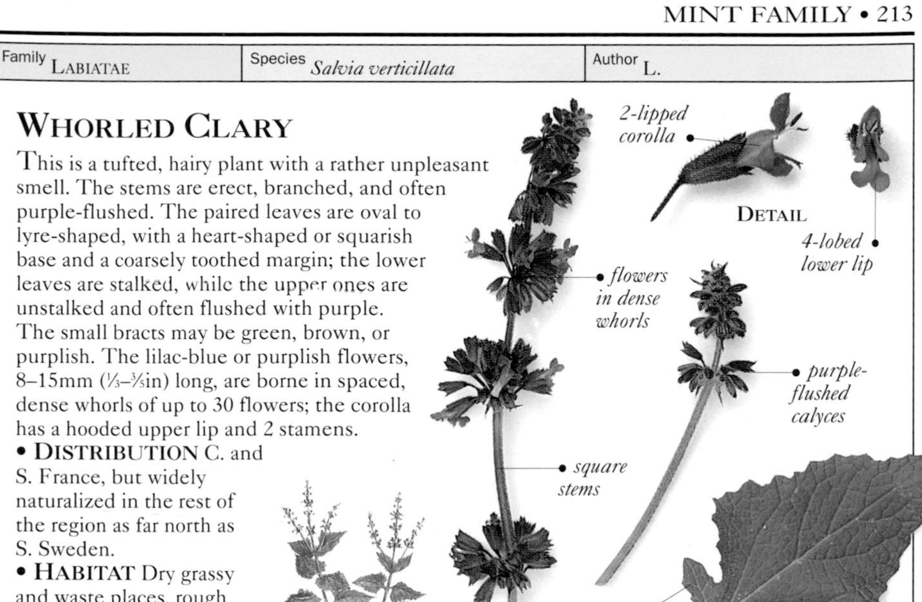

Habit Perennial	Height 40–80cm (16–32in)	Flowering time May–Aug

Family LABIATAE	Species *Salvia nemorosa*	Author L.

WILD SAGE

This hairy plant has square, branched, erect stems without glands. The leaves are oblong or oval with a heart-shaped base; the lower leaves are long-stalked; the upper are short-stalked or unstalked. The bracts are small, the lower ones being leaf-like and green, but often flushed with violet. The violet-blue, rarely pink or white, flowers, 8–12mm (⅓–½in) long, are borne in loose whorls of up to 6; the corolla is 2-lipped and contains 2 stamens. The fruit consists of 4 small nutlets hidden at the base of the peristent calyx.

- **DISTRIBUTION** C. France to S. Germany southwards; naturalized rarely in places in Britain, N. France, and S. Scandinavia.
- **HABITAT** Grassy sites like meadows, and bare and waste ground.

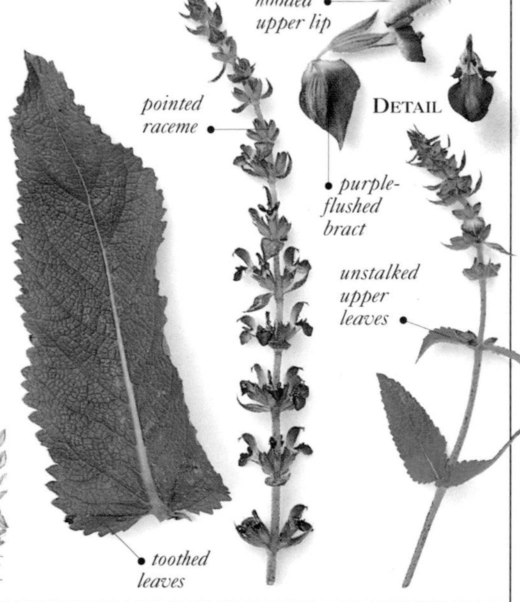

Habit Perennial	Height 40–60cm (16–24in)	Flowering time June–Aug

POTATO FAMILY

Family SOLANACEAE	Species *Atropa belladonna*	Author L.

DEADLY NIGHTSHADE

This hairless plant has a thick, branched, green stem. The dull green leaves, up to 20cm (8in) long, are elliptical to oval. The flowers are brownish violet or greenish, 25–30mm (1–1⅕in) long, and solitary in the upper leaf-axils; the broad corolla-tube has 5 stamens inside. The many-seeded berry is 15–20mm (⅗–⅘in) long. The plant is poisonous.

• **DISTRIBUTION** Britain to Belgium and Germany southwards; naturalized further north and in Ireland.

• **HABITAT** Damp, shaded places, woodland, copses, banks, pathways, rocky sites; mainly on calcareous soils.

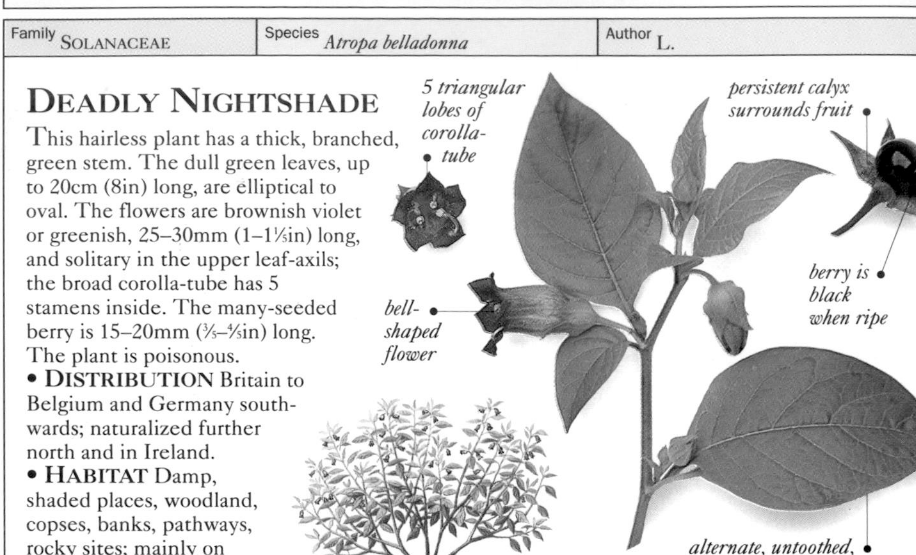

Habit Perennial	Height 1–2m (3¼–6½ft)	Flowering time June–Sept

Family SOLANACEAE	Species *Hyoscyamus niger*	Author L.

HENBANE

Rather evil-smelling, this stickily hairy plant has erect, branched, or sometimes unbranched, stems. The alternate leaves, up to 20cm (8in) long, form a loose rosette in the first year, and are quite soft, oval to oblong, and lobed to coarsely toothed; only the basal leaves are stalked. The pale yellow flowers, 20–30mm (⅘–1⅕in) long, are borne in one-sided, branched spikes; the funnel-shaped calyx enlarges as the fruit develops and becomes stiff and papery; the corolla is deeply lobed. The many-seeded fruit opens by a small lid. The plant is poisonous.

• **DISTRIBUTION** Throughout, except for the far north; rare in N. Britain.

• **HABITAT** Disturbed, bare, and cultivated land, coastal shingles, and farmyards.

Habit Annual or biennial	Height 40–80cm (16–32in)	Flowering time May–Sept

Family SOLANACEAE	Species *Solanum nigrum*	Author L.

BLACK NIGHTSHADE

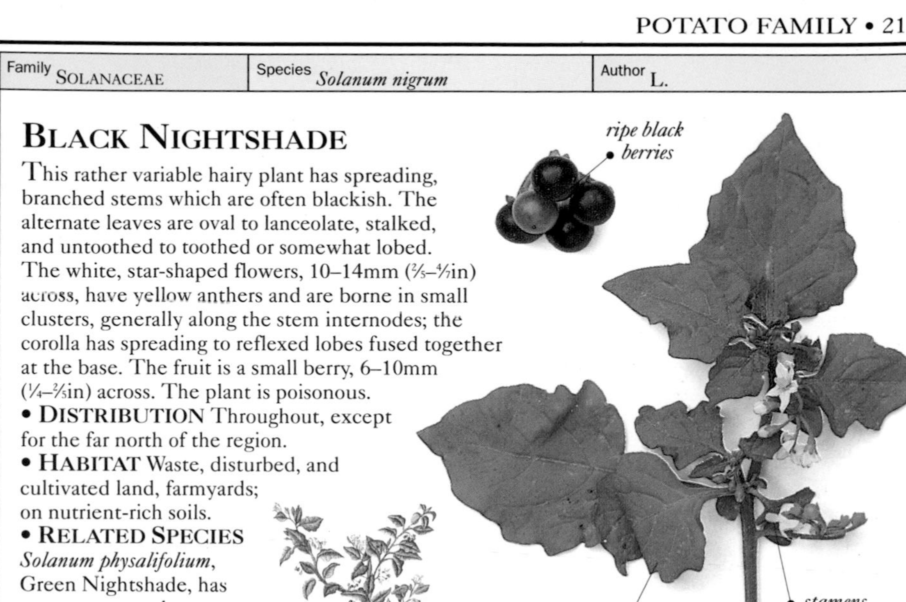

This rather variable hairy plant has spreading, branched stems which are often blackish. The alternate leaves are oval to lanceolate, stalked, and untoothed to toothed or somewhat lobed. The white, star-shaped flowers, 10–14mm (2/5–4/7in) across, have yellow anthers and are borne in small clusters, generally along the stem internodes; the corolla has spreading to reflexed lobes fused together at the base. The fruit is a small berry, 6–10mm (1/4–2/5in) across. The plant is poisonous.

• **DISTRIBUTION** Throughout, except for the far north of the region.

• **HABITAT** Waste, disturbed, and cultivated land, farmyards; on nutrient-rich soils.

• **RELATED SPECIES** *Solanum physalifolium*, Green Nightshade, has green stems and green to purple-brown fruit. It is naturalized in Britain and Belgium.

Habit Annual	Height 30–70cm (12–28in)	Flowering time June–Oct

Family SOLANACEAE	Species *Solanum dulcamara*	Author L.

BITTERSWEET

This is a scrambling, or sometimes trailing, rather robust, hairy or hairless plant, with green stems that become woody and brown. The alternate leaves are arrow- or heart-shaped, stalked, untoothed, and mostly 3- to 5-lobed, although sometimes unlobed and oval. Borne in loose, branched clusters, the purple, rarely white, flowers are 10–15mm (2/5–3/5in) across; the corolla has 5 spreading to reflexed, pointed lobes; the stamens are yellow. The fruit is an oval berry 8–12mm (1/3–1/2in) long, and is bright red when ripe. The plant is poisonous.

• **DISTRIBUTION** Throughout, except for the far north.

• **HABITAT** Damp places in woods, scrub, fens, marshes, ditches, river and lake margins.

stamens in an erect cone

clustered, pendent berries

nodding flowers

5-lobed leaf with large end lobe

Habit Perennial	Height 1–4m (3¼–13ft)	Flowering time June–Sept

Family SOLANACEAE	Species *Datura stramonium*	Author L.

THORNAPPLE

This robust, usually hairless plant has an unpleasant smell. The stiff stems are erect and usually branched. The leaves, up to 18cm (7in) long, are oval to elliptical with the margin usually lobed or coarsely and jaggedly toothed. The white, occasionally pale purple, flowers, 5–10cm (2–4in) long, are erect; the corolla has a long tube and 5 spreading, triangular lobes. The fruit, 35–70mm (1⅖–2⅘in) long, splits lengthwise. The plant is very poisonous.

• **DISTRIBUTION** Naturalized throughout the region, except for Ireland and the far north.

• **HABITAT** Cultivated, disturbed, and waste land, in farmyards, on rubbish tips, and along field margins.

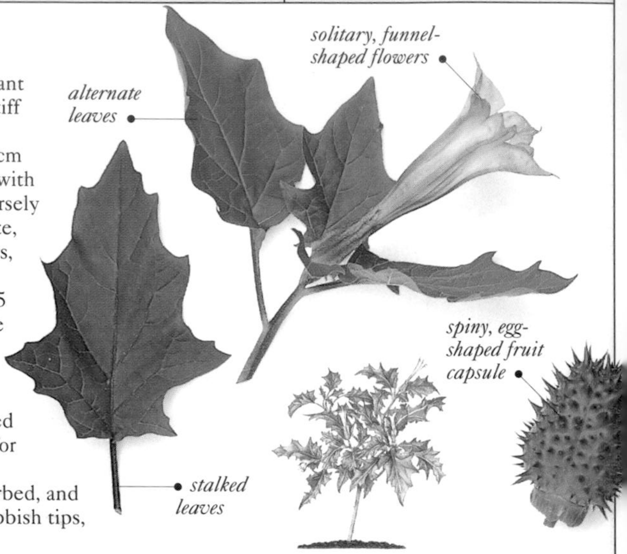

alternate leaves

solitary, funnel-shaped flowers

spiny, egg-shaped fruit capsule

stalked leaves

Habit Annual	Height 70–150cm (28–60in)	Flowering time July–Oct

FIGWORT FAMILY

Family SCROPHULARIACEAE	Species *Gratiola officinalis*	Author L.

GRATIOLE

This hairless, patch-forming plant has erect, square, hollow stems with a creeping and rooting base. The pairs of leaves are lanceolate to linear, pointed at the apex, slightly toothed, and half-clasping the stem; the leaf surface is covered in small, semi-transparent dots. Borne in leafy racemes, the flowers, 10–18mm (⅖–⅗in) long, are white veined and flushed with purple; the calyx is deeply divided into 5 narrow teeth; the tubular corolla is weakly 2-lipped with the lower lip 3-lobed and the upper slightly 2-lobed. The fruit is a small, many-seeded capsule.

• **DISTRIBUTION** Holland to Germany southwards. Often local.

• **HABITAT** Wet marshes, meadows, river and stream margins, and ditches; rarely found in large numbers.

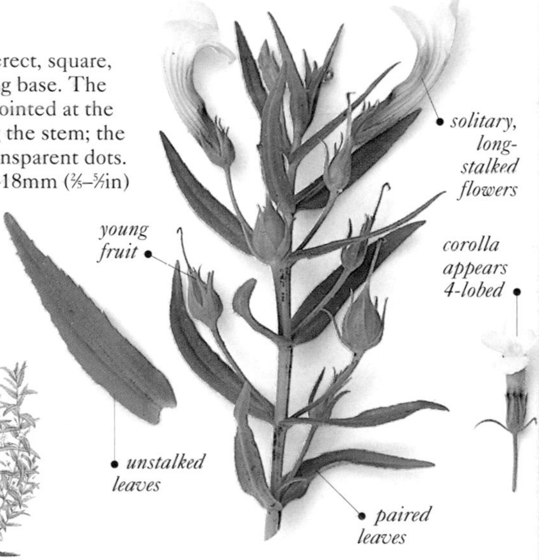

solitary, long-stalked flowers

young fruit

corolla appears 4-lobed

unstalked leaves

paired leaves

Habit Perennial	Height 15–50cm (6–20in)	Flowering time May–Oct

Family SCROPHULARIACEAE	Species *Verbascum thapsus*	Author L.

GREAT MULLEIN

Whitish or greyish with soft hairs, this plant forms a large leaf-rosette in the first year and puts up a stiff, generally unbranched, leafy flower stem in the second. The leaves are oblong to elliptical, with an untoothed or slightly toothed margin and a narrowly winged stalk. The yellow flowers, 12–35mm (½–1⅖in) across, are borne in a narrow, crowded spike; the calyx is woolly; the corolla has 5 spreading, rounded lobes.
• **DISTRIBUTION** Throughout the region, except for the far north.
• **HABITAT** Rough, dry grassland and waste sites, banks, stony places, roadsides, and hedgerows.
• **RELATED SPECIES** *Verbascum phlomoides*, Orange Mullein, has larger, orange-yellow flowers and unwinged leaf bases. It is native in France and Germany and naturalized in S. England, Belgium, and Holland.

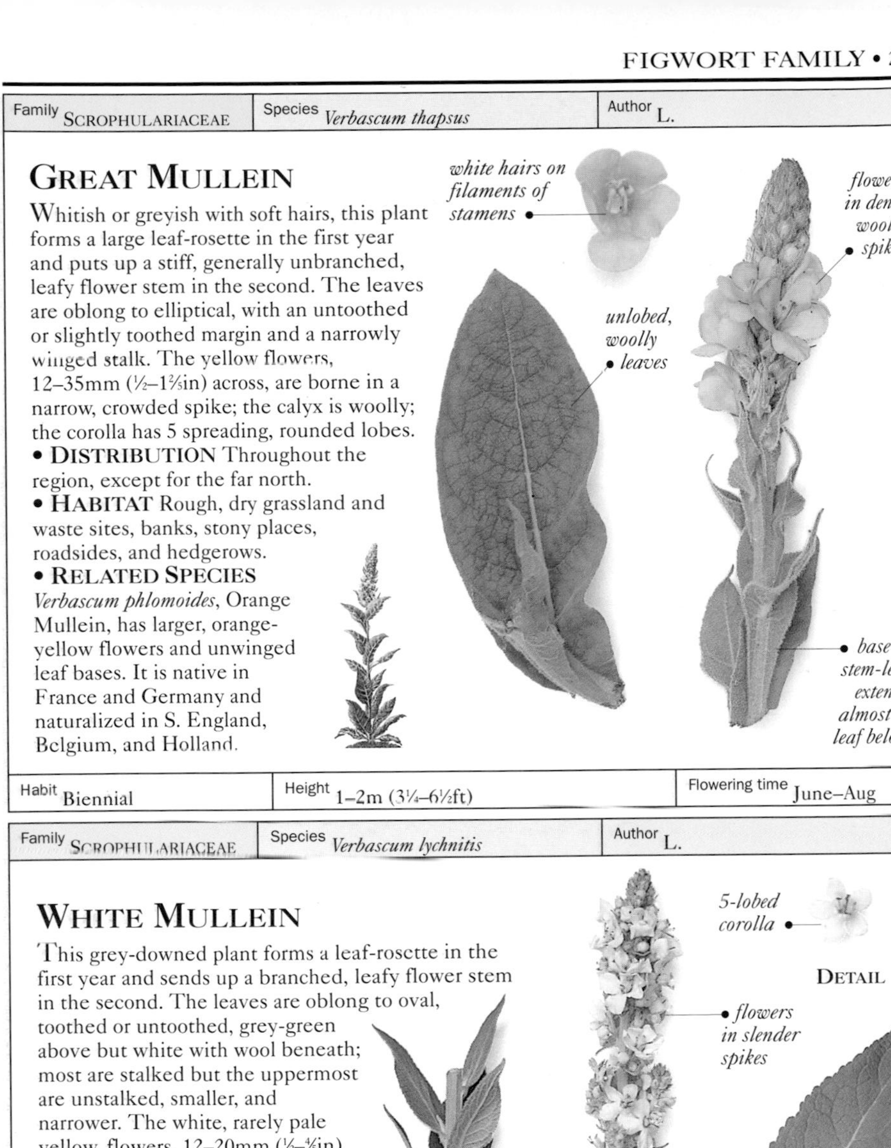

Habit Biennial	Height 1–2m (3¼–6½ft)	Flowering time June–Aug

Family SCROPHULARIACEAE	Species *Verbascum lychnitis*	Author L.

WHITE MULLEIN

This grey-downed plant forms a leaf-rosette in the first year and sends up a branched, leafy flower stem in the second. The leaves are oblong to oval, toothed or untoothed, grey-green above but white with wool beneath; most are stalked but the uppermost are unstalked, smaller, and narrower. The white, rarely pale yellow, flowers, 12–20mm (½–⅘in) across, are borne in branched spikes; the corolla has 5 rounded, spreading lobes. The fruit is a small capsule.
• **DISTRIBUTION** Britain to Denmark and Germany southwards; naturalized elsewhere.
• **HABITAT** Grassy places, hedgerows, scrub, rocky places, railway embankments; mostly calcareous soils.

5-lobed corolla

DETAIL

flowers in slender spikes

unstalked, alternate stem-leaves

stalked lower leaves

Habit Biennial	Height 1–1.5m (3¼–5ft)	Flowering time July–Aug

Family SCROPHULARIACEAE	Species *Verbascum nigrum*	Author L.

DARK MULLEIN

A non-mealy plant, Dark Mullein has basal leaf tufts and erect, leafy flower stems. The alternate leaves, green above but paler beneath, are thinly hairy and oval to oblong, with a toothed margin and often a heart-shaped base. The yellow flowers, 18–25mm (5/7–1in) across, have a slightly cupped corolla with spreading lobes, and are borne in slender, branched or unbranched spikes. The fruit is a small, many-seeded capsule.

• **DISTRIBUTION** Throughout, as far north as S. Sweden, but absent from Ireland; in Britain, confined mainly to the centre and south.

• **HABITAT** Dry grassy and rocky places, embankments, and hedgerows; on calcareous or sandy soils.

Habit Perennial	Height 70–120cm (28–48in)	Flowering time July–Oct

Family SCROPHULARIACEAE	Species *Mimulus guttatus*	Author DC.

MONKEY-FLOWER

This rather fleshy, patch-forming, bright green plant is hairless in the lower parts but glandular-hairy in the upper. The stem is hollow and branched or unbranched. The paired leaves are oval and irregularly toothed, and all but the lowermost are unstalked. Borne in leafy racemes, the bright yellow flowers, 25–45mm (1–1⅘) long, have small red spots in the throat, which is closed by 2 bosses on the lower lip. The fruit capsule is enclosed within the persistent calyx.

• **DISTRIBUTION** A naturalized plant throughout the region, except for the far north. Native to North America.

• **HABITAT** Wet places including marshes, flushes, river, stream, and lake margins; widely cultivated in gardens.

• **RELATED SPECIES** *Mimulus luteus*, Blood-drop Emlets, has open-throated flowers heavily blotched with red. It is naturalized in N. Britain; native to Chile.

2-lobed upper lip
2-lipped corolla
ridged calyx
3-lobed lower lip
square stem
paired leaves

Habit Perennial	Height 30–70cm (12–28in)	Flowering time July–Sept

Family SCROPHULARIACEAE	Species *Scrophularia nodosa*	Author L.

COMMON FIGWORT

This rather robust, hairless plant is glandular in the inflorescence. The stems are erect, branched, and not winged on the angles. Mostly paired, the leaves are oval to lanceolate with a heart-shaped base and a sharply and finely toothed margin; only the lower leaves are stalked. The bracts are mostly linear; the lowermost are leaf-like. Borne in loose panicles, the weakly 2-lipped, flowers, 7–9mm (2/7–3/8in) long, are green with a purplish brown upper lip, or purplish brown all over; the calyx-lobes have membranous margins. The fruit is a 2-parted capsule.

• **DISTRIBUTION** Throughout, except for the far north.

• **HABITAT** Damp places, open woodland, hedgerows, marshy ground, meadows, and stream and river banks; generally on rich deep soils.

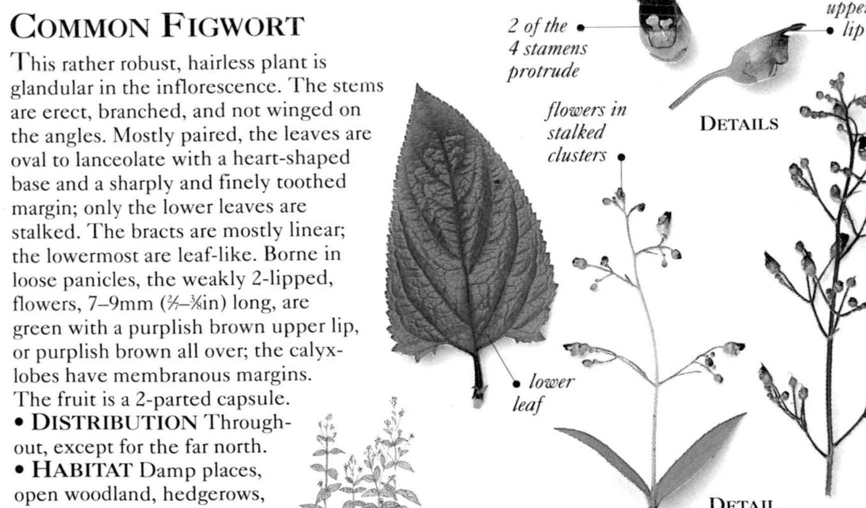

Habit Perennial	Height 60–100cm (24–40in)	Flowering time June–Sept

Family SCROPHULARIACEAE	Species *Scrophularia vernalis*	Author L.

YELLOW FIGWORT

This softly hairy, tufted plant has a glandular inflorescence. The erect stems are branched or unbranched. The opposite leaves are stalked, oval, and mostly have a heart-shaped base and a blunt to pointed apex; the upper leaves are smaller and narrower than the lower. The bracts are small and leaf-like. Borne in airy panicles, the flowers are greenish yellow or dull yellow and 6–8mm (¼–⅓in) long; the calyx has 5 oval lobes half the length of the corolla. The fruit is a 2-parted capsule containing numerous small seeds.

• **DISTRIBUTION** France and S. Germany, but naturalized in Britain and N. Europe as far as S. Sweden.

• **HABITAT** Woodland clearings, coppices, hedgerows, waste and cultivated land; primarily in the mountains to an altitude of 1,800m (5,900ft).

Habit Perennial	Height 30–60cm (12–24in)	Flowering time Apr–June

Family SCROPHULARIACEAE	Species *Scrophularia auriculata*	Author L.

WATER FIGWORT

This more or less hairless plant has stiff, branched, square stems which have a narrow wing on the angles. The inflorescence is glandular. The paired leaves are stalked and often have a pair of small lobes at the base. The pointed bracts are mostly linear and not leaf-like. The greenish or purplish brown flowers are 8–10mm (⅓–⅜in) long; the calyx-lobes are oval with a membranous margin, and are under half the length of the corolla. The 2-parted fruit capsule is many-seeded.

• **DISTRIBUTION** Britain, Ireland, Holland, Belgium, France, and Germany.

• **HABITAT** Wet sites, river, stream, lake, and canal margins, marshes, swamps, fens, ditches, chalk woodland, and occasionally moist cultivated land.

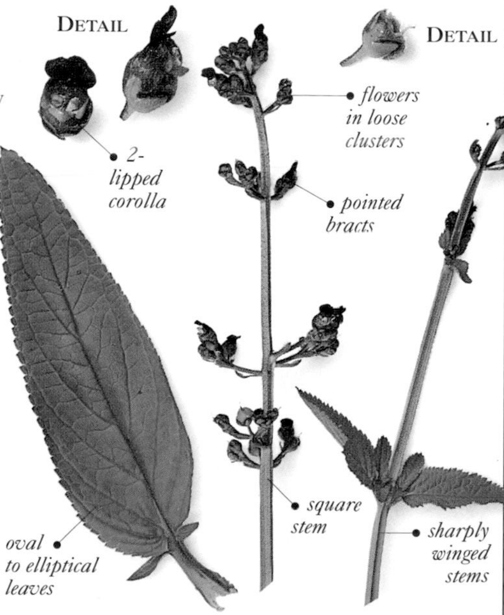

Habit Perennial	Height 70–120cm (28–48in)	Flowering time June–Sept

Family SCROPHULARIACEAE	Species *Antirrhinum majus*	Author L.

SNAPDRAGON

Tufted, branched, and rather soft-leaved, this plant has rounded stems and, while usually hairless below, is sticky with glandular-hairs in the upper parts, especially in the inflorescence. The leaves are linear to elliptical or lanceolate, short-stalked or unstalked; the lower leaves are usually opposite, the upper alternate. The fragrant 2-lipped flowers, 33–45mm (1⅕–1⅘in) long, are pink, purple, or occasionally yellow or bicoloured; the calyx has 5 elliptical lobes; the corolla has a closed "mouth" which bees have to push open. The conical fruit capsule contains many seeds which escape by 3 pores near the top.

• **DISTRIBUTION** Widely naturalized in Britain, Belgium, France, and Germany. A native plant of the Mediterranean region.

• **HABITAT** Rocky places, old walls, abandoned cultivation, railway embankments, waste ground, and arable fields.

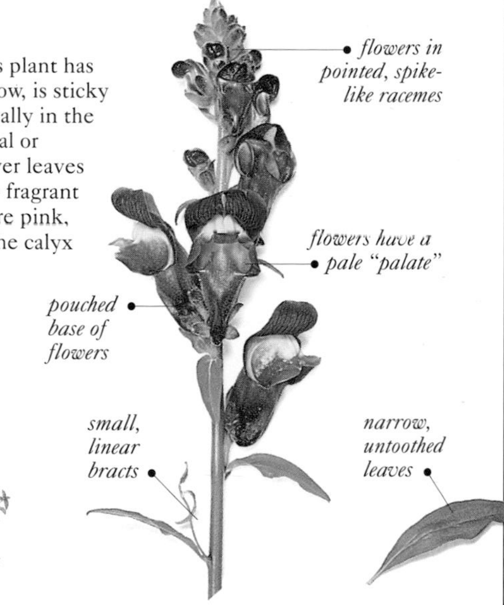

Habit Perennial	Height 40–100cm (16–40in)	Flowering time June–Sept

Family SCROPHULARIACEAE	Species *Misopates orontium*	Author (L.) Raf.

LESSER SNAPDRAGON

Also known as *Antirrhinum orontium*, this plant has thin, rounded, sparsely branched stems which are hairy or hairless in the lower part, but glandular-hairy and sticky in the upper. The linear to elliptical leaves are mostly unstalked; the lower leaves are opposite, the upper alternate. The bracts are leaf-like. The bright pink, rarely white, flowers, 10–15mm (⅖–⅗in) long, are scarcely stalked; the calyx has 5 linear lobes; the corolla has a closed "mouth" and a pouched base. The many seeds of the fruit escape through 3 terminal pores.

• **DISTRIBUTION** Britain, Holland, Belgium, and France; a naturalized plant in Germany; absent or only casual in Scotland and Ireland.

• **HABITAT** On cultivated, disturbed, or waste land, in rocky habitats, and along railway embankments; generally at low altitudes.

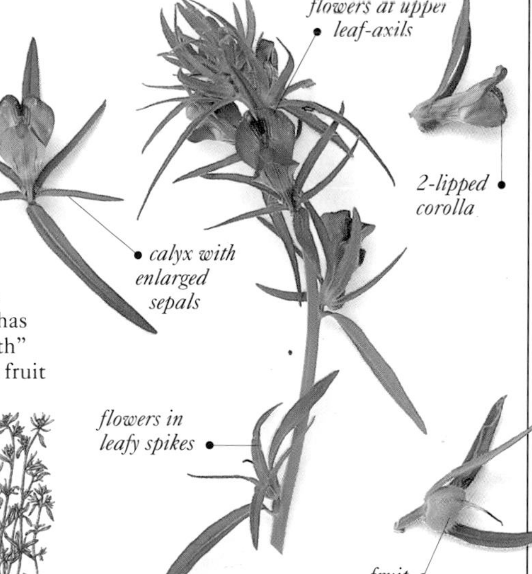

Habit Annual	Height 20–50cm (8–20in)	Flowering time July–Oct

Family SCROPHULARIACEAE	Species *Linaria vulgaris*	Author Miller

COMMON TOADFLAX

This variable, tufted plant has a creeping rhizomatous rootstock and erect, round flowering stems which are hairless or sticky with glandular-hairs in the upper parts. The rather crowded, linear or narrow-elliptical leaves are slightly fleshy and grey-green. The bracts are leaf-like. The flowers are 18–33mm (5/7–1 1/3in) long, and often have orange bosses on the lower lip; the corolla has a closed "mouth". The fruit capsule contains many small seeds that escape through irregular slits located near its apex.

• **DISTRIBUTION** Throughout the region, except for the Faeroes, Iceland, and Spitsbergen.

• **HABITAT** Grassy places, meadows, embankments, roadsides, hedgerows, and rough and waste ground.

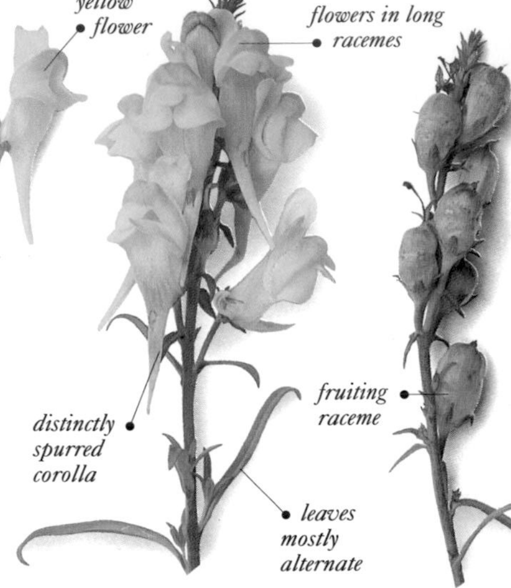

Habit Perennial	Height 40–80cm (16–32in)	Flowering time July–Oct

Family SCROPHULARIACEAE	Species *Linaria purpurea*	Author (L.) Miller

PURPLE TOADFLAX

A rather robust plant, its slender, erect stems are mostly branched in the upper parts, and hairless. The leaves are grey-green; the lower are whorled, but the upper are alternate. The bracts are leaf-like but shorter. The purplish violet to mauve snapdragon-like flowers are 9–15mm (3/8–5/8in) long; the corolla has a closed "mouth". The fruit capsule opens by several slits close to the apex.

• **DISTRIBUTION** Widely naturalized in Britain, occasionally on mainland Europe.

• **HABITAT** Cultivated and waste land, old walls, embankments.

• **RELATED SPECIES** *Linaria repens*, Pale Toadflax, has white to pale lilac flowers with darker veins and a shorter spur. It is native in Belgium, France, and Germany and is naturalized in Britain, Ireland, Holland, and Scandinavia.

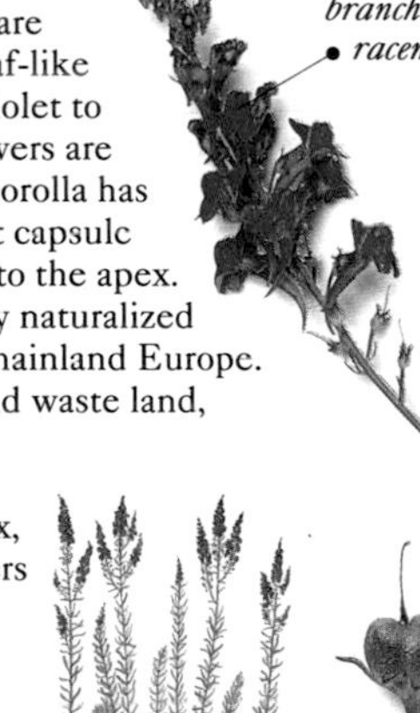

Habit Perennial	Height 60–100cm (24–40in)	Flowering time June–Aug

Family SCROPHULARIACEAE	Species *Kickxia elatine*	Author (L.) Dumort.

SHARP-LEAVED FLUELLEN

Also known as *Linaria elatine*, this plant has thin, branched, mostly hairy stems. The alternate leaves are untoothed; the lower ones are stalked, while the upper are often unstalked and bract-like. In the leaf-axils, the solitary flowers, 7–10mm (2/7–⅖in) long, are yellow with a purple or bluish upper lip. The fruit capsule opens by 2 valves near the apex.

• **DISTRIBUTION** Throughout the region, except for the Faeroes, Iceland, and Norway.

• **HABITAT** Light arable soils and other cultivated land.

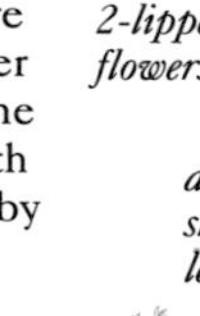

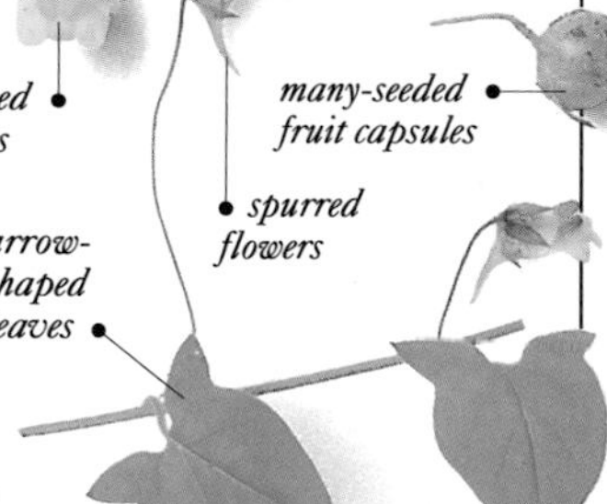

Habit Annual	Height 5–20cm (2–8in)	Flowering time July–Oct

Family SCROPHULARIACEAE	Species *Cymbalaria muralis*	Author P. Gaertn., Mey. & Scherb.

IVY-LEAVED TOADFLAX

The numerous thin stems of this sprawling plant are hairless and often flushed with purple. The rather fleshy, stalked leaves are rounded to kidney-shaped and have 5 to 9 broad triangular lobes but are otherwise untoothed. The flowers, 9–15mm (⅜–⅗in) long, are lilac to mauvish violet with a pale yellow patch on the lower lip. The small fruit capsule opens by irregular slits close to the apex.

• **DISTRIBUTION** Naturalized in the region as far north as C. Scandinavia. A native plant of S. Europe and W. Asia.

• **HABITAT** Rocky places, old walls, pavements, woods; generally in shade.

Habit Perennial	Stem length Up to 60cm (24in)	Flowering time May–Sept

Family SCROPHULARIACEAE	Species *Erinus alpinus*	Author L.

FAIRY FOXGLOVE

This tufted, hairy plant bears leaf-rosettes and leafy flowering stems. The basal leaves are oblong, coarsely toothed, and stalked; the upper are smaller and unstalked. The purple, purplish pink, or rarely white flowers, 6–9mm (¼–⅜in) across, are borne in clusters that elongate as the many-seeded fruit capsules develop.

• **DISTRIBUTION** Mountains of France and Germany; naturalized in N. Britain.

• **HABITAT** Rocky places, cliffs, and old walls, to an altitude of 2,400m (7,900ft).

Habit Perennial	Height 5–18cm (2–7in)	Flowering time May–Oct

Family SCROPHULARIACEAE	Species *Digitalis purpurea*	Author L.

FOXGLOVE

Robust, hairy, and greyish, this plant develops a large leaf-rosette in the first year and an erect leafy flower stem in the second; the stem is unbranched or slightly branched. The leaves, up to 40cm (16in) long, are oval to lanceolate; the lower ones narrow into a winged stalk; the upper are smaller and unstalked. The drooping, funnel-shaped, lipped flowers, 40–55mm (1⅗–2⅕in) long, are pink or purple with darker spots or rings inside, or plain white. The capsule expels the seeds through 3 slits near the apex. The plant is poisonous.

• **DISTRIBUTION** Throughout the region, as far north as C. Sweden.

• **HABITAT** Woodland, hedgerows, river banks, and scrub; on acid soils.

DETAIL

fruit is a many-seeded capsule

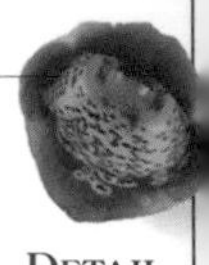

darker spots

DETAIL

tapered, spike-like raceme

softly hairy leaves

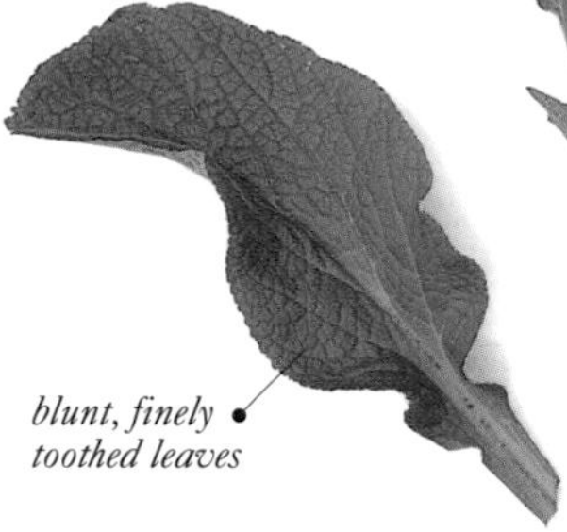

blunt, finely toothed leaves

Habit Biennial or perennial	Height 1–2m (3¼–6½ft)	Flowering time June–Sept

Family SCROPHULARIACEAE	Species *Digitalis lutea*	Author L.

SMALL YELLOW FOXGLOVE

This slightly hairy plant develops a loose leaf-rosette in the first year and flowering stems in the second and subsequent years; the stems are hairless or slightly hairy. The leaves are lanceolate to oblong, toothed, and often broadest above the middle; only the lowermost leaves are stalked. The relatively small flowers are pale yellow, or occasionally whitish, 15–22mm (⅗–⅞in) long, and have no markings; the corolla has 5 pointed lobes. The fruit capsule opens by 3 slits close to the apex.

• **DISTRIBUTION** Belgium, France, and Germany; rarely naturalized in S. England.

• **HABITAT** Woodland margins, rocky places, screes, embankments, roadsides, and old walls; on limy soils.

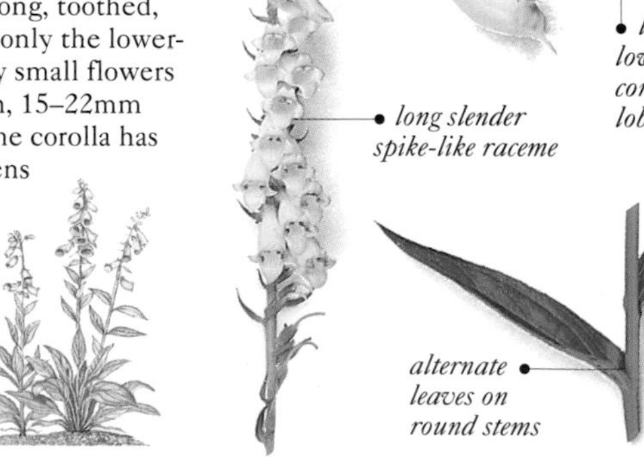

Habit Biennial or perennial	Height 60–100cm (24–40in)	Flowering time June–Aug

Family SCROPHULARIACEAE	Species *Veronica beccabunga*	Author L.

BROOKLIME

Robust, hairless, and rather fleshy, this plant has prostrate to ascending stems that root at the lower nodes. The leaves are oval to oblong or elliptical and short-stalked. The pale to dark blue, rarely pink, flowers, 5–8mm (⅕–⅓in) across, bear only 2 stamens and are borne in paired racemes at the base of the upper leaves. The small fruit capsule is rounded with a slight notch at the top.

• **DISTRIBUTION** Throughout the region, except for Spitsbergen.

• **HABITAT** River, stream, and lake margins, fens, marshes, flushes, ditches, and occasionally on wet meadows.

• **RELATED SPECIES** *Veronica anagallis-aquatica*, Blue Water Speedwell, has scarcely toothed, paler, longer leaves, and pale blue flowers with violet lines. It is absent from the far north.

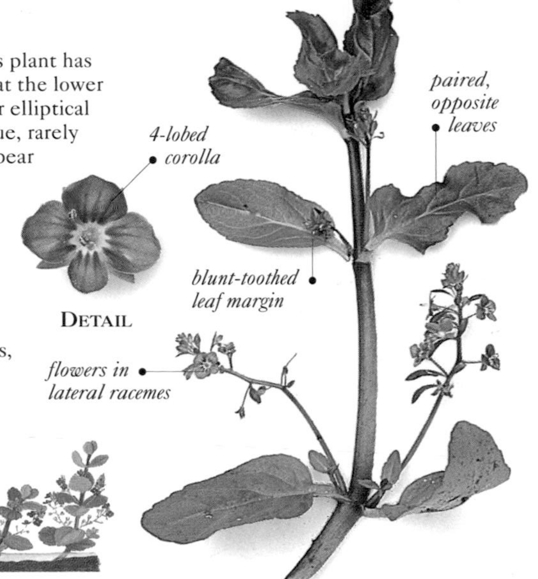

Habit Perennial	Height 20–60cm (8–24in)	Flowering time May–Sept

Family SCROPHULARIACEAE	Species *Veronica chamaedrys*	Author L.

GERMANDER SPEEDWELL

This hairy plant has spreading to sprawling stems that root at the lower nodes. The leaves are oval to almost triangular; the lower leaves are short-stalked, the upper ones usually unstalked. The bright blue flowers, 9–12mm (⅜–½in) across, have 2 stamens and are borne in loose, generally paired, lateral racemes. The small fruit capsules are heart-shaped and shorter than the persistent sepals.

• **DISTRIBUTION** Throughout the region, except for the far north; locally common.

• **HABITAT** Woodland, coppices, thickets, grassy habitats, hedgerows, embankments, and damp stony ground; to an altitude of 2,250m (7,400ft).

• **RELATED SPECIES** *Veronica montana*, Wood Speedwell, has pale lilac-blue flowers, paler, stalked leaves, and stems that are hairy all round. It inhabits damp woodland throughout, except for N. Scandinavia and Iceland.

DETAIL

4-lobed corolla

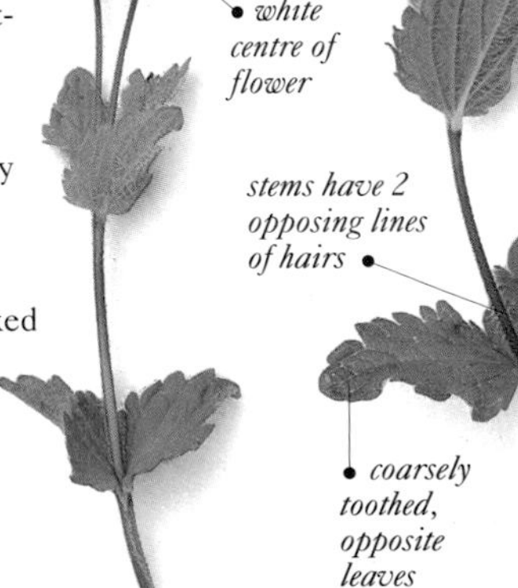

coarsely toothed, opposite leaves

Habit Perennial	Height 20–40cm (8–16in)	Flowering time Mar–July

Family SCROPHULARIACEAE	Species *Veronica serpyllifolia*	Author L.

THYME-LEAVED SPEEDWELL

This variable, creeping, sparsely hairy plant has slender stems rooting at the nodes. The opposite leaves are oval to elliptical, with a toothed or untoothed margin and a short stalk. The pale blue or white flowers, 6–8mm (¼–⅓in) across, generally have darker lines on the upper petal; the corolla has 4 lobes and 2 stamens. The fruit is a small, hairy, heart-shaped capsule.

• **DISTRIBUTION** Throughout.

• **HABITAT** Cultivated, waste, and bare ground, grassy places, and open woodland; generally at low altitudes.

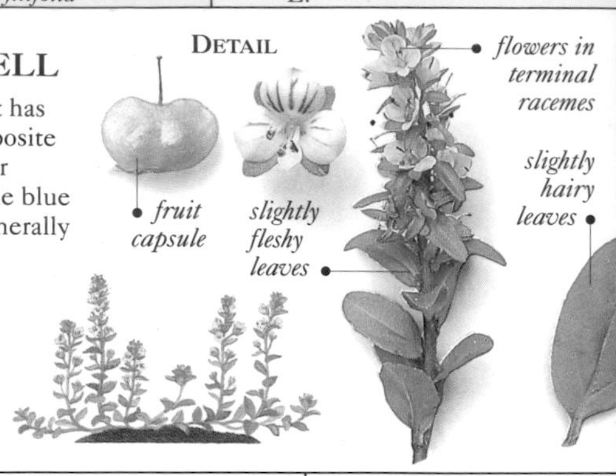

Habit Perennial	Height 10–30cm (4–12in)	Flowering time Mar–Oct

Family SCROPHULARIACEAE	Species *Veronica persica*	Author Poiret

COMMON FIELD-SPEEDWELL

This spreading, hairy plant has thin, branched, prostrate to sprawling stems. The oval leaves are mostly alternate, although the lowermost are usually opposite. The bright blue flowers, 8–12mm (⅓–½in) across, are solitary on slender stalks; the corolla has 4 lobes and 2 stamens. The fruit is a capsule.

• **DISTRIBUTION** A naturalized plant throughout the region, except for the far north.

• **HABITAT** Common on cultivated, waste, and disturbed land.

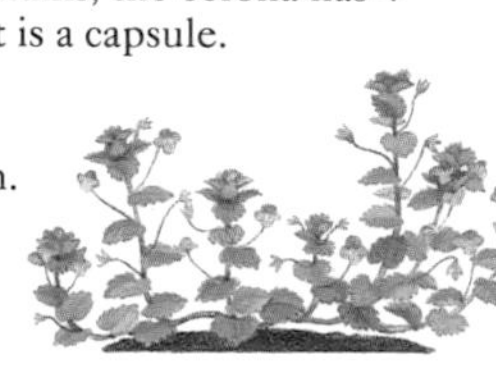

Habit Annual	Height 5–20cm (2–8in)	Flowering time Year-round

Family SCROPHULARIACEAE	Species *Veronica arvensis*	Author L.

WALL SPEEDWELL

This hairy plant has erect to spreading stems. The oval leaves are opposite or alternate; only the lower are short-stalked. Bracts are leaf-like. The flowers, 2–3mm (1/12–⅛in) across, have 2 stamens. The small heart-shaped fruit capsule has a hairy margin.

• **DISTRIBUTION** Grows throughout the region, except for the far north.

• **HABITAT** Dry open places, banks, old walls, grassy slopes, heaths; acid or calcareous soils.

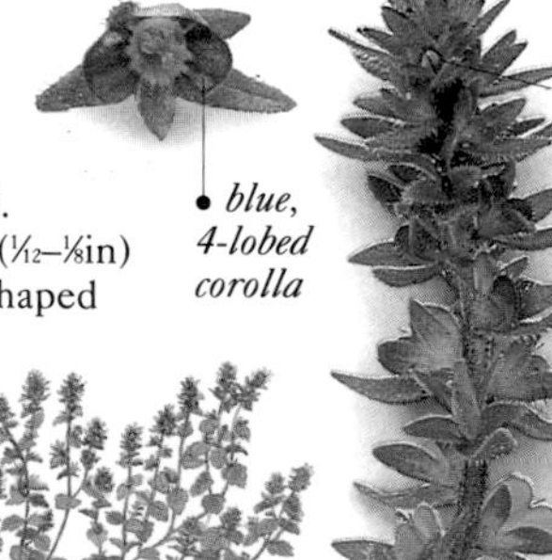

Habit Annual	Height 5–30cm (2–12in)	Flowering time Mar–Oct

Family SCROPHULARIACEAE	Species *Veronica officinalis*	Author L.

HEATH SPEEDWELL

This tufted and hairy plant has spreading to ascending stems which often root down at the lower nodes and are hairy all round. The rather small, paired leaves are oblong to elliptical, often broadest above the middle, stalked, and toothed. The flowers, 5–9mm (⅕–⅜in) across, are lilac-blue or lilac, have darker veins, and are borne in solitary or paired, long-stalked racemes. The bracts are linear. The small fruit capsule is heart-shaped, hairy, and longer than the sepals.

• **DISTRIBUTION** A native plant throughout the region; absent from Spitsbergen.

• **HABITAT** Open woods, heaths, and grassy places; on well-drained soils to an altitude of 2,150m (7,050ft).

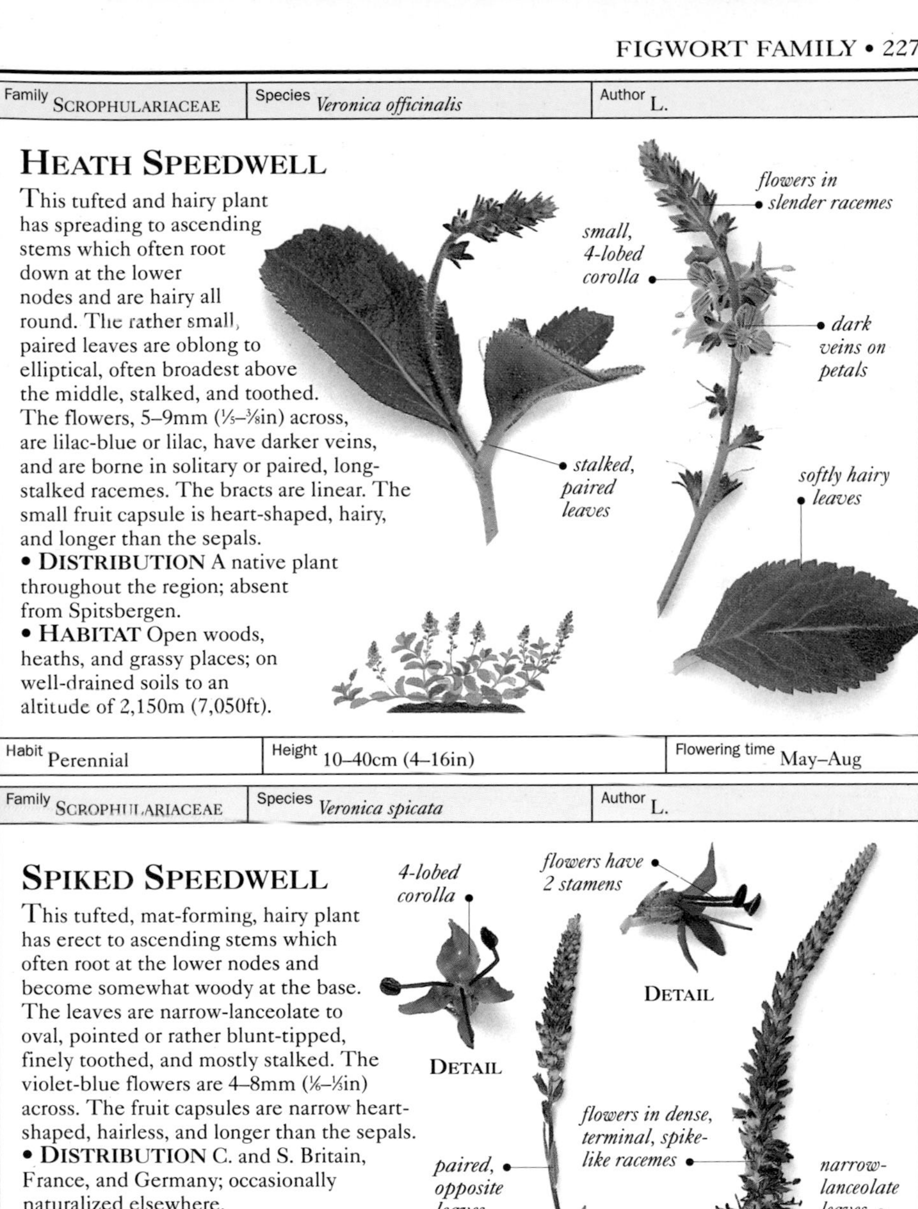

Habit Perennial	Height 10–40cm (4–16in)	Flowering time May–Aug

Family SCROPHULARIACEAE	Species *Veronica spicata*	Author L.

SPIKED SPEEDWELL

This tufted, mat-forming, hairy plant has erect to ascending stems which often root at the lower nodes and become somewhat woody at the base. The leaves are narrow-lanceolate to oval, pointed or rather blunt-tipped, finely toothed, and mostly stalked. The violet-blue flowers are 4–8mm (⅙–⅕in) across. The fruit capsules are narrow heart-shaped, hairless, and longer than the sepals.

• **DISTRIBUTION** C. and S. Britain, France, and Germany; occasionally naturalized elsewhere.

• **HABITAT** Woodland margins, grassy places, and rocky ground; often on calcareous or basic soils.

• **RELATED SPECIES** *Veronica longifolia*, Garden Speedwell, is a much taller plant, with deeply and sharply toothed, pointed leaves, and lilac or pale blue flowers often borne in branched racemes.

4-lobed corolla

flowers have 2 stamens

DETAIL

DETAIL

paired, opposite leaves

flowers in dense, terminal, spike-like racemes

narrow-lanceolate leaves

Habit Perennial	Height 20–60cm (8–24in)	Flowering time July–Oct

Family SCROPHULARIACEAE	Species *Melampyrum cristatum*	Author L.

CRESTED COW-WHEAT

This finely hairy, erect, often branched plant is semi-parasitic on the roots of many herbs. The leaves are narrow-lanceolate to lanceolate, untoothed or sharply toothed towards the base, and pointed. The leaf-like bracts have a sharply toothed, purplish, expanded base. Borne in dense 4-sided spikes, the flowers, 12–16mm (½–⅝in) long, are pale yellow with a purple upper lip or with purple and darker yellow areas; the corolla has a closed "mouth". The small fruit capsule opens along one margin only.

• **DISTRIBUTION** Scattered throughout the region, except for the far north; in Britain, confined to C. and E. England.

• **HABITAT** Dry places, grassy and rocky sites, open woodland, and woodland margins.

2-lipped corolla
DETAIL
paired, unstalked leaves
bracts
erect stem
toothed bract-base
DETAIL

Habit Annual	Height 30–50cm (12–20in)	Flowering time June–Sept

Family SCROPHULARIACEAE	Species *Melampyrum pratense*	Author L.

COMMON COW-WHEAT

This variable, hairless or slightly hairy plant is semi-parasitic on a number of herbs or shrubs. The stems are generally branched. The leaves are oval to linear, tapered to a pointed tip, untoothed, and mostly unstalked. The bracts are similar to the leaves. The bright yellow flowers, 10–18mm (2/5–5/7in) long, are often marked with purple or red. The small 4-seeded fruit capsule splits along one side.

• **DISTRIBUTION** Throughout the region, except for the far north.

• **HABITAT** Woodland, scrub, and heaths.

• **RELATED SPECIES** *Melampyrum sylvaticum*, Small Cow-wheat, has very short, often golden or brownish yellow flowers, with a downturned lower lip. The fruit is 2-seeded. It grows in similar habitats in uplands and mountains.

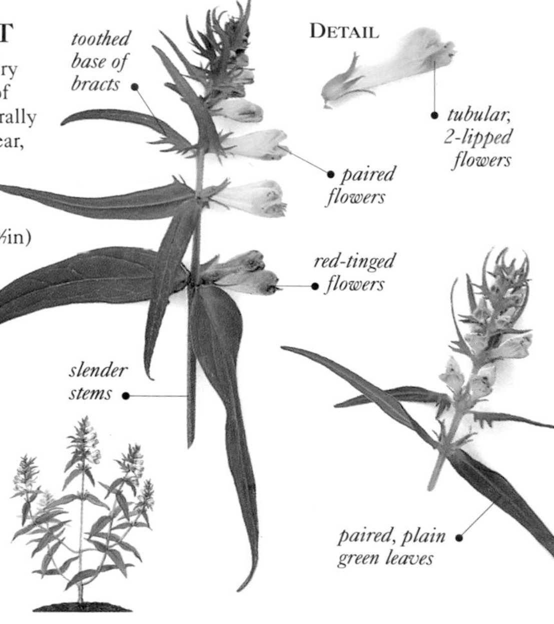

Habit Annual	Height 15–35cm (6–14in)	Flowering time June–Aug

Family SCROPHULARIACEAE	Species *Parentucellia viscosa*	Author (L.) Caruel

YELLOW BARTSIA

A glandular-hairy plant, Yellow Bartsia has erect, usually unbranched stems. The paired, unstalked leaves are oval to lanceolate, with a pointed apex and coarsely toothed margin. The leaf-like bracts decrease in size up the stem. The yellow, rarely white, flowers are 16–24mm (⅝–1in) long; the corolla has an open "mouth", a hooded upper lip, and a 3-lobed lower lip. The hairy fruit capsule contains numerous small seeds.

• **DISTRIBUTION** Britain, Ireland, and France; naturalized in Belgium, Holland, and Denmark.

• **HABITAT** Damp, acid grassy places, often close to the sea.

• **RELATED SPECIES** *Parentucellia latifolia* is a stockier plant, with smaller reddish purple flowers. It inhabits sandy and stony sites from N.W. France southwards.

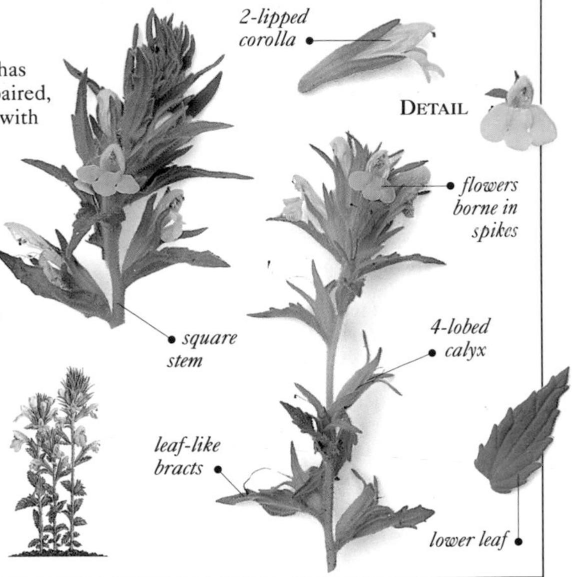

2-lipped corolla
DETAIL
flowers borne in spikes
square stem
4-lobed calyx
leaf-like bracts
lower leaf

Habit Annual	Height 30–50cm (12–20in)	Flowering time June–Sept

Family SCROPHULARIACEAE	Species *Odontites vernus*	Author (Bellardi) Dumort.

RED BARTSIA

This is a very variable, hairy, frequently purple-flushed plant, with erect, more or less square, often branched stems. The paired leaves are lanceolate to narrow-lanceolate or narrow-oblong. The bracts are similar to the leaves and mostly longer than the flowers. The flowers, 8–10mm (⅓–⅖in) long, are reddish pink or occasionally white, and often have protruding stamens; the corolla has an open "mouth". The hairy fruit capsule contains few seeds.

• **DISTRIBUTION** Throughout the region, except for the far north.

• **HABITAT** Grassy places, meadows, pastures, scrub, roadsides, waste places, sea shores, and saltmarshes; on lowland and in the mountains to 1,800m (5,900ft).

• **RELATED SPECIES** *Odontites jaubertianus*, French Bartsia, has linear, untoothed or slightly toothed leaves. The flowers are yellow tinged with pink. It grows on gravelly rough ground and is native in France but naturalized in S. England.

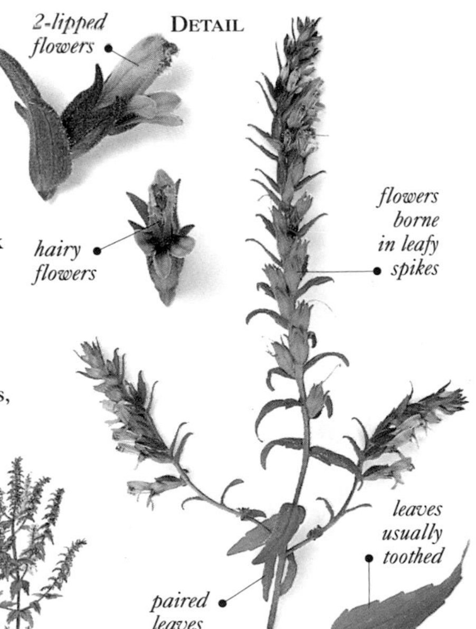

Habit Annual	Height 25–50cm (10–20in)	Flowering time July–Oct

Family SCROPHULARIACEAE	Species *Euphrasia nemorosa*	Author (Pers.) Wallr.

WIND EYEBRIGHT

Often flushed with purple, this short plant has a slender, erect stem, generally with up to 9 pairs of ascending lateral branches. The leaves are elliptical to lanceolate to almost triangular, deep green or purplish green, usually hairy, and with deep marginal teeth; the uppermost leaves are generally larger than the lower. The bracts are similar to the leaves but smaller. The 2-lipped flowers, 5–7.5mm (⅕–⅖in) long, are white or pale lilac, often with a bluish upper lip. The small fruit capsule is oblong and slightly shorter than the sepals.

• **DISTRIBUTION** Grows throughout the region, except for the far north.

• **HABITAT** Grassy places, heaths, open woodland, and sand dunes; often gregarious.

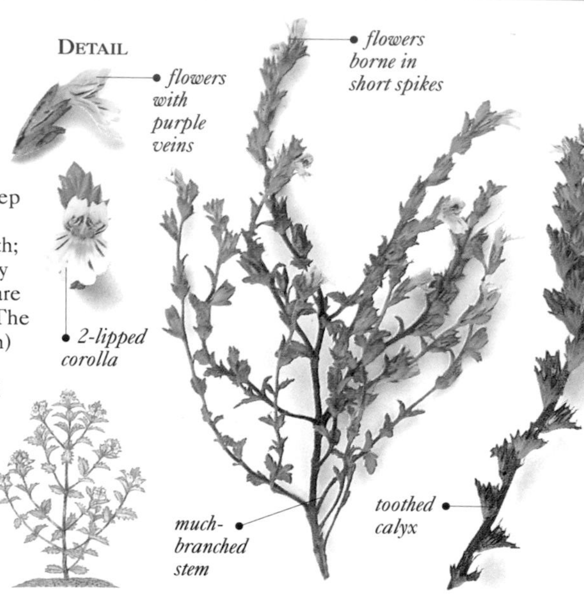

Habit Annual	Height 10–25cm (4–10in)	Flowering time June–Sept

Family SCROPHULARIACEAE	Species *Pedicularis sylvatica*	Author L.

LOUSEWORT

This is a tufted, hairy or hairless plant. The erect, unbranched stems are numerous and often have 2 opposing lines of hairs. The leaves are lanceolate in outline, 2-pinnately lobed, and fern-like. The bracts are similar to the leaves but shorter. The pink or white flowers are 20–25mm (⅘–1in) long, and are borne in rather loose spikes; the calyx is hairless; the upper lip of the corolla has 2 small teeth near the apex. The many-seeded fruit capsule is enclosed within an inflated calyx.

• **DISTRIBUTION** Throughout, except for the far north, the Faeroes, and Iceland.

• **HABITAT** Damp sites, heaths, moors, open woodland; generally on peaty soils.

• **RELATED SPECIES** *Pedicularis palustris*, Marsh Lousewort, is taller, with more open spikes; the calyx is 2-lipped and hairy. It grows in wetter habitats but has a similar distribution.

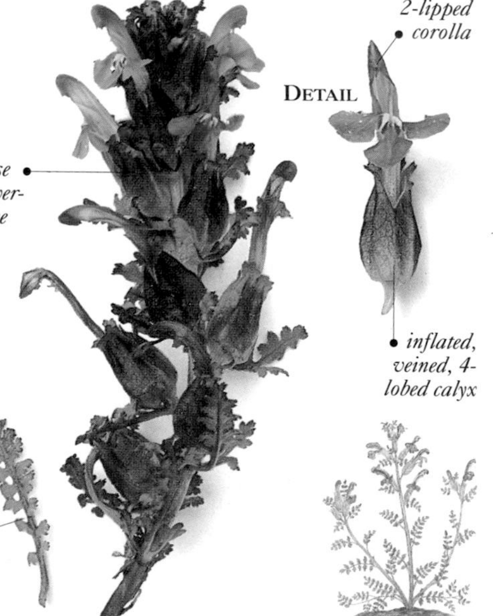

Habit Biennial or perennial	Height 10–25cm (4–10in)	Flowering time Apr–July

Family SCROPHULARIACEAE	Species *Rhinanthus minor*	Author L.

YELLOW RATTLE

This variable, erect, rather stiff-stemmed plant is semi-parasitic on the roots of various herbs; the thin stem is branched or unbranched. The dark green leaves are oblong to narrow-lanceolate, 5–15mm (⅕–⅗in) wide, coarsely toothed, and unstalked. Borne in leafy spikes, the flowers, 13–15mm (½–⅗in) long, are yellow or brownish with violet or white teeth on the upper lip; the calyx is green or reddish with rounded short teeth, and enlarges and dries when the plant is in fruit; the corolla has a more-or-less open "mouth". The fruit capsule contains many seeds, which become loose and rattle within the capsule and the dried calyx and are eventually released by wind action.

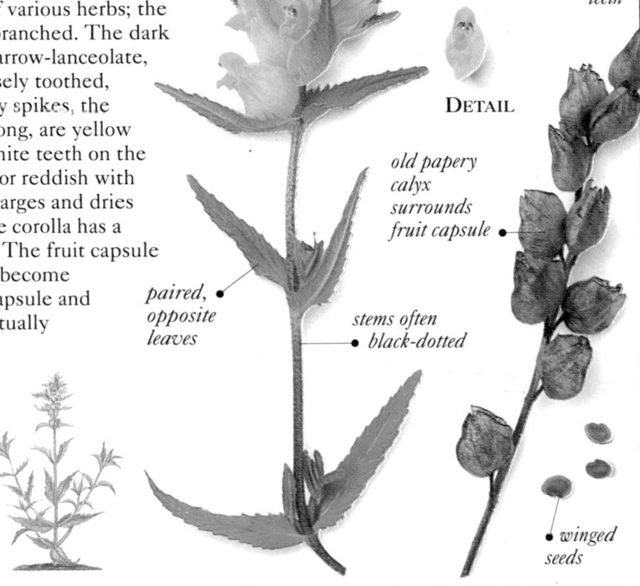

• **DISTRIBUTION** Throughout the region, except for Spitsbergen.

• **HABITAT** Grassy places, meadows, downs, pastures, fens, heaths, roadsides, and orchards; on basic and calcareous soils.

Habit Annual	Height 20–50cm (8–20in)	Flowering time May–Sept

Family SCROPHULARIACEAE	Species *Lathraea clandestina*	Author L.

PURPLE TOOTHWORT

This low parasitic plant is almost stemless and flowers at ground level, forming small tufts on the roots of trees. The fleshy scale-leaves are kidney-shaped, whitish or brownish, alternate or opposite, and clasp the short stem. The bracts are similar to the leaves. The violet flowers, 40–50mm (1⅗–2in) long, have a tubular calyx with 4 short, equal lobes, and a 2-lipped, open-mouthed corolla with a reddish purple lower lip and a hooded upper lip which surrounds the stamens. The fruit is a few-seeded capsule which explodes when ripe to disperse the seeds.

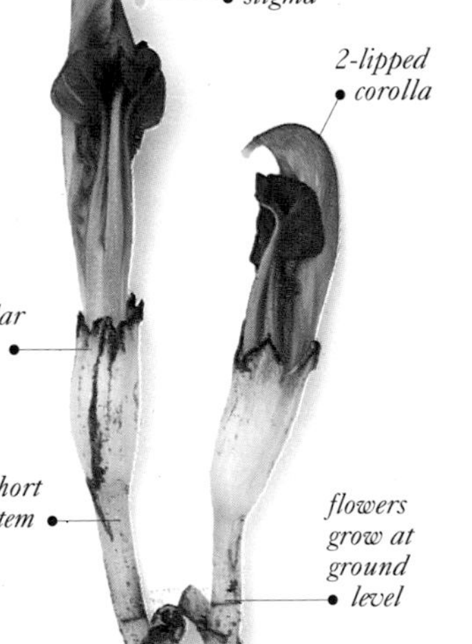

• **DISTRIBUTION** Scattered localities in Belgium and France; naturalized in Britain and Ireland and also widely cultivated in gardens.

• **HABITAT** Parasitic on the roots of various deciduous trees, particularly those of alders, willows, and poplars.

Habit Perennial	Height 4–6cm (1⅗–2⅖in)	Flowering time Apr–May

BROOMRAPE FAMILY

Family OROBANCHACEAE	Species *Orobanche minor*	Author Smith

COMMON BROOMRAPE

This very variable, erect plant is parasitic on the roots of other plants and has no green leaves. The stem is yellowish, often tinged with red or purple, glandular-hairy, and swollen at the base. The alternate scale-leaves are oval to lanceolate and pointed. The bracts are similar to the leaves and roughly equal in length to the flowers. The flowers, 10–18mm (⅖–⅝in) long, are pale yellow, usually tinged with purple, and are borne in spikes that elongate as the flowers open; the stigma is purple. The fruit capsule contains many small seeds.
• **DISTRIBUTION** Throughout much of the region, except for the far north; probably only naturalized in Ireland, Denmark, and Sweden.
• **HABITAT** Meadows and other grassy places, roadsides, and hedgerows; parasitic on clovers (*Trifolium*) and various members of the daisy family, as well as other herbs.

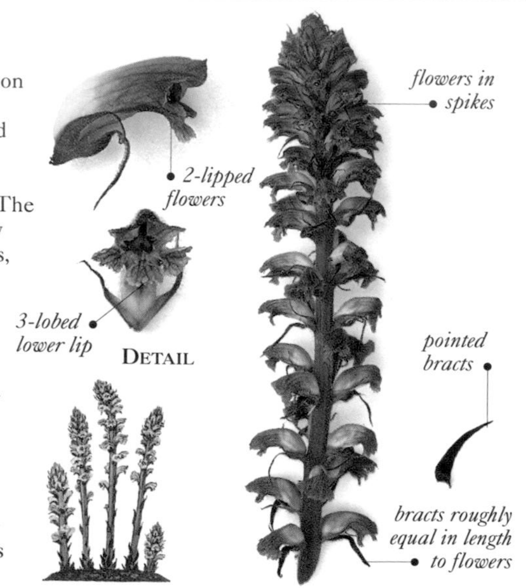

Habit Perennial	Height 30–60cm (12–24in)	Flowering time June–Sept

Family OROBANCHACEAE	Species *Orobanche purpurea*	Author Jacq.

YARROW BROOMRAPE

Lacking chlorophyll, this parasitic plant has no green leaves. The stiff stem is glandular-hairy, usually branched, and greyish or bluish. The scale-leaves are narrow-lanceolate, pointed, and mainly on the lower part of the stem. Bracts and bracteoles are present and appear as 3 bracts to each flower. Borne in fairly dense spikes, the bluish violet flowers, 18–25mm (⅘–1in) long, are generally white underneath; the corolla has a hooded upper lip and a 3-lobed lower lip; the stigma is white or pale blue. The fruit capsule is many-seeded.
• **DISTRIBUTION** Throughout, except for Ireland, N. Scandinavia, and Iceland; in Britain, confined to a few scattered localities in S. England.
• **HABITAT** Rough grassy places; primarily parasitic on *Achillea millefolium*, Yarrow (see p.252).

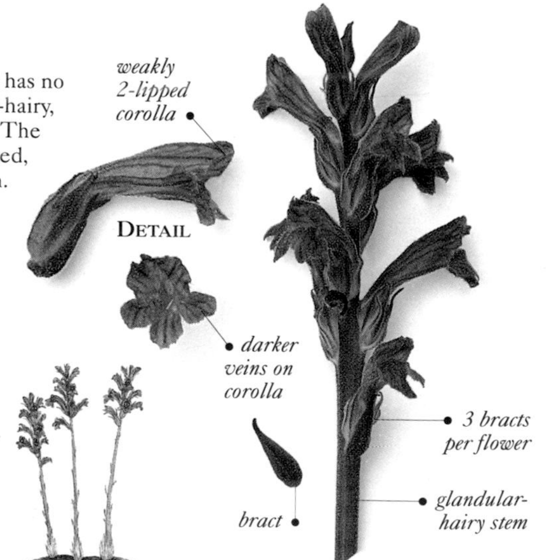

Habit Perennial	Height 25–45cm (10–18in)	Flowering time June–July

Butterwort Family

Family Lentibulariaceae	Species *Pinguicula vulgaris*	Author L.

Common Butterwort

This pale greenish yellow plant has a single basal leaf-rosette and solitary flowers. The fleshy leaves are oblong to elliptical, with inrolled, untoothed leaf margins; the upper surface is sticky with glands. The flowers, 15–20mm (3/5–4/5in) across, are violet with a white patch in the throat, and have a straight or slightly curved spur, 3–6mm (1/8–1/4in) long. The fruit is a small many-seeded capsule.

• **Distribution** Throughout, but rare or absent in much of S. Britain and S. Ireland.

• **Habitat** Bogs, moors, wet heaths, wet rocks, ditches; up to 980m (3,200ft).

• **Remark** The plant is insectivorous, trapping and partly digesting small insects and spiders on the sticky upper surface of the leaves.

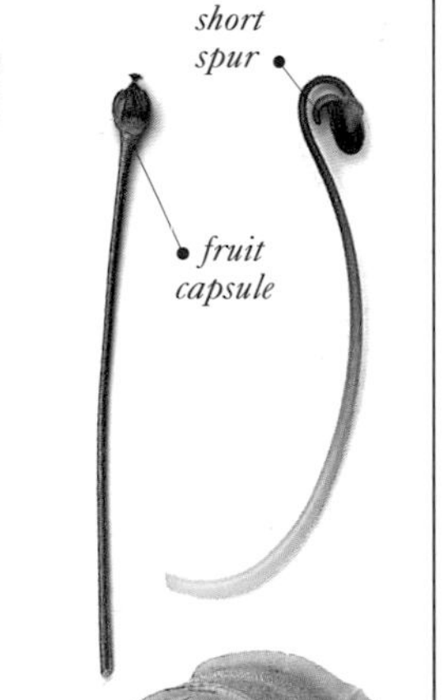

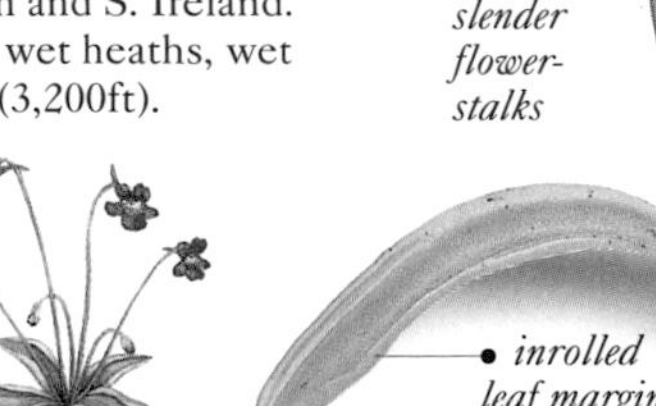

Habit Perennial	Height 5–18cm (2–7in)	Flowering time May–July

Plantain Family

Family Plantaginaceae	Species *Plantago lanceolata*	Author L.

Ribwort Plantain

This is an extremely variable, hairy or sometimes hairless plant, with all the leaves borne in a basal tuft or rosette and with leafless flower-stalks. The stalked leaves are lanceolate to linear-lanceolate, with an untoothed or very slightly toothed margin and 3 to 5 prominent rib-like veins. The tiny flowers are greenish or brownish, and are borne in a long and slender rat's-tail-like spike which often appears to be almost black with pale yellow anthers; the stalk bearing the spike is ridged. The fruit is a small capsule containing many seeds.

• **Distribution** Throughout most of the region, except for the far north.

• **Habitat** Grassy places, fields, meadows, embankments, roadsides, and cultivated and waste land; often gregarious and usually on neutral or chalky soils.

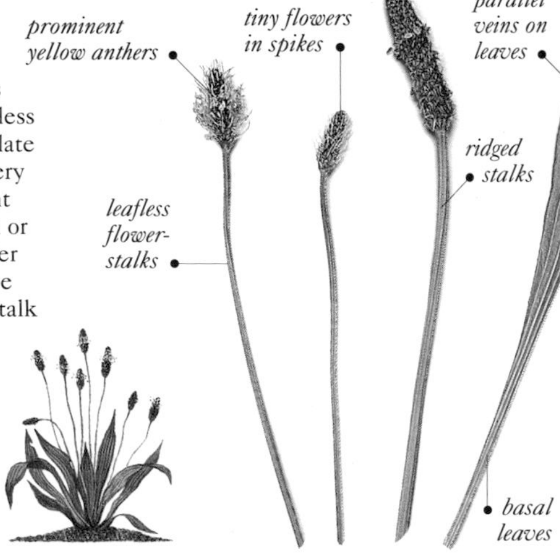

Habit Perennial	Height 20–50cm (8–20in)	Flowering time Apr–Oct

Family PLANTAGINACEAE	Species *Plantago major*	Author L.

GREATER PLANTAIN

This very variable, hairy or more or less hairless plant has a basal rosette of leaves and leafless flower-stalks. The leaves often form a rather flat, ground-hugging rosette, and are thick, dark green, oval to broadly elliptical with a rounded or heart-shaped base, with 5 to 9 main veins; the leaf margin can be toothed or untoothed. The tiny greenish yellow flowers are borne in a dense and slender spike above the foliage; the anthers are pale purple to yellowish or brownish. The fruit is a small capsule containing many seeds.

• **DISTRIBUTION** Throughout the region, except for Spitsbergen; naturalized in Iceland.

• **HABITAT** Grassy cultivated and waste places; often in large colonies, especially on lawns.

• **REMARK** Subsp. *intermedia* grows in damp saline coastal areas; it has a similar distribution.

Habit Perennial	Height 10–35cm (4–14in)	Flowering time June–Oct

Family PLANTAGINACEAE	Species *Plantago coronopus*	Author L.

BUCK'S-HORN PLANTAIN

Usually a hairy plant, Buck's-horn Plantain has one or several, often rather flat or spreading, basal leaf-rosettes, with lanceolate to linear leaves that are mostly pinnately lobed, more rarely unlobed, and sometimes deeply and finely divided. The yellowish brown flowers are borne in slender spikes up to 40mm (1⅗in) long, occasionally more, on unridged stalks; the anthers are pale yellow. The fruit is a small many-seeded capsule.

• **DISTRIBUTION** Throughout, except for the far north.

• **HABITAT** Coastal sands and gravels or short turf; rarely grows inland.

• **RELATED SPECIES** *Plantago maritima*, Sea Plantain, has unlobed leaves and longer spikes. Its distribution and habitats are similar, but it also grows on mountains inland.

tiny flowers in dense spikes
leafless flower-stalks
finely divided, narrow leaves
slender leaf-stalks

Habit Annual or perennial	Height 10–25cm (4–10in)	Flowering time May–July

MOSCHATEL FAMILY

Family ADOXACEAE	Species *Adoxa moschatellina*	Author L.

MOSCHATEL

This delicate, hairless plant is patch-forming, spreading by means of creeping rhizomes. The leaves are pale green; the basal leaves are long-stalked and twice-trifoliate, with oval to oblong, toothed, leaflets; the single pair of stem-leaves are like the basal but less divided, and short-stalked. The small flowers are in clusters, 6–8mm (¼–⅓in) across, of usually 5 flowers; the upper flower is 4-parted, the others are 5-parted. The small greenish fruit is rarely produced.

• **DISTRIBUTION** Grows throughout, except for Holland and the far north.

• **HABITAT** Shady places on damp soils, woodland, coppices, scrub, and rocky places.

small, terminal flower clusters

DETAIL

long-stalked basal leaf

thin, erect, unbranched stem

Habit Perennial	Height 6–15cm (2⅖–6in)	Flowering time Apr–May

HONEYSUCKLE FAMILY

Family CAPRIFOLIACEAE	Species *Lonicera periclymenum*	Author L.

HONEYSUCKLE

A vigorous deciduous climber, Honeysuckle is a hairy or hairless plant with twining stems which become woody with age. The oblong to elliptical leaves are dark green above and bluish green beneath; the lower leaves are stalked; the upper are unstalked but not fused together. The flowers, 35–55mm (1⅖–2⅕in) long, are creamy white changing to yellow, and sometimes purple-flushed; the slender corolla tube has a 4-lobed upper lip and one-lobed lower lip. The ripe berries are red.

• **DISTRIBUTION** Throughout, as far north as C. Scandinavia.

• **HABITAT** Woodland, coppices, hedgerows, rocky places, and cliffs.

• **RELATED SPECIES** *Lonicera caprifolium*, Perfoliate Honeysuckle, has its upper leaves fused together below the flowers. It has a similar distribution but is naturalized.

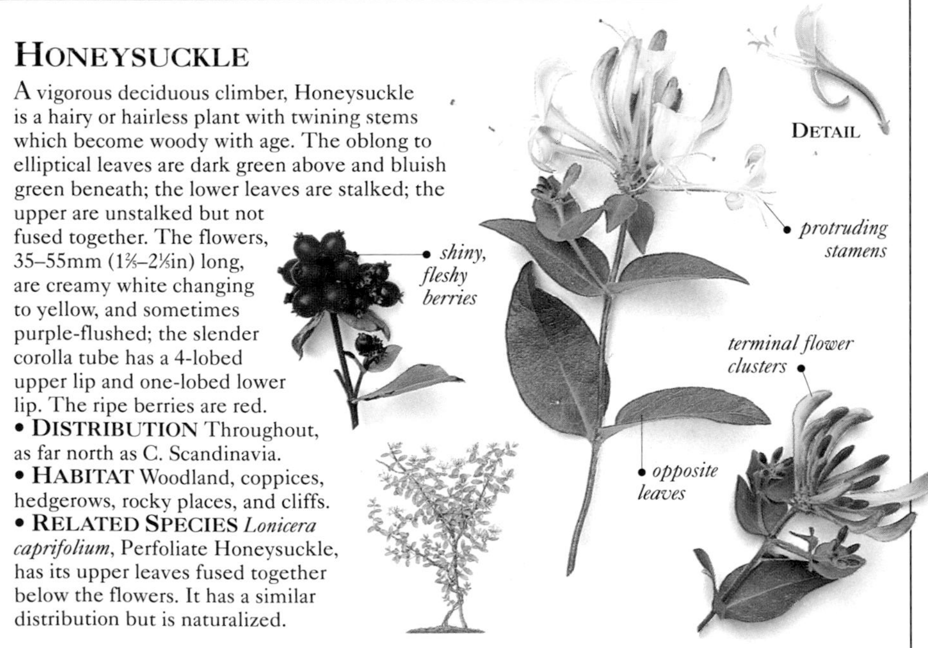

Habit Climbing shrub	Height 2–6m (6½–20ft)	Flowering time June–Oct

Family CAPRIFOLIACEAE	Species *Sambucus ebulus*	Author L.

DWARF ELDER

This spreading, patch-forming, hairless herb has vigorous underground rhizomes and erect stems. The large, stalked, pinnate leaves have 5 to 13 lanceolate to elliptical leaflets. The stipules are conspicuous, oval, toothed, and leaflet-like. The scented, white flowers are borne in branched, flat-topped clusters up to 16cm (6¼in) across, and have 5 sepals, 5 petals, and protruding stamens. The fruit is a small fleshy berry.

• **DISTRIBUTION** Britain, and Belgium to Germany southwards; naturalized elsewhere, particularly in Denmark and S. Sweden.

• **HABITAT** Hedgerows, woodland margins, rough ground, and waste places.

DETAIL

5-petalled flowers

small flowers in broad, flat heads

paired leaves

ripe black fruit

sharply toothed leaflets

Habit Perennial	Height 80–150cm (32–60in)	Flowering time July–Aug

VALERIAN FAMILY

Family VALERIANACEAE	Species *Valerianella locusta*	Author (L.) Laterr.

COMMON CORNSALAD

This is a variable, often small, hairless plant. The leaves are pale green; the lower leaves are broadly oval to more-or-less spoon-shaped, untoothed, and usually stalked; the upper leaves are oval to lanceolate, untoothed or slightly toothed. The tiny flowers are pink or bluish and are borne in small umbel-like clusters on thin, branching stems. The small rounded fruit, only 2mm (1/12in) across, is smooth or faintly ridged.

• **DISTRIBUTION** Throughout, but mainly coastal in the north of its range.

• **HABITAT** Cultivated, waste, and disturbed land, sparsely grassy places, rocky areas, wall-tops, and sand dunes.

• **REMARK** Also known commonly as Lamb's Lettuce and sometimes grown as a salad crop for its edible young leaves.

Habit Annual	Height 5–20cm (2–8in)	Flowering time Apr–June

Family VALERIANACEAE	Species *Valeriana officinalis*	Author L.

COMMON VALERIAN

The hairless stems of this variable plant are generally branched in the upper part. The pinnate leaves have linear to lanceolate or oval, toothed leaflets; the lower leaves are long-stalked, while the upper are short-stalked, smaller, and have fewer leaflets. The pink or white flowers, 2.5–5mm (1/10–1/5in) long, are borne in broad panicles or rounded clusters; the calyx consists of 5 tiny teeth; the corolla has a thin, slightly spurred or pouched tube with 5 spreading lobes and 3 stamens. The non-splitting fruit may be hairy or hairless.

• **DISTRIBUTION** Britain, Ireland, France, Belgium, Holland, Denmark, and Iceland.

• **HABITAT** Dry or damp grassy places such as meadows, pastures, and fens.

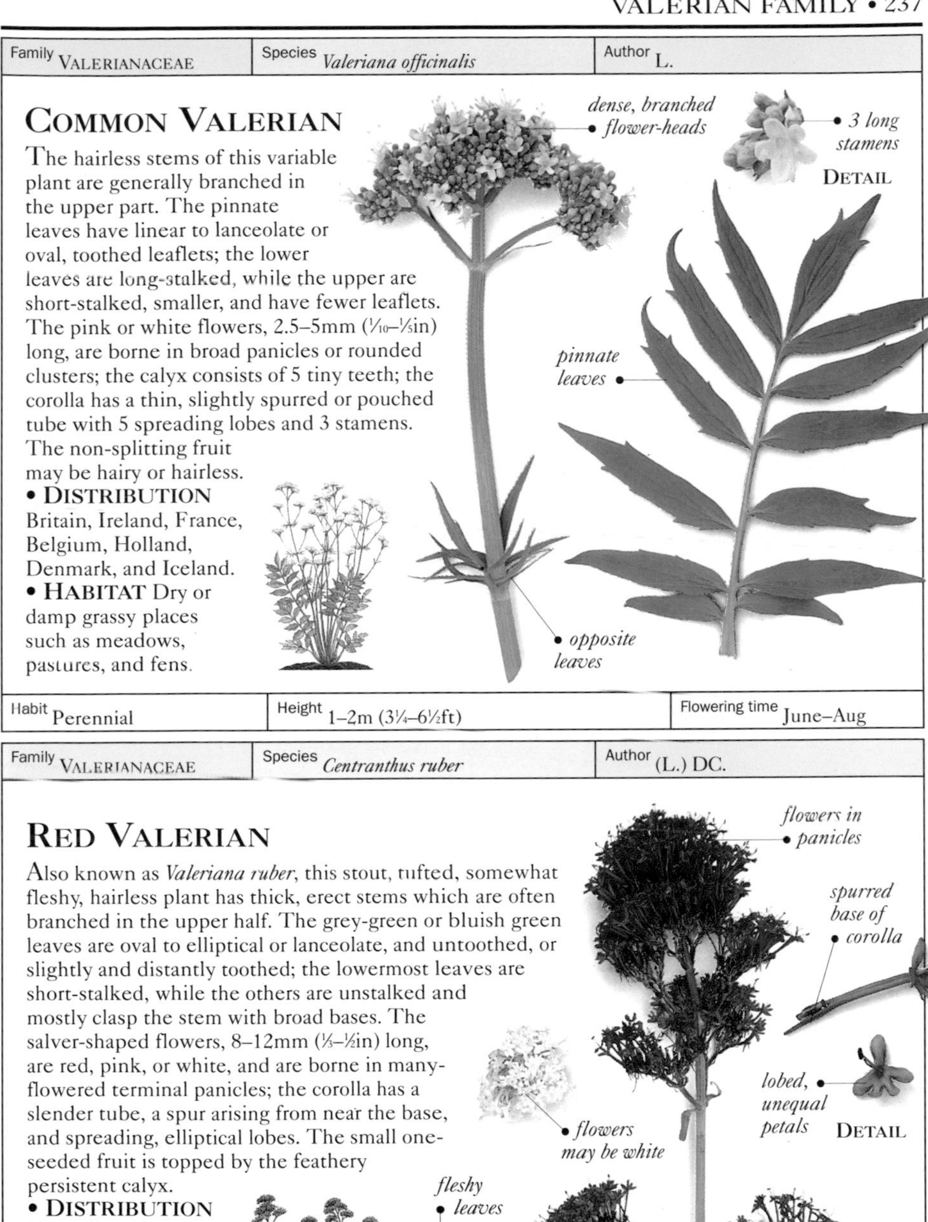

Habit Perennial	Height 1–2m (3¼–6½ft)	Flowering time June–Aug

Family VALERIANACEAE	Species *Centranthus ruber*	Author (L.) DC.

RED VALERIAN

Also known as *Valeriana ruber*, this stout, tufted, somewhat fleshy, hairless plant has thick, erect stems which are often branched in the upper half. The grey-green or bluish green leaves are oval to elliptical or lanceolate, and untoothed, or slightly and distantly toothed; the lowermost leaves are short-stalked, while the others are unstalked and mostly clasp the stem with broad bases. The salver-shaped flowers, 8–12mm (1/3–1/2in) long, are red, pink, or white, and are borne in many-flowered terminal panicles; the corolla has a slender tube, a spur arising from near the base, and spreading, elliptical lobes. The small one-seeded fruit is topped by the feathery persistent calyx.

• **DISTRIBUTION** Naturalized in Britain, N. Ireland, France, and Holland.

• **HABITAT** Dry, sunny sites, coastal rocks and cliffs, old walls, sandy places.

Habit Perennial	Height 50–80cm (20–32in)	Flowering time June–Aug

TEASEL FAMILY

Family DIPSACACEAE	Species *Dipsacus fullonum*	Author L.

WILD TEASEL

This plant forms a basal rosette of leaves in the first year and puts up stiff flowering stems in the second; the stems are erect, angled, and prickly. The leaves are oblong-elliptic to lanceolate, and usually untoothed; the basal leaves are stalked and wither by flowering time; the stem-leaves fuse around the stem to form a cup that fills with water. The bracts are linear, curved, and spiny. The flower-heads, 30–80mm (1⅕–3⅕in) long, are oblong, with the pinkish purple to lilac flowers opening progressively up the head. The fruit is a small achene.

• **DISTRIBUTION** Britain, Ireland, Belgium, Holland, France, Germany, Denmark.

• **HABITAT** Grassy places, meadows, embankments, roadsides, hedgerows, woodland margins, and river- and stream-banks; generally growing on clay soils.

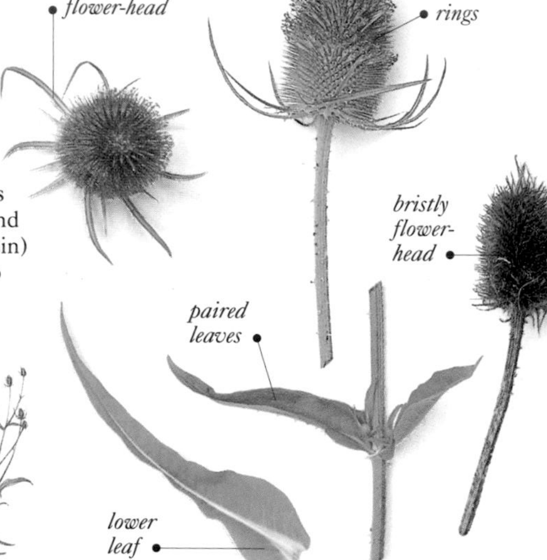

Habit Biennial	Height 1–2m (3¼–6½ft)	Flowering time July–Aug

Family DIPSACACEAE	Species *Dipsacus pilosus*	Author L.

SMALL TEASEL

Daintier than most teasels, this species forms a leaf-rosette in the first year and flowers in the second. The stiff stem is usually branched. The leaves are hairy; the basal are oblong, toothed, and stalked, while the stem-leaves are oval to elliptical, with a pair of basal lateral leaflets, short-stalked, and sometimes slightly prickly. The bracts are linear and prickly, forming a small ruff at the base of the flower-head. The bristly flower-heads, 15–20mm (⅗–⅘in) across, have white flowers; the funnel-shaped corolla has 4 short lobes and 4 protruding stamens.

• **DISTRIBUTION** Native in England and Wales, and on mainland Europe as far north as S. Sweden.

• **HABITAT** Damp sites, open woodland, hedgerows, and streamsides.

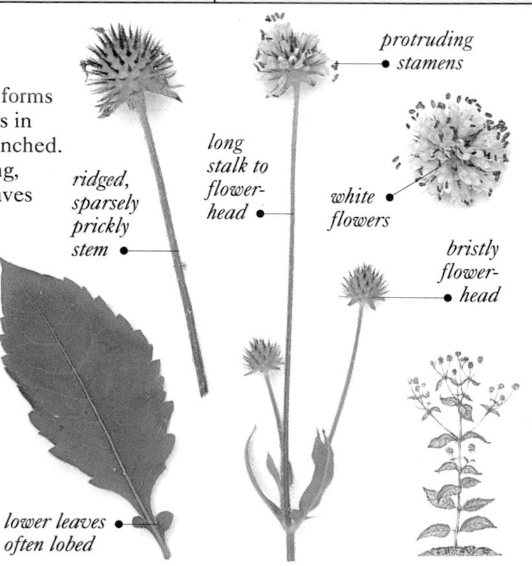

Habit Biennial	Height 80–150cm (32–60in)	Flowering time Aug–Sept

Family DIPSACACEAE	Species *Succisa pratensis*	Author Moench

DEVIL'S-BIT SCABIOUS

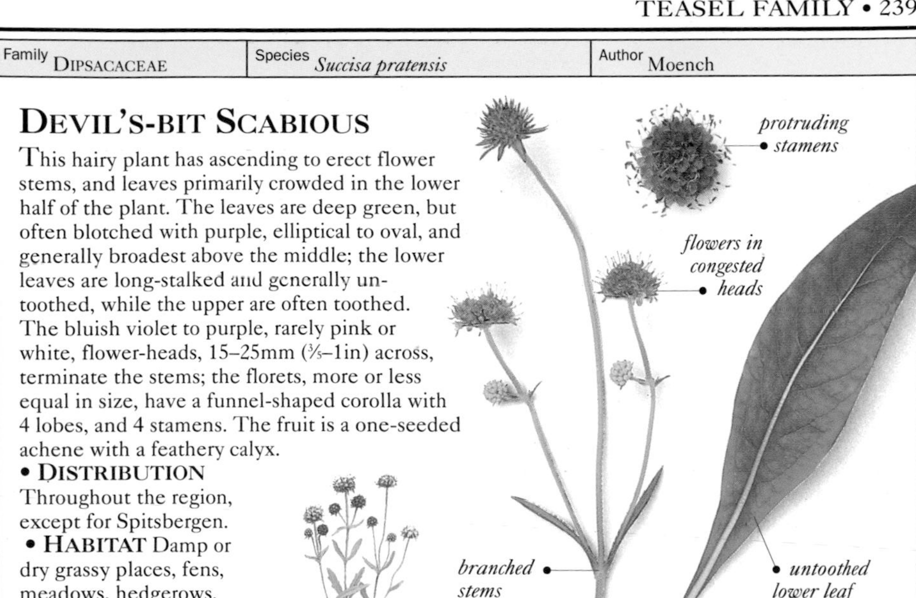

This hairy plant has ascending to erect flower stems, and leaves primarily crowded in the lower half of the plant. The leaves are deep green, but often blotched with purple, elliptical to oval, and generally broadest above the middle; the lower leaves are long-stalked and generally untoothed, while the upper are often toothed. The bluish violet to purple, rarely pink or white, flower-heads, 15–25mm (3/5–1in) across, terminate the stems; the florets, more or less equal in size, have a funnel-shaped corolla with 4 lobes, and 4 stamens. The fruit is a one-seeded achene with a feathery calyx.

• **DISTRIBUTION** Throughout the region, except for Spitsbergen.

• **HABITAT** Damp or dry grassy places, fens, meadows, hedgerows, open woodland, heaths; on both calcareous and slightly acid soils.

Habit Perennial	Height 50–100cm (20–40in)	Flowering time July–Oct

Family DIPSACACEAE	Species *Scabiosa columbaria*	Author L.

SMALL SCABIOUS

A tufted, hairy plant, Small Scabious has much-branched ascending to erect stems. The lower leaves are oval to lanceolate, lobed or unlobed, and long-stalked, while the upper leaves are narrower and more finely pinnately dissected. The bracts are narrow, lanceolate, and pointed. The flower-heads, 20–40mm (4/5–1 3/5in) across, are bluish lilac; the corolla is funnel-shaped, with 4 spreading lobes and 4 stamens. The one-seeded fruit is adorned by a feathery persistent calyx.

• **DISTRIBUTION** Throughout the region as far north as S. Sweden, but absent from Ireland.

• **HABITAT** Dry grassy places, meadows, downs, embankments, roadsides, and coastal areas; on calcareous soils.

• **REMARK** Coastal forms growing in exposed places may be very dwarf.

bracts shorter than florets

bristly fruit-head

outer florets larger than central florets

upper leaf

lower leaf

Habit Perennial	Height 10–70cm (4–28in)	Flowering time July–Aug

Family DIPSACACEAE	Species *Knautia arvensis*	Author (L.) Coulter

FIELD SCABIOUS

Rather robust and hairy, this plant has branched, often purple-spotted stems, with basal leaf-rosettes. The lower leaves are pinnately lobed; the basal are sometimes undivided and spoon-shaped; the upper are smaller and less divided. The linear-lanceolate bracts are roughly as long as the florets. The bluish lilac flower-heads, 20–40mm (⅘–1⅗in) across, terminate the stems.

• **DISTRIBUTION** Throughout the region, except for the far north; often local in the north of its range.

• **HABITAT** Grassy places, embankments, hedgerows, and open woodland; mainly on light, neutral to calcareous, well-drained soils.

ruff of bracts below flower-head

enlarged, 4-lobed outer florets

lanceolate terminal leaflet

flower-head in bud

branched stem

pinnately lobed basal leaves

stalked basal leaves

paired, unstalked upper leaves

Habit Perennial	Height 50–100cm (20–40in)	Flowering time July–Sept

BELLFLOWER FAMILY

Family CAMPANULACEAE	Species *Campanula rapunculoides*	Author L.

CREEPING BELLFLOWER

Sparsely hairy or hairless, this stoloniferous plant is patch-forming, with stiff and slender, generally unbranched, stems. The deep green, toothed leaves are variable: the basal are heart-shaped and long-stalked; the upper are oval to lanceolate and unstalked. The bracts are leaf-like and decrease in size up the inflorescence. The violet-blue, rarely white, bellflowers, 20–30mm (⅘–1⅕in) long, are borne in a slender, somewhat tapered spike with the lowermost flowers opening first; the calyx, with narrow spreading lobes, is much shorter than the corolla; the corolla is 5-lobed and edged with hairs. The pendent fruit capsules release seed through narrow slits when ripe.

• **DISTRIBUTION** Mainland Europe except for the far north; naturalized in Britain and Ireland.

• **HABITAT** Grassy places, woods, embankments, hedgerows, and rocky places; widely grown in gardens.

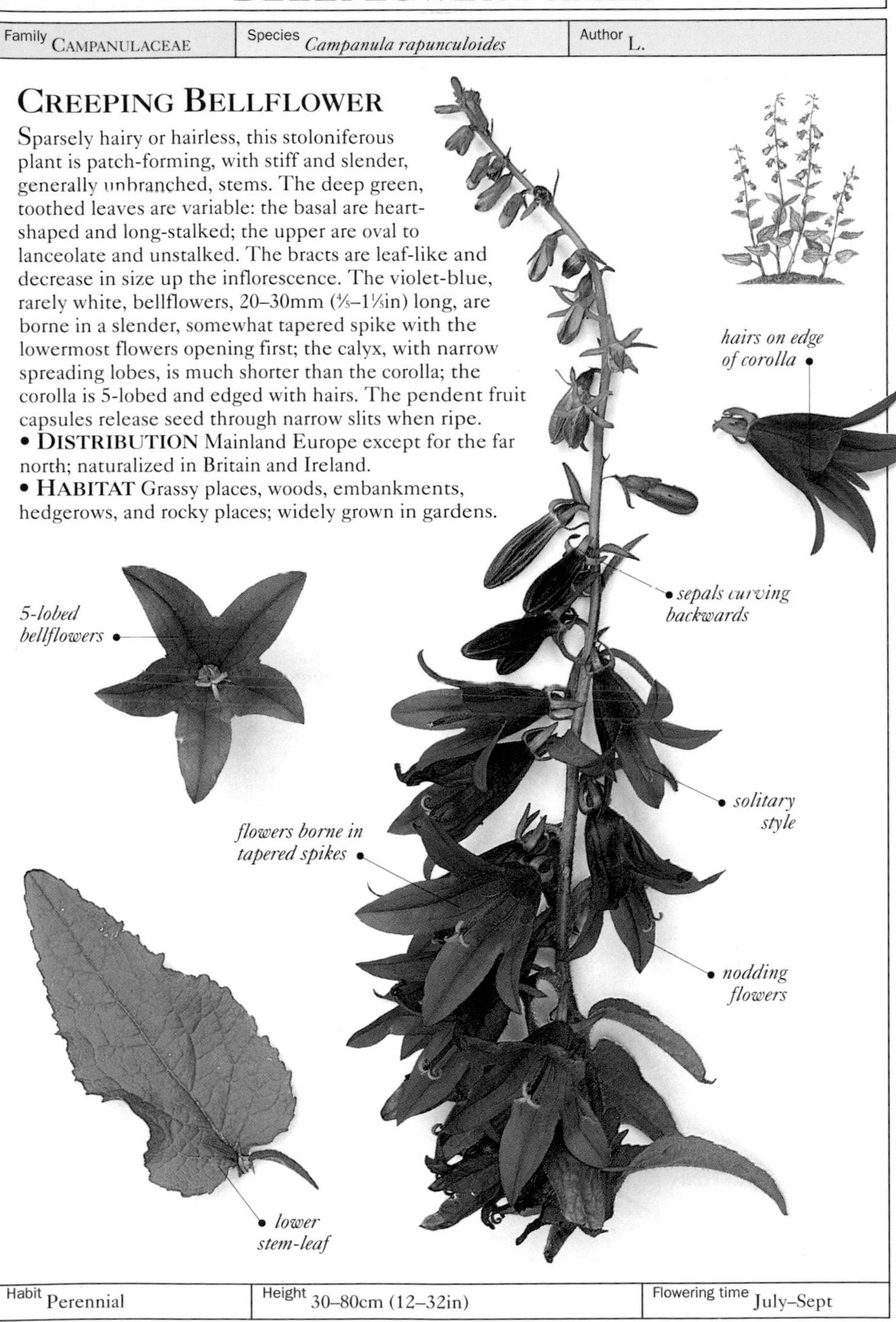

Habit Perennial	Height 30–80cm (12–32in)	Flowering time July–Sept

Family CAMPANULACEAE	Species *Campanula trachelium*	Author L.

NETTLE-LEAVED BELLFLOWER

This rather robust, hairy plant has stiff, angled, bristly stems. The leaves, deep green on top but paler beneath, are broad-lanceolate; the lower leaves are stalked and often slightly heart-shaped at the base; the upper are unstalked. The pale blue to violet-blue flowers are 25–50mm (1–2in) long. The fruit capsule is pendent.

• **DISTRIBUTION** Throughout, except for the far north; scarcer in N. Britain and Ireland.

• **HABITAT** Woodland margins, hedgerows, and scrub; on calcareous soils.

• **RELATED SPECIES** *Campanula latifolia*, Giant Bellflower, has most stem-leaves narrowed at the base and unstalked. Its habitats are moister. Its distribution is similar, but it is very rare in S. England and scarce in the north of its range.

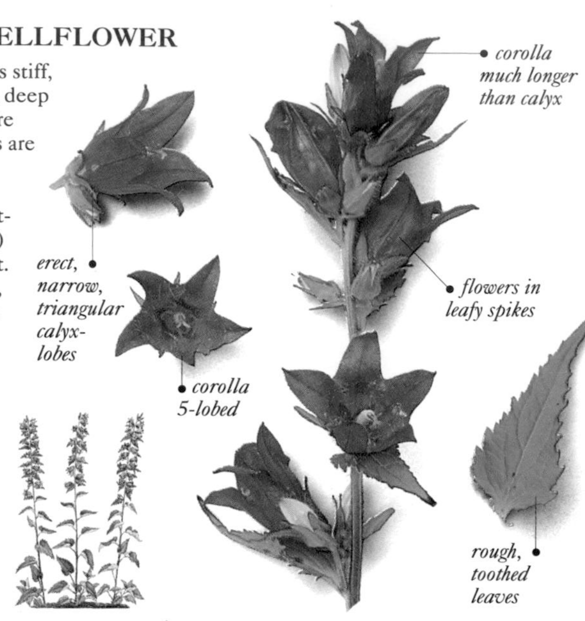

Habit Perennial	Height 40–80cm (16–32in)	Flowering time July–Sept

Family CAMPANULACEAE	Species *Campanula rotundifolia*	Author L.

HAREBELL

This very variable, hairless or slightly hairy plant has creeping stolons and is often patch-forming. The thin, erect to ascending stems produce a white latex when cut (as do most of the Campanulaceae). The basal leaves are round to oval or lanceolate, toothed, and stalked, while the middle and upper stem-leaves are narrower, often linear, untoothed, and unstalked. The pale to bright blue, occasionally white, bellflowers, 12–20mm (½–⅘in) long, are borne in airy, often few-flowered, panicles; the calyx-lobes are linear and spreading. The fruit capsule is pendent.

• **DISTRIBUTION** Throughout, except for parts of the far north.

• **HABITAT** Grassy places, meadows, heaths, commons, downs, embankments, roadsides, rocky places, and sand dunes; on acid or calcareous soils to 2,200m (7,200ft).

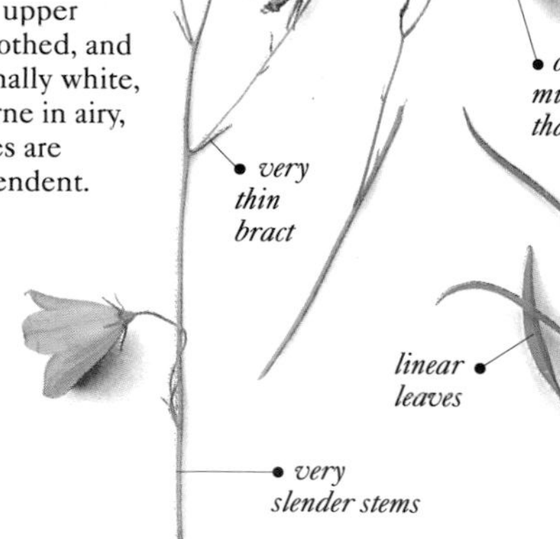

Habit Perennial	Height 20–50cm (8–20in)	Flowering time July–Sept

Family CAMPANULACEAE	Species *Phyteuma orbiculare*	Author L.

ROUND-HEADED RAMPION

This is a variable, hairless or slightly hairy, tufted plant, with erect flowering stems. The lower leaves are elliptical to lanceolate with a rounded or slightly heart-shaped base, and are toothed; the upper leaves are narrow-elliptical to linear, and generally untoothed. The bracts, immediately beneath the flower-head, are oval, and toothed or not. The flower-heads, 10–20mm (⅖–⅘in) across, are violet-blue or deep blue; the corolla is strongly incurved in bud, splitting almost to the base when open. The many-seeded fruit capsule splits by 2 or 3 lateral pores when ripe.

• **DISTRIBUTION** Native in S. England, France, and Germany.

• **HABITAT** Grassy places, meadows that are often closely grazed, and embankments; always growing on calcareous soils.

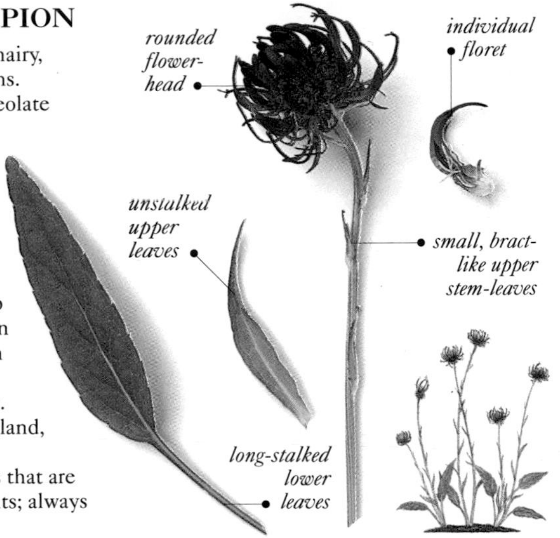

rounded flower-head

individual floret

unstalked upper leaves

small, bract-like upper stem-leaves

long-stalked lower leaves

Habit Perennial	Height 20–50cm (8–20in)	Flowering time June–Aug

Family CAMPANULACEAE	Species *Jasione montana*	Author L.

SHEEP'S BIT

This is a tufted, rather variable, hairy plant, with erect to ascending flower-stems. The leaves are grey-green; the lower oblong to lanceolate, with a wavy, untoothed margin, and often short-stalked; the upper narrower and unstalked. The oval to lanceolate bracts are untoothed, forming a ruff below the flower-head. The pale blue flower-heads, 5–30mm (⅕–1⅕in) across, terminate the stems. Each flower has a corolla with 5 spreading, narrow lobes, 5 stamens, and a protruding style. The fruit capsule opens by 2 valves at the apex.

• **DISTRIBUTION** Throughout the region, except for the Faeroes, Iceland, and parts of the far north.

• **HABITAT** Dry grassland, beaches, heaths, rocky places, cliffs, and coastal rocks and shingles; on light acid soils to 1,700m (5,600ft).

Habit Perennial	Height 20–50cm (8–20in)	Flowering time May–Aug

DAISY FAMILY

Family COMPOSITAE	Species *Eupatorium cannabinum*	Author L.

HEMP-AGRIMONY

This robust, tufted, hairy plant bears stiff, erect stems. The leaves are paired, palmately lobed, and toothed; the lower leaves are often 5-lobed and stalked, the middle and upper ones are mainly 3-lobed, short-stalked or unstalked, and the uppermost are sometimes undivided. The bracts are like the uppermost leaves and decrease in size up the stem. The small pinkish purple or pink, rarely white, flowers, 2–5mm (1/12–1/5in) across, are aggregated into broad heads that attract bees and butterflies; the florets are all tubular with 5 short teeth.

• **DISTRIBUTION** Throughout the region, except for the far north; scarce in Scotland.

• **HABITAT** Damp, open or shaded places in woodland, river, stream, and pool margins, and ditches; at low altitudes.

Habit Perennial	Height 90–150cm (36–60in)	Flowering time July–Sept

Family COMPOSITAE | Species *Solidago virgaurea* | Author L.

GOLDENROD

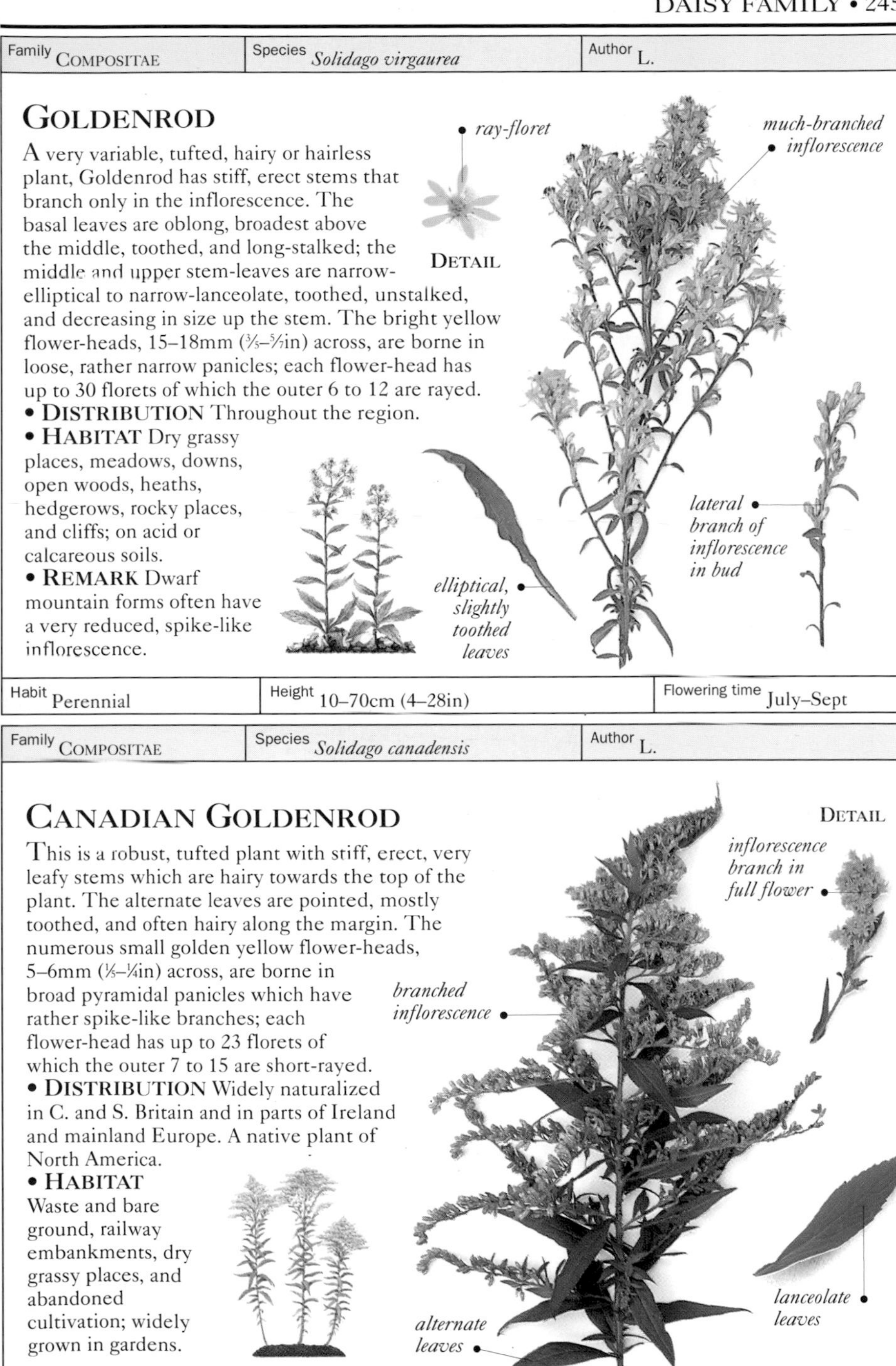

A very variable, tufted, hairy or hairless plant, Goldenrod has stiff, erect stems that branch only in the inflorescence. The basal leaves are oblong, broadest above the middle, toothed, and long-stalked; the middle and upper stem-leaves are narrow-elliptical to narrow-lanceolate, toothed, unstalked, and decreasing in size up the stem. The bright yellow flower-heads, 15–18mm (3/5–5/7in) across, are borne in loose, rather narrow panicles; each flower-head has up to 30 florets of which the outer 6 to 12 are rayed.

• **DISTRIBUTION** Throughout the region.

• **HABITAT** Dry grassy places, meadows, downs, open woods, heaths, hedgerows, rocky places, and cliffs; on acid or calcareous soils.

• **REMARK** Dwarf mountain forms often have a very reduced, spike-like inflorescence.

Habit Perennial | Height 10–70cm (4–28in) | Flowering time July–Sept

Family COMPOSITAE | Species *Solidago canadensis* | Author L.

CANADIAN GOLDENROD

This is a robust, tufted plant with stiff, erect, very leafy stems which are hairy towards the top of the plant. The alternate leaves are pointed, mostly toothed, and often hairy along the margin. The numerous small golden yellow flower-heads, 5–6mm (1/5–1/4in) across, are borne in broad pyramidal panicles which have rather spike-like branches; each flower-head has up to 23 florets of which the outer 7 to 15 are short-rayed.

• **DISTRIBUTION** Widely naturalized in C. and S. Britain and in parts of Ireland and mainland Europe. A native plant of North America.

• **HABITAT** Waste and bare ground, railway embankments, dry grassy places, and abandoned cultivation; widely grown in gardens.

Habit Perennial | Height 1–2m (3¼–6½ft) | Flowering time Aug–Oct

Family COMPOSITAE	Species *Bellis perennis*	Author L.

DAISY

This familiar little hairy plant has all its leaves crowded into basal rosettes. The leaves are oval to elliptical or occasionally spoon-shaped, generally widest above the middle, irregularly toothed or untoothed, and stalked. The solitary flower-heads, 15–25mm (⅗–1in) across, have numerous narrow white ray-florets often tipped or flushed with red or purple, and a disc of yellow tubular florets. The achenes are plain with no feathery attachment.

- **DISTRIBUTION** Most of the region.
- **HABITAT** Short grassy places such as lawns, downs, commons, roadsides, and railway embankments.
- **REMARK** Cultivated forms with large white, pink, or red double flowers sometimes become naturalized.

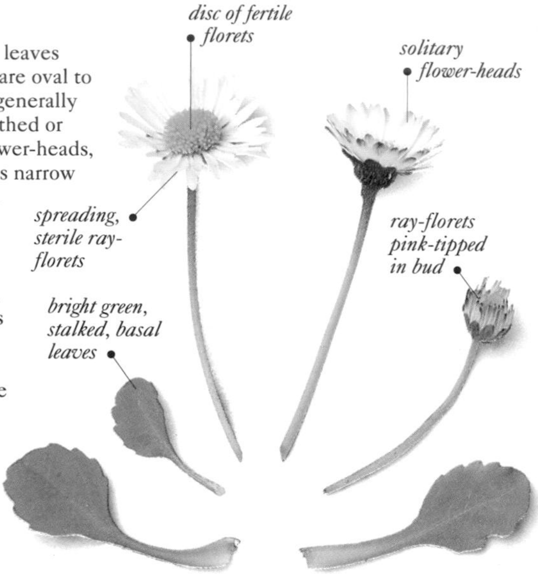

disc of fertile florets

solitary flower-heads

spreading, sterile ray-florets

ray-florets pink-tipped in bud

bright green, stalked, basal leaves

Habit Perennial	Height 4–12cm (1⅗–4¾in)	Flowering time Year round

Family COMPOSITAE	Species *Aster tripolium*	Author L.

SEA ASTER

This is a rather fleshy, hairless, patch-forming plant. Often reddish or purplish, the stems are erect or ascending from a branched base. The alternate leaves are round in cross-section and untoothed; only the lower leaves are stalked. The flower-heads, 8–20mm (⅓–⅘in) across, have a small yellow disc and up to 15 long bright blue or purple ray-florets; the ray-florets are sometimes absent.

- **DISTRIBUTION** Throughout the region, except for the far north.
- **HABITAT** Coastal areas, especially salt marshes, and occasionally rocky places and cliffs or saline areas inland.
- **RELATED SPECIES** *Aster linosyris*, Goldilocks Aster, has linear, pointed leaves and dense, yellow, rayless flower-heads. It grows on limestone cliffs throughout the region as far north as S. Sweden; in Britain it is confined to the west.

mauve ray-florets

yellow disc-florets

DETAIL

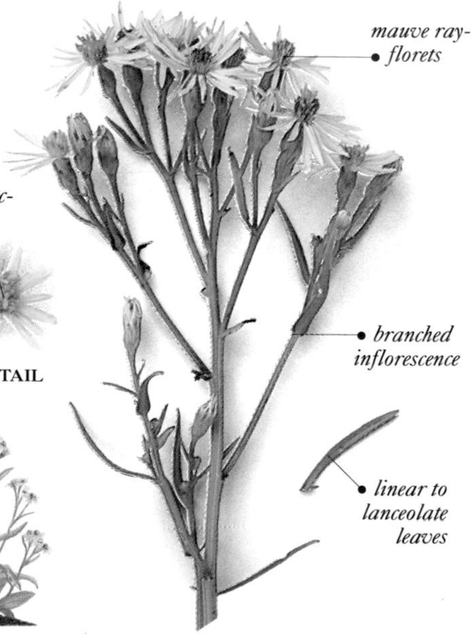

branched inflorescence

linear to lanceolate leaves

Habit Perennial	Height 20–70cm (8–28in)	Flowering time July–Oct

Family COMPOSITAE	Species *Aster novi-belgii*	Author L.

MICHAELMAS DAISY

This robust, tufted plant has stiff stems lined with hairs. The oval to lanceolate or narrow-lanceolate leaves are mostly slightly toothed; the lower leaves are short-stalked. Borne in clusters, the flower-heads, 25–40mm (1–1⅗in) across, have purple, mauve, violet-blue, or rarely white, rays around a yellow disc.

• **DISTRIBUTION** Widely naturalized in the region, except for the far north. Native to North America.

• **HABITAT** Waste land, rough ground, and river banks.

• **RELATED SPECIES** *Aster lanceolatus*, Narrow-leaved Michaelmas Daisy, has narrower leaves which taper to the base and do not clasp, and mauve or white rays.

Habit Perennial	Height 80–150cm (32–60in)	Flowering time Sept–Oct

Family	Species	Author
COMPOSITAE	*Erigeron karvinskianus*	DC.

WALL DAISY

Also known as *Erigeron mucronatus*, this slender little daisy has spreading to ascending, branched, slightly hairy stems that form an intricate tuft. The alternate leaves are lanceolate to oval, and untoothed or with a pair of lobe-like teeth; the uppermost leaves are smaller and narrower. The small daisy flowers, 12–15mm (½–⅗in) across, have white ray-florets and a yellow "eye", the former usually becoming pink and finally purple with age. The fruit consists of a small achene with a pappus of simple hairs.

• **DISTRIBUTION** Naturalized in S. Britain (including East Anglia) and parts of W. France. Native to Mexico.

• **HABITAT** Walls, pavements, dry banks, and rocky places.

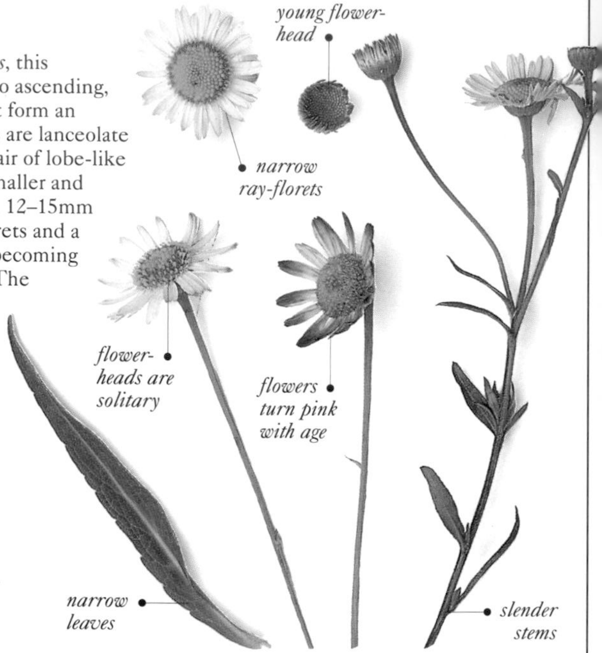

young flower-head

narrow ray-florets

flower-heads are solitary

flowers turn pink with age

narrow leaves

slender stems

Habit	Height	Flowering time
Perennial	20–50cm (12–20in)	June–Sept

Family	Species	Author
COMPOSITAE	*Conyza canadensis*	(L.) Cronq.

CANADIAN FLEABANE

Also known as *Erigeron canadensis*, this rather variable, hairy plant has slender, but erect, stiff stems. The green leaves are alternate, stalked, linear to elliptical or oblong, with an untoothed margin; the lowermost have often withered and fallen by flowering time. The small daisy flowers, 2–5mm (1/12–⅕in) across, are white or occasionally pinkish, with a pale yellow disc and rather short ray-florets. The fruit consists of a small achene with a pappus of simple hairs.

• **DISTRIBUTION** Naturalized throughout, except for Scotland, Ireland, and the far north. Native of North America.

• **HABITAT** Waste, bare, and cultivated land, embankments, roadsides, old walls, and sand dunes; primarily growing on rather poor, dry soils.

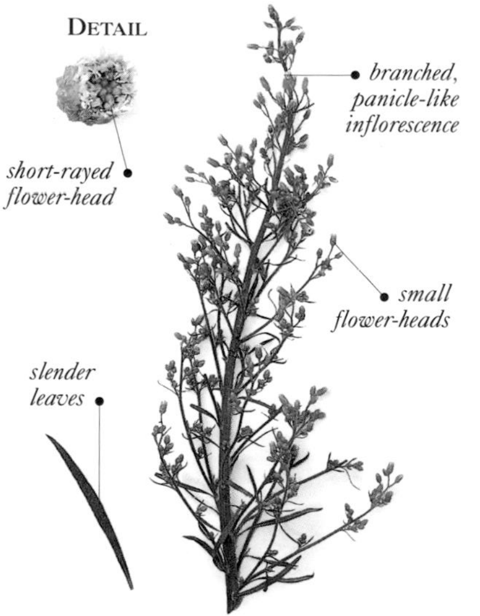

Habit	Height	Flowering time
Annual	50–100cm (20–40in)	July–Sept

Family COMPOSITAE	Species *Inula conyza*	Author (Griess.) Meikle

PLOUGHMAN'S SPIKENARD

This tufted, hairy plant has erect, rather purplish stems. The alternate leaves are elliptical to lanceolate or narrow-oval; the lowermost leaves are long-stalked, while the upper are unstalked but do not clasp the stem. The dull yellow flower-heads are 9–11mm (3/8–3/7in) across and are borne in flat-topped clusters; the outer florets of the flower-heads have very short and rather inconspicuous rays. The outer flower-bracts are oval and green, while the inner are narrow, pointed, and purplish. The achenes have a feathery top.

• **DISTRIBUTION** England, Wales, Denmark, Belgium, Holland, France, and Germany.

• **HABITAT** Rocky places in open scrub and woodland, rocky slopes and cliffs, grassy and rather bare places; generally on calcareous soils at low altitudes.

Habit Perennial	Height 60–120cm (24–48in)	Flowering time July–Sept

Family COMPOSITAE	Species *Inula crithmoides*	Author L.

GOLDEN SAMPHIRE

A rather succulent, hairless plant, Golden Samphire has erect stems which are sometimes slightly spreading at the base, and are branched and somewhat woody towards the bottom. The alternate leaves are linear to narrow-elliptical, often widest above the middle, narrowed to the base but not obviously stalked, and untoothed or with a 3-toothed apex. The golden yellow flower-heads, 15–28mm (3/5–1 1/8in) across, have narrow, spreading rays surrounding a wide disc, and are borne in a few-flowered, flat-topped, branched cluster. The flower-bracts are green, linear, pointed, and erect.

• **DISTRIBUTION** S. and W. Britain, S. and S.E. Ireland, and France; scattered and often very local; mainly a Mediterranean plant.

• **HABITAT** Coastal rocks, sands, and shingle, cliffs, salt marshes, and coastal ditches; often growing with *Aster tripolium*, Sea Aster (see p.246).

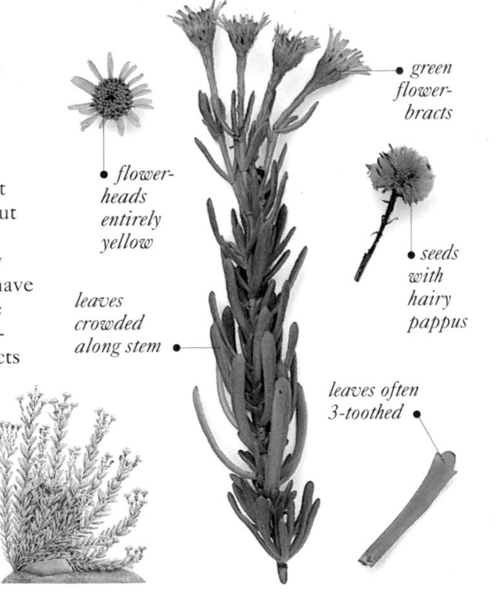

Habit Perennial	Height 20–100cm (8–40in)	Flowering time July–Sept

Family COMPOSITAE	Species *Antennaria dioica*	Author (L.) Gaertner

MOUNTAIN EVERLASTING

This low mat-forming plant has spreading, slender, branched stolons. The stems and undersides of the leaves are covered in a down of white hairs. The alternate leaves are oval to spatula-shaped, with an untoothed margin and often a notched apex; the basal leaves are borne in a loose rosette. The small flower-heads, 6–12mm (¼–½in) across, are borne in clusters of up to 8, and male and female flowers are borne on separate plants; the male flowers have white flower-bracts, while the female have pink ones. The fruit is a small achene with a pappus of simple hairs.

• **DISTRIBUTION** Throughout, except for the far north.

• **HABITAT** Mountain meadows and grassy places, heaths, moors, and rocky slopes; on base-rich or calcareous soils, to an altitude of 3,000m (9,850ft).

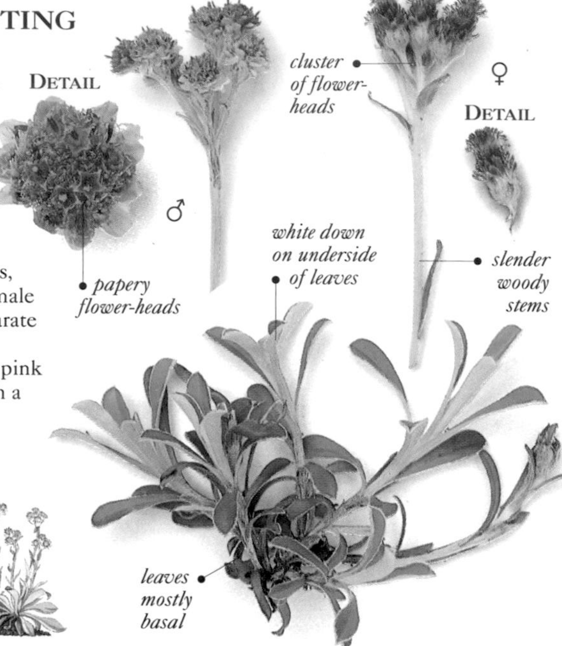

Habit Perennial	Height 8–20cm (3⅕–8in)	Flowering time May–July

Family COMPOSITAE	Species *Pulicaria dysenterica*	Author (L.) Bernh.

COMMON FLEABANE

The erect stems of this densely hairy stoloniferous plant are rather stiff and are usually branched above. The alternate leaves are variable: the basal are oval with a narrowed base and have generally withered by flowering time; the stem-leaves are heart- or arrow-shaped and unstalked; all leaves are green above and greyish beneath. The flower-heads, 15–30mm (⅗–1⅕in) across, are yellow, daisy-like, and borne in branched clusters; the ray-florets are numerous and rather short; the flower-bracts are linear and downy. The fruit is a small achene with a pappus of scales and simple hairs.

• **DISTRIBUTION** Throughout the region, except for the far north.

• **HABITAT** Damp places along rivers and streams, ditches, marshes, and wet meadows; sometimes along hedgerows.

Habit Perennial	Height 50–100cm (20–40in)	Flowering time Aug–Sept

Family COMPOSITAE	Species *Bidens tripartita*	Author L.

TRIFID BUR-MARIGOLD

Hairy or almost hairless, this variable plant has erect, branched stems. The opposite, elliptical to oval, coarsely toothed leaves mostly have one, occasionally 2, basal pairs of leaflets, similar to, though smaller than, the main leaflet. Borne in branched clusters, the solitary yellowish flower-heads, 10–25mm (⅖–1in) across, usually lack ray-florets. The fruit is a small barbed achene which attaches itself to soft materials like clothing and fur.

• **DISTRIBUTION** Throughout the region, except for the far north.

• **HABITAT** Damp places in fields and marshes, or mud by ponds and rivers.

• **RELATED SPECIES** *Bidens cernua*, Nodding Bur-marigold, has larger nodding flower-heads with or without ray-florets, and leaves that are not lobed. Its distribution and habitats are similar to the above.

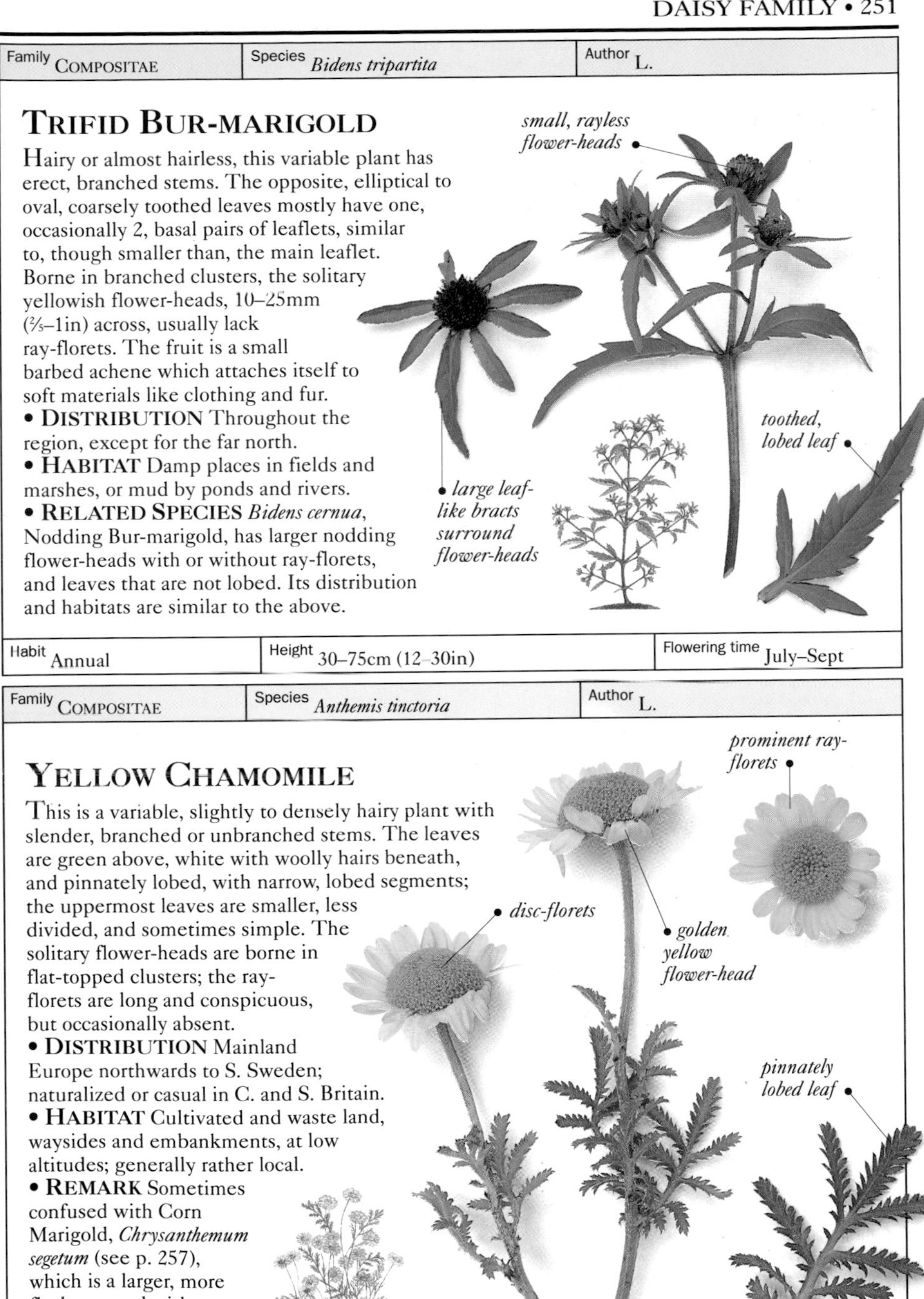

Habit Annual	Height 30–75cm (12–30in)	Flowering time July–Sept

Family COMPOSITAE	Species *Anthemis tinctoria*	Author L.

YELLOW CHAMOMILE

This is a variable, slightly to densely hairy plant with slender, branched or unbranched stems. The leaves are green above, white with woolly hairs beneath, and pinnately lobed, with narrow, lobed segments; the uppermost leaves are smaller, less divided, and sometimes simple. The solitary flower-heads are borne in flat-topped clusters; the ray-florets are long and conspicuous, but occasionally absent.

• **DISTRIBUTION** Mainland Europe northwards to S. Sweden; naturalized or casual in C. and S. Britain.

• **HABITAT** Cultivated and waste land, waysides and embankments, at low altitudes; generally rather local.

• **REMARK** Sometimes confused with Corn Marigold, *Chrysanthemum segetum* (see p. 257), which is a larger, more fleshy annual with very different leaf-lobing and broader ray-florets.

Habit Perennial	Height 20–50cm (8–20in)	Flowering time July–Sept

Family COMPOSITAE	Species *Achillea millefolium*	Author L.

YARROW

Hairy and patch-forming, this plant spreads by means of rooting stolons. The flowering stems are stiff, erect, and unbranched. The deep green or grey-green, finely divided, feathery leaves are basal or alternate, cut into numerous narrow pinnate segments, and give off a strong smell when crushed. The small, white, pink, or occasionally red flower-heads, 4–6mm (⅙–¼in) across, are borne in dense, broad, flat-headed corymbs; the outer heads have a few short rays. The fruit is an achene with no pappus.

- **DISTRIBUTION** Throughout the region, except for Spitsbergen.
- **HABITAT** Grassy places, especially meadows, embankments, roadsides, grassy heaths, and hedgerows.
- **RELATED SPECIES** *Achillea distans*, Tall Yarrow, is much taller, with flatter leaves and larger flower-heads, 5–10mm (⅕–⅖in) across. It is naturalized in England and perhaps elsewhere in the region.

Habit Perennial	Height 40–80cm (16–32in)	Flowering time July–Oct

Family COMPOSITAE	Species *Achillea ptarmica*	Author L.

SNEEZEWORT

This is a patch-forming, slightly hairy plant which spreads by woody stolons. The flowering stems are stiff, erect, angular, and unbranched. The flat leaves are lanceolate to narrowly elliptical, pointed, finely toothed, scarcely hairy, and unstalked. The flower-heads are white with a greenish white disc, 12–18mm (½–⅝in) across, and borne in loose, branched clusters. The achenes have no pappus of hairs.

• **DISTRIBUTION** Throughout, except for the far north; naturalized in Iceland and parts of the north of its range.

• **HABITAT** Damp grassy places, meadows, pastures, marshes; on heavy, acid soils.

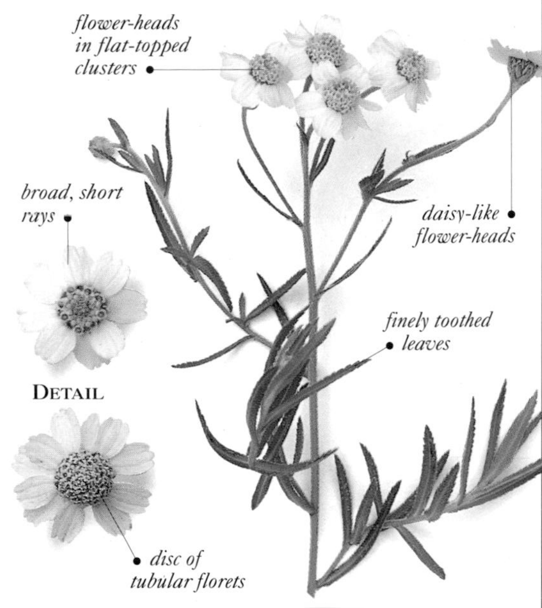

Habit Perennial	Height 30–60cm (12–24in)	Flowering time July–Sept

Family COMPOSITAE	Species *Otanthus maritimus*	Author (L.) Hoffsgg. & Link

COTTONWEED

This plant generally forms large, low patches and has rather stout spreading and ascending stems which are branched in the upper part. The alternate leaves are thick and fleshy, woolly, and unstalked, with an untoothed or shallowly toothed margin. Borne in small dense clusters, the button-like yellow flower-heads, 7–10mm (¼–⅜in) across, are globose and have no ray-florets; the flower-bracts are elliptical, closely overlapping, and white-woolly like the leaves. The achenes have no pappus of hairs.

• **DISTRIBUTION** S.W. Ireland (where it is now very rare) and France; formerly present in parts of coastal England. It is a common species further south in the Mediterranean coastal region, where it can form substantial colonies, especially on dunes.

• **HABITAT** Coastal sands, primarily on dunes and shingle.

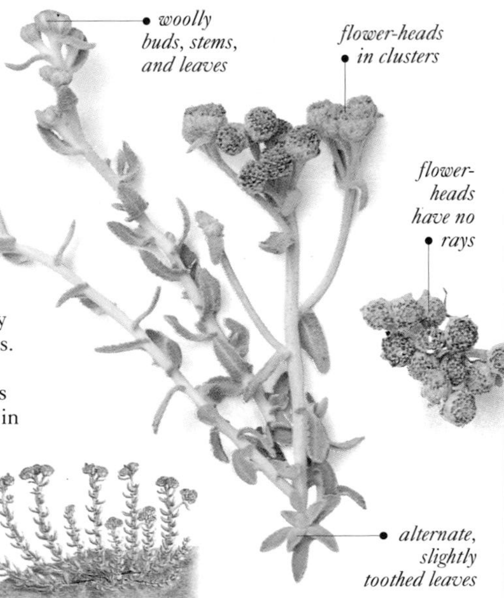

Habit Perennial	Height 20–30cm (8–12in)	Flowering time Aug–Oct

Family COMPOSITAE	Species *Matricaria maritima*	Author L.

SEA MAYWEED

This very variable plant is also known as *Tripleurospermum maritimum*. Plants range from spreading to erect and are faintly scented when crushed. The stems are hairless and usually branched. The alternate leaves are rather fleshy and pinnately cut into numerous short and narrow divisions which may be blunt or pointed at the tip. The daisy flower-heads, 15–50mm (⅗–2in) across, are white with a yellow disc, solitary, and long-stalked; the ray-florets are long and spread widely or are reflexed. The flower-bracts are few, elliptical, and plain green or with a dark margin.

• **DISTRIBUTION** Throughout the region, except for most of the far north; often growing in extensive colonies.

• **HABITAT** Coastal sands, shingle, and rocks, cliffs, old walls, and occasionally waste or bare ground close to the coast; on dry, well-drained soils.

Habit Biennial or perennial	Height 20–60cm (8–24in)	Flowering time July–Sept

Family COMPOSITAE	Species *Chamomila suaveolens*	Author (Pursh) Rydb.

PINEAPPLE MAYWEED

Also known under the names *Matricaria discoidea* and *M. matricarioides*, this sweetly pineapple-scented plant often forms extensive colonies. Plants are hairless, with erect to ascending, usually well-branched stems. The alternate, bright green leaves are cut into numerous thread-like divisions. The yellowish green flower-heads, 5–8mm (⅕–⅓in) across, are rayless and have a prominent conical disc; the corolla is 4-lobed. Achenes have a pappus of hairs.

• **DISTRIBUTION** Naturalized in much of the region, except the far north. Native to N.E. Asia.

• **HABITAT** Cultivated, waste, and disturbed land, bare places, farm tracks, and pathways.

• **RELATED SPECIES** *Chamomilla recutita*, Scented Mayweed, has sweetly scented foliage, and flower-heads with or without white rays; the disc florets are 5-lobed. Its habitats and distribution are similar to the above but it is less common.

Habit Annual	Height 10–35cm (4–14in)	Flowering time May–Nov

Family COMPOSITAE	Species *Tanacetum vulgare*	Author L.

TANSY

This is an almost hairless, strongly aromatic, patch-forming plant, spreading by means of vigorous underground stolons. The stems are stiffly erect, becoming rather woody with age. The leaves are alternate, unstalked, deep green, and pinnately divided into lanceolate to elliptical, toothed segments. The small, yellow, pin-cushion-like flower-heads, 7–12mm (2/7–1/2in) across, have no ray-florets and are aggregated into branched, rather flat-topped clusters. The flower-bracts are elliptical and closely overlap one another. The achenes have no pappus of hairs.

• **DISTRIBUTION** Throughout the region, except for the far north, but rather scarce in the north of its range; a naturalized plant in Ireland.

• **HABITAT** Grassy places, open scrub, roadsides, cultivated land, and often riverbeds; on a variety of soil types, especially calcareous ones.

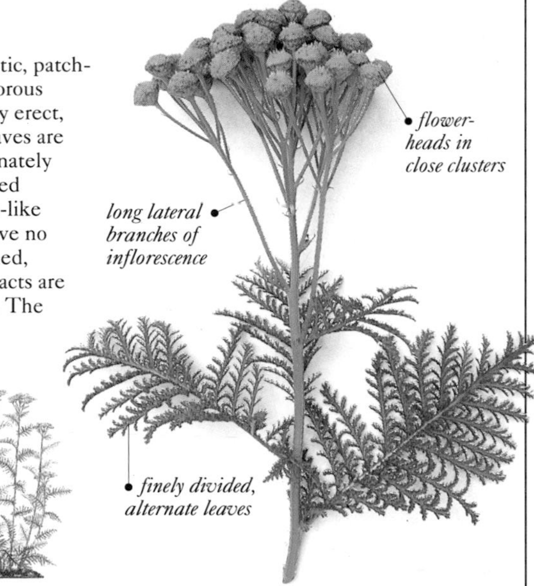

Habit Perennial	Height 80–120cm (32–48in)	Flowering time July–Sept

Family COMPOSITAE	Species *Tanacetum parthenium*	Author (L.) Schultz-Bip.

FEVERFEW

This is a tufted, strongly aromatic, and almost hairless plant, with stiff erect stems branched in the upper part. The alternate yellow-green to bright green leaves are oval to oblong and pinnately divided into broad lobed or toothed segments; most leaves are stalked. The flower-heads, 10–25mm (2/5–1in) across, have short, blunt, white rays surrounding a yellow disc and are borne in large, more or less flat-topped, clusters. The achenes lack a pappus of hairs.

• **DISTRIBUTION** Naturalized throughout, as far north as S. Sweden. Native to S.E. Europe.

• **HABITAT** Cultivated and waste land, hedgerows, roadsides, embankments, old walls, and areas close to habitation.

• **RELATED SPECIES** *Tanacetum macrophyllum*, Rayed Tansy, has more numerous, smaller flower-heads measuring 8–15mm (1/3–3/5in) across. It is naturalized in Britain, Denmark, and Germany. Like Feverfew, it is native to S.E. Europe.

Habit Biennial to perennial	Height 40–70cm (16–28in)	Flowering time July–Sept

Family COMPOSITAE	Species *Leucanthemum vulgare*	Author Lam.

OX-EYE DAISY

This familiar daisy is also known as *Chrysanthemum leucanthemum*. The plant is patch-forming, with spreading, short, leafy shoots and erect flowering stems. The basal leaves are oval and stalked, while the stem-leaves are smaller and narrower with unstalked clasping bases. The solitary flowers, 25–50mm (1–2in) across, are white with a central yellow disc and are borne on branched or unbranched, somewhat ridged stems.

- **DISTRIBUTION** Throughout; naturalized in the Faeroes and Iceland.
- **HABITAT** Grassy places, particularly meadows, embankments and verges, scrub, hedgerows, waste ground, and open woodland; mostly on base-rich soils.
- **RELATED SPECIES** *Leucanthemum* x *superbum* (syn. *L. maximum*), Shasta Daisy, has larger flowers, up to 75mm (3in) across, and is widely cultivated and naturalized in the region.

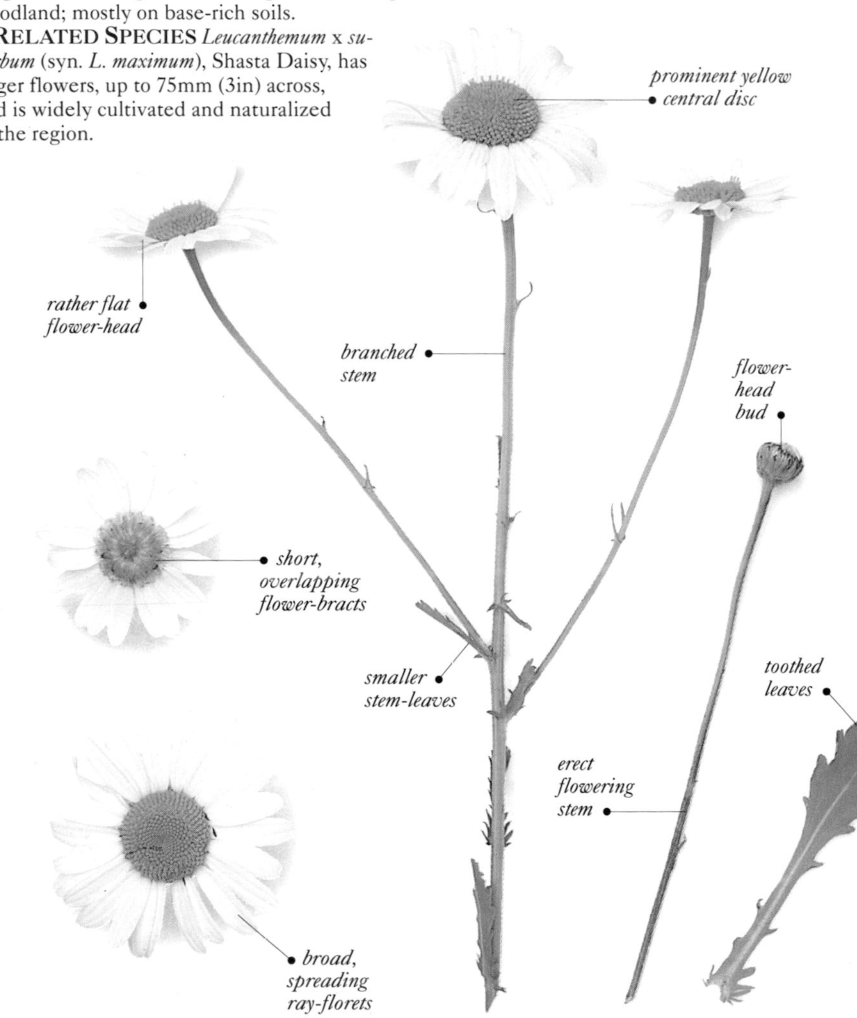

Habit Perennial	Height 40–80cm (16–32in)	Flowering time May–Sept

Family COMPOSITAE	Species *Chrysanthemum segetum*	Author L.

CORN MARIGOLD

This greyish plant is erect, usually branched, and somewhat fleshy. The alternate leaves are oblong, deeply and sharply toothed or lobed, and clasp the stem with small-lobed bases; the uppermost leaves are smaller and sometimes untoothed. The flower-heads, 35–55mm (1⅖–2⅕in) across, are solitary, with a flat disc and long, broad ray-florets. The achenes have no pappus of hairs.

• **DISTRIBUTION** Native throughout the region as far north as N. Scandinavia, but probably only naturalized in Britain.

• **HABITAT** Arable land, especially cornfields; waysides, waste places, and road verges; declining in many areas due to modern farming practices.

• **RELATED SPECIES** *Chrysanthemum coronarium*, Crown Daisy, has leaves with finer divisions, and cream, yellow, or bicoloured flower-heads. It is native to S. Europe but is naturalized or casual in Britain and elsewhere in the region.

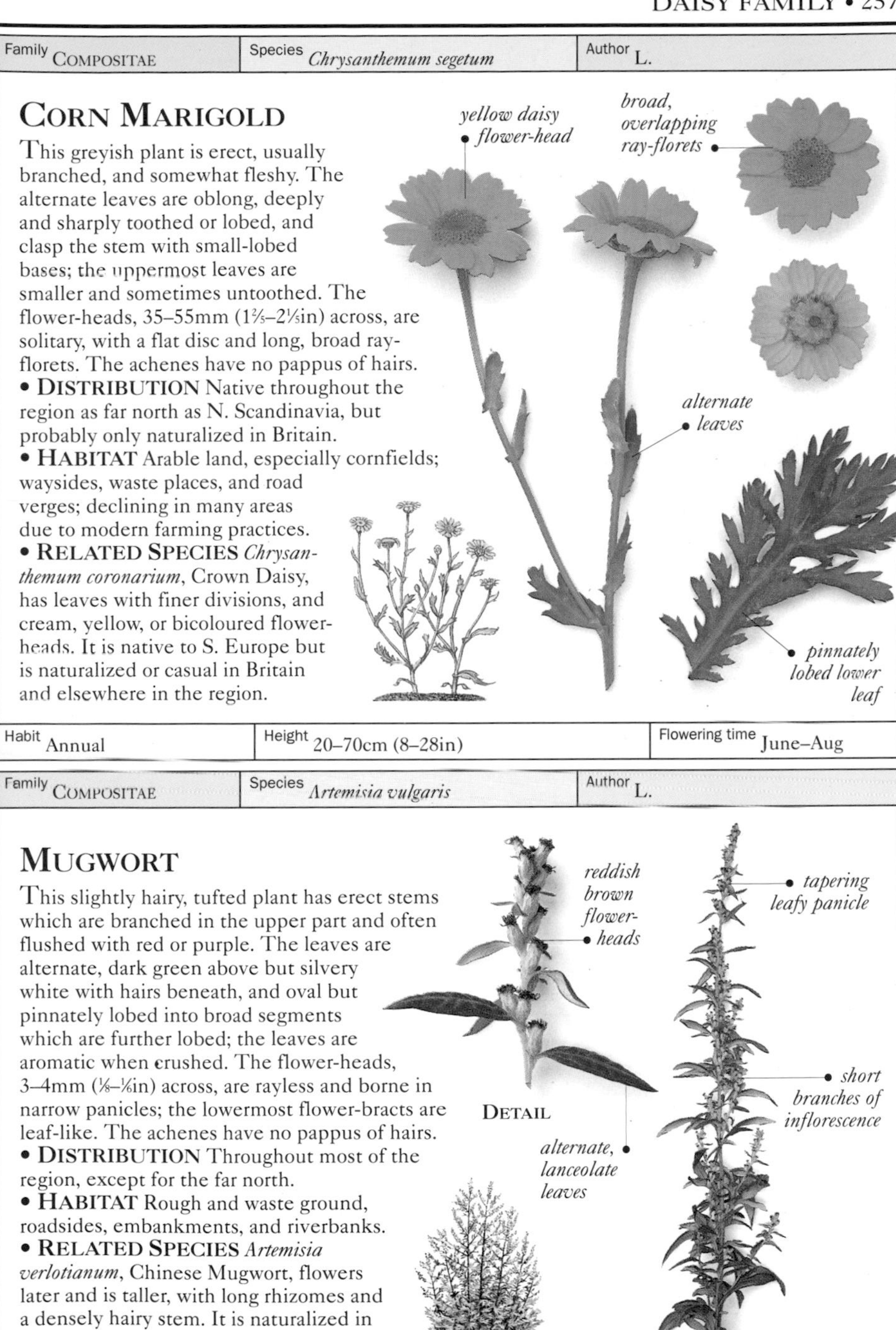

Habit Annual	Height 20–70cm (8–28in)	Flowering time June–Aug

Family COMPOSITAE	Species *Artemisia vulgaris*	Author L.

MUGWORT

This slightly hairy, tufted plant has erect stems which are branched in the upper part and often flushed with red or purple. The leaves are alternate, dark green above but silvery white with hairs beneath, and oval but pinnately lobed into broad segments which are further lobed; the leaves are aromatic when crushed. The flower-heads, 3–4mm (⅛–⅙in) across, are rayless and borne in narrow panicles; the lowermost flower-bracts are leaf-like. The achenes have no pappus of hairs.

• **DISTRIBUTION** Throughout most of the region, except for the far north.

• **HABITAT** Rough and waste ground, roadsides, embankments, and riverbanks.

• **RELATED SPECIES** *Artemisia verlotianum*, Chinese Mugwort, flowers later and is taller, with long rhizomes and a densely hairy stem. It is naturalized in S. Britain, Belgium, France, and Germany.

Habit Perennial	Height 80–150cm (32–60in)	Flowering time May–Sept

Family COMPOSITAE	Species *Petasites fragrans*	Author (Vill.) C. Presl.

WINTER HELIOTROPE

This low, robust, spreading and patch-forming, hairy plant has thick, rather fleshy rhizomes. The heart-shaped to kidney-shaped leaves have a toothed margin, are hairless and shiny green above, paler and hairy beneath, and appear at the same time as the flowers. The vanilla-scented, pink or pinkish white flower-heads are relatively few and are borne in a broad raceme, with male and female flower-heads born on separate plants; male flower-heads have mostly tubular florets with few rays, while the female have many short rays. The fruit clusters are a series of small "clocks".

• **DISTRIBUTION** Naturalized in Britain, Belgium, Holland, France, and Denmark.

• **HABITAT** Cultivated and waste land, damp places along streams, rivers, and ditches, open woodland, hedgerows, and embankments.

loose racemes of flower-heads

♀

reduced, leaf-like bracts

long-stemmed, kidney-shaped leaves

Habit Perennial	Height 15–40cm (6–16in)	Flowering time Nov–Mar

Family COMPOSITAE	Species *Petasites hybridus*	Author (L.) P. Gaertn., Mey. & Scherb.

BUTTERBUR

This patch-forming, hairy plant spreads by means of stout rhizomes. Appearing after the flowers, the leaves, up to 90cm (36in) across, are rounded with a heart-shaped base, irregularly toothed or somewhat lobed, and grey with hairs beneath. The white or pale pink flower-heads are usually flushed with purple and are borne in dense erect racemes or panicles; male and female flowers are on separate plants. The fruit is a typical "clock".

• **DISTRIBUTION** Britain to Holland and Germany southwards, and occasionally naturalized further north.

• **HABITAT** Damp places.

• **RELATED SPECIES** *Petasites japonicus*, Japanese Butterbur, has green bracts and cream or white flower-heads. It is naturalized in Britain, Holland, and Denmark.

Habit Perennial	Height 70–150cm (28–60in)	Flowering time Mar–May

Family COMPOSITAE	Species *Tussilago farfara*	Author L.

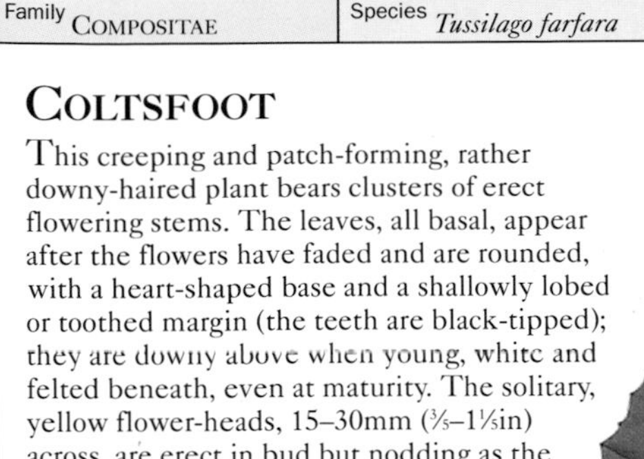

COLTSFOOT

This creeping and patch-forming, rather downy-haired plant bears clusters of erect flowering stems. The leaves, all basal, appear after the flowers have faded and are rounded, with a heart-shaped base and a shallowly lobed or toothed margin (the teeth are black-tipped); they are downy above when young, white and felted beneath, even at maturity. The solitary, yellow flower-heads, 15–30mm (⅗–1⅕in) across, are erect in bud but nodding as the flowers fade; flower-stems have numerous overlapping, often purplish, scales.

• **DISTRIBUTION** Throughout the region, except for the far north.

• **HABITAT** Damp sites on cultivated land, meadows, roadsides, ditches, riverbanks, embankments, screes, woodland margins; sometimes on coastal dunes or shingle.

Habit Perennial	Height 10–25cm (4–10in)	Flowering time Feb–Apr

Family COMPOSITAE	Species *Doronicum pardalianches*	Author L.

LEOPARD'S-BANE

This robust, hairy, patch-forming plant has bright green stems and foliage and spreads by short leafy stolons. The leaves are alternate and generally slightly toothed, although occasionally untoothed; the basal leaves are long-stalked, while the stem-leaves are smaller, narrower, usually oval to lanceolate, and unstalked. The bright yellow daisy flower-heads, 30–50mm (1⅕–2in) across, or occasionally larger, are borne mostly in clusters of 3 to 8, each with numerous narrow rays.

• **DISTRIBUTION** Belgium to France and Germany southwards; naturalized in Britain.

• **HABITAT** Woodland, coppices, hedgerows, cultivated and waste land; primarily on calcareous soils.

• **RELATED SPECIES** *Doronicum plantagineum*, Plantain-leaved Leopard's-bane, has larger, mostly solitary, flowers, and basal leaves narrowed at the base. It is native in France; naturalized in Britain and Holland.

Habit Perennial	Height 50–80cm (20–32in)	Flowering time June–July

Family COMPOSITAE	Species *Senecio squalidus*	Author L.

OXFORD RAGWORT

The stems of this rather variable, hairy or hairless plant are usually well-branched. The deep green leaves are pinnately lobed, with the narrow lobes further lobed or toothed; the lower leaves are stalked, while the upper ones are unstalked and clasp the stem. Borne in flat-topped clusters, the flower-heads, 15–25mm (⅗–1in) across, have roughly 13 ray-florets. The achenes have a pappus.

• **DISTRIBUTION** Naturalized widely in England, Wales, France, and Denmark.

• **HABITAT** Dry disturbed, waste, and cultivated land, railway lines and embankments, old walls, and derelict building sites.

• **RELATED SPECIES** *Senecio cambrensis*, Welsh Groundsel, has leafier inflorescences and smaller flower-heads, 6–12mm (¼–½in) long, with rays that soon recurve. It is native in W. Britain.

Habit Annual or perennial	Height 20–50cm (8–20in)	Flowering time Apr–Dec

Family COMPOSITAE	Species *Senecio vulgaris*	Author L.

GROUNDSEL

This variable, usually erect plant is very finely hairy or occasionally hairless, with simple or somewhat branched stems. The bright green, slightly shiny leaves are pinnately lobed and toothed; the lower leaves are stalked, while the upper are unstalked and clasp the stem with lobed bases. Borne in branched clusters, the yellow oblong flower-heads are either rayless and 4–5mm (⅙–⅕in) across (var. *vulgaris*), or larger with 6 to 12 short yellow rays which soon recurve after the flowers open (var. *denticulatus*); flower-bracts are often black-tipped, the outer ones being much shorter than the inner.

• **DISTRIBUTION** Throughout the region, except for Spitsbergen.

• **HABITAT** A widespread weed of cultivated, waste, and disturbed land, and of waysides, road verges, railways, and other open habitats.

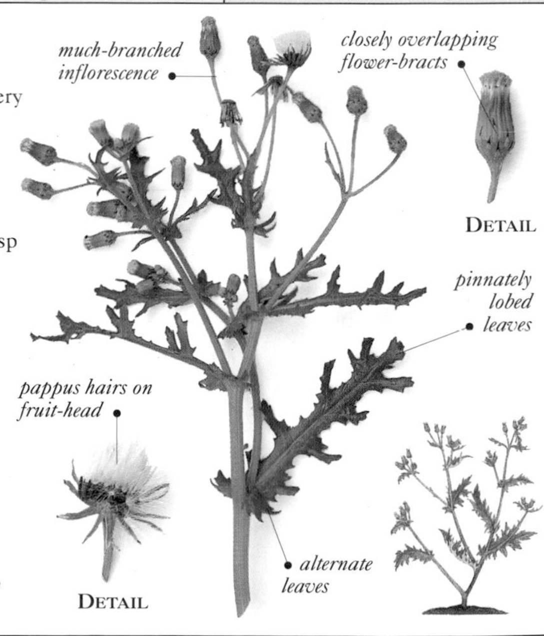

Habit Annual	Height 10–45cm (4–18in)	Flowering time Year round

Family COMPOSITAE	Species *Senecio jacobaea*	Author L.

COMMON RAGWORT

This is a rather robust, often tufted, hairy or practically hairless plant. The dark green, alternate leaves are oblong and pinnately lobed; the lower leaves are stalked and often withered by flowering time, while the upper are smaller, often more divided, and clasp the stem with unstalked bases. The bright yellow, daisy-like flower-heads, 15 25mm (3/5–1in) across, are borne in large, branched, flat-topped clusters, each flower-head with 12 to 25 long ray-florets; the few flower-bracts are even, overlapping, and black-tipped.

• **DISTRIBUTION** Throughout, except for the far north.

• **HABITAT** A widespread weed of cultivated and waste land, meadows, pastures, river embankments, and roadsides; also on sand dunes and coastal shingles.

• **REMARK** Very poisonous to livestock.

Habit Biennial or perennial	Height 80–150cm (32–60in)	Flowering time June–Nov

Family COMPOSITAE	Species *Carlina vulgaris*	Author L.

CARLINE THISTLE

This prickly plant has a stout, branched or unbranched stem. The leathery, alternate leaves are narrow-oblong and are cottony with hairs, especially on the underside. The flower-heads, 15–40mm (⅗–1⅗in) across, are borne in groups of 2 to 5 or are solitary; all florets are tubular and yellowish or purplish brown, and are surrounded by yellowish, linear, stiff, pointed flower-bracts. The fruit is an achene with a pappus of feathery hairs.

• **DISTRIBUTION** Throughout the region, except for the far north.

• **HABITAT** Dry grassland and meadows, downs, fixed sand dunes, and cliff-tops; on calcareous or sandy soils.

• **REMARK** The plant has a basal leaf-rosette in the first year only.

conspicuous flower-bracts spread widely apart

thistle-like flower-head

wavy, spiny leaf margin

feathered seeds on fruit-head

densely leafy stems

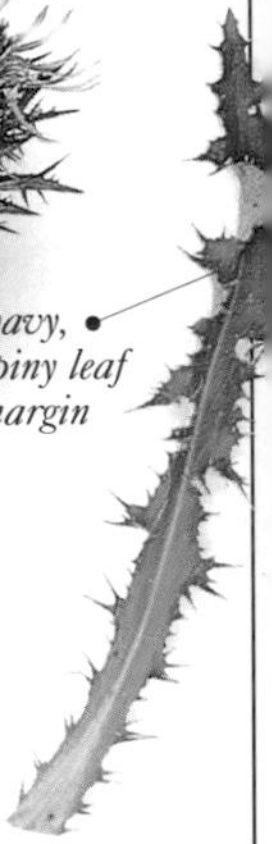

Habit Biennial	Height 20–60cm (8–24in)	Flowering time July–Sept

Family COMPOSITAE	Species *Arctium lappa*	Author L.

GREATER BURDOCK

This erect, robust plant is hairy to almost hairless, with stout branched stems. The basal leaves, up to 50cm (20in) long, are rough, with a heart-shaped blade and an untoothed or slightly toothed margin. The flower-heads, 20–25mm (⅘–1in) across but larger in fruit, are reddish purple, occasionally white, and are enclosed by shiny, golden green flower-bracts which have a conspicuous hooked tip. The fruit is an achene with a pappus of rough, yellowish hairs; seeds spread by hooked bract-tips which attach readily to fur and clothing.

• **DISTRIBUTION** Throughout, except much of the far north.

• **HABITAT** Wood-land clearings, hedge-rows, waste ground.

Habit Biennial	Height 80–150cm (32–60in)	Flowering time July–Sept

Family COMPOSITAE	Species *Serratula tinctoria*	Author L.

SAW-WORT

This rather variable, thistle-like plant is clump-forming, hairless or slightly hairy, with slender, but stiff, erect flowering stems which are usually branched above. The dark green leaves are alternate; the basal and lower leaves are pinnately lobed and stalked, while the upper are much smaller, unlobed, and stalkless. The flower-heads, 15–20mm (⅗–⅘in) across, are purple, or rarely white, with male and female flowers on separate plants; the florets are not rayed but have 5 narrow lobes; the flower-bracts are erect, purplish, and closely overlapping. The achenes have a pappus of hairs.

• **DISTRIBUTION** Throughout, except for most of the far north.

• **HABITAT** Rough grassland and meadows, scrub, open woodland, tracksides, heaths, and cliffs; on acid and calcareous soils. Coastal plants may be very dwarf, as small as 10cm (4in).

florets all tubular

cluster of flower-heads at stem tops

finely toothed leaf

round stem

slightly lobed base of leaf

Habit Perennial	Height 10–70cm (4–28in)	Flowering time June–Aug

Family COMPOSITAE	Species *Carduus crispus*	Author L.

WELTED THISTLE

Also known as *Carduus acanthoides*, this common thistle is extremely prickly, with erect stems that are adorned with spiny wings, except immediately beneath the flower-heads. The leaves are lanceolate to oblong, pinnately lobed, and a rather dull deep green above but paler with whitish cottony hairs beneath; only the lowermost leaves are stalked. The flower-heads are reddish purple, 10–25mm (⅖–1in) across, erect, and solitary or borne in small clusters; the florets are all tubular and 5-lobed. The achenes have a pronounced pappus of simple hairs.

• **DISTRIBUTION** Throughout the region as far north as S. Sweden.

• **HABITAT** Grassy places, meadows, fields, roadsides, embankments, hedgerows, stream and ditch margins, and also waste ground; mostly growing on soils with a high lime content.

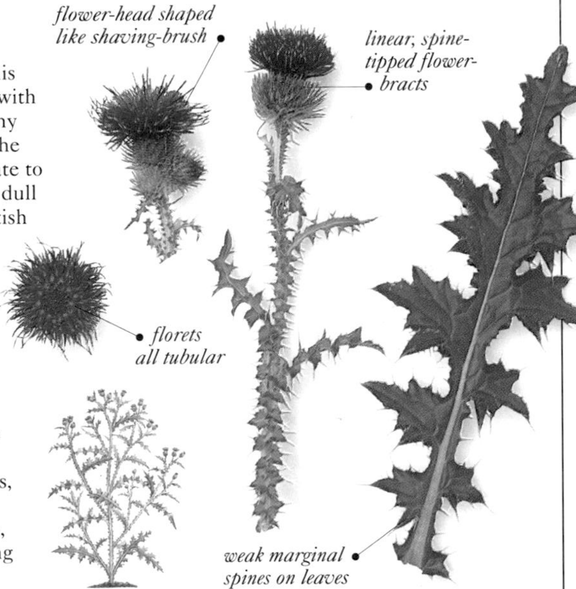

Habit Biennial	Height 1–2m (3¼–6½ft)	Flowering time June–Aug

Family COMPOSITAE	Species *Carduus nutans*	Author L.

MUSK THISTLE

Sometimes also commonly called Nodding Thistle, this imposing and rather cottony plant has erect stems that are adorned with narrow, spiny wings, except immediately below the flower-heads. The alternate leaves are deeply pinnately lobed, and woolly on the veins beneath. The flower-heads are solitary or clustered, half-nodding, bright reddish purple, and 30–50mm (1⅕–2in) across; all the florets are tubular and 5-lobed. The outer flower-bracts are recurved. The achenes have a pappus of simple hairs.

• **DISTRIBUTION** Throughout the region as far north as S.E. Norway, but rare in most of Scotland and Ireland.

• **HABITAT** Grassy places especially meadows and pastures, arable land, roadsides, and river and road embankments; generally on calcareous soils.

Habit Biennial	Height 80–150cm (32–60in)	Flowering time May–Sept

Family COMPOSITAE	Species *Carduus tenuiflorus*	Author Curtis

SLENDER THISTLE

This rather slender, very spiny plant, without stolons, has spiny wings running up the stems as far as the flower-heads. The leaves are alternate, deep green above but white with cottony hairs beneath, elliptical to lanceolate, with a lobed and spiny margin. The pink flower-heads are clustered and only 6–10mm (¼–⅜in) across. The narrow, oval flower-bracts have a curved spine at the tip.

• **DISTRIBUTION** Britain to Holland southwards; naturalized in parts of Scandinavia; in Britain, common only near the coast.

• **HABITAT** Grassy and waste places, roadsides, and open ground.

• **RELATED SPECIES** *Carduus pycnocephalus*, Plymouth Thistle, has unwinged flower-stalks; flower-heads are solitary or 2 or 3 together. It is naturalized in S.W. England; casual elsewhere in the region.

Habit Annual or biennial	Height 30–70cm (12–28in)	Flowering time May–Aug

Family COMPOSITAE	Species *Cirsium eriophorum*	Author (L.) Scop.

WOOLLY THISTLE

This generally stout, hairy plant has erect stems which are branched in the upper part. The large leaves are oblong to elliptical in outline and pinnately lobed. The reddish purple flower-heads, 25–50mm (1–2in) across, have 5-lobed tubular florets. The numerous flower-bracts are narrow, spine-tipped, and covered in cobwebby hairs; the outer bracts are spreading to recurved. The fruit is an achene with a feathery pappus.

• **DISTRIBUTION** Britain, Belgium, Holland, France, and Germany; scarce in N. Britain and Ireland.

• **HABITAT** Dry grassy sites, downs, scrub, embankments, roadsides, and railways; on calcareous soils.

Habit Biennial	Height 80–150cm (32–60in)	Flowering time July–Sept

Family COMPOSITAE	Species *Cirsium vulgare*	Author (Savi.) Ten.

SPEAR THISTLE

This very common thistle is robust and very spiny, with stiff stems. The dull green alternate leaves are paler underneath, with the upper surface covered in small, sharp bristles. The purple flower-heads, 20–40mm (⅘–1⅗in) across, are borne in panicles or flat-topped clusters. The flower-bracts are narrow and taper to a straight spine at the tip.

• **DISTRIBUTION** Throughout the region, except for parts of the far north.

• **HABITAT** Grassy, waste, and disturbed ground, roadsides, embankments, and farmland; frequently on rich fertile soils.

• **RELATED SPECIES** *Cirsium dissectum*, Meadow Thistle, is perennial with softer spines. The stems are not winged at the top.

Habit Biennial	Height 80–150cm (32–60in)	Flowering time July–Oct

Family COMPOSITAE	Species *Cirsium palustre*	Author (L.) Scop.

MARSH THISTLE

This thistle has narrow spiny wings along the whole length of its stems. The spiny, narrow-lanceolate to oblong leaves are hairy on the upper surface; only the lowermost leaves are stalked. The flower-heads 10–20mm (⅔–⅘in) across, are purple, or rarely pink or white; all florets are tubular and 5-lobed. The oval flower-bracts have a weak spine-tip, are not spreading, and are often purple-tinged. The achenes have a feathery pappus.

• **DISTRIBUTION** Throughout, except for the far north.

• **HABITAT** Damp places, meadows, fens, and wet woods.

flower-heads in clusters of 2 to 8

pinnately lobed leaf

very spiny leaf margin

branches in upper part of stem

Habit Biennial	Height 1–2m (3¼–6½ft)	Flowering time July–Sept

Family COMPOSITAE	Species *Cirsium arvense*	Author (L.) Scop.

CREEPING THISTLE

This is a spreading, spiny plant. The stems are erect, branched towards the top, have no spiny wings, and are usually hairy. The oblong to lanceolate, alternate leaves are hairless above but usually cottony beneath. The flower-heads, 15–25mm (⅗–1in) across, are purple, pink, or lilac, and are solitary or in clusters of up to 5; the florets are all tubular and 5-lobed. The flower-bracts are erect, lanceolate with a short spine-tip, and often flushed with purple.

• **DISTRIBUTION** Throughout the region, except for Spitsbergen.

• **HABITAT** Cultivated land, waste places, bare ground, fields, pastures, meadows, open woodland, and roadsides.

fruit-head with feathery pappus

tubular florets

pinnately lobed, spiny leaves

alternate leaves

Habit Perennial	Height 60–120cm (24–48in)	Flowering time June–Sept

Family COMPOSITAE	Species *Cirsium acaule*	Author (L.) Scop.

DWARF THISTLE

Also known as *Carduus acaulos*, this prickly plant bears leaves in dense basal rosettes. The short stem, never more than 10cm (4in) long, is wingless and sparsely hairy. The leathery leaves are oblong in outline, deeply pinnately lobed, and have stout spines on the margins; the upper leaf surface is deep green, but the lower suface is paler. The flower-heads, 20–40mm (⅘–1⅗in) across, are purple and are solitary or in clusters of 2 or 3; the florets are narrow and tubular, with 5 spreading linear lobes. The fruit is an achene topped by a feathery pappus.

• **DISTRIBUTION** Throughout, as far north as C. Scandinavia; absent from N. Britain and Ireland.

• **HABITAT** Grassland, especially grazed pastures on calcareous soils.

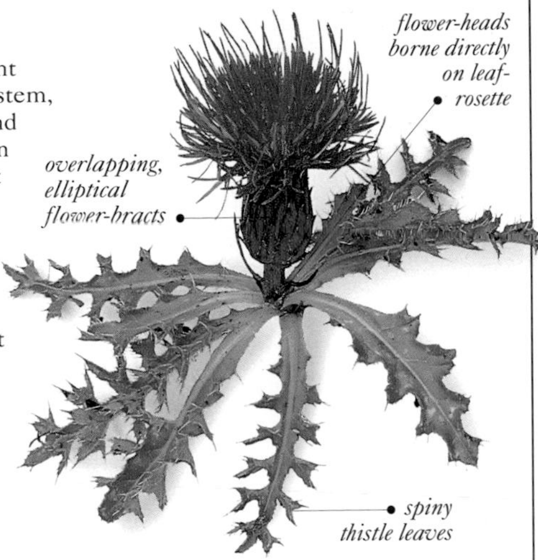

Habit Perennial	Height 5–13cm (2–5in)	Flowering time June–Sept

Family COMPOSITAE	Species *Onopordon acanthium*	Author L.

COTTON THISTLE

Also known as Scotch Thistle, this plant has an overall greyish or whitish appearance. The stout, erect stems are branched in the upper part. The large leaves are borne in a rosette in the first year and alternate along the stem in the second; they are oval to lanceolate, coarsely toothed to shallowly lobed, with a spiny undulating margin and, like the stems, are covered in white, cottony hairs. The solitary purple or white thistle-heads, 30–50mm (1⅕–2in) across, are surrounded by spreading bracts ending in a stiff yellowish spine.

• **DISTRIBUTION** Holland to Germany southwards; naturalized in Britain and S. Scandinavia.

• **HABITAT** Hedgerows, embankments, roadsides, waste places, and cultivated land; often grown in gardens.

spreading, cottony, linear bracts

pappus of unbranched hairs

spiny wings along entire length of stem

purplish florets

Habit Biennial	Height 1.5–2.5m (5–8ft)	Flowering time July–Sept

Family COMPOSITAE	Species *Centaurea scabiosa*	Author L.

GREATER KNAPWEED

This tufted, erect knapweed is rough with bristles and has stiff stems branched in the upper part. The leaves are grey-green; the lower are short-stalked and pinnately lobed, with many narrow, oval to linear segments; the upper leaves are much reduced and sometimes unlobed, but often with a few short basal lobes. The purple flower-heads, 30–50mm (1⅕–2in) across, are solitary, with the outer florets much larger than the inner; all florets have 5 narrow lobes joined below into a slender tube; the flower-bracts are closely overlapping and are green with a black or brown bristly margin.

• **DISTRIBUTION** Throughout the region, except for the far north.

• **HABITAT** Rough grassland, road verges, embankments, scrub, and cliffs; mostly on calcareous soils.

spreading, sterile outer florets

involucre of bracts having shed fruit

pinnately lobed lower leaves

unlobed upper leaf

Habit Perennial	Height 80–120cm (32–48in)	Flowering time July–Sept

Family COMPOSITAE	Species *Centaurea nigra*	Author L.

COMMON KNAPWEED

This variable, tufted, stiff-stemmed plant is rough with hairs. The stems are branched or unbranched and thickened immediately below the flower-heads. The alternate leaves are greyish green and elliptical to oval; the lower are stalked and slightly toothed, while the upper are usually untoothed and unstalked. The flower-heads, 20–40mm (⅘–1⅗in) across, are purple or reddish purple and are solitary or borne in branched clusters; the flower-bracts have an expanded and deeply fringed dark brown or black apex; the outer florets are sometimes enlarged.

• **DISTRIBUTION** Throughout, as far north as C. Scandinavia; generally common.

• **HABITAT** Grassy places, especially meadows, road verges, scrub, and railway embankments.

Habit Perennial	Height 50–100cm (20–40in)	Flowering time June–Sept

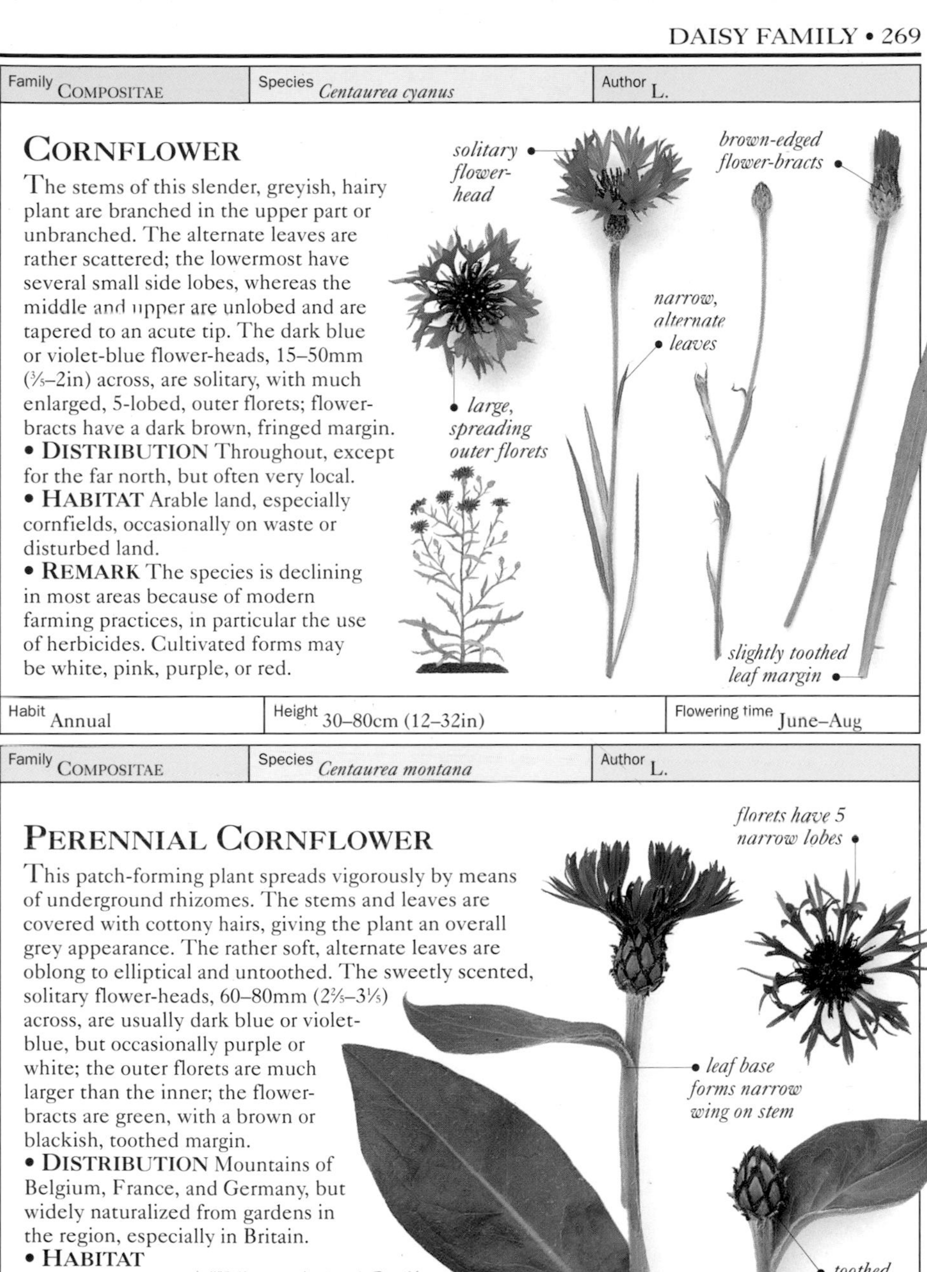

Family COMPOSITAE	Species *Centaurea cyanus*	Author L.

CORNFLOWER

The stems of this slender, greyish, hairy plant are branched in the upper part or unbranched. The alternate leaves are rather scattered; the lowermost have several small side lobes, whereas the middle and upper are unlobed and are tapered to an acute tip. The dark blue or violet-blue flower-heads, 15–50mm (3/5–2in) across, are solitary, with much enlarged, 5-lobed, outer florets; flower-bracts have a dark brown, fringed margin.

• **DISTRIBUTION** Throughout, except for the far north, but often very local.

• **HABITAT** Arable land, especially cornfields, occasionally on waste or disturbed land.

• **REMARK** The species is declining in most areas because of modern farming practices, in particular the use of herbicides. Cultivated forms may be white, pink, purple, or red.

Habit Annual	Height 30–80cm (12–32in)	Flowering time June–Aug

Family COMPOSITAE	Species *Centaurea montana*	Author L.

PERENNIAL CORNFLOWER

This patch-forming plant spreads vigorously by means of underground rhizomes. The stems and leaves are covered with cottony hairs, giving the plant an overall grey appearance. The rather soft, alternate leaves are oblong to elliptical and untoothed. The sweetly scented, solitary flower-heads, 60–80mm (2 2/5–3 1/5) across, are usually dark blue or violet-blue, but occasionally purple or white; the outer florets are much larger than the inner; the flower-bracts are green, with a brown or blackish, toothed margin.

• **DISTRIBUTION** Mountains of Belgium, France, and Germany, but widely naturalized from gardens in the region, especially in Britain.

• **HABITAT** Dry grassy, open places, hedgerows, waste ground, and abandoned cultivation.

Habit Perennial	Height 30–70cm (12–28in)	Flowering time June–Aug

Family COMPOSITAE	Species *Silybum marianum*	Author (L.) Gaertner

MILK THISTLE

Large and imposing, this thistle-like plant is hairless or slightly hairy and forms a big leafy rosette at first, before the stiff flowering stems appear. The oblong leaves are pinnately lobed and are shiny deep green conspicuously variegated with white along the veins above, and sometimes also with white blotches; the upper leaves are unstalked and clasp the stem with broad bases. The solitary flower-heads are purple and 40–50mm (1⅗–2in) across; the flower-bracts are stiff, curved, spiny, and overlap in the lower half.

• **DISTRIBUTION** France, but naturalized or casual in Britain and parts of Holland, Belgium, and Germany.

• **HABITAT** Cultivated and waste land, roadsides, scrub, and embankments; sometimes forming extensive colonies.

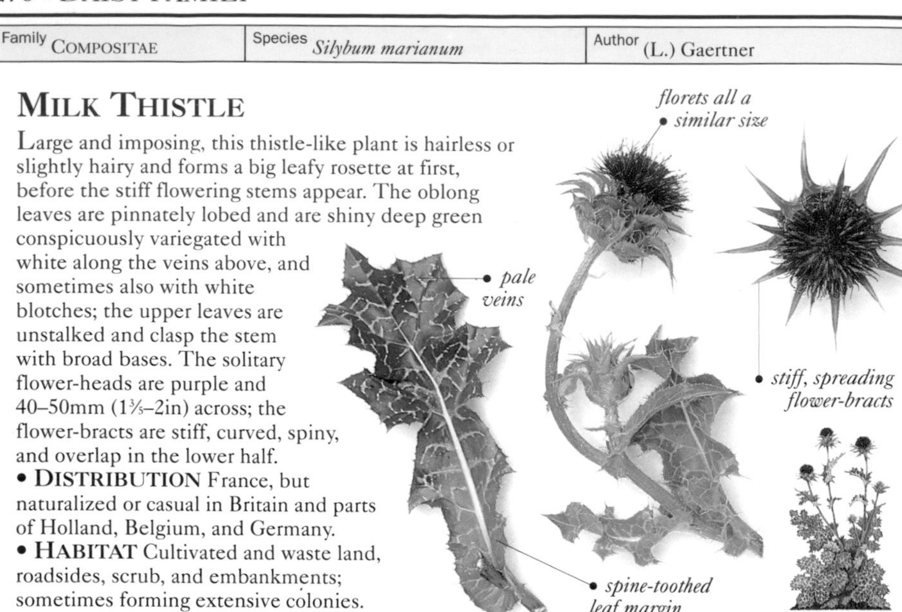

Habit Annual or biennial	Height 60–120cm (24–48in)	Flowering time June–Aug

Family COMPOSITAE	Species *Cichorium intybus*	Author L.

CHICORY

This rather robust, somewhat hairy or hairless plant has stiff, ridged stems, and produces a white latex when cut. The basal leaves are pinnately lobed to coarsely toothed, while the upper leaves are much smaller and untoothed, often with a slightly wavy margin. The flower-heads are bright blue, more rarely pink or white, and 25–40mm (1–1⅗in) across; they open in bright light and have relatively few broad and strap-like, spreading rays that are toothed at the tip; the flower-bracts are green and few, the inner being narrower than the outer. The achenes have no feathery pappus.

• **DISTRIBUTION** Throughout the region, except for the far north, but probably not native everywhere.

• **HABITAT** Grassy and waste places, fields, road verges, hedgerows, and embankments; mostly on calcareous soils. Widely cultivated for use as a salad crop.

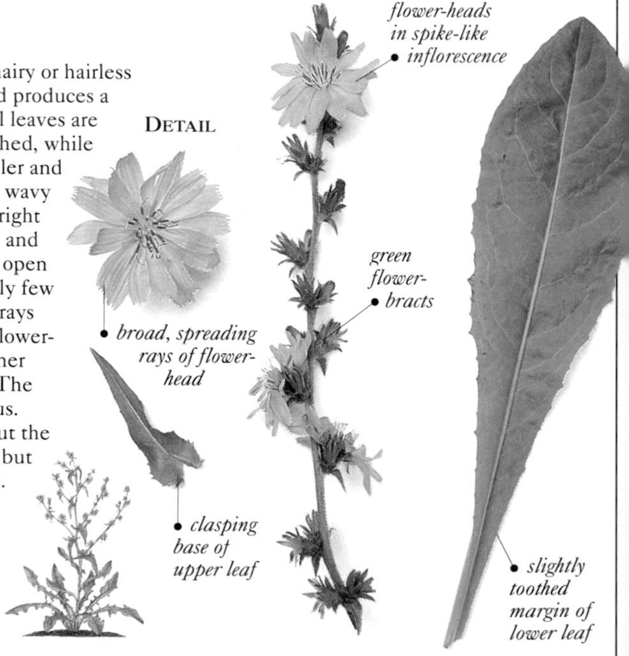

DETAIL

flower-heads in spike-like inflorescence

broad, spreading rays of flower-head

green flower-bracts

clasping base of upper leaf

slightly toothed margin of lower leaf

Habit Perennial	Height 60–100cm (24–40in)	Flowering time July–Oct

Family COMPOSITAE	Species *Tragopogon pratensis*	Author L.

GOAT'S-BEARD

Often rather robust and usually hairless, this plant has erect, unbranched or slightly branched stems that produce a white latex when cut and are somewhat swollen beneath the flower-heads. The long linear-lanceolate leaves are channelled and tapered to a fine tip. The flower-heads are pale yellow, 18–40mm (⅔–1⅗in) across, and solitary, with the spreading rays somewhat shorter than the linear flower-bracts. The fruit-head is a characteristic "clock" forming a whitish ball up to 12cm (4¾in) across; the achenes have a long slender beak that terminates in a feathery pappus.

• **DISTRIBUTION** Throughout, except for the far north.

• **HABITAT** Rough grassy places, meadows, embankments, road verges, hedgerows, and occasionally sand dunes.

• **REMARK** *Tragopogon pratensis* subsp. *minor* has smaller, paler flowers, and bracts that are much longer than the rays. It is common in Britain and W. France.

spreading ray-florets

stem swells slightly below flower-head

single row of flower-bracts

"clock" of feathered achenes

flower-bud

narrow, alternate leaves

ridged stem

basal leaf

Habit Annual to perennial	Height 40–75cm (16–30in)	Flowering time June–July

Family COMPOSITAE	Species *Hypochaeris glabra*	Author L.

SMOOTH CAT'S-EAR

The stems of this hairless, or rarely slightly prickly, plant are slender, usually branched, and somewhat thickened towards the flower-heads. Borne mostly in basal rosettes, the shiny pale green leaves are pinnately lobed to toothed. The flower-heads, 10–15mm (⅖–⅗in) across, are pale or bright yellow.

• **DISTRIBUTION** Throughout the region, except for the far north; local and decreasing.

• **HABITAT** Open grassy sites, meadows, roadsides, embankments, and sand dunes; mostly on light, well-drained, sandy or gravelly soils.

• **RELATED SPECIES** *Hypochaeris radicata*, Cat's-ear, is perennial, with generally hairy leaves and larger flower-heads. Its distribution and habitats are similar but it is more common.

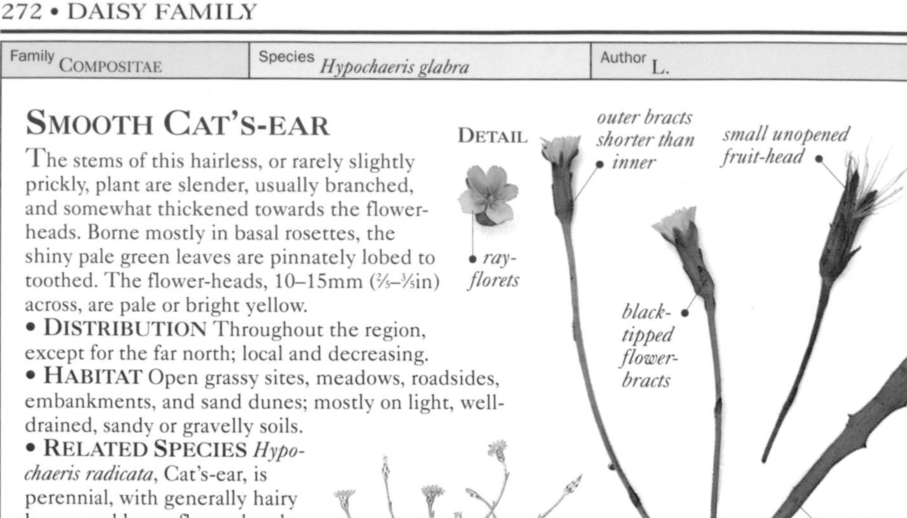

Habit Annual	Height 20–40cm (8–16in)	Flowering time June–Oct

Family COMPOSITAE	Species *Sonchus arvensis*	Author L.

PERENNIAL SOW-THISTLE

This vigorous, patch-forming, and somewhat bristly plant has a far-reaching rhizomatous rootstock and produces copious amounts of white latex when cut. The greyish leaves are alternate; the lower are stalked, while the middle and upper are unstalked and clasp the stem with a heart-shaped base. The yellow flower-heads are 40–50mm (1⅗–2in) across, and are clustered on stiff stems; the florets are all rayed. The flower-bracts are linear, pointed, and covered with sticky yellowish glands.

• **DISTRIBUTION** Throughout the region, except for the far north.

• **HABITAT** A widespread weed of cultivated land; also on waste land, ditches, and coastal sands and shingle.

Habit Perennial	Height 80–150cm (32–60in)	Flowering time July–Oct

Family COMPOSITAE	Species *Lactuca virosa*	Author L.

GREAT LETTUCE

The erect stem of this hairless plant is branched in the inflorescence, produces milky latex when cut, and is flushed with maroon or black. The alternate leaves are pinnately lobed, with a finely toothed, slightly prickly margin, but also with prickles on the underside along the midrib; the upper leaves are held horizontally. The yellow flower-heads are 9–11mm (3/8–3/7in) across. The fruit, a maroon to black achene, has a hairy pappus.

• **DISTRIBUTION** Britain to Holland and Germany southwards; always local.

• **HABITAT** Cultivated, waste, and disturbed land, river banks, gravelly sites, and cliff-tops.

• **RELATED SPECIES** *Lactuca serriola*, Prickly Lettuce, is more prickly, has greenish white stems, and olive-grey achenes. It grows throughout, except for Ireland, Scotland, and the far north.

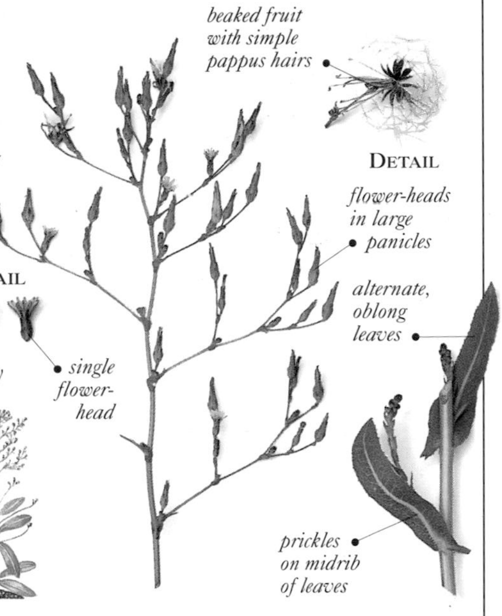

beaked fruit with simple pappus hairs

DETAIL

flower-heads in large panicles

alternate, oblong leaves

DETAIL

ray-florets only

single flower-head

prickles on midrib of leaves

Habit Annual or biennial	Height 1–2m (3¼–6½ft)	Flowering time July–Sept

Family COMPOSITAE	Species *Taraxacum officinale*	Author Weber

COMMON DANDELION

Extremely variable and widespread, this plant forms a basal rosette of leaves and has solitary, scapose flowers; leaves and scapes exude a white latex when cut. The leaves are elliptical to oblong or almost linear, pinnately lobed, or sometimes unlobed, and usually have broadly winged stalks; they often form large coarse rosettes, and are a bright shiny green, never spotted. The flower-heads are 25–50mm (1–2in) across; florets usually have a brownish or greyish violet stripe on the underside. The flower-bracts are dark blue-green. The fruit is a "clock".

• **DISTRIBUTION** Throughout the region, except for Spitsbergen.

• **HABITAT** Grassy meadows, pastures, lawns, roadsides, embankments, river and stream margins, open woodland, and scrub.

• **REMARK** This plant represents a complex group of closely related species.

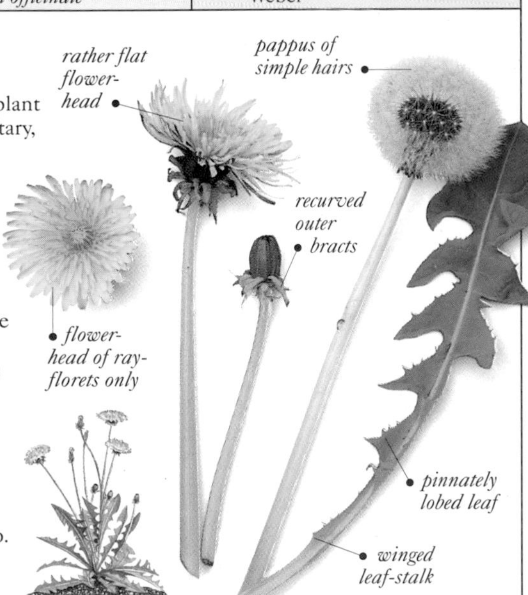

Habit Perennial	Height 5–40cm (2–16in)	Flowering time Mar–Oct

Family COMPOSITAE	Species *Lapsana communis*	Author L.

NIPPLEWORT

This slender-stemmed, erect, and hairy annual may have branched or unbranched stems, and forms a loose leaf-rosette at first; stems and leaves do not produce a latex when cut. The pale green leaves are rather variable. The lower leaves are stalked, oval to elliptical, toothed, and often have several small basal lobes, while the upper are lanceolate, toothed or not, and the uppermost are small and bract-like. The yellow flower-heads are small, 10–20mm (⅖–⅘in) across, and are borne in a loose panicle; the florets all have rays and are toothed at the tip. The flower-bracts are lanceolate, erect, and green. The achenes have no pappus.

• **DISTRIBUTION** Throughout.

• **HABITAT** Cultivated, waste, and disturbed land, open woodland and scrub, roadsides, and old walls; a rapid-growing and often tiresome weed of gardens. Sometimes growing in large numbers and producing copious amounts of seed.

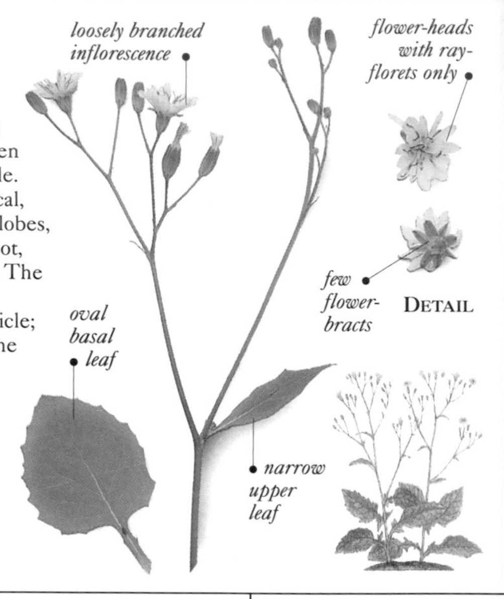

Habit Annual, rarely biennial	Height 20–90cm (8–36in)	Flowering time May–Oct

Family COMPOSITAE	Species *Picris echioides*	Author L.

PRICKLY OXTONGUE

This bristly plant has well-branched stems; the bristles are hooked at the apex and arise from a pimple-like base on the stems and leaves. The alternate leaves are elliptical to oblong, with a wavy margin; the lower leaves are stalked; the upper clasp the stem with unstalked bases. The flower-heads, 20–25mm (⅘–1in) across, have ray-florets only. The flower-bracts are erect; the outer are heart-shaped and much broader than the inner. The achenes have a pappus.

• **DISTRIBUTION** Naturalized from Britain, Ireland, Holland, and Germany southwards.

• **HABITAT** Rough grassy places, disturbed and waste land, streamsides; on heavy soils, especially near the sea.

• **RELATED SPECIES** *Picris hieracioides*, Hawkweed Oxtongue, has narrower, usually toothed leaves, and narrower flower-bracts with black hairs. It grows throughout, except for the far north.

Habit Annual or biennial	Height 40–80cm (16–32in)	Flowering time June–Nov

Family COMPOSITAE	Species *Crepis capillaris*	Author (L.) Wallr.

SMOOTH HAWK'S-BEARD

This rather slender, hairless or slightly hairy plant has stems branched close to the base or above. The alternate leaves are shiny green and lanceolate, with a shallowly to deeply pinnately lobed margin. Most leaves are clustered near the bottom of the plant; the basal leaves are narrowed at the base and stalked, while the upper clasp the stem with narrow basal-lobes. The rather dandelion-like flower-heads, 10–15mm (⅖–⅗in) across, are yellow; the florets are all rayed and usually reddish beneath. The fruit is a small beaked achene with a pappus of simple white hairs.

• **DISTRIBUTION** Britain to Holland and Germany southwards, but naturalized in parts of Scandinavia.

• **HABITAT** Grassy, waste, and cultivated land, roadsides, embankments; often gregarious.

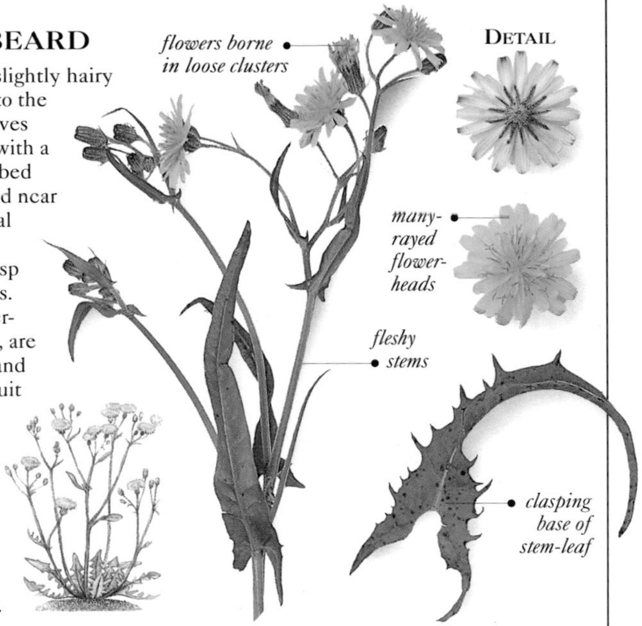

flowers borne in loose clusters

DETAIL

many-rayed flower-heads

fleshy stems

clasping base of stem-leaf

Habit Annual or biennial	Height 30–75cm (12–30in)	Flowering time June–Nov

Family COMPOSITAE	Species *Pilosella officinarum*	Author F. Schultz & Schultz-Bip

MOUSE-EAR HAWKWEED

Also known under the name *Hieracium pilosella*, this widespread plant has a spreading stoloniferous habit, with the stem and the leaf undersurface covered in soft woolly hairs. The leaves are all borne in basal rosettes and are elliptical to oblong, untoothed, and white-felted beneath. The dandelion-like flower-heads are lemon-yellow and 20–30mm (⅘–1⅕in) across; the florets are all rayed, the outer rays often striped red below. The fruit is a small achene with a brittle, brownish pappus.

• **DISTRIBUTION** Throughout the region, except for the far north.

• **HABITAT** Cultivated and waste ground, meadows, pastures, roadsides, sand dunes, and rocky sites; on dry acid or chalky soils.

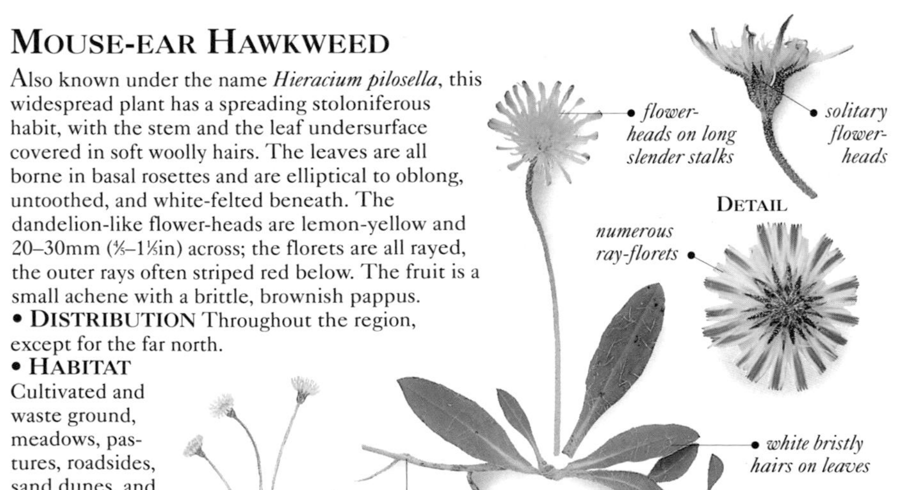

Habit Perennial	Height 10–30cm (4–12in)	Flowering time June–Sept

Family COMPOSITAE	Species *Pilosella aurantiaca*	Author (L.) F. Schultz & Schultz-Bip.

FOX AND CUBS

Often called *Hieracium aurantiacum*, this familiar plant is covered in blackish hairs and forms a mat of bluish green leaves which spread by means of slender, rooting stolons. The stems are scarcely leafy. The leaves are elliptical to lanceolate, untoothed, and mostly stalked; upper stem-leaves are few, smaller, and often bract-like. The flower-heads are orange-brown or orange-red and 13–15mm (½–⅗in) across; the flower-bracts are linear and closely overlap one another. The fruit is a small achene with a brittle, brownish pappus.

• **DISTRIBUTION** France, Germany, and S. Scandinavia; widely naturalized in much of the rest of the region.

• **HABITAT** Grassy places, meadows, roadsides, cultivated and waste land, embankments, and old walls; widely grown in gardens.

Habit Perennial	Height 25–60cm (10–24in)	Flowering time June–Aug

Family COMPOSITAE	Species *Hieracium vulgatum*	Author Fries

COMMON HAWKWEED

This is a very variable, hairy plant with the leaves mostly crowded close to the base. The stem is thin, erect, and branched in the upper part. The leaves are oval to lanceolate with a coarsely toothed margin; the upper leaves are smaller and unstalked. The bright yellow flower-heads, 20–30mm (⅘–1⅕in) across, are borne in a flat-topped cluster; the flower-bracts are white-haired as well as glandular. The fruit is a small achene with a brittle, brownish pappus.

• **DISTRIBUTION** Throughout the region, except for the far north and Iceland.

• **HABITAT** Rocky and grassy places, open woodland, heaths, embankments, cliff-tops.

• **REMARK** This is a complex species or, more accurately, group of closely related species in which some authors recognize several hundred separate microspecies.

Habit Perennial	Height 20–80cm (8–32in)	Flowering time June–Aug

MONOCOTYLEDONS

WATER-PLANTAIN FAMILY

Family	Species	Author
ALISMATACEAE	*Sagittaria sagittifolia*	L.

ARROWHEAD

This semi-aquatic, hairless plant often forms large tufts. The long-stalked aerial leaves are shaped like an arrowhead, with long, triangular basal lobes and an untoothed margin; when present, the floating leaves are elliptical and long-stalked; the submerged leaves are ribbon-like. The white flowers, 20–26mm (4/5–1in) across, have a distinctive purple centre, 3 sepals, 3 petals, and many purple anthers. They are borne in whorls in racemes or panicles, with male and female flowers on the same plant. The fruit consists of a collection of achenes.

• **DISTRIBUTION** Throughout the region, except for the far north.

• **HABITAT** Shallow freshwater: lakes, ponds, canals, slow-moving streams and rivers, and marshes.

• **RELATED SPECIES** *Sagittaria latifolia*, Duck-potato, has plain white flowers with yellow anthers. It is naturalized in Jersey, France, and Germany.

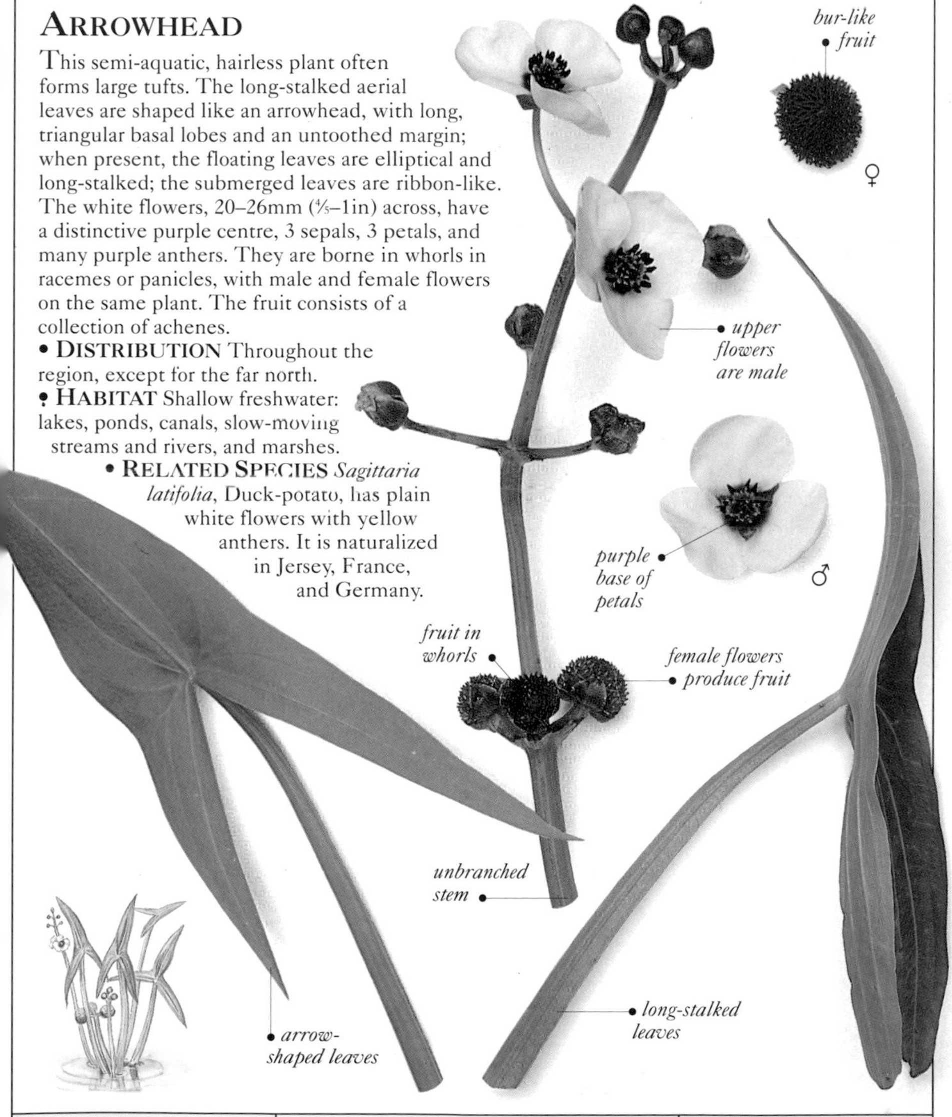

bur-like fruit

♀

upper flowers are male

purple base of petals

♂

fruit in whorls

female flowers produce fruit

unbranched stem

arrow-shaped leaves

long-stalked leaves

Habit	Height	Flowering time
Perennial	60–100cm (24–40in)	July–Aug

Family ALISMATACEAE	Species *Alisma plantago-aquatica*	Author L.

WATER-PLANTAIN

This semi-aquatic, hairless plant forms tufts. The leaves are basal and long-stalked, mostly aerial, elliptical to oval, pointed, and with a rounded to slightly heart-shaped base. The flowers, 6–10mm (¼–⅖in) across, have 3 petals and 3 shorter sepals; the many anthers are yellow. The fruit consists of a collection of single-seeded, beaked achenes.

• **DISTRIBUTION** Throughout the region, except for the far north.

• **HABITAT** Shallow fresh water: lakes, ponds, slow-moving river and stream margins, ditches, and marshes.

• **RELATED SPECIES** *Alisma lanceolatum*, Narrow-leaved Water-plantain, has lanceolate to narrow-elliptical leaves and slightly larger purplish pink flowers. It has similar habitats and distribution.

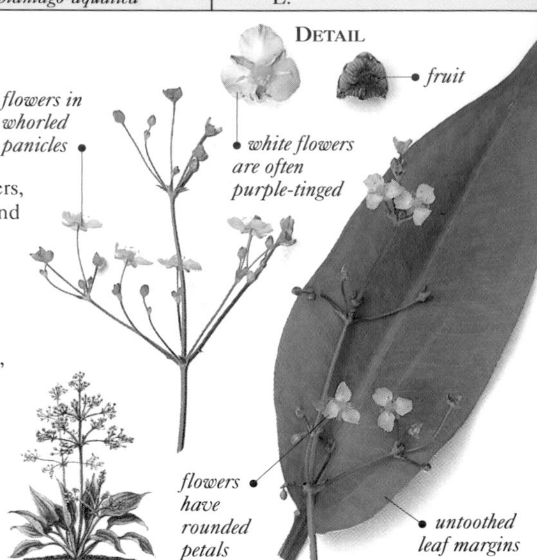

Habit Perennial	Height 40–100cm (16–40in)	Flowering time June–Aug

FLOWERING RUSH FAMILY

Family BUTOMACEAE	Species *Butomus umbellatus*	Author L.

FLOWERING RUSH

Rather stout and often tufted, this hairless plant has a creeping rhizomatous stock. The scapes are erect. The leaves are all basal, linear, triangular in cross-section in the lower half, with a broadened sheathing base. Borne in large umbel-like heads that rise above the leaves, the flowers, 16–26mm (⅝–1in) across, are pale to deep pink with darker veins, and have 3 sepals and 3 petals; the sepals are stained with green on the outside. The fruit consists of 6 reddish purple follicles fused together at the base.

• **DISTRIBUTION** Local throughout much of the region, except the far north; often naturalized.

• **HABITAT** River, canal, and stream margins, lakes, ponds, and ditches.

Habit Perennial	Height 80–150cm (32–60in)	Flowering time July–Aug

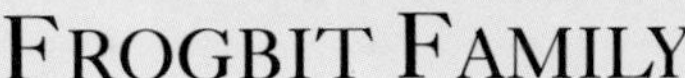

FROGBIT FAMILY

Family HYDROCHARITACEAE	Species *Hydrocharis morsus-ranae*	Author L.

FROGBIT

This aquatic plant has long horizontal runners which give rise to tufts of leaves and roots at intervals. The leaves, mostly on the water surface, are heart-shaped to kidney-shaped and deep green, often flushed with bronze. The flowers, 18–20mm (5/7–4/5in) across, are in clusters of 2 to 4 or occasionally solitary; male and female flowers are on separate plants; the 3 sepals are half as long as the 3 petals. The fruit is a small capsule.

• **DISTRIBUTION** Throughout; not the far north.

• **HABITAT** Freshwater ponds, lakes, canals, ditches; never in fast-flowing waters.

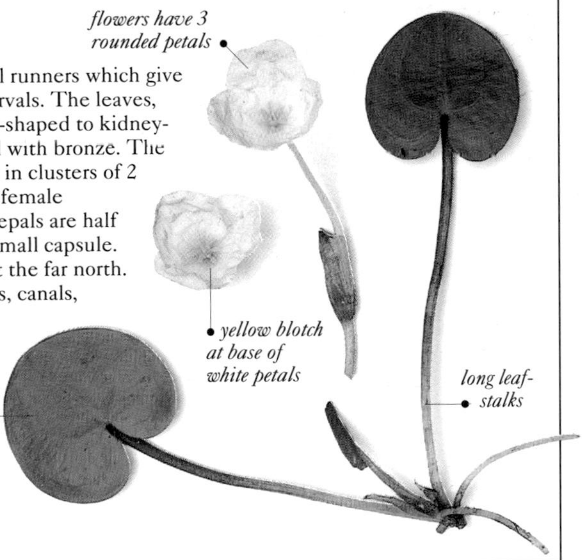

flowers have 3 rounded petals

yellow blotch at base of white petals

long leaf-stalks

untoothed kidney-shaped leaves

Habit Perennial	Stem length 1m (3¼ft) or more	Flowering time July–Aug

CAPE PONDWEED FAMILY

Family APONOGETONACEAE	Species *Aponogeton distachyos*	Author L. f.

CAPE PONDWEED

This hairless, aquatic plant has a tuberous rootstock and floating leaves. The stems are fleshy and spongy, usually branched, and root into the mud. The floating leaves are elliptical to oblong with an untoothed margin, long-stalked, and have a sheathing base. The white flowers, 10–12mm (2/5–½in) long, are borne in Y-shaped clusters just above the surface of the water; each flower has one or 2 petal-like tepals and up to 18 stamens. The fruit consists of a cluster of 3 follicles, each containing many small seeds.

• **DISTRIBUTION** Naturalized in scattered localities in Britain and France, and possibly elsewhere within the region. A native plant of South Africa.

• **HABITAT** Lakes, ponds, occasionally ditches; cultivated in gardens.

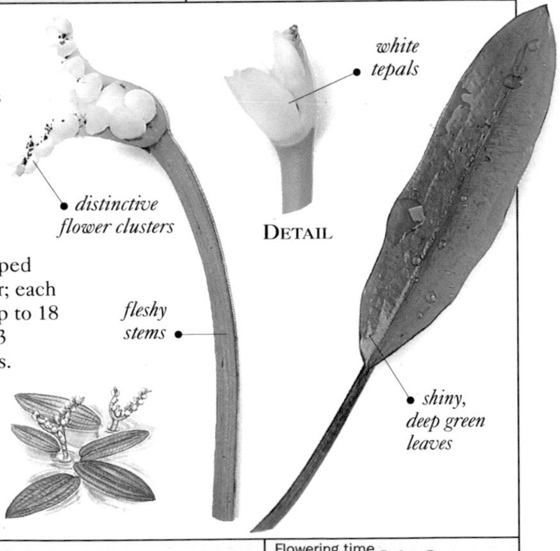

distinctive flower clusters

white tepals

DETAIL

fleshy stems

shiny, deep green leaves

Habit Perennial	Height Water surface	Flowering time July–Oct

Pondweed Family

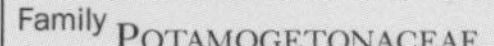

Family POTAMOGETONACEAE	Species *Potamogeton natans*	Author L.

Broad-leaved Pondweed

This is a vigorous and hairless aquatic plant. The stems are fleshy, somewhat spongy, and generally branched. The floating leaves are oval to elliptical, with a long stalk and a sheathing base; the submerged leaves are linear and under 3mm (⅛in) wide. The green flowers, 3–4mm (⅛–⅙in) across, are borne in a dense spike on a thick stalk just above the water surface; each flower has 4 sepals but no petals. The fruit consists of 4 small nutlets, each 3–4mm (⅛–⅙in) long.

• **Distribution** Throughout the region, except for Spitsbergen.

• **Habitat** Lakes, ponds, ditches, slow-moving rivers and streams; generally growing in water rich in nutrients.

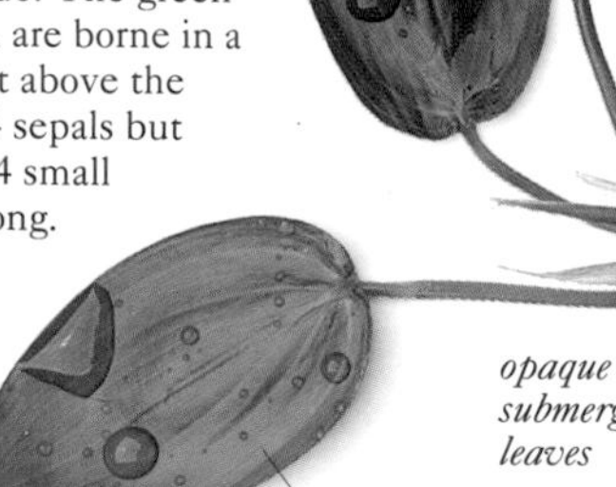

Habit Perennial	Height Water surface	Flowering time May–Sept

Lily Family

Family LILIACEAE	Species *Narthecium ossifragum*	Author (L.) Hudson

Bog Asphodel

This is a rather variable, tufted, rhizomatous plant with deep green fans of leaves. The leaves are fleshy, sword-shaped, and often flushed with orange; the stem-leaves are few and smaller than the basal leaves and are often bract-like. Borne in stiff racemes, the greenish yellow or orange-yellow flowers, 10–16mm (⅖–⅝in) across, are star-shaped, with 6 petal-like tepals; the stamen filaments are densely hairy. The fruit is a small, narrow-oblong, orange, 3-parted capsule.

• **Distribution** Most of the region, except for the far north; absent or rare in C. and E. England.

• **Habitat** Acid moors, bogs, and heaths, moist peaty and mossy places; mostly in the hills and mountains to an altitude of 1,600m (5,250ft).

Habit Perennial	Height 15–45cm (6–18in)	Flowering time July–Sept

Family LILIACEAE	Species *Anthericum liliago*	Author L.

St. Bernard's Lily

The flowering stems of this tufted and hairless plant are erect, rather stiff, and usually sparsely branched in the inflorescence. The fleshy, linear leaves are all basal, flat or somewhat channelled, and taper to a fine point. The bracts are membranous, linear, and tapered. The white flowers are star-shaped and 20–35mm (⅘–1⅖in) across; the 6 tepals are all similar and petal-like. The fruit is a 3-parted capsule containing numerous seeds.

• **DISTRIBUTION** France, Belgium, Germany, and S. Scandinavia.

• **HABITAT** Rocky and grassy calcareous slopes on hills and mountains to 1,800m (5,900ft); generally found growing in limestone areas. Cultivated in gardens.

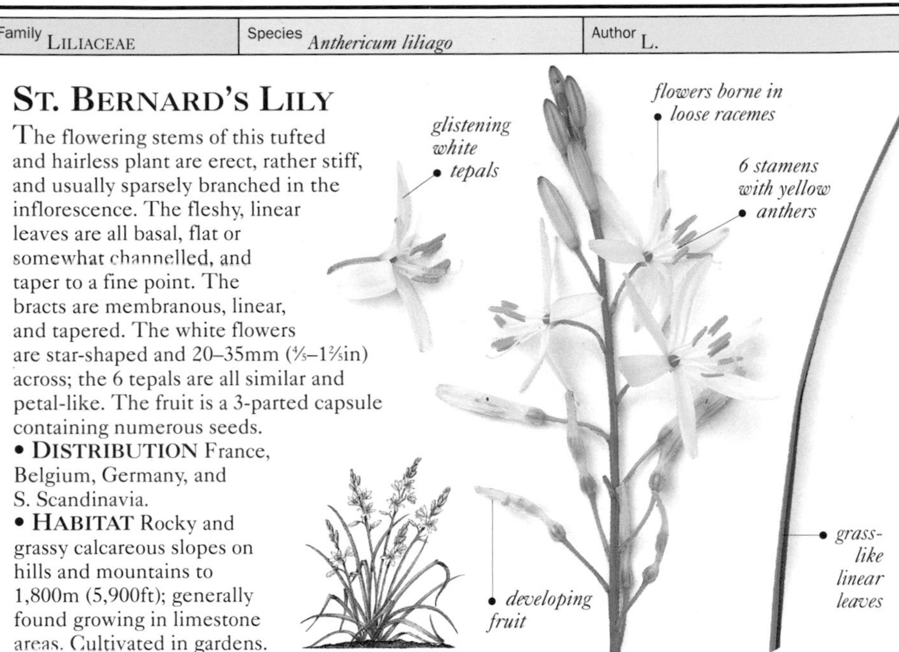

Habit Perennial	Height 30–70cm (12–28in)	Flowering time May–July

Family LILIACEAE	Species *Colchicum autumnale*	Author L.

Meadow Saffron

This is a hairless plant with a large underground corm. It flowers in the autumn before the leaves appear. The leaves, 2 to 4 clustered together on a short stem close to ground level, are deep glossy green and broad-lanceolate, with an untoothed margin. The crocus-like flowers are pink, pinkish lilac, or occasionally white, and 40–60mm (1⅗–2⅖in) long, with a long tube-like stalk; the 6 tepals are all similar and petal-like; the 6 stamens have yellow anthers. The fleshy 3-parted fruit capsules nestle in the centre of the leaf clusters. The plant is poisonous.

• **DISTRIBUTION** England and Wales to France and Germany southwards; naturalized in S. Ireland, the Channel Islands, and S. Scandinavia.

• **HABITAT** Damp meadows and pastures, roadsides, and open woodland; on neutral or calcareous soils.

goblet-shaped pink flowers

broad leaves appear in spring

flowers appear in autumn

long flower-tube

Habit Perennial	Height 10–40cm (4–16in)	Flowering time Aug–Oct

Family LILIACEAE	Species *Fritillaria meleagris*	Author L.

SNAKESHEAD LILY

This hairless, bulbous plant is solitary or clump-forming. The leaves are slightly channelled, tapered to the tip, and decrease in size up the stem. The solitary, occasionally paired, pendent flowers, 30–45mm (1$\frac{1}{5}$–1$\frac{4}{5}$in) long, are purple or pink with conspicuous chequering, or white or creamish with greenish markings; the 6 tepals are all similar. The flower-stalk gradually lengthens and becomes erect as the fruit capsule develops. The capsule contains numerous disc-like seeds.

• **DISTRIBUTION** S. England, Holland, France, and Germany; widely cultivated in the region and sometimes naturalized.

• **HABITAT** Damp grassy places, especially river meadows and pastures; generally declining due to modern farming practices.

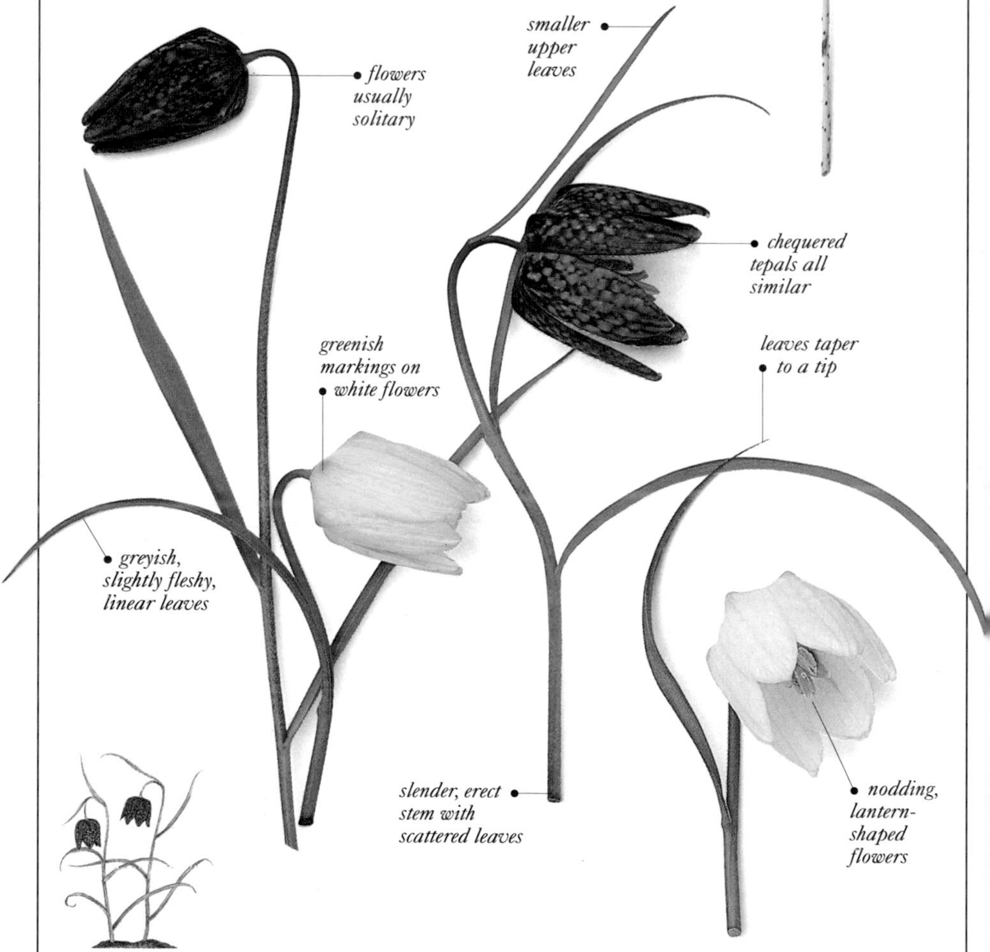

Habit Perennial	Height 25–50cm (10–20in)	Flowering time Apr–May

Family LILIACEAE	Species *Ornithogalum angustifolium*	Author Boreau

STAR-OF-BETHLEHEM

Formerly known as *Ornithogalum umbellatum*, this hairless and bulbous plant has basal leaves and scapose inflorescences. The deep green, linear leaves have a pale white stripe running along the grooved middle; they are generally rather limp and flop on the ground at maturity. The star-shaped flowers, 28–44mm (1 1/12–1 4/5in) across, are glistening white and are borne in a pyramidal raceme, with the lower flowers on longer stalks than the upper ones. The bracts are linear-elliptical and whitish. The fruit capsule is erect, 3-parted, and contains numerous seeds.

- **DISTRIBUTION** Britain and western Europe; naturalized in Ireland and parts of Scandinavia.
- **HABITAT** Grassy places, meadows, hedgerows, open woodland and scrub, and waste and cultivated land; often rather local and often on sandy soils.

6 stamens

green stripe on back of tepals

6-parted flower

one bract to each flower

pale central stripe on linear leaves

Habit Perennial	Height 10–30cm (4–12in)	Flowering time Apr–June

Family LILIACEAE	Species *Ornithogalum nutans*	Author L.

DROOPING STAR-OF-BETHLEHEM

Often forming extensive colonies, this is a hairless, bulbous plant with basal leaves only and scapose inflorescences. The grass-like leaves are bright green or greyish green with a narrow white central stripe on the upper surface. The bracts are longer than the flower-stalks and are membranous. Borne in one-sided racemes, the nodding, bell-shaped flowers, 15–30mm (3/5–1 1/5in) long, have 6 white tepals which have a broad grey-green stripe on the reverse and eventually spread widely apart; each flower has 6 stamens. The fruit consists of a small 3-parted capsule containing many seeds.

- **DISTRIBUTION** Widely naturalized in the region, except for parts of Scandinavia and the far north. Native to C. and E. Europe.
- **HABITAT** Grassy meadows, open woodland, scrub, grassy roadsides, and cultivated land; often grown in gardens and sometimes escaping to become naturalized locally.

broad grey-green stripe along tepal reverse

bract

flowers have 6 tepals

spike of drooping flowers

leafless inflorescence

linear leaf

Habit Perennial	Height 30–60cm (12–24in)	Flowering time Apr–May

Family LILIACEAE	Species *Tulipa sylvestris*	Author L.

WILD TULIP

This is a more or less hairless plant, with an underground bulb and a solitary, leafy stem. The rather fleshy leaves are alternate, lanceolate to elliptical, or almost linear, untoothed, somewhat channelled along the centre, and deep green on the outer surface but grey-green on the inner one. The large yellow flowers are solitary, 36–70mm (1⅖–2⅘in) long, and more or less goblet-shaped, with 6 petal-like tepals; the outer 3 tepals are usually flushed with green, pink, or crimson on the outside and are sometimes recurved. The fruit consists of a 3-parted capsule containing numerous flat seeds.

• **DISTRIBUTION** Native to C. and S. France; naturalized in C. and S. England and in S.E. Scotland; probably only naturalized in the rest of Europe as far north as S. Sweden.

• **HABITAT** Meadows, grassy and rocky places, and copses; growing at low altitudes.

• **REMARK** This plant rarely sets seeds, increasing instead by means of underground stolons from the parent bulb.

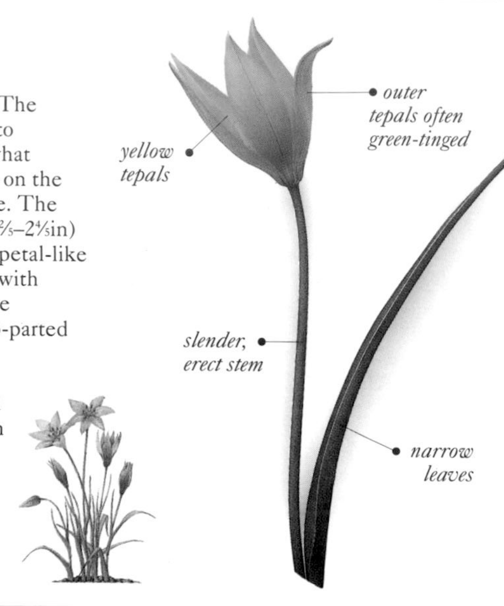

Habit Perennial	Height 20–50cm (8–20in)	Flowering time Apr–May

Family LILIACEAE	Species *Scilla autumnalis*	Author L.

AUTUMN SQUILL

This small, hairless, bulbous plant produces flowers in the autumn before the leaves appear. The 5 to 10 leaves are all basal and thread-like, deep green, and usually ascending to erect, appearing after the flowers have faded. The plant has no bracts. The small, star-shaped flowers, 6–10mm (¼–⅖in) across, are lilac to pinkish blue, occasionally white, and are borne in short racemes on erect scapes; the 6 tepals are all similar and petal-like; the 6 stamens have dark blackish purple anthers. The small fruit capsule is 3-parted and contains numerous seeds.

• **DISTRIBUTION** S. England and France; extinct in Wales.

• **HABITAT** Dry grassy and rocky places, cliff-tops, commons, and dunes; usually fairly close to the sea and generally local; sometimes found in large colonies.

Habit Perennial	Height 25–50cm (10–20in)	Flowering time Apr–June

Family LILIACEAE	Species *Scilla non-scripta*	Author (L.) Hoffmanns

BLUEBELL

Also known as *Endymion non-scriptus* and *Hyacinthoides non-scripta*, this flower often forms extensive colonies. The plant is hairless and has a bulbous stock which is frequently clump-forming. The bright green leaves are all basal, linear-lanceolate, and have a distinct keel beneath. The bracts, 2 per flower, are membranous and are often coloured like the flowers. The tubular, bell-shaped flowers are violet-blue, rarely pinkish or white, 14–20mm (⁴⁄₇–⁴⁄₅in) long, and borne in slender racemes that are arched or nodding at the apex; the tepals, 6 per flower, are all similar and petal-like. The fruit is a small 3-parted capsule.

• **DISTRIBUTION** Native in W. France and the whole of the British Isles; naturalized elsewhere in N.W. Europe.

• **HABITAT** Woodland, copses, scrub, hedge-banks, and heaths, sometimes along sea-cliffs.

• **RELATED SPECIES** *Scilla hispanica*, Spanish Bluebell, has erect racemes and broader bells. It is widely grown in gardens and naturalized in Britain and France; native to Spain and Portugal.

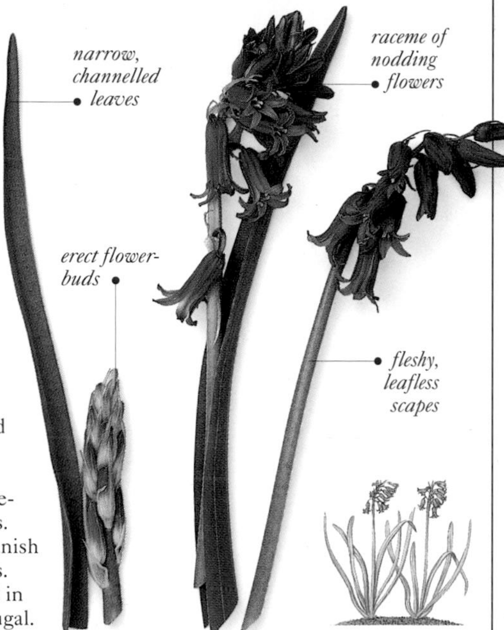

Habit Perennial	Height 25–50cm (10–20in)	Flowering time Apr–June

Family LILIACEAE	Species *Scilla verna*	Author Hudson

SPRING SQUILL

This is a small, hairless plant, with a bulbous stock. It may be solitary or several may grow together, but it often forms large scattered colonies. Borne at the same time as the flowers, the rather bright green leaves, generally 2 to 7 per bulb, are all basal, linear, thread-like, and often rather curly. The bracts, one per flower, are membranous and often longer than the flower-stalks. The small, star-shaped flowers, 10–16mm (²⁄₅–⁵⁄₈in) across, are usually violet-blue, rarely white, and are borne in short racemes on a long, leafless scape; the 6 tepals are all similar and petal-like. The fruit consists of a small 3-parted capsule.

• **DISTRIBUTION** E. Ireland, Britain (mainly W. and N.E.), the Faeroes, France, and Norway; mostly close to the coast.

• **HABITAT** Rocky and grassy places, especially short grass along cliff-tops, usually on non-calcareous soils; up to an altitude of 2,000m (6,550ft).

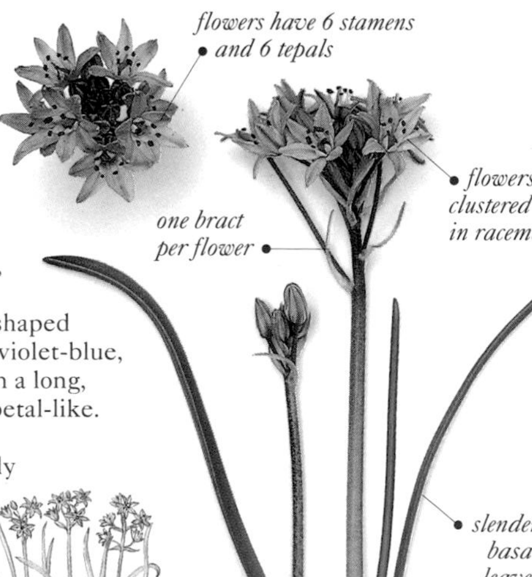

Habit Perennial	Height 5–15cm (2–6in)	Flowering time Apr–June

Family LILIACEAE	Species *Muscari neglectum*	Author Guss. ex Ten.

GRAPE HYACINTH

Also known under the names *Muscari atlanticum* and *M. racemosum*, this is a very variable, hairless, bulbous, and often clump-forming plant. The 3 to 6 bright green leaves are all basal, linear, and channelled, often with a reddish base. The small blackish blue to deep violet-blue flowers, 3.5–7mm (1/7–2/7in) long, are bell-shaped and borne in dense scapose racemes; the 6 tepals are fused together and are revealed only by 6 tiny white teeth at the mouth of the flower. The fruit is a 3-parted, many-seeded capsule.

• **DISTRIBUTION** E. England (scarce), France, and Germany; occasionally naturalized elsewhere in the region.

• **HABITAT** Grassy places, meadows, hedgebanks, abandoned cultivation, and rocky mountain slopes.

• **RELATED SPECIES** *Muscari armeniacum*, has more oblong bright blue flowers. It is naturalized locally in the region; native of E. Europe and W. Asia.

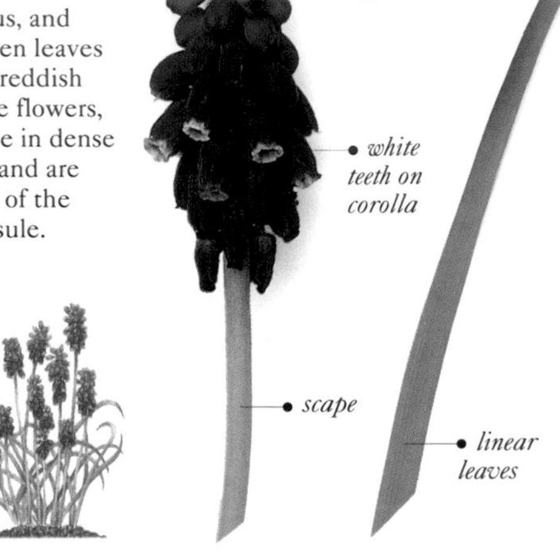

Habit Perennial	Height 15–30cm (6–12in)	Flowering time Mar–May

Family LILIACEAE	Species *Muscari comosum*	Author (L.) Miller

TASSEL HYACINTH

This is a very variable, hairless, bulbous plant with basal leaves and scapose inflorescences. There are usually between 3 and 5 rather floppy, linear leaves which are channelled along the centre and tapered to the tip. The flowers are borne in a dense raceme that slowly elongates as successive flowers open; the lower fertile flowers are bell-shaped, 5–9mm (1/5–3/8in) long, and pale brown with cream or yellowish teeth, while the uppermost flowers are sterile and form a conspicuous bright bluish violet, sometimes white, tassel at the top of the raceme. The fruit is a small 3-parted capsule.

• **DISTRIBUTION** France and Germany; naturalized in Britain and parts of N. Europe.

• **HABITAT** Grassy, cultivated, and waste ground, roadsides, and occasionally sand dunes; widely cultivated in gardens.

• **REMARK** The bulbs are eaten in some Mediterranean countries.

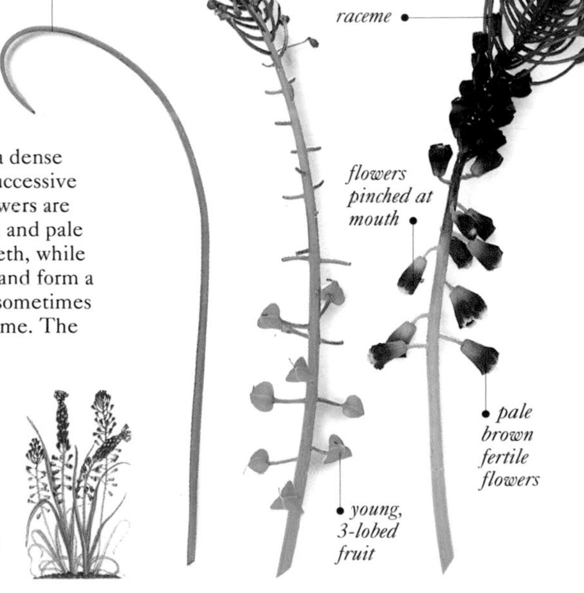

Habit Perennial	Height 30–60cm (12–24in)	Flowering time May–June

Family LILIACEAE	Species *Allium triquetrum*	Author L.

THREE-CORNERED GARLIC

Smelling powerfully of garlic when crushed, this hairless, often clump-forming, bulbous plant has basal leaves and scapose inflorescences; the scapes are 3-cornered. The 2 to 5 linear, rather floppy, fleshy, greyish green leaves are tapered to the apex. 2 spathes, equalling the umbel in length, surround the flowers in bud. The white, bell-shaped flowers, each 10–18mm (⅖–⅗in) long, droop in a one-sided umbel; the 6 tepals are equal and separate, with a greenish midvein; 6 stamens are hidden inside the flower. The small fruit capsule is 3-parted and contains numerous small seeds.

• **DISTRIBUTION** Naturalized in Ireland, France, and S. Britain, including Wales; very common in Cornwall (England). A native plant of S.W. Europe.

• **HABITAT** Grassy places, hedgerows, woodland margins, coppices, stream-banks; mainly on rather moist heavy soils.

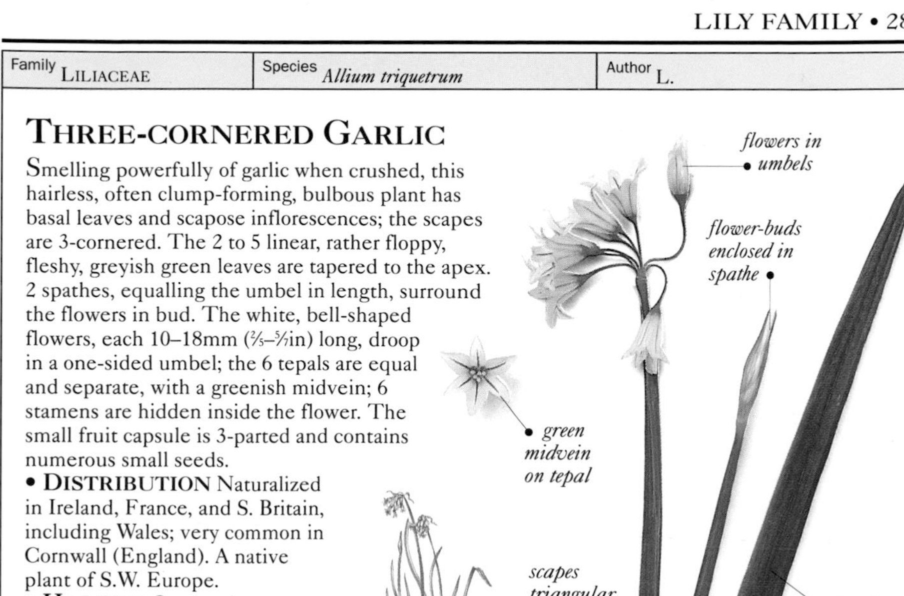

Habit Perennial	Height 25–45cm (10–18in)	Flowering time Apr–June

Family LILIACEAE	Species *Allium ursinum*	Author L.

RAMSONS

Also known as Wild Garlic, this strong-smelling, bulbous plant has basal leaves and scapose inflorescences. The 2 or 3 leaves are bright green, broadly to narrowly elliptical, and flat, with a strong garlic smell when crushed. The white, star-shaped flowers are 12–20mm (½–⅘in) across, and are borne in loose umbels at the end of a ridged or triangular scape; the 6 petal-like tepals are similar and spread widely apart. The 2 spathe valves are more or less equal in length, but are shorter than the umbel. The fruit consists of a small 3-parted capsule containing numerous black seeds.

• **DISTRIBUTION** Throughout the region, as far north as S. Scandinavia.

• **HABITAT** Woodland, especially deciduous woods, scrub, coppices, hedgerows, partially shaded meadows and banks, and other damp habitats; mainly growing on base-rich soils; often forming extensive colonies.

Habit Perennial	Height 25–45cm (10–18in)	Flowering time Apr–June

Family LILIACEAE	Species *Allium ampeloprasum*	Author L.

WILD LEEK

This is a very variable, often rather stout, semi-bulbous, hairless plant which smells of onion when crushed. The 4 to 10 strictly alternate, fleshy leaves are grey-green, linear, channelled above and keeled beneath, and up to 40mm (1⅗in) wide. The spathe is solitary and papery and quickly falls as the flowers begin to open. The flowers are pale purple, pinkish, or whitish, bell-shaped, 4.5–5mm (⅙–⅕in) long, and borne in a dense, globose umbel up to 90mm (3⅗in) in diameter; tepals are all similar and petal-like. The fruit is a small 3-parted capsule.

• **DISTRIBUTION** France, W. Britain, and Ireland, but widely naturalized (from cultivated plants) and locally casual in parts of the region.

• **HABITAT** Rocky and grassy places, waste ground, rubbish tips; often close to the sea.

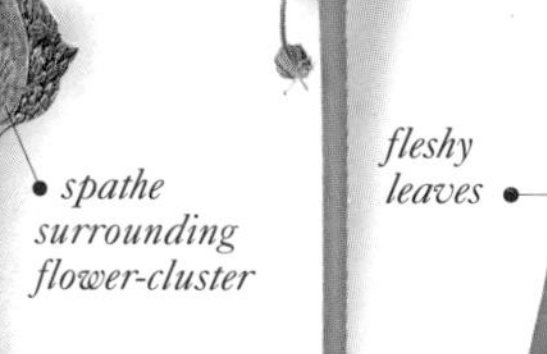

Habit Biennial or perennial	Height 80–200cm (32–80in)	Flowering time July–Aug

Family LILIACEAE	Species *Allium sphaerocephalon*	Author L.

ROUND-HEADED LEEK

This rather variable, bulbous plant has a slender stem and smells strongly of onion when crushed. The 2 to 6 leaves are linear and thread-like, hollow but with a slight groove on the upper surface, with their bases usually sheathing the lower half of the stem. The 2 spathes surrounding the head of flowers are membranous, short-beaked, and persistent. The flowers are reddish purple to pink, occasionally greenish or whitish, bell-shaped, 3.5–5.5mm (⅐–¼in) long, and borne in a dense, globose umbel, with the uppermost flowers opening first; each flower has 6 similar, petal-like tepals and 6 protruding stamens. The fruit is a small 3-parted capsule.

• **DISTRIBUTION** Belgium and Germany southwards, also in Britain (rare and confined to Gloucestershire); naturalized from cultivation elsewhere.

• **HABITAT** Open rocky and grassy places; generally in limestone regions.

Habit Perennial	Height 50–80cm (20–32in)	Flowering time June–Aug

Family LILIACEAE	Species *Convallaria majalis*	Author L.

LILY OF THE VALLEY

This is a low, hairless plant, forming patches by means of thin underground stolons. The short, erect stems are unbranched, usually bear just 2 leaves, and have green or violet sheaths at the base. The rather dull, deep green leaves are elliptical to oval, with an untoothed margin and numerous parallel veins. The small, drooping, bell-shaped flowers, 5–9mm (⅕–⅜in) long, are white but may sometimes be flushed with pink; they are borne in stiff one-sided racemes and are very fragrant. The fruit is a fleshy berry which turns bright red when ripe and is poisonous.

• **DISTRIBUTION** Growing throughout much of the region, except for Ireland, N. Scotland, and the far north.

• **HABITAT** Woodland, limestone pavement, hedgerows, mountain meadows; to 2,300m (7,550ft) altitude. Widely grown in gardens and often naturalizing close to cultivation.

Habit Perennial	Height 15–25cm (6–10in)	Flowering time May–June

Family LILIACEAE	Species *Polygonatum multiflorum*	Author (L.) All.

SOLOMON'S-SEAL

This rather robust, hairless plant forms patches by means of thick and fleshy rhizomes. The stems are rounded, erect, and arched at the apex. The leaves are lanceolate to elliptical, with an untoothed margin and parallel veins. The unscented, nodding flowers, 9–20mm (⅜–⅘in) long, are borne at the leaf-axils in clusters of 2 to 6, although the uppermost are often solitary. The small fleshy berries are bluish black when ripe.

• **DISTRIBUTION** Throughout the region, except for Ireland, Scotland (occasionally naturalized), and the far north.

• **HABITAT** Woodland, copses, hedgerows; generally on calcareous soils.

• **RELATED SPECIES** *Polygonatum odoratum*, Angular Solomon's-seal, has larger, solitary or paired, scented flowers, and 4-sided stems. It inhabits calcareous woods as far north as C. Scandinavia.

Habit Perennial	Height 40–80cm (16–32in)	Flowering time May–June

Family LILIACEAE	Species *Paris quadrifolia*	Author L.

HERB PARIS

A low growing, often patch-forming, hairless plant, Herb Paris spreads by means of underground rhizomes and bears no basal leaves. The deep green leaves, usually 4 but occasionally 5 or 6, are borne in a single whorl located halfway up the stem, and are broadly oval to elliptical and untoothed, with 3 to 5 principal veins. The solitary star-shaped flower is yellowish green, with a blackish ovary 35–55mm (1⅖–2⅕in) across, and usually has 4 lanceolate, pointed sepals, 4 thread-like petals, and 8 stamens. The fruit capsule is black and splits irregularly to reveal the shiny bright red seeds. The plant is poisonous.

• **DISTRIBUTION** Throughout the region, except for Ireland and the far north; usually very local.

• **HABITAT** Moist humus-rich woodland and shady habitats over calcareous soils; often associated with ancient woodland.

8 stamens

flowers with 4 petals and 4 sepals

blackish ovary

DETAIL

usually 4 stem-leaves in a whorl

Habit Perennial	Height 20–40cm (8–16in)	Flowering time May–June

Family LILIACEAE	Species *Ruscus aculeatus*	Author L.

BUTCHER'S BROOM

This hairless, rather rigid and tough, patch-forming plant spreads by short underground rhizomes. The stems are erect and branched in the upper part. The leaves (actually short flattened branches called cladodes) are deep green to brown, oval to elliptical, and up to 30mm (1⅕in) long. The flowers, 4–5mm (⅙–⅕in) across, are dull green with purple spots, solitary or paired, each with 6 tepals; male and female flowers are distinct and generally borne on separate plants. The fruit is 10–15mm (⅖–⅗in) in diameter.

• **DISTRIBUTION** C. and S. Britain and France; naturalized elsewhere in the region.

• **HABITAT** Woodland, scrub, hedgerows, sea cliffs, and rocky places; generally on dry calcareous soils.

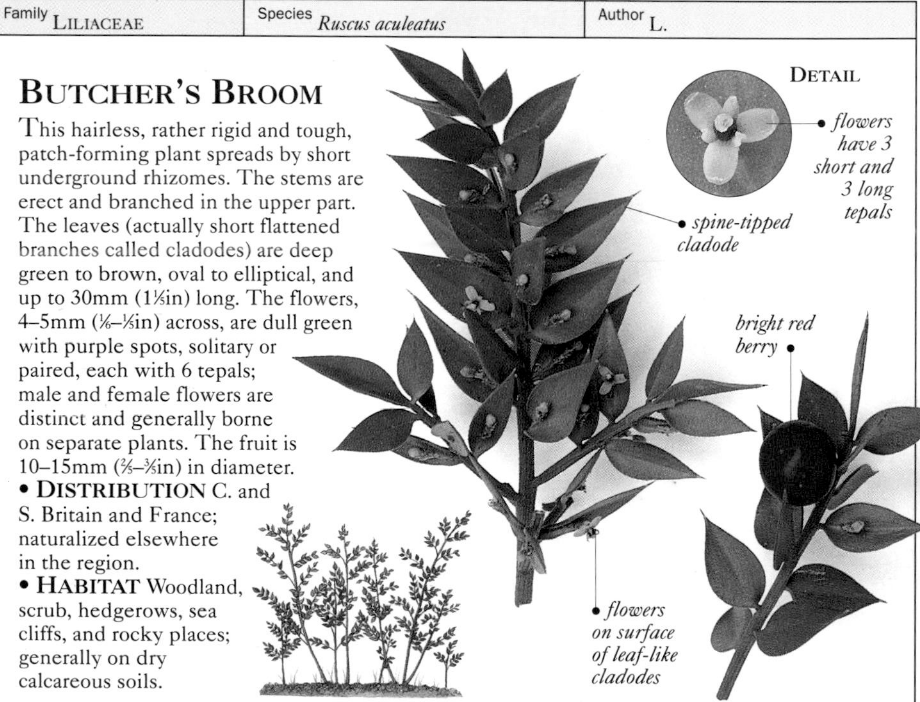

Habit Perennial	Height 40–75cm (16–30in)	Flowering time Jan–Apr

DAFFODIL FAMILY

Family AMARYLLIDACEAE	Species *Leucojum aestivum*	Author L.

SUMMER SNOWFLAKE

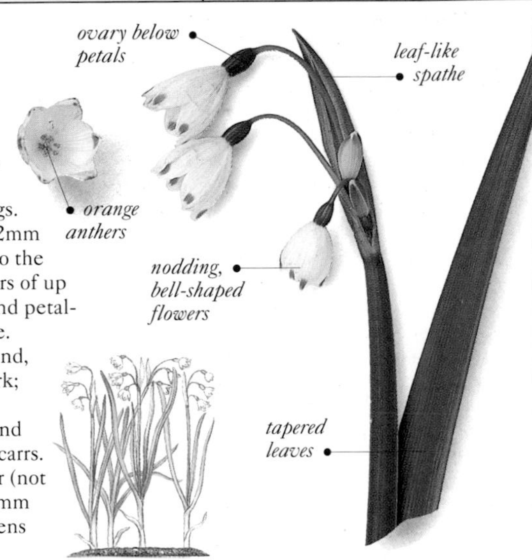

This is a hairless, bulbous plant, with basal leaves, and flowers borne on scapes. The daffodil-like leaves are bright green, rather fleshy, strap-shaped, and about the same length as the scapes or shorter; the scapes have 2 narrow wings. The nodding, bell-shaped flowers, 13–22mm (½–⅞in) long, are white with green tips to the tepals, and are borne in one-sided clusters of up to 6 flowers; the 6 tepals are all similar and petal-like. The fruit is a small 3-parted capsule.

• **DISTRIBUTION** S. England, S. Ireland, mainland Europe as far north as Denmark; naturalized elsewhere from gardens.

• **HABITAT** Moist places along rivers and streams, marshes, wet meadows, willow carrs.

• **REMARK** Subsp. *pulchellum* has fewer (not more than 4) and smaller flowers, 10–15mm (⅖–⅗in) long. It is naturalized from gardens in Britain and elsewhere in the region.

Habit Perennial	Height 25–50cm (10–20in)	Flowering time Apr–June

Family AMARYLLIDACEAE	Species *Leucojum vernum*	Author L.

SPRING SNOWFLAKE

This small, hairless, and bulbous plant is solitary or clump-forming. The 2 or 3 bright green, rather fleshy, basal leaves, up to 15mm (⅗in) wide, are strap-shaped, and are only partly developed at flowering time. The scape has 2 narrow wings, and one or 2 papery spathes at the top which enclose the flowers in bud. The nodding, white, bell-shaped flowers, 15–25mm (⅗–1in) long, have green or yellowish tips to the tepals, and are usually solitary, rarely paired; the 6 tepals are all similar to each other and petal-like. The fruit consists of a small 3-parted capsule.

• **DISTRIBUTION** Native in Belgium and Holland southwards; rarely naturalized in S. England, Ireland, Holland, and Denmark.

• **HABITAT** Woodland and copses, meadows, and occasionally hedgerows; widely cultivated in gardens.

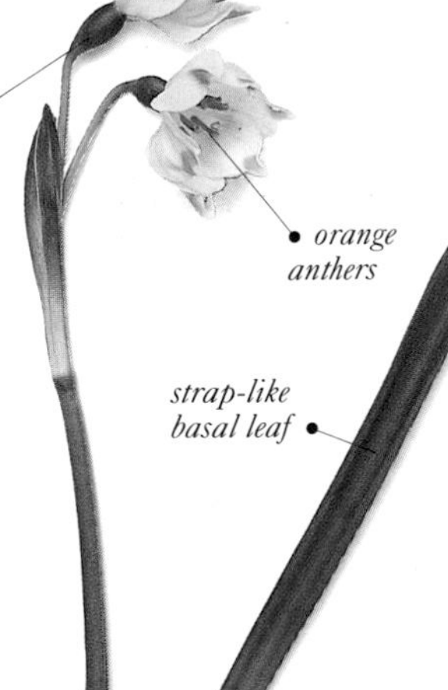

Habit Perennial	Height 15–35cm (6–14in)	Flowering time Feb–Mar

Family AMARYLLIDACEAE	Species *Galanthus nivalis*	Author L.

SNOWDROP

This small, hairless, and bulbous plant, is often clump-forming. The grey-green, linear leaves are basal, and the plant generally has only 2; these are held flat against one another in bud and are only partly developed at flowering time. The solitary nodding flower is borne on a slender scape with the ovary located below all the other flower parts; the 3 oval, white sepals eventually spread widely apart, while the petals, half the length of the sepals, scarcely spread and have a green mark close to the notched apex. The fruit consists of a small 3-parted capsule.

• **DISTRIBUTION** Widely naturalized as far north as S. Sweden; probably not native anywhere in the region.

• **HABITAT** Woodland, coppices, scrub, hedgerows, churchyards, meadows, and streambanks.

• **REMARK** The double-flowered cultivar, *Galanthus nivalis* 'Flore Pleno', is occasionally naturalized.

spreading sepals

green markings on petals

double flower

nodding flower

linear leaf

usually only 2 leaves

Habit Perennial	Height 10–20cm (4–8in)	Flowering time Jan–Mar

Family AMARYLLIDACEAE	Species *Narcissus poeticus*	Author L.

PHEASANT'S-EYE DAFFODIL

This hairless, bulbous, often clump-forming plant bears basal leaves and solitary, scapose flowers. The 2 to 5 leaves are slightly fleshy, somewhat grooved, and 6–10mm (¼–⅖in) wide. The fragrant flowers, 40–50mm (1⅗–2in) across, have 6 tepals and a small central cup or corona which is yellow with a wavy brown or orange rim. The many-seeded fruit capsule is 3-parted.

• **DISTRIBUTION** C. and E. France, but widely naturalized in Britain, Belgium, and Germany.

• **HABITAT** Damp lowland and mountain meadows, and other grassy places.

• **REMARK** The hybrid between this species and *Narcissus pseudonarcissus* (see opposite), called *Narcissus* x *incomparabilis*, produces solitary flowers with yellow or whitish tepals and a deep yellow or orange cup. It is naturalized or spontaneous in similar regions.

spreading, white, elliptical tepals

wavy orange rim on corona

papery spathe below flower

linear, grey-green leaves

long scape

Habit Perennial	Height 40–70cm (16–28in)	Flowering time Apr–June

Family AMARYLLIDACEAE	Species *Narcissus pseudonarcissus*	Author L.

DAFFODIL

This very variable, hairless, often clump-forming plant bears basal leaves and solitary, scapose flowers. The leaves, 6–12mm (¼–½in) wide, are grey-green, rather fleshy, and generally 2 to 5 in number. The large flowers have pale yellow tepals and a deep yellow corona; the tepals are elliptical and often somewhat twisted. The papery spathe, immediately below the flower, is pale brown. The fruit capsule is 3-parted and many-seeded.

• **DISTRIBUTION** Britain, France, Holland, and Germany; also widely naturalized in the region and beyond.

• **HABITAT** Meadows, woodland, coppices, river-banks, roadsides, hedgerows, and abandoned cultivation.

• **REMARK** Several cultivated forms and hybrids, many more vigorous and in a wider range of colours, are sometimes naturalized.

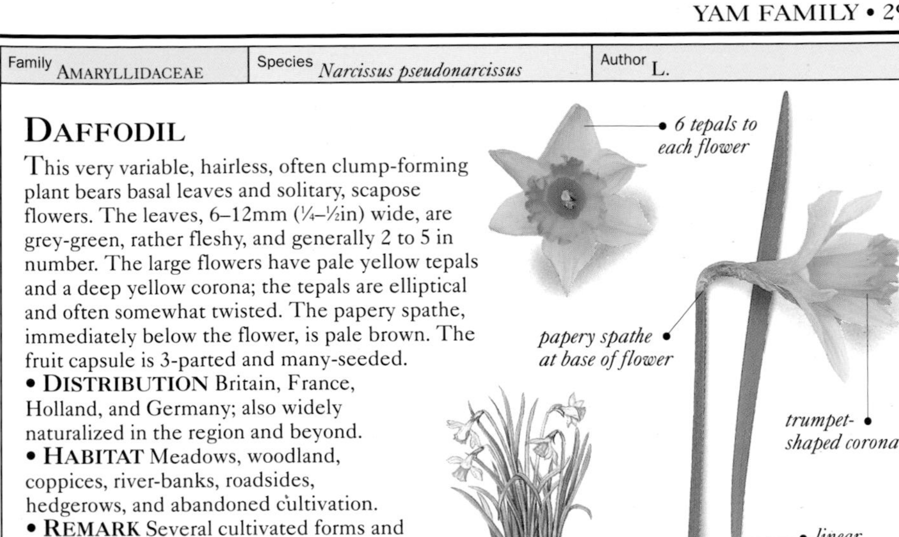

Habit Perennial	Height 30–50cm (12–20in)	Flowering time Mar–May

YAM FAMILY

Family DIOSCOREACEAE	Species *Tamus communis*	Author L.

BLACK BRYONY

This vigorous, climbing, hairless plant has long, twining stems and produces annual shoots from a tuberous rootstock. The shiny, bright green, alternate leaves are heart-shaped, long-stalked, and untoothed. The greenish yellow flowers are only 3–6mm (⅛–¼in) across; male flowers are in long slender racemes; the female are on separate plants in small lateral clusters. The fruit is a cluster of fleshy red berries which persist on the stems into late autumn and early winter. The plant is poisonous.

• **DISTRIBUTION** C. and S. Britain, Belgium, France, and Germany; naturalized in N. Britain and Ireland.

• **HABITAT** Woodland, scrub, coppices, hedgerows, and fences; at low altitudes.

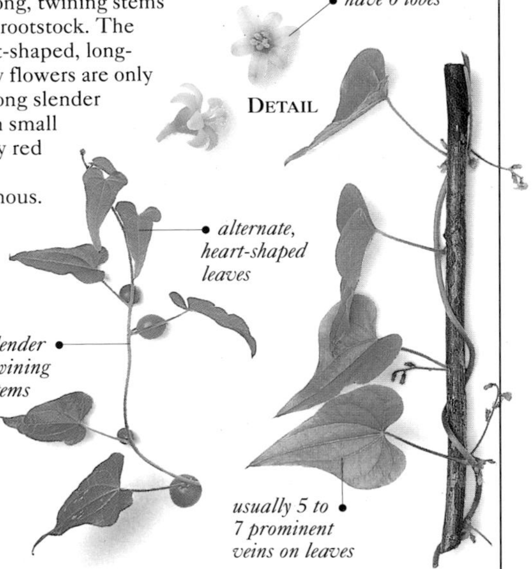

flowers usually have 6 lobes

DETAIL

alternate, heart-shaped leaves

slender twining stems

shiny, bright red, ripe berries

DETAIL

usually 5 to 7 prominent veins on leaves

Habit Perennial	Height Up to 4m (13ft)	Flowering time May–Aug

IRIS FAMILY

Family IRIDACEAE	Species *Iris germanica*	Author L.

BEARDED IRIS

This robust, more or less hairless plant, is patch-foming and spreads by means of rhizomes at ground level. The stems are thick and are generally branched in the upper part. The alternate, sword-shaped leaves, 20–35mm (⅘–1⅖in) wide and borne in flattened fans, are tapered to the tip and grey-green. The fragrant flowers, 80–110mm (3⅕–4⅖in) across, are bluish violet to purple, occasionally white tinged with blue; the outer 3 tepals (falls) droop and have a wide blade with a yellow "beard" in the centre; the inner 3 tepals (standards) are not bearded. The fruit is a large, rather fleshy, 3-parted capsule.

• **DISTRIBUTION** Native origin uncertain, but naturalized from gardens throughout much of the region, except for the north.

• **HABITAT** Roadsides, embankments, walls, waste places, and rubbish tips.

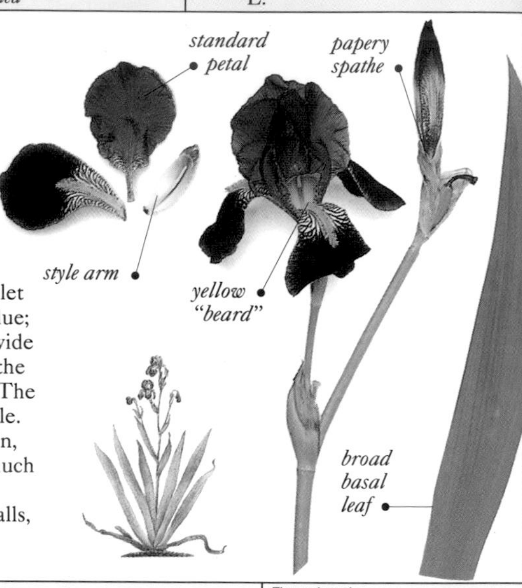

Habit Perennial	Height 40–90cm (16–36in)	Flowering time May–July

Family IRIDACEAE	Species *Iris foetidissima*	Author L.

STINKING IRIS

This tough, hairless plant forms large tufts in time and spreads by means of short underground rhizomes. The stem is erect to arching. The deep green leaves, up to 25mm (1in) across, are mostly basal and have an unpleasant smell when crushed. The dull violet flowers, 55–80mm (2⅕–3⅕in) across, are flushed with pale yellow; outer tepals (falls) are lightly veined, with a narrow-oblong blade; inner tepals (standards) are smaller and narrower than the falls. The fleshy, 3-parted fruit capsules split to reveal rows of striking bright red seeds.

• **DISTRIBUTION** S. England, S. Wales, and France; naturalized in Ireland and Scotland.

• **HABITAT** Woodland, hedgerows, embankments, and clifftops; generally on calcareous soils and most frequent near the coast.

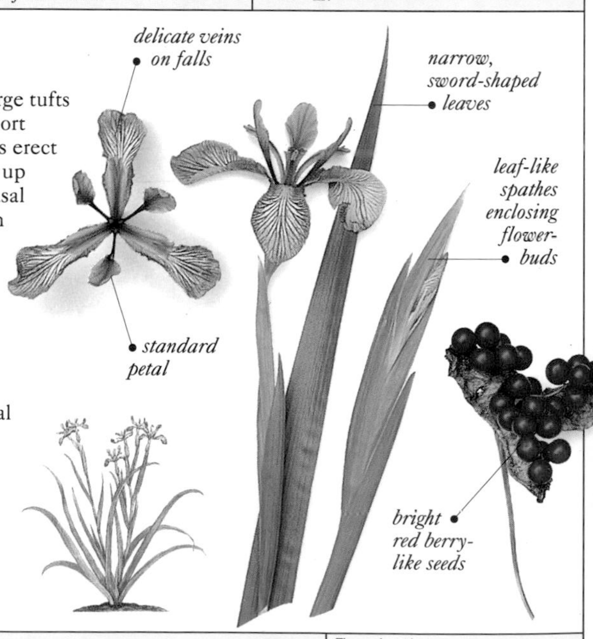

Habit Perennial	Height 40–70cm (16–28in)	Flowering time May–July

Family IRIDACEAE	Species *Iris pseudacorus*	Author L.

YELLOW FLAG

This is a stout, clump-forming, hairless plant, spreading by means of thick rhizomes. The sword-shaped, bright grey-green leaves form narrow fans, each 10–30mm (⅖–1⅕in) wide and with a prominent raised midrib. The showy yellow flowers are 7–10cm (2⅘–4in) across and are borne on thick, somewhat leafy stems, which generally have several short branches; the fall petals have a broad oval blade marked with green dots and veins, while the erect standard petals are unmarked, smaller, and narrower. The large, oblong, drooping fruit capsules are 3-parted and contain numerous seeds which are ranked closely together.

• **DISTRIBUTION** Throughout the region, except for Iceland and Spitsbergen.

• **HABITAT** Wet places such as marshes, swamps, bogs, the margins of rivers, lakes, and ponds, ditches, fens, coastal freshwater pools, and seepage areas.

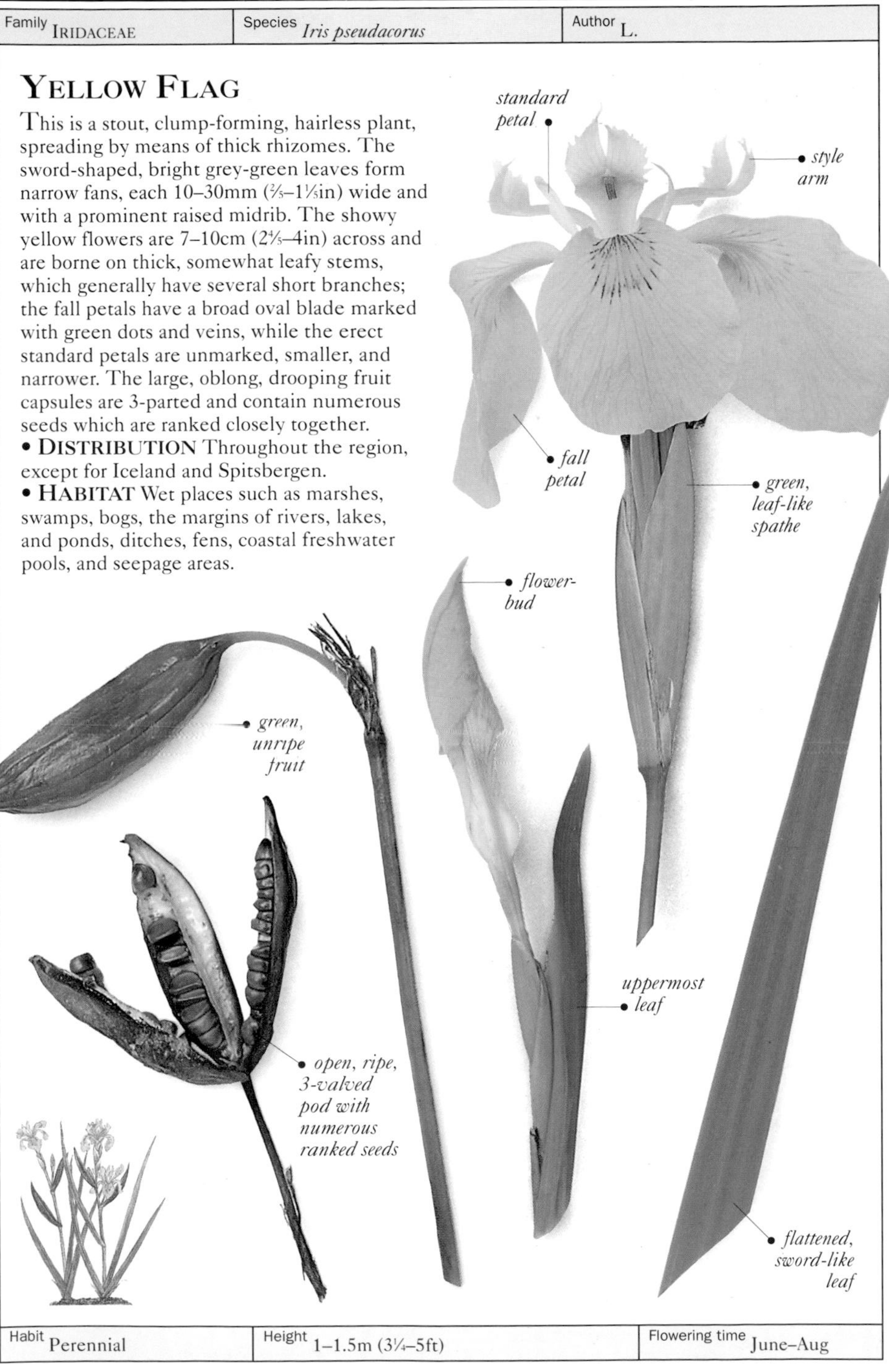

Habit Perennial	Height 1–1.5m (3¼–5ft)	Flowering time June–Aug

Family IRIDACEAE	Species *Crocosmia* x *crocosmiflora*	Author (Lemoine) N.E.Br.

MONTBRETIA

A hybrid between *Crocosmia pottsii* and *C. aurea* (both South African species), this vigorous, clump-forming, corm-rooted, and hairless plant spreads by means of short stolons. The stems are stiff and erect, and are usually branched in the upper part. The grass-like, rather pale green leaves are alternate and 5–20mm (1/5–4/5in) wide. The orange flowers, 25–55mm (1–2⅕in) long, are borne in horizontal to spreading, 2-sided spikes; the corolla is tubed below but has 6 lobes in the upper half; the stamens, only 3, protrude with the style.

• **DISTRIBUTION** Widely naturalized from gardens in Britain, Ireland, France.

• **HABITAT** Woodland, hedgerows, waste ground, abandoned cultivation, and river and lake margins.

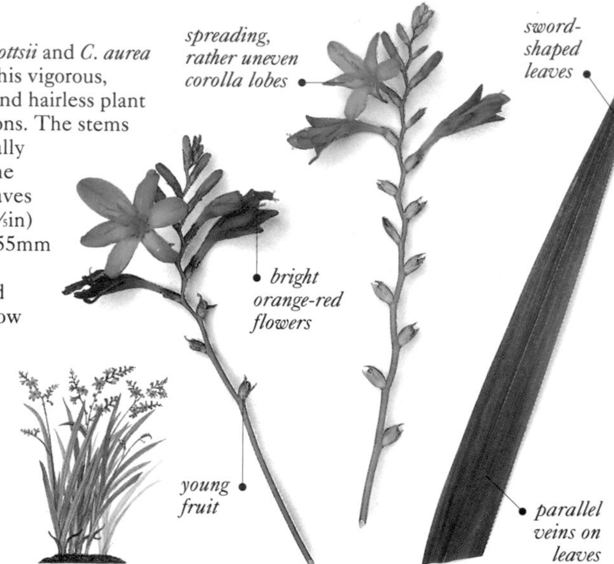

Habit Perennial	Height 50–60cm (20–24in)	Flowering time July–Sept

BUR-REED FAMILY

Family SPARGANIACEAE	Species *Sparganium erectum*	Author L.

BRANCHED BUR-REED

This is a very variable, often rather robust, hairless plant, spreading by means of creeping rhizomes. The stiff, erect stems are branched in the upper part. The strap-shaped leaves are triangular in cross-section and are usually erect but may occasionally be floating and ribbon-like. The inflorescence consists of rounded clusters of flowers, the lowermost clusters being female, the others male, and most being borne on lateral branches; the perianth consists of 3 or 4 scale-like segments in the female flowers, and one to 6 in the male. The dry, one-seeded fruit is borne in bur-like clusters.

• **DISTRIBUTION** Throughout, except for the far north.

• **HABITAT** Freshwater places such as lake, pond, river, and canal margins, marshes, and ditches.

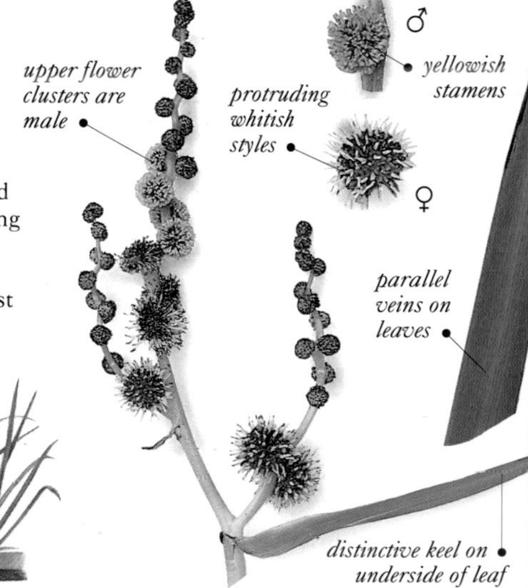

Habit Perennial	Height 80–150cm (32–60in)	Flowering time July–Aug

ARUM FAMILY

Family ARACEAE	Species *Arum maculatum*	Author L.

LORDS AND LADIES

Also commonly called Cuckoo Pint, this hairless, rather fleshy plant forms patches by means of underground dividing tubers. The leaves have an untoothed but frequently slightly undulating margin and are bright shiny green above, often with small black blotches. The small flowers are borne in dense, fleshy spikes enclosed within the spathe, with the male above the female; the spathe is yellowish or greenish, and streaked, spotted, and flushed with purple. The ripe fruit is bright orange-red.

• **DISTRIBUTION** Britain to Holland and Germany southwards.

• **HABITAT** Woodland, scrub, hedgerows; sometimes on cultivated land.

spathe envelops flower-spike

unopened spathe

shiny succulent berries

DETAIL

long leaf-stalk

arrow-shaped leaves

Habit Perennial	Height 15–35cm (6–14in)	Flowering time Apr–May

REED MACE FAMILY

Family TYPHACEAE	Species *Typha latifolia*	Author L.

REED MACE

Also called Bulrush, this robust, tufted plant has creeping rhizomes. The stems are stiff and erect. The greyish green leaves are up to 20mm (⅘in) wide. Minute flowers are borne in very dense cylindrical spikes, with the yellow male flowers immediately above the reddish brown female. The spikes disperse in a mass of fluffy wind-borne seed.

• **DISTRIBUTION** Throughout much of the region, except for the far north.

• **HABITAT** Wet places such as river, stream, and canal margins, ditches, marshes, wet meadows, and reed swamps.

• **RELATED SPECIES** *Typha angustifolia*, Lesser Reed Mace, has leaves up to 6mm (¼in) wide. Male and female flowers are separated by a length of stem.

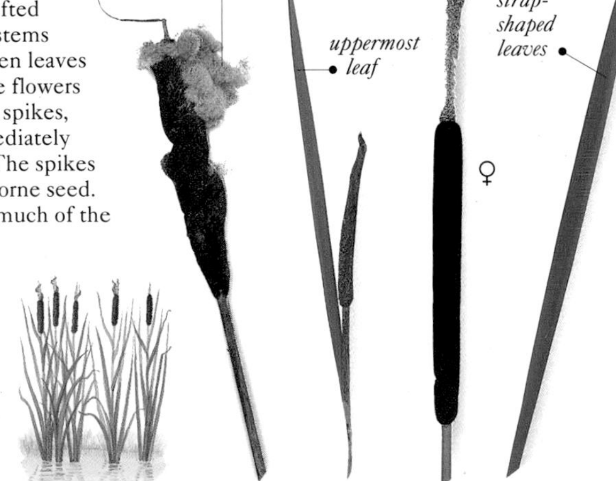

Habit Perennial	Height 1.5–3m (5–10ft)	Flowering time July–Aug

ORCHID FAMILY

Family ORCHIDACEAE	Species *Epipactis atrorubens*	Author (Hoffm.) Besser

DARK RED HELLEBORINE

The erect, leafy stem of this rhizomatous plant is solitary and unbranched, often violet- or purple-tinged, and hairless or downy. The 5 to 10 alternate leaves are oval to lanceolate with a pointed apex, and are borne in 2 opposing rows. The fragrant half-nodding flowers are borne in long spikes; the sepals and petals are similar, deep purple-red, and spreading. The lip, 5.5–6.5mm (¼–⅟₄in) long, is 2-parted: the lower part green and cup-shaped; the upper part heart-shaped, the same colour as the sepals, and with a pointed tip which curves under. The hairy fruit capsule is 3-parted.

• **DISTRIBUTION** Throughout the region, except for the far north, but often very local; absent from S. Britain.

• **HABITAT** Open woodland, downland, limestone cliff-edges and screes, and sand dunes; on calcareous soils.

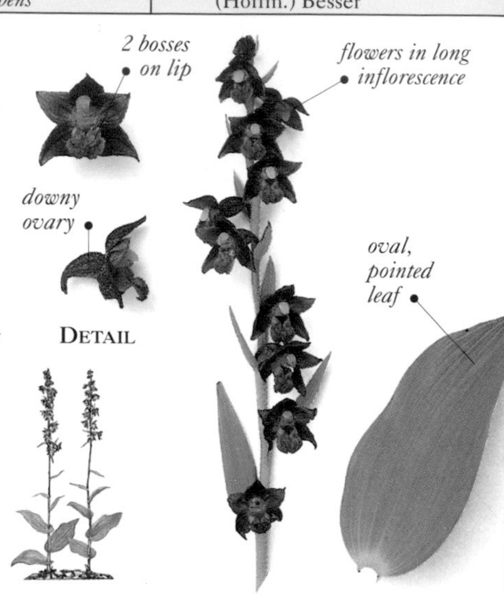

Habit Perennial	Height 20–35cm (8–14in)	Flowering time June–July

Family ORCHIDACEAE	Species *Epipactis palustris*	Author (L.) Crantz

MARSH HELLEBORINE

This is a patch-forming, rhizomatous plant with erect stems which are leafy and purplish in the lower part and hairy in the upper. The alternate leaves are oval to lanceolate, about 3 to 8 in number, and decrease in size up the stem. Borne in a long spike, the flowers have spreading sepals and petals; the sepals are greenish with faint purple or brownish stripes, while the petals are white with a pink base; the lip has a rather cupped lower half which is white with a yellow blotch and purple lines, while the upper half is white with a frilly margin. The fruit is a hairy, 3-parted, pendent capsule.

• **DISTRIBUTION** Throughout the region, except for the far north.

• **HABITAT** Wet or damp places such as marshes, flushes, fens, and dune slacks; on calcareous or base-rich soils.

• **REMARK** This plant has become scarcer, especially inland, due to the destruction of its habitat by drainage and water pollution.

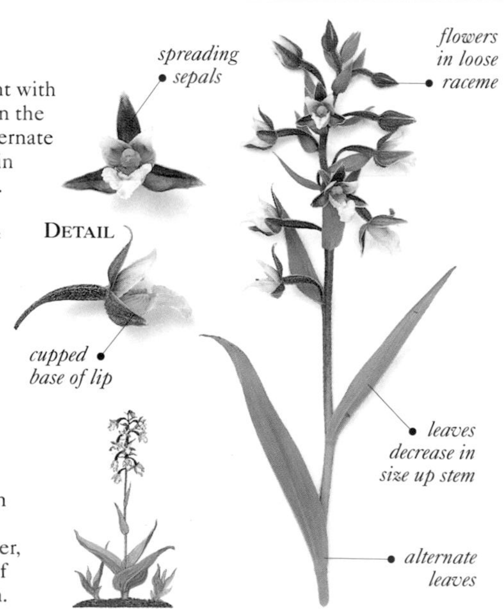

Habit Perennial	Height 30–55cm (12–22in)	Flowering time July–Aug

Family ORCHIDACEAE	Species *Cephalanthera longifolia*	Author (L.) Fritsch

NARROW-LEAVED HELLEBORINE

This hairless plant has short rhizomes and bears a solitary or several erect stems; the stems have 2 to 4 basal sheaths which are whitish with a green tip. The leaves are alternate along the stem, dark green, lanceolate to linear, and tapered. The bracts are mostly shorter than the ovaries. The white flowers are borne in spikes of 3 to 20 flowers, with the sepals and petals similar and pointed; the lip, 10–16mm (⅖–⅝in) long, is forward projecting and constricted in the middle, with orange or yellow ridges.

• **DISTRIBUTION** Throughout, except for the far north; rather local and rare.

• **HABITAT** Woodland, often of beech, and shady sites; generally on chalky soils.

• **RELATED SPECIES** *Cephalanthera damasonium*, White Helleborine, has broader, oval leaves, longer bracts, and cream flowers. It grows in similar habitats throughout, as far north as S. Sweden.

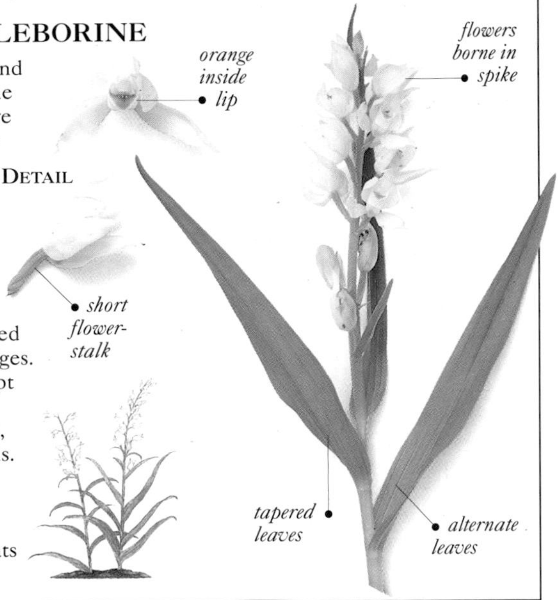

orange inside lip

DETAIL

short flower-stalk

flowers borne in spike

tapered leaves

alternate leaves

Habit Perennial	Height 40–60cm (16–24in)	Flowering time May–June

Family ORCHIDACEAE	Species *Cephalanthera rubra*	Author (L.) Rich.

RED HELLEBORINE

This is a rhizomatous plant. The stem, usually solitary, is erect, often tinged with purple, hairy in the upper part, with several brownish sheaths close to the base. The alternate leaves are deep green and elliptic-oblong to lanceolate. The bracts are leaf-like and longer than the ovaries, decreasing in size up the inflorescence. The flowers are bright pink to pinkish purple and are borne in long, loose spikes of up to 12, or occasionally more, flowers; the sepals and petals are similar to each other, finely pointed, and often spread widely; the lip, 17–22mm (⅔–⅞in) long, is constricted in the middle, the upper half having 7 to 9 narrow, yellow ridges. The ovary is hairy.

• **DISTRIBUTION** Throughout the region as far north as S. Sweden; in Britain, very rare and confined to S. England.

• **HABITAT** Open woodland, often of beech, copses, and other semi-shaded habitats, but only flowering in sunny glades.

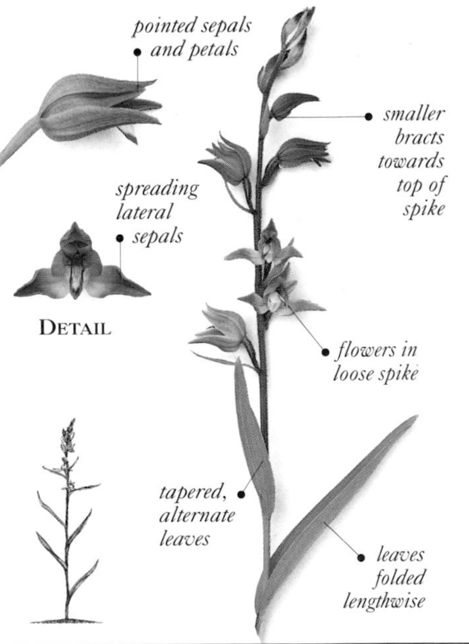

Habit Perennial	Height 40–60cm (16–24in)	Flowering time June–July

Family ORCHIDACEAE	Species *Listera ovata*	Author (L.) R. Br.

COMMON TWAYBLADE

This rhizomatous plant has one pair of leaves towards the base. The solitary stem is erect, hairy in the upper part, with brownish sheaths near the base. The leaves are oval with prominent ribs. The numerous small greenish yellow flowers are borne in a long, loose spike; the sepals and petals are elliptical, and the lip, 7–15mm (2/7–3/5in) long, is pendent, strap-like, notched at the tip, and has no basal spur.

• **DISTRIBUTION** Throughout, except the far north.

• **HABITAT** Woodland, scrub, hedgerows, and fields; occasionally on marshy ground, moorland, or dune slacks.

• **RELATED SPECIES** *Listera cordata*, Lesser Twayblade, has heart-shaped leaves, and reddish green flowers in low spikes. It inhabits coniferous woodland and damp heather moors in the uplands of the region.

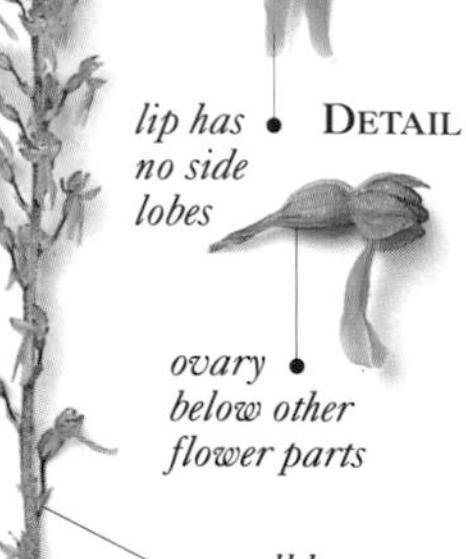

Habit Perennial	Height 20–70cm (8–28in)	Flowering time May–July

Family ORCHIDACEAE	Species *Platanthera bifolia*	Author (L.) Rich.

LESSER BUTTERFLY ORCHID

This is a tuberous-rooted, hairless plant with a solitary erect stem. The 2 basal leaves are subopposite, elliptical to oblong, and bright green in colour; the stem-leaves are much smaller and bract-like. The bracts are narrow-lanceolate and somewhat longer than the ovaries. The fragrant flowers are white with a green flush and are borne in cylindrical spikes; the lip is linear, 6–12mm (1/4–1/2in) long, and extends backwards into a very long, narrow spur; the pollinia are parallel to each other.

• **DISTRIBUTION** Throughout the region, except for the far north.

• **HABITAT** Woodland, scrub, grassy places, and heaths; mostly on calcareous soils.

• **RELATED SPECIES** *Platanthera chlorantha*, Greater Butterfly Orchid, is larger in all its parts. The flowers have a strong, rich fragrance; the lip is 10–16mm (2/5–5/8in) long; the pollinia are diverging. Its distribution and habitats are similar to those of the above but it occurs mostly on alkaline soils.

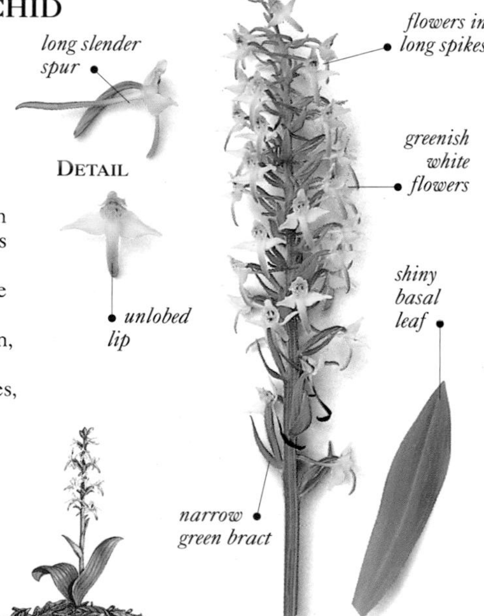

Habit Perennial	Height 30–50cm (12–20in)	Flowering time June–July

Family ORCHIDACEAE	Species *Spiranthes spiralis*	Author (L.) Chevall.

AUTUMN LADY'S-TRESSES

This tuberous-rooted plant has solitary, erect, glandular-hairy stems bearing several overlapping scale-leaves. The basal leaves, in a rosette to one side of the flowering stem, are bluish green and oval to elliptical. The fragrant white flowers, 4–6mm (⅛–¼in) long, are in a slender spike; the sepals and petals are slightly spreading, and the lip is yellowish green with a wavy margin.

• **DISTRIBUTION** Confined mainly to the west and south of the region, north as far as Denmark.

• **HABITAT** Dry grassy places, including dunes; sometimes on old lawns.

• **RELATED SPECIES** *Spiranthes aestivalis*, Summer Lady's-tresses, is taller and has linear-lanceolate leaves around the base of the flowering spikes. The flowers are slightly larger. It inhabits bogs in the west of the region; rare or extinct in Britain.

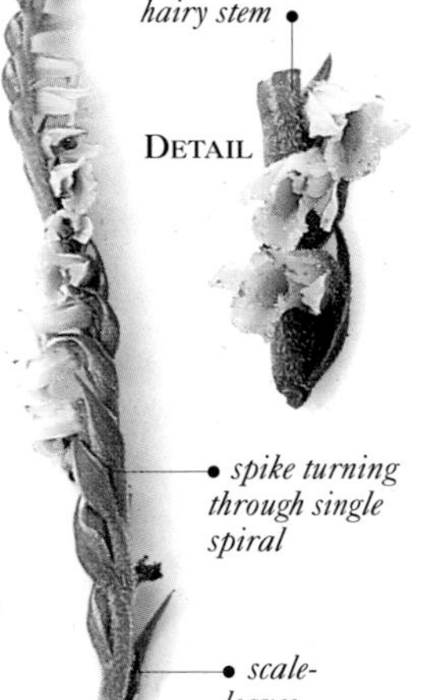

Habit Perennial	Height 8–15cm (3–6in)	Flowering time Aug–Sept

Family ORCHIDACEAE	Species *Gymnadenia conopsea*	Author (L.) R. Br.

FRAGRANT ORCHID

This is a rather variable, hairless, tuberous-rooted plant with one or several erect stems which bear many brownish basal sheaths. The 4 to 8 alternate, plain mid-green leaves are linear-lanceolate, grooved, and decreasing in size up the stem, with the uppermost leaves small and bract-like. The bracts are longer than the ovaries. The vanilla-scented flowers are borne in a cylindrical spike and range in colour from pink to purple or lilac-purple, or are occasionally white; the lateral sepals are spreading, while the upper sepal and petals are held close together to form a hood; the 3-lobed lip, 3.5–6mm (⅐–¼in) long, extends backwards into a long and slender, down-pointed spur.

• **DISTRIBUTION** Throughout the region, except for the far north.

• **HABITAT** Grassy places, scrub, and fens; often on calcareous soils.

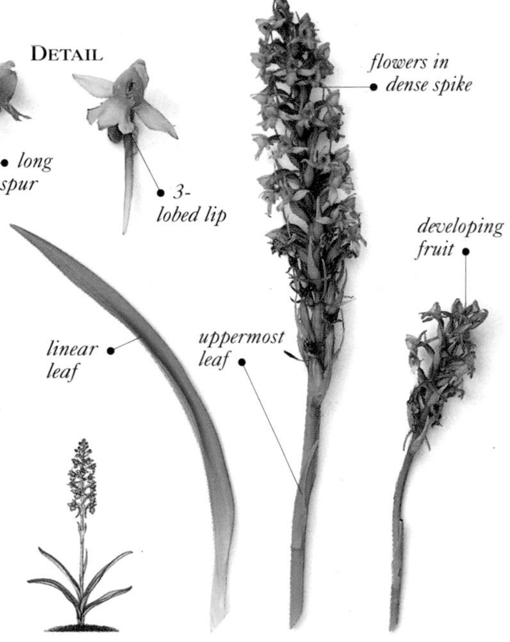

Habit Perennial	Height 20–45cm (8–18in)	Flowering time June–July

Family ORCHIDACEAE	Species *Dactylorhiza fuchsii*	Author (Druce) Soó

COMMON SPOTTED ORCHID

This is a very variable, tuberous-rooted, hairless plant. The 7 to 12 lanceolate to linear, alternate leaves are shiny, deep green, and keeled beneath; the uppermost leaves are small and bract-like. The bracts are linear and longer than the ovaries. The pink, reddish purple, or white flowers are borne in a spike; the deeply 3-lobed lip, 7–11mm (2/7–3/7in) long, is patterned with dots and looping lines.

• **DISTRIBUTION** Throughout the region, except for the far north.

• **HABITAT** Woodland, scrub, grassland, meadows, marshes, and fens; mostly on calcareous soils.

• **RELATED SPECIES** *Dactylorhiza maculata*, Heath Spotted Orchid, has circular spots on the leaves, a shallowly lobed, broad-triangular lip, and grows in damper acid habitats over a similar range.

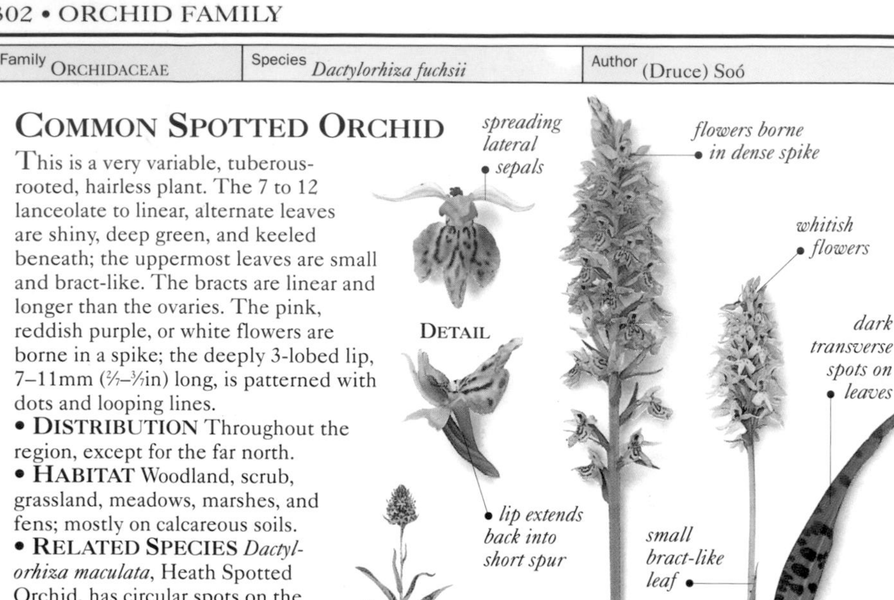

Habit Perennial	Height 25–50cm (10–20in)	Flowering time June–early Aug

Family ORCHIDACEAE	Species *Dactylorhiza praetermissa*	Author (Druce) Soó

SOUTHERN MARSH ORCHID

This hairless and tuberous-rooted plant is solitary or clump-forming. The stems are erect and unbranched. The alternate leaves, generally 3 to 7 in number, are lanceolate to narrow-elliptical, usually plain green, but occasionally with dark rings, not spots, on the upper surface; the lowermost leaves are up to 25mm (1in) wide. The flowers are pale to mid-purplish pink in colour and are borne in a dense spike above the foliage; the wing-like lateral petals spread upwards; the lip, 10–12mm (2/5–1/2in) long, is shallowly 3-lobed or more or less unlobed and is marked with dots and broken lines. The fruit is a many-seeded, 3-parted capsule.

• **DISTRIBUTION** England, Wales, and mainland Europe as far north as S. Scandinavia.

• **HABITAT** Wet meadows, marshes, fens, and bogs; on slightly acid to calcarcous soils.

• **REMARK** Southern Marsh Orchid hybridizes with Common Spotted Orchid and Heath Spotted Orchid (see above).

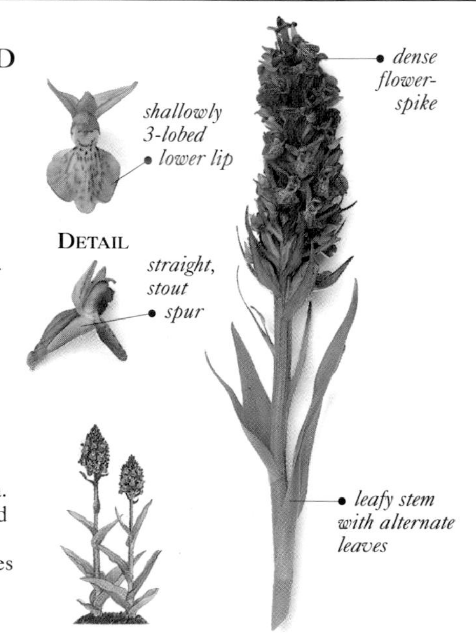

Habit Perennial	Height 30–50cm (12–20in)	Flowering time May–July

Family ORCHIDACEAE	Species *Anacamptis pyramidalis*	Author (L.) Rich.

PYRAMIDAL ORCHID

Variable and hairless, this orchid is a tuberous-rooted plant and may bear either a solitary or several stems. The plain, rather pale green leaves are lanceolate and decrease in size up the stem; the uppermost leaves are bract-like. The pale to deep pink, purplish pink, occasionally white, flowers are borne in a dense spike that is pyramidal at first but which gradually lengthens to become cylindrical; lateral sepals are spreading; the lip is deeply 3-lobed, 6–8mm (¼–⅓in) long, and extends backwards into a slender, downward pointing, somewhat curved spur.

• **DISTRIBUTION** Throughout the region, except for the far north. One of the most common orchids in the region.

• **HABITAT** Grassy places, downland, pastures, scrub, open woodland, roadsides, and coastal dunes; mostly found growing on calcareous soils.

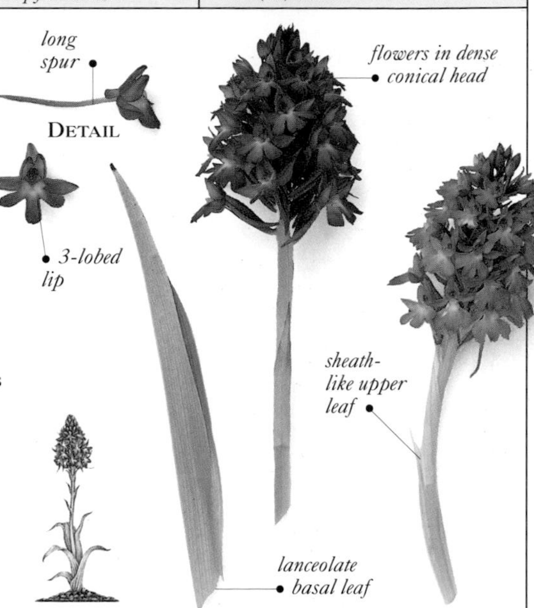

Habit Perennial	Height 30–60cm (12–24in)	Flowering time June–Aug

Family ORCHIDACEAE	Species *Orchis purpurea*	Author Hudson

LADY ORCHID

This is an imposing, tuberous-rooted, hairless plant with a solitary erect stem. The 3 to 6 basal leaves are borne in a loose rosette and are shiny, deep green, unspotted, and elliptic-oblong; the upper leaves are smaller and partly sheathe the stem. The small and rather insignificant bracts are shorter than the ovaries. The flowers are fragrant and are borne in a broad cylindrical spike; the sepals and petals form a close, brownish purple hood, and the 3-lobed lip, 10–15mm (⅖–⅗in) long, is white or pale pink dotted with purple, with a broad, notched, skirt-like central lobe and arm-like lateral lobes.

• **DISTRIBUTION** S. England (rare), Denmark, and Germany southwards.

• **HABITAT** Grassy places such as meadows, woodland and woodland margins, coppices, scrub, and road verges; on calcareous soils.

Habit Perennial	Height 40–70cm (16–28in)	Flowering time May–June

Family ORCHIDACEAE	Species *Orchis militaris*	Author L.

MILITARY ORCHID

This hairless, tuberous-rooted plant usually has a solitary stem. The leaves are glossy green; the lower 3 to 5 are spreading and oval to lanceolate, while the upper few are erect, smaller, and sheathe the lower part of the stem. The pink to pinkish purple flowers are manikin-like and are borne in a rather dense cylindrical spike. The sepals and petals of each flower form a close, ash-grey, pointed hood; the rather flat lip, 12–15mm (½–⅗in) long, has 2 "arms" and 2 "legs" and is spotted with deep red-purple or pink; the spur is short and downcurved. The fruit is a 3-parted, oblong capsule containing numerous minute seeds.

• **DISTRIBUTION** Throughout, as far north as S. Sweden; in Britain, very rare and confined to S.E. England and the Chilterns, where it is protected.

• **HABITAT** Open calcareous grassland and scrub; more rarely in woodland glades or fen meadows.

sepals and petals form • *hood*

DETAIL

flowers borne in spike •

• *short spur*

Habit Perennial	Height 30–60cm (12–24in)	Flowering time May–June

Family ORCHIDACEAE	Species *Orchis mascula*	Author (L.) L.

EARLY-PURPLE ORCHID

This hairless, tuberous-rooted plant has a solitary, often purple-tinged, erect stem. The 3 to 5 basal leaves are oblong and plain green or with elongated blackish purple blotches or spots. The bracts are lanceolate and equal the ovaries in length. The purple, occasionally pink or white, flowers have an unpleasant smell; the wing-like lateral sepals spread upwards; the lip is shallowly 3-lobed, 6–8mm (¼–⅓in) long, and spotted in the centre; the spur is long and upward pointing.

• **DISTRIBUTION** Throughout the region, except for the far north.

• **HABITAT** Woodland, coppices, scrub, grassy places, and road verges.

• **RELATED SPECIES** *Orchis morio*, Green-winged Orchid, has all sepals and petals held close together; lateral sepals are greenish with purple veins. It prefers grassland in similar regions.

DETAIL

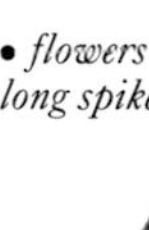

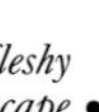

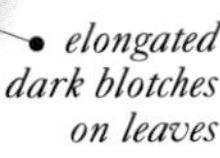

Habit Perennial	Height 20–50cm (8–20in)	Flowering time Apr–June

Family ORCHIDACEAE	Species *Orchis palustris*	Author Jacq.

ORCHIS PALUSTRIS

This slender, rather elegant orchid is tuberous-rooted, hairless, and produces a single or several stems which are often purplish. The 3 to 8 leaves are plain green and lanceolate to linear, with a long tapered apex. The bracts are often purplish and are equal in length to, or longer than, the ovary. Borne in a long, rather loose spike, the purple flowers have wing-like lateral sepals that spread widely, a 3-lobed lip, 7–9mm (²⁄₇–³⁄₈in) long, with the lobes more or less equal, and a long and upward pointing spur.

• **DISTRIBUTION** Germany, N.W. France, and S. Sweden.

• **HABITAT** Wet marshy places, meadows, and lake margins.

• **RELATED SPECIES** *Orchis laxiflora*, Loose-flowered Orchid, has darker flowers with the spur broadened at the tip; the lip has 3 unequal lobes. It inhabits similar habitats in S.W. Britain (Jersey), France, Belgium, and Germany.

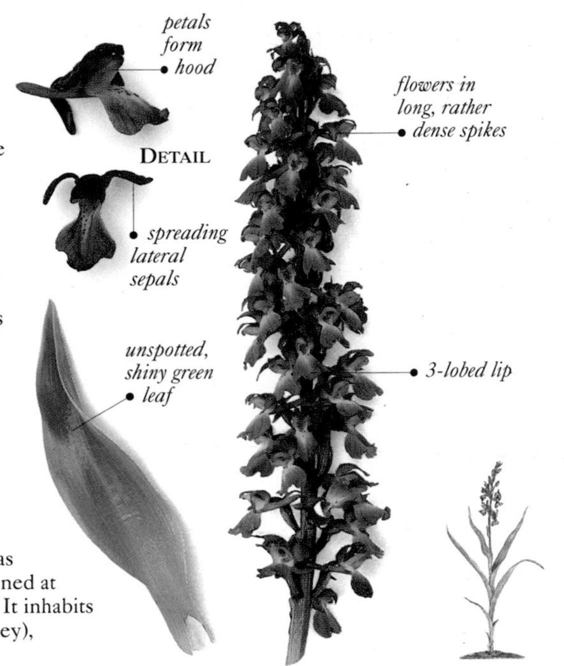

Habit Perennial	Height 30–70cm (12–28in)	Flowering time May–June

Family ORCHIDACEAE	Species *Aceras anthropophorum*	Author (L.) Aiton f.

MAN ORCHID

This is a slender, hairless, tuberous-rooted plant, with a solitary erect stem. The leaves are narrow-oblong to elliptical; the upper leaves are smaller than the lower and are bract-like. Borne in a long and narrow spike, the small, manikin-like flowers are green but are often flushed with reddish brown; the sepals and petals are held close together to form a small hood; the lip, 12–15mm (½–⅝in) long, is pendent, with narrow pointed "arms" and "legs", and lacks a spur (by which it differs from the closely related genus *Orchis*).

• **DISTRIBUTION** England, Belgium, Holland, France, and Germany; often very local.

• **HABITAT** Dry grassy places such as downs, dunes, road verges, scrub, and more rarely along woodland margins; on calcareous soils.

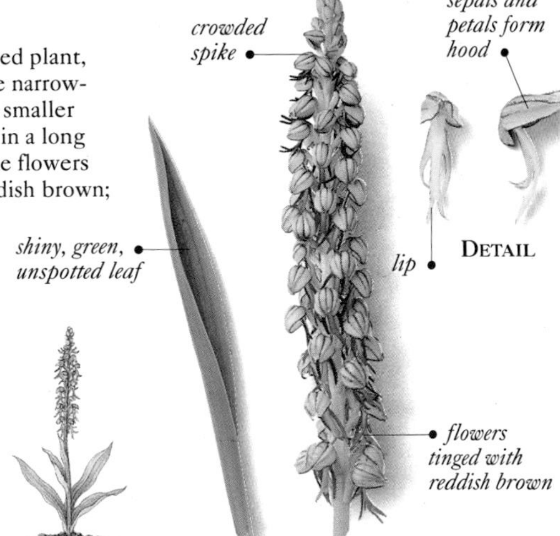

Habit Perennial	Height 20–40cm (8–16in)	Flowering time May–June

Family ORCHIDACEAE	Species *Himantoglossum hircinum*	Author (L.) Sprengel

LIZARD ORCHID

This large and imposing plant is hairless and tuberous-rooted, with a solitary erect, rather stout stem. The 4 to 6 lowermost leaves are elliptical to oblong and are often partly withered by flowering time; the upper leaves are smaller and narrower. The bracts are narrow and often slightly longer than the ovaries. The foul-smelling flowers are borne in a long, tapered spike; the small sepals and petals form a hood with the lip dangling below; the lip, 30–50mm (1⅕–2in) long, is coiled in bud, ribbon-like, with 2 short "arms" close to the top, notched at the end, and spotted with purple; the spur is short and downturned.

• **DISTRIBUTION** S.E. England (rare), Holland to Germany southwards.

• **HABITAT** Grassy places such as scrub and woodland margins, road verges, and grassy sand dunes.

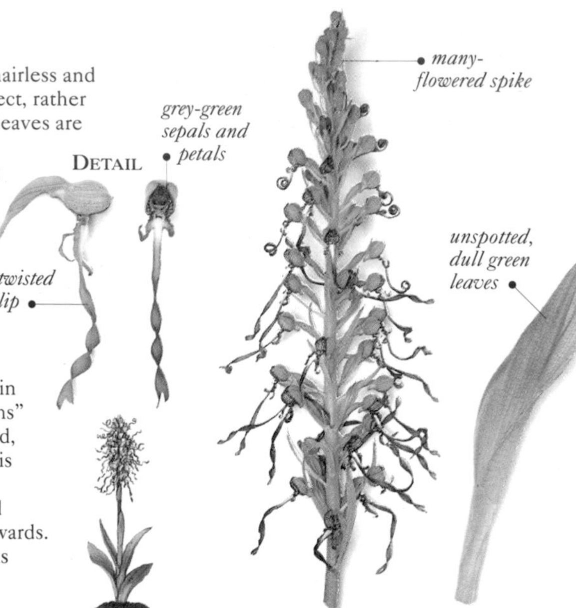

Habit Perennial	Height 50–90cm (20–36in)	Flowering time June–July

Family ORCHIDACEAE	Species *Ophrys apifera*	Author Hudson

BEE ORCHID

This is a variable, slender, almost hairless, tuberous-rooted plant, with a solitary erect stem. The oval to lanceolate, grey-green leaves are mainly close to the base of the plant and form a loose rosette; the upper leaves are smaller and sheathe the stem. The 2 to 11 unspurred flowers are borne in a loose spike; the pink, purple, occasionally white, sepals spread widely apart, while the petals are about a third the length and are narrower; the lip is 10–13mm (⅖–½in) long, reddish brown, and remarkably bee-like, with hairy side-lobes and a shield-shaped orange-brown central zone, called the speculum, enclosed by a yellowish pattern.

• **DISTRIBUTION** England, Wales, Ireland, Belgium, Germany, and France.

• **HABITAT** Grassy places, meadows, pastures, scrub, road verges and embankments, and grassy sand dunes; mostly on calcareous soils.

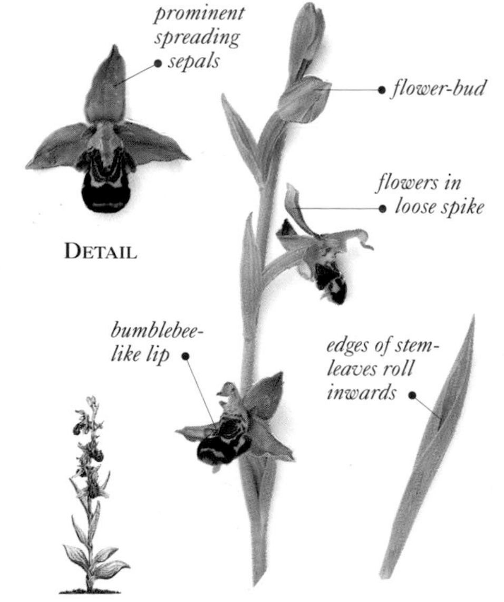

Habit Perennial	Height 25–45cm (10–18in)	Flowering time May–June

Family ORCHIDACEAE	Species *Ophrys fuciflora*	Author (Crantz) Moench

LATE SPIDER ORCHID

Also known as *Ophrys holoserica*, this almost hairless, tuberous-rooted plant produces a solitary erect stem. The leaves, mainly basal, are plain green and elliptical to oval. Borne in a loose spike, the 2 to 10 pink, purple, or whitish flowers have widely spreading sepals and a spider-like lip which is 9–13mm (⅜–½in) long, mostly pale to dark brown, and has hairy side-bosses and a small forward-pointing tip. The shiny central zone of the lip, called the speculum, is violet or blue outlined with yellow, and consists of an H- or X-shape or of 2 parallel lines.

• **DISTRIBUTION** S.E. England (rare), Belgium to Germany southwards.

• **HABITAT** Grassy places, meadows, pastures, scrub, and road verges.

• **RELATED SPECIES** *Ophrys sphegodes*, Early Spider Orchid, has yellowish green to brownish green sepals and petals. It grows in S.E. England (although rare), and Belgium to Germany southwards. Its habitats are similar to those of the Late Spider Orchid.

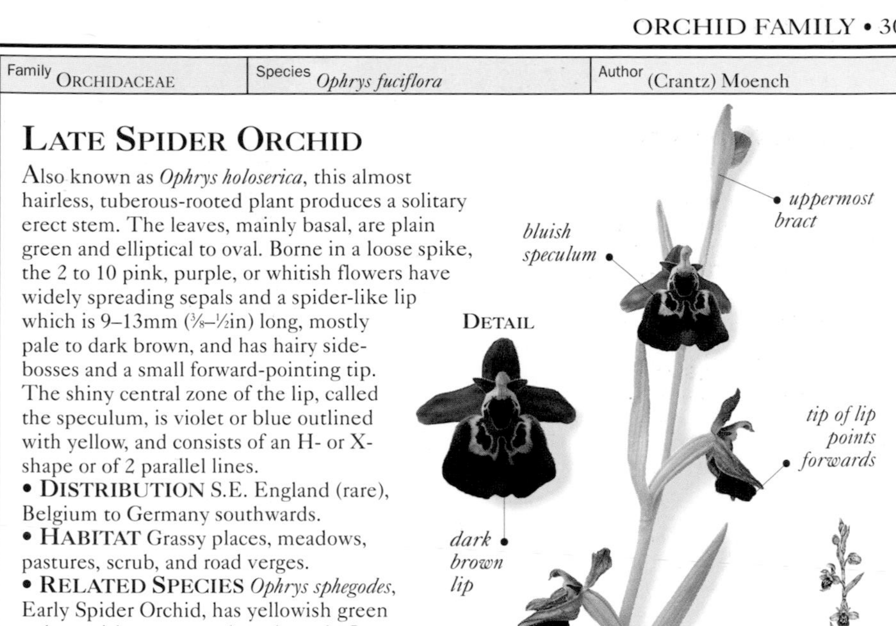

Habit Perennial	Height 20–40cm (8–16in)	Flowering time June–July

Family ORCHIDACEAE	Species *Ophrys insectifera*	Author L.

FLY ORCHID

This is a very slender, more or less hairless, tuberous-rooted plant. The leaves are mostly borne close to the base of the plant and are plain green and narrow-lanceolate; the upper leaves are smaller than the lower and are bract-like. The bracts are narrow and roughly equal the ovary in length. The small flowers are borne in a loose spike; the sepals are green and spread widely apart, while the lip, 9–10mm (⅜–⅖in) long, is narrow, 3-lobed, deep violet-brown, or occasionally greenish or whitish, with a shiny, deep violet zone, called the speculum, close to the base.

• **DISTRIBUTION** Throughout, except for the far north and Scotland; often local.

• **HABITAT** Woodland, coppices, scrub, grassy places, fens, and lake margins; generally in shady places on calcareous soils.

• **REMARK** Difficult to spot because it is often well camouflaged among other plants.

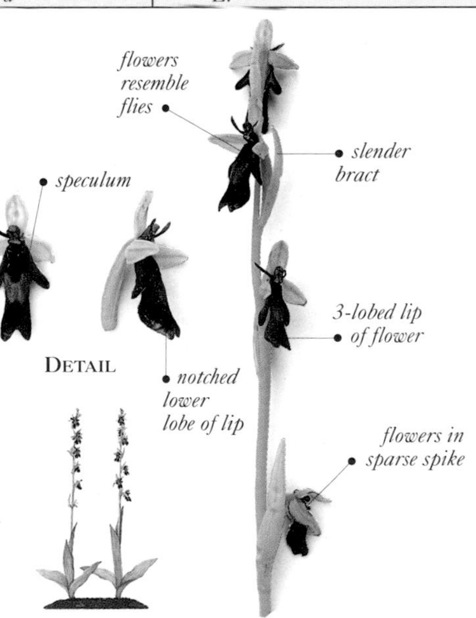

Habit Perennial	Height 40–60cm (16–24in)	Flowering time May–June

GLOSSARY

Terms for parts of a plant are explained on pp.12–19. Below, words written in **bold** type are defined elsewhere in the glossary.

• **AXIL**
Angle between the stem and the leaf or lateral branch.

• **BASE-RICH/BASIC**
Soils or rocks rich in basic elements such as lime.

• **BEAK**
Small projection like a bird's beak.

• **BRACTEOLE**
A secondary bract; above a bract or on a lateral branch.

• **BULB**
The swollen base of leaves forming a solid fleshy organ.

• **BULBIL**
A small **bulb** located on the stem in the **axil** of leaves or bracts.

• **BURR (BUR)**
A prickly, spiny, or hooked seed-head or **flower-head**.

• **CALCAREOUS**
Soils or rock high in calcium; limy.

• **CARPEL**
Basic unit of the female reproductive part of the flower containing the unfertilized seeds; may be solitary to many, fused or separate.

• **CARR**
A copse or woods on boggy land.

• **CASUAL**
Not **native** and only occurring from time to time.

• **CLAW**
Narrow basal part of sepal or petal.

• **CLEISTOGAMOUS**
Flowers that do not open but do self-pollinate and produce seeds.

• **CORM**
The swollen, often fleshy, base of an erect underground stem.

• **DISC-FLORET**
One of the **florets** in the disc-like centre of a flower-head.

• **DUNE SLACK**
A damp depression between dunes, often saline.

• **FLORET**
A small or individual flower.

• **FLOWER-HEAD**
Formal arrangement of tightly clustered **florets**, e.g. daisy-head.

• **GLABROUS**
Without hairs.

• **GLAND**
A small, often rounded, organ that secretes oils or other substances; usually on leaves, stems, or hairs.

• **GLAUCOUS**
Bluish green or greyish blue.

• **HERBACEOUS**
Perennials with growth dying down to ground level each year, usually in the autumn.

• **INVOLUCRE**
A ring of crowded bracts; often overlapping, often surrounding the base of **flower-heads**.

• **KEEL-PETAL**
The basal pair of petals in a peaflower that are united along the lower margin.

• **MEALY**
With a floury texture; generally refers to surface of leaves or stems.

• **LIP**
Petal or petals (sometimes sepals) forming a distinctive lobe.

• **LOCAL**
Restricted to particular localities.

• **NATIVE**
A plant belonging naturally to a country or region; having colonized by natural means.

• **NATURALIZED**
An alien (non-**native**) plant that has become established in a country or region by accident or by human intervention.

• **NECTARY**
A nectar-secreting organ in flowers, often a modified sepal, petal, or stamen.

• **OCHREA**
A sheath-like organ formed from stipules united around the stem.

• **PARASITIC**
Plants without chlorophyll that live on other plants.

• **PERIANTH**
A general term for the sepals and petals when they are not clearly differentiated.

• **PERSISTENT CALYX**
Remaining attached and not falling away; often present around fruit.

• **POLLINIA**
Pollen that is aggregated into formal masses; refers to orchids.

• **PROCUMBENT**
Trailing along the ground.

• **RAY/RAY-FLORET**
Outer **floret** of a **flower-head** such as a daisy; often strap-shaped.

• **RECURVED**
Turned or bent back.

• **REFLEXED**
Turned back upon itself.

• **REFUGIO**
Biologically a place where wildlife can survive.

• **RHIZOME**
A swollen, often horizontal, surface or underground stem.

• **RUNNER**
A general term for a **stolon**.

• **SCALE-LEAVES**
Small leaves resembling scales.

• **SCAPE**
A flowering stem in which the leaves are usually all basal with none on the stem.

• **SEPTUM**
A wall separating the cells of an ovary and fruit.

• **SPATHE**
An enveloping or encircling bract, sometimes leaf-like; small or large.

• **SPECIES AGGREGATE**
A group of closely related species that are often difficult to separate by easy visual means.

• **SPECULUM**
A mirror-like area, often shield-shaped; refers to the **lip** of orchids.

• **SPUR**
A cylindrical or pouch-like appendage to sepals or petals.

• **STANDARD PETAL**
The uppermost petal, especially of peaflowers.

• **STAMINODE**
A sterile stamen, often modified into a petal or **nectary**.

• **STIGMATIC RAYS**
A stigma that forms a star with radiating branches.

• **STOCK**
The base of a plant from which the stems arise.

• **STOLON**
A slender trailing stem, generally above ground, usually producing new plants and sometimes rooting down.

• **SUBOPPOSITE**
Not quite opposite.

• **TEPAL**
Term for sepals and petals when they are not differentiated but resemble petals.

• **TERNATE**
A compound leaf with three leaflets.

• **TUBER**
Swollen root or underground stem.

• **WING-PETAL**
The lateral petals of a flower; refers to peaflowers or orchids.

INDEX

D

F

G

H

I

N

O

P

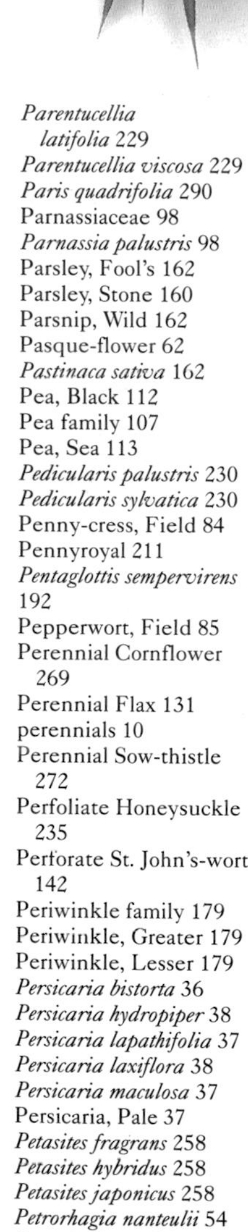

R

T

U

V

W

YZ

ACKNOWLEDGMENTS

The author would like to thank Christine Grey-Wilson for her careful reading of the proofs, and David Burnie for helpful suggestions in the preparation of this work.

Dorling Kindersley would like to thank: Jim Marks and Mustafa Sami for organizing the referencing and commissioning of the illustrations; Murdo Culver for researching the references for the illustrators; Michael Allaby for compiling the index; Damien Moore, Lucinda Hawksley, and Charlotte Davies for editorial assistance; Mark Bracey, Deborah Myatt, Alison Shackleton, Ann Thompson, and Colin Walton for additonal design assistance; and Lesley Riley for proofreading. Special thanks are also due to the following for their help to the photographer: Francis Rose; Joyce Pitt; John Fisher; Rose Murphy; Royal Botanic Gardens, Kew; The Royal Horticultural Society, Wisley; Chelsea Physic Garden, London; John Mitchell of the Royal Botanic Gardens, Edinburgh; Anne Bebbington of Juniper Hall Field Studies Centre, Dorking; Steve Richardson of the Arundel Wildfowl Trust, Arundel.

All photographs are by Neil Fletcher, except: Dorling Kindersley/ Geoff Dann: 7b (wildflower garden). Dr. Alan Dunkley: 24b. Christopher Grey-Wilson: 23b (Alpine). Derek Hall: 8 (Clematis); 288b; 303b; 307t. Dorling Kindersley/ Colin Keates: 24 (camera, notebook/pencils). Dorling Kindersley/Tim Ridley 24 (tape measure). Matthew Ward: 109t.

Illustrations by: Laura Andrew: 48t; 95t; 98b; 117b;184t; 234t. Evelyn Binns: 74b; 80m; 83m; 88t; 109t; 186b; 202t; 205; 210t; 245t; 255t; 255b; 256; 262b; 293b. Peter Bull: 40b; 43b; 43t;46b; 57b; 57t; 62t; 67b; 71b; 72m; 72b; 75t; 78t; 79t; 82b; 85t; 87b; 91; 96b; 97t; 97m; 110t; 113b; 123t; 124t; 130t; 132b; 134b; 139; 141b; 142t; 171b; 78b; 187b; 208b; 208t; 212b; 213b; 219t; 223t; 224b; 230t; 238b; 239b; 241; 257t; 260t; 260b; 261; 277; 272t; 279t; 280t; 285t; 285b; 287; 288t; 291t; 293t; 297t; 300t. Julia Cobbold: 87t; 107b; 153b; 154t; 209t; 304b. Joanne Cowne: 54t; 68t; 101b; 120b; 138b; 191b; 196t; 242b; 251b; 273t; 273b. Ruth Hall: 79b; 150b; 190t; 205b; 215t; 259t. Tim Hayward: 41t; 41b; 152b; 154b; 174t. Philippa Lumber: 44t. Stephen Mclean: 63t. David More: 77t; 106t; 156t. Tricia Newell: 39t; 42t; 47t; 48b; 49t; 50t; 54b; 60b; 65t; 65b; 66t; 67t; 72t; 75; 83t; 90t; 92t; 93t; 94m; 94b; 97b; 98t; 99b; 100b; 107t; 108t; 113t; 115t; 119b; 121t; 112b; 124t; 128t; 132t; 135t; 136; 137b; 138b; 141t; 147b; 148b; 155t; 162b; 166b; 177t; 181t; 189t; 190b; 192t; 193t; 194t; 194b; 195b; 197b; 201b; 202b; 203t; 210t; 211; 212t; 230b; 231t; 232b; 233b; 235t; 235b; 240; 243t; 243b; 248t; 254b; 264b; 274t; 274b; 275b; 276b; 282; 288; 289b; 294b; 294b; 295; 299t; 305t. Sue Oldfield: 68b. Liz Pepperell: 106b; 178t; 181m; 246t; 252; 257b; 262t. Valerie Price: 69t; 71t; 89t; 116t; 148t; 159t; 163b; 188; 214b; 216t; 238t. Elizabeth Rice: 37t; 37b; 38t; 47m; 58b; 75b; 105b; 146t; 279b; 301b. Michelle Ross: 38b; 46t; 61; 63b; 77b; 100t; 101t; 103t; 104t; 125t; 137t; 142b; 152t; 167t; 167b; 176b; 193b; 206b; 207t; 221t; 237t; 288b; 290t; 290b; 305b. Helen Senior: 35b; 45b; 51b; 52b; 53t; 78b; 81b; 83b; 84t; 85b; 86b; 88b; 102b; 105t; 109b; 110t; 110b; 111t; 111b; 114t; 116b;121b; 123b; 127b; 128b; 129t; 130b; 131t; 133t; 134t; 135b; 142b; 143t; 143b; 144t; 144b; 145t; 145m; 145b; 150t; 156b; 160t; 172t; 173t; 173b; 175; 176t; 176b; 180t; 180b; 182b; 184b; 186t; 197t; 209b; 215b; 216b; 221t; 224; 226b; 226t; 228t; 231b; 237b; 241; 242t; 247; 248b; 249b; 259b; 263b; 265t; 265b; 267t; 268t; 268b; 269b; 276t; 278b; 291b; 294t. Jenny Stear: 34t. Rebekah Thorpe: 217t. Anthea Toorchen: 126. Barbara Walker: 34b; 45t; 73t; 108b; 143t; 146b; 151t; 158t; 169t; 169b; 179t; 185; 189b; 201t; 206t; 219b; 233t; 251t; 270t; 286b. Wendy Webb: 214t. Ann Winterbotham: 41t; 44b; 47b; 49m; 50b; 53b; 55t; 56t; 56b; 59t; 60t; 62b; 64b; 70t; 73b; 74t; 80b; 82m; 95t; 97t; 99t; 102t; 103b; 104b; 118t; 119t; 120t; 133b; 140t; 147t; 149t; 149b; 155b; 157t; 159b; 161t; 162t; 163t; 164t; 164b; 165t; 166t; 168b; 170t; 171b; 172; 182t; 187t; 191t; 195t; 196b; 198; 199b; 200t; 200b; 204b; 210b; 217b; 218; 220b; 220t; 222t; 222b; 223b; 225t; 226t; 226m; 226b; 227t; 227b; 228b; 229b; 232t; 236b; 239t; 244; 245b; 250b; 253t; 263t; 269t; 272b; 283b; 292t; 296t; 296b; 297b; 298t; 298b; 301t; 302t; 302b; 304t; 306t; 307b. Debra Woodward: 36b; 118b; 199t; 271; 289t.

Additional artwork: Mark Bracey and Dorling Kindersley Cartography Department: 6. Stephen Dew: 13b. Janos Marffy: airbrushing 8; 10–11. Liz Pepperel: 25–33.
Endpaper illustrations by Caroline Church.